THE SPREAD OF ISLAMIKAZE TERRORISM IN EUROPE

The Spread of Islamikaze Terrorism in Europe

The Third Islamic Invasion

RAPHAEL ISRAELI
Hebrew University of Jerusalem

VALLENTINE MITCHELL
LONDON • PORTLAND, OR

First published in 2008 by Vallentine Mitchell

Suite 314, Premier House,   920 NE 58th Avenue, Suite 300
112–114 Station Road,   Portland, Oregon,
Edgware, Middlesex HA8 7BJ   97213-3786

www.vmbooks.com

Copyright © 2008 Raphael Israeli

British Library Cataloguing in Publication Data

Israeli, Raphael
  The spread of Islamikaze terrorism in Europe : the third Islamic invasion
  1. Terrorism - Religious aspects - Islam 2. Terrorism - Europe 3. Islamic fundamentalism - Europe
  I. Title
  303.6'25'088297'094

ISBN 978 0 85303 733 0 (cloth)
ISBN 978 0 85303 734 7 (paper)

Library of Congress Cataloging-in-Publication Data
A catalog record has been applied for

All rights reserved. No part of this publication may be reproduced, stored in or introduced into a retrieval system or transmitted in any form or by any means, electronic, mechanical, photocopying, recording or otherwise, without the prior written permission of the publisher of this book.

Printed by Biddles Ltd, King's Lynn, Norfolk

To Ruth and Michael Shiloh
who defied duress and vanquished it,
on their attaining the delights of retirement.

To the members of my Research Group
on Religious Actors in Political Conflicts (RACA)
at the Truman Institute, Hebrew University,
and to my collaborators across Europe,
for their inspiration and collegiality.

Contents

Acknowledgements		ix
Introduction: Events in their Context		1
1.	The New Demographic Balance in Europe and its Consequences	54
2.	Britain: Leading the Way	93
3.	France's Domestic Turmoil	174
4.	Germany's Dilemmas	227
5.	The Cartoon Affair and the Failure of Dialogue and Coexistence	277
6.	*Quo Vadis*, Europe?	363
Bibliography		453
Index		485

Acknowledgements

This volume is a sequel to this author's *Islamikaze: Manifestations of Islamic Martyrology* (London: Frank Cass, 2003), where this very term was first coined and the ideological and organizational setting was laid out for the September 11 (2001) events and their aftermath. Since then, mainly due to the extraordinary security measures adopted in the US, which were much maligned by those whose acts of terror had caused the tightening of security in the first place, not one more significant terrorist event has occurred on US soil, at least for now. Conversely, European allies of the US, including some of those who reneged on their alliance and elected to cut deals with the terrorists, and even more so Asian countries, many of them among the fifty-seven Islamic Conference member-states, who thought they were immune to such horrors, have become the immediate and repetitive victims thereof.

The title *The Spread of Islamikaze Terrorism in Europe: The Third Islamic Invasion* refers to the historical sequel whereby the first invasion into Europe was made by the Arabs in the eighth century from the south, when they conquered Spain, Portugal and half of France, before they retreated after the Charles Martel victory in 732 near Poitiers, and the eight centuries of Muslim rule in Andalusia that ended with their final retreat from Granada in 1492 under the relentless advance of the Spanish *reconquista*. After they were repulsed from the Iberian Peninsula in the fifteenth century, they launched the second invasion by the Ottomans from the East which led to the fall of Constantinople into their hands and went as far as the gates of Vienna before it was arrested and thwarted in 1683, and ultimately concluded with the break-up of the Ottoman Empire during the First World War. The current third invasion is being achieved by immigration and the demographic inundation of Europe, together with a campaign of *da'wa* to propagate Islam, aided by a terrorist wave to intimidate the West.

International terrorism has not been limited to the confines of the Islamist struggle against the West in the international arena, but has expanded into the domestic scene of Islamic countries where local Islamist oppositions aspire to seize power from current illegitimate regimes that are usually supported by the West. This is the genesis of the Bali, Casablanca, Istanbul, Sinai, Amman, Riyadh and Jeddah acts of terror that were primarily directed against visiting aliens after September 11, in order to destroy the tourist source of income or the economic base of those hated regimes. More ominously, many a home-grown Islamist, who was allowed to sow lethal propaganda in western democracies where he had initially sought asylum from oppression in his land of origin, has used his familiarity with his adoptive land to turn it into his personal jihadist battleground. This is the background for September 11 and then the Madrid (March 2004) and London (July 2005) horrors.

Due to limitations of space, this volume includes only the three largest states in Europe: Britain, France and Germany. The rest of Europe will be tackled in a separate volume, tentatively entitled *The Islamic Challenge in Europe*. In unison, they will hopefully provide a comprehensive picture of how entangled Europe and Islam have become, in all appearance to the detriment of the continent, and an awakening call to shake it out of its slumber.

I am grateful to the late Mr Frank Cass for having raised some of these questions and suggested that they should be tackled. This volume is dedicated to his memory. I am also very much obliged to a host of friends, colleagues and collaborators in England, France, Germany and Scandinavia, who have relentlessly assisted in the collection of these materials, but I remain alone responsible for any errors of fact or misinterpretation thereof.

Jerusalem
Autumn 2007

Introduction:
Events in their Context

For too long the world had accepted as a 'natural' calamity the Palestinian hijackings and attacks of the 1970s and 1980s which inaugurated this era of international terrorism. Instead of confronting and uprooting the terrorists, western governments and passengers accepted with staggering docility to be stripped and searched at airports, to have their otherwise sacrosanct privacy encroached and trampled upon in public, to pay ever-increasing air fares in order to cover security costs, and to repeat the mantra that a 'solution of the Palestinian conflict will resolve the problem'. After September 11, America decided to fight terrorism independently of the Palestinian problem; Madrid elected to yield to the terrorists' demands; London 'changed the rules' only after it was rocked by a series of attacks on its public transportation; and the rest have yet to follow.

After the van Gogh murder in the Netherlands in 2004 and the anti-Denmark outburst of Muslim rage following the cartoon affair of early 2006, the public debate was turned on its head. Previously, far from recognizing that the fight against terrorism in Iraq, Afghanistan and worldwide was launched by the US as a defensive measure, after it was attacked on its home territory, America's detractors in Europe and the Muslim world claimed, on the contrary, that it was American offensive moves in those countries which prompted terrorism, exactly as it was Israel's 'injustices' towards the Palestinians that had triggered terrorism in the first place. Cause and effect were reversed. So, instead of joining the US in its universal struggle against terrorism, thus also ridding themselves of its menace, they blamed the violence on American and Israeli policies, thus unwittingly becoming its unwilling accomplices and its unsuspecting next victims. But the cartoon affair has dramatically demonstrated that the general Muslim wrath against the West had just been compressed until Muslims were confident that their presence there constituted a critical mass, numerous enough to instil fear of potential civil disorder in European governments. The fear of an American reaction, which was finally brought to bear in Afghanistan and Iraq, was mitigated in the past by America's willingness to absorb atrocious behaviour from Syria, Iran and Egypt or the havoc of the 1973 oil price rise. The Arabs are constantly testing the limits of what America will endure, simultaneously aware that America ignores misdemeanours aplenty to secure uninterrupted oil exports for the West. Thus America (and other western countries) are seen to favour totalitarian rulers in the Middle East, fearful of the regimes that may replace them – the 'devil they know' approach. No American president wishes to be responsible for creating another Iran, after the ignominious behaviour of Jimmy Carter *vis-à-vis* the Shah.

The waves of recriminations of the Muslim world against the West and Israel, which have also been expressed in the rise of Muslim parties in Turkey, Egypt, Jordan and the Palestinian Authority; the unbridled desire of the Iranians to go nuclear; and the thug-like rhetoric of their President Ahmadinejad against western values and Jews in general, to the point of blatantly denying the Shoah (Holocaust), are indications of the spreading anti-western antagonism amongst Muslims. Their zeal is directed not only against Israel and the West, but aims primarily to remove from power their own (selectively) western-allied regimes which are regarded as American stooges. As the major Egyptian paper, *al-Ahram,* put it, 'religious identity has replaced nationalist ideology',[1] and that applies not only in Muslim countries but also amidst Muslim minorities throughout their diasporas. Muslim terrorism will continue to rise in both Europe and the Muslim world, hence the relevance of the present volume as a sequel to the saga of 9/11 and its aftermath. Nevertheless, the basic data on Islam by both scholars and politicians are replete with distortions, reflecting their eagerness to depict a more benign and less menacing picture of the Islamic rise than demonstrated by empirical evidence. This is done through two distinctions that have become conventional wisdom among both critics and proponents of Islam. One is the artificial bifurcation between the so-called 'Islamists' or radicals, the supposed minority who defame all Muslims by their violent deeds and wage war against the West and Israel; and the majority itself, which is viewed as 'peace-loving' and shuns violence in favour of coexistence. The other artificial, and equally spurious, distinction wants us to believe that Judaeophobia, which is an attenuated version of anti-Semitism, posing as anti-Zionist and anti-Israel, has nothing to do with anti-Semitism; and that while Islam as a whole carries no traces of anti-Semitism, its present anti-Jewish manifestations are no more than a much less lethal and vastly less threatening Judaeophobia. It is clear that these 'scientific' distinctions, though they are pursued by some scholars of reputation, and may have some empirical merit to them, have much more to do with political correctness and a degree of sheepish *dhimmi*-like submissiveness, or fear of being accused of racism, than with historical reality.

It is unconvincing to say that Muslims are merely anti-Israel and anti-Zionist and not anti-Semitic, when Jews in the diaspora are habitually attacked for no reason whatsoever today, or were historically mistreated, beaten, massacred or forced to convert until compelled to leave Islamic lands, apart from the fact that they were Jews. French Jews, British Jews or Belgian Jews are all citizens of the countries in which they reside, and cannot influence the policies of the Israeli Government even if they wished to do so. To attack them because of opposition to Israeli policies is gratuitous and is undeniably an expression of innate Islamic anti-Semitism. The equivalent in Jewish attitudes would be for Jews to attack their Muslim fellow-citizens in Europe every time an Arab or Muslim country defames, vilifies or demonizes (or indeed physically attacks) Jews in the media or school curricula, or subjects them to economic boycotts individually or collectively, all of which happen on a sustained, daily basis. But that would be a case of 'Islamophobia' (or anti-Muslim bigotry, which is what the accusers imply), and the fact that it does not happen proves firstly that such bigotry is a figment of the Muslims' imagination (bandied about precisely to combat the very notion of their pervasive anti-Semitism); and secondly that Jews do distinguish between right and wrong, and have never lost their sense of justice and civilized behaviour despite the relentless provocations of Muslims, and not only radicals, against them. When partial processes of liberalization are adopted, as in Algeria, Jordan, Egypt, and lately the Palestinian territories, namely when people are given the opportunity to express themselves freely, it is invariably political Islam that gains votes, and since it is a popular vote, it cannot be said to represent 'radicals', exactly as it cannot be claimed that the 60 per cent of Palestinians who voted for Hamas are all 'Islamists'.

If, as some claim, only a small percentage of Muslims are 'radical', 'fundamentalist' or simply 'Islamists', while the majority are 'peace-loving', what explains the teeming crowds who erupt violently in Cairo, Gaza, Karachi, Teheran or Kabul at every manufactured 'provocation'? What happens to those supposedly peace-loving majorities if they are not represented by the violent crowds? And when Muslim columnists, including western-educated degree-holders, write in the mainstream journals of the Muslim world, including in 'moderate' and 'pro-western' countries, about genocidal designs against Jews and Israel, virulent recriminations against the West, and expressions of joy after 9/11 or every time a bus or a restaurant explode in the West with dozens of victims, are they representative of 'radicals' or of 'Islamists', or of 'Judaeophobic' individuals who avoid blatant anti-Semitism? Where then is the difference between peace-loving Muslims and 'Islamists'? While there are theological differences of nuance between Sunnis and Shi'as, and within the Sunnis between the four Schools of Law (*madhahib*), for instance between the puritanical Wahhabis of the Hanbali cult and the more lenient Hanifites on matters of shari'a law, there appears to be unanimity among them with regard to jihad wars, the denigration of Jews and the contempt and hostility towards the West, because they all draw from the same medieval Abu Yussuf and Ibn Taymiyya and the more modern Hasan al-Banna, Sayyid Qut'b or Abu al-Ala' al-Mawdudi. Understandably, not every Muslim would observe to the letter the strictest prescriptions of these scholars, but at the same time no sweeping, authoritative alternative to them has emerged to challenge them, let alone replace them.

The 'insurgency' in Iraq where Muslims are killing each other mercilessly clearly illustrates the falsity of this artificial bifurcation. The fighting is between the different sects of Islam, the Shi'a and Sunni, and between different clans within the sects – with each vying for power and supremacy over members of their own sects and over the opposing sect – rather than between 'Islamists' and 'moderates'. The same holds true for other Muslim lands where massacres, oppression and repression are relentless but largely unreported in the western media. (The killings in Iraq would have received only minimal exposure if it were not for the allied forces.) Unless a physical or even a theological war starts in earnest between 'Islamists' and 'moderates', non-Muslims can only view Islam as a single political ideology.

Those referred to as Islamists regard themselves as plain Muslims, who are perhaps more zealous than others and wish to fulfil Muslim goals here and now. But are they so distinguishable from other Muslims that they deserve to be treated in a class of their own or as if they observe a different Islam? All religious Muslims venerate the great masters of radical Islam like Hasan al-Banna, Sayyid Qut'b, Mawdudi and Yusuf al-Qaradawi, even if they are not categorized as 'radical'. The latter relate to the masses of common Muslims the way activists or militants in a political party refer to the rank and file of sympathizers who only vote on election day, but are not involved in any day-to-day politics. But we do not distinguish between 'radical' and 'common' party members. Yes, they differ, in both cases, as far as the degree of commitment, activity and observation are concerned, but we cannot set them apart ideologically, and they continue to belong to the same core of belief and conviction. For if there were a 'liberal' or 'moderate' tendency in Islam, it would be evinced by theologians of Islam who would stand up courageously and battle against the ideas and theses of the 'Islamists'. However, while truly moderate and daring individuals of Muslim descent (and sometimes conviction) do exist, principally in the safety of the West, we cannot discern any significant trend of moderation and 'peace-loving' inclination which rallies behind it masses of Muslims. So, what is erroneously dubbed 'moderate' or non-Islamist Islam, is actually the silent majority which is, unfortunately, more likely than not to partake in the outbursts of jubilation when Jews or Israel are harmed, to watch a blatantly anti-Semitic series on television which depict Israelis (and Americans for that matter) as blood-suckers, conspiracy plotters and children-killers, and to avidly absorb genocidal statements by their leaders and clerics and reiterate their belief in the same nonsensical slogans and conspiracy theories that are circulated in their media. One year after September 11, Dan Rather of CBS News undertook a worldwide survey of Muslim (not Islamist) reactions to those horrific events. From a sample of eight Muslim countries, between Morocco and Pakistan, where he polled the literate population in remote villages in each one of these countries, the overwhelming majority of the populace, which was not 'radical', spelled out their conviction that the horror was 'of course' perpetrated by Jews, Mossad and other such delusive fairy tales.

Did the Palestinians suddenly become 'Islamists' when the radical Hamas won the elections? No. They remained as Muslim as they were before the elections. They burst into unabashed joy when September 11 happened, much to Arafat's embarrassment, prompting him to send his security forces to disband those 'radicals' to avoid further disgrace. Why did they do that? Because they were indoctrinated by their school textbooks, which assured them of the imminent victory of Islam against the 'corrupt and tyrannical' West. They are jubilant when Israeli and western families are shown torn into pieces, and they re-enact harrowing scenes of explosions against Israel, exhibiting cardboard buses or restaurants alight and limbs flying around, with huge crowds of children, passers-by, shopkeepers, students and policemen applauding and rejoicing. Even their universities and school plays stage such re-enactments. Could they all be 'Islamists'? No. In their eyes, Israelis and the West are perceived as the enemies of Islam (not of Islamists). One should therefore rejoice at their defeat, and because they are not defeated often enough for the Muslims' taste, few Muslim can skip the delight of replaying that defeat and savouring it in slow motion. Another question is why America and Israel are particularly targeted and their national flags usually accompany each other, when a Muslim frenzy of burning and destruction occurs in any part of the globe. The answer is threefold: first, both of these countries stand out as the consummate representatives of strength, modernity, prosperity and success, thereby accentuating the impotence and backwardness of the Islamic world. That is the true source of the 'humiliation' that Muslims reiterate so often and so intensely, for the very existence of that successful world is a provocation, daily reminding Muslims of their failure and the extent to which they lag behind. The potency of feelings of humiliation should not be underestimated in these 'shame and honour-based' societies. Along with Israel, which became independent in 1948, several Arab states achieved independence from the Europeans in the first half of the twentieth century: Egypt in 1922; Iraq in 1932; Lebanon in 1943; Syria in 1946 and Jordan in 1946. Saudi Arabia, which was not a European colony, was founded in 1932. On any measure of development, Israel has left the Arabs far behind. According to the CIA *World Factbook*, Egypt's GDP per capita (purchasing power parity) was an estimated $4,200 in 2006. The equivalent figure for the oil-rich Saudis was $13,600, while Israel's figure of $26,800 was not far behind Britain's $31,800.

Secondly, since no one in the West fears an American or an Israeli bomber attacking the local transport system, their Muslim detractors have worked overtime to portray them as threats – knowingly pandering to the liberal-left 'blame America first' brigade. They exploited divisions in the western political spectrum, and the liberals were duly manipulated into castigating their own governments even if it meant ignoring their own security. That hardly a day goes by without one Muslim leader or preacher articulating the death and destruction they plan for non-Muslims leaves the ideological liberals unmoved. Thirdly, their dream of rectifying the situation by creating a *Pax Islamica* to encompass the entire universe, has been scuttled principally by Israel in its immediate vicinity and by America worldwide, for the US is the only power able and willing to confront them and impede their goal of establishing a world Caliphate. These frustrations are shared by Muslims in general, regardless of whether one categorizes them as 'Islamists' or otherwise. A Muslim-born author, Ibn Warraq, who renounced Islam, put the matter succinctly:

> Islam is a totalitarian ideology that aims to control the religious, social and political life of mankind in all its aspects; the life of its followers without qualification; and the life of those who follow the so-called tolerated religions to a degree that prevents their activities from getting in the way of Islam in any way. And I mean Islam, I do not accept some spurious distinction between Islam and 'Islamic fundamentalism' or 'Islamic terrorism'. The terrorists who planted bombs in Madrid; those responsible for the deaths of more than two thousand people on September 11, 2001, in New York and Washington, DC; and the ayatollahs of Iran were and are all acting canonically; their actions reflect the teachings of Islam, whether found in the Qur'an, in the acts and sayings of the prophet, or Islamic law based on them. Islamic law, the shari'a, is the total collec-

tion of theoretical laws that apply in an ideal Muslim community, one that has surrendered to the will of God. It is based, according to Muslims, on divine authority that must be accepted without criticism, without doubts and questions. It is an all embracing system of duties to God, and it controls the entire life of the believer and the Islamic community. Islamic law intrudes into every nook and cranny of the life of an individual, who is not free to think for himself. Given the totalitarian nature of Islamic law, Islam does not value the individual, who has to be sacrificed for the sake of the Islamic community. Collectivity has a special sanctity under Islam. Under these conditions, minorities are not tolerated. Expressing one's opinion or changing one's religion – the act of apostasy – is punishable by death.[2]

Pierre Rehov interviewed several failed Islamikazes for his documentary 'Suicide Killers',[3] which left viewers shaken by their calmness and the certitude of their convictions. Hassan, 16, was frustrated because he was caught before he could blow himself up among a crowd of Israeli civilians: 'If I had been killed, my mother would call it a blessing. My family and seventy relatives would have gone to paradise, and that would be a great honour for me.' Rehov identifies two psychological factors which are key to the formation of the terrorist mindset, both of which he argues are inherent in Islamic belief and practice – a high degree of sexual frustration and a deep sense of humiliation and wounded pride. The terrorists rarely speak of nationalist grievances but constantly emphasize their religious mandate. A sense of shame is another major motivating factor. 'It is bad enough that the infidel West is superior in technology and wealth, but to have been defeated by Jews, whom Muslims have held in contempt for centuries, is the utmost humiliation', he said. 'Young Muslim men are raised in a highly restrictive atmosphere riddled with sexual guilt and taboos. They grow up without a natural relationship to women, whom they hold in deep contempt.' The fantasy of martyrs receiving seventy-two virgins in paradise is part of that culture. Crucially, Rehov dismissed the argument that Islamic moderates will eventually rein in extremists if given proper support by the West. 'All Muslims, even in countries like Egypt and Tunisia, believe that Islam will prevail worldwide in the end, because that's the word of God. Moderates believe that this will happen sometime in the future. The extremists think that it will happen in their lifetimes, and they want to be part of the victory. It's just a difference in the timing, not in the ultimate outcome.'[4]

The father of suicide bomber Tareq Hamid was ecstatic as he praised his son's 'martyrdom operation' on the Hamas TV network, saying that when his son was about to perform the terrorist attack, he called his friends and told them:

> I swear by Allah that I saw the black-eyed virgins of paradise on the hood of my car. Some people claim that all these young mujahideen [participants in a jihad] who blow themselves up are desperate people. These claims are wrong. These are lies and clear Zionist propaganda. All the mujahideen I came to know are the finest of Palestinian society. The only thing they need is to reach paradise by means of defence and martyrdom for the sake of Allah.[5]

The transatlantic airline plot which was intercepted in Britain in August 2006 resulted in significant changes in western terminology concerning Islamic terrorism. President Bush used the term 'Islamic fascists' to describe groups such as al-Qa'ida. He used the fifth anniversary of the September 11 attacks to remind Americans of the nature of the fight against radical Islam. 'It's been called a clash of civilizations', Bush said. 'It is a struggle for civilization.' The metamorphosis of Bush's war rhetoric was urged by Senator Rick Santorum who chided those who talk about a war on terror. 'I would say that we have a messaging problem, and that we in this country for a variety of different reasons have chosen not to identify the enemy and do it with consistency', Santorum said. 'Some say we're fighting a war on terror. That's like saying World War II was a war on blitzkrieg. In World War II we fought Nazism and Japanese imperialism. Today we are fighting against Islamic fascism.'[6]

Dr Yaron Brook, head of the Ayn Rand Institute (ARI) in California, also believes 'War on Terror' is a title that dooms the West to failure. Ayn Rand is an educational institute and resource centre entrusted with spreading Objectivism, the formal name of the philosophy of the controversial twentieth-century novelist-philosopher. 'You don't fight a tactic', said Brook. 'Terrorism is a tactic, and I believe we have to look at the ideological source of terrorism in order to identify the true enemy.' He defines this source as Islamic totalitarianism, which he describes as an expansionist philosophy that seeks to spread Islam by the sword. Brook believes the enemy's identity has been blurred or ignored by government leaders and the intelligentsia. 'We don't have the guts, the courage, the self-esteem to even identify who the enemy is. We couch it in terms of terrorists who happen to be Muslims who are "hijacking a great religion". We're afraid to say "Islamic anything": Islamic fascism, totalitarianism, whatever you want to call it.' The fear stems, he said, from the trend of multiculturalism, in which all cultures are morally equal, and moral relativism. But, he said, the most damaging idea to the cause of the West is the opposite of Rand's virtue of selfishness: altruism, which Rand didn't define as good-hearted kindness and generosity, but as the idea that one must sacrifice his own interests for the sake of others. Altruism, said Brook, leads to pacifism because 'self-defence is a very selfish act. It's a very self-interested act to defend one's own life, especially in war.' Most importantly, when you're filled with self-doubt and don't believe that your values are better than anyone else's, you cannot fight or win. 'I believe victory is possible, it just takes something we're not willing to do.' That 'something' is to wage war with little restraint and without apology against Islamic totalitarianism. 'If you want to win, innocents will die. There is no way to get around it. There was no war in which innocents didn't die, and there won't be.'[7]

Brook applies Rand's philosophies to Israel. 'We view what happens in Israel as an indicator of what will happen in the rest of the world. To the extent America abandons Israel, it abandons itself.' Israel is a beacon of civilization in a barbaric, backward area, he said. 'Israel represents, despite its flaws, the values of the West: individual rights, free speech, freedom of the press, equality before the law and the rule of law.' Objectivism upholds values generally associated with western culture – individualism, reason and science – but its distinctive development is a moral ideal of 'selfishness', whereby someone's own happiness is a moral responsibility. ARI was founded in 1985, after Rand's death, to pave the way for a philosophical and cultural renaissance in the US and to reverse what ARI sees as anti-reason, anti-individualism and anti-capitalist trends in today's culture. It concentrates on American domestic issues, but Israel figures prominently in its work. 'The West turning against Israel', which Brook said Ayn Rand saw occurring in the late 1960s and early 1970s, 'was the West committing suicide.'

It does not help that many western legislators are insular, voting on issues about which they know very little. Gary Streeter, the Tory MP for South West Devon, and chairman of his party's international office and its human rights commission and a member of the all-party parliamentary Friends of Islam group, confessed he did not know the difference between a Sunni and a Shi'a. He was one of thirty Middle East 'experts' from the world of politics questioned over Iraq, Iran and other countries in the region by the *Sunday Times*. Streeter, once private secretary to former Prime Minister John Major, also failed to identify Mahmoud Ahmadinejad as President of Iran, as did Khalid Mahmood, the Labour MP for Birmingham Perry Bar. Many of those quizzed by the paper 'did not know their Hamas from their Hizbollah'. Both Sarah Teather, the Liberal Democrat MP for Brent East, and Sally Keeble, Labour member for Northampton North, thought Hizbollah was an organization based in 'Palestine'. Asked if al-Qa'ida was Sunni or Shi'a, Brian Iddon, Labour MP for Bolton South East and secretary of the Britain–Palestine parliamentary group, said: 'Well, it attracts all sorts.' The survey mirrors similar questions posed to politicians in Washington. Jeff Stein, a columnist on Congressional Quarterly, asked Silvestro Reyes, a congressman chosen to chair the House intelligence committee in the new Democrat administration, whether the followers of Osama Bin Laden were Sunnis or Shi'as. Reyes guessed wrongly that they were primarily Shi'as. Stein said: 'It's been five years since these Muslim extremists flew hijacked airliners into the World Trade Centre. Is it too much to ask that our intelligence overseers know who they are?' Streeter later told the *Sunday Times*: 'It is not the proper role for journalists to try to be our judge and jury but to get on with the news.'[8]

Noting that the term 'Islamofascism' was introduced by the French Marxist writer Maxine Rodinson to describe the Iranian Revolution of 1978, Roger Scruton observed that the word has caught on, not least because it provides a convenient way of announcing that you are not against Islam but only against its perversion by the terrorists. He added: 'But this prompts the question whether terrorism is really as alien to Islam as we should all like to believe.' Scruton interprets the readiness of Muslims to take offence as a sign of the deep-down insecurity of their psyche in the modern world. He continued:

> In the presence of Islam, you have to tread carefully, as though humouring a dangerous animal. The Qur'an must never be questioned; Islam must be described as a religion of peace – isn't that the meaning of the word? – and jokes about the prophet are an absolute no-no. If religion comes up in conversation, best to slip quietly away, accompanying your departure with abject apologies for the Crusades.

While Scruton agrees that 'it is wrong to give gratuitous offence to people of other faiths', he adds that 'it is right to respect people's beliefs, when these beliefs pose no threat to civil order'.

> Although Islam is derived from the same root as *salaam*, it does not mean peace but submission. And although the Qur'an tells us that there shall be no compulsion in matters of religion, it does not overflow with kindness toward those who refuse to submit to God's will. The best they can hope for is to be protected by a treaty (*dhimma*), and the privileges of the *dhimmi* are purchased by onerous taxation and humiliating rites of subservience. As for apostates, it remains as dangerous today as it was in the time of the prophet publicly to renounce the Muslim faith. Even if you cannot be compelled to adopt the faith, you can certainly be compelled to retain it ... Ordinary Christians, who suffer a daily diet of ridicule and scepticism, cannot help feeling that Muslims protest too much, and that the wounds, which they ostentatiously display to the world, are largely self-inflicted.[9]

After September 11, a talk show was held by al-Jazeera (representing what is known as 'moderate' and 'peace-loving' Islam) where the question of whether Bin Laden was a terrorist or a hero was posed to the panellists and viewers. The only moderate participant, a Tunisian, was mocked and ridiculed by his co-panellists and the moderator for daring to dissent from the otherwise unanimous opinion which crowned Bin Laden as a hero. Viewers who called or e-mailed from the entire Islamic world were almost unanimous in agreement. That was not a poll among Islamists, but among the rank and file of Muslims, most of whom were supposedly the educated owners of home computers. Yet, their reaction was 'Islamist' in substance. So, where is the distinction? Yes, there are Islamikaze[10] activists who are ready to blow themselves up for the cause of Islam solely to kill westerners and Jews. But they are few in number, who are recruited, trained, financed, indoctrinated and dispatched by a vast infrastructure of Muslim states, organizations, 'charities' and individuals, and surrounded by the sympathy and admiration, often adulation, of the vast masses of the Muslim public and the mainstream press in countries that are clients of the US or signatories of peace treaties with Israel. Who then is an Islamist among all these layers of activists and supporters, and who is the 'moderate' and 'peace-loving'?

In the US and Europe, it was found that several Muslim intellectuals, leaders and clerics, who gained favour with the authorities and access to the highest echelons of power, for their supposed 'moderation', and their openness to 'dialogue', were later arrested for illicit fund-raising for Muslim terrorist organizations, for incitement to terrorism or for suppressing women's rights. Were they suddenly transformed from 'moderates' to 'radicals'? No. They were the same Muslims who were perceived previously as moderate when they acted or refrained from acting in a certain way, who became Islamists when they were caught red-handed while engaging in subversive acts. In both instances they acted as Muslims in the name of Islam; it is western and westernized Muslim scholars who attached to them those epithets which they themselves never recognized. Similarly, clerics and other Muslims who dub the Jews 'descendants of pigs and monkeys' (basing themselves on a Qur'anic verse), or cite the *hadith* (sayings and traditions of Muhammad) which claims that on the 'Day of Judgement' Jews will hide behind rocks and trees (with the latter acquiring the magical power of denouncing them and inviting Muslims to come and kill them), are not exactly setting themselves apart from Islamists by being less anti-Semitic and merely 'Judaeophobic'. All Muslims who cite these passages, and they do so regularly and perennially, are making blunt anti-Semitic and genocidal statements against the Jews, and no amount of rhetorical manoeuvring can mitigate that fact.

It seems that the fictional distinction that is drawn between Islam and Islamism, which is usually made either by western scholars and politicians or by Muslims who live in the West, emanates more from a culture of political correctness or an instinct of self-defence and survival than from a sober observation of reality. As far as westerners are concerned, the artificial distinction also emanates from the comfort inherent in dealing with mirror-images of themselves. Those Muslims who can be influenced, or have merely learned to use conciliatory vocabulary, are labelled 'moderates'. Yet an obsessive and uninformed search for 'moderates' precludes the emergence of genuine non-radicals. In Muslim countries themselves it is often hard to distinguish between Islam and Islamism, inasmuch as Palestinian, Saudi, Egyptian and Pakistani clerics who belong to the 'moderate' establishment often issue fatwas and deliver sermons that are every bit as 'extremist' as the 'radical' ones. Neither imported nor home-trained Muslim clerics in the West make any effort to distance themselves from 'Islamists'. Western scholars and politicians, who need to cater to Islam, for electoral or other worldly perks, on the one hand, but cannot overlook the impatience of their own people with violent Islam on the other, find shelter in that distinction which allows them to claim that the Islam they support or defend is 'moderate', while the violence emanates solely from the 'extremist Islamists'. At the same time politicians and scholars critical of Islam need that distinction to shelter themselves from accusations of 'racism', as if multicultural and multiracial Islam were a 'race', or of anti-Muslim bias and hatred. Muslim scholars and public figures who live in the West resort to that distinction in order to avoid a blanket condemnation of Islam of which they are part, and to escape suspicions by their co-religionists that they 'sold out' to the West or that they committed an act of 'treason' against their culture and religion. Many of them find it more expedient to claim that they are 'secular Muslims', a notion that is unacceptable to Islam in all its nuances, and some of them convert to Christianity in order to feel free to criticize their previous religion. According to a Channel 4 documentary, approximately 3,000 British Muslims have converted to Christianity.[11]

The fact is that throughout the Muslim world, the legitimacy of Israel is challenged, the Holocaust is denied systematically, as evidenced by the popularity there of such Holocaust deniers as Robert Faurisson, Roger Garaudy or David Irving, the prohibition of *Schindler's List* on their screens and the violent declarations of the Iranian President on both scores. This is a common denominator for most Muslims. There is no differentiation between 'radicals' and 'moderates' here, with anti-Semitic or Judaeophobic stereotypes current among them all, with rare exceptions. That is why they contradict themselves on the Shoah, denying it on the one hand and wishing Hitler had brought his annihilation plan to completion on the other; urging a 'scholarly, free and objective' research of the Holocaust, in order to prove that it never was. Similarly, the acceptance and dissemination of the *Protocols of the Elders of Zion,* the blood libel, the claimed poisoning of wells or the distribution of AIDS-infected gum to Palestinian children and other conspiracy theories featuring Jews, are recurring themes in Palestinian (not only Hamas) as well as other mainstream Muslim writings and propaganda. Genocidal threats against the Jews abound not only in Bin Laden's statements and in Ahmadinejad's delusions, but also in columns of Egyptian, Jordanian, Saudi, Pakistani and other newspapers of the respected mainstream. Is this Judaeophobia of the 'moderates' or plain anti-Semitism of the 'Islamists'? Words have a significance, and it is imperative to streamline our vocabulary. Otherwise we are under the permanent threat of losing our ability to express what we mean or to comprehend what we are told.

The aftermath of the airline plot in Britain in 2006 produced a new-found willingness to use the word 'terrorist', in contrast to Israel's enemies who apparently belong to a 'resistance force' or are confusingly called 'operatives', 'militants' or 'gunmen'. Westerners who become human shields for terrorists by placing themselves in the way of Israel's defensive action are 'activists'. These words are deliberately vague. The *raison d'être* of news broadcasters is to inform the public, but they do a great disservice when they resort to words devoid of meaning in the name of political correctness. Misuse of words such as 'militant' and 'activist', especially when the latter is preceded by 'peace', have not only degraded language but limited western understanding of the issues at stake. So instead of seeing Israel's latest war as a seamless extension of the West's war against Islamofascism, Israel is perceived as an aggressor.

Matters are further complicated and made less comprehensible to western minds by the paranoia and conspiracy theories that permeate the Muslim world, amongst both modern and western-educated or traditionalist and obscurantist Muslims. Those theories that are rampant even among Muslims in the West, maintain that world leaders who support Israel are Jewish (like Presidents Reagan and Bush), that the UN, of all places, is a tool of the Jews who utilize it for their world dominion, and that the major events that shook the world, like the world wars, revolutions and September 11, are all the fruit of Jewish imagination and execution. Their minds are so permeated with these nonsensical theories that they become impervious to logical, rational debate that is open to argument and discussion. Blair pointedly criticized those Muslims who have been quick to level charges of Islamophobia and oppression against Britain and the US, telling them: 'It's not just your methods that are wrong, your ideas are absurd. Nobody is oppressing you. Your sense of grievance isn't justified ... Some of what is written on this is loopy-loo in its extremism.'[12]

Therefore, the difficulty of dealing with Muslim minds consists not only of removing the mountains of pure delusion that stifle their thinking, but also of persuading them that the very attempt to counter-argue those futilities is not part of the world conspiracy that is supposedly being woven against them. It is possible to explain their imaginary picture of the world by their need to project onto their enemies the analytical shortcomings that bewitch them, but it is impossible to move them out of the illusory scenarios that they have constructed around themselves, to which they cling with a tenacity that defies and contradicts western comprehension. The result is that even when Muslims initiate and launch an act of violence, they blame the West, and label it, or what led to it, as an act of aggression of which they are the victims and which deserves their retaliation.

Much mirth has flowed from the publication of lists naming those who were caught rewriting *Wikipedia*, the online encyclopaedia that 'anyone can edit'. The WikiScanner site, which links amendments back to the computers that make them, found that a Syrian state computer added to the entry on JFK: 'By the way, the prime suspect involved in the assassination was Mossad.'[13] This obsession with Israel instead of their own economic development goes some way towards explaining why Syria's GDP per capita was an estimated $4,100 in 2006.

As long as the Muslim anti-western and anti-Semitic discourse was internal, little attention was paid to it in the outside world. But since the end of the first Afghanistan War (1979–89) which also signalled the end of the Soviet Empire, the Cold War and the return of the mujahideen to their Muslim home countries, tremendous energies were released by the 'Afghanis', namely the foreign battle-hardened graduates of the war in Afghanistan, which were channelled both domestically (in Algeria, Saudi Arabia, Sudan, Lebanon, Egypt, Jordan, Pakistan and Taleban Afghanistan), and internationally to wage a worldwide jihad, led by Bin Laden's al-Qa'ida, but carried out simultaneously on Arab, American, African, Asian and European soil. Rising oil prices allowed some oil-producing countries and their rulers to finance the spread of a puritanical and violent brand of Islam and to absorb some of the unemployed Afghani mujahideen, while the others were drawn to the battlefields of Iraq, Lebanon, Bosnia, Chechnya and the Palestinian territories, or became mercenaries of violence in America and Europe. The Danish cartoon affair (2006) proved a golden opportunity for Muslim regimes who began to feel the heat of terrorism, to redirect the rage and fury of the masses outwardly against the West and Israel, regardless of whether we define them as radicals or moderates, anti-Semitic or Judaeophobic, for western institutions were attacked in Libya, Egypt, the Palestinian territories, Syria and Lebanon, and the boycott of Danish products was launched by Saudi Arabia and other Gulf states which are usually considered 'moderate' and 'pro-western'.

A new study by the US Institute for Peace (USIP) of polling data from fourteen different Muslim countries found that support for a role for Islam in politics strongly correlates with more likely support for terrorism. *Correlates of Public Support for Terrorism in the Muslim World*, by Ethan Bueno de Mesquita of Washington University in St Louis,[14] also found that support for terrorism is dispersed in the Muslim world. Perhaps more surprisingly, people who perceive Islam to play a large role in the politics of their home country are also more likely to support terrorism. The USIP study rebuts the claim of Islamic apologists that support for terrorism is driven by people living under dictatorships. The author discovered that the perceived threat to Islam by their home government had very little impact on the respondents' support for terrorism, but instead, 'those who believe the US and the West pose such a threat are particularly likely to support terrorism'. Respondents in these Muslim countries who believed they had some degree of freedom of speech were found to be more likely to support terrorism. The author explains that 'when people perceive themselves to have freedom of expression, they are more inclined to admit their support for terror'. Support for terrorism is constant across education groups. Perception of the state of the country's economy was uncorrelated with support for terrorism, undercutting the argument that Islamic terrorism is driven by poverty. Age is negatively correlated to support for terrorism, meaning that the older one gets, the less likely one will justify the use of terrorism. The author explains that although people may support terrorism it is because they perceive there to be a threat to Islam from the US. But the relationship could also work the other way. Terrorism is, among other things, a tool of propaganda. One of the key messages of Islamic terrorists is anti-Americanism. Thus, if terrorism is an effective tool of propaganda, people who support terrorism end up having strongly anti-American sentiments because they are persuaded by the terrorists' message. Another, related, explanation argues that people who support terrorism have a psychological need to justify this support. As a result, they adopt views that 'rationalize' their support for terrorism. Thus anti-Americanism does not cause support for terror, but support for terror causes anti-Americanism.[15] Just as important is the role played not only by the terrorist groups but also by Muslim governments in their constant and relentless incitement of hatred against America. This is just as true of the Egyptian Government, the recipient of approximately $50 billion in US aid since 1979, as it is of Kuwait, which was rescued from Saddam Hussein in 1991.

There is another factor which affects the Muslim hatred of America, highlighted by Professor Bernard Lewis's distinction between the western and Muslim outlook on the collapse of the Soviet Union. While the West views it as a consequence of the Reagan administration's decision to confront it and engage it in an arms race that proved ruinous to the Soviet economy, for Muslims it was an Islamic victory in a jihad. Bin Laden wrote at the time that Muslims had defeated the more dangerous of their two main enemies, and that defeating the effeminate Americans would prove easier. This perception was encouraged by the weak or non-existent

American responses to a series of attacks, including the embassy hostage crisis in Teheran in 1979, the bombing of the marine barracks in Lebanon in 1983, the World Trade Centre in New York and US troops in Mogadishu in 1993, the US military office in Riyadh in 1995, the US military housing in Khobar in 1996, the American embassies in Kenya and Tanzania in 1998 and the USS Cole off Yemen in 2000 (and this list is by no means exhaustive). Lewis summarized the three stages of the ideology of al-Qa'ida as the expulsion of 'infidels' from Islamic countries; conquest of lost Islamic lands, namely countries where Islam once ruled, including Spain, Portugal, Sicily and Israel; and then Islam taking over the world.[16] The personnel from the Council on American–Islamic Relations (CAIR), one of the most vocal in the US, are normally reticent about the organization's agenda but sometimes inadvertently reveal their ambitions. The *San Ramon Valley Herald* reported that CAIR's long-serving chairman, Omar Ahmad, told a crowd of California Muslims on 4 July 1998, 'Islam isn't in America to be equal to any other faith, but to become dominant. The Qur'an ... should be the highest authority in America, and Islam the only accepted religion on earth.'[17]

The theme of converting the world to Islam is recurring. Bin Laden's latest video portrayed him incongruously sounding like an anti-globalization protester, with his adoption of left-wing vocabulary. He referred to 'the reeling of many of you under the burden of interest-related debts, insane taxes and real estate mortgage' and blamed 'global warming and its woes' on 'emissions of the factories of the major corporations'. Mohamed el-Sayed, of the Ahram Centre for Political and Strategic Studies in Cairo, said Bin Laden's words were proof the West cannot appease al-Qa'ida by withdrawing from Iraq. The message 'uses iconic language that suggests: "The only way to get peace is to convert to Islam." He's in a state of constant, unending war until he Islamizes the world.' [18]

Muslim relations with Russia and China illustrate the irrationality of their hatred of the West. True, politics does throw up strange bedfellows, but an alliance by people who supposedly live and die by their religious tenets with two ungodly, atheistic powers should logically be anathema. If anything, the Qur'an enjoins them to offer protection to the Jews and Christians, the 'people of the book', albeit as subjugated categories. But the Qur'an vilifies atheists, and urges

Muslims to launch wars against them. Moreover, logic dictates that Muslims should shun governments who are today actively persecuting and oppressing their fellow-Muslims. Russia has killed upwards of 100,000 in a still unresolved war against the Muslims of Chechnya, while China persecutes its Muslim Uighur minority intermittently. Yet, Muslim governments from the 'fundamentalists' of Iran to their like-minded brethren of Hamas, the Wahhabis of Saudi Arabia to the more secular Gulf Sheikhdoms or Egypt, do not think twice about conducting, indeed even coordinating, high-level diplomatic and trade relations with Russia and China. Having a principled foreign policy, based on 'Islamic values', is something no Muslim government can be accused of. On the contrary, the moral of their dual policy is that they have admirably learned to reserve their 'principles' for the self-torturing West, which bends over backwards to appease their every whim, and still is always found wanting. After 9/11, the West was excoriated, from liberals within and Muslims without, for initially introducing some degree of 'ethnic profiling' as a security measure for airlines. China, on the other hand, banned all Muslims and especially Arabs from travelling on its airline for some time, without so much as a whispered censure from Muslims or their governments.

'Jihad' is often inadequately translated as 'holy war', but its full original meaning is important. It refers to offensive warfare against non-Muslims to spread Islam and extend Islamic rule. It is therefore more extensive than the word 'Crusade', at which Muslims are wont to take such acute offence. The Crusades were medieval Christian military expeditions which set out to recover the Holy Land from Muslims. Unlike jihad, which in the early years of Islam led to the military conquest of lands as far as India to the east and Spain to the west – forcibly Islamizing the breadth of North Africa in the process at the expense of the indigenous Copts and Berbers amongst others – the Crusades were limited to their era and limited geographically.

The centrality of Spain in the jihadi plans for Europe today is barely reported. An Islamic conference in the Spanish city of Granada called on Muslims around the world to help bring about the end of the capitalist system. The call came at a conference titled 'Islam in Europe' attended by about 2,000 Muslims. The keynote speaker was Umar Ibrahim Vadillo, leader of the worldwide Muslim group known as Murabitun.[19] Vadillo said America's economic interests had become the religion of the world and that people slavishly adjusted their lifestyles to suit the capitalist model. But he said capitalism cannot sustain itself and is bound to 'collapse'. Vadillo, a Spanish Muslim, called on all followers of Islam to stop using western currencies such as the dollar, the pound and the euro and instead to return to the use of the gold *dinar*. He said the introduction of the gold *dinar* to the world's economies would be the single most unifying event for Muslims in the modern era, after which the capitalist structure would fall and it would make the Wall Street crash of 1929 seem 'minor by comparison'.[20]

When Gustavo de Arístegui, foreign affairs spokesman for Spain's conservative Partido Popular, published *The Jihad in Spain: The Obsession to Reconquer al-Ándalus*,[21] Yusuf Fernandez, the spokesman for the Spanish Federation of Islamic Religious Entities, branded him an 'enemy of Islam'. There followed death threats against the Spanish politician on encrypted jihadist websites based in Saudi Arabia. In an interview in 2006, Arístegui asserted that the Islamofascists' obsession with reconquering Spain should be a concern for all westerners, and that they want to overthrow governments that they consider anti-Islamic, corrupt, and above all apostate, believing they are obliged to do so; reconquer any country or territory that has at any time in its history been under the domain of Islam; re-establish the Caliphate; and lastly, extend their domain and power over the whole world. The symbolism of Spain is extremely important to them, but it is not just Andalucía as some believe. What he calls the *síndrome andalusí* extends to other parts of Europe. Their goal is to recover four-fifths of the Iberian Peninsula, parts of southern France, half of Italy, all the Balkans, and definitely all the islands of the Mediterranean. He continued: 'Ayman al-Zawahiri said in his book *Knights Under the Banner of the Prophet*[22] that Europe had become a spiritual vacuum that only Islam could fill and that Europe is the new frontier of Islam, the new land of conquest, and above all the new battleground of the global jihad.' They think that when Europe actually becomes a continent with a very important Muslim minority, it will be a very easy target and its land very easy to conquer. Arístegui dispels the myth that 'medieval Spain was a perfect and peaceful coexistence between the three most important monotheistic religions. Muslims only tolerated Jews and Christians when they were very powerful and not so much when they were not so powerful. It had a lot to do with the political and historical moment.' In addition to the re-Islamization of the mosque of Córdoba, the Muslims have adopted the policy of the 'foot in the threshold'.[23] 'They believe that conquering a neighbourhood, then a town, then a city, then a province, and then a region will eventually lead to the reconquest of the whole country.' Arístegui adds that 'there is a part of the University of al-Azhar in Egypt that is obsessed with a very clear strategy to reconquer land that was once under the domain of Islam'. For Arístegui, multiculturalism and political correctness are the most tried systems for coexistence in Europe and both have failed miserably. Multiculturalism is in many ways a return to the Middle Ages, he said. 'It means in fact that whoever is a Christian, a Jew, or a Muslim is going to be ruled by laws and courts of justice that are Christian, Jewish or Muslim. This is preposterous. It is very much like the communities in which the Ottoman Empire was divided up into.' Significantly, he adds:

> The western left has chosen to see radical Islamism as the only enemy capable of confronting the West, the United States, and its allies. They truly believe that it is in many ways their ally. If you are to observe the way that Venezuela, Bolivia and other countries dominated by populist regimes have acted, you will see that they vote consistently with countries like Iran or Syria, which are very anti-western. Political correctness and the obsession of the left with radical Islamism are deactivating the self-defence capabilities of western democracies. By not denouncing radicals and the movements that are clearly linked to radical associations, institutions, and even terrorist organizations, the West is getting closer to being dominated by them.[24]

Although Arístegui does not think that Islam will conquer Spain, he says the fight will gradually become more difficult and extensive because Spanish society today is not willing or ready to confront the threat. People have become prosperous in a very short time. Spain has a per capita income of around $28,000 a year. People want to pay their mortgages, go out on Friday night, take up to thirty days off from work each year, buy nice cars, and generally enjoy the good life. While some people are aware of the huge danger that Islamism represents for a large part of the world, they don't believe it is capable of jeopardizing their way of life or their liberties and freedoms. He quoted Joschka Fischer, the German Foreign Minister from 1998 to 2005, who said that if by any chance Israel were to be defeated, the next in line would definitely be Spain.[25] Many Muslim clerics, however, expect Rome to be conquered next, in keeping with Muhammad's 'prophecy' in the *hadith*. Speaking on al-Jazeera, Yusuf al-Qaradawi said: 'Constantinople was conquered, and the second part of the prophecy remains, that is, the conquest of Romiyya. This means that Islam will return to Europe ... The conquest need not necessarily be by the sword ... Perhaps we will conquer these lands without armies. We want an army of preachers and teachers who will present Islam in all languages and in all dialects.'[26]

So keen are Muslims to see Israel destroyed that they are willing to countenance the destruction of a large proportion of their own people in the process. In an interview on ANB TV in June 2007, Abd al-Bari Atwan, editor of the London-based *al-Quds al-Arabi* newspaper, was speculating on possible Iranian action in a war with the West. He said: 'It will burn the oil wells, block the Straits of Hormuz, attack the bases in the Gulf, and Allah willing, it will attack Israel as well. If the Iranian missiles strike Israel – by Allah, I will go to Trafalgar Square, and dance with delight if the Iranian missiles strike Israel.'[27] Since Israel is only nine miles wide across her waist within the 1967 armistice borders, any strike on Israel would inevitably hit the West Bank too and kill hundreds of thousands of Bari Atwan's fellow-Palestinians, and leave their 'sacred' al-Aqsa mosque in ruins.

Israel's importance as a bulwark against further Islamic encroachment in Europe is a recurring theme in jihadi discourse. Labelling Christians and Jews according to their day of worship, it is commonplace to hear jihadis speak of attacking the 'Sunday people' after defeating the 'Saturday people'. This theme was aired by a former British Conservative government minister, Michael Portillo, who commented on the refusal by George Bush and Tony Blair to support UN calls for a quick ceasefire between Israel and terrorists in Gaza and Lebanon in the summer of 2006, thereby risking both diplomatic isolation and criticism at home. In an article entitled 'The bloody truth is that Israel's war is our war', Portillo wrote that the same considerations that shape Israel's actions are equally applicable to the West:

> Critics of Israel point out that bombing Lebanon provides fresh grievances for Palestinians and other Muslims. That is undoubtedly so, and it is exactly what Hamas, Hizbollah, Syria and Iran would wish. Israel is forced to choose between looking feeble (which will increase its vulnerability) or playing into its enemies' hands through 'disproportionate' action. Before we criticize Israel we should at least understand that dilemma and be aware that if we stoke up anti-Israeli feeling we dance to a devilish tune.[28]

Noting that for Israelis only the prospect of security justifies the trading of captured land, he said the Israeli Government was elected to make peace and did not depart from that course of its own volition. On both the borders with Gaza and Lebanon, Israeli soldiers were killed and others kidnapped. Its struggle against Hizbollah fits into a complex global jigsaw of battles against terrorism, and for the West to turn against Israel and America would be perverse and potentially suicidal. Israel's three attempts at accommodation since 1993 have been based on the premise that only Israeli concessions can displace Palestinian despair. Israeli concessions indeed enhance Palestinian hope, but not of a reasonable two-state solution – rather a hope that they will actually be able to destroy Israel. The Iranian–Syrian–Hizbollah–Hamas axis is quite explicit about a genocidal objective. When they speak of 'ending Israeli occupation' they mean of Tel Aviv. It is time to recognize that the Israeli–Palestinian issue will likely not be the first matter settled in the decades-long war that Islam has declared on the US, Israel and the West. It will more likely be one of the last.[29] Now that Israel has withdrawn from Gaza, and Hamas has ousted Fatah from the strip, human rights groups and ordinary Gazans say Hamas is committing exactly the same crimes as its Fatah predecessors, whose corruption and brutality were supposedly one of the main reasons why support for Hamas grew. By their own behaviour, the Palestinians daily prove that conflict in the Middle East will not be resolved by a peace treaty with Israel. Palestinian political culture cannot produce peace internally, let alone externally.³⁰

It is often claimed that fighting between Muslims and non-Muslims leads to further radicalization. Yet there is another consideration when assessing radicalization, often repeated by Muslim clerics the world over. For them, all publicity is good publicity, even when it makes others recoil in horror. A Palestinian-born US Muslim cleric who teaches at Georgetown University, Yahya Hendi, said 9/11 had spurred Americans to know more about Islam, and Muslims to affirm their US identity. 'There are serious efforts being made among the second and third generation to become part of the political establishment', he said. 'Last year we elected the first Muslim to Congress and I expect that by 2015 there will be three or four as well as at least thirty mayors.' He said he did not feel there was general animosity towards Muslims in American society, and that he encouraged Muslims to join intelligence bodies like the CIA and FBI. Islam has some 17,000 converts a year.³¹ Far from fearing that 9/11 may have had a negative effect on Muslims and the way they are perceived by the rest of society, he saw the publicity generated for Islam in a positive light, since it encouraged non-Muslim Americans to study the religion – leaving open the possibility of an increase in conversion or 'submission' to it. The attacks throughout the West have also made the Muslims more assertive, encouraged by the insistence of western governments that Islam is a 'peaceful' religion that has been 'hijacked' by an extremist minority. For yet other Muslims, the 'success' of these attacks served as an added motivation for recruitment to the jihadi cause.

Discussion of any Muslim dispute in the world is reduced into something that has less to do with the Muslims than with Israel. The epicentre of the war on terrorism may be *focused* on Israel, but this isn't Israel's war. Islamic violence is prevalent throughout the world, demonstrating a sustained aim at civilization itself. It receives minimal coverage in the welter of 24/7 news, but when viewed together, the threats, attacks, intercepted attacks, diplomatic manoeuvres or inaction all confirm Islam's unity of intent.³² On any one day, stories abound of al-Qa'ida attacks in Iraq, Somalia, Nigeria, Kenya, Tanzania, Indonesia, the Philippines and Afghanistan; genocide by the Arab Sudanese Government-backed Muslim militiamen against the black Africans of Darfur or until recently the Christians and animists in the south; attacks or intercepted attacks in America, Canada, India and Europe; beheadings of Buddhist monks in Thailand by Muslim terrorists; Syrian Government-backed terrorists battling the Lebanese army; Hamas and Fatah taking time out from attacking Israel by killing each other, as well as innocent bystanders, in Gaza; blood-curdling threats from Iran against Britain, America and Israel, or hostage-taking of naval personnel to ridicule Britain; and last but not least, the ongoing repression of their own populations by Muslim governments across the Middle East and northern Africa.

While each conflict is unique and rooted in its own history, the common thread is obvious. It is the culmination of a century's worth of failed political systems that were driven by morally bankrupt ideologies, led by cruel dictators, or both. In the 1930s, German-style fascism appealed to Arabs in Palestine and Egypt, to the extent that the Palestinian leader Hajj Amin al-Husseini formed an alliance with Hitler and actively promoted the Holocaust with the aim of killing the Jews in the entire Arab world. Soviet-style communism had sympathetic governments in Afghanistan, Algeria and Yemen. Ba'athism took hold in Syria and Iraq. The secular Egyptian dictator Gamal Abdel Nasser promised a new pan-Arabism that would do away with colonial borders that divided the 'Arab nation'. Then there is the more pragmatic authoritarianism that survives in the petrol-monarchies in the Gulf. Unlike fascism or communism, the appeal of Islam is that it has local roots. Huge oil profits filter throughout the Muslim world, allowing Islamic leaders and terrorists to act on their rhetoric. In today's world, militias can easily acquire everything from shoulder-held anti-aircraft missiles to rocket-propelled grenades. With such weapons, and on their own turf, the terrorists can neutralize western jets and tanks. They are encouraged by the hesitation of the West, and its fears over terrorism or oil supplies and prices. They have also waged a brilliant propaganda war, adopting the role of victims of western 'imperialism' and 'racism'.[33]

In his own inimitable fashion, Victor Davis Hanson offered an assessment of why 'much of the region is so unhinged – and it's not because of our policy in Palestine or our efforts in Afghanistan and Iraq':

Introduction: Events in their Context

First, thanks to western inventions and Chinese manufactured goods, Middle Easterners can now access the non-Muslim world cheaply and vicariously. To millions of Muslims, the planet appears – on the internet, DVDs and satellite television – to be growing rich as most of their world stays poor. Second, the Middle East either will not or cannot make the changes necessary to catch up with what they see in the rest of the world. Tribalism – loyalty only to kin rather than to society at large – impedes merit and thus progress. So does gender apartheid. Religious fundamentalism translates into rote prayers in madrassas while those outside the Middle East master science and engineering. Without a transparent capitalist system – antithetical to both shari'a and state-run economies – initiative is never rewarded. Corruption is. Meanwhile, mere discussion in much of the region of what is wrong can mean execution by a militia, government thug or religious vigilante.

It is not surprising that they resort to the monotonous scapegoating of America or Israel and retreat into fundamentalist extremism. Almost daily, the killing of westerners is justified because of a cartoon, a papal paragraph or, most recently, a British knighthood awarded to novelist Salman Rushdie. The terrorism of Bin Laden, Hamas, Hizbollah and the Taleban is as much about nihilist rage as it is about blackmailing western governments to grant concessions. Meanwhile, millions of others simply flee the mess, immigrating to either Europe or the US. These reactions to failure often lead to circumstances that can defy logic. The poor terrorists of Arafat's old party, Fatah, expect sympathy for having been out-terrorized by Hamas, and demand more western aid to compensate for what has been squandered or stolen. Muslims flock to Europe to enjoy a level of freedom and opportunity long denied at home, and promptly castigate their adopted continent as decadent. They then clamour for shari'a law, importing with them the intolerance that they escaped and simultaneously negating the rationale behind their migration.[34]

In a major foreign policy speech to the Los Angeles World Affairs Council in August 2006, Tony Blair highlighted several pertinent points about the nature of the war facing the West:

> This is war, but of a completely unconventional kind. 9/11 in the US, 7/7 in the UK, 11/3 in Madrid, the countless terrorist

attacks in countries as disparate as Indonesia or Algeria, what is now happening in Afghanistan and in Indonesia, the continuing conflict in Lebanon and Palestine, it is all part of the same thing. What are the values that govern the future of the world? Are they those of tolerance, freedom, respect for difference and diversity or those of reaction, division and hatred? ... We are fighting a war, but not just against terrorism but about how the world should govern itself in the early twenty-first century, about global values ... Ever since September 11th, the US has embarked on a policy of intervention in order to protect its and our future security. Hence Afghanistan. Hence Iraq. Hence the broader Middle East initiative in support of moves towards democracy in the Arab world ... Of course the fanatics, attached to a completely wrong and reactionary view of Islam, had been engaging in terrorism for years before September 11th. In Chechnya, in India and Pakistan, in Algeria, in many other Muslim countries, atrocities were occurring. But we did not feel the impact directly ... We rather inclined to the view that where there was terrorism, perhaps it was partly the fault of the governments of the countries concerned. We were in error. In fact, these acts of terrorism were not isolated incidents. They were part of a growing movement ... It has an ideology, a world-view, it has deep convictions and the determination of the fanatic. It resembles in many ways early revolutionary communism.[35]

Blair emphasized that the fanatics ran the risk that fellow Muslims would reject their fanaticism if they merely fought against other Muslims (as in Algeria, where it is estimated that 250,000 were slaughtered):

They realized they had to create a completely different battle in Muslim minds: Muslim versus Western. This is what September 11th did. Still now, I am amazed at how many people will say, in effect, there is increased terrorism today because we invaded Afghanistan and Iraq. They seem to forget entirely that September 11th predated either. The West didn't attack this movement. We were attacked. Until then we had largely ignored it.[36]

Australia's Foreign Minister Alexander Downer warned European politicians that anti-American feeling in Europe is playing into the hands of al-Qa'ida, and criticism of America's conduct in Iraq could inadvertently provide an incentive for terrorist attacks. 'People in the West, and not only in Europe, blame America for a suicide bomber in a market in Baghdad', he said. 'That only encourages more horrific behaviour. Every time there is an atrocity committed, it is implicitly America's fault, so why not commit some more atrocities and put even more pressure on America?' Downer added: 'The al-Qa'ida leadership has said on many occasions that more than 50 per cent of the battle is a battle in the media. The more you can get media denigration of America, the more that the war against terrorism is seen to be an indictment of America, the better for those who started this war.' He added that populist attacks on Washington 'might play well in some political constituencies in Europe, but that's no excuse'.[37]

The Middle East Media Research Institute (MEMRI) reported that an Islamist website instructs mujahideen in using popular US web forums to foster anti-war sentiment among Americans. The 'media jihadis' have increased their efforts to expose as broad a western audience as possible to their jihad films, which purport to document the growing success of the mujahideen in Iraq and Afghanistan. They have posted jihad films on video-sharing websites such as YouTube, hoping that such films will tip public opinion in the West against the war. A member of the al-Muhajirun website with the username al-Wathiq Billah (meaning, significantly, 'The one who puts his trust in Allah'), instructed mujahideen in how to infiltrate popular American forums and to use them to distribute jihad films and spread disinformation about the war. The following are excerpts:

> Raiding American forums is among the most important means of obtaining victory in the fierce media war ... and of influencing the views of the weak-minded American ... Obviously, you should post your contribution ... as an American ... You should invent stories about American soldiers you have [allegedly] personally known ... who were drafted to Iraq and then committed suicide while in service by hanging or shooting themselves ... [Use any story] which will break their spirits, oh

> brave fighter for the sake of God ... Your concern should
> [only] be introducing topics which ... will cause [them to feel]
> frustration and anger towards their government ..., which will
> ... render them hostile to Bush ... and his Republican Party.[38]

Just as Islam attracts some alienated Muslim youth in the West as an oppositional ideology more than for its religious value, the leftists in Europe defend Islam because it has replaced Marxism as the only belief system which unsettles the existing social equilibrium. Britain's Stop the War coalition, which has organized over a dozen nationwide protests and hundreds of smaller events, was largely forged by two small, intensely committed bodies – the far-left Socialist Workers Party (SWP) and the Muslim Association of Britain, which is close to the Muslim Brotherhood. These tiny groups have coordinated street protests by up to a million people. But in many other places, too, Muslim grievance has been attached to a broader anti-capitalist or anti-globalist movement whose leitmotif is loathing of the Bush administration. An Italian Marxist involved in the 'Social Forum' movement, which organizes groups opposed to the existing world order, puts it this way: Almost everybody in the movement shares the belief that 'capitalism and militarism' (both epitomized by America) are the main challenges to human welfare. If political Islam can blunt American triumphalism, then so much the better – even from the viewpoint of those who would never dream of donning a headscarf or upsetting a minority.

The argument of a new school of leftists is that parts of the international left are now making as colossal a mistake as they did over Soviet or Chinese communism. They have let hatred of America and capitalism blind them to darker forces. Two sorts of people have stressed this point: European ex-Marxists, embarrassed by their errors over Stalin, and dissident ex-Muslims from the Islamic world who have fled to the West and fear their hosts will 'go soft' on their persecutors. Norman Geras, a Manchester-based political scientist who still calls himself, with qualifications, a Marxist, said that by studying the rise of Nazi Germany, he realized both the power and the limits of Marxist ideas: they help explain the economic forces that brought Hitler to power, but cannot explain certain 'egregious forms of evil' – such as the regime of Saddam

Hussein, whose downfall was an absolute imperative. Nick Cohen, a peppery writer for Britain's centre-left media, has listed the sins of the Islamic–leftist compact. Political Islam, he says, is not just a disaster for many causes (like feminism and gay rights) that the left cherishes; it also overturns the Enlightenment idea that diversity of opinion is desirable. Paul Berman, a professor at New York University, is one of several Americans of liberal background who have joined the British denunciation of Islamofascism. He says the left's refusal to take sides in the internal battles of Muslim countries (between dissidents and oppressors) reflects an 'angelic blindness' which mistakes violent reactionaries for charming exotica.[39]

Nick Cohen published a book about the latest moral disorder afflicting his fellow-leftists, wrote Martin Ivens in the *Sunday Times*. Fashionable anti-Americanism, and hatred of the Bush administration and Tony Blair, had so warped opponents of the war in Iraq, Cohen argued, that they want the Islamic terrorists to win. In *What's Left? How Liberals Lost Their Way*, Cohen asked, 'Why do leftist papers publish defences of suicide bombers?' and answered that the failure of socialism freed them to go along with any movement, however far right it may be, 'as long as it is against the status quo and America'. The triumph of the liberal-left social agenda in the West (human rights, gay rights, women's emancipation) left a gap. But these causes are, apparently, not for export. Supporting these values outside the West was considered the equivalent of 'moral imperialism'.

Although Cohen is not Jewish, his surname seems to be enough to damn him in some quarters. Since he wonders why the left doesn't devote anything like the same attention to, say, Robert Mugabe's Zimbabwe as Israel, he is presented in some quarters as a stooge of the American neo-cons. Cohen supported the war in Iraq because he loathed Saddam Hussein's fascist regime. He told his interviewer: 'The idea that liberals would want Iraq to fail to give Bush and Blair bloody noses appals me. They just don't care about the consequences for the people.' Cohen's diagnosis of the left-wing pathology is brutal. 'This is rage without a programme. Also, don't forget the element of fear – one response when confronted by psychopaths is that you hope they can be appeased.' He also chides the 'parochialism' of the liberal left. 'It is difficult to defend your country against foreign threats if you are a critic of the status quo.'[40]

When one examines the spread of Islam into Europe one must take stock of all these considerations. It is not enough to account for Muslim immigration into the Old Continent and its transformation at their hands, but one must also go into the dialectic between European counter-measures after the major terrorist acts and the Muslim worldview which regards such defensive measures as aggression, persecution, and racism against the ever-docile and always 'poor', helpless, innocent and 'victimized' Muslim who had just come to seek work. When Europeans idolize multiculturalism as a way to 'enrich' their culture and celebrate the fake 'difference' between moderate Islam of the mainstream and the violent few, the Muslims regard that as an attempt to dilute Islam in order to dominate and eliminate it. Only their unrestricted and violent activity against local Jews in Europe, and recognition of their own mores and norms, such as wearing the veil, forcing marriage on their women or pursuing 'honour killings', would be regarded as fair and acceptable behaviour of the host countries towards them. In other words, not satisfied with full equality of opportunity, freedom of speech and of religious observance, Muslims demand special privileges for themselves, like the prerogative to train terrorists or incite violence against fellow-citizens, because in their skewed view of democratic society, only too much freedom and *laissez-faire,* even at the detriment of the host state and society, is enough freedom for them. When they burn down a Jewish synagogue in Berlin or Paris, they expect their adopted countries to accept that as a matter of course, and they are often aided in that belief by the local extreme-left or extreme-right, or church organizations that boost Muslim demands due to their common anti-Semitism or in order to appear as 'progressive' multiculturalists.

And then one has to consider not only the direct victims of terrorism, those who perished instantly, but those left behind, either wounded or maimed, or otherwise traumatized by the horror he or she watched or was affected by. There is no denying that pacific Muslims who shun violence and terror are also suffering from the adverse effects that terrorism has on their reputation, on their collective consciousness, on the circumspect conduct of their neighbours, colleagues and passers-by when they are identified as Muslims. But their justified grievances have to be directed to their co-religionists who by their behaviour have soiled the Muslim collective. What of individuals of the host cultures of Europe, who see their hospitality and liberal welcome of asylum seekers rewarded by terrorism? George Psaradakis, 50, the driver of the bus blown apart by one of the London bombs on 7/7, spoke a year later about the devastating effect on his life and how he has been left permanently traumatized by the outrage. He saw some horrific sights as people lay on the road after being caught up in the blast, some obviously dead. 'Another bomb exploded inside me – it was carnage, too gruesome to go into detail. It was death – I could feel it, I could smell it. Most of the people I saw were young, they had been so full of life. I felt devastated because they had been under my care.'[41]

All these facets of Muslim terrorism, which require not only objective reporting of what they are, and also an attempt to comprehend the mechanics, temptations, motivations and aspirations evinced by the terrorists themselves, have to be supplemented by the role the media play in the diffusion of this comprehension among the masses. The media, in spite of the paradox involved, create immediacy but also inaccuracy inasmuch as reports sometimes prove premature and have to be reversed or corrected. Very often a stand is taken by certain media towards terrorism, either leaning towards 'understanding' the terrorists, at times censuring them, often without preserving the equilibrium between report and comment, fact and emotion, sympathy and criticism, manipulation and straightforward information, supplying the terrorists with what Margaret Thatcher had termed the 'oxygen of publicity', or choking them by the lack thereof. Ideological writing is resorted to, that patronizingly relies on a political agenda in order to 'educate' and influence readers, instead of selfless and honest striving to inform them; in short, this is the difference between good journalism and journalistic spins. Are the media actors on the scene or merely a mirror of events? Consider the following excerpt from a leading article in a major British medium:

> Strangely, the story didn't appear on the BBC News website last night. But apparently the internet and digital TV have supplanted what is now called the 'mainstream media' to the extent that BBC1 has lost a million viewers in the past year. Technology is responsible for a dual phenomenon. We are

seeing a mass opening up as people are able to contribute directly to the reporting and discussion of news, whether through the internet or (as on July 7 last year) using camera and video-phones. But we are also seeing a closing down. The proliferation of news outlets means we increasingly receive narrow-casting rather than broadcasting: news tailored not for everyone, but for us and people like us. These developments are entwined – we cannot have the one without the other. But they do make the idea of a monolithic state broadcaster seem sadly twentieth century.[42]

As an organization which operates on a compulsory licence fee from the taxpayer, it is worth focusing on the BBC as an example of the invidious media bias. A claim can be made that it is the compulsory nature of the fee that facilitated the BBC's departure from the integrity and impartiality which should inform its output. Antony Jay, a BBC employee during the 1950s and 1960s, believes the public's attitude to the BBC has changed with the BBC's own report on impartiality that effectively admitted to an institutional 'liberal' bias among programme makers. There is growing general agreement that the culture of the BBC is the culture of the 'chattering classes', which is found also in *The Guardian*, Channel 4, the Church of England, academia and showbusiness. Jay himself was part of this media liberal consensus: 'We were anti-industry, anti-capitalism, anti-advertising, anti-selling, anti-profit, anti-patriotism, anti-monarchy, anti-empire, anti-police, anti-armed forces, anti-bomb, anti-authority. Almost anything that made the world a freer, safer and more prosperous place – you name it, we were anti it.' Noting that he was 9 years old when the Second World War broke out, Jay offered a description of life during the 1940s: 'I spent my early years in a country where every citizen had to carry identification papers. All the newspapers were censored, as were all letters abroad; general elections had been abolished: it was a one-party state. Yes, that was Britain – Britain from 1939 to 1945.'[43]

Jay asserts that since 1963 the country's institutions have been the villains of the media liberals – the police, armed services, courts, political parties and multinational corporations. This hostility to institutions is not shared by the majority of the electorate. The BBC's own 2007 report on impartiality found that 57 per cent of poll respondents said that 'broadcasters often fail to reflect the views of people like me'. Crucially, Jay wrote that members of a small and close-knit 'metropolitan media arts graduate' tribe met at work and socially, reinforcing their uniformity of views.

> We saw ourselves as part of the intellectual elite, full of ideas about how the country should be run. Being naive in the way institutions actually work, we were convinced that Britain's problems were the result of the stupidity of the people in charge of the country. This ignorance of the realities of government and management enabled us to occupy the moral high ground. We saw ourselves as clever people in a stupid world, upright people in a corrupt world, compassionate people in a brutal world, libertarian people in an authoritarian world.[44]

The BBC itself admitted that it is dominated by trendy, left-leaning liberals who are biased against Christianity and in favour of multiculturalism. A leaked account of an 'impartiality summit' called by then-BBC chairman Michael Grade, revealed that executives would let the Bible be thrown into a dustbin on a TV comedy show, but not the Qur'an, and that they would broadcast an interview with Bin Laden if given the opportunity. Further, it disclosed that the BBC wants Muslim women newsreaders to be allowed to wear veils when on air. In contrast, there was criticism of TV newsreader Fiona Bruce, who had worn a necklace with a cross. BBC executives also admitted the corporation is dominated by homosexuals and people from ethnic minorities and is anti-American and anti-countryside. One veteran BBC executive said: 'There was widespread acknowledgement that we may have gone too far in the direction of political correctness. Unfortunately, much of it is so deeply embedded in the BBC's culture, that it is very hard to change it.' Washington correspondent Justin Webb said that the BBC is so biased against America that deputy director general Mark Byford had secretly agreed to help him to 'correct' it in his reports. Webb added that the BBC treated America with scorn and derision and gave it 'no moral weight'. Former BBC business editor Jeff Randall said he complained to a 'very senior news executive', about the BBC's pro-multicultural stance but was given the reply: 'The BBC is not neutral in multiculturalism: it believes in it and it promotes it.' Randall said he once wore Union Jack cufflinks to work but was rebuked with: 'You can't do that, that's like the National Front!'[45]

Against this background, it is easy to see why the BBC feels entitled to spend thousands of pounds of licence payers' money to block the release of a report which is believed to be highly critical of its Middle East coverage. The corporation is mounting a High Court action to prevent the release of the *Balen Report* under the Freedom of Information Act, despite the fact that BBC reporters often use the Act to pursue their journalism. The action has increased suspicions that the report, which is believed to run to 20,000 words, includes evidence of anti-Israeli bias in news programming. The document was compiled by Malcolm Balen, a senior editorial adviser, in 2004.[46]

The Archbishop of Algeria was quoted by *The New York Times* as remarking that when satellite dishes first appeared in Algeria, they were typically positioned to receive French broadcasts. Now the majority receive programming from the Persian Gulf. 'If you watch western television, you live in one universe, and if you watch Middle Eastern television, you live in another altogether.' The Middle Eastern broadcasts depicted the West in a negative light. To address this problem, the US established its own Arabic-language satellite television station, al-Hurra ('The Independent') in 2004. But stations like al-Jazeera and al-Arabiyya, based in the Gulf states, dominate the region. The BBC World Service plans to start an Arabic television service, building on the huge audience it has had for its radio broadcasting for over sixty years. But the World Service in English, though dominated by a 'liberal' agenda, is one thing, and the World Service in Arabic is another entirely. If the BBC's Arabic TV programmes resemble its radio programmes, then they will be just as anti-western as anything that comes out of the Gulf. The Arabic service not only shields Arab leaders from criticism but avoids topics they might find embarrassing: human rights, the role of military and security forces, corruption, discrimination against minorities, censorship, poverty and unemployment. By contrast, the words and deeds of western leaders, particularly the American President and the British Prime Minister, are subject to minute analysis, generally on the assumption that behind them lies a hidden and disreputable agenda. When the British arrested two dozen people alleged to have been plotting to blow up airlines crossing the Atlantic, a BBC presenter centred a discussion on the theory that these arrests had taken place because Blair, embarrassed by opposition to Britain's role in the conflict between Hizbollah and Israel, wanted to distract the public while at the same time associating Muslims with terrorism. The British taxpayer funds these broadcasts, many of which are produced in Cairo rather than in London.[47]

In August 2007, the BBC dropped plans to screen a fictional terrorist attack by Muslim extremists in the hospital drama 'Casualty'. Senior executives had discussed the plotline but were overruled by the corporation's editorial guidelines department amid fears it would cause offence. The opening episode will now focus on the bloody aftermath of an explosion caused by animal rights extremists. Yet a BBC spokesman dismissed as 'ludicrous' suggestions that the corporation was too frightened to deal with an Islamic plotline. Lord Tebbit, the former Conservative Party chairman whose wife was paralysed by an IRA terrorist attack in Brighton in 1984, condemned the climb-down. 'People were perfectly free during the violence in Northern Ireland to produce dramas about terrorism for which presumably they might have been accused of stereotyping IRA terrorists or even suggesting that all Catholics were terrorists. What is the difference here?'[48] On the same day, it was reported that the BBC was forced to remove statements from its website referring to Jesus as a 'bastard' after receiving complaints from religious groups. Critics claimed the remarks remained on BBC Radio Five Live's online message board for several weeks before the corporation took them down. Critics also said anti-Semitic remarks were allowed to stay on the message board for more than a month. One posting said: 'Zionism is a racist ideology where Jews are given supremacy over all other races and faiths.' The BBC said the Jesus remarks were on the site for 'a matter of days not weeks', and the statement on Zionism did not merit removal. Offensive remarks are usually removed within minutes by moderators after complaints.[49] Anti-Muslim comments vanish instantly.

The BBC's coverage of Islamic affairs has been unsatisfactory for many years. In its international and domestic news reporting, the corporation has consistently come across as naive and partial, rather than sensitive and unbiased. Its reporting of Israel and Palestine, in particular, tends to underplay the hate-filled Islamic ideology that inspires Hamas and other factions. In its coverage of

British Muslims, it has presented Islam on its own terms, as if only Muslims had the authority to describe their religion; and it has only scratched the surface of one of one of the biggest newsworthy stories: the penetration of Muslim youth by Islamic supremacist groups. According to *The Daily Telegraph*, the corporation has even helped this to happen by giving a platform to Islamic 'moderates' who belong to hard-line sects. It has been left to Channel 4 to conduct undercover investigations in radical mosques and to commission an opinion poll revealing that almost a quarter of British Muslims believe that the government helped stage 7/7. *The Daily Telegraph* concluded:

> We live in a world in which, although the vast majority of Muslims are not terrorists, the vast majority of terrorists are Muslim. Younger BBC programme-makers are aware of this awkward fact; the problem lies with an older generation of executives stuck in a PC timewarp. *Casualty* is fiction, but that is no excuse for constructing a politically acceptable parallel universe. To ban a storyline featuring Islamic terrorists not only misrepresents reality; it is also an insult to licence-payers whose family, friends or colleagues were blown to pieces on July 7 – and not by animal rights activists.[50]

In Britain, Abu Hamza may be behind bars, and Omar Bakri Mohammed in exile, but the 'preachers of hate' continue to ply their trade. Video footage depicted Muslim preachers exhorting followers to prepare for jihad, to hit girls for not wearing the hijab, and to create a 'state within a state'. Many of the preachers are linked to the Wahhabi strain of Islam practised in Saudi Arabia, which funds a number of Britain's leading Islamic institutions. Preachers in some mosques which are unthinkingly labelled as 'moderate' urged followers to reject British laws in favour of shari'a. Mosque leaders claimed they were unaware such views were being disseminated. At the Sparkbrook mosque, run by UK Islamic Mission, an organization that maintains forty-five mosques in Britain and which Blair has said 'is extremely valued by the government for its multifaith and multicultural activities', a preacher was captured on film praising the Taleban. In response to the news that a British Muslim soldier was killed fighting the Taleban, the speaker declared: 'The hero of Islam is the one who separated his head from his shoulders.' Another preacher said Muslims cannot accept the rule of non-Muslims. 'You cannot accept the rule of the kafir', declared Dr Ijaz Mian. 'We have to rule ourselves and we have to rule the others.' 'Kufr' is a derogatory term for non-Muslims meaning 'blasphemy', and together with 'kafir' (blasphemer, singular) and 'kuffar' (blasphemers), recurs repeatedly in Muslim discourse. The year-long investigation also recorded a deputy headmaster of an Islamic high school in Birmingham telling a conference at the Sparkbrook mosque that he disagrees with using the word democracy. 'They should call it ... kuffrocracy, that's their plan.' The Darul Uloom school conveniently claimed it no longer employed the teacher. At the Islamic bookstore at Regent's Park Mosque in central London, DVDs of a preacher called Sheikh Yasin are sold, in which he accuses missionaries from the World Health Organization and Christian groups of putting the 'aids virus' in the medicine of African people. Another DVD on sale features Sheikh Feiz, a Saudi-trained preacher. Feiz says: 'Kafir is the worst word that can ever be written, a sign of infidelity, disbelief, filth, a sign of dirt.' A satellite broadcast from the Grand Mufti of Saudi Arabia, Sheikh Abdul Aziz al-Sheikh, beamed into the Green Lane mosque suggests that Muslim children should be hit if they don't pray: 'When he is 7, tell him to go and pray, and start hitting them when they are 10.' Another preacher is heard saying that if a girl 'doesn't wear hijab, we hit her'.[51]

Ghayasuddin Siddiqui, who heads the 'Muslim Parliament' in London, called for the imams and mosque leaders filmed by Channel 4 to be questioned about extremism. He also expressed concern about a Muslim primary school teacher who was secretly filmed while he delivered a diatribe against Jews, Christians and 'filthy non-Muslim doctors'. Murtaza Khan, an Islamic Studies teacher at al-Noor Muslim primary school in Ilford, Essex, said: 'For how long do we have to see our mothers, sisters and daughters having to uncover themselves before these filthy non-Muslim doctors? We should have a sense of shame.' A CD of Khan's speeches is on sale at a mosque in London. The school confirmed that it was investigating the remarks but said: 'We have always found him to be a dedicated and committed teacher throughout his employment. He has never expressed religiously or racially intolerant views whilst teaching at al-Noor.'[52] Siddiqui himself has not always been reliable in confronting radicalization. He once claimed the government's work since 7/7 to forge links with Muslim youth had been undermined by its own foreign policy, elaborating: 'Many in the British Muslim community are convinced that the war on terror is a war against Islam and Muslims.' Not for the first time, nor will it be the last, Muslim leaders have enunciated the right message to the British public, while reserving their incitement for Muslim audiences in private.[53]

The television investigation for the Channel 4 'Dispatches' programme, 'Undercover Mosque', was as significant for its contents as for the way it was ignored by the political establishment and media. In *The Observer*, Henry Porter wondered what the reaction would have been if an Anglican clergyman had made similar statements. When they are made in British mosques and recorded by a secret camera, there is no reaction. Porter asserts that the standards that most British institutions live by simply do not apply to the missionaries of Saudi fundamentalism who, as demonstrated beyond doubt by this documentary, are attempting to poison relations between Muslims, Christians and Jews in Britain and to establish what amounts to a separate community under shari'a law. This is akin to saying that so little is expected of the ignorant fundamentalists that they are unworthy of being held to account. Their outrageous behaviour has put them beyond the pale of civilized society. Normal society is at a loss as to how to deal with them, and finds it easier to disregard them by leaving them to their parallel existence, however primitive they are and oppressive to their women. While the programme was not a portrait of the whole of Muslim Britain, it represents a significant part which cannot be ignored. The loathing and violence of the language used by these preachers about the 'kuffar', namely the rest of British society, has become a dangerous habit and a very great threat. Porter rightly fears the growth of an alternative account of reality among radicalized youth, a parallel truth almost uncontested within British Muslim society.[54]

An 'alternative account of reality' is precisely what has made conflicts involving Muslims elsewhere in the world so intractable. Whether in Kashmir or Kosovo, 'Palestine' or Thailand, the historical narrative has been rewritten and accepted as gospel. Whenever their 'new history' remains unchallenged by a confrontation-averse West, thanks to relentless bullying and threats and acts of terrorism, a new

Introduction: Events in their Context 41

layer of outrageous 'facts' is added to the narrative until ignorance of history becomes so widespread that it is well-nigh impossible to recover the truth. No lie is too egregious for the fertile Muslim mind, to the extent that it is now the 'received wisdom' that all the prophets of the Old and New Testaments have been posthumously declared to be Muslim. The inconvenient fact that Islam appeared on the scene some 600 years after Jesus Christ, by which time both Testaments had existed for many centuries, is completely overlooked.

Henry Porter comments on the 'other truth' proffered by Muslims in relation to their widespread denials that their co-religionists were responsible for 9/11, 7/7 or the Madrid bombings, noting that 'there is no limit to the paranoia and fantasy to be found on Islamist websites'. If these denials are unchallenged each and every time they are invoked, experience demonstrates that they will sooner or later become 'established facts'. Porter believes that 'a reflexive sense of persecution is beginning to disable people's reason in these communities', but it would be more accurate to point out that 'reason' has been jettisoned a long time ago in favour of the more politically productive practice of *taqqiya* (dissimulation or deception to advance Islam). It is very revealing that Muslims have a word dedicated to deceiving non-Muslims in their vocabulary. Porter highlights the findings of the Arab Human Development Report, written by Arabs and published under UN auspices in 2002, portraying societies crippled by the lack of political freedom and knowledge. As Pervez Hoodbhoy, a Muslim physicist, commented: 'High-quality, mind-opening education is virtually non-existent. Half of Arab women cannot read or write. The entire Arab world translates about 330 books annually, one fifth the number that Greece translates ... in the thousand years since the reign of Caliph al-Ma'mun, the Arabs have translated as many books as Spain does in just one year.' These facts offer a sad reflection of the closing of the Arab mind.[55]

The Crown Prosecution Service (CPS) and the West Midlands Police took the bizarre decision to complain about the programme to the television regulator, Ofcom. Writing in *The Daily Telegraph*, Charles Moore asked: 'Why is it the business of the CPS or the police to make complaints, which are nothing to do with the law, about what appears on television? Aren't they supposed to be fighting crime, not acting as television critics?' The material for the programme was collected from British mosques, mainly in Birmingham. It showed film, DVDs and internet messages from Islamist sermons and speeches. One preacher says that all Jews will be killed at the end of time, and makes a snorting noise as if imitating a pig. One pronounces that woman is 'deficient' and that homosexual men should be 'thrown off the mountain' and another that children should offer themselves for Islamic martyrdom. The CPS and the West Midlands Police decided that charges for crimes of racial hatred could not be brought against the preachers and their comments had been 'broadcast out of context'. They also announced that they had investigated the programme itself for stirring up racial hatred – but decided not to press charges. They did not acknowledge that the organizations and individuals depicted in 'Undercover Mosque' were given a right of reply. The preachers shown in the programme have not claimed that they did not say the words attributed to them, but complain about the 'context'. Charles Moore examined the issue of 'context':

> The context is, according to many of the preachers, that they are talking not about Britain now, but about the Islamic state that they seek. They are not, therefore, they say, urging the breaking of existing laws ... But even if we accept that it is true, is it reassuring? The Islamic state envisaged by most of those featured is not an ideal, imaginary kingdom of heaven where the lion shall lie down with the lamb. It is, as one of the speakers explains, a concept for the here and now, a concept of 'political dominance'. According to Sayyid Mawdudi, one of the ideological fathers of all this stuff, Islam is an 'international revolutionary party'. There are branches of this ideology in many countries, of which Hamas is the best known. They hold that all states – including Muslim ones – which do not implement shari'a law are illegitimate.

On the programme, Sheikh Hasan, from 'a major mosque in east London', explains how this Islamic state would operate. There would be 'the chopping off the hands of the thieves', 'flogging of the drunkards', 'jihad against the non-Muslims'. Another speaker, trained in Riyadh and operating from Derby, rejects the existing order – 'King, Queen, House of Commons ... you have to dismantle it' and rejoices in the day when, in Britain, 'every woman will be covered'. A fellow in the Green Lane mosque in Birmingham explains the punishment coming to the apostate when right rule is established: 'Kill him in the Islamic state.' Crucifixion will be an approved method of death, he adds.

> Similarly, the line about killing all the Jews at the end of the world is not invented by the preacher who says it, though the smirk and the noise of the pig are all his own. The words come from one of the *hadith*, the traditionally accepted records of Muhammad additional to the Qur'an: 'Allah's apostle said, The hour will not be established until you fight with the Jews, and the stone behind which a Jew will be hiding will say, "Oh Muslim! There is a Jew hiding behind me, so kill him."' Does that context make you feel better?

Moore concludes:

> What security agencies call 'thematic analyses' show that, at present, the problems of Islamist extremism are particularly acute, especially in prisons and universities, in the West Midlands area. Yet the West Midlands police and the Crown Prosecution Service decide that the target of their wrath should be not people who want to undermine this country, but some journalists who want to expose them. Are they fit to protect us?[56]

Paul Goodman, the shadow community cohesion minister, wrote to Jack Straw, the Justice Secretary, saying the decision caused 'widespread concern' and warned that it could encourage extremists:

> This decision raises serious questions about media freedom in Britain, and about whether public authorities tasked with upholding the rule of law are now, as a matter of policy, giving special assistance to those who seek to undermine the rule of law, and the pluralist, liberal, democratic culture which both underpins it and guarantees community cohesion ... It's hard to avoid the conclusion that this is a politically motivated referral, driven by the mistaken belief that the best

means of dealing with separatist extremists is to appease them.[57]

People do not simply read or view or listen to the media but respond to them, and their opinions must be heeded lest the medium lose its constituency. A case in point was the anniversary of the London bombings when bereaved relatives and survivors reacted angrily after a video of one of the London bombers was broadcast. The statement of one of the Islamikaze terrorists, Shehzad Tanweer from Leeds, was released and was obviously designed to cause 'maximum hurt and distress' to the victims' families. Tanweer is seen in the video wearing a headscarf and jabbing his finger at the camera. 'What you have witnessed now is only the beginning of a string of attacks that will continue and become stronger', he says. The video, which also features a statement from Ayman al-Zawahiri, al-Qa'ida's second in command, was broadcast by al-Jazeera, which does not shrink from torturing families of the victims of terrorism. Tanweer's statement was cut with footage of unidentified people experimenting with explosives and images of an unidentified man circling points on a map of London. Scotland Yard subjected the video to the same scrutiny brought to bear on footage previously released on Mohammad Sidique Khan, Tanweer's fellow terrorist. Nader Mozakka, whose wife Behnaz died in the tube attack near King's Cross, said the video and its timing were 'abhorrent', adding: 'It is like a smack in the face – the timing especially.' Jacqui Putnam, 55, who was on the tube at Edgware Road, said the video seemed designed to taint the first anniversary of the attacks. 'Nothing is going to overshadow this anniversary', she said. 'We are just going to mourn the dead and show they are not going to intimidate us. Whatever they think the reaction will be, it won't be. These people don't understand us, which is why they thought they could frighten people off the Underground.' Like Khan, Tanweer used Islamic jihadi rhetoric on his video to intimidate viewers, knowing that it would be broadcast. He threatened more attacks until troops leave Afghanistan and Iraq and British support for the US and Israel ceases.[58]

When conscientious and knowledgeable journalists dare to confront and ask the right questions, interesting reporting results, which sheds light on events and informs the populace. BBC1's John Ware

Introduction: Events in their Context

presented a 'Panorama' programme where a robust confrontation with his Muslim panellists generated an immensely revealing and instructive trove of information. Iqbal Sacranie, then secretary general of the Muslim Council of Britain (MCB), said he did not believe in double standards, and if affiliates of the MCB, like Markazi Jamiat Ahl-e-Hadith (Central Association of the People of Hadith), want to say that the ways of Jews and Christians are 'based on sick or deviant views', it is merely part of the 'diversity that exists in the community'. This is the man who campaigned for the government to imprison people for seven years for inciting religious hatred. Yet at a time when Islamic fanatics were blowing up commuters, he was unconcerned by his own members holding people of other faiths in moral contempt. He also considered that death was 'too easy' for Salman Rushdie and that *The Satanic Verses* should be banned. According to him, 'We respect the freedom of expression but we expect freedom of expression to be exercised with responsibility.' Different standards apply, though, when the freedom is exercised by one of the MCB's affiliates. For Sacranie, Hamas leader Sheikh Yassin, the architect of the suicide-bomb campaign in Israel, was a 'renowned Islamic scholar'. Together with Inayat Bunglawala, MCB media secretary, Sacranie was recruited by the government to root out Islamic extremists. Only months before 9/11, Bunglawala was a propagandist for Bin Laden. Naturally, the MCB has accused the BBC of Islamophobia in screening Ware's 'Panorama' investigation into the ideology of supposedly moderate community leaders. Writing in *The Observer*, Andrew Anthony noted that:

> The last time I checked my dictionary, 'phobia' meant 'fear' and it would seem entirely rational, if I were a Jew or a Christian, to fear anyone who called me sick or deviant. No doubt, by Sir Iqbal's reckoning, such logic is Islamophobic rather than, say, an example of the diversity that exists in the community. But then the MCB's standard response to any form of criticism is to shout 'Islamophobia' at the top of its voice. It's to Ware's and the BBC's credit that they were not deterred by such shameless victim posturing. Sacranie has been at the forefront of many political campaigns of late and Ware gave him the kind of grilling that politicians routinely receive on 'Newsnight'. He responded with all the incoherence

and evasion of a man who has grown used to an easy ride from the media. One outraged 'liberal' critic has since accused Ware of McCarthyism. However, there's a much better word to describe what Ware did in 'Panorama'. It refers to the dogged process of finding out facts, scrutinizing inconsistencies and asking difficult questions. It's called journalism.[59]

Islamic organizations regularly accuse non-Muslims of 'Islamophobia' if they are criticized, while they freely criticize several aspects of western society. The individual freedoms and equality within the West are unknown in Muslim countries, which are under the grip of gender apartheid and repressive or corrupt rule. A culture which allows men to dictate women's lives with regard to their dress, behaviour and marriages, and subjects them to 'honour killing' and female genital mutilation, is not entitled to claim moral superiority. The death of a girl aged 12 in Egypt during the operation in June 2007 (which is performed to tame a girl's sexual desire and maintain her 'honour') sparked a public outcry and prompted the government to officially ban the procedure which is widespread throughout Egypt. Another death was uncovered when 13-year-old Karima Rahim Massoud's father applied for a death certificate in August, insisting his daughter had died from natural causes, reported the independent daily *al-Masry al-Youm*. Clerics insist the practice has nothing to do with Islam, but like the government, have done little to stop it. When performed without any anaesthetic, the mutilation can lead to death through shock from immense pain, excessive bleeding or infections. The first attempt at sexual intercourse will often be extremely painful. Depending on the extent of the mutilation, a second cut may be needed, sometimes performed by the husband with a knife.[60]

In one of his last articles before his untimely death, Tashbih Sayyed, a Pakistani émigré who moved to America, made a heartfelt plea to fellow-Muslims to appreciate the fear that terrorism has engendered in the West:

> As an American Muslim who grew up loving his religion, I do not feel any happiness, nor do I see anything positive in realizing that the world now fears Muslims ... I do not want to be feared; I want to be respected, accepted and loved. I am afraid

that Muslim extremism is pushing this world to a point from where its rescue will be almost impossible. I do not see anything good in the situation. The fact that the world fears Muslims speaks volumes about the image of my co-religionists.[61]

Israel's UN ambassador accused 'moderate' Muslim and Arab leaders of standing by in 'eerie silence' while Islamic extremists terrorize people around the world. 'We live in a world where when Christians kill Muslims, it's a Crusade. When Jews kill Muslims, it's a massacre. When Muslims kill Muslims, it's the weather channel. Nobody cares', Dan Gillerman told reporters at a press lunch in New York.[62] Islamic reformers are not immune to the charge of 'Islamophobia' either. Tawfik Hamid has preached a reformed interpretation of Islam to inculcate peace and respect for human rights, pointing out the violent teachings of Salafism and the imperative of westerners to protect themselves against it.[63] He said that it was perfectly rational to fear those who explode themselves to kill others. But this fear does not translate into general hostility, and the level of restraint displayed by westerners despite the Islamic atrocities to date has been remarkable. Daniel Pipes made an interesting additional observation: 'I have argued that terrorism generally obstructs the progress of radical Islam in the West by stimulating hostility to Muslims and bringing Islamic organizations under unwanted scrutiny. I must admit, however, that the evidence from Britain – where the July 7 terrorism inspired more self-recrimination than it did fury against jihad – suggests that violence can also strengthen lawful Islamism.'[64]

Tawfik Hamid is critical of western 'progressives' for actively and passively defending Islamic terrorists, frequently citing the need to examine 'root causes'. It is true that terrorism is only the manifestation of a disease and not the disease itself. But the root causes are quite different from what they think:

> As a former member of Jama'ah Islamiya, a group led by al-Qa'ida's second in command, Ayman al-Zawahiri, I know firsthand that the inhumane teaching in Islamist ideology can transform a young, benevolent mind into that of a terrorist. Without confronting the ideological roots of radical Islam it will be impossible to combat it. While there are many ideological 'rootlets' of Islamism, the main tap root has a name –

Salafi Islam, a violent, ultra-conservative version of the religion. It is vital to grasp that traditional and even mainstream Islamic teaching accepts and promotes violence. Shari'a, for example, allows apostates to be killed, permits beating women to discipline them, seeks to subjugate non-Muslims to Islam as *dhimmis* and justifies declaring war to do so. It exhorts good Muslims to exterminate the Jews before the 'end of days'. The near deafening silence of the Muslim majority against these barbaric practices is evidence enough that there is something fundamentally wrong. The grave predicament we face in the Islamic world is the virtual lack of approved, theologically rigorous interpretations of Islam that clearly challenge the abusive aspects of shari'a. Unlike Salafism, more liberal branches of Islam, such as Sufism,[65] typically do not provide the essential theological base to nullify the cruel proclamations of their Salafist counterparts.[66]

Tawfik believes western intellectuals, who claim to support human rights, have become obstacles to reforming Islam. Political correctness obstructs unambiguous criticism of shari'a's inhumanity. They find socio-economic or political excuses for Islamic terrorism such as poverty, colonialism, discrimination or the existence of Israel. He contends that there is no incentive for Muslims to demand reform when western 'progressives' pave the way for Islamic barbarity. The mantra of western politicians and scholars that Islamic extremism is caused by the Arab–Israeli conflict is irrational. The murder of over 150,000 innocent people in Algeria during the 1990s, their slaying of hundreds of Buddhists in Thailand, or the brutal violence between Sunni and Shi'a in Iraq, have nothing to do with the Arab-Israeli conflict. Tawfik continues:

Western feminists duly fight in their home countries for equal pay and opportunity, but seemingly ignore, under a façade of cultural relativism, that large numbers of women in the Islamic world live under threat of beating, execution and genital mutilation, or cannot vote, drive cars and dress as they please. The tendency of many westerners to restrict themselves to self-criticism further obstructs reformation in Islam. Americans demonstrate against the war in Iraq, yet decline to

Introduction: Events in their Context 49

demonstrate against the terrorists who kidnap innocent people and behead them. Similarly, after the Madrid train bombings, millions of Spanish citizens demonstrated against their separatist organization, ETA. But once the demonstrators realized that Muslims were behind the terror attacks they suspended the demonstrations. This example sent a message to radical Islamists to continue their violent methods.

Worst of all, perhaps, is the anti-Americanism among many westerners. It is a resentment so strong, so deep-seated, so rooted in personal identity, that it has led many, consciously or unconsciously, to morally support America's enemies. Progressives need to realize that radical Islam is based on an anti-liberal system. Well-meaning interfaith dialogues with Muslims have largely been fruitless. Participants must demand – but so far haven't – that Muslim organizations and scholars specifically and unambiguously denounce violent Salafi components in their mosques and in the media. Muslims who do not vocally oppose brutal shari'a decrees should not be considered 'moderates'.

He concludes:

When westerners make politically-correct excuses for Islamism, it actually endangers the lives of reformers and in many cases has the effect of suppressing their voices. Tolerance does not mean toleration of atrocities under the umbrella of relativism. It is time for all of us in the free world to face the reality of Salafi Islam or the reality of radical Islam will continue to face us.[67]

In the West, 'dialogue' is a process entered into in good faith to achieve consensus towards a common goal. But to Muslims, dialogue is *the* goal, since it serves to convince them that they qualify as equals of the West. They get the recognition that they crave, but without ceding any of their principles. Since they also believe that their religion is superior to any other (on the grounds that Islam constitutes the 'final revelation' and therefore supersedes any belief system that came before), they enter a dialogue in the full expectation that their western interlocutors will accede to their demands as of right. It does not occur to them that the West sometimes gives in patronizingly, when it is believed that the Muslims have reached the limits of their reasoning powers; at other times, the West may give way out of fear of further terrorism, but there is nothing noble or indeed lasting about gaining 'respect' on such terms. A variant of the enthusiasm for 'dialogue' is that for 'engagement'. The House of Commons' Foreign Affairs Committee published a report in August 2007 which concluded that Britain's refusal to speak to Hamas is counterproductive and jeopardizes 'peace'. 'Given the failure of the boycott [of Hamas] to deliver results, we recommend the government should urgently consider ways of engaging politically with moderate elements within Hamas', the all-party group of lawmakers said.[68] The very notion of 'moderate elements within Hamas' is an oxymoron since the goal of the destruction of Israel is inscribed into the Hamas covenant, but even the reasoning behind the parliamentarians' logic is flawed. Muslims in Europe and abroad have learned from experience that the short attention-span of their western interlocutors translates into impatience for results, and all they need do is maintain their intransigence and wait for the West to buckle. But if the boycott of Hamas did not persuade them to recognize Israel and renounce terrorism, why do the parliamentarians believe that 'engaging' with Hamas will? On the contrary, it will provide the precise vindication for its recalcitrance that Hamas seeks. Europeans would be better advised to heed the unambiguous words of those whom they seek to 'engage'. The former Palestinian Authority Foreign Minister Mahmoud al-Zahar of Hamas said that recognizing Israel contradicts the Qur'an.[69] Perhaps the parliamentarians believe that non-Muslims can persuade Muslims to override the Qur'an by 'engagement'.

Many books have been written, with specialized monographs of events, country by country, that analyse the future that awaits Europe; attempts to detect the motivations of the terrorists or the suffering of their victims; the anatomy of major attacks like September 11, Madrid 2004 or London's 7/7; the socio-economic dislocations of the immigrants which are supposedly at the base of the growing wave of terror which threatens to submerge all Europe; or else the self-satisfied delusions of western governments who elect to sink in their illusory 'multiculturalism' instead of taking stringent measures to rescue their societies and preserve their patrimonies. But all this remains theoretical and incomprehensible to many western minds which are not accustomed to thinking in apocalyptic terms, or to imagining the unimaginable, before the next disaster strikes. For this reason, this book will rather concretize the threats and exemplify the impending disaster, if nothing is done to stem them. Western governments, whose most cherished goal is re-election, still tend to act as firemen who rush to extinguish fires and provide immediate satisfaction to their prospective voters, while avoiding long-term solutions of fire-prevention that are most costly both financially and electorally. Unless national Churchills emerge, ready to sacrifice short-term interests and instil long-term blood-and-sweat struggles to face Muslim world terrorism, an assortment of petty and myopic Chamberlains will continue to govern our chanceries and lead us from bad to worse.

NOTES

1. 'Beyond the Vacuum', *al-Ahram Weekly*, 13–16 April 2006.
2. Ibn Warraq, 'The Genesis of a Myth', in Robert Spencer and Andrew G. Bostom, *The Myth of Islamic Tolerance: How Islamic Law Treats Non-Muslims* (Amherst, MA: Prometheus Books, 2005), p. 13.
3. Pierre Rehov interviewed several failed Islamikazes for his documentary 'Suicide Killers'.
4. Tom Tugend, 'Letting suicide bombers speak for themselves', *The Jerusalem Post*, 26 November 2006.
5. Steven Stalinsky, 'Hamas TV Prepares For Intifada III', *The New York Sun*, 12 April 2007, citing a MEMRI report.
6. Ken Herman, 'Bush insists on "Islamic fascists"', *The Atlanta Journal-Constitution*, 12 August 2006.
7. Orit Arfa, 'The Nexus', *The Jerusalem Post*, 12 July 2007.
8. Maurice Chittenden and Tom Baird, 'MPs don't know their Sunnis from Shi'ites', *Sunday Times*, 7 January 2007.
9. Roger Scruton, 'Islamofascism – Beware of a religion without irony', *Opinion Journal*, 20 August 2006.
10. This term, a combination of Islam and the Japanese kamikaze of WWII, is borrowed from the title of this author's book *Islamikaze: Manifestations of Islamic Martyrology* (London: Frank Cass, 2003).
11. 'Dispatches, Unholy War', Channel 4, 17 September 2007.
12. R. James Woolsey and Nina Shea, 'What About Muslim Moderates?', *Opinion Journal*, 15 July 2007.
13. Rhys Blakely, 'The week on the web', *The Times*, 1 September 2007.
14. Ethan Bueno de Mesquita, *Correlates of Public Support for Terrorism in the Muslim World* (St Louis, MO: Washington University in St Louis, 2006).
15. Patrick Poole, 'New Study: Political Islam Correlated to Support for Terrorism, *American Thinker*, 15 June 2007.
16. Bernard Lewis, 'Was Osama Right? Islamists always believed the U.S. was weak. Recent political trends won't change their view', *Opinion Journal*, 16 May 2007.
17. Daniel Pipes and Sharon Chadha, 'CAIR: Islamists Fooling the Establishment', *Middle East Quarterly*, Spring 2006.
18. Tim Shipman, 'US loner helps bin Laden to taunt Bush', *Sunday Telegraph*, 9 September

2007.
19. Murabitun have traditionally been considered as pioneers, who 'camp' on the frontiers of Islam, ready to fight and defend it and repulse its enemies. Hence *ribat* (the encampment), which constituted the nucleus for military, and then regular, cities of Islam. Rabat, Morocco, is one of them.
20. Mark McCallum, 'Muslim call to thwart capitalism', BBC News, 12 July 2003.
21. Gustavo de Arístegui (foreign affairs spokesman for Spain's conservative *Partido Popular*), *The Jihad in Spain: The Obsession to Reconquer al-Ándalus* (Madrid: Plaza Edición, 2005).
22. Ayman al-Zawahiri, 'Knights Under the Banner of the Prophet', US Army CGSC *Military Review*, 85, 1 (January 2005).
23. Aaron Hanscom, 'A Fatwa in Spain', *FrontPageMagazine.com*, 4 September 2006.
24. Ibid.
25. Ibid.
26. 'Sunni Sheikh Yusuf al-Qaradawi and Other Sheikhs Herald the Coming Conquest of Rome', al-Jazeera Television, 24 January 1999, cited by MEMRI, Special Dispatch Series, 447, 6 December 2002.
27. Abd Al-Bari Atwan, editor-in-chief of *al-Quds al-Arabi*: MEMRI TV Clip, 1506, 27 June 2007.
28. Michael Portillo, 'The bloody truth is that Israel's war is our war', *Sunday Times*, 23 July 2006.
29. James Woolsey, 'West Bank Terrorist State – The folly of Israeli Disengagement', *Opinion Journal*, 29 May 2006.
30. James Taranto, 'Best of the Web', *Opinion Journal*, 27 August 2007.
31. Andrew Hammond, 'Muslims Gaining Strength in United States – Cleric', *Reuters*, 5 August 2007.
32. Ibid.
33. Victor Davis Hanson, 'Why Radical Islam – and Why Now?', victorhanson.com, 26 December 2006.
34. Victor Davis Hanson, 'Endemic Madness', *The Washington Times*, 23 June 2007.
35. Tony Blair's Speech to the Los Angeles World Affairs Council, *The Times*, 1 August 2006.
36. Ibid.
37. David Blair, 'Anti-Americanism Helps Fuel Terror, Warns Australia', *The Daily Telegraph*, 9 February 2007.
38. 'Islamist Website Instructs Mujahideen in Using Popular US Web Forums to Foster Anti-War Sentiment among Americans', MEMRI, Special Dispatch Series, 1508, citing http://www.mohajroon.com/vb/showthread.php?t=48233, 20 March 2007.
39. 'Muslims and socialists – With friends like these', *The Economist*, 8 February 2007.
40. Martin Ivens meets Nick Cohen, 'You've lost it, Guardianistas', *Sunday Times*, 4 February 2007.
41. 'Bus Driver Speaks of his Mental Torment', *The Daily Telegraph*, 7 July 2006.
42. 'News from Everywhere', *The Daily Telegraph* Leader, 8 July 2006.
43. Antony Jay, 'Confessions of a BBC liberal', *Sunday Times*, 12 August 2007.
44. Ibid.
45. Simon Walters, 'We are Biased, Admit the Stars of BBC News', *Mail on Sunday*, 21 October 2006.
46. Chris Hastings and Beth Jones, 'BBC Mounts Court Fight to keep "Critical" Report Secret', *Sunday Telegraph*, 15 October 2006.
47. Frank H. Stewart, 'The Biased Broadcasting Corporation', *The New York Times*, 15 March 2007.
48. Nicole Martin, 'BBC drops Casualty Suicide Bomb Plotline', *The Daily Telegraph*, 20 August 2007.
49. Nicole Martin, 'Anger over Jesus quote left on BBC website', *The Daily Telegraph*, 20 August 2007.
50. 'Terror Victims are BBC Licence-payers too', *The Daily Telegraph* Leader, 20 August 2007.
51. Jamie Doward, 'Revealed: Preachers' Messages of Hate – Muslim Worshippers are

being Urged by Radical Clerics to Ignore British law', *The Observer*, 7 January 2007.
52. Tom Harper, 'TV "Preachers of Hate" Escape Police Action', *Sunday Telegraph*, 21 January 2007.
53. Jon Ungoed-Thomas, 'The "Hearts and Minds" Battle for British Muslims that Failed', *Sunday Times*, 13 August 2006.
54. Henry Porter, 'Tolerating Intolerance is still this Country's Besetting Sin', *The Observer*, 4 February 2007.
55. Ibid.
56. Charles Moore, 'Stirring up Racial Hatred – not the Medium', *The Daily Telegraph*, 11 August 2007.
57. 'Channel 4 TV Complaint "Politically Motivated"', *The Daily Telegraph*, 17 August 2007.
58. John Steele, 'Suicide bomber's video won't frighten us, say July 7 families', *The Daily Telegraph*, 7 July 2006.
59. Andrew Anthony, 'A Muslim at Bay: Panorama Programme, BBC1', *The Observer*, 28 August 2005.
60. 'Egyptian Girl Dies from Circumcision', *The Jerusalem Post*, citing *AP*, 12 August 2007.
61. Tashbih Sayyed, 'The Plea of a Genuine Muslim Moderate', *FrontPageMagazine.com*, 6 October 2006.
62. 'Gillerman accuses Moderate Muslims of Silence in Face of Islamic Terrorism', *Ynetnews*, citing *AP*, 22 May 2007.
63. Tawfik Hamid, 'How to End Islamophobia', *Opinion Journal*, 25 May 2007.
64. Daniel Pipes, 'Piggybacking on Terror in Britain', *The New York Sun*, 29 August 2006.
65. This is the mystic aspect of Islam, the word itself deriving from *suf* (wool), the rough woollen tunics worn by early ascetics. Sufism is predicated on the direct knowledge of God through experience and devotion rather than only through the shari'a precepts and their intellectual perception. As the inner dimension of Islam, Sufism complements the shari'a, which is the outer manifestation or 'clothing' of the faith. Sufis are divided into many orders, all derived from chains of masters, going back to the first companions of the prophet. They were instrumental in spreading the faith in remote areas of Islamdom.
66. Tawfik Hamid, 'The Trouble With Islam – Sadly, mainstream Muslim teaching accepts and promotes violence', *Opinion Journal*, 3 April 2007.
67. Ibid.
68. 'UK Panel tells Brown Boycott of Hamas is Counterproductive', *Haaretz*, citing *Reuters*, 13 August 2007.
69. 'Zahar: Qur'an Forbids Recognizing Israel', *The Jerusalem Post*, 20 April 2007.

CHAPTER ONE

The New Demographic Balance in Europe and its Consequences

The Muslim world, which consists of some fifty-seven Muslim-majority countries spanning the two continents of Asia and Africa, comprises about 1.3 billion believers (20 per cent of the total world population), making it after Christianity (33 per cent) the second-largest faith.[1] Islam spread since its inception, as did other faiths, by conquest, missionary work or expanding trade from the core areas of Islam in the Middle East to the Far East and the coasts of Africa. While it was extending its rule into others' territories it necessarily came into armed conflict with the prevailing cultures, including the Zoroastrians of Iran, the Berbers in North Africa, the Hindus of the Indian subcontinent or the Jews and the many Christian denominations of the Middle East and Europe. But since the arrest of the Muslim Ottomans at the gates of Vienna by the Europeans in the late seventeenth century, and the defeat of the Muslim Moghuls in India by the British in the nineteenth century, a reversal in the fortunes of Islam has unfolded. Thenceforth, Islamic might would be in the descent and European and western power on the ascent. As Islamdom contracted, independent Judaeo-Christian and Hindu nations emerged in the Balkans, in India and in the Levant, and the remaining Islamic world was colonized by Europe, until its re-emergence as independent nation-states after the world wars.

Colonization had its long-term effects nonetheless, inasmuch as modernization, both in thought and in effect, has set in and begun gnawing at the monopoly of Islam in those societies. As a result, the elites of those emerging new nations took to western culture and learned the languages, the mores, the civilizations, the institutions and the thought of their occupiers and remained tied to them long after their emancipation from their rule. So, after attaining independence, many formerly colonized populations moved to the metropolis of their previous occupiers and established Muslim communities there. Some of the newcomers were more at home in the ambience of their newly adopted cultures than in their original homes where they had become alienated. Others went in search of better economic opportunities, still others came for study periods or to seek political asylum, but then were reluctant to relinquish the freedom, prosperity and tranquillity of the West and return to the poverty, oppression and turmoil of their own countries. Compared to the immense populations of their original homelands, these were tiny trickles of privileged individuals or families who were intent on adapting to their new environments, to adopt their new countries and cultures as their own and to take the necessary steps to merge into the host cultures of their choice. Their limited numbers on the one hand, and their dispersion among the general population on the other, were inbuilt guarantees that in no time they would integrate into the mainstream and assimilate completely.

But the reconstruction of the ravages of war after the Second World War and the economic and technological revolutions that these societies underwent, coupled with the very slow pace of reproduction of European populations, where both men and women were seeking careers rather than raising families, brought about an acute shortage of manpower. Previous colonies, where manpower was available which required relatively limited cultural adaptation, became the unlimited sources for unqualified labourers, who little by little at first, and then in droves, replenished the slacking pool of workers in Europe. Vast countries like the US, Canada and Australia, which had been founded as immigrant societies in the first place, also absorbed much of this massive migration from Muslim countries. This growing movement of populations now came to encompass not only adventurers and seekers of new economic opportunities, but also increasing numbers of 'political refugees', some of whom were genuine asylum seekers from the oppressions of their regimes at home. Many of them, however, learned to abuse the generosity, concern for human rights and openness of the West, to escape from 'justice' in their own countries or to use their countries of asylum as launching pads for political struggle against their home regimes. Eventually, some of the migrants would turn against their adoptive countries and launch terrorist campaigns against them. They studied the vulnerabilities of western societies, and gradually detected how to exploit them.

These new immigrants gained local citizenship after the requisite period of residency which varies from one country to another. No sooner had they raised their status from temporary immigrants to permanent residents or fully-fledged citizens, than they began to make their impact on their adoptive countries in different areas:

1. Under the humanitarian heading of 'family reunion', they secured immigration rights for many of their relatives back home, thus markedly increasing their numbers; for many of the radical Muslims, this has become a sort of 'soft jihad' to encourage Muslim immigration into their new adoptive countries and increase their influence through sheer numbers.
2. Due to their social and religious needs, they developed Muslim communities in certain localities throughout Europe, where their numbers created local majorities that no candidate for elections could ignore; the growth of the communities required the construction of mosques and Muslim cultural centres, some of which were and remain innocent houses of prayer, while others grew into secret lodges of subversion and undercover nests for incitement and recruitment of radical youth.
3. Muslim communities, side-by-side with their irreproachable cultural activities, soon also engaged in illicit avenues of civil disobedience and criminal activities, and sometimes in radical incitement against the state; as a result, prisons in Europe are saturated with Muslim inmates out of proportion to their numbers in the general population.
4. Muslim communities have imported the Middle Eastern conflict into their host countries, with the related acts of violence and an unbridled anti-Semitic campaign against local Jewish communities which had otherwise lived undisturbed.
5. Muslim individuals, and some of their leaders, make no secret of their intent to transform Europe in accordance with their blueprint instead of adapt to it. They demand, and in some cases achieve, in the name of multi-ethnicism and multiculturalism, their own school systems, in their own native languages, financed by the host state and in the long run to its own detriment.
6. European countries adopted multiculturalism, and increasingly multilingualism, not as the implementation of the chosen social

ideal of cross-fertilizing different cultural groups by allowing them to enrich each other, but as an imposed reality whereby they have abdicated their role to absorb the newcomers and integrate them into the existing systems. Immigrants dictate their own visions of 'integration', which means in effect separatism, secession, or an eventual takeover when demography runs its course.

Undoubtedly, the problem of demography is the most pressing for Europe. Generally speaking, the 1.3 billion Muslims of the world are distributed into three major blocks: about one third in the Middle East and Africa, with the Arabs constituting over half of them; another 150 million in Turkey and Iran and the rest in black Africa, principally Nigeria and the Horn of Africa. The other third encompasses the Indian subcontinent with its three major components of Pakistan, India and Bangladesh with between 125 and 160 million each, and smaller Muslim populations in Afghanistan and Central Asia. The rest are concentrated in East and Southeast Asia, with about half in Indonesia, the largest Muslim country, Malaysia and Muslim minorities in Thailand, Burma and the Philippines, and the Muslims of Russia and China (about twenty-five million in each). The inroads of Islam into the western societies of Europe, America and Australia are quite a new phenomenon, and as their numbers increase, either via immigration (legal or illegal) or by natural growth, their proportion in the general population and their awakening to their Muslim identity deter their integration. There are already areas of France, Belgium and the Netherlands, and also Germany and Britain, where Muslim children constitute the majority of the school population, a situation that is pregnant with disaffection and can potentially lead to unrest.

There is another consideration to take into account in a discussion of immigration, namely the effect on host societies. A study by Robert Putnam, a Harvard University academic, has suggested that people living in more ethnically diverse areas show lower levels of trust not only between ethnic communities but also within them. In highly multicultural communities, people tend to have fewer close friends, watch more television, and have lower expectations of local and national government leaders. They also vote less frequently. 'The inhabitants of diverse communities tend to withdraw from collective life and to distrust their neighbours, regardless of their skin colour', Professor Putnam told *New Scientist* magazine. The findings emerged from an analysis of the US Social Capital Community Benchmark Survey, in which more than 30,000 Americans from different social groups and areas were asked in 2000 about their activities and how much they trusted one another.[2]

While the demographic trends in Europe seem irreversible, in view of the European population's reluctance to perpetuate itself, on the one hand, and its pressing needs for manpower to replace its ageing and retiring segments of society on the other, a reassessment of immigration policies is in the offing with regard to asylum seekers who do not necessarily respond to the labour needs of the host countries. In May 2006, Austria's Interior Minister Liese Prokop announced that 45 per cent of Muslim immigrants were 'unintegratable', and suggested that these people should 'choose another country'. In the Netherlands, one of Europe's most integrated Somali refugees and a critic of Islam, Ayaan Hirsi Ali, resigned her seat in parliament and immigrated to the US in the wake of criticism that she faked details on her asylum application to the Netherlands in 1992. France's lower house of parliament passed a strict new immigration law. Indeed, recent rumblings from the top echelons of governments across Europe suggest that the continent is rethinking its once-vaunted status as a haven for refugees as it becomes more suspicious that many immigrants are coming to exploit its social benefits and democratic principles. 'The trend today in Europe is more and more to try to control immigration flow', says Philippe De Bruycker, founder of the Odysseus Network, an academic consortium on immigration and asylum in Europe. 'At the same time we still say we want to respect the right of asylum and the possibility of applying for asylum. But of course along the way we create obstacles for asylum seekers', he acknowledged.[3]

Hirsi Ali – who was elected to parliament in 2003 – was informed by her own political party that her Dutch citizenship was in question. Immigration Minister Rita Verdonk, who had long promised a tough stance on immigration, said 'the preliminary assumption must be that – in line with case law of the Dutch Supreme Court – [Hirsi Ali] is considered not to have obtained Dutch nationality'. At issue were inconsistencies in Hirsi Ali's application for asylum in 1992 – giving a false name and age, and saying she was fleeing from Somalia's civil war and not from a forced marriage. She had publicly admitted to the inconsistencies in 2002, but a TV documentary heightened public scrutiny of her. She had been under twenty-four-hour protection from death threats since the murder in November 2004 of Theo van Gogh, the director of a film she wrote. Her case, heatedly debated across Europe in the aftermath of Verdonk's announcement, was seen as particularly ironic. But it also highlighted the dramatic change in Europe since the turn of this century.[4]

In the years following the Second World War, the US and Europe vowed to follow the Geneva Conventions and create safe havens for refugees. Yet such ideals were hard to uphold after massive influxes of workers in the 1960s and early 1970s were halted during an economic downturn. These immigrant populations swelled with family reunifications, yet often remained economically and socially distinct from the societies that they had adopted. The image of the immigrant began to change, and distinctions between those who came for work and those who came for safety began to blur. Now, according to Jean-Pierre Cassarino, coordinator for the Return Migration to the Maghreb (hosted by the Robert Schuman Centre for Advanced Studies in Florence), 'asylum seekers are viewed as potential cheaters'. Today, in once-homogenous Europe, tensions between immigrants and native Europeans are increasing. The perception that an ever increasing number of newcomers – who neither speak the language of their adopted country nor accept its cultural mores – are changing the culture, has increased support for ideas once only advanced by far-right political parties. 'France, Austria, and the Netherlands all have had very significant electoral success of the far-right parties', says Michael Collyer, a research fellow in European migration policy at the University of Sussex. Collyer points to the success in France of the strict new immigration law introduced by Interior Minister Nicolas Sarkozy to institutionalize 'selective' immigration, giving an advantage to privileged immigrants of better economic and education status who are more 'integratable'. It would also change the rights of family reunification for workers already in the country; speed up the expulsion of undocumented (another politically-correct euphemism for illegal infiltrators) immigrants who are discovered or whose applications for asylum are rejected; lengthen the amount of time it takes to apply for permanent residency status for married couples; and toughen visa requirements. Most controversially, Sarkozy announced deportations for undocumented immigrant schoolchildren. 'We speak of the need to fight immigration but we don't have a clear position on whether we need immigrants', says De Bruycker, noting the precipitous dip in population growth in EU countries in the last half century. He adds that a series of recent incidents have affected the image of immigrants in the European mind: the brutal murder of a young Jewish man, Ilan Halimi, on the outskirts of Paris in February 2006, for example, by a band of Muslim immigrant youths; or the murder of a Malian woman and a Flemish child in Antwerp in May 2006 by the son of a founder of Belgium's most far-right party. 'In Europe, we are still unable to accept that we are a continent of immigration', says De Bruycker.[5]

The basic datum when one considers demographic growth in the Islamic world is that, beyond its expansion into new areas, such as western democracies, it has sustained a consistent internal growth of 3 per cent for many years, amounting to a doubling of the total population every generation of twenty-five years. With this breakneck pace of the birth rate on the one hand, that is due to tradition, prohibitions on birth control and the general trend in the developing world where the rich get richer and the poor more children, and the decreasing mortality due to health improvements on the other, there is a virtual population explosion in the Islamic world. Countries like Iran, Turkey and Egypt, which boasted in the 1980s populations of 35–40 million each, have doubled in size since. Indonesia, Pakistan, India and Bangladesh, where the Muslim populations were already high in the 1980s, attaining 100 million in Indonesia and the 70–80 million mark for the rest, have also doubled since. Smaller-sized countries like Saudi Arabia, Syria, Morocco and Algeria have also doubled their populations (from 10–15 to 20–30 million), and the Palestinians of the West Bank and Gaza (from 1.6 to 3.2 million). This trend does not seem to relent, so that in general, the three-quarter billion Muslim population of the 1980s has soared to 1.3 billion. Moreover, since most of this population is young, the rapid demographic growth in these countries will continue apace as the innumerable populations of children come of age.

Caution must be added nonetheless insofar as demographic

statistics in these countries are not always reliable, although the trends are clear. Moreover, while European statistics on incoming Muslim legal immigrants are reliable, the countless illegal migrants tend to baffle the arithmetic and leave data of this massive human movement in the dark. The lack of statistics in the Muslim countries on emigration further complicates the calculations that demographers have attempted thus far. One thing is certain: if the immense surpluses of Muslim manpower (who are mostly uneducated and unskilled) do not find outlets in the rich Gulf States (which prefer trained Arab workers in their education system and bureaucracy), they find their way into western democracies as 'political refugees', as manpower for manual jobs that Europeans are reluctant to do, or as illegal migrants who easily slip through the porous European borders. When Europe began to tighten its control of the borders following the major terrorist attacks of Madrid and London in 2004–05, the large Muslim population of Europe was already difficult to supervise due to the lax and liberal freedom of movement of Europeans across the entire expanse of the Union. Another source of demographic growth of the Muslim population in the West is domestic proselytization, which though not massive at this point, produces some of the most devout and radical Muslims, and potential recruits for terrorism.

It is believed that France's Muslim population has reached approximately 10 per cent. In the Netherlands, Belgium and Scandinavia, the figure is still under 10 per cent. In the large-population countries such as Germany, Britain, Italy and Spain, though Muslims can be counted in the millions, they are more diluted among the massive preponderant Christian environment than in France, and do not transcend a few percentage points. However, Muslim visibility and public prominence seem out of proportion to their real numbers for several reasons:

1. They are usually concentrated in the large cities and clustered together in certain neighbourhoods, which in the eyes of the members of the host culture appear to have slipped out of their own jurisdiction. In many areas of, for example, Paris, Marseille, Malmo and Berlin, local Europeans feel as strangers (in French '*dépayses*') in their own countries.
2. Due to the background of the unskilled immigrants, who are

usually uneducated, they feel alienated inasmuch as many of them preserve their languages and mores, are different in dress, food and way of life, and they build up a high degree of frustration which occasionally explodes in violent demonstrations.

3. Alienation, poverty and frustration often lead many of the youth among the immigrant Muslim population to crime. In all European countries which absorbed Muslim immigrants, statistics illustrate the sad story of Muslim prison inmates out of proportion to their rate in the population. Such statistics are not often publicized for fear of accusations of 'bigotry' or 'racism'. The host countries are driven to frustration when their generosity in welcoming the immigrants and supporting their training and welfare, often turned into permanent burdens instead of the relief of manpower shortages.

4. Muslim alienation has tended not only to lead them to build their own enclaves within their host societies, where even the forces of order sometimes do not dare to enter, but it makes them insensitive to the general host population, something which in turn boosts the Europeans' reluctance to absorb them into their culture. For example, mosques which call for prayer at odd hours, when recurring and perennial, may turn previously quiet neighbourhoods into areas of friction. Or when naturalized Muslims demand, in the name of their new citizenship, that the cross that garnishes the national flags of their host countries be eliminated because it hurts their feelings, their shelter societies are stunned by what seems to them as a presumptuous demand.

5. The phenomenon of growing numbers of converts into Islam in major European countries such as France and Britain (some 60,000 in each in the past decade), plays a growing role in the visibility of the Muslim community. Sarah Joseph, a British convert who now promotes Islam, makes the astonishing claim that between 10,000 and 50,000 people in the UK convert each year.[6] Comparisons are inevitably made with the fact that not only are Christians banned from missionary work in Islamic countries, but individuals who convert are liable to be executed for apostasy. Shortly after 7/7, *Le Monde* reported on a study of converts by the intelligence service Renseignements Généraux (RG) in 'Les conversions à l'islam radical inquiètent la police française'

(French police worried about conversions to radical Islam). Looking at 1,610 French converts, it found that 83 per cent were male, one-third have police records and a tenth converted in prison. Tablighi Jama'at and the Wahhabis were behind 28 and 23 per cent of the conversions.[7]
6. From time to time, scandals like forced marriages of young Muslim women in Europe, or their murder to protect the 'honour' of the family, the Rushdie affair of 1989, terrorism and violent demonstrations as in the cartoon affair of 2005–06, all tend to raise the profile of Islam in Europe and make it seem particularly menacing.

On the other hand, several factors militate against an even faster rise of Muslim communitarian identity and demographic growth in Europe, as discussed in Amitai Etzioni's seminal work:[8]

1. The large numbers of Muslims who have assimilated over the past generation or two in their European environment, especially among the young who have been absorbed by the local educational systems, have grown ignorant of their original cultures and languages, and are more interested in developing successful careers than in spreading Islam or responding to its call. These Muslims, whose rate among their community is hard to ascertain, would be unlikely to stand to be counted as Muslims, although intermarriage rates remain very low.
2. Precisely due to the ascendance of militant Islam in Europe and the West in general, with the attending violence that sometimes accompanies its assertion of its identity and its manifestation of disaffection and discontent, the more assimilated and quietist Muslims who are reluctant to be identified with their radical kin, distance themselves from them and elect to blend unnoticed into the general population.
3. Unlike the radical militants who do not hide their intent to Islamize European societies, by peaceful means if possible, through conversions and recruiting for terrorist operations, if necessary, the non-observant Muslims on the contrary seem to have reconciled to the idea of integrating into their adoptive societies and state their intentions to maintain peace and to focus on their personal concerns. While the radicals have not

established their own Muslim political parties, since their numbers are not large enough to make an electoral impact, non-observant Muslims indicate their will to adapt via affiliation to the existing political system.

As long as Islam lived within the traditional boundaries of Islamdom, its tensions and frictions with the West remained outside the domain of the western public, except for politicians, diplomats, merchants and military men who had to deal with it. Misunderstood, shunned, demonized as it may have been in the eyes of Europeans, it was remote and lay beyond the horizon. Similarly, when Muslim visitors arrived in the West from the turn of the twentieth century, for study or business, they were for the most part respectful, even admirers, of its culture and modernity. They adopted the low-profile demeanour of a student who wished to learn and a self-effacing attitude of awe towards everything western which was deemed superior. But with the rise of fundamentalist Islam in the past few decades, and the increase of Muslim immigration into the West which brought them into permanent contact with western societies, Muslims learned to face up to their host societies and even to confront them in debate. Their increasing self-confidence and self-assertion taught them that they could debate the West on a par, without being arrested, humiliated or even imprisoned or executed, as in their home countries. For the Europeans, the clash of civilizations which took place on the borders of Christendom moved into their own heartland and they were ill-equipped to face it, on the psychological or the societal levels. Convinced that their open and democratic societies would prevail and entice the new immigrants to abandon their roots and identity, they were shocked to discover that over the years, far from bridging the gap that yawned between them and their unintegrated immigrants, it had on the contrary widened, and the differences grew into clashes, the complaints into demands, the debates into explosions of violence. So much so, that once westerners realized that they were obliterating their traditionally homogeneous societies in favour of multiracial, multireligious and at times even multilinguistic ones, the social contract which held them together previously began dissipating, much to the chagrin of local nationalist parties and to the frustration of the rest.

The explosion of the cartoon controversy throughout the world in early 2006 did not make matters easier for the Europeans, who saw their goodwill and hospitality towards Muslims 'rewarded' by violent demonstrations around the globe, as if cartoons of the prophet could be a real reason for this eruption of outrage, and not an opportunistic pretext to air Muslim anger and frustration. This will not facilitate the entry of Turkey into the EU either, primarily for demographic reasons. The opponents of Turkey within the Union were reluctant to admit her following the success of the Islamic Party in the 2002 elections, realizing that the so-called Islamic fundamentalism almost invariably translates into discord and trouble for Europe. Bringing Turkey in would mean not only freedom of movement for Turkish labour and nationals throughout Europe, but also spreading the message of Islam, and not necessarily only of the benevolent kind, into all corners of the continent. With numbers approaching or exceeding 10 per cent of the population in some Western European countries, frictions are already difficult; how much more so if the seventy-five million-strong nation should join, raising the rate of Muslims to 20–25 per cent (out of a total population of 480 million in all twenty-seven members of the EU).[9]

The rapid growth of the Muslim population on the one hand, and the shrinkage of the European family unit on the other, would mean that in the next generation or two Europe may become half Muslim. If that is the will of the Europeans, then there is no faster or more efficient way to achieve that goal than admitting Turkey; but if they intend to preserve their Christian heritage and European culture, their technological advancement and modern lifestyle, Islamization of their societies is not the most hopeful avenue to pursue. Already second thoughts about Turkey have begun to take root in the EU. Britain, the most ardent proponent of Turkish integration, agreed to suspend talks between the parties, when it realized that Turkish oppression of the Kurds continues unabated, women are still discriminated against and Turkish school textbooks, which are monitored by the Union, contain thousands of cases of racism and human rights abuses, notably negative portrayals of Greeks, Jews, Kurds and Armenians.[10]

There is a lesson to be learned from the example of Malaysia, enthusiastically cited, alongside Turkey, as 'a moderate Islamic nation'. Hardline Islamic law could be introduced across Malaysia under reforms proposed by the country's chief justice. Ahmad Fairuz told an Islamic conference in Kuala Lumpur that fifty years of independence from Britain had failed to free Malaysia from the 'clutches of colonialism', and shari'a should be 'infused' into the gaps created by abolishing common law. Malaysia's non-Muslim Chinese and Indian communities, who constitute 40 per cent of the population, are alarmed at creeping Islamization. Prime Minister Abdul Badawi denied what the British-authored constitution has said for fifty years – that Malaysia is a secular state. Shari'a law already operates in some Malaysian states and is occasionally applied to non-Muslims, as in July 2007 when Islamic officials forcibly separated a Hindu-Muslim couple with six children after twenty-one years of marriage. The majority ethnic Malays are defined as Muslim by law and forbidden from converting. Racial tensions are already high due to official discrimination in favour of Malays, who enjoy better employment opportunities, preferential loans and lower house prices.[11] The issue of 'colonialism' was raised in an interesting exchange between an Arab and a Chinese official, revealing more vividly than anything else why China has made great economic strides while the Muslim world is going backwards. Barry Rubin, the director of Global Research in International Affairs (GLORIA) at the Interdisciplinary Centre in Herzliya, Israel, wrote that on more than one occasion, Arab friends told him about discussions they have had with people in China. One conversation went like this: 'How do you feel about having been the victims of western imperialism for so many years?' the Chinese official was asked. 'We got over it and moved on with our lives', was the response.[12]

In Malaysia, Chinese and Indians feel increasingly treated like second-class citizens. They complain that Islamic religious schools are much better funded than theirs and that a system of affirmative action favours Malays for university places. None of this discrimination against non-Muslims stops Malaysia from being in the forefront of attacks on 'apartheid' in Israel. Chinese or Indians who want to marry a Malay must convert to Islam. In 2007 a Malay woman called Lina Joy attempted to have Malaysia's courts recognize her conversion to Christianity, but failed and fled into hiding. Some hardliners have even called for the execution of apostates.

Every state has a religious department with Saudi-style moral enforcers. Unmarried couples found sharing hotel rooms are hunted down by the enforcers. Couples caught sitting too close together on park benches are fined £285 in the city's shari'a court under a provision called *khalwat*, loosely translated as 'close proximity'. Couples have been forced into marriage after being caught together and moral enforcers sometimes target foreigners.[13]

There is nothing virtuous about the 'enforced virtue' as practised in Iran or Saudi Arabia or Malaysia. Far more admirable are people elsewhere in the world who choose to live virtuous lives without coercion. 'Virtue' as enforced by the Saudi religious police, the *mutawayyin* (under the control of a government agency called the Authority for the Promotion of Virtue and the Prevention of Vice) is the very opposite of virtue. In March 2002, the BBC reported that Saudi Arabia's religious police stopped schoolgirls from leaving a blazing building because they were not wearing correct Islamic dress. According to the *al-Eqtisadiah* daily, firemen confronted police after they tried to keep the girls inside because they were not wearing the headscarves and *abayas* (black robes) required by the kingdom's strict interpretation of Islam. One witness said he saw three policemen 'beating young girls to prevent them from leaving the school because they were not wearing the *abaya*'. Fifteen schoolgirls were allowed to perish in the name of Saudi 'virtue'.[14]

Demography has a long-term effect on the prospects for coexistence in countries where Muslims are in the minority, because of the inbuilt contradiction between the requirement of Muslims to live under Islamic rule (since only there the law of Allah can be brought to bear), and the grim necessity for many Muslims to escape from the persecutions of their Muslim regimes by seeking refuge in the West. Believers who live in non-Muslim lands must either regard their stay there as temporary, doing their best to live their Muslim life undisturbed in the interim, or return to the 'Abode of Islam' as soon as they can, or try to turn their country of residence into a Muslim one by seizing power. For this reason, the existence of Muslim minorities under non-Islamic rule has always alternately pursued these trajectories and driven the Muslim guest culture into a state of mind varying from a quietist acceptance of a permanent minority status to violent rebellion. The response of the Muslim minority depends in no small measure on the perceived threat posed to it by the majority host culture. Whenever coexistence seemed feasible, as was the case with Muslim minorities in the West before the rise of fundamentalism among them, they could say that so long as they could perform the obligations of their faith without inhibition, they could consider themselves as living within enclaves of the 'Abode of Islam', a state of affairs they could bear indefinitely. Once perceived oppression made their lives as Muslims untenable, and they diagnosed their position in consequence as residents in the 'Abode of War', they were set on a collision course with their hosts, and conflict ensued.

To this rather simplistic scheme one ought to introduce three more variables: first, the general Muslim environment, which when rising and embracing the road of militancy can draw behind it Muslim minorities who are fascinated by its power which compensates for their feelings of oppression, underprivileged status and hopelessness in tackling the requirements of modern life. Secondly, the demographic data of the minority come into play, to wit, the larger the minority, to the point of constituting local majorities in certain areas, the more it feels self-confident to challenge the majority. Indeed, in areas where large concentrations of Muslims are clustered together, they feel strong enough to advance demands and to resort to violence or to threaten the use of violence if their demands are not fulfilled. Thirdly, the nature of the regime under which they live plays its part. If the regime is oppressive as in their own countries of origin, they would be less inclined to rebel, knowing what their punishment would entail; but under the liberal democratic rule of the West, it is easier for them to act to undermine it and paradoxically seek its destruction although, or because, it gives them more leeway. This is the case with Muslims in the liberal democracies of the West.

Majority–minority relations in general are by nature dynamic and their fortunes usually hinge on the infringements upon the uneasy balance between the two parts of the equation. When the minority becomes or is perceived as a demographic, economic or political menace to the majority, for example, fears and suspicions increase, followed by oppression on the part of the majority and self-imposed isolation by the minority, ultimately leading to alienation, conflict, separation, rebellion and secession. All the while both parties test the boundaries of cohabitation and coexistence and attempt to limit the autonomy of the minority on the one hand and pushing it to its utmost on the other. The collision course is the result of the failure of the parties or one of them to stop on the verge of the precipice and instead rush to trigger a violent explosion. These modalities come in cycles: material acculturation of the minority (in speech, dress, manners, mores, customs) goes a long way to condition it to become more sensitive to its environment and to the interests of the host culture. So the next time it rebels it finds that it has accumulated more affinities with the majority than ever before. More than it states its rejection of the majority, its rebellion proclaims its fear lest it be engulfed by it. Following periods of assimilation into the majority, voices of renewal are raised, warning the minority that unless it revives its roots it runs the imminent danger of total disappearance. Revival – religious, ethnic, cultural, linguistic or otherwise – breeds opposition and rejection by the majority culture, sometimes leading to violent rebellion and attempts at secession by the minority and its brutal repression, so as to remove the perceived threat that it poses to the majority, and back to square one. During this trajectory from quietism to violence, the minority people often embrace multi-identities, in periods of assimilation emphasizing the majority culture, in eras of conflict asserting their own ethno–cultural–religious–linguistic distinctiveness. Like the modalities of coexistence themselves, identities also vary, combining various components from the composite menu from which they are constantly called to choose.

These rules apply to Muslim minorities the world over, as their current predicament in non-Muslim lands readily illustrates. One more element is needed nonetheless to explain the mechanics of these dynamics, and that is charismatic leadership, without which the transition from quietism to rebellion is difficult. For if acculturation, assimilation, quietism and a passive mood towards the majority require no leadership, just indifference and a societal *laissez-faire,* the traumatic crossover to rebellion, violence and upheaval which require risk-taking and a revolutionary spirit, depend much on a political or religious leader who commands authority and attracts followers. In the case of Muslim minorities the actor is more likely to be religious or to combine religion and politics due to the inextricability of the sacred and the profane, the holy and the secular in Islamic political tradition. A distinction is called for nevertheless between the activity of religious actors in Islamic-majority countries and Muslim-minority ones. If a certain convergence of events is what provides the religious actor with the opportunity to act, it goes without saying that in situations of Muslim-minority existence the field of friction between the Muslim guest culture and the majority host culture is usually wider and more thorny than in homogeneous Muslim countries. For, granted that within Muslim entities too there are wide-open possibilities for conflict, as strife abounds on behalf of the Muslim majority towards non-Muslim minorities (Sudan, Iran, Nigeria), or between different Muslim sects and factions (Afghanistan, Pakistan, the Gulf States, Iraq and Egypt), the situation is different when Muslim minorities are concerned. The reason is that within Muslim-majority states it is the official government which conducts the repression against other factions or minorities, and while the oppressed (for example, the Gama'at or the Muslim Brotherhood in Egypt, Syria and Jordan) usually produce charismatic leaders who lead the resistance as religious actors, the latter seldom challenge the state's legitimacy. Their goal is to remove the regime, alter its policies, or gain a share of power within the state apparatus. However, since Muslims are required to live in Islamic lands, their presence under non-Islamic rule poses insoluble problems which end in crisis and unrest. Under such a convergence of events, where the plight of the Muslim minority is identified as 'religious', only recognized religious actors who arise to meet the challenge are capable of dealing with it for the most part.

There was a time when Muslim minorities were quite limited in numbers and scope of dispersion, usually as a result of interaction with the colonial powers who encouraged a certain number of 'natives' to tread their cultural ways in their own metropolitan centres, and some of them intermarried and stayed. However, the large waves of Muslim immigrants since the mid-twentieth century to the Americas, Australia and Europe, and more so the opening labour markets in the West to Muslim 'guest workers', coupled with important movements of conversion to Islam as a result of intense Muslim *da'wa* (mission), has dramatically increased the numbers of Muslim migrants to those countries. Moreover, the 'guests' have come to regard themselves as permanent residents with all attending privileges of citizenship and social benefits. In an interesting twist, not only don't they regard any longer their presence outside the realm of Islam as temporary, embarrassing and calling for justification, but with the birth in place of the second and third generations, who grow to learn the languages, cultures and ways of their new habitats, the process of their acculturation into their new homelands has accelerated. As long as their rate in the general populations of their new countries remained negligible, and the socio-political environment was liberal (as in the US, Canada, Australia, Israel and Europe), then social pluralism and individual freedom of worship were advocated by the Muslim minorities. Under oppressive regimes like the Soviet or the Chinese, the Muslims were quick to adopt material acculturation into their host society, with all the trappings of language, dress, education and participation in the elites and social customs. The core of the faith was kept almost intact, however, with the Muslim calendar, festivals, dietary laws, worship and places of prayer preserved to the extent possible. This was easier in areas where Muslim minorities were more sizeable and commanded the critical mass necessary to entertain communal life, and much more difficult when the Muslim population was so sparse as to render any public display of Muslim identity impractical.

These situations of rebellious guest cultures, who no longer accept their minority status, can give rise to violence that is aimed either at secession or various forms of autonomy, or grows into an irredentist claim when the minority dwells in adjacent proximity/territorial continuity to their mother country where the main bulk of their people is located (the Kurds in Turkey, Iran, Iraq and Syria, the Hungarians of Transylvania and Voivodina, the Sudeten Germans and the Arabs of Israel, the Turkic-Muslim population of Eastern Turkestan). Such claims, which may be bolstered especially when the minority becomes too sizeable to govern, or grows into a local majority in its area of residence, gain currency when the demographic growth of the minority is so much faster than that of the host culture as to arouse hopes of a 'democratic' takeover by the one-man one-vote device that worked in Zimbabwe and South Africa. In other words, minorities of this sort, be they national or religious, do not seek to merge through integration as in Brazil and create a race-less society where no value is given to skin-colour, creed or original culture, but to dominate through subjugation of the others when their numbers so allow. In these situations religious actors find a fertile ground to act, by advocating demographic growth in their communities, denigrating the majority culture so as to discourage acculturation into it, creating an atmosphere of separateness and strife, inventing irredentist claims and mobilizing their community to obey them in the pursuance of these ambitions.

When Muslim minorities become frustrated by the unworkability of a pluralistic society, as in Cyprus, the Philippines, Israel, China and increasingly within European countries, either because they believe they are discriminated against or their expectations are not met, they become antagonistic to their host society. Such antagonism becomes much more likely when they perceive the majority as having transgressed the limits of previous coexistence and encroached upon their freedom of worship or conduct. In such cases, they use western vocabulary (freedom, tolerance, democracy, human rights) to impress upon their hosts that while they wish to play by the rules of their adoptive countries, it is the latter who violate them. In more extreme cases, as with some Muslim fundamentalist leaders (religious actors *par excellence*) in London, they claim that they came to Europe in order to change it, not to be reshaped by it, or they reject western attitudes (like the banning of the veil in French schools, or freedom of expression during the cartoon affair). This sets the Muslim minority, especially the fundamentalist elements in its midst, on a collision course with the host authorities. Militant elements among this disaffected minority may seek political or cultural autonomy (the British 'Muslim Parliament', or various national or international Muslim associations, or organizations of imams and mosque leaders, or the heads of the Arab Local councils in Israel, or the demand for autonomy and for an 'Arab' or 'Muslim' university and other separate institutions). In India Muslims had conquered the land and subjugated Hinduism, but when Muslim power was eroded by the British, Islam sought and achieved separation from the Hindus, rather than submit to the democratic rule of modern India that would have allowed the Hindus to exercise political domination over the Muslims. When the majority of Indian Muslims established their own state (Pakistan), their *'ulama* (Islamic scholars) spoke of the reinstitution of shari'a as their state law. There was no alternative to this arrangement if one bears in mind the fact that Islam is incompatible with other political ideologies. Abu al-Ala' al-Mawdudi, the prominent Indian Muslim modernist expressed it this way: 'To be a Muslim and adopt a non-Muslim viewpoint is only meaningless. "Muslim nationalist" and "Muslim Communist" are as contradictory terms as "Communist Fascist" and "chaste prostitute".[15]

Thus, as Orthodox Muslims see it, and much more so the fundamentalists among them, Islam is ideally an either/or affair. Either Islamic law and institutions are given full expression and dominate state life or, failing that, if the state is non-Islamic, Muslims should try to reverse the situation or leave. In practice, however, things are not so clear-cut. As long as an appearance of peace and accommodation can be maintained, the minority Muslim community, although entertaining a vague hope for the fulfilment of its political aspirations at some future time, can contain the discrepancy between dream and reality, and the tension between the two can remain unresolved. But if persecution of the minority is intensified, for example in non-democratic countries, to the point where no real Muslim life can be ensured, and when a practical opportunity arises, the minority Muslims are likely to seize it and proclaim either a separate Muslim entity or a Muslim state regardless of whether the Muslim population is a majority or a minority in the territory in question. For an Islamic state can encompass either. Muslims have experienced both a Muslim majority under non-Islamic rule as in Christian Valencia where Muslims outnumbered the Christians four to one,[16] or the modern Muslim colonies under Christian rule, and a Muslim minority rule in Hindu-majority India and the Umayyad Muslim rule over a Christian-majority state in the Iberian Peninsula. It is Muslim rule, then, that defines the borders of the 'Abode of Islam', not Muslim majorities or minorities. In recent years the enhanced stature of Islam has led the Muslim centre to take a keener and deeper interest in the minorities on its periphery. This renewed interest has been manifested in the resolutions of the Organization of the Islamic Conference (OIC) which bring together delegates from fifty-seven Muslim-majority countries in a Muslim-only 'United Nations'. More interest has been taken by remote Muslim communities in participating in the pilgrimage to Mecca, where two million people from all nationalities share their fellowship with their brothers and enhance the identity of the universal umma. These are the building blocks of Muslim-minority discontent and rebellion, which in our days may lead to what is termed 'terrorism'.

The subtitle of Walter Laqueur's book, *The Last Days of Europe*:

Epitaph for an Old Continent,[17] does not leave much room for doubt about his fears. When Europe's boom ended after the OPEC oil shock in 1973, he wrote, governments stopped issuing work visas although immigration continued. Relatives flowed in legally, through family reunification laws, and illegally, as immigrant smuggling became a major business. Chain migration through family reunification transported entire extended families, even whole villages, thus creating serious barriers to assimilation. There followed a flood of asylum seekers, to whom the authorities were quite liberal in their approach, even though the majority migrated for economic rather than political reasons. All asylum seekers, legitimate or otherwise, were supported by a powerful lobby, the human rights associations and churches that provided legal and other aid. In contrast, illegal immigrants to most non-European countries were returned to their countries of origin within days. Laqueur believes that we now face 'the end of Europe as a major player in world affairs'.[18]

The historian David Starkey observed that without even pondering the consequences, Europe effectively imported a significant community amounting to about one in twenty-five of the population who are at a different stage of religious development (in fact it is more than 4 per cent and closer to 7 or 8 per cent). Founded in the seventh century, Islam is 600 years younger than Christianity. In Islamic time, it is still AD 1400. They haven't had a Reformation, let alone an Enlightenment. And they treat their religion with the same kind of passion that Europeans did when they burnt heretics.[19] The Afghan-born US ambassador to the UN expressed a variation on Starkey's theme. Dr Zalmay Khalilzad told the Austrian daily *Die Presse* that 'The [Middle East] is going through a very difficult transformation phase. That has strengthened extremism and creates a breeding ground for terrorism. Europe was just as dysfunctional for a while. And some of its wars became world wars. Now the problems of the Middle East and Islamic civilization have the same potential to engulf the world.' He referred to the Islamic world as a slow starter. 'They started late. They don't have a consensus on their concept. Some believe they should return to the time of the prophet Muhammad. It may take decades before some understand that they can remain Muslims and simultaneously join the modern world.'[20] In his book *Sacred Causes,*

Michael Burleigh asks why no one questioned the implications of introducing large Muslim populations into a secularizing West. Absolute tolerance, Burleigh believes, makes western societies particularly vulnerable to those who play by other rules, particularly when self-doubt hobbles western leaders.[21]

It is instructive to compare the post-Second World War Muslim immigration with the wave of Jewish migration to both Western Europe and the US at the beginning of the twentieth century. Jews entered Western Europe by the tens of thousands, not by the millions. They also made great efforts to integrate, above all seeking a good secular education for their children. There was no welfare state in those days – no social workers, subsidized housing, free medical services or social security. Immigrants survived according to their own initiative, whereas the modern welfare state has removed the incentives for success that used to force cultural integration. Laqueur writes that many of the early Bangladeshi immigrants were reluctant to accept government assistance, viewing welfare payments as dishonourable. But social workers turned welfare dependence into a way of life for them. Laqueur argues that the fundamental problem of Muslim assimilation is cultural, and that the term 'barbarian' can be applied with justice to the actions of some lawless young Muslim men. He also takes seriously the possibility of a violent Muslim revolution in Europe. He rejects the cultural blindness of economic elites who see immigration in strictly market terms, or the suggestion that racism or 'Islamophobia' explain the failure of Muslim integration. He rejects economic explanations for the decline of Europe, insisting that the erosion of strong families, relativism, and a loss of faith in the future are at the root of Europe's problems. Laqueur is impatient with the delusion which portrays Europe as the world's emerging 'soft superpower', a continent destined to lead the world through its exemplary combination of benevolence and justice. He ridicules the notion that the hard-eyed powers of the world will, on the basis of sheer inspiration, come to emulate European rule of law. Yet Laqueur's account could be read to make the point that Europe's delusional belief in its ability to lead the world without force rests on a misplaced conviction of its own moral superiority. This same self-confidence helps explain why Europe's elites discounted the cultural challenge of immigration. The assumption was that liberal modernism's superiority would be seen, acknowledged, and therefore eventually adopted by Muslim immigrants. It is a characteristic weakness of liberal democracy to assume its own universal appeal, while taking democracy's cultural prerequisites for granted. Yet Europe's immigrants lack the cultural pre-requisites for democracy and market capitalism – as demonstrated by the widespread fraud in postal voting in parts of the UK, when large numbers of voting forms were handed over to local Muslim activists.[22]

Despite the initial naive days of Muslim immigration, when it was a matter of course to assume that Muslim minorities would integrate painlessly into the much more prosperous nations where they made their new homes, difficulties began to emerge from the outset, which were dismissed as pangs of acculturation. But as the years elapsed, the Muslim communities grew, and their radicalism came to the surface, the illusion of integration began to fade, substituted by the illusory vision of multicultural societies, which made cultural concessions to the immigrants in order to accommodate them and make them partners of the system, not its clients. But that too, far from satisfying the newcomers, whose growing numbers gave them the necessary self-confidence to defy the system and even start acting against it, only further increased their sense of alienation. The Europeans, in turn, sensing that their liberalism had turned against them, began to try to back-pedal, but it was too late, and the collision course became inevitable. A European survey published in April 2006 found that the degree of anti-Muslim bias was 'dangerously high', and 'may lead to a vicious circle of isolation and radicalization of the immigrant youth'. The vocabulary of the survey, which avoided pronouncing the word 'Muslim', substituting for it instead 'immigrant youth', 'suburb youth', 'immigrant population' or 'unemployed youth', evinced a refusal to admit that Europe was already dragged into a vicious circle. Beate Winkler, the head of the European Monitoring Centre on Racism and Xenophobia, told 100 European imams convened in Vienna to discuss integration, that European countries had enough laws to foster integration, and that real issues are often avoided. The Europeans attending the conference agreed that attitudes towards Islam had hardened since 9/11 and subsequent attacks. Winkler suggested that Europe could help by supporting mosque construction, providing time for religious broadcasts and assuring proper education of imams and Islamic religious teachers. On the other hand, she demanded that work be actively conducted against Muslim extremism, 'honour killings', forced marriages, spousal abuse and self-imposed isolation in order to help solve other issues arising from halal butchering or the wearing of headscarves.[23]

Sometimes, the heightened fear of Muslim immigration can cause individual harm to innocent families uninvolved with violence or subversion. A case in point was cited in *The Washington Post*.[24] Eight-year-old Andrianina Ralison of Bourg-La-Reine, France, was described by his teacher as one of the top achievers in class. Scheduled to be deported to his native Madagascar after school ended in July 2006, together with his law-abiding family, he asked his mother, 'Why don't they want us here?' Many teachers, classmates and parents rebelled against the political consensus to crack down on illegal immigrants, which involved deportation of entire families. Teachers at a school in central France hid students from police, even at the risk of being fined. Other schools went on strike to protest the sudden evictions. Local town halls run by socialist officials who opposed the government's increasingly hard-line approach supported many of the families in their legal appeals to remain in the country. Sarkozy, architect of the new assault on illegal immigration, relented and declared a temporary amnesty for families with children in school and agreed not to deport them until the end of the school year of 2005/6. Richard Moyon, founder of the Education Without Borders Network, a teachers' association that organizes protests as part of its efforts to assist youngsters threatened with deportation, noted that, 'One of the roles of a teacher is to teach kids the ideals of the republic – freedom and equality. How can teachers explain what freedom and equality are when you've got in front of your eyes this kind of example of children seeing their friends deported?'[25]

However, one of the principles of the republic is also to abide by the law; hence the imperative of seizing those who have entered illegally and deporting them. Otherwise, the entire concept of border control and of legal migration would collapse. Following pressure from Moyon's group and sympathetic politicians, the Interior Ministry issued new voluntary guidelines to the local governing authorities that decide whether to grant residency papers to illegal immigrants. Families were given more favourable consideration if their children had spent at least a year in French schools, were born in France or arrived at a young age and spoke French fluently. The French Government estimates that illegal immigrants number between 200,000 and 400,000, of whom 50,000 are children. In the past few years, French authorities stepped up raids on city streets and at subway stations in immigrant neighbourhoods, pressured employers to stop hiring illegal workers and rejected larger numbers of applications from illegal immigrants seeking visas. Deportations increased by nearly 70 per cent, from 11,692 in 2003 to 19,489 in 2005. In contrast to the US, where many illegal immigrants slip through porous southwestern borders, or Spain, where thousands of Africans have arrived on leaky boats, most immigrants arrive in France on tourist visas. While the US screens tourist visas from applicants in developing nations, France historically has been lenient in granting them to citizens of impoverished former colonies in the Middle East and Africa where cultural and linguistic ties with France remain.[26] These immigrants for a while entertained the illusion of being integrated in the culture of their choice, only to see themselves rejected and deported.

A warning by the former director of the Israeli Mossad, Ephraim Halevy, that by the middle of the century, major cities in Germany will have a Muslim majority and so will many member districts of the Russian Federation, further unsettled the Europeans. Halevy spoke of Islamic terror, saying it is 'the main problem of the world today', adding that, 'We are in the middle of WWIII, and I see no end to it.' Halevy also addressed the issue of Hamas to illustrate how the European security establishments can contain their own terrorists, saying it is 'a young movement, consisting of only 19-year olds, and it is a ruthless enemy of Israel. The success of the Israeli defence establishment in fighting this organization is immense.'[27] He implied that while the immigration and growth of the Muslim populations in Europe was unstoppable, to the point of becoming local majorities over time, their terrorist threat was manageable and controllable. While Europeans are certainly concerned about the ability of their governments to protect them in their own lands from Muslim terrorism in the short run, they are much more worried about what will become of their nations, cultures and religions in the long run, should the waves of immigration not subside.

Even those jihadis who had left Europe to go to Iraq and other battlefields have been readmitted to their European homes. So, while the Saudis are constructing a fence along their Iraqi border to keep out returning jihadis, the Europeans allow them back thanks to their 'human rights' pieties. The returnees are highly motivated and battle-hardened, and therefore dangerous. As far back as October 2005, Iraqi Interior Minister Bayan Jabr warned that intercepted correspondence between Abu Musab al-Zarqawi, then leader of al-Qa'ida in Iraq, and other figures in the movement had revealed a decision to send large numbers of Islamist volunteers back to their countries of origin to wage 'holy war'. Baltazar Garzon, a judge who has led inquiries into al-Qa'ida in Spain, said: 'I cannot say how many cases we are talking about, but it is a question of logic. Up until now, inquiries were focused on volunteers travelling to Iraq. Now we are beginning to get indications that they have begun to return.' Hundreds of jihadi volunteers from almost every country in Europe have travelled to Iraq, via Syria, Egypt, Turkey or Iran. Once there, they have participated in the anti-US 'resistance' (their code for terrorism), often to commit Islamikaze attacks. In 2005, the International Institute for Strategic Studies in London estimated the number of foreign volunteers in Iraq to be at least 1,000. In May 2006 the head of France's domestic security service, Pierre de Bousquet, indicated that at least nine French Muslims had been killed in Iraq. Claude Moniquet, director of the Brussels-based European Strategic Intelligence and Security Centre, said: 'It is pretty much impossible to organize the surveillance of several hundred people across Europe. Effective surveillance of one person requires an absolute minimum of twelve to fifteen officers. Multiply that by several hundred, and you need thousands. And even then, we're talking about a makeshift operation.'[28]

Much has been written about the role of demographics to explain violent behaviour in the Muslim world, which is just as often directed internally as externally. There are religious, political and cultural reasons for this violence, the latter being aggravated by temperament, ostentatiously expressed through public displays of anger and emotion. For political scientists, the percentage of young men in a society is a crucial factor. Gary Fuller, director of population studies at the University of Hawaii, refers to a 'youth bulge' when youths aged 15–24 make up 20 per cent or more of the population. Samuel Huntington, author of *The Clash of Civilizations*,[29] has argued that a huge reservoir of young men aged 15–30 provides a natural pool of instability and violence. Gunnar Heinsohn, a social scientist and genocide researcher at the University of Bremen, has taken this factor further. Since its publication in 2003, his *Sohne und Weltmacht: Terror im Aufstieg und Fall der Nationen* (Sons and World Power in the Rise and Fall of Nations),[30] has become something of a cult book. In Heinsohn's view, when youths aged 15–29 make up more than 30 per cent of the population, violence tends to happen; when large percentages are under 15, violence is often imminent. There are sixty-seven countries in the world with such 'youth bulges' now and sixty of them are undergoing some kind of civil war or mass killing. The 'causes' in the name of which that violence is committed can be immaterial. Of the twenty-seven biggest youth-bulge nations, thirteen are Muslim. Between 1988 and 2002, 900 million sons were born to mothers in the developing world and a careful demographer could almost predict the trouble spots. Iraq had five million people in 1950 but has 25 million now, in spite of a quarter-century of wars. Since 1967, the population of the West Bank and Gaza has grown from 450,000 to over three million, 47 per cent of whom are under 15. Gangland slayings between Hamas and Fatah in the Palestinian territories defy civilized norms and political common sense. 'It's very ironic but I'm relieved the Israelis have started a bombing campaign. The gunmen killing each other on the streets were forced to go into hiding', said Mai, a Gaza housewife, referring to strikes aimed at halting rocket attacks on Israel in June 2007. President Mahmoud Abbas said the threat posed by internal bloodshed rivaled the dangers presented by 'Israeli occupation'. Legislator Nasser Jum'a, once a leading member of Fatah's al-Aqsa 'Martyrs Brigades', said ordinary Palestinians were so fed up with the armed groups 'they now wish the Israeli occupation would take over in Gaza or hope for the return of Jordanian rule in the West Bank' to get rid of them.[31]

If Heinsohn is right, then Palestinian violence of recent years is not explained by Israeli 'occupation' (which ended in August 2005 in Gaza) or poverty (the most violent parts of the Muslim world are not the poorest). It is just violence for its own sake. The Israeli withdrawal has not concentrated Palestinian minds on developing a functioning society with efficient public utilities and services, but divided society along factional lines. The problem is that no society can provide enough respectability and satisfaction for such large numbers of young men, even if there were enough ordinary jobs. It only adds to the rage of young men that sexual relationships outside marriage are unthinkable. At the same time, a degree of social standing is needed in order to get married at all. Envy against older, inheriting brothers is unleashed, as is ambition. Military heroism presents itself as a time-honoured way for younger sons to wrest a position of respectability from an otherwise indifferent society – using an ideology that turns even death into an achievement, which they perversely label 'martyrdom'. It is not uncommon for sons from the same family in Gaza to fight for different factions. Societies with a glut of young men become temperamentally different from 'singleton societies' such as Europe's, where the prospect of sending an only child to war is almost unthinkable. Huntington's original clash of civilizations thesis might be reformulated to suggest that the presence of a youth bulge contributes to the willingness of a society to justify violence on religious or moral grounds, writes Heinsohn. The Palestinian population explosion can partly be blamed on European financial aid to the Palestinian Authority. He argues that had Europe made it clear back in the 1990s that the EU would no longer help subsidize ten-children families, perhaps Palestinian women would today be having two children, just like their Algerian counterparts. The Islamic youth bulge worldwide won't start to shrink until 2015. Against such demographic threats, America and Canada are the only geographic entities even theoretically capable of shielding themselves. Heinsohn contends that by 2030 many of Europe's more savvy non-Muslim youth will have already left for sanctuary in the US, and that in future America will leave its fortress only if its security is directly threatened. The Israeli fortress is already being built, in the shape of the security barrier. While the key to reducing violence is to reduce birth rates, such an option is unlikely because of religious opposition among traditional Muslims.[32]

For *The Economist*, 'America's debate on immigration may be painful, but Europe's is dysfunctional.'[33] As the American Senate was passing its version of an immigration bill, Spain was calling on the EU to help it stem a flood of migrants from West Africa to the Canary Islands. The EU sent patrol boats and aircraft to the seas which thousands have crossed (and where hundreds have died) in the hope of getting into Europe. Britain and France are reforming their immigration laws. Britain and Italy are fretting over the deportation of immigrant criminals. Six countries favour European 'integration contracts', or tests of would-be citizens' knowledge of their host countries as a precondition for getting passports. But if both sides of the Atlantic are experiencing similar upheavals, there is a big difference between their debates. The American version is out in the open, with tumultuous demonstrations clogging the streets. Politicians, lobbyists and interest groups cram the talk shows. In Europe, debate exists, but it is distorted and submerged. After second-generation immigrants staged their riots in France in late 2005, the Prime Minister downplayed the riots' significance. Questions about the impact of immigration merge into issues such as asylum, and even Islamic terrorism. 'The big difference in the way Europeans and Americans look at immigration', argues Kathleen Newland of the Migration Policy Institute in Washington, DC, 'springs from the fact that America protects its welfare system from immigrants but leaves its labour markets open, while the EU protects its labour markets and leaves its welfare system open.' Immigrants to Europe are welcomed with welfare benefits but cannot get jobs (their unemployment rate is far higher than average). America makes it easy even for illegal immigrants to get jobs but stops even legal ones claiming means-tested welfare benefits or subsidized housing. The result is that in America political debate centres on illegal immigration, and there is no sense that legal immigrants impose burdens on others. This obviously emanates from the fact that America is basically composed of immigrants, while Europe had a homogeneous culture and tradition. To take one example, Sweden's highly-developed and generous welfare state was sustainable only under the conditions which obtained previously – namely with a homogenous population committed to an unwavering Protestant work ethic, and always opting for a negotiated consensus to avoid public conflict. Therefore in Europe, even legal immigrants are often seen as sponging on others through welfare receipts; and the fact that some have taken jobs, which would not otherwise be done so cheaply, is forgotten. In Europe, says Danny Sriskandarajah of Britain's Institute for Public Policy Research, it is harder to talk about immigration as an economic issue. Politically, the debate is different, too. In America, immigration is a mainstream issue, and splits both parties. With few exceptions, European parties most willing to raise immigration as a political issue lie outside the mainstream – notably (though not only) far-right parties such as France's National Front and the Danish People's Party. The Netherlands is an exception: there, the politics of immigration entered the mainstream after two critics of multiculturalism were murdered. Britain is a partial exception, too: both Labour and Conservatives have espoused the cause of immigration control. But for the most part, big parties of the centre-left and centre-right have not made deep reform of immigration a high priority. Because immigration has been the preserve of the fringe, Europe's debate about it is bedevilled with accusations of racism, harming those who want to impose controls: they are tainted by association. But paradoxically, it does not help those who back immigration and benefit from it either (such as employers of immigrant labour). Moreover, there is less political representation of immigrants in European countries. Unlike America, which has two dozen congressmen with Latino backgrounds, hardly any of the 36,000 mayors in France are immigrants. Europe's black economy is large, making it harder for migrants to integrate through normal (legal) employment channels. Europeans harbour fears of globalization and immigrants are the most visible sign of that process. Nearly every government accepts that there is a need for European, as well as national, immigration policies now that most internal EU border controls have been removed. In the absence of agreements on such policies, governments are rewriting their own. Lastly, none of the usual engines of integration work well in Europe: churches, the military, jobs, schools.[34]

Francis Fukuyama wrote that Europe's multicultural model was based on group recognition and group rights. Out of a misplaced sense of respect for cultural differences and imperial guilt, it ceded too much authority to cultural communities to define rules of behaviour for their own members. But liberalism cannot be based on group rights because not all groups uphold liberal values. The civilization of the European enlightenment, of which contemporary liberal democracy is the heir, cannot be culturally neutral since liberal societies have their own values regarding the equal worth and dignity of individuals. Cultures that do not accept these premises do not deserve equal protection in a liberal democracy. Members of immigrant communities and their offspring deserve to be treated equally as individuals, not as members of cultural communities. There is no reason for a Muslim girl to be treated differently under the law from a Christian or Jewish one, whatever the feelings of her relatives. Multiculturalism was seen as a kind of ornament to liberal pluralism that would provide ethnic food, colourful dress and traces of distinctive historical traditions to societies often seen as numbingly conformist and homogeneous. Cultural diversity was something to be practised largely in the private sphere, where it would not lead to any serious violations of individual rights or otherwise challenge the liberal social order. By contrast, some contemporary Muslim communities are making demands for group rights that contradict liberal principles of individual equality, in addition to ambitions to challenge the secular character of the political order as a whole. This clearly intrudes on the rights of other individuals in society and pushes cultural autonomy well beyond the private sphere.[35]

Alarming analyses, that have the virtue of offering a new, more realistic perspective, must be heeded too. They are not written by 'Islamophobes', but by strategists and demographers who envision a dark future for Europe should the present trends continue. Some make outlandish suggestions, but they also consider the policy of multiculturalism as the means through which Islam returned and kept its separate identity, instead of integrating into existing cultures. Rather than speaking about pluralism, which would have allowed various groups from different backgrounds to rally around a social contract composed of common core values, in order to maintain a shared state and societal entity, multiculturalism has encouraged immigrants to demand that their own values, which are often contradictory with the host culture, gain equal footing (in the Netherlands this was dubbed the 'pillars of Dutch society'). This process unsurprisingly brings about the disintegration of society, causing frictions and competition between the various groups for state resources, instead of rallying them together for the common good. While policymakers are still grappling with how to assimilate immigrants, these analyses suggest that 'assimilation was becoming redundant', in other words that the problem of assimilation has come and gone before politicians have even acknowledged its existence.

At a conference in June 2006, one of Britain's most senior military

The New Demographic Balance in Europe and its Consequences 85

strategists warned that western civilization faces a threat on a par with the barbarian invasions that destroyed the Roman Empire. In an apocalyptic vision of security dangers, Rear Admiral Chris Parry said future migrations would be comparable to the Goths and Vandals while North African 'barbary' pirates could be attacking yachts and beaches in the Mediterranean within ten years. Europe, including Britain, could be undermined by large immigrant groups with little allegiance to their host countries. Parry, head of the Development, Concepts and Doctrine Centre at the British Ministry of Defence, is charged with identifying the greatest challenges that will frame national security policy in the future. Parry pointed to the mass migration which disaster in the Third World could unleash. 'The diaspora issue is one of my biggest current concerns', he said. 'Globalization makes assimilation seem redundant and old-fashioned … [the process] acts as a sort of reverse colonization, where groups of people are self-contained, going back and forth between their countries, exploiting sophisticated networks and using instant communication on phones and the internet.' Third World instability would lick at the edges of the West as pirates attacked holidaymakers from fast boats. Parry is not claiming all the threats will come to fruition, but what may happen if dangers are not addressed by politicians. He foresees wholesale moves by the armed forces to robots, drones, nanotechnology, lasers, microwave weapons, space-based systems and even 'customized' nuclear and neutron bombs. Lord Boyce, the former Chief of the Defence Staff, welcomed Parry's analysis. 'Bringing it together in this way shows we have some very serious challenges ahead', he said. 'The real problem is getting them taken seriously at the top of the government.'[36]

Parry identified the most dangerous flashpoints by overlaying maps showing the regions most threatened by factors such as agricultural decline, booming youth populations, water shortages, rising sea levels and radical Islam. He predicts that as flood or starvation strikes, the most dangerous zones will be Africa, particularly the northern half; most of the Middle East and Central Asia as far as northern China; a strip from Nepal to Indonesia; and perhaps eastern China. He pinpoints 2012 to 2018 as the time when the current global power structure is likely to crumble. Rising nations such as China, India, Brazil and Iran will challenge America's sole superpower status. This will take the form of 'irregular activity' such as terrorism, organized crime and 'white companies' of mercenaries in lawless areas. The effects will be magnified as borders become more porous and some areas sink beyond effective government control. Parry expects the world population to grow to about 8.4 billion in 2035. By then some 68 per cent of the population will be urban, with some giant metropolises becoming ungovernable. In an effort to control population growth, some countries may be tempted to copy China's 'one child' policy. This, with the widespread preference for male children, could lead to a ratio of boys to girls of as much as 150 to 100 in some countries. This will produce dangerous surpluses of young men with few economic prospects and no female company. 'When you combine the lower prospects for communal life with macho youth and economic deprivation you tend to get trouble, typified by gangs and organized criminal activity', said Parry. 'When one thinks of 20,000 so-called jihadists currently fly-papered in Iraq, one shudders to think where they might go next.' The competition for resources may lead to a return to 'industrial warfare' as countries with large and growing male populations mobilize armies, even including cavalry, while acquiring high-technology weaponry from the West. The subsequent mass population movements could lead to the 'Rome scenario'. The Western Roman Empire collapsed in the fourth and fifth centuries as groups such as Ostrogoths, Visigoths, Suevi, Huns and Vandals surged over its borders. The process culminated in the sack of Rome in 455 by the Alans and Vandals, in an invasion from North Africa. Parry estimated there were already more than seventy diasporas in Britain. In the future, he believes, large groups that become established in Britain and Europe after mass migration may develop 'communities of interest' with unstable or anti-western regions. Any technological advantage developed to deal with the threats was unlikely to last. 'I don't think we can win in cyberspace – it's like the weather – but we need to have a raincoat and an umbrella to deal with the effects', said Parry. Some of the consequences would be beyond human imagination to tackle.[37]

Other researchers believe that the demographic drowning of Europe by and in Islam, if the co-optation of Turkey came to pass, might oblige the Continent to 'adapt its societies to Islam'. One of them is Franck Fregosi, an expert in contemporary Islam in Europe at the Law and Religion Research Centre at Strasbourg's Robert Schuman University. Fregosi is studying the processes of Islam's institutionalization, organization and handling in a European context. He is also looking at the multiple forms of religious authority and the Islamic authorities in France and analyses present relations between Islam and European society. He attributes the European uneasiness about Islam to the al-Qa'ida attacks and the '9/11 effect'. The manifestations of this obsession are different in the various European countries. Fregosi believes that demographically speaking, European Islam is a reality. European Muslims have strong roots in Europe because not all of them are first-generation immigrants. Many living in Europe today were actually born within European borders. Yet their identity also stems from the history peculiar to each country. German Muslims are of Turkish origin while French Muslims mostly have roots in North Africa. Many British Muslims hail originally from the Indian subcontinent. These communities define themselves partly by their differing countries of origin. For example, Turkish Muslims living in Germany see themselves as a separate community without substantial ties binding them to French North African Muslims.

Yet there is also a notion of European solidarity for some Muslims. Young French girls suspended from a state school in Alsace for wearing their hijab had no qualms about going to Belgian schools instead. They belonged to a Turkish radical Muslim group which is largely based in Germany. Thanks to such Islamic links, European Muslims cross European borders a great deal and in this sense are ahead of other Europeans. Nevertheless, he believes we cannot really talk of a European Muslim community. In reality it is made up of small fiefdoms which compete to attract members from the Muslim population. In France, for instance, large Muslim federations do not unite a large majority of the immigrants despite the existence now of the French Muslim Council. In several French cities there are many different mosques, each with its own small separate community. Spanish Muslim communities have similarly failed to establish enough common ground to draw up a religious education programme. Some writers and observers contend that this religion is pluralistic in its practice and theoretical interpretations and should remain so, for there is always a risk with standardization. The challenge for Fregosi is not so much one of adapting Islam to European society but of adapting European society to Islam, thus fulfilling the dream, indeed the demand, of Muslim leaders. The rationale is that discriminatory attitudes against the Muslim community increase Muslim frustration and harden the resolve of certain groups who turn to radicalism, and European mentalities and bureaucracies therefore need to change.[38] This *dhimmi*-like attitude towards Islam will certainly facilitate the Islamization of the continent, much to the chagrin of strategists like Parry.

Muslim governments have little incentive to control the migration of their citizens, not least because they usually send cash home. These governments typically show concern about their citizens only when they have migrated. Then these people are no longer volatile proof of their own failures, but victims of some wealthy foreign government's indifference. The only lasting solution is for failed societies to encourage family planning and develop their own economies to keep more of their own people home. Ironically, the more western elites ignore their own laws, allow unassimilated ethnic ghettos, and profit from an exploitative labour market, the more their own nations will begin to resemble the very places immigrants fled from.[39] The fact that migration is all in one direction is an unspoken admission by the Muslims that their societies are inferior to the West. Should they succeed in their goal of constituting the majority in their new homes and eventually transforming the West into *Dar al-Islam*, they will effectively be importing their failed political culture and thereby neutralizing the very reason that attracted them to the West in the first place.

Since the problematic immigrants to Europe originate from Muslim lands, it is instructive to examine citizenship laws in the Muslim countries themselves. As a rule, the acquisition of citizenship by both Arabs and foreigners is difficult and complex in all Arab countries. With Shi'ites comprising 70 per cent of its population of 700,000, Bahrain is ruled by the minority Sunni. Only 62 per cent of the population are citizens (with the same ratio of Shi'ites and Sunnis), and the rest are foreigners or are stateless. To ameliorate the Sunnis' minority status, Bahrain eased the citizenship laws for Sunni Arabs, who were even imported from places such as Syria, Jordan and Egypt. Sunni Arabs can obtain Bahraini citizenship much more easily than Bahraini Shi'ites who have been living in the country for many years, without any civil status.

Only 45 per cent of Kuwaiti residents are citizens. Kuwait stopped granting citizenship to foreigners in 1966. Even Kuwaiti residents who were not counted in the 1965 census could not obtain citizenship until an amendment to the law was passed recently. Kuwaiti women who marry foreigners lose their citizenship until such time as they divorce or are widowed. Their children are not entitled to citizenship nor to citizenship rights such as voting or running for office. They can obtain only a temporary driving licence; they cannot attend government schools or obtain official government documents; they cannot have a job in government offices and they must pay for their health care, which is provided free to citizens. In 2005, Kuwait slightly amended its citizenship law, so that residents who have 'performed lofty deeds on behalf of the country' may request citizenship. In effect, the Kuwaiti Interior Minister arbitrarily decides who will receive citizenship. The United Arab Emirates does not grant citizenship to foreign citizens, Arabs or not, unless it is someone with ties to the government.

The acquisition of citizenship by Palestinian residents of these countries is extremely difficult for a number of reasons. First, the Palestinians have long been regarded as troublemakers and Arab governments fear the terrorism that Palestinians may bring to their shores. Second, the Arabs do not wish to see a settlement of the Palestinian issue. Their value lies in maintaining their 'refugee' status *ad infinitum*, so that they remain a festering sore to confront Israel on international platforms. The hundreds of thousands of Palestinians living in their domain would happily accept citizenship, as they have done in many western countries. No other people anywhere in the world are considered refugees after the second generation, except for the Palestinians – to further the Arabs' political agenda against Israel. Thus has the Palestinian 'refugee problem' been inoculated against a solution.

An amendment to the Saudi Citizenship Law in 2004 permits Saudi residents who have been in the country for over ten years and work in professions that the country needs – primarily doctors, engineers and technicians – to apply for citizenship. This was the first time that an Arab country – with the exception of

Jordan – has been ready to grant citizenship to Palestinians, albeit with restrictions. The Arab League has determined that the children of Palestinian refugees could reside, work and study in Arab countries as if they were citizens, but they would be unable to acquire citizenship. Until 1978, Egyptian authorities granted equal rights to Palestinian refugees (although they needed renewable permits), even if they did not receive citizenship. But after Anwar Sadat's visit to Israel, Palestinians acquired the status of foreigners. The children of an Egyptian woman who married a Palestinian were now classified as Palestinians, although this regulation has been relaxed. In addition, it costs approximately $200 every time children's residency permits are renewed, and medical care has to be paid for as if they were foreigners. The justification given for not granting citizenship to Palestinian children was that Egypt did not want to cause the 'loss of the Palestinian identity' of the children. Jordan, which granted citizenship to Palestinian refugees who arrived there from the West Bank (which Jordan had ruled until 1967, instead of forming a Palestinian state), does not grant it to Palestinians who fled to the Gaza Strip (ruled by Egypt until 1967, again at the expense of a Palestinian state). The result is that Jordanian women who marry Palestinian residents of Gaza cannot obtain Jordanian citizenship for their husbands and children.

In a salutary lesson for Europe, the deputy speaker of the Bahraini parliament, Abd al-Hadi Marhoun, remarked:

> We must carefully assess the threat on the threshold of the identity of the nation and the citizen, his ability to support himself and the future of coming generations. We cannot legislate laws to create an artificial mosaic using force. Human beings and societies are not metals or chemical substances or natural colours that can be melted and reformed – this situation [of artificially granting citizenship] will lead to separation and social and ethical divides that will never be repaired.

And he was referring to granting citizenship to Muslim Arab residents of a Muslim Arab country. This difficulty explains, perhaps, why Israel's restrictions on granting citizenship to Palestinian spouses of Israelis hardly reverberated in the Arab world. Europe, too, may have to stop conferring automatic citizenship to everyone born on the continent.[40]

Between 1970 and 1980, the developed world took about one million migrants a year from poor countries. According to the UN, at least 2.2 million migrants will arrive in the developed world every year from now until 2050. Britain's population will rise from sixty million to approaching sixty-nine million by 2050 – almost entirely because of immigration. The latest figures from the UN's population division predict a global upheaval without parallel in human history over the next four decades. There will be billions more people in Africa, Asia and the Middle East. Of these, tens of millions will migrate to Europe and America, while the indigenous populations of most western countries will either stagnate or decline. The gap in wealth and opportunity between the rich and poor worlds will be the most significant 'pull factor' behind this change. But the pressure exerted by rapidly rising populations in developing countries will also be an important underlying cause. This massive population growth will lead to land degradation on a huge scale and place an immense strain on the limited water resources of poor countries.[41]

NOTES

1. World population statistics, 6.6 billion, *CIA World Factbook*, July 2007 estimate.
2. Mark Henderson, 'People in Ethnically Diverse Area less Trusting of Others', *The Times*, 30 August 2007.
3. Sarah Wildman, 'Europe Rethinks its Safe Haven Status', *The Christian Science Monitor*, 24 May 2006.
4. Ibid.
5. Ibid.
6. Robert Smith, 'Islam will be Dominant UK Religion', *Gulf Daily News* (Bahrain) 10 March 2004.
7. Daniel Pipes, 'More Converts to Terrorism', *FrontPageMagazine.com*, 7 December 2005.
8. Amitai Etzioni, *From Empire to Community* (New York: Macmillan, 2004).
9. Eurostat, the Statistical Office of the European Communities. In January 2006, the population of the EU twenty-five was estimated at 453.5 million. The addition of the two 2007 accession countries with a further 29.3 million raised the new EU total to 482.8 million. http://epp.eurostat.ec.europa.eu/cache/ITY_OFFPUB/KS-NK-06-016/EN/KS-NK-06-016-EN.PDF
10. Anthony Browne and Suna Erdem, 'Education Clash holds up EU Talks', *The Times*, 8 April 2006.
11. Thomas Bell, 'Malaysia Considers Switch to Islamic Law', *The Daily Telegraph*, 1 September 2007.
12. Barry Rubin, 'The Region: East and West', *The Jerusalem Post*, 5 August 2007.

13. Nick Meo, 'Islam's War on Sin Dims Bright Lights in a Nation Torn between Cultures', *The Times*, 18 August 2007.
14. 'Saudi Police "Stopped" Fire Rescue', BBC News, 15 March 2002.
15. Abu al-Ala' al-Mawdudi, *Nationalism in India* (Malihabad, 1948), pp.5–11.
16. Robert Burns, *The Crusader Kingdom of Valencia* (Cambridge, MA: Harvard University Press, 1967), p.303.
17. Walter Laqueur, *The Last Days of Europe: Epitaph for an Old Continent* (New York: Thomas Dunne Books, 2007).
18. Stanley Kurtz, 'European Lessons – The Last Days of Europe show how Immigration is at the Root of Europe's Current Problems', *National Review*, 6 June 2007.
19. David Starkey, 'Henry was Wrong. Put Religion back in its Box – Our Outdated Link between Church and State is Dangerous in a Fundamentalist Era', *Sunday Times*, 12 November 2006.
20. 'US Envoy to UN: ME Conflicts could lead to Conflagration', *The Jerusalem Post*, 27 August 2007.
21. Cited by William Anthony Hay, 'Misplaced Faith', *Opinion Journal*, 22 February 2007.
22. Kurtz, 'European Lessons'.
23. *Reuters*, cited by *Haaretz*, 8 April, 2006.
24. Molly Moore, 'With End of French School Year Comes Threat of Deportation', *The Washington Post*, 15 June 2006.
25. Ibid.
26. Ibid.
27. Ahiya Raved, 'Ex-Mossad Chief warns of Muslim European Cities and of World War Three', in his address at the Technion in Haifa, Israel, 4 June 2006.
28. 'Jihadists' Return Worries Europe', *The Washington Times*, citing *AFP* 18 May 2006.
29. Samuel Huntington, *The Clash of Civilizations* (New York: Free Press, 2002 New Edn).
30. Gunnar Heinsohn, *Sohne und Weltmacht: Terror im Aufstieg und Fall der Nationen* (Zurich: Orell Füssli Verlag, 2003).
31. Wafa Amr, 'Palestinians say fed up with Gunmen', *Reuters*, 7 June 2007.
32. Jonas Attenhofer, 'Youth Bulge Violence', *The Jerusalem Post*, 10 April 2007; Christopher Caldwell, 'Youth and War, a Deadly Duo', *Financial Times*, 5 January 2007.
33. 'Talking of Immigrants: America's Debate on Immigration may be Painful, but Europe's is Dysfunctional', *The Economist*, 1 June 2006.
34. Ibid.
35. Francis Fukuyama, 'The Wrong Kind of Freedom Endangers the West', *Sunday Times*, 28 January 2007.
36. Peter Almond, 'Beware: the New Goths are Coming', *Sunday Times*, 11 June 2006.
37. Ibid.
38. Philippe Jacque, 'The Challenge is to Adapt our Societies to Islam', *Café Babel, The European Magazine*, 16 December 2004 (translated from French by Veronica Newington).
39. Victor Davis Hanson, 'A Borderless World – The Immigration Problem is Global', *National Review*, 31 May 2007.
40. Zvi Bar'el, 'The Arab Version of the Citizenship Law', *Haaretz*, 1 June 2005.
41. David Blair, 'UN Predicts Huge Migration to Rich Countries', *The Daily Telegraph*, 15 March 2007.

CHAPTER TWO

Britain: Leading the Way

The most immediate sequel of the July 7 2005 attacks in London was disarray. Both the Prime Minister and his chief of police were flabbergasted that young Britons who were born and educated in Britain and benefited from the country's generous welfare allowances could commit such a horrendous 'crime' against their country. Unlike regular criminals who take risks for economic gain, the terrorists in London were not seeking any benefit for themselves. They were ideological terrorists, who sought a political or religious goal. And as those young people did not act alone, but were indoctrinated, organized, financed, trained and dispatched by a Muslim terrorist group, the issue at hand was no longer the arrest and incarceration of individual violators of the law in order to maintain public order and safety, but one of a wide-ranging soul-searching of the British anti-terrorist apparatus with a view to stemming what was finally perceived as a real and concrete threat to national security. A revision was needed of the legal loopholes which had allowed the ideologues of terrorism to feel free in London, of the necessary security arrangements to safeguard public transportation and public institutions, to educate the complacent public to become more alert, to monitor Muslim centres of incitement and to be more wary of provocative imams, like Abu Hamza al-Masri and Omar Bakri Mohammed, who had been allowed to roam the country at will, to recruit young Britons for training camps in Afghanistan and to instil their poisonous jihadism into the minds of mindless people.

The major showpiece of the new policy was Abu Hamza's arrest and trial, which ended in conviction. Abu Hamza, whose real name is Mostafa Kamel Mostafa, was dubbed 'The Hook' by the media, due to his hook-like prosthesis which replaced the two hands he lost in a minefield 'work accident' in Afghanistan years back. He had a criminal record in Egypt and was a fugitive from the Egyptian legal system, but no one in Britain questioned his 'right' to obtain a visa of entry into Britain. No one inquired about the circumstances of his serious injury, which might have clarified his Afghani and violent background. As Amir Taheri pointed out,[1] Abu Hamza was given a three-month visa, after which no one expelled him, even as he began working illegally as a club bouncer. In May 1980, barely ten months after he arrived in Britain to dodge national service in Egypt, he entered into a bigamous marriage with a British woman of Catholic Spanish origin, in order to gain a permit to stay permanently. Their four-year marriage produced a son who, some years later, was involved in terrorist escapades in the Yemen. Taheri also makes the point that while the British denied the Egyptian owner of Harrods, Muhammed Fayed, a British passport despite the decades he spent in London and his contribution to its economy, Abu Hamza, the terrorist and Muslim radical who lived off the British social welfare system, easily obtained one. Back from Afghanistan, he promoted himself as a Muslim scholar though he was never trained to be one, and took over illicitly the Finsbury Park mosque which he turned into a hotbed of hostility and incitement, again without questions being asked. Encouraged by his success, he started recruiting for terrorist activities, leading demonstrations and making fiery speeches to his followers, without any interference by the British authorities. *The Suicide Factory*, serialized in *The Times*, points out that he pleaded guilty at a magistrates' court to overstaying his visitor's visa. He was given a conditional discharge followed by permission to remain, but had his immigration status been investigated, he could have been deported. Abu Hamza was later placed in the Belmarsh top security prison in south London after being sentenced to seven years for incitement to murder and racial hatred.[2]

It was announced in August 2007 that Abu Hamza may be freed from prison in 2008 after James Ujaama, an al-Qa'ida informer, said he was no longer prepared to testify against him. This may lead to the collapse of the American request for Abu Hamza's extradition now going through British courts. He will qualify for parole in 2008 and may go free. Ujaama, a Muslim convert from Seattle, was charged with trying to set up the Oregon camp with Abu Hamza and Haroon Rashid Aswat, another Briton. After his arrest in 2003 Ujaama struck a deal with the FBI: he promised to testify against Abu Hamza and Aswat and was allowed to plead guilty to a lesser charge of aiding the Taleban, which left him with a reduced sentence. But while on supervised release,

Ujaama fled on a false passport to Belize, where he was arrested in December 2006. The more serious terror-related charges against him have been reinstated, and he faces a thirty-year sentence. According to court transcripts, Ujaama said: 'Part of the reason I left the US was to avoid having to ... give testimony in the criminal matters against Abu Hamza and others.'[3] The wife of Abu Hamza complained about her husband's treatment in prison. In a letter to a London-based Islamic organization, al-Maqreze Centre for Historical Studies, Nagat Mostafa, said her husband claimed to be the victim of racist bullying and Islamophobia in Belmarsh. Prison officers, meanwhile, gave warning of the threat of extremists 'radicalizing' inmates. Steve Gough, the vice-chairman of the Prison Officers' Association, said: 'If you go to Belmarsh you'd see twenty going to Friday prayers a few years ago. Now you'll see 150. Put it this way, we're a power station and you don't want us to explode. The radical Muslims make the IRA look like kittens.'[4]

Instead of pursuing betterment and trying to bring themselves up to the level of the general population by adapting, assimilating and working hard, many Muslim immigrants have resorted to self-pity and victimhood which together make them impervious to criticism and self-criticism, the prerequisites for advancement. For any suggestion for improvement is interpreted as 'racism' and 'Islamophobia', and that sentiment of resentment by the Muslim populace is reflected in the statements of its leadership. Tony Blair repeatedly said that moderate Muslims are not doing enough to tackle the problem of extremism in their communities. He called for a more 'fundamental' debate, where extremists' views and ideology were condemned – not just their methods. Blair said there was an impression Muslim leaders sympathized with extremists' grievances but disagreed with their actions. Speaking before the Commons Liaison Committee, Blair said: 'In the end, government itself cannot go and root out the extremism in these communities. I profoundly disagree that the problem here is that the government hasn't acted.'[5]

Detailed media coverage of 7/7 and subsequent terrorist plots became routine in the British media. Though cynics claimed that such stories were encouraged by the British Government to justify the draconian measures belatedly adopted to curb terrorism, there is no doubt that public awareness of the imminent dangers posed by terrorism had been considerably raised. For example, the debate in Britain as to whether the half a million illegal immigrants should be granted an 'amnesty' and allowed to apply for work permits, raised the issue of the additional tax money that the project would cost. The Institute for Public Policy Research argued that the forced deportation of illegal migrants is neither feasible nor desirable, because most of them cannot be found and the cost of deporting them would be too high, based on the calculation of £11,000 per individual, or a total of £4.7 billion. The head of the institute said that though 'no one likes illegal immigration, the subject is an extremely difficult one for politicians to tackle. We are not going to deport hundreds of thousands of people from the UK, for otherwise our economy would shrink and we would notice it immediately in uncleaned offices, dirty streets and unstaffed pubs.'[76] In other words, the controversy no longer involved the celebrated moral values and liberalism of the British, but on the practicality and cost of their application. The choice offered to the British populace is either to risk their security or endure uncleaned offices and streets. The option of cleaning them themselves, and the idea that life itself and a secure environment are more important than a clean one, never occurred to those who pass the responsibility from government to research institutions, and offer no real exit from the crisis. The novel idea of issuing identity cards to all British citizens, who were never accustomed to this level of invasion of their privacy, might be enforced despite the strong opposition to it. That would take time to implement, even if the illegal immigrants, for whom this measure is primarily intended, could all be located and identified. One of the major inhibitions in Britain towards 'regularization' of immigration has been the political correctness involved in discussing immigration, religion, race, discrimination and the harsh measures necessary to halt the imminent dangers which the country faces. It took a foreigner, Sri Lankan refugee Johannes Shanmugam, who finally spelled out the ingratitude of many of the Muslim refugees who were given asylum in Britain, and yet do not cease criticizing their benefactors. He announced the foundation of a Political Correctness Corrective Party, and declared: 'We are so scared in this country of offending minority people that we have come full circle and got into an absurd situation. Is it all right for me to serve a black pudding, should Blackpool be renamed, where is it going to end?' And, referring to Muslims without himself daring to mention them by name, he added: 'I do think we must curb immigration. I can say this because I am dark-skinned ... We need to have a civilized political debate. You can't go around waving placards and threatening to behead someone just because you disagree with them."[7]

During the summer of 2006, Tony Blair's Government admitted it had no policy for controlling the size of Britain's population. He refused to estimate the number of illegal immigrants in Britain, although a study calculated there could be up to 570,000. He agreed with an MP's suggestion that the issue was 'political dynamite', adding that it was difficult to give objective facts on the benefits and 'disbenefit' of migration. Migration on the whole was positive and with benefit to countries but had to be controlled. Allowing all illegal migrants to stay would encourage many more to come, he said.[8] *The Daily Telegraph* reported that thousands of failed asylum seekers were paid millions of pounds to return to their home countries because it is cheaper than trying to deport them. An offer under which rejected applicants, or those who agree to withdraw their asylum request, are paid £2,000 in cash and £1,000 'benefits in kind', was taken up by almost 2,000 people in the first four months of 2006. The £2,000 cash payment was introduced in January 2006 in addition to a £1,000 resettlement grant in an effort to encourage more prospective refugees to abandon their attempts to stay in the country. Only those who applied for asylum before 1 January 2006 were eligible for the enhanced package and they had to leave between 1 July and the end of December 2006.[9]

New immigration proposals were published in March 2007, including reducing the length of a visitor's visa to three months and raising the age for a marriage visa. Among the proposals were further measures to ensure that foreigners do not travel to Britain unless entitled to do so. Britons sponsoring visits by overseas relatives will be fined at least £1,000 if their relatives overstay or work illegally. Britons who support a sponsored family vistor's visa will also be expected to maintain and accommodate their family members during the visit, and fund non-emergency medical care. All visitors will be made to take out medical insurance. Immigration overstayers will have their bank accounts frozen and families of overstayers will be barred from bringing in other relatives in future. Universities and employers will be banned from bringing in people in future if foreigners they have sponsored fail to return home. The measures are planned as the government prepares for a huge increase in the number of people heading for Britain. In 2005–2006 two million visas were granted to non-EU visitors. The plan also proposed raising the minimum age for a marriage visa from 18 to 21, in an attempt to stop forced marriages. It will largely affect people from the Indian subcontinent and will mean 3,000 fewer people coming to Britain each year. A US-style visa-waiver programme will be introduced, with all countries outside the EU being assessed as to whether their citizens should require a visa to visit Britain.[10] The Conservative Party wants to make it harder for Britons to marry foreigners in order to protect vulnerable young women from abuse. Of the 41,560 spouses and fiancées who came to Britain in 2005, 39 per cent travelled from the Indian subcontinent. More than 104,000 grants of settlement were made to spouses and dependents, an increase of 17 per cent on the previous year. Both husband and wife must be over 18 and wait two years before the foreign partner is given the right to stay in Britain. The Tories claim that there is strong anecdotal evidence that men are abusing the probationary period, serially marrying, and then abandoning, young women to collect dowry money.[11]

In May 2006 it emerged that more than 230 foreigners identified by MI5 and Scotland Yard as suspected terrorists were allowed to stay in Britain as asylum seekers. While their applications were processed, all were entitled to state benefits such as free housing and legal aid to pursue their claims that they would be persecuted in their home countries. The figures made a mockery of an announcement by Tony Blair after 7/7 that the government would automatically refuse asylum to anyone engaged in terrorism. The disclosure increased pressure on John Reid, the Home Secretary, who already faced claims that he misled the public over the affair of five Nigerians who were arrested while working as illegal immigrants at the Home Office, where they had worked for years. The figures on terrorist suspects reignited the debate over Britain's 'porous borders'. The Tories called for a US-style national border police to stop dangerous terrorists and criminals from entering the country.[12]

Blair's decade-long tenure in government has been the most demographically disastrous in British history. British citizenship has been granted to nearly one million foreign nationals since Labour assumed power in 1997. A record 161,000 obtained citizenship in 2005, a 15 per cent increase on 2004, and a further 214,000 lodged applications, representing an increase of 64 per cent. About half the new citizens in 2005 were people who qualified through being resident in the country for five years or more and around 20 per cent became British through marriage. The remainder were mainly dependent children. The rate of overseas settlement in Britain is four times greater than in the mid-1990s. In the late 1960s, about 75,000 new citizens a year were accepted for citizenship but this fell to about 50,000 after new laws were introduced in 1971. For about twenty-five years the annual figure remained near or below this level, falling to a low point of 37,000 in 1997, the year Labour took office. Since then, there has been a spectacular increase, with the rate of growth accelerating every year. The scale of new settlements is a principal driver behind the increase in Britain's population. The government asserted there was no limit to the numbers who can enter, but ministers put in place a new points-based work permit system designed to restrict settlement to highly-qualified immigrants. However, Sir Andrew Green, the chairman of MigrationWatch UK, countered: 'Immigration on this scale is changing the nature of our society without public consent. It is no longer acceptable.' The figures showed that 30 per cent of new citizens in 2005 were born in Africa and 19 per cent were from the Indian subcontinent.[13]

Perversely, the more terrorism suspects are arrested, the more they seem to multiply, particularly when those who have returned from combat training in camps in Pakistan, Afghanistan and elsewhere are included. James Hart, Police Commissioner for the City of London, warned that shortages of resources and trained surveillance teams were undermining attempts to monitor all suspects. He therefore had to make intelligent guesses about whom to watch, so the security of the nation amounted to a lottery. MI5 has drawn up a 'thermal map' of terror hotspots across Britain. The threat was believed to be particularly acute in the Manchester area, where police disclosed that several suspected would-be suicide bombers were stopped at the airport *en route* for Iraq in 2006. As a result of these warnings, MI5 has received funds to establish offices in Manchester, Liverpool, Leeds, Birmingham and Glasgow with others planned for Wales and the south-west.[14]

The British media made an effort to provide their readership with insights into the souls of British Muslims who are caught between the resentment of terrorism by the population and their own concern not to lose what they achieved in British society. Mustafa Kurtuldu, who survived the underground explosions in London, avowed to be himself the 'victim of extremist' (he dare not say Muslim) terrorism. He said that his family originates from many places, all Muslim or Muslim-minority, such as Turkey, Macedonia and Cyprus, and therefore he could fit nowhere. He intimated that though he was born in Britain, he was never captivated by nationalism of any sort, because a place of birth was not something one could choose. So, he found shelter for his uncertain identity in religion, which taught him to be open and tolerant. He admitted that though he had always felt a foreigner in Britain, July 7 helped him make the choice after he emerged from a wrecked underground train. In fact the choice had been made for him. He implied that all the questioning that he was subjected to, from both the police and the media, centred around one essential issue: 'Who are you Mustafa? Are you choosing Britain, the country where you were raised, educated and employed, or are you going to choose your brothers of faith, those murderers who killed innocent people?' His answer was a little convoluted:

> I like living here. One does generally have more freedom to practise one's religion than in other countries, particularly some Muslim countries. But I have always faced barriers and have suffered from an extreme racial and religious prejudice in the places where I have studied and worked. I would like the terrorists' supporters to show me some proof from the Qur'an or the *hadith* where the prophet Muhammad took an innocent life as an act of revenge … On July 7 only innocent people died and only innocent people suffered … Yes, innocent people suffer everyday in Iraq, Afghanistan and Chechnya, but retaliation like this is never the way … The new terror laws do scare me, but they were passed only because of what happened.[15]

Mustafa posed as the victim of terrorism, having escaped almost unscathed while tens of others had died. He implied that the western soldiers and other security forces who fight the war against terrorism, including those who protect him in his London shelter, are also terrorists, and the suffering people of the Muslim world ought to be understood when they resort to violence. If he had some knowledge of Islam, he would know how many times his prophet, and not only him, did take revenge on innocent people (remember the Jews of Medina and Khaybar, as examples). So he cannot hide behind the model of the prophet, who is repeatedly cited to justify the acts of modern terrorism. What has changed in him, according to his own reckoning is that he no longer trusts people as he used to. But he did not specify what sort of people ought not to be trusted: the Muslims who committed the act of terror to which he almost fell victim, or the British who came to his rescue, or his friends and colleagues who became more circumspect after the July 7 events. In conclusion, he admitted that he was 'British by definition', because this adjective referred to those born in, or citizens of, Britain. At the same time, he emphasized his Muslim identity, though he denied support for any sort of terrorism, 'whether the terrorists wear army uniform or not, or represent a state or not. They are all terrorists for me.' Evidently, he adopts the classic Muslim definition of terrorism that regardless of the reprehensible means used by anyone to annihilate indiscriminately innocent civilian passengers or bystanders, the main consideration is the goal that may justify terrorism, for those who are 'aggressed' have no choice but to retaliate in kind.[16]

Within Britain, the public remained puzzled by the direction the country was taking in the face of the traumas that the wave of Islamic terrorism sank it in and the dilemmas it was confronted with. Reverend Julie Nicholson admitted her anger and said she was undergoing a test of faith after she lost her daughter in the London bombings. Less than two years before the attacks on 7/7, she had become a parish priest. Confronted with an event that shook her world to its foundations, she found she could no longer reconcile her priestly function with her refusal to forgive the killers. Reverend Nicholson said: 'I did not feel there was any integrity in standing in front of a group of people week by week leading them through words of peace, reconciliation and forgiveness when I felt so distanced from those things myself.' Torn by the collision of faith and rage, she resigned from St Aidan's in Bristol. She has not quit the priesthood, although her faith became nuanced by doubt.[17]

'In terms of forgiveness for this act, I don't think it's incumbent on me to offer it', she said. 'It's not mine to give. I think forgiveness is a cheap grace.' In a BBC documentary she allowed the cameras to follow her to the Edgware Road subway station at the mouth of the tunnel where her daughter died. 'If I stand looking at the tunnel in Edgware Road, that's when I feel consumed with rage and bitterness', she said. 'But we should be outraged at what's going on in the world. Anger is not negative.' She was tempted to ask a priest where God was at that moment, but she had never believed in a God so omnipotent as to control all events. For her BBC documentary, London Underground agreed to halt a train briefly at the place where her daughter died. The moment was entwined with her musings on the

Pieta – the Christian vision of Mary cradling Jesus after his crucifixion. After the bombing, she said, 'physically holding and cradling' her daughter was impossible. But she had wanted for months to enter the tunnel 'and just stand a moment at that place where my daughter's life ended ... I feel that going into the tunnel and just pausing for a moment was as close as I could be to that moment where her life ended in that place. I feel that on a spiritual and emotional level I have cradled her, I have expressed what I needed to express of the Pieta.'[18]

The clerical leaders of Britain seem to be more sober than their political counterparts, for they have no constituency to compete for, and some of them have abandoned the 'let us all be friends' ideology. Indeed, on the sad anniversary of the London attacks, Jewish and Christian leaders called for renewed efforts to combat terrorism, although its Muslim origin was left unstated. The Archbishop of York, Dr John Sentamu, said: 'We need to show young people that there are far more worthy ideals to stake their lives on. We must out-imagine terrorism and that means believing and living a faith which will attract all idealists.' The Chief Rabbi, Dr Jonathan Sacks, in the *Jewish Chronicle*, said that the issues raised by the bombings were still unresolved. Campuses, professional groups and charities were being hijacked for sectarian political ends. He wrote: 'We have now reached a situation in which conflicts far away have been imported into Britain, poisoning the atmosphere of trust and civility on which a liberal democracy depends.'[19] What Sacks probably had in mind was the inflammatory anti-Israeli rhetoric of many Muslims in Britain, since they now regarded it as their duty to support any of their co-religionists in the world, regardless of whether it had anything to do with the British Government. In other words, not content with voicing their protests *against* the government for their perceived persecution and discrimination, they now wish to protest *to* the government and the Jewish community in Britain, for what is happening in the Middle East between Israel and the Arabs.

Radical Muslims in Britain, for example, have been critical of Hamas for failing to carry out a 'real' Islamic holy war. A number of British-based Muslim organizations have called on followers to wage a jihad on Israel. 'What the Jews are doing in Palestine today will no doubt disturb any true Muslim', a statement authored by Abdul Aziz al-Dimashqi said on the website of the Saved Sect group. 'However, what hurts us equally as much is to see the Muslims in Palestine calling for an independent Palestinian state, Palestinian constitutions, man-made law, democracy, freedom and so on. Hamas have no intention of establishing the shari'a, and are only concerned with having their own nationalistic state', the statement said. Calling on Muslims around the world to answer the call for jihad, the statement concluded: 'If a terrorist is a person who resists occupation, calls for the implementation of Islam and fights for his rights, then we are terrorists.' In an earlier statement, the same group said that 'Israel is a cancer, Islam is the answer', usefully spelling out that the conflict with Israel has its origins in religion and not territory. During protests against the Danish cartoons of Muhammad, members of the organization held similar signs declaring that 'Europe is a cancer.'

'The only solution and divine method to liberate Muslim land is jihad. Jihad, in shari'a, means fighting, not boycotting Coca-Cola or Fanta, and definitely not voting for man-made laws as suggested by many hypocrites', the Saved Sect declared. The organization also said that jihad was a means to bring about its long-term vision of an enormous Islamic state occupying the whole of the Middle East. 'The Khilafah [Caliphate, or Islamic state] is undoubtedly the permanent solution for the Muslim umma', the statement said. In pro-jihad forums used by British Muslims, anti-Israel hatred peppers discussions. 'I'm so fed up with these dirty, filthy Israeli dogs. May Allah curse them and destroy them all, and may they face the same fate as Banu Qurayzah!' wrote one contributor on the Muntadaa Islamist forum. Qurayzah was the name of a seventh-century Jewish tribe living in the Arabian Peninsula whose members were killed by Islam's prophet.[20]

Melanie Phillips's new book, *Londonistan*,[21] was another occasion to air in public the deteriorating social situation in London in particular and Britain in general. The term Londonistan was coined to describe a town which had become the major European centre for the promotion, recruitment and financing of Islamic terror and extremism. The exponents of violent jihad have always rather liked Britain for its extraordinary latitude to the most deranged Islamist dissidents from Saudi Arabia, Egypt, Afghanistan and the Maghreb, a latitude buttressed by supra-national legislation. It was one reason, often cited by Abu Hamza, why London had never suffered a Muslim terrorist attack until July 2005. Phillips describes the network of poisonously rabid and dangerous Islamist individuals, cheerfully claiming their state benefits whilst urging their followers, via their sermons or the internet, to wage war against Britain. The creed of multiculturalism takes much of the blame for the bizarre doublethink and intellectual vapidity of the liberal establishment in allowing Britain's famous tolerance to be so abused:

> As multiculturalism thus unwittingly fomented Islamist radicalism in the sacred cause of diversity it simultaneously forbade criticism of Muslim practices such as forced marriages or polygamy, or the withdrawal of children to be sent for long periods to Pakistan. Even to draw attention to such practices was to be labelled a racist ... And so, as British identity was steadily eviscerated by multiculturalism, real human rights abuses on British shores were studiously ignored and its victims left abandoned in its name.

Phillips does not make the politically convenient mistake of absolving the ideology of Islam from blame, although she clings to the view (supported by plenty of apologists for Islam, such as Karen Armstrong) that it is an ideology which has been perverted somewhere along the way. Her most impressive chapter deals with the false dichotomy presented, out of political expediency, by the government that Muslims can be conveniently divided into 'moderate' and 'radical' camps, despite the fact that both camps are more or less agreed upon the ideology; it is only the plan of action which differs.[22]

Another reviewer of Phillips's book illuminated other aspects of her findings, though some consider her an alarmist, while others believe she has understated the peril that the Londonistan phenomenon poses to the US and to Europe, both of which owe a profound debt to the British culture that is now in such disarray. When Daniel Johnson worked together with Phillips for the London *Daily Telegraph*, Iqbal Sacranie and Inayat Bunglawala, from the Muslim Council of Britain (MCB), came to see them several times. They strongly objected to the reporters' use of the phrase 'Islamic terrorism', and demanded that Osama Bin Laden be described not as an Islamic or even an Islamist terrorist but as an international one. To mention Islam in connection with terrorism, these lobbyists insisted, was Islamophobic. Their demands were rejected despite hints that Muslim readers might boycott the *Telegraph*; but the state has been more responsive. Editors must now tread carefully because the law now punishes Islamophobia as a 'hate' crime. He says that when Americans express anger or frustration at Europe's response to the global threat of Islamism, they generally make an exception for one country: Great Britain. The strong British presence in Iraq and Afghanistan, Blair's staunch support of Bush, the legacy of a common history, culture, and language; these have reassured Americans that the US has at least one ally across the Atlantic on which it can depend. If the book by Phillips is right, however, this is a dangerous illusion. A successful columnist and broadcaster, and at one time the news editor of the left-wing *Guardian*, Phillips reveals a very different Britain from the heroic nation that defied Hitler. She compares the mood today with that of the 1930s, the era of appeasement. Senior officials and their cultural cheerleaders still refuse to accept that they are confronted by a murderous, expansionist Islamic ideology, or that their own capital city has been transformed (in a term coined by the western intelligence community during the 1990s) into Londonistan. For Phillips, Britain is a nation in denial about Islam, about terrorism, about Israel, and above all about itself. *Londonistan* is, first and foremost, about the identity crisis provoked by the terrorist attack on London's transportation system in July 2005. As the British people learned to their horror, the 'suicide bombers' were not foreigners radicalized by suffering or oppression but British-born, with good families and good prospects. They differed from most of their contemporaries in only one respect: they were young Muslims who had repudiated not just British values but the elementary codes of humanity. The leader of the bombers, Mohammad Sidique Khan, left behind a surreal video in which, speaking in a Yorkshire accent, he blamed his act of mass murder on British atrocities against his people, meaning the Muslim umma. He owed allegiance not to Britain but to Islam. How many others might there be like Khan, biding their time before turning on their fellow citizens? Officials estimate that some 16,000 British Muslims actively engage in or support terrorism (not counting unknown numbers of foreigners resident in the country). Of these, some 3,000 have been trained at al-Qa'ida camps in Pakistan or Afghanistan.[23]

No less terrifying for Johnson is the fact that even the supposedly mainstream elements in the British Muslim community have become more radical in their political theology. As Phillips shows in a pitiless unmasking, many of the 'moderate' Muslims to whom the British authorities regularly pay obeisance are themselves hard-line Islamists, differing only by degree from more notorious recruiters for jihad. Of particular interest to Phillips is Sir Iqbal Sacranie, then secretary general of the MCB. Sacranie was knighted at the same time as Britain's Chief Rabbi Jonathan Sacks, evidently for reasons of multicultural balance, though there is no intellectual or moral comparison between Sacks, one of Britain's most respected religious leaders, and Sacranie, who rose to prominence by supporting Ayatollah Khomenei's fatwa against Salman Rushdie in 1988. The MCB was founded in November 1997, shortly after Tony Blair came to power. Though he was the government's chief Muslim interlocutor, Sacranie had an avowedly anti-Zionist and anti-Semitic agenda: he justified Hamas 'suicide bombings', boycotted Holocaust commemorations, and harassed pro-Israel politicians. When his equivocal attitude to terrorism was exposed by a BBC documentary, Sacranie accused his critics of being part of a 'Zionist conspiracy'. The real wonder, according to Phillips, is not so much that Sacranie and his followers had aired their detestable views, but that their propaganda had been granted legitimacy by British officialdom. Shortly before the 2005 bombings, Sir Ian Blair, London's police commissioner, declared: 'There is nothing wrong with being an Islamic fundamentalist ... Bridges will be built.' Even after the attack, the worst terrorist episode in London's history, an assistant police commissioner could tell the nation, 'Islam and terrorists are two words that do not go together.' Shortly afterward, the police, for fear of raising tensions, persuaded the government to abandon its request for new powers to close down extremist mosques, as well as its plans to outlaw one of the most dangerous Islamist organizations, Hizb ut-Tahrir. British security agencies do not understand Islamic jihad, Phillips argues, because they instinctively recoil from the idea of a war of religion. Having grown up in the shadow of Irish terrorism, they believe that, like the Irish Republican Army, the Islamists can eventually be induced, with the right package of concessions, to end their armed struggle. To Phillips, this is nonsense: there is no deal to be made with those who want to turn Britain into an Islamic republic.[24]

A historian's view of Muslim disengagement from British society was offered by Charles Moore, former editor of *The Daily Telegraph*. He argued that multiculturalism is not new in British history, and compares Jewish waves of immigration into Britain with its Muslim newcomers. He wrote that 350 years ago, Britain began to be a multiracial society. Driven out in 1290, 1656 marked the return of Jews to England. In the intervening centuries, Jews came to Britain on business, but they were not permitted to reside there or practise their religion. Their status was that of Christians (and Jews) in Saudi Arabia today. In 1656, Cromwell let 300 of them return. Though the Jewish community has never been enormous in Britain (at present, it is somewhere between 250,000 and 400,000), it has achievements out of proportion to its size.[25]

The Jews overcame prejudices that at first excluded them absolutely and later accepted them only on qualified terms (Jews could not sit in Parliament until the mid-nineteenth century, for example). The key reason is to be found in one of the earliest reports of Jews in England after their return. In 1663, Samuel Pepys visited a synagogue in London (something very unusual for a gentile at that time) and described the service which he witnessed. He did not like it, but noted that the Jews said a special prayer for the King. In other words, they accepted the civil power as part of their religious duty. No believing Jew will obey a civil law that forces him to disobey his religious law, but if there is no conflict, his religion teaches him that he must obey the law of the land. In *Pirkei Avot* (Ethics of the Fathers), which brings together rabbinical wisdom over the centuries, Jews are told: 'Pray for the welfare of the government, for, without the fear of it, people will swallow one another alive.' Even the most cursory study of Jewish life shows that it is full of disputes. There are splits between orthodox and reformed Jews, and within orthodoxy. There are thousands of secular Jews who feel very Jewish, but refuse to have their Jewishness defined by religion. There is ceaseless, often angry argument: when you read the Christian Gospels, you find that one of the most common scenes is of learned men quarrelling. That is still the case in Jewish culture. But because of this basic agreement among Jews about the status of the secular law, the effect of these quarrels on the wider society is minimal.[26]

Moore asserts that if Judaism were an aggressive religion, seeking to lay down its law for all mankind, then the *Dayan* (religious judge), who adjudicates on the endless delicate points of Jewish law, could acquire menacing power. Like the Ayatollah Khomeini in Iran after 1979, the *Dayan* could tell people to kill in the name of God. Instead, by policing the difference between the precise duties of Jews and the duty to society at large, this scholar helps define the space necessary for people with beliefs quite at variance with those of the majority to live harmoniously among them. In this sense, people can be 'fundamentalist' and yet perfectly at home in a society which is not. For 2,000 years, Jews have developed a subtle understanding of the difference between the ideal society that would exist if God's laws prevailed everywhere and the world as it is. The Jewish concept of *mitzvah* (the obligation to perform a good deed) means a good deed done for its own sake. There is also the idea of '*chesed*', which is man's kindness to all men. Thus does a potentially very closed community open itself out. In the past half-century, Muslims have come where the Jews came earlier, and in much larger numbers. They have also experienced the unhappiness that comes when one's religion is misunderstood or derided. But unlike the Jews, too many of their leaders tend to teach them that such slights must be avenged, that existence as a minority is just a temporary misfortune, not a state to be lived with, and that the law of England is virtually no law at all. If that attitude continues, society is reduced to a conflict about who will swallow whom alive. To avoid that is a huge and urgent task.[27]

The British willingness to be over-accommodating towards Islamic sensibilities has had the perverse effect of making integration less likely. A Staffordshire theme park, Alton Towers, was booked by Islamic Leisure for a 'Muslim fun day' on 17 September 2006, many months after a young British couple had booked the venue for their wedding celebration. Tickets were available only through Islamic Leisure, and the event was advertised on the website belonging to the Muslim Public Affairs Committee (MPAC). Special provisions were negotiated, including segregated adult ride zones, a ban on alcohol, music and gaming machines, halal food stalls and prayer areas, and women had to be covered in accordance with religious custom. The couple contacted the organizers of the Muslim fun day, who confirmed their wedding party would have to adhere to their terms and conditions. Yaseen Patel, director of Islamic Leisure, said women would have to wear clothing that covered up their bodies, although they would not have to wear the Muslim headscarf.[28] Although the organizers eventually cancelled the event, Rod Liddle of the *Spectator* parodied the plans, providing a glimpse of how impatient people had become with the 'special treatment' given to Muslims alone. And quite apart from the antagonism the proposed event engendered within the 'godless kufr press', it also caused problems for devout Muslims, some of whom considered it inappropriate to disport themselves in such a temple of decadence: 'even if the best of the decadence will have been expunged for twenty-four hours'. Liddle reported the fervent debate taking place on the message board of MPAC. Wasn't this haram? (prohibited by Islam), one correspondent asked, haram being a word from the Qur'an, 'meaning the sort of naughty behaviour which Allah really, really hates'. Another insisted that as Muslims they should not have fun. One blogger pointed out that the prophet never went to leisure parks and that the money is going to a 'kufr' enterprise. The majority of remarks complained that women were to be allowed to the park at all, never mind being segregated from the men and forced to don the usual sackcloth and ashes. Integration was the reason given by one MPAC spokesman for the event taking place, but to describe such a staggeringly insular event as something which will improve integration is hardly credible.[29]

When Sacranie once remarked that homosexuality was damaging to society, Britain's champion of gay rights, Peter Tatchell, complained that the British beleaguered minorities should stick together, the implication being that both Muslims and gays were similarly oppressed by the straight, white, male, Christian hegemony – as if the Islamic distaste for homosexuality were a mere aberration, and that beyond this inconvenient difference of opinion there was a unity of purpose and aspiration shared by these two discriminated-against communities. Liddle concluded:

> If being thrust up ... in a boob tube on the dodgems offends, then close your eyes and think of England, or Allah; whichever does the job. Hell, those of us who find not the remotest succour in Allah have to do much the same thing. In this crowded island we are all afflicted with distaste for some of our fellow men and women from time to time, even if that distaste is not always dignified as being God-given. But to ring-fence an entire day at a public leisure complex because you cannot face being anywhere near the rest of us; that is as eloquent a statement of separateness, of apartheid, as you could wish to get. It says, simply: We find you repulsive to the degree that we cannot share our space with you. We abhor you and the way you live your lives. In which case the rest of us may find it all too easy to respond: Well, clear off, then.[30]

A radical Muslim, who ousted a cleric from his mosque on the south coast with a campaign of violence, said he believes Tony Blair is a 'legitimate target' for terrorists. Abubaker Deghayes, who now runs the mosque in Brighton and whose brother Omar is a detainee at Guantanamo, told an undercover reporter that he endorsed the views of George Galloway, the Respect MP, who said an attack on the Prime Minister by a 'suicide bomber' could be morally justified. Deghayes said he prayed for Allah to support anyone who attacked Blair. Court documents show Deghayes took over the mosque using violence, intimidation and threats. Dr Abduljalil Sajid, chairman of the Muslim Council for Religious and Racial Harmony, and a government adviser on Islam, was forced out as head of the mosque by Deghayes and his supporters. Sussex Police Special Branch held a number of meetings with Sajid about extremist elements at the site, but no overt action was taken. Police sources have confirmed that in the past, extremist literature had been found at the site and that some of those attending the mosque were suspected of having fought as mercenaries abroad. The Charity Commission, which has jurisdiction over the mosque because it is run as a charity, said it did not know how the mosque was receiving and spending money and added that it was operating in breach of legal requirements. On Fridays, it can attract 100–200 worshippers. Deghayes also said he was unconcerned about British troops being killed in Iraq because the issue was 'all clear in international law. Under international law anybody who's been invaded, they are entitled to self-defence.' But he urged his interviewer to be careful with whom he discussed his views for fear of prosecution. Deghayes said: 'Don't talk openly, like Tony Blair [is] an open target. Now you can be taken in for glorifying terrorism. [Even] among Muslim Brothers ... there are *munafiqs* [hypocrites]. There are spies, all sorts of people.' Deghayes insisted he had understood Galloway to mean Blair was a legitimate political target. Deghayes, who is from Libya but now has British citizenship, said he was personally opposed to violence.[31]

How does a mosque that was mainstream ('moderate' in government parlance) become 'radical'? Isn't it the same congregation of believers? If the imam was 'radical', why did he get British citizenship? If he implied a threat to the life of the Prime Minister, why wasn't he arrested? If the mosque was in breach of the law, why was no one interrogated or arrested? David Courtailler, a convicted supporter of al-Qa'ida who is connected to a number of terrorists responsible for the Madrid bombings and 9/11, converted to Islam at the Brighton mosque days before travelling to Afghanistan. Courtailler, who received a four-year prison sentence in 2004 for aiding terrorists, was given £1,000 by Omar Deghayes to travel to a jihad training camp in Afghanistan, according to records from his Paris trial. Activists criticized the lack of evidence to justify holding Omar Deghayes, saying his incarceration is a case of mistaken identity. According to court records, his older brother Abubaker Deghayes orchestrated a sustained campaign of intimidation against Sajid. Deghayes, 38, became aggressive towards those running the Brighton mosque after they were sceptical about his plan to start an Islamic primary school on the site in 1996. He told the trustees he wanted to give Muslim children an education away from 'western influences' and 'misleading ideologies', but the scheme was rejected. In May 1997 Brighton county court found Sajid had been assaulted four times by Deghayes in December 1996 and January 1997 and threatened with a knife by one of his supporters.

Injunctions were issued to prevent Deghayes and his supporters approaching Sajid but he was forced out of the mosque, followed by the trustees of the Sussex Muslim Society charity, which operates it. Deghayes wrote to the Charity Commission in 1996 stating that he and his followers were in charge but regulators at the commission said they had not been properly elected and were not entitled to run the charity. The Charity Commission closed the case in 2004 when new elections were promised, although by then all the charity's ties with the original trustees had been severed. Charity Commission records indicate that since 1998 the charity has filed incomplete and sporadic accounts. No accounts for the past four financial years have been received. The takeover of the mosque is similar to the coup executed at the Finsbury Park mosque in north London by Abu Hamza, who drove out the trustees and imam using violence and slander so he could use the site to expound his extremist rhetoric. Abu Hamza also spent some time living at the Brighton mosque in the late 1980s. Rafique Miah, one of the trustees before the takeover, said: 'Abubaker came in as a worshipper. Then he started to take over. When we told Abubaker, this is England, we have to follow the law, he would say "British law under my foot".'[32]

The number of mosques which preach radical views is unknown, since they are not monitored. Even those clerics who have established relationships with officialdom cannot always be labelled 'moderate', as illustrated by the case of Sajid. His 'moderate' credentials notwithstanding, he was involved in controversy on a visit to Australia in October 2006, when he defended as 'a great scholar' the

Australian imam, Sheikh Taj Din al-Hilali. The latter likened immodestly dressed women to meat that attracted predators and suggested that they were to blame for being attacked by men. 'If you take out uncovered meat and place it outside on the street ... and the cats come and eat it, whose fault is it, the cats or the uncovered meat? The uncovered meat is the problem', he said. Sajid, a senior figure in the MCB, said that 'loose women like prostitutes' encouraged men to be immoral. Referring to the thrust of the Sheikh's argument, he said: 'So what is wrong in it? Who will object to that?'[33]

A recurring feature of all speeches made by jihadis is that they are replete with threats. This is a reflection of the primitive societies from which they originate, which function by instilling fear. This has been the pattern of Muslim terrorist behaviour: to explain their terrorist acts as 'retaliation' for what their victims supposedly did to them, and if the enemy yields, then they find other reasons or rationalizations for continuous terror. Terrorist cells had operated in Britain (and the US and the rest of Europe for that matter) well before the Twin Tower attacks, before there were any westerners in Afghanistan or Iraq and before any Muslim terrorist suspect was put in prison. If anything, the reverse happened: while terrorists were concocting their schemes and justifying their actions with quotations from the Qur'an, western countries were naively listening to their inflammatory incitement and plots and doing nothing to stop them.

Britain's anti-terrorist laws, which followed the rising threats, were accompanied by their abrogation in courts which feared the erosion of civil rights.

> December 2001: as a result of the terrorist attacks on the US in September, the Anti-terrorism, Crime and Security Act 2001 was adopted, which allows suspected foreign terrorists to be detained indefinitely. Requires Britain to opt out of Article 5 of the Human Rights Convention, the right to liberty.
>
> December 2004: Law lords rule opt-out unlawful because it was 'disproportionate to terrorist threat and discriminated against foreigners'.
>
> March 2005: Prevention of Terrorism Act 2005 replaces detention with control orders for British and foreign suspected terrorists.
>
> April 2006: less than one year after the London bombings of July 2005, the High Court rules part of the 2005 Act is

incompatible with the Human Rights Convention. But it remains in force.

June 2006: High Court quashes control orders under 2005 Act.

July 2006: Government to appeal against April ruling.[34]

The ambience of permissiveness of the courts was mirrored in some British media. The BBC rejected a call made by an independent panel studying charges of bias in its coverage of the Israeli–Palestinian conflict to change its editorial policies on the use of the word 'terrorist'. Using the word 'terrorist' to describe attacks on civilians, BBC management argued in a paper released on 19 June 2006, would make the 'very value judgements' it had been asked to eschew. The independent panel found the BBC's reporting from Israel did 'not consistently constitute a full and fair account of the conflict but rather, in important respects, presents an incomplete and in that sense misleading picture'. However, the thirty-eight-page report commissioned by the BBC's governors found that apart from 'individual lapses' there 'was little to suggest systematic or deliberate bias' in its reporting. They recommended a senior manager be appointed to oversee BBC coverage of the Middle East, that its reporting provide a 'full and fair' account of the 'complexities' of the conflict, that its complaints procedure be revised, and that it reform its use of language. The report recommended that the BBC describe violent attacks upon civilians that had the intent of causing terror for political or ideological reasons 'whether perpetrated by state or non-state agencies' as 'terrorism'. After all, if they refuse to refer to terrorists by what they are, they are only serving the agenda of those who use violence for political ends, whether in Britain or elsewhere. In addition, this refusal confuses the population at home instead of clarifying the issues involved. If everyone is the same, and there is more than one 'truth', how can those unacquainted with the minutiae distinguish between the aggressors and the victims? It is worth noting that this broadcasting group is publicly funded, by means of a compulsory television licence that each television-owning household has to pay whether or not they watch the BBC.[35]

The BBC management stated that they do permit the use of the word 'terrorist', but cautioned its reporters 'against its use without attribution'. However, appointing a senior manager to provide 'more secure editorial, planning, grip and oversight' in its Middle East coverage would add an extra layer of management that 'could undermine the independence and accountability of BBC editors'. The BBC conceded that more could be done to 'explain the complexities of the conflict' and tackle its viewers' 'high level of incomprehension'. Trevor Asserson, director of BBCWatch, however, noted the only way for the BBC to put 'its house in order' was to 'improve its systems; senior editors must be given the responsibility of systematically imposing impartiality and an independent complaints system must be set up that tells the BBC when it fails'.

In the face of the criticism directed towards them, many Muslims in Britain perennially hurl abuses at the government and society which have given them shelter and showered them with benefits. The counter-attacks, in 'self-defence', Muslims would argue, are energetically voiced by British converts to Islam, who readily become the most vociferous apologists for their new faith of which they know little, or by liberals and politicians of all tendencies, whose coalition with the jihadis may serve their agendas. Yvonne Ridley, the former journalist who was kidnapped by the Taleban during the US-led invasion of Afghanistan in 2001, stated that Muslims in east London should stop cooperating with the police after the 'terror raid' by police against Muslim suspects in which a man was shot. Ridley, who is now an activist with George Galloway's Respect Party, said the community was being 'terrorized' by the Metropolitan Police and should end all contact with the force. But a senior officer said good relations on the ground were vital to ensuring difficult issues were handled in a sensitive way.[36]

Muslim leaders have also expressed disquiet about the effect on race relations of the anti-terror raid on an alleged chemical bomb factory, after more than 250 police burst into a house in June 2006 in Forest Gate, east London but failed to find any evidence. One of two brothers was accidentally shot, prompting Ghayasuddin Siddiqui, leader of the Muslim Parliament, to warn that if the police were found responsible for another 'bungled shooting' it could have 'a devastating impact' on racial harmony. He claimed there was no evidence of extremism in the area around Forest Gate. Identity politics has become so entrenched in Britain that no one even questioned why Muhammad Abdul Bari, the newly elected secretary general of the MCB, felt it necessary to visit Forest Gate. The Archbishop of Canterbury does not visit every place where Christian criminals are arrested or pursued. The visit gave backing to the suspects, which would have been entirely inappropriate if their guilt had been proven.³⁷

Abdul Bari replaced Sacranie as head of the MCB in June 2006. He said the news that a 23-year-old east London Muslim had been shot in a terrorism raid left him stunned, continuing the state of denial of his predecessor. 'I am chairman of the East London Mosque and I come from Bangladesh – I know the families in the area well. The children may squabble in the playground and there are occasional drugs – but not terrorists.' He added: 'After 9/11 and 7/7, this area prided itself on being mature. We don't rant and rave.' Assuming the mantle of a police operations expert at Forest Gate, he complained that the police had completely overreacted. In the aftermath, the media published a photograph apparently showing a third brother from the raided household standing next to a man wearing a fake bomb at a demonstration. Abdul Bari insisted: 'The man involved in the Danish cartoon protests was only a half-brother they barely knew.' As the public has come to expect from Muslim leaders after every arrest, Abdul Bari maintained that those who knew the brothers in the Bangladeshi community said they were good boys. But if the Muslim community abounds with good boys, where do the terrorists in England and those who fight for al-Qa'ida in Iraq come from?³⁸

'Muslims are frightened now', he said. 'Many are still poor, undereducated and unemployed and they are finding life increasingly difficult. It is a nightmare, particularly for the young.' But who asked them to come to England to live in misery and oppression? They could have stayed in Bangladesh and enjoyed its prosperity and freedom. 'The young are rebelling. They become demotivated; some turn to drugs, others become more religious.' He continued: 'An increased interest in religion does not, however, turn them into extremists and terrorists', without explaining what it is that motivates them. All immigrant groups face the same problems of adjustment as the Muslims, but they do not strap bomb-belts onto themselves. Abdul Bari added: '7/7 was committed by idiots and the devout were against the man who dressed up as a "suicide bomber" to protest at those cartoons.' Had the bombers been arrested before exploding themselves, he may well have described them as 'good boys'. It is interesting to note, too, that the devout were apparently against the man who dressed up as a bomber, but did not condemn the death and destruction wrought worldwide by those who were protesting against some cartoons. Asked by the interviewer if he would not agree that many in Britain see Muslim fundamentalism as the biggest threat of the next few years, he replied: 'Extremism is a threat, but on all sides: Christian, Muslim, Jewish. It is objectionable when people talk about Islamic terrorists; those who terrorize people are not being Islamic in any way.' It is precisely because such statements are never challenged that Muslim extremists can continue to hide behind lame self-justifications. Christians and Jews do not express their 'extremism' by threatening or bombing anyone, and are therefore hardly comparable. Nor do they support or justify acts of terror. When Britain was attacked by IRA terrorists, the bombers were referred to as Irish. True, they were not labelled 'Catholic terrorists', because that is not how they identified themselves. They were acting in the name of a limited political cause, a united Ireland, and not as representatives of their religion. Islamic terrorists, in contrast, identify themselves first and foremost by their religion, invoking their *Allah* every time they behead a man or kill and maim those unfortunate enough to be near them when they self-implode. A refusal to name the identity of these terrorists (instead of resorting to such platitudes as 'youths', 'ethnics', 'minorities', 'communities' or 'Asians') results in unnecessary confusion, and therefore impedes the likelihood of formulating a workable counterterrorist strategy. The nature of the problem must be stated clearly and concisely at all times. Abdul Bari wants to promote the activities of British mosques and to work with the imams, saying, 'They do a tremendous job; but, in Britain, they are seen as nasty men with claw hooks.' There was at least one that answered that description, even if Abdul Bari now prefers to disown him. Abdul Bari ignores the mosque incitement against the country and society that gave him and all his fellow-Muslims shelter. There have been too many instances of incendiary sermons recorded by undercover reporters for him to be so complacent.

As the new secretary general, he wants to encourage Muslims to help Britain to become a better place. 'We want to help fight hooliganism, drugs and broken families; we want the British to become better neighbours. Muslims can give and teach Britain so much: looking after the elderly, enduring marriages, respect, strong faith, no alcohol.' There is no hint of humility in the interview. Far from teaching the British 'to become better neighbours', his co-religionists have increased crime rates, as can be seen from their over-representation in the prison system. He neglects to mention forced or polygamous unions or 'honour killings' when he praises the endurance of Muslim marriages. He cites 'respect, strong faith, no alcohol' as attributes of Muslim societies, but does not say in which parts of the Muslim world these attributes made Islamic societies a better place to live. He and other Muslims voted with their feet by leaving such societies in favour of setting up their homes in 'decadent' Britain.

Referring to the schoolgirl in Luton who demanded to wear the jilbab, he said: 'We supported her right to wear what she wanted. It was wrong for her to lose out on an education just because of her dress. As Muslims, we are far more shocked by pupils' short skirts, but we don't complain. That is another thing the British could learn: modesty is very attractive.' But modesty is the last quality on the minds of Muslim leaders, including Sacranie, Abu Hamza or Omar Bakri, who demean unbelievers and boast of the superiority of their own creed. Their absolute certainty about their own moral rectitude as well as the 'truth' of their religion is acutely irritating in a liberal society. As for sartorial modesty, Abdul Bari evidently views it as a virtue, even when it is enforced. Nor can the shrouding of women in black gowns from head to toe, with only an eye-slit for navigating the streets, be considered in any way attractive. In Saudi Arabia, where such gowns are strictly enforced by gangs of otherwise underemployed 'virtue police', women are disparagingly referred to by men as 'BMOs', or Black Moving Objects.[39] A western society prizes gender equality above narrow notions of modesty and virtue, and the fact that a strict dress code is enforced on women but not on men will never be acceptable. Without a hint of irony, Abdul Bari notes that he likes British dress: 'I feel comfortable in shirts and suits.'

Asked if he liked anything about Britain, he replied: 'The education system is superb, compared to Bangladesh. Children are allowed to think.' He also admires Britain's dynamism, pluralism and tolerance. 'We may have graffiti and bottles thrown at Muslims but, after 9/11, no Muslims were killed. For all its faults, we do feel grateful to this country.' He believes all Muslims must learn English. Before long, however, he contradicted the very qualities he was praising in England. He does not think that Muslims should adopt too many British practices; Britain should espouse many more Muslim traditions, such as arranged marriages. He warms to his theme. 'Pre-marital sex is wrong, cohabitation is wrong; by the time you get married, you are bored. There is no mystery. Muslim marriages tend to be more successful, more of a partnership', ignoring their hierarchical nature and the Qur'anic licence for men to beat their wives. He is also critical of gambling, and admits that non-Muslims are unlikely ever to forswear alcohol. While he wants the Archbishop of Canterbury to be more active in promoting moral issues, the Prince of Wales is regarded as 'a hero to the Muslim community'. Abdul Bari also thinks that there should be more faith schools and that British children should be encouraged to attend Muslim establishments – despite his earlier praise for the British education system. In other words, his goal is to integrate British children into Islamic culture, rather than the other way round.

Now, suddenly, Muslim schools are better: 'They have more discipline, more respect, better exam results, children work hard, there are fewer mini-skirts, there is less bad behaviour, the teachers can get on with their jobs.' The reason that scholarly achievements in the Muslim world are so wanting applies also to Muslim schools in the West: children are expected to learn the Qur'an by heart, and that ethos permeates the attitude to all education. Abdul Bari said that Muslim schools would teach all religions, although it is no secret that Muslims regard other religions as inferior. He also spoke of teaching British values. The same immigrants who are undermining British values in the public sphere now wish to teach British children what these values are![40]

Taheri predicted that the understanding that Blair attempted to develop with the Muslims would fail since it was based on a fundamental contradiction. Moments after the Muslim attacks, the Prime Minister declared that the tragedy had nothing to do with Islam. And yet he immediately invited the self-styled 'leaders of the Muslim community' to Downing Street to discuss the matter. They cited the classical recommendations of better schools, more jobs, improved PR, and help for those suffering from an 'identity crisis'. However, there is no such thing as a Muslim community in Britain. There are over 100 communities with different ethnic, cultural and linguistic backgrounds, different understandings of Islam, and distinct social and religious structures, although they have two points in common. The first is a general attachment to a broad, though never defined, idea of Islam. That attachment is deliberately kept implicit and vague, or else it could lead to conflict amongst them. The second point is that they all realize that while delving into theological matters would divide them, focusing on political issues, such as Palestine and Kashmir, could offer a degree of unity *vis-à-vis* non-Muslims. The result has been an excessive politicization of Islam in Britain as its religious aspects are de-emphasized. Islam must decide whether it wants to be a religion or a political movement in the West. The current British policy of treating Islam as a special case, a political movement that is also a faith, is harmful for Britain and the Muslims too.[41]

Taheri continued his inimitable analysis in a second column:

> There is a new game in British politics. Called 'Muslims Are Angry', this new game is designed to force Prime Minister Tony Blair out of office. The game starts with the assertion that 'the British Muslim community' is 'seething with anger' against Blair, because of his foreign policy. It then proceeds to assert that it was Muslim anger that caused the terrorist attacks in London and the plots nipped in the bud since. The game concludes with the claim that unless Britain reshapes its foreign policy, no one in the UK would be safe from terrorism by 'Angry Muslims'. Many Britons who otherwise look sane and sober play the sinister game without questioning its premise.

Taheri goes on to ask some pertinent questions: 'How would one explain terrorist attacks in Spain, where the socialist Prime Minister wears the Palestinian scarf, in Germany that has stayed out of the Iraq war, and in Turkey that is, after all, a Muslim state governed by an Islamist party? Today no fewer than forty-six of the fifty-seven Muslim majority countries face the same kind of terrorism that Britain is facing. Is that also the fault of Tony Blair?' Taheri sees Britain as the one non-Muslim nation with the closest ties to the Muslim world. It is the main trading partner of most Muslim nations; the main destination for Muslims seeking further education abroad; attracts the largest number of Muslim visitors to the West; and attracts more than half of all investments that Muslims make outside Islamic countries. Proportionate to its Muslim population, Britain has twice as many mosques as the Islamic Republic of Iran. Britain is one of a handful of countries where all Muslim sects are fully free to practise their faith, run their schools, develop their culture, operate their media, and propagate their ideas.[42]

Taheri listed some of Blair's policies which benefited Muslims, including doubling the number of Muslims coming to the UK for higher education since 1997; reinstating the elected Muslim

President of Sierra Leone, after he was toppled by his mainly Christian enemies; sending troops to Bosnia-Herzegovina to protect its Muslim population from being massacred by Serbs and Croats; sending troops to prevent genocide against Albanian Muslims in Kosovo; pressing for 20,000 UN troops to be sent to Darfur to stop the genocide there; helping several Muslim states become members of the World Trade Organization, often in the face of reticence from the US and the EU; encouraging the North Atlantic Treaty Organization (NATO) to admit eight Muslim states in a special partnership; continuing to keep British troops in Cyprus to prevent a Muslim–Christian civil war; joining the campaign that ended the murderous rule of the Taleban in Afghanistan in 2001 which enabled the Afghan people to establish a government of their choice; persuading the Bush administration to commit itself to the creation of a Palestinian state alongside Israel – something that no previous US administration had done; and finally, saving the people of Iraq from the most murderous regime in recent Arab history. Perhaps Blair's detractors would have preferred to retain Saddam Hussein and his cousin 'Chemical Ali' in office, to enable them to resume gassing the Kurds and massacring any Iraqi Arab who disagreed with them. Blair's critics also complain that he has been too close to George Bush. Yet America and Britain have been instrumental in securing G8 participation in $60 billion in new aid to Africa, and Muslims comprise roughly half the beneficiaries of this aid. On the key issues of importance in the international arena, Britain has been at odds with the Bush administration over more than half. Blair sided with Bush when there was a choice between the US, as a democratic ally, and a criminal regime that acted as the enemy of its own people and of humanity. Blair sided with the US over Milosevic, Mullah Omar, Bin Laden, Saddam Hussein and Abu Musab al-Zarqawi. One can only question the true motives of those who would have sided with any of these characters. Blair's critics are free to oppose his foreign policy, wrote Taheri. But they should say why they do so and what they would do instead. The threat of terrorism is no argument for change; it is a call to surrender.[43]

In an age when political correctness invariably trumps the truth, the contribution by non-politicians to a public debate can be invaluable. In a letter to the *Sunday Telegraph*, the novelist Frederick Forsyth wrote:

In the struggle for the minds of young British Muslims, the

media use euphemisms and wholly inaccurate buzzwords. Terrorists are terrorists, not militants. Preachers of hatred are not 'fundamentalist', because that means 'one returning to the basis'; Qur'anic scholars are adamant that Islam is not based in hatred. Young men whose minds are twisted and perverted are not being 'radicalized' because 'radical' means pertaining to the root, and Qur'anic scholars are adamant that Islam is not rooted in mass murder. And a youth who is so twisted that he commits suicide and kills as many women and children as possible is not a martyr but a heretic, for the Qur'an denounces both as crimes. The words are: preachers of hatred, brain-washing, indoctrination, mass murder, heresy and eternal damnation.[44]

When the BBC reporter John Ware investigated the MCB for a 'Panorama' programme in 2005, he was surprised to discover the views of some of the affiliated groups. Muhammad Abdul Bari, then deputy secretary general of the MCB, opened a new Islamic centre in east London in 2004, and chose the prominent Saudi cleric Sheikh Abd al-Rahman al-Sudayyis, imam of Islam's most important mosque in Mecca, as the guest of honour. Al-Sudayyis has said that 'the worst of the enemies of Islam are those whom he made monkeys and pigs – the aggressive Jews and the oppressive Zionists, and those that follow them. The callers of the Trinity and the Cross worshippers [by which Sudayyis meant Christians], the poison of their ideas and the followers of secularism.' Ware also found that Ahl-e-Hadith, another MCB affiliate with forty-one branches across Britain, advised its website readers to 'Be different from the Jews and Christians. Their ways are based on sick or deviant views concerning their societies. Imitating the "kuffar" leads to a permanent abode in hellfire.' Yet Sacranie, then secretary general of the MCB, was surprisingly reluctant to condemn Ahl-e-Hadith, saying it was part of the 'diversity of the Muslim community in the UK. It may be an objectionable view, but the fact is that it exists within the community.' Sacranie has also been very reluctant to condemn the claim, made by many of the more extremist Muslim preachers, that the 'War on Terror' is actually a 'War on Islam'. Ware put it to him that it was his 'responsibility, as leader of the Muslim community in effect in Britain – to disabuse the Muslim population of Britain of the notion that, whatever is going on in Iraq, it is not a war against Islam'. Sacranie replied that 'in terms of the motives – nobody knows about it, we don't know about it'.⁴⁵

The government gave the MCB almost £150,000 over the previous two years, while the Foreign Office funded a conference in Istanbul, flying 180 leaders, including Yusuf al-Qaradawi, from Europe, Egypt and Saudi Arabia to a luxury hotel in the city. Although the conference condemned terrorism, it should be emphasized that the Islamist definition of terrorism does not accord with that of the West. The categories of terrorism which they approve of are referred to as 'resistance' and therefore permitted. The opinions of Qaradawi, who is Professor of Sunni Studies at the University of Qatar, are widely disseminated, whether from his website or his weekly programme on al-Jazeera, which is watched by around forty million worldwide. In common with other clerics who know they are quoted by the western media, he varies his opinions to suit the audience receiving them. He has condemned 9/11 but supported suicide bombing, even where the victims are women and children, as 'heroic martyrdom'. He describes suicide bombings as 'permissible and commendable' in Islam. 'These are not suicidal operations, and the heroes who carry them out don't embark on this action out of hopelessness and despair, but are driven by an overwhelming desire to cast terror and fear in the hearts of the oppressors.' The Washington Institute for Near East Policy think-tank described him in 2001 as a 'Jekyll and Hyde figure'. The MCB, however, described him as 'a voice of reason and understanding'. Qaradawi believes homosexuality is a 'sexual perversion' for which the penalty should be death, and the only matter left for debate is whether participants should be thrown from a high cliff or flogged to death. Banned from the US, he founded the European Council on Fatwa and Research, with headquarters in Dublin, to spread his influential opinions into the very heart of the 'decadent' West.⁴⁶

Muslim leaders challenged a leading Church of England bishop to back up his claims that extremist imams are indoctrinating British children. The Bishop of Rochester, Michael Nazir-Ali, whose father converted from Islam, called on the government to impose rigorous checks on foreign Muslim clerics. He warned that Britain may be too weak to resist Islamic fundamentalism 'unless there is some reclaiming of the moral and spiritual tradition which created this country'. Bishop Nazir-Ali proposed filtering out imams who might incite extremism. Responding to the bishop's claims that extremist preachers were operating in mosques, the MCB spokesman, Bunglawala, said: 'If he has any evidence he should take that to the police. We are not aware of any extremist imams indoctrinating children.' The bishop also expressed concerns in relation to the declared wish of the Prince of Wales to become 'Defender of Faith' as King, rather than 'Defender of the Faith'.[47] Nazir-Ali said he believed that some Muslims had a 'dual psychology' in which they desired both 'victimhood and domination'. It would therefore always be impossible to satisfy all their demands. 'Given the world view that has given rise to such grievances, there can never be sufficient appeasement and new demands will continue to be made', adding that 'their complaint often boils down to the position that it is always right to intervene when Muslims are victims, as in Bosnia or Kosovo, and always wrong when the Muslims are the oppressors or terrorists, as with the Taleban or in Iraq'. Failure to counter these beliefs had allowed radical Islam to flourish in Britain and stricter checks should be made to exclude extremist clerics from the country.[48] After lobbying from Muslim groups, the government retreated from proposals to toughen entry requirements. Plans to require foreign clerics to sit a test on civic values a year after arriving were cancelled along with the introduction of a requirement to speak English to conversational level.[49]

The death-knell of the multiculturalist experiment was sounded in a speech by Tony Blair in December 2006, overturning more than three decades of Labour enthusiasm for the idea. Blair did not want to dilute religious identity but said that all British citizens had a duty to integrate. He set out a series of proposals designed to strike the 'right balance' between integration and diversity. First, all future grants to ethnic and religious groups would be assessed against a test of promoting cohesion and integration. Faith schools would have to meet new guidelines on respect for other religions, and firm action was pledged against madrassas that fail to comply with their legal requirements. According to Blair, 'very good intentions got the better of us. We wanted to be hospitable to new groups. We wanted, rightly, to extend a welcome and did so by offering public money to entrench their cultural presence. Money was too often freely awarded to groups that were tightly bonded around religious, racial or ethnic identities.' To address the complaint from Muslim women that they are barred from even entering certain mosques, Blair asked the Equal Opportunities Commission to produce a report on how the problem of discrimination in mosques could be overcome. Visiting preachers would have to have a proper command of English and would be banned if their presence is judged not to be in the public good. In addition, the age at which a person can get permission to enter the UK to marry may be raised from 18. Blair continued:

> If you come here lawfully, we welcome you. If you are permitted to stay here permanently, you become an equal member of our community and become one of us. Then you, and all of us, who want to, can worship God in our own way, take pride in our different cultures after our own fashion, respect our distinctive histories according to our own traditions; but do so within a shared space of shared values in which we take no less pride and show no less respect.[50]

The Labour Muslim MP Shahid Malik was horrified to find that Islamic holidays and shari'a formed part of Kelly's discussions with Muslim leaders, while the press coverage was understandably focused on the airline plot. 'Out of touch with reality, frightened to propose any real solutions for fear of "selling out", but always keen to exact a concession – a sad but too often true caricature of some so-called Muslim leaders', he wrote in the *Sunday Times*. He cringed as he listened to the demands made by Syed Aziz Pasha, secretary general of the Union of Muslim Organizations of the UK and Ireland, who told Kelly: 'If you give us religious rights, we will be in a better position to convince young people that they are being treated equally along with other citizens.' Malik considered the call for special public holidays for Muslims as unnecessary, impracticable and divisive. Most employers already allow their staff to take such days out of their annual leave. And what about special holidays for Sikhs, Hindus, Jews? If all such requests were accommodated, then society would become fractured. Malik quoted the Islamic scholar Muhammad ibn Adam, who said: 'It is necessary by shari'a to abide by the laws of the country one lives in, as long as the law doesn't demand something that is against Islam.' British laws do not force Muslims to do something against shari'a and Muslims enjoy the freedom to worship and follow their religion. Malik compared the freedoms in Britain to the strictures in Muslim countries: the shari'a regime in Saudi Arabia bans women from driving; Turkey is a secular country where women are forbidden to wear the hijab; in Tunisia, civil servants are forbidden to wear a beard.[51]

In October 2006, the government finally withdrew its support from the MCB, after accusing it of failing to lead the fight against religious extremism. This led to the inevitable accusation that the government was trying to engineer a subservient 'state-sponsored Islam'. Ruth Kelly attacked the MCB for boycotting Holocaust Memorial Day, criticizing police anti-terrorist operations and 'sitting on the sidelines' in the campaign against extremists. Abdul Bari, secretary general of the MCB, was invited to hear Kelly's speech, which was delivered to a Muslim audience, but refused to attend. Ministers had previously viewed the MCB, which represents 400 organizations and hundreds of mosques around the country, as the most important Muslim voice in Britain. Kelly said that in future she would engage with and give funding to organizations that represented young Muslims and Muslim women and which were taking a 'proactive leadership role in tackling extremism and defending our shared values'. Kelly also attacked groups which criticized British foreign policy as anti-Muslim and denigrated the police.[52] Abdul Bari complained to Kelly, claiming that a 'drip feed' of ministerial statements had 'stigmatized' the entire Muslim community, and accused her of pandering to an 'Islamophobic' agenda.

Although it is rare for the head of MI5 to speak out in public, Dame Eliza Manningham-Buller said, after the trial of Dhiren Barot: 'More and more people are moving from passive sympathy towards active terrorism through being radicalized or indoctrinated by friends, families, in organized training events here and overseas.' Young teenagers, some still at school, are being groomed to be suicide bombers. Five major conspiracies in Britain had been thwarted since 7/7, and ninety-nine defendants were awaiting trial in thirty-four cases. Polls say that up to 100,000 British citizens consider that the London attacks were justified. And al-Qa'ida is quick to take advantage, admitting that half its war is waged through the media. Her comments came in an address to a discreet audience from the Mile End Group, an academic organization run by Peter Hennessy, Professor of Contemporary British History at Queen Mary, University of London. She said the methods used by terrorists had become more sophisticated. 'Today we see the use of home-made improvised explosive devices. Tomorrow's threat may, and I suggest will, include the use of chemical, bacteriological agents, radioactive materials and even nuclear technology.'[53] Sir Ian Blair, the Metropolitan Police Commissioner, addressed the Reform Club Media Group in October 2006. Although the meeting was conducted under Chatham House rules (whereby no one attending is supposed to attribute what is said), one person revealed that Sir Ian said the British people should 'brace themselves for a truly appalling act of terror', and that following this act of barbarism 'people would be talking quite openly about internment'.[54]

Muktar Said Ibrahim, the leader of the 21/7 bomb plot, came to the UK at the age of 14 to escape civil war in Eritrea. His family settled into a council house in suburban Stanmore in 1992. At 15, he indecently assaulted a girl, dropped out of college and began stealing to fund his cannabis addiction. He was soon convicted of two robberies and it was while serving a five-year sentence that he fell under the influence of older inmates who were strict Muslims. After his early prison release in 1998, he lived in hostels while claiming a £56.20-a-week jobseeker's allowance. Yassin Omar, who came to Britain from Somalia in 1992 as an 11-year-old refugee, was taken into foster care and at 18 was given a council flat as a 'vulnerable young adult'. Friends said he spent most of his time in bed and never looked for work. The 26-year-old relied instead on the £25,000 in housing benefit and £13,000 in income support he received in the six years before his arrest. Father-of-three Hussain Osman used forged documents to gain entry to the UK in 1996. He claimed he was Somalian, making him eligible for asylum, although he was Ethiopian. He was given a housing association flat in south London, where he lived on benefits with his family. Ramzi Mohammed, 25, came to the UK in 1998 from Somalia. In 2003, he moved out of the house he shared with his girlfriend because they were not married, which was 'un-Islamic'. He quit his job at a bar because it involved alcohol, and lived on benefits in a council flat in west London, spending his time distributing Islamic literature. Two of the four bombers, including Muktar Ibrahim, applied for, and were granted, UK citizenship.[55]

The four 21/7 bombers were imprisoned for life for conspiracy to commit murder and have been told they will serve a minimum of forty years. The two other defendants, Adel Yahya and Manfo Asiedu, face a retrial after the jury failed to reach a verdict in their cases. The judge said: 'What happened on July 7 in 2005 is of considerable relevance to this sentencing. I have no doubt that they were both part of an al-Qa'ida-inspired and controlled sequence of attacks.' The men all denied the charges, claiming the devices were not intended to go off and were meant as a protest against the Iraq War. The court had heard how the gang used explosives made of hydrogen peroxide and chapatti flour in an attempt to kill commuters, and that the authorities had only ever come across improvised explosive devices made from hydrogen peroxide and organic substances on two occasions: July 7 and July 21.[56] The most unforgettable image for Britons of 21/7 will remain that of Ibrahim and Mohammed being drawn out of the latter's flat wearing only their underpants after officers threw CS gas canisters inside, when Muktar Ibrahim repeatedly shouted, 'I know my rights.'

The conviction of four refugees for terrorist offences once again exposed the porous nature of Britain's borders. The bombers came to the country as children or young adults in the early 1990s from Eritrea and Somalia. Although one applied, they were never granted political asylum, which requires that they have a genuine fear of persecution in their own country. They were not returned home because their countries were deemed unsafe. They were given what is called 'Exceptional Leave to Remain' in the country, which allows someone to stay legally for four years at the Home Office's discretion. This can then be translated into 'Indefinite Leave to Remain' and eventually into a grant of citizenship. Mukthar Ibrahim was convicted as a teenager for a number of robberies and an assault. Yet he was still given a British passport. The rules then allowed a foreign national to qualify for citizenship if the offences were committed as a juvenile. They were considered 'spent' after five years. The law has recently been changed so that the condition applies to juvenile convictions as well. Ibrahim used his British passport to travel to Pakistan. Usually his departure would not have been noted because embarkation controls were dismantled in 1998. But he was stopped by Special Branch, acting on intelligence. He was on bail for a public order offence, but there was no legal way he could be stopped from leaving. While he was away a warrant was issued for his arrest for jumping bail. When he came back into the country, he was subject to a low-level investigation by MI5 about his trip to Pakistan but was deemed not to pose a threat. The government says its plans for electronic border checks – both in and out – will help secure the frontier. But these are not due to come until 2014. The rules for letting people stay have been made stricter and it is possible now to remove British citizenship from someone who is considered a threat – though it has not been done yet and the individual has to have an alternative citizenship. Ministers say ID cards will make a difference, but since the July 7 bombers were all British passport holders and used their own names it is not clear how. Sir Andrew Green, chairman of MigrationWatch, said: 'We have been saying for five years that the government has lost control of the borders. This is dramatic evidence that we were right.'[57]

A bleak picture of a generation of young British Muslims radicalized by anti-western views and misplaced multicultural policies was shown in a survey by the think tank Policy Exchange, published in January 2007. The study found disturbing evidence of young Muslims adopting more fundamentalist beliefs on key social and political issues than their parents or grandparents. Forty per cent of Muslims between the ages of 16 and 24 said they would prefer to live under shari'a law in Britain, in contrast to 17 per cent among those over 55. Shari'a allows a man to have four wives, and imposes a death penalty for leaving Islam. In some countries, people found guilty under shari'a law face beheading, stoning (for adultery), the amputation of a hand (for theft) or being lashed. For young Muslims raised in Britain to favour shari'a law indicates that it is not enough to be raised in a free-thinking society to value personal freedoms. MCB spokesman Bunglawala cited the Muslims' 'emotional attachment' to shari'a, just as Christians are attached to the Ten Commandments – which is hardly an appropriate comparison.

The study also found a significant minority who expressed backing for Islamic terrorism. One in eight young Muslims said they admired groups such as al-Qa'ida that 'are prepared to fight the West'. Turning to issues of faith, 36 per cent of the young people believed that a Muslim who converts to another religion should be 'punished by death', in contrast to 19 per cent among those over 55. Three out of four young Muslims would prefer Muslim women to 'choose to wear the veil or hijab', compared to only a quarter of over-55s. Support was also strong for Islamic schools, according to the *Populus* survey of 1,000 people commissioned by Policy Exchange. Forty per cent of younger Muslims said they would want their children to attend an Islamic school, compared to only 20 per cent of over-55s.

Britain's foreign policies were a key issue among the Muslim population as a whole, with 58 per cent arguing that many of the world's problems are 'a result of arrogant western attitudes'. However, knowledge of foreign affairs was sketchy, with only one in five knowing that Mahmoud Abbas was the Palestinian President! Ignorance on matters on which they actively campaign and protest is particularly astounding. The Policy Exchange report, *Living Apart Together: British Muslims and the paradox of multiculturalism*, says there is strong evidence of a 'growing religiosity' among young Muslims, with an increasing minority firmly rejecting western life. Munira Mirza, the lead author of the report, said: 'The emergence of a strong Muslim identity in Britain is, in part, a result of multicultural policies implemented since the 1980s which have emphasized difference at the expense of shared national identity and divided people along ethnic, religious and cultural lines.' Shahid Malik, the Muslim Labour MP for Dewsbury, said: 'This report makes very disturbing reading and it vindicates the concern many of us have that we're not doing enough to confront this issue.'[58]

The poll found that 86 per cent of Muslims feel that 'my religion is the most important thing in my life'. Despite widespread concerns about Islamophobia, 84 per cent believe they have been treated fairly in Britain, while 28 per cent believe that the authorities go over the top in trying not to offend Muslims. Mirza cautioned:

> We should be wary of treating the entire Muslim population as a monolith with special needs that are different to the rest of the population. There is considerable diversity amongst Muslims, with many adopting a more secular approach to their religion and a majority feeling they have as much, if not more, in common with non-Muslims in Britain as with Muslims abroad. There is clearly a conflict within British Islam between a moderate majority that accepts the norms of western democracy and a growing minority that does not.

Meanwhile, a call by the leader of the Conservative Party, David Cameron, for a new 'crusade for fairness', was described as 'extraordinarily sloppy' by Osama Saeed, of the Muslim Association of Britain. He said that it risked undermining his central message, adding: 'It is not a nice word and nice things do not happen on the back of crusades.'[59] But neither do 'nice things' happen on the back of jihad. It would be wrong to let the Muslim minority in the country dictate the vocabulary in a public debate. While the historical connotations of 'crusade' have been left behind (it is now understood simply to mean a 'campaign' or 'struggle'), the militaristic associations of 'jihad' are still very much with us.

Soon after the army began a recruitment drive for Muslims in the West Midlands, nine men were arrested in dawn raids across Birmingham in January 2007 by police investigating a plot to kidnap a British Muslim soldier. Eight were British men of Pakistani descent and one was Pakistani. It is notoriously difficult to recruit Muslims to the armed forces and police because of their reluctance to swear allegiance to a state of non-Muslims. Muslims serving in the armed forces, Civil Service and the police are regarded as targets for British-based terrorists after detectives foiled an alleged plot to kidnap and behead a soldier home on leave from Iraq. The plan was to force the soldier, under torture, to denounce his role in the army and behead him on camera. Like Kenneth Bigley, the British contractor murdered after being seized in Baghdad in September 2004, the hostage was allegedly to be paraded in an orange boiler suit similar to the uniforms worn by inmates at Guantanamo. The plan was to be carried out within seventy-two hours because the plotters knew that the kidnapping would result in an intensive police search. The intention was to announce the time of the execution, film it and then post it on a website with a warning that other British Muslim 'collaborators' would face a similar fate. Police believe that the kidnappers were also planning to abduct Muslim civil servants and others perceived as working for the British military machine. Police are investigating possible links to terror training camps in Pakistan. Eight homes and four commercial premises, including two bookshops, an internet café and a general store, were raided.[60]

Defence chiefs launched an urgent investigation into how the suspected Islamic terrorists obtained a list of names and addresses for twenty-five serving British Muslim soldiers. A priority was to ensure that no Ministry of Defence 'mole' provided the cell with such top-secret personal information. It was felt new security provisions were needed to protect the 330 Muslims serving in the armed forces and their families. The threat to kill Muslim troops as 'traitors' would also damage a drive to recruit more young male and female Muslims into the armed forces.[61] Al-Qa'ida leaders in Pakistan and Iraq instructed dozens of their followers in Britain to carry out a series of kidnappings and beheadings, according to intelligence uncovered by MI5. (However, al-Qa'ida's leaders in Iraq had previously called a halt to filmed beheadings because they alienated many Muslims.) Several suspects were personally acquainted with the Muslim soldier, a corporal in military intelligence. Those involved in the plot were supplying equipment and computer hardware to al-Qa'ida camps in Afghanistan. One of the suspects had recently returned from a trip to Pakistan.[62]

In January 2007, the government decided to establish a 'joint information unit', to counter disinformation issued by Islamic terrorists. It signalled a change of approach to the war on terrorism, with ministers placing more emphasis on influencing opinion in the Muslim world rather than relying on military action. Since 9/11, senior al-Qa'ida figures have issued a stream of videos claiming responsibility for atrocities and warning of even more devastating attacks unless the West changes its foreign policy. Al-Qa'ida also launched an internet broadcasting channel as a recruitment tool. The channel was heavily advertised in password-protected jihadist websites across the world, including those based in Britain. The channel, Sawt al-Khilafa (Voice of the Caliphate), shows programmes and footage of attacks on American and British troops in Iraq and Afghanistan, and mujahideen operations in Chechnya and central Asia as well as speeches by Bin Laden and incendiary preachers. The aim of the new British unit was to coordinate well-argued public 'rebuttals' of such propaganda messages, but it faces an impossible task. Resources would be better spent on inflicting a decisive defeat on the jihadists.[63]

The British Council, the state-funded cultural body, decided to close half of its public offices in Europe by March 2008 and shift its attention to Muslim countries in the Middle East and Central Asia. £7.5 million, nearly a third of the public money it spends in Europe, will be diverted to countries stretching east from Saudi Arabia to Kazakhstan so that it can play its part in the war. It will scrap traditional arts activities on the Continent, such as orchestral tours and artistic commissions, in favour of projects designed to prevent Muslim youths from being indoctrinated by extremists sympathetic to al-Qa'ida. The initiatives include a £20 million scheme to combat radicalization of Muslim youths in Pakistan and other predominantly Muslim states. A scheme to strengthen European identity among European Muslims is planned.[64]

In February 2007, the government launched a £5 million fund to fight Islamic extremism at the community level in a 'battle for hearts and minds'. Such battles are destined to fail because the onus is wrongly placed on the host country to win the 'hearts and minds' of the immigrants. Nevertheless, Ruth Kelly said local authorities would bid for the money to back local initiatives aimed at halting the radicalization of young Muslims. The so-called Preventing Violent Extremism Pathfinder Fund will be available to around fifty local authorities to work with Muslim communities to devise new approaches to fight extremism. Asked whether the fund could also be used to tackle non-Islamic extremism, a spokeswoman for Communities and Local Government said: 'No. That threat is the main threat to the UK at the moment.' Of course it was a hypothetical question, but a useful one, eliciting from a government spokesman an admission that *all* terrorism is emanating from one faith alone. At a question-and-answer session with Select Committee chairmen, Tony Blair added a note of realism: 'Winning hearts and minds is not just about reaching out to people. It is also sometimes about standing up to them and saying, "Your value system is a value system that is wrong".'

Kelly admitted that, 'In the past, government relied too much on traditional leadership organizations.' This initiative reinforced her previous conviction that mainstream Muslim organizations, including the MCB, had been lackadaisical in confronting extremists. Local schemes backed by the new fund could include programmes to work with young people seen as vulnerable to extremist messages – those excluded from councils, schools and mosques, for example. Khurshid Ahmed, chairman of the British Muslim Forum, said that the initiative could be effective in highlighting the value of smaller projects to local councils. But he added: 'If it's expected to deliver the whole agenda, it's peanuts money.'[65] This constant sense of entitlement from the very community which has spawned the terrorists is less than endearing. That Muslim organizations have access to sufficient resources is beyond doubt, and it was confirmed in July 2007 by the Muslim peer Lord Ahmed. Discussing the need to train imams for British mosques, he pointed out that training could be funded by the Muslim community, adding: 'Mosque committees have plenty of money – cost is not a problem.'[66]

British Muslims themselves have their own ideas about what would help them integrate. They think a British Mufti – a single leader for their religion to act as their voice – should represent them alongside other religious leaders such as the Archbishop of Canterbury, the Catholic Archbishop of Westminster and the Chief Rabbi. They believe this would help to ease tensions between Muslims and other groups, and ensure a more positive image in the media. But divisions between Muslims would make the creation of a British Mufti difficult. While 57 per cent of Sunnis are in favour, the proportion falls to just 30 per cent among Britain's Shi'ite Muslims.[67] It is precisely because there are profound theological divisions amongst Muslims that they focus excessively on foreign policy issues.

A new organization, representing former Muslims who fear for their lives because they have renounced their faith, was launched in June 2007. The Council of Ex-Muslims of Britain intends to campaign against Islamic states that still punish Muslim apostates with death under shari'a law. It also aims to become the voice of non-religious ex-Muslims. The council is led by Iranian-born Maryam Namazie, an outspoken human rights activist, following the formation of similar branches across Europe. Namazie, a left-wing feminist who was awarded the title of 'Secularlist of the Year' in 2005, has herself faced death threats. In Islam, apostasy is called *ridda* (turning back) and it is considered by Muslims to be a profound insult to God, which deserves harsh punishment. Apostasy is punishable by death in a number of countries, including Saudi Arabia, Yemen, Iran, Sudan and Afghanistan. In other parts of the world apostates can be shunned by family and friends. Namazie said: 'We are establishing the alternative to the likes of the MCB because we don't think people should be pigeonholed as Muslims or deemed to be represented by regressive organizations like the MCB.' She said the new council will start with a membership of twenty-five British ex-Muslims who are prepared to be named and pictured publicly.[68]

Blair left office at the end of June 2007. His twelve-point counter-terrorist strategy in the aftermath of 7/7 was reviewed by Philip Johnston in *The Daily Telegraph*:

New grounds were created for deporting undesirables, closing bookshops, and negotiating memorandums of understanding with countries to take deportees. However, no firebrand clerics have been ejected though Omar Bakri has been prevented from returning from Lebanon. Others, like Abu Hamza, are in prison or facing trial for allegedly fomenting racial hatred. Police and immigration officials have compiled a list of more than 120 undesirables. Only three countries – Lebanon, Jordan and Libya – have signed memorandums. Talks continue with other countries, including Algeria.

Condoning or glorifying terrorism here and abroad became an offence. There have been no convictions, although one person has been charged.

Asylum was automatically refused to anyone who has participated in terrorism anywhere, and a provision has been included in the Immigration, Asylum and Nationality Bill.

Procedures to strip citizenship were to become simpler and more effective. Provisions were included in the Immigration, Asylum and Nationality Act to replace one of the existing criteria for deprivation of citizenship – that a person concerned 'has done anything seriously prejudicial to the vital interests of the UK'.

A maximum time limit was to be set on future extradition cases involving terror suspects, but there has been no time limit for speeding up the process. Rashid Ramda, who had been waiting ten years for extradition, has been removed to France. Other alleged terrorists sought by the Americans are still here nine years after their arrest.

A new pre-trial process in court procedure was to be introduced, and the detention of terrorist suspects before charging was to be significantly extended. A decision has yet to be made on whether to allow more sensitive evidence, including that from tapping phones, to be produced in court. The government wanted to extend detention without charge to ninety days but was defeated in Parliament, which agreed an extension to twenty-eight days.

Control orders for those who are British nationals and cannot be deported was to be extended. Approximately eighteen control orders have been issued, but their provisions have been challenged in the courts, and about half the suspects are on the run.

Court capacity to deal with control orders and other related issues was to be expanded. The Ministry of Justice is still reviewing the way terrorist trials are handled.

Hizb ut-Tahrir and its successor organization al-Muhajirun were to be proscribed. HuT is still operating. Al-Muhajirun has been banned but it has reformed into other groups. The criteria for banning groups was expanded in the Terrorism Act 2006.

New thresholds were to be set for citizenship, and a commission on integration was to be established with the Muslim community. Citizenship provisions were introduced in the Immigration, Asylum and Nationality Act. Commissions involving community spokesmen were set up but ministers were not happy with the way they worked. New powers to close mosques were dropped after objections from religious leaders and police.

Plans were introduced for securing borders, new visa controls, and biometric visas. Embarkation controls are to be reimposed in 2009. New technology for immigration controls should be introduced over the next five years.[69]

The atrocities planned for London and Glasgow in June 2007, just as Gordon Brown became Prime Minister, involved the use of car bombs to cause indiscriminate civilian casualties – a technique honed in Baghdad to deadly effect. They have led to restrictions on car access, parking, movement within city centres and at airports and stations. For many, the most dreadful discovery was that those who were arrested were doctors, supposedly imbued with a vocation to save lives. The standard claim that this is a perversion of Islam has by now become impossible to sustain, as a familiarity with Islamic theology and texts reveals:

> The discovery gives the lie to assertions that Islamist extremism is the result of poverty, deprivation, injustice or the West's pursuit of policies in Iraq, the Palestinian territories and the wider Muslim world that are somehow inimical to Islam. This is patently not so. Al-Qa'ida has often recruited men who are educated, come from a middle-class background and who, in some cases, have personal experience of western values, learning and the western way of life. What is clear, however, is that this perversion of Islam cannot be written off simply as Wahhabi fanaticism or a Muslim equivalent of liberation theology. It does indeed have its roots in narrow fundamentalism, as those who have been temporarily seized by its spurious religious message have bravely admitted. But it is better understood as a cult, and one that appeals especially to the frustrations and rage of young Muslim men. In earlier times, the social restrictions of conservative societies, especially on relations between men and women, would have been largely accepted by men who had little outlet for their emotions. But in the digital age, the contrast with more liberal societies is quickly apparent and often agonizing. The result is a prurient interest in the tawdriest aspects of western life and a subsequent self-loathing, confusion and misogyny that blames women and western society for undermining Muslim 'purity'. Their frustrations are exploited by the politically ambitious, using causes such as Iraq and the Palestinians as motivators.[70]

Thoughts were subsequently turned to confronting the terrorists in earnest. Apart from further boosting the budgets of the intelligence agencies, legislation to control the 'terror trail' between Britain and Pakistan was called for. Britain formerly had rules that prevented British citizens in Northern Ireland from coming to the mainland without permission. Something similar will be required to deal with the route to and from Pakistan. It will be necessary to suspend whatever sections of the Human Rights Act may be required and derogate from the entirety of the European Convention on Human Rights if that cannot be avoided. A balance always has to be struck between security and liberty, but the age of the car bomber means it has to be assessed again.[71] The bungled car bombings reinforced the view that British Islamists are relative amateurs. Nor are their motives understood. The restoration of the medieval Caliphate sounds too much like a fairy tale straight out of *The Thousand and One Nights*. The western mindset cannot comprehend the irrationality of the Caliphate dream, nor appreciate that it is non-negotiable. It is far more logical to view jihad as a Muslim reaction to 'western interference' in their own countries, which can be brought to a swift conclusion by a withdrawal from Iraq and Afghanistan. To recognize the single-minded goal of jihad is to admit that the ongoing war has no forseeable end.

The two doctors, Bilal Abdulla, 27, and Kafeel Ahmed, 27, who were in the Jeep at Glasgow Airport, were trained in Baghdad where medicine is one of the most sought-after professions of the wealthy middle classes. Three other suspects are also doctors, including Kafeel's brother Sabeel, Mohammed Haneef, 27, from India, and Mohammed Asha, 26, a Jordanian brain surgeon. The backgrounds of the alleged terrorists came as no surprise to Ed Husain, a former member of Hizb ut-Tahrir.

> Al-Qa'ida is filled with people who are graduates from medical and engineering colleges. They regard scripture like a textbook, manual or medical handbook. In their minds, there is no room for any humanity-based nuance or even alternative arguments. They have the arrogance of their advanced education, consider themselves to be above the rest, and to be absolutely right ... They are intent on cleansing the entire world and putting in its place their own puritanical creed.

More alarmingly, he adds: 'You are wrong if you think that they are from a small minority. They are a vocal minority with significant numbers.'[72]

Several leading British Muslims have already stated that the change of tone that has marked Gordon Brown's premiership is 'helpful' in gaining the support of Muslim communities in Britain. Ahmed Versi, the editor of *Muslim News*, remarked that 'Tony Blair used to use the phrase "Islamic terrorism" ... it made the whole [Islamic] community feel they were being targeted.' Versi is pleased that Brown decided to drop phrases including 'Islamic terrorism' and the 'war on terror'. Jacqui Smith, the new Home Secretary, said it was 'unacceptable to hold any one community responsible' for the attempted outrages, something Versi agreed with, because, in his view, what motivates the terrorists is not Islam but British foreign policy.[73] Ed Husain, who renounced Islamism in favour of what he now thinks of as orthodox, traditional Islam, said:

> The MCB's insistence that there is a duty to help the police is very welcome. The trouble is, they are still wedded to a version of Islam that is, at the very least, hospitable to the extremists. None of the leading members of the MCB have condemned the hard-line anti-western ideology of figures such as Sayyid Qut'b, the Egyptian radical fundamentalist who developed, in the early Sixties, the theological justification for violence in the name of establishing an Islamic state (Qut'b was executed by the Egyptian Government in 1965). It would be a very powerful signal if the MCB said that Qut'b's hatred of the West and of democracy, and his endorsement of violence as the means to replace secular government with theocracy, had no Qur'anic justification. But no one from the MCB seems willing to make that move.

The MCB has also failed to condemn suicide bombing by Hamas against Israel. 'It is a very short step from accepting that there is a theological justification for "martyrdom" operations in Israel', states Husain, 'to accepting that there is a justification for perpetrating the murder of civilians here. I know. I have been down that road.'
Hassan Butt also spent several years as an extremist before becoming aware that the people with whom he was working were 'evil'. His family have rejected him for what they see as his 'treachery'. Butt believes many imams who preach at mosques in Britain

> refuse to broach the difficult and often complex truth that Islam can be interpreted as condoning violence against the unbeliever, and instead repeat the mantra that 'Islam is peace', and hope that all of this debate will go away. This has left the territory open for radicals ... I know, because [when] I was a recruiter, I repeatedly came across those who had tried to raise these issues with mosque authorities, only to be banned from

their grounds. Every time this happened ... it served as a recruiting sergeant for extremism.

Tellingly, Husain said, 'One of the main reasons I was recruited to Islamism was because I was ignorant. Like most Muslims born in Britain, I knew nothing of Islamic traditions and I couldn't read Arabic. The extremists had the field to themselves.'[74]

Gordon Brown banned ministers from using the word 'Muslim' in connection with the terrorism crisis, and dropped the phrase 'war on terror', as part of another attempt to improve community relations and avoid offending Muslims. Adopting a more 'consensual' tone than existed under Tony Blair provoked claims that ministers are indulging in yet more political correctness.[75] The deputy secretary general of the MCB, Daud Abdullah, urged everyone to cooperate with police in their hunt for the car bombers. But when asked whether Muslim extremists might be behind the attacks, he hastily added: 'Such incidents create tensions and suspicions. Let's not create a hypothetical problem ... it can be the work of Muslims, Christians, Jews or Buddhists.' London Mayor Ken Livingstone, meanwhile, added some humour of his own when speaking to BBC Radio: 'In this city, Muslims are more likely to be law-abiding than non-Muslims and less likely to support the use of violence to achieve political ends than non-Muslims.' When, a few days later, it became untenable to deny Muslim responsibility for the car bomb incidents, Muslim leaders condemned the attempted attacks. 'We acknowledge that there is radicalization taking place in our community', said Daud Abdullah. In an article in *The Daily Telegraph* aptly titled, 'Offering sanctuary threatens our safety', Philip Johnston wrote:

> In the past few months, more than a dozen Islamist fanatics have been brought before the courts for plotting mass murder and many more accused are on remand. Those sceptics who suspected that the government was exaggerating the scale of the threat – and those Muslims who complained about the number of arrests in their communities – have had their answer.[76]

Gordon Brown announced a new unified border police force to handle both customs and passport checks at all UK ports and airports by October 2007. The Border Force would bring together officers from the immigration service and Customs. Such a force has long been demanded by the Tories and was recommended by a Commons committee five years ago. Brown told MPs that the failed car bomb attacks in London and Glasgow were the fifteenth attempted terror assault on British soil since 2001. To counter the terrorist threat he announced a variety of measures including a review on the question of whether police should be able to use intercept evidence in court. The package also included: a new system of electronic exit controls at UK borders from 2009, so that passports can be checked against the 'warnings index' in real time; from March 2008, biometric visas will be extended to all visa applicants; the UK watchlist of suspects to be linked to the Interpol database of lost and stolen documents; and a consultation on tightening bail conditions and travel restrictions in any cases where people are suspected of involvement with terrorism.[77] Brown also proposed that police should be allowed to question suspects after they are charged. The leader of the opposition, David Cameron, raised the biggest obstacle to possible deportations – the European Convention on Human Rights (ECHR), or the way it has been interpreted by British courts. Article 3 makes it impossible to remove people who may be a threat to Britain, to countries which may be a threat to them. In *The Daily Telegraph*, Philip Johnston posed a question: 'Why should the terrorist threat require the civil liberties of British people to be circumscribed by measures such as identity cards while foreign nationals who pose the threat are protected by human rights laws?'[78]

Elsewhere, Michael Burleigh asked why Britain scrupulously adheres to the Human Rights Act, when her allies systematically flout the European Convention on Human Rights. On much of the continent they don't allow civil liberty lawyers to turn terrorism into a risk-free activity. The Socialist Interior Minister of Spain organized a campaign of assassinating ETA terrorists across the border in France during the 1990s. France deported ETA suspects to places such as Papua New Guinea, and has since been repatriating radical Islamist clerics. The Germans deported a Turkish imam on grounds of national security, even though he had lived in Germany for thirty years. The former German Interior Minister, Otto Schily, once a lawyer for Baader-Meinhof defendants, cryptically remarked of the jihadis: 'Those who love death can have it.' Burleigh continued:

> While we agonize about twenty-eight or fifty-six days custody, it is not uncommon for terrorist suspects in France to be held in

preventive detention for four or five years before their case goes to court. The use of intelligence intercept evidence in courts is being debated here, but the Italian security services have long made transcripts of this material available, so revealing the lying cynicism with which, for example, Milan-based Arab jihadis regard European asylum laws ... If Mr Brown's anti-terrorism measures seem ignorant of what our fellow Europeans practise routinely, they also reflect an outmoded habit of separating domestic and foreign policy. Why is foreign aid not contingent upon warning recipient states that they will forfeit it if clerics they subsidize preach hatred of the West? Why aren't we helping Afghanistan or Pakistan to build secular alternatives to the Saudi-financed madrassas where children are brainwashed with cartoon Jew killers? If this is a neo-Cold War, why are we failing to help the four fifths of Muslims who are not from the Middle East to assert themselves against that demented region?[79]

The intelligence agencies are monitoring every Muslim who travels from Britain to Mecca on pilgrimage in a wider effort to piece together intelligence on suspected al-Qa'ida terrorist activity. Over 100,000 British Muslims had to be monitored following evidence that British Islamic terrorists visited the city before carrying out attacks in Britain and abroad. The importance of the intelligence operation was one of the reasons given by spy chiefs for maintaining ties with Saudi Arabia when the Saudi Government was threatening to break off intelligence ties over a bribery investigation by the Serious Fraud Office (SFO) into BAE. Dr Ghayasuddin Siddiqui, leader of the Muslim Parliament, demonstrated a complete lack of understanding about this laborious step: 'It is absolutely wrong that people who are going to Mecca for entirely religious purposes should be monitored by the security services. It is a sad commentary on Britain's relations with Saudi Arabia.' The Mecca operation was launched after 7/7, when MI5 discovered that at least two of the suicide bombers had made the trip.[80] Omar Khayam, who dressed as a suicide bomber at a rally threatening terror attacks, cleans carriages unsupervised for rail giant First Group. Furious train drivers claimed the safety of staff and passengers was being put at risk and one of them said: 'We cannot believe this man is employed in a job giving him access to locked places on trains where bombs could be hidden and never be found. He has keys that could be passed on to others for the electrical cupboards in carriages. It is a risk too far.' Khayam had been filmed dressed as a bomber at the controversial demonstration outside London's Danish Embassy, while demonstrators around him called for new UK terror attacks.[81]

After all the new limitations on immigration, the new legislation, the security checks and the arrests, hundreds of al-Qa'ida members are still roaming the streets of British cities. Lord Stevens, the former Metropolitan Police Commissioner, said MI5 had suggested a figure of 2,000 terrorism suspects and their supporters as being active in Britain but the true number was 'probably nearer 4,000'. Lord Stevens also gave warning that al-Qa'ida-linked extremists were already trying to infiltrate the police and the security services and that dozens had already been weeded out.[82] Most are not involved in plotting attacks but the security service is alarmed at the increasing speed with which groups move from radicalization to action. It is struggling to monitor all the networks and is unable to keep all the people under constant surveillance. Security chiefs revealed that up to 4,000 Islamic extremists have attended terrorist training camps in Afghanistan before returning to Britain. It demonstrates how Gordon Brown's plans for tighter checks on people entering Britain will come too late to keep out many dangerous individuals. Afghanistan was the centre for al-Qa'ida terrorist training between 1996, when the Taleban regime came to power, and October 2001, when America and Britain invaded. MI5 and MI6 are working on the assumption that al-Qa'ida ordered them to return to establish autonomous terrorist 'sleeper cells'. A US intelligence report says that al-Qa'ida has regrouped along the Afghan-Pakistan border and is now in a stronger position that it was before 9/11.[83]

Another depressing impact on British society has been the growing numbers of foreign inmates in its prisons. Foreign prisoners now make up almost one in six of Britain's prison population and are costing the taxpayer almost £400 million a year. The explosion in the number of overseas inmates has caused an overcrowding crisis, pushing the total above 80,000. Figures published by the Home Office show there are now 12,122 foreign prisoners. The overcrowding crisis has led to calls for fewer and lesser sentences to be handed down by the courts. But if there were not so many foreign inmates, there would not even be a crisis. The annual cost per prisoner place was £32,888 in 2005–06.[84] The mismanagement of foreigners in the prison system became clear with the revelation that a man about to stand trial for terrorist offences was able to remain in Britain despite serving a prison sentence for armed robbery, although he should have been considered for deportation on his release in 1998. In 2004, he was even granted British citizenship. A lack of detailed records by the Home Office led to the release of 1,023 foreign prisoners without deportation moves being initiated, an omission which contributed to the dismissal of Home Secretary Charles Clarke in Blair's Government reshuffle in May 2006. Clarke had revealed that some seventy-nine were involved in the most serious crimes, while five out of the 1,023 prisoners released between 1999 and March 2006 had gone on to commit more crimes. Somalian Mustafa Jama was allowed to stay in Britain just months before he was implicated in the murder of PC Sharon Beshenivsky in Bradford in November 2005.[85]

The high number of Muslim prisoners, relative to their numbers in the population, has presented several challenges. They are mostly of Pakistani descent, and the relative absence of people of subcontinental origin who follow other religions is equally striking. Secondly, Islamic proselytizing is prevalent in British prisons. More often than not, this is the prisoner's first experience of reading abstract theological principles. Thirdly, prisoners as a group are susceptible to religious conversion. Most criminals give up crime in their 30s. The majority give up spontaneously but some are seeking a pretext to do so. Religion provides them with that pretext; and by conversion, they do not feel that they have simply surrendered unconditionally to society, meekly accepting its law-abiding norms after years of flouting them. They feel they have actively chosen a new life. Islam answers more than one of the needs of such people. Many prisoners prefer life in prison to life outside, which is one motive for recidivism. Prison imposes boundaries on them that they are unable to impose on themselves. Islam, with its daily rituals and its list of prohibitions, is ideally suited to those who are seeking to contain their own lives. It has one other great advantage: it is feared by society at large. Among the majority of young Muslim men in prison, however, the extent of their secularization can hardly be exaggerated. The same phenomenon has been noticed in France, where a much higher proportion of the prison population, rising to as much as 60 per cent, is Muslim. The prisoners are not religiously observant, and share the interests of their white and black counterparts. Their one difference is that, thanks to their cultural inheritance, their abuse of women is systematic rather than unsystematic as it is with the whites and blacks. A small number among them will be susceptible to conversion. And the zeal of converts is usually greater than the zeal of those who were born into the faith. A general sense of grievance and of a grave injustice that they believe has been done them provides the tipping point into radicalism. By injustice they do not mean that they did not do what they were accused of having done. Their justice is an ideal state of affairs which includes an effortlessly acquired supply of women and BMWs: for them, much zealotry is, in the view of Theodore Dalrymple, disappointed and embittered materialism.[86]

The Prison Service has no strategy to tackle extremist recruitment, and is rendered helpless to stop it by circumstances ranging from language barriers to bureaucracy. Britain has the greatest number of terrorist suspects of any European country. It is a myth that they are kept separate from the rest of the prison community. The majority reside in high-security institutions, but remain on normal wings because of lack of resources. As early as 2000 Jack Straw, then Home Secretary, was told that radical imams were operating in prisons.[87] A Muslim preacher once described as Bin Laden's 'right-hand man in Europe', Abu Qatada, may be attempting to radicalize fellow prisoners at a Worcestershire gaol. The Prison Officers Association is worried because its members cannot understand what Abu Qatada is saying when he is seemingly praying in Long Lartin prison, where he is fighting expulsion from Britain. Steve Gough, the vice-chairman of the association, said: 'People ... who have the ability to radicalize and have got a proven track record to radicalize, need a new type of control that we're not ready for and the government doesn't appear to have put any thought into.' The association is calling for interpreters to monitor about 320 terror-related inmates in British prisons.[88]

In attracting prison converts to radical Islam, Muslim literature in English has been known to play a part. This includes Wahhabi-funded English-language translations of the Qur'an to which certain interpolations have been added. According to testimony given in September 2006 to the US Senate Homeland Security and Governmental Affairs Committee by a one-time American convert to Islam, who has since renounced Islam for Christianity, Saudi 'charities' for which he worked distributed to US prisoners Wahhabi/Salafi English translations of the Qur'an which contain explanatory footnotes that propagate the most incendiary versions of Islam. For example, when he worked for a now defunct Saudi organization called al-Haramain, it distributed to prisons an English translation of the Qur'an that contained the following explanatory footnote about the meaning of 'jihad':

> Al-jihad (holy fighting) in Allah's cause (with full force of numbers and weaponry) is given the utmost importance in Islam and is one of its pillars (on which it stands). By jihad Islam is established, Allah's word is made superior ... and his religion (Islam) is propagated. By abandoning jihad (may Allah protect us from that) Islam is destroyed and the Muslims fall into an inferior position; their honour is lost, their lands are stolen, their rule and authority vanish. Jihad is an obligatory duty in Islam on every Muslim, and he who tries to escape from this duty, or does not in his innermost heart wish to fulfil this duty, dies with one of the qualities of a hypocrite.

Also included in this Wahhabi English-language edition of the Qur'an was a twenty-two-page appendix by a former Saudi Arabian chief justice, entitled 'The Call to Jihad'. According to its former employee, al-Haramain kept a database with particulars of the more than 15,000 inmates with whom it had had dealings while they were in prison, which included details of their release dates and the addresses to which they planned to return upon release.[89] Rival groups of Muslim inmates created a potentially explosive situation over the interpretation of the Qur'an in Britain's biggest prison. Some Muslim inmates were also pressurizing fellow Muslim prisoners to adopt extremist beliefs and lifestyles. The row concerns the way the Qur'an is interpreted within the Sunni Muslim sect and not between Sunni and Shi'a Muslims. The rising number of Muslim inmates in Wandsworth means that the existing mosque is too small, but measures to deal with the problem have been criticized. A report disclosed that 'inherent' tensions among Muslims are exacerbated because they have to walk through the Christian chapel to reach their place of worship.[90] Some of the crimes committed by Muslims are novel for British law, since they relate to mores and customs in Muslim countries, for example in the case of so-called 'honour killings'. Azhar Nazir, 30, and his cousin, 17, used four knives to cut Samaira Nazir's throat and repeatedly stab her after she fell in love with an Afghan asylum seeker from what they regarded as an unsuitable caste. Samaira, 25, had rejected suitors lined up to meet her in Pakistan and was attacked by her father, brother and cousin in the family home in Southall, Middlesex. She was then held down as a scarf was tied around her neck and her throat was cut in three places. Nazir's daughters, aged 2 and 4, were screaming and were splattered with blood. He denied murder but told police that his sister had to be stopped. The father was also charged with the murder but fled to Pakistan. The court was told that Nazir and his father ran a successful grocery store on Southall Broadway. The son also owned a recruitment company, which supplied workers for the Hilton hotel chain and had made Samaira a director. She was articulate and had studied travel and tourism at Thames University, but clashed with her family when she told them that she wanted to marry Mr Mohammad.[91]

'Honour killings' in Britain have been linked with extremist groups abroad by the Crown Prosecution Service (CPS). The CPS told a BBC investigation that Islamist terror groups were behind the murder five years ago of Heshu Yones, 16, who was stabbed to death by her father, Abdalla Yones, who had associations with a Kurdish nationalist organization. In a further case, a woman received a death threat from her family. The threat is said to have originated in an Egyptian terrorist group. Nazir Afzal, from the CPS, said that such killings were not confined to the older generation and that a second generation of youths were continuing the tradition. 'We know they are bizarre and outdated but they get their identity from those traditions and they feel very strongly that how you treat your women is a demonstration of your commitment to radicalism and extremist thought', he told BBC Radio. According to the UN Population Fund, 5,000 women a year die in 'honour killings'. There were twelve such murders recorded in the UK last year.[92] Police are re-examining 2,000 deaths and murders dating from 1996 to establish whether they involve 'honour killings'.[93]

Mohammed Riaz, 49, killed his wife and four daughters aged 3 to 16 in their sleep by setting their home alight because he could not bear them adopting a westernized lifestyle. Riaz, who had spent the evening drinking, set himself on fire and died two days later. He found it abhorrent that his eldest daughter wanted to be a fashion designer, and that she and her sisters were likely to reject the Muslim tradition of arranged marriages. Riaz, who came from the

North West Frontier region of Pakistan, met his Anglo-Pakistani wife when her father sent her to the sub-continent to find a husband. After an arranged marriage, she developed a career as a community leader in Accrington while he took on a series of low-paid jobs, held back by a lack of English. Mrs Riaz allowed the girls to express themselves in a more western way and began to work with women who felt suppressed by Asian culture. Many saw her as a role model for young Asian women.[94]

While Muslim organizations incessantly complain about 'hate' crimes against their community, the authorities deliberately downplay instances of Muslim 'hate' crimes against whites. Three Asian men were found guilty and imprisoned for life for the murder in March 2004 of Kriss Donald, a schoolboy who was killed in a shockingly brutal racially-aggravated attack. Imran Shahid, his brother Zeeshan Shahid, and Mohammed Faisal Mushtaq, were convicted of the abduction, assault and murder of the 15-year-old. All three had spent time in custody for previous offences. As he was pulled into a vehicle in Glasgow, Donald is said to have pleaded: 'I'm only 15, what did I do?' Sentencing Imran Shahid to twenty-five years behind bars, the judge said the leader of the killing was 'not fit to be at liberty in a civilized society'. The victim was stabbed thirteen times and set alight with petrol while he was still alive.[95]

The Muslim presence has left its mark on unexpected aspects of life in the UK. Muhammad could soon become the most popular boy's name in the country, as more and more Muslim parents choose to name their sons after their prophet. When all the different spellings of the name are added up, the name was second only to Jack in the registration of boys' births in 2006. It was given to 6,010 babies that year, compared to 6,928 children who were called Jack. The Muslim birth rate is about three times higher than the national average. Reaz Ahmed, from the Islamic Community Centre in Tottenham, north London, said: 'In the Qur'an the prophet said, If you do not love me more than your parents or your children, or anybody else in the world, then your faith will not be fulfilled.'[96] *Time Out* published an article by Michael Hodges suggesting that the total Islamization of the city would bring many advantages. Writing in the *City Journal*, Theodore Dalrymple remarked that regardless of his motives for writing such an article, Hodges did not consider the effect it may have on Hindus and Sikhs, 'of whom there are large numbers in London, and for whom a joke about an Islamic takeover would not be so amusing'. Dalrymple continued:

> Opinion is divided as to whether Hodges's article was, in fact, merely satirical. I think that it was: his suggestion that regular Islamic prayer would lessen osteoarthritis points to satire, as does his proposed transformation of pubs into juice bars, to the great benefit of public health. His eulogy of *zakat*, the Muslim 2.5 per cent tax earmarked for the poor, could be taken as a plea for lower taxes, since all social democracies exact far higher taxes for the purpose. The problem with deciding whether the article is purely satirical or not is that it so exactly reproduces some of the Islamists' claims. Here, for example, it lauds Muslim race relations: 'Under Islam all ethnicities are equal. Once you have submitted to Allah you are a Muslim – it doesn't matter what colour you are. End of story.' This is about as accurate a depiction of the actual situation in Muslim countries as the old Communist claim that everyone was economically equal in the Soviet Union. But it is a claim that Islamists make nevertheless, and the gullible often believe it … So many concessions have already been made to Islamism in Britain that joining an irresistible tide might seem a sensible precaution, or an astute positioning for the future … So is London's future Islamic? I do not think so, even if Mohammed does become the commonest British name. Islamism's intellectual resources are so slight as to be negligible, and its pretensions ridiculous. To state its claims is to refute them: perhaps that was Hodges's intention.[97]

Rising immigration and older mothers have fuelled an increase in the number of children women are having in England and Wales. Figures released by the Office of National Statistics show the average number of children has increased to 1.87, the highest rate since 1980. Almost 150,000 children born in the UK in 2006 had mothers who were not born here, accounting for 21.9 per cent of all live births. The number of children born to mothers born outside the UK is 77 per cent higher than it was a decade ago.[98] In London, 53 per cent of births in 2006 were to mothers who were not born in Britain.[99] Professor Ludi Simpson, from Manchester University, forecast that Leicester will become the first minority white city by 2019, followed by Birmingham in 2024, and Luton and Slough in the 2030s. A population map, prepared by experts at Leeds University, shows that the proportion of whites in all parts of the country will fall between 2001 and 2020. The biggest reduction will be in Greater London, where 64 per cent of people will be white by 2021, down from 71 per cent in 2001.[100]

In order to be seen to be treating all faiths equally, regardless of the risks they pose, British officialdom has taken some bizarre decisions. Under legislation passed in 1994, ministers who are not ordained cannot get a work visa. Every year, the Methodist Church in the US sends fourteen probationer ministers to England for a year, but for the first time in 2006, they were barred by the Home Office under the 1994 legislation. Church leaders accused the Home Office of an attack on religious freedom. Although probationer ministers in the Methodist Church are fully trained, they cannot be ordained until they have served a set of churches for two years. Dr Paul Glass, Superintendent Methodist Minister for Wakefield, said: 'This rule is meant to be for unqualified Islamic students. You could not imagine somebody less like a terrorist than a young American Methodist minister.' Lord Griffiths, Minister of Wesley's Chapel in Central London, pointed out that 'If ever there was a law with unintended consequences, this surely has to be it.'[101]

Increasingly, Christian congregations feel they are being squeezed between twin threats: from secularism and from Islamic extremists. Regular Sunday church attendance declined by 2 per cent in the Church of England in 2005. About 1.7 million Britons worship monthly at an Anglican church, while about 1.2 million go to church weekly.[102] Police often refuse to act against Islamic extremists, who abuse Britain's freedom by preaching hatred and incitement against the West, while the culture of political correctness and an over-zealous espousal of human rights leaves Christianity exposed to attack. Simon Calvert, from the Christian Institute, compiled a dossier of incidents of discrimination and attacks on Christians. He is worried about the police's role. 'They increasingly think it is their business to tell Christians what they can and cannot say', he said. It is an issue that is causing concern in the Evangelical Alliance, which represents 1.2 million British Christians. 'A lot of people get the distinct impression that there are certain minorities that are protected more by our laws than others', said Dr Don Horrocks, its head of communications. Colin Hart, of the Christian Institute, pointed out: 'It is noticeable that police never arrest Muslims who make remarks about homosexuality.' Two pensioners, Joe and Helen Roberts, from Fleetwood,

Lancashire, were quizzed by police for more than an hour after they asked if they could put Christian pamphlets next to gay rights literature on display at their town hall. Police told them that their request was close to a 'hate' crime and said they wanted to 'educate' them out of their belief that homosexuality was wrong. Similarly, the author Lynette Burrows received a warning from the Metropolitan Police for suggesting, on radio, that gay people did not make ideal adoptive parents. When Sacranie said, during a Radio 4 broadcast in January 2006, that homosexuality was harmful, police initially prevaricated, and then dropped the matter after a cursory investigation. And then there was the case of the young Muslim who dressed as a suicide bomber and paraded in London in February 2006, six months after the 7/7 bombings in which fifty-two were murdered by real suicide bombers. Police did not arrest him on the day, but arrested two counter-demonstrators.

The cause for such a difference in treatments, many believe, lies with Christianity itself, with its own over-eagerness to encompass multifaith movements. Damian Thompson, the editor-in-chief of *The Catholic Herald*, said: 'The fact that Christians are persecuted and harassed, while Muslim extremists are left alone to spread their propaganda, can be partly attributed to the incredible wimpishness of Anglican and Catholic bishops in Britain, who have spent decades wringing their hands and apologizing for the sins of Christianity.' He added: 'Much of the damaging appeasement of extreme Muslims can be traced back to the multifaith movement embraced so vigorously by the liberal clergy in the seventies and eighties. Offending Muslim sensibilities frightens Church leaders far more than acts of terrorism.' An astonishing example of the church's liberalism was demonstrated when a Church of England priest who converted to Hinduism was allowed to continue to officiate as a cleric. Reverend David Hart said his switch of faiths would be 'read in the spirit of open exploration and dialogue, which is an essential feature of our shared modern spirituality'. Dr Patrick Sookhdeo, of the Institute for the Study of Islam and Christianity, believes that 'any society must be based on its values. And for the UK they are Judaeo-Christian. The pluralism of the seventies and eighties marginalized Christianity. Then secularism came along and effectively neutralized it. So, now we have a moral/spiritual vacuum and anything that is seen to be Christian can be attacked.' Dr Sookhdeo is a convert from Islam to Christianity – for which the penalty is death. 'It is true that Islam is the only religion that does not allow its followers to leave. It is a one-way street', he said.¹⁰³

To the surprise of many, the Church of England launched an astonishing attack on the government's drive to turn Britain into a multifaith society, saying that the attempt to make minority 'faith communities' more integrated has backfired, leaving society 'more separated than ever before'. The criticisms were made in a confidential Church document, entitled *Cohesion and Integration – A briefing note for the House* [of Bishops]. It challenges the 'widespread description' of Britain as a multifaith society and even calls for the term 'multifaith' to be reconsidered. It claims that divisions between communities have been deepened by the government's 'schizophrenic' approach to tackling multiculturalism. While trying to encourage interfaith relations, it has actually given 'privileged attention' to the Islamic faith. Written by Guy Wilkinson, the interfaith adviser to the Archbishop of Canterbury, Dr Rowan Williams, the report lists a number of moves made by the government since 7/7 to win favour with Muslims. These include 'using public funds' to fly Muslim scholars to Britain, shelving legislation on forced marriage and encouraging financial arrangements to comply with Islamic requirements. One bishop said it was the first time the Church had launched such a defence of the country's Christian heritage. The paper argues that the effort invested in trying to integrate Muslims since the London bombings has had no positive impact on community relations and that the Commission on Cohesion and Integration seems doomed to fail. Bishops were dismayed that no Christian denomination was represented on the commission. The 2001 census showed that 72 per cent of Britons describe themselves as Christian. 'It could certainly be argued that there is an agenda behind a claim that a 5 per cent adherence to 'other faiths' makes for a multi-faith society', says the document.¹⁰⁴

In a startling warning to the government, senior church and political figures backed a report advocating force to protest against policies that are 'unbiblical' and 'inimical to the Christian faith'. The report from the Evangelical Alliance said 'violent revolution' should be regarded as a viable response if government legislation encroaches further on basic religious rights. The report, entitled *Faith and Nation*, was published amid growing concern that people are being prevented from expressing their faith. The government's attempt to introduce religious hatred laws highlighted the growing threat to religious liberty. Proposals to ban proselytizing in publicly-funded Christian projects could ultimately lead to Christians being prevented from teaching others about the Bible. This would 'be unambiguously recognized by Christians as perpetrating evil that has to be resisted by deliberate acts of defiance'. While it has always been expected that the greatest threat to Britain's security will come from Muslim extremists, the report caused alarm to government ministers as it revealed disquiet among the Christian population. Significantly, it came from the Evangelical Alliance – a mainstream organization representing 1.2 million Christians. The organization acknowledged that 'resisting evil in the modern state' can take many different forms. Before resorting to force, Christians would normally first turn to dialogue. Active forms of resistance to the state may encompass civil disobedience involving selective, non-violent resistance or, ultimately, violent revolution. Mike Morris, the executive director of the Evangelical Alliance, said that the report reflected the breadth of submissions they had received. The Evangelical Alliance raised the debate at a time when religious liberty issues became prominent following the row over Muslim women's right to wear the veil and BA's decision to suspend Nadia Eweida for breaching its uniform policy by wearing a cross.[105]

Britain's anti-terrorist efforts are not only directed at the home front but are also connected to the Iraq War in which Britain has high stakes. Anti-terrorist police who arrested eight Libyans in a series of dawn raids in May 2006 believe they may have thwarted a wave of suicide bomb attacks on British and US forces in Iraq. The suspects, picked up at the end of an investigation in Manchester, were held on suspicion of either encouraging al-Qa'ida or helping to fund some of its atrocities. But intelligence sources said that some of them may have been planning to fly out to Iraq as suicide bombers. Some were regarded as so dangerous that police and Home Office officials sought their immediate deportation. The men were arrested during coordinated raids on nineteen addresses in five force areas. Two of the men were previously named as having terrorist links on a United Nations website. One of them, Tahir Nasuf, 44, worked for the Sanabel Relief Agency, which raises money for Muslims in poor parts of the world. The US Treasury department has claimed that Sanabel is a front for the Libyan Islamic Fighting Group, which in turn is said to have links with al-Qa'ida. In February 2006 the UN froze the assets of both Nasuf and the Sanabel agency. Some of the intelligence is believed to have surfaced in June 2005 when police raided the Manchester home of a suicide bomber who had blown himself up in an attack four months earlier. The man, a 41-year-old French national of North African origin, was the first person to travel from Britain to attack coalition troops in Iraq. He had spoken to friends at a mosque of his desire to fight jihad, or 'holy war'. The bomber was unknown to MI5 but fits the profile of the 'jihadists' who went to fight for the greater Muslim cause in Bosnia, Chechnya and Afghanistan. Security sources suspect there is a European network that supplies fighters and suicide bombers to Iraq. Police also raided the offices of the Sanabel Relief Agency in Sparkbrook, Birmingham.[106]

Up to 150 Islamic radicals had travelled from Britain to Iraq to join up with a 'British brigade' established by al-Qa'ida leaders to fight coalition forces. Senior security sources said leaders of the Iraqi insurgency set up a 'foreign legion' composed entirely of westerners to fight alongside the insurgents in the war against British and American forces. Security sources say dozens of cases have been unearthed where suspected would-be 'suicide bombers' have been stopped at British airports while they were en route to Iraq. One said: 'Greater Manchester police frequently interdict individuals whom they believe are going to Iraq and other locations in order to carry out "suicide" attacks. Conventional charges, such as passport irregularities, are used to prevent them leaving the country. But this leaves police with the problem of returning potential "suicide bombers" to the Manchester community.'[107]

The Guardian reported a secret high-level Metropolitan Police document which concluded that Muslim officers are more likely to become corrupt than white officers because of their cultural and family backgrounds. The document caused outrage among ethnic minorities within the force, who labelled it racist and proof that there is a gulf in understanding between the police force and the Muslim community. The document was written as an attempt to investigate why complaints of misconduct and corruption against Asian (who dares to say Muslim?) officers are ten times higher than against their white colleagues. The main conclusions of the study, commissioned by the Directorate of Professional Standards and written by an Asian detective chief inspector, delicately and tactfully stated: 'Asian officers and in particular Pakistani Muslim officers are under greater pressure from the family, the extended family ... and their community against that of their white colleagues to engage in activity that might lead to misconduct or criminality.' The report argued that British Pakistanis live in a cash culture in which 'assisting your extended family is considered a duty' and in an environment in which large amounts of money are loaned between relatives and friends. The first version was considered so inflammatory when it was shown to representatives from the staff associations for Black, Hindu, Sikh and Muslim officers, that it had to be toned down, thus diluting its value in the process. There are 31,000 officers in the Met – 7 per cent, or 2,170, are Black and minority ethnic; among these an estimated 300 are Muslim.[108]

Terror in Britain, terror directed abroad and terror among Muslims within Europe, by bomb, by Islamikaze attacks or by murder in the family, do not exhaust the entire gamut of evil planned by terrorists. Some of these terrorist cells were suspected of planning terrorism by gas or other weapons of mass destruction which, by their nature, cannot be directed at anyone in particular and are calculated to harm masses of civilians. MI5 operatives suspect that al-Qa'ida sympathizers intended to produce a nerve agent – probably sarin – and release it in a confined space to maximize the number of casualties. The sarin attack on three railway lines in the Japanese capital killed twelve people and injured more than 5,000 in March 1995. The plan was to be implemented on the anniversary of 7/7, providing a rallying call to al-Qa'ida sympathizers to continue their jihad against the West. Police and MI5 officers had reason to believe that the bomb factory they were tipped to find in Forest Gate was of such a type, and therefore they had to act. Had there been no July 7, Forest Gate would not have happened either. They questioned the two men after the raid, and then released them since they had insufficient evidence.[109]

Indeed, British security has been alerted by a wide assortment of potential and actual terrorists, of every hue. A Pakistani-born British national, Iaz Ali, was arrested by the Shin Bet (Israel Security Agency). He admitted to having served as an official representative of Islamic Relief Worldwide (IRW), a Birmingham-based organization established in 1984 and suspected of funding Hamas activity. Ali told Shin Bet investigators that he had served as the organization's representative in the Gaza Strip since December 2005 and mainly worked on money transfers from abroad and to Hamas institutions which had been outlawed by Israel. On his computer, Shin Bet found incriminating documents allegedly proving IRW's relationship with illegally-run Hamas charities in Nablus, Saudi Arabia and Britain. IRW representatives in Israel sometimes operated out of Hamas offices and served as an integral part of the Palestinian terror organization, security officials said. Following negotiations with Ali's lawyer, the Shin Bet agreed to deport him to the UK without the option of returning to Israel.[110]

Charles Moore, the former editor of *The Daily Telegraph*, has joined the dots, using the evidence all around him, of Islamic subversion of the West – and has highlighted the common threads between Israel's predicament and that of Europe. His most valuable contribution is to alert the champions of human rights that their doctrinal one-sidedness sacrifices national security and poses existential threats to nation states, for the sake of protecting the 'rights' of criminals and terrorists who are bent on destroying those same systems that protect them. Suffice it to scan the daily European press to appreciate how suffocating, detrimental, all-enveloping, suicidal and corrupt the European edifice has become. Disbursing funds in all directions, including terrorist organizations such as Hamas, on 'human rights' grounds, gives the unelected bureaucrats unmerited power accompanied by delusions of grandeur.

In Moore's view, the Human Rights Act is for Tony Blair's Government what the ERM (Exchange Rate Mechanism of the European Monetary System) was for John Major's – the humiliating failure of its most sacred doctrine. The thing it was most sure it was right about turned out to be what it got most wrong. Major argued that almost all the experts thought Britain should go into it, so he could not be much blamed when the exit came on 16 September 1992. Blair found himself in a similar position. He was a barrister, married to a human rights barrister, and in 1997 was moving in circles where everyone he met thought that the European Convention on Human Rights should be incorporated into British law. All the New Labour people, and all the Matrix Chambers people who were doing well by doing good, and most of the judges, and anyone else who considered himself 'civilized', hoped that the long, dark night of Tory Government was coming to an end. 'Europe', in the form of the ECHR and the Euro and the European Court of Justice and all the rest of it, was the future. The High Court in Britain had finally passed judgement in the case of the Afghans who hijacked an internal flight in Afghanistan in 2000, and were subsequently involved in a four-day stand-off at Stansted Airport. The judges ruled that they had a right to remain in Britain, even though they violently grabbed a plane to get to British soil in the first place, because Article 3 of the Human Rights Convention says that they cannot be sent anywhere where they might face torture. Blair said this decision was 'an abuse of common sense'. But in upholding such an abuse, as when quashing laws to protect Britain from terrorism, the judges are only doing what the law tells them, and the person most responsible for passing the law is Blair.[111]

Moore predicts that the collapse of the human rights edifice is near certain. In popular conversation now, 'human rights' in Britain is the subject of mockery, and viewed as a system by which judges defend bad people from the consequences of their actions and impose unreasonable duties upon good people. Every nasty school pupil knows that his human rights can be invoked if the teacher gets too angry with him; every conscientious teacher knows that twenty years of unblemished conduct will count for nothing in his favour if he can be shown to have breached a child's human rights. Every grumpy prisoner, second-rate employee, suspected terrorist, mixed-up transsexual, Muslim schoolgirl who wants to wear the most extreme forms of religious attire – these, and countless others, know that they can get lawyers, attention, legal aid and often, money, out of 'human rights'. Because the laws regard most of those rights as being universal, one does not have to be a British citizen to qualify for them. All one has to do is get inside the perimeter fence to obtain rights to religious freedom, social security, privacy, founding a family, paid holidays and free health treatment. This is accompanied by the delay that so much law involves, the public expense of keeping claimants and their dependants, the fees for people like Mrs Blair, and the virtual breakdown of all administrative systems – policing, immigration, criminal justice, prisons, deportation, extradition – which relate to the problems involved. If Britain were to repeal the Human Rights Act and withdraw from the European Convention on Human Rights, asserts Moore, it would suffer no ill consequences beyond the pursed lips of its continental partners. He believes Britain is entitled to do it and should do it. The demand for human rights laws originally grew with the realization that government had too much unchecked power and that Parliament was failing in its duty to provide those checks. But Britain cannot cure the oppressiveness of its domestic legislation by putting itself under the judgement of a foreign court (in Strasbourg) and making that Strasbourg system part of its own law. That court is, in the literal sense of the word, irresponsible, and Britain must regain responsibility.

But no one could have imagined that during Blair's administration the Muslim population in Britain would grow enormously, or that the self-effacing Islam of the initial years of immigration would gradually abuse the rights it was granted. Approximately 45,000 Muslims were granted citizenship in 2005, out of a total of 161,000 new citizens. As Islam grew, its demands and expectations increased, commensurate with the government's unwillingness and inability to resist them. A *Guide to Islam* was launched in London, claiming that the publication of the controversial novel *The Satanic Verses* has had a more lasting impact on British Muslims than the rise of al-Qa'ida, September 11 and the London bombings. The implication is that only what supposedly hurts the soul of the Muslims is important, never mind the death and havoc wreaked on others. The publication from the British Council and the Association of Muslim Social Scientists said that Salman Rushdie's 1989 work of fiction led to the MCB being established and therefore had a huge influence on Muslims. A third significant event for them was the election of the Labour Government in 1997 which brought the first Muslim MPs to Parliament. The guide, written by Ehsan Masood, said: 'Of these three, it is the aftermath of *The Satanic Verses* that has so far had the most lasting impact.' Asked about his conclusions, Masood said: 'Al-Qa'ida, terrorism and the London bombings are still fairly recent. In the fullness of time they will probably have the most long-lasting impact. But sixteen years have passed since *The Satanic Verses* and we're still seeing the impact now.' The book, designed for journalists and diplomats, gives an overview of politics, education, Muslim women, charity, the media and culture amongst British Muslims, trying to present the acceptable face of Islam. It describes efforts to reduce extremism in Muslim communities, and gives a definition and brief history of 'Islamophobia'.[112]

As with the pattern established by many guides written before and since, non-Muslims make every effort to understand and empathize with Muslims, while the reverse is not even considered. It would be quite a challenge to find books explaining Christianity or Judaism, let alone the non-monotheistic religions, to Muslims. There is an underlying logic attached to the absence of such guides – Islam is an actively proselytizing faith, whose adherents will settle for any and all means to spread their creed. In a perverse way, they seek to exploit the newly-generated interest in Islam (and hence books on Islam) following 9/11 to convert non-Muslims, exploiting the fact that the rise of secularism and materialism in the West has created a spiritual vacuum in many impressionable minds. Many have never been taught the basic tenets of Christianity, and Christian worship is out of favour in state schools – where multiculturalism is the reigning deity, accompanied by acute sensitivity to all faiths except for the established church. While most people are aware that Christmas celebrates the birth of Christ, many are clueless about the significance of Easter. An April 2007 survey of 1,000 adults in the UK showed that those aged between 15 and 24 were least likely to know the religious meaning of Easter. One in ten in that age group did not know why Easter Sunday was celebrated, and one in six had no idea of the significance of Good Friday.[113]

An American writer, Stephen Schwartz, put the jihadist threat into perspective, saying that Britain had emerged as the apparent main target for jihadist terror in Europe because a million or more Sunnis of Pakistani background, who comprise the main element among British Muslims, also include the largest contingent of radical Muslims in Europe. Their jihadist sympathies embody an imported ideology, organized through mosques and other religious institutions, rather than a 'home-grown' phenomenon. The threat has little to do with British policies, poverty, discrimination or Islamophobia. Dr Irfan Ahmed al-Alawi, head of the UK Islamic Heritage Foundation and a British Muslim adversary of the extremists, put it well at a Washington conference on Euro-Islam in June 2006. He declared, 'Students who graduate from the Muslim schools in England and those who become extremists have the same brainwashing done to them as the Taleban. There is extremist Islam within the UK – yes, there is – and we should clean out our own house.' Islam in the UK is overwhelmingly influenced by imams and other religious officials born in Pakistan and trained in that country or in Saudi Arabia. Pakistani Sunni mosques in Britain are major centres for jihadist preaching, finance, incitement and recruitment. Schwartz believes the Islamic picture in the UK is much darker than that in Germany or even France, and criticizes the leaders of British Islam, exemplified by MCB, who have assumed a posture of truculence, obstruction and indignation when any suggestion is made that jihadist sympathies infect their ranks. British politicians and media exacerbate this problem when they are baffled over Muslims and converts raised to be British but turning out anti-British. The problem is not British society. British Muslim youths who enlist for jihad act not out of negative experiences of British culture or politics, but as tools in a deliberate process of indoctrination, carefully pursued by imams and agitators mainly imported from Pakistan with Saudi backing.[114]

Schwartz recounted his experience of official British relations with radical Islam at two colloquia held to address 'discrimination against European Muslims' (terrorism is a subject off the agenda at such affairs). One was called in Warsaw by the Organization for Security and Cooperation in Europe (OSCE) in 2005, and the other was sponsored by the UK Foreign Office and the Saudi-financed Organization for the Islamic Conference (OIC) at Wilton Park in May 2006. At the former conclave, dominated by British Muslims, a London Metropolitan Police representative reassured his audience that British law enforcement would go out of its way to avoid 'stereotyping' and Islamophobia, which he defined as presuming that suspects in terror conspiracies might be found among Muslims. The Brighton-based Pakistani imam Dr Abduljalil Sajid, of the obscure Muslim Council for Religious and Racial Harmony, chose to rebuke Tony Blair for an alleged assault on civil rights after the London bombings of July 2005. Imam Sajid entertained delegates with anecdotes of how he harassed Blair, acting out his insistence that Islam and terrorism are completely unconnected. To many Muslims present, the bombings and the radicalism that inspired them were nothing compared with their need to defy British and other western authorities. Sajid later came to prominence while on a speaking tour of Australia in October 2006, shortly after a sermon given by the leading Australian Muslim cleric Sheikh al-Hilali, in which al-Hilali likened immodestly dressed women to meat that attracted predators. Abduljalil Sajid defended al-Hilali as 'a great scholar' and said that the sermon had been taken out of context. Referring to the thrust of the Sheikh's argument, he said: 'So what is wrong in it? Who will object to that?'[115]

Britain faces a choice between accepting more 'Islamization' of society or facing a backlash as Britons grow increasingly troubled by the dilution of the majority culture. Tablighi Jama'at, an ultra-orthodox Muslim sect (established in India in 1927, but now most prominent in Pakistan), was planning to build Europe's largest mosque beside the London 2012 Olympic Park in Newham on an eighteen-acre site purchased for £1.6m in 1996. It would rival the two ancient churches of St Paul's Cathedral and Westminster Abbey. It would also serve as a vivid reminder that attendance in Christian churches is in decline, while Islam has assumed greater prominence. 'Islam is actually the most practised religion in Britain', claimed

Massoud Shadjareh, chairman of the London-based Islamic Human Rights Commission. The mosque complex, known as the London Markaz (centre), was originally intended to accommodate 40,000 worshippers, to be increased to 70,000 if necessary. The site also envisaged an Islamic garden and a religious boarding school with places for 500 pupils, library, exhibition spaces and restaurants. In comparison, Britain's largest Christian place of worship is the Anglican Cathedral in Liverpool, which accommodates 3,000. The two largest mosques now are in Morden, south London, which holds 10,000 people, and the London Muslim Centre in east London, which holds a similar number.[116] Arun Kataria, a spokesman for the Church of England, disputed the contention that Islam is now the most practised religion in Britain. He cited figures showing that 1.7 million Britons visit an Anglican church during the course of a month, in comparison to the country's official Muslim population of over two million. Other studies have shown that weekly attendance in Anglican churches has plunged below one million. But there is little dispute that the percentage of British Muslims who worship in mosques is much greater than the percentage of Christians who go to church. Incidentally, Hinduism is also growing in Britain. Greater London is said to be home to about fifty Hindu temples, including the Shri Swaminarayan Mandir, the first traditional Hindu temple built outside of India in more than 800 years. The temple, which opened in 1995, and adjoining prayer hall can accommodate more than 2,500 people. On each of the two holiest days of the year, 50,000 people pass through the temple doors. Of course, no one has any reason to fear the growth of Hinduism, since no Hindu has been caught inciting or perpetrating terrorist attacks in the West.[117]

Not one of the fifty-seven Muslim countries in the world, where there are religious minorities, would dream of declaring itself a multicultural state. On the contrary, Islam is declared, recognized and practised as the 'state religion'. The approach is clear: once a Muslim foothold has been acquired in a city, Muslims claim multiculturalism as the rationale for spreading their faith – on the basis of parity with the dominant culture. Writing in *The Daily Telegraph*, Philip Johnston noted that Abu Izzadeen, the firebrand Muslim, had berated then-Home Secretary John Reid for 'daring' to visit a Muslim area, suggesting that part of London was off-limits for a British minister. Alan Craig, a Newham councillor representing the Christian People's Alliance, is concerned about the community and security impact of the mosque. 'Although permission has not yet been given, Muslims are moving into the area in preparation. The Savile Town area of Dewsbury where Tablighi Jama'at is currently based is now more than 90 per cent Muslim. This part of London has always been a very diverse community and that is how it should be kept. We can't have one group taking over.' Craig believes the local community would be denied a say, since the council has not consulted local people. In an irony not lost on Craig, the Kingsway International Christian Centre, the biggest evangelical church in Europe with 12,000 worshippers on a Sunday, is coming down to make way for the Olympic stadium.[118]

Britain, like the rest of Europe, has been desperately trying to restore self-confidence in its culture, and to salvage what remains of it by installing entry tests for new immigrants. But a third of immigrants are failing the new citizenship test amid complaints that some of the questions are too obscure. New entrants must get 75 per cent of the twenty-four multiple-choice questions correct within forty-five minutes to qualify for citizenship. The test was introduced in November 2005 as one of the last hurdles in gaining citizenship, and has created a new industry for consultants promising to coach immigrants through the process. There have been claims of corruption, with one official allegedly sitting the test on an immigrant's behalf. Of the 82,375 candidates who took the exam in the first nine months, 56,615 walked out with a pass while 25,760 failed, giving an overall pass rate of 68.7 per cent. Before migrants take the test they must study *Life in the United Kingdom: A Journey to Citizenship*. The book was subjected to ridicule when historians complained that it was riddled with errors. The test can be repeated as often as necessary.[119] In 2006 Barnet College in north London was temporarily closed after allegations that an Albanian gang had arranged for applicants to pass the test with the help of a staff member with the gang charging up to £700 per pass. In 2007, four men were arrested in a community training centre over claims of a nationwide scam to help immigrants achieve citizenship. It is believed that test passes may have been offered for sale from the City Wide Learning Centre in Broomhall Street, Sheffield. Monitoring revealed that applications to take the test in Sheffield were being received from throughout the country, as far away as London.[120]

When jihadists in London openly and freely distribute leaflets in the streets calling for shari'a law in Britain, the Muslim radical threat becomes more and more concrete. In the context of the demonstrations against Forest Gate, the sister of the two arrested brothers called upon the demonstrators to maintain calm, lest the police use any unrest as a pretext to inflict another trauma on the community and portray it in a negative light. 'More brothers and sisters as a result, could be arrested, this will have an adverse affect in proving both of my brothers' innocence', she said. Many of those who attended wore long *thobes* (gowns), the traditional attire in the Gulf, and masked their faces, as did a handful of women protestors wearing burqas. Anjem Choudary, former UK head of al-Muhajirun, told demonstrators: 'We have a right to defend ourselves. We will defend ourselves as a community, our lives, our honour. Cowardice and Islam cannot be in the heart of a Muslim at the same time.' Muslim community leaders invariably invoke their 'rights', but seldom do they urge their followers to fulfil their duties as citizens, to inform police of impending terrorism, to keep public order and to do something positive for their country of asylum. Protestors waved placards against police tactics and shouted: 'Hands off Muslims. Tony Blair is a terrorist and Tony Blair, watch your back.' For direct threats like that people would be prosecuted in most countries. In Britain, however, the 'human right' to free speech takes precedence, even if laced with direct threats to the life of an incumbent Prime Minister. In a chilling aside, a statement put out by al-Ghuraba', followers of Ahl al-Sunnah Wal Jama'a, said that the killing of Muslims was the price Britons have to pay because of the 'real terrorists in our midst'. In an apparent *non sequitur*, the statement added: 'After all, imagine what would happen if a nuclear device were to be unleashed onto the streets of Britain or if our water supply were suddenly poisoned killing millions of us.' A boy aged 10, from Tunisia, handed out leaflets headlined: 'Police Target Muslims: Will You Be Next?'[121]

The impertinence continues apace. Muslims produce murderers from their midst; the government responds by extending to them courtesies no other minority receives; they then have the effrontery to claim that the body set up by the government to accommodate them lacks independence from the government. Indeed, the Mosques and Imams National Advisory Body, set up by the Home Office after 7/7 as a platform for Muslims, has been criticized by them for lacking independence from the government. The concerns have been raised by Khurshid Ahmed, of the British Muslim Forum, who founded the Leicester Islamic Foundation and has been a senior figure in Jama'at-e-Islami, and Ibrahim Mogra, who heads the MCB's Mosque and Community Affairs. Britain's Muslims have come to regard their new asylum as a milking cow, which produces human rights, social benefits, education and health, job opportunities and even mosques where they can pour forth their inflammatory slogans against the state and its institutions, and free demonstrations where they can proffer threats against the society they live in and demand more rights. But none of them speaks about any obligation to the country or any gratitude to the home they freely chose. So many groups, front 'charities', institutions and organizations have been established – each controlling a number of sub-groups with Arabic and Urdu names – that it is very difficult for the layman to establish their true identities and causes, to identify the sources of support they receive from abroad, their sources of funding at home, who serves whom and the overlap between them all. There is another source of confusion which serves these groups well. The fact that their names are difficult for people to remember, and moreover tend to be spelt differently in various publications, allows them to evade identification.

No wonder then that it is disconcerting when Muslims decide to launch yet another organization, this time for children. Voices have been raised over plans to set up Islamic Scout groups in Scotland. The Islamic Society of Britain (ISB) claims separate Scout troops are necessary as some parents are 'uncomfortable' with the idea of sending their children to groups seen as predominantly Christian. But critics of the plan say the move could drive a wedge between young Muslims and others. Individual Muslims have been welcomed by the Scout Association for more than thirty years, but in recent years Islamic groups have been launched in England. Glasgow, Edinburgh, Dundee and Aberdeen are all expected to follow. Sajid Quayum, of the ISB, said: 'Scouting values are good strong values and that is why we want to go down that route rather than just starting Muslim youth clubs. Having our own groups will give us the flexibility to include Muslim values and teachings as well as general scouting values.' He did not elaborate on what Islamic values have to do with scouting values, which raises the suspicion that under the innocent scouting label, they plan in fact to develop Muslim youth groups, devout to their community, organized and disciplined, which can be diverted to other purposes. Quayum's own experiences as a Sea Scout in Glasgow convinced him that it is best for Muslims to go it alone. 'It can be a little bit daunting joining a group where you are the only non-white face. I still enjoyed my time in the Scouts but I would have been far more comfortable if the opportunity to join a group which was more open to Muslim ideals had been available.' The discomfort he displays at being amongst whites is never questioned. Quayum, who helped launch the Islamic community station Radio Ramadan in Glasgow in 2003, stresses Muslim Scout groups would be open to youngsters of all background, presumably to introduce them to Islam, and denies the move will foster division.[122]

Patrick Sookhdeo canvassed the opinions of Muslim clerics in Britain on the row over the Danish cartoons, and they believed that the British Government capitulated to them, because the cartoons were not published in the UK. 'It's confirmation of what they believe to be a familiar pattern: if spokesmen for British Muslims threaten what they call "adverse consequences" – violence to the rest of us – then the British Government will cave in. I think it is a very dangerous precedent.' Sookhdeo believes that 'in a decade, you will see parts of English cities which are controlled by Muslim clerics and which follow, not the common law, but aspects of Muslim shari'a law. It is already starting to happen – and unless the government changes the way it treats the so-called leaders of the Islamic community, it will continue.' Sookhdeo was brought up as a Muslim in Guyana, the only English colony in South America, and attended a madrassa there, and converted to Christianity at university. He believes British Muslims will isolate themselves to a much greater extent over the next decade. The government, he says, is 'fundamentally deluded about the nature of Islam'. In an interview in February 2006, Sookhdeo noted Blair unintentionally revealed his ignorance when he said, in an effort to conciliate Muslims, that he had 'read through the Qur'an twice'. He thought he was saying something which showed how seriously he took Islam:

> every Muslim knows that you cannot read the Qur'an through from cover to cover and understand it. The chapters are not written to be read in that way. Indeed, after the first chapter, the chapters of the Qur'an are ordered according to their length, not according to their content or chronology: the longest chapters are first, the shorter ones are at the end. You need to know which passage was revealed at what period and in what time in order to be able to understand it – you cannot simply read it from beginning to end and expect to learn

anything at all. That is one reason why it takes so long to be able to read and understand the Qur'an: the meaning of any part of it depends on a knowledge of its context – a context that is not in the Qur'an itself.

This ignorance of Islam led to the unsuccessful attempts to conciliate it. Sookhdeo wondered why a book called *The Noble Qur'an: a New Rendering of its Meaning in English*, is openly available in Muslim bookshops, although it calls for the killing of Jews and Christians, and it sets out a strategy for killing the 'infidels' and for warfare against them. He thinks the explanation is that the government does not take Islam seriously, and that ministers see Islam through the prism of their own secular outlook. 'They simply do not realize how seriously Muslims take their religion. Islamic clerics regard themselves as locked in mortal combat with secularism.' He continued:

> Islamic clerics do not believe in a society in which Islam is one religion among others in a society ruled by basically non-religious laws. They believe it must be the dominant religion – and it is their aim to achieve this. That is why they do not believe in integration. In 1980, the Islamic Council of Europe laid out their strategy for the future – and the fundamental rule was never dilute your presence. That is to say, do not integrate. Rather, concentrate Muslim presence in a particular area until you are a majority in that area, so that the institutions of the local community come to reflect Islamic structures. The education system will be Islamic, the shops will serve only halal food, there will be no advertisements showing naked or semi-naked women, and so on.
>
> The next step will be pushing the government to recognize shari'a law for Muslim communities – which will be backed up by the claim that it is 'racist' or 'Islamophobic' or 'violating the rights of Muslims' to deny them shari'a law.
>
> There's already a Shari'a Law Council for the UK. The government has already started making concessions: it has changed the law so that there are shari'a-compliant mortgages and shari'a pensions. Some Muslims are now pressing to be allowed four wives: they say it is part of their religion. They claim that not being allowed four wives is a denial of their religious liberty.

There are Muslim men in Britain who marry and divorce three women, then marry a fourth time – and stay married, in shari'a law, to all four.

Sookhdeo outlined a plan of action for the government: it should try to engage with the Muslim majority and not with the unelected, self-appointed 'community leaders'; it should reject faith-based schools, because they are a block to integration; English must remain the language of education; finally, the government must insist that all newcomers accept the secular basis of British law and society. That is a non-negotiable condition of being here. Otherwise, Islamic communities within Britain will form a state within a state and religion will occupy an ever-larger place in political life.[123]

It is often best left to observers from afar to place events in their proper perspective. An Indian columnist, Kanchan Gupta, writing in an Indian paper, commented on a conference in January 2007 called 'World Civilization–Clash of Civilizations', in which the host, London's Mayor Ken Livingstone, debated with the Middle East scholar Daniel Pipes. According to Gupta's down-to-earth world view, some weird notions of multiculturalism and its merits were voiced, including bizarre assertions by a certain Salma Yaqoub that Islamist terror attacks like those witnessed on 7/7 are actually 'reprisal events' and hence need to be understood rather than condemned. Livingstone, who had previously outraged fellow-Britons by hosting Yusuf al-Qaradawi, was in his element defending the indefensible. He quoted John Stuart Mill, advising the gathering, 'live as you wish as long as you do not hurt anyone'. As Gupta noted, 'If only Britain's rapidly growing community of radical Islamists, most of them immigrants from Pakistan and Bangladesh who are seeking to recreate in their adopted country the bigotry that has brought their home countries to rack and ruin, would have lived by that dictum, the world would have been a safer place.' British Muslim terrorists are known to have been involved in acts of terrorism in as many as fifteen countries, and in Gupta's opinion, neither at home nor abroad do they wish to allow others to live in peace, let alone live in open societies free of the burdens imposed by Islamic orthodoxy and its preachers. Gupta concluded:

> Abu Hamza al-Masri may not be preaching at Finsbury Park mosque anymore, but that does not mean Friday prayers in

London and across Britain have become a tame affair. On the contrary, having tasted victory by forcing Mr Blair and his government on the backfoot and getting away with taunting mainstream British society with which they refuse to integrate, Britain's Muslims are now preparing for the big push. To pretend otherwise would be plain stupid.[124]

A humourous note was injected into British politics in July 2007, when a 'sacred' Hindu bull called Shambo was executed by lethal injection despite protests by Hindus in Britain and abroad. The Welsh Assembly wanted the animal to be put down because it was infected with tuberculosis. Writing in the *Spectator*, Rod Liddle asked:

> I wonder too if the members of the assembly would have dared to make their decision if it were Muslims rather than Hindus who chose to revere cattle? And what would have happened if they did? By now there would be priests set alight from Jakarta to Rabat, effigies burnt, fatwas issued. Cardiff airport would be missing an international departure gate. The assembly would probably have come up with a compromise: okay, the bull lives but it has to wear a burqa when it goes out. I suppose Britain's Hindus can console themselves with the thought that having their sensibilities trampled on suggests they are a community with whom the rest of us feel at ease and can thus victimize with impunity.[125]

As in other parts of Europe, the rise in anti-Semitism in Britain has been inexorably connected with the demographic and militant expression of Islam. Soon after *The Times* revealed that conflict in the Middle East had led to a surge in anti-Semitism, an All-Party Parliamentary Inquiry into Anti-Semitism reported a sinister 'symbiotic' relationship had developed between far-right groups and Islamist extremists who are united in their hatred of all things Jewish. The inquiry, chaired by former Minister for Europe Denis MacShane, uncovered calls for the killing of Jews in the name of a radical ideology or extremist religion and the demonization of Jews through conspiracy myths and Holocaust denial. It found that Arabic translations of *Mein Kampf* and *The Protocols of the Elders of Zion* were stocked in Arabic bookshops in London. Of particular concern to the inquiry was anti-Semitism on campuses, with literature being distributed that called for the killing of Jews and the destruction of Israel. Criticism of Israel is being used as a pretext for fomenting hatred against Jews in Britain. There was a tendency to compare Israeli policies to those of the Nazis, and to hold Jews collectively responsible for the actions of Israel. The committee was sent material broadcast on Arab and Iranian television in which children are incited to engage in jihad against Jews. It referred to 'anti-Semitic discourse', defined as a 'widespread change in mood and tone when Jews are discussed, whether in print or broadcast, at universities, or in public or social settings'. It recommended that an interdepartmental task force be set up to combat anti-Semitism, involving local government. It called for more research into the correlation between attacks on Jews in Britain and events in the Middle East, adding that all police forces should be required to record anti-Semitic incidents. The conclusions drawn by the fourteen-member panel of MPs support the findings of a study published by two Yale University professors, which reported that anti-Israel sentiments were a predictor of anti-Semitism.[126]

Figures compiled by the police illustrate that Jewish people are four times more likely to be attacked because of their religion than Muslims. One in 400 Jews compared to one in 1,700 Muslims are likely to be victims of 'faith hate' attacks every year. The figure is based on data collected over three months in 2006 in police areas accounting for half the Muslim and Jewish populations of England and Wales. The crimes range from assault and verbal abuse to criminal damage at places of worship. Police forces started recording the religion of 'faith hate' crime victims on the instruction of the Association of Chief Police Officers (ACPO), which wanted a clear picture of alleged community tensions around the country, following reports of Muslims being attacked after 9/11 and 7/7. The Crown Prosecution Service (CPS) said that the large rise expected after 7/7 had not materialized, and that not a single person accused of an anti-Semitic crime had been prosecuted on a charge of religiously aggravated offending. Iain Duncan Smith, the former Tory leader, who sat on the All-Party Parliamentary Inquiry into Anti-Semitism in September, said it was 'perverse' that not all police forces recorded anti-Semitic incidents. The ACPO directive was ignored by most forces, whose systems are not designed to record religion, though they routinely record ethnicity. Information on 'faith hate' crimes obtained by the *Sunday Telegraph* showed that in London and

Manchester, where Muslims outnumber Jews by four to one, anti-Semitic offences exceeded anti-Muslim offences.[127]

Denis MacShane gave a presentation at a special conference on anti-Semitism in Berlin in November 2006, where he said a 'witches brew' of Islamic fundamentalists, left-wing intellectuals and neo-Nazis is causing a new resurgence of anti-Semitism to spread across Western Europe. There is an unorthodox alliance between several distinct groups: an organized ideological Islamism across Europe, which is openly anti-Semitic and subscribes to the appalling statements by the President of Iran that Israel should be wiped off the face of the earth; the 'soft' anti-Semitism from Muslim intellectuals, who are often religious, and include the Muslim Brotherhood who claim there is Zionist or Jewish control over the media and politics (the 1930s vocabulary of the 'Jewish conspiracy' has been replaced today by the 'Jewish Lobby'); the traditional right-wing anti-Semitism; and finally, the left, encompassing both the far left and the legitimate left's hatred of Israel – a distorted association of Israel and America as the twin demons that have caused all the world's problems. MacShane claimed that the solution was for Europeans to demonstrate 'a robust defence of Israel's right to exist', and an insistence on 'the separation of faith from politics', so fundamentalists who claimed their actions were part of God's will are instantly discredited. He concluded: 'Fighting anti-Semitism is part of a common struggle against intolerance and demagoguery. It is a noble political cause to fight.[128]

The government introduced guidelines to tackle anti-Semitism in British universities. Campus authorities should record all complaints of anti-Semitism made by students, including statements or speeches. University vice-chancellors are warned not to tolerate academics whose critical views of Israel 'cross the line' from personal interest or activism to abuse of power. There is particular concern about so-called Islamic anti-Semitism, with radical Muslim clerics, or their followers, being allowed to preach anti-Jewish hatred in universities. Phil Woolas, the Communities Minister, said: 'We are very worried about Islamic anti-Semitism on campuses. In this country we tend to see it as something of the past. It is not.' Although the government did not announce legislation, Woolas said it had not been ruled out. Police forces must now keep records of anti-Semitic attacks, the Foreign Office will be required to raise the issue with Arab countries such as Egypt and Jordan, which produce some of the most extreme anti-Semitic material, and a taskforce will be set up to combat anti-Semitism. Denis MacShane said: 'During our evidence sessions we heard of Jewish students having anti-Semitic graffiti scrawled on their doors, and of extremist Muslim groups being invited to speak on campuses. There are also attempts to ban people from putting forward Israel's case in debates on the Middle East.' His report found that Jewish students felt 'isolated and unsupported', and that pro-Palestine debates were being used as a 'vehicle for anti-Jewish language'.[129]

The government announced that the CPS is to investigate why fewer than one in ten anti-Semitic incidents results in prosecution. The review follows criticism by MPs that the judicial system is failing Jews, who are more vulnerable to attacks and abuse than at any time for a generation. Police forces are also overhauling their procedures for recording such incidents after MPs complained that many were 'complacent'. Ministers are to urge the police to use the Public Order Act 1986, which outlaws the spread of racial hatred, where there is enough evidence to bring prosecutions against Islamic extremists for speeches on campuses. According to the figures from Jewish groups, there were 594 anti-Semitic incidents in Britain in 2006, up 31 per cent from 2005. More than a fifth of the incidents, which included 112 assaults and seventy attacks on properties, took place during the thirty-four-day war between Israel and Hizbollah in Lebanon in July and August 2006.[130]

British police will begin recording anti-Semitic crimes as racist attacks starting in 2008. The government also pledged additional funds to monitor anti-Semitic incidents in the country. 'Anti-Semitism has not been taken as seriously as other forms of hatred in some parts of our society', Iain Wright, the parliamentary Under-secretary of State for Communities and Local Government, said during a discussion of Britain's All-Party Inquiry into Anti-Semitism in July 2007. Wright also reiterated the government's opposition to an academic boycott of Israel, which repeatedly rears its head in Britain, calling it 'anti-Jewish in principle'.[131]

NOTES

1. Amir Taheri, 'Abu Hamza: Unanswered Questions', *Arab News*, 18 February 2006.
2. Sean O'Neill and Daniel McGrory, 'Blunders that left Abu Hamza free', *The Times*, 30 May 2006.
3. Abul Taher, 'Hamza may go Free as Witness Backs Down', *Sunday Times*, 19 August 2007.
4. Ben Leapman, 'Abu Hamza Bullied in Prison, says wife', *Sunday Telegraph*, 29 July 2007.
5. 'Blair calls on Moderate Muslims to do more to Combat Terror', *The Daily Telegraph*, 4 July 2006.

6. Toby Helm, 'Amnesty Call for 500,000 Immigrants', *The Daily Telegraph*, 31 March 2006.
7. Simon de Bruxelles, 'Refugee's Counter to Political Correctness', *The Times*, 31 March 2006.
8. George Jones, 'Blair admits he has no Policy on Population', *The Daily Telegraph*, 5 July 2006.
9. Philip Johnston, 'Asylum Cheats get £3,000 to go Home', *The Daily Telegraph*, 6 June 2006.
10. Richard Ford, 'Visa Rules will Raise Marriage Age to 21', *The Times*, 29 March 2007.
11. Francis Elliott, 'Tory move to Protect Young Foreign Brides', *The Times*, 25 May 2007.
12. David Leppard, 'More than 230 Terror Suspects free to stay in Britain', *Sunday Times*, 21 May 2006.
13. Philip Johnston, '1 Million new British Citizens under Blair', *The Daily Telegraph*, 24 May 2006.
14. David Leppard, '400 Terror Suspects on loose in UK', *Sunday Times*, 9 April 2006.
15. Mustafa Kurtulu, interviewed by *Times Online*, 30 March, 2006.
16. Ibid.
17. Alan Cowell, 'A Suicide Bomb, a Dead Daughter and a Test of Faith', *The New York Times*, 6 May 2006.
18. Ibid
19. Ruth Gledhill, 'Faiths Unite against Terrorism', *The Times*, 7 July 2006.
20. Yaakov Lappin, 'UK Islamists: Make Jihad on Israel', *Ynetnews.com*, 2 July 2006.
21. Melanie Phillips, *Londonistan: How Britain is Creating a Terror State Within* (London: Gibson Square, 2006).
22. Rod Liddle, 'When Toleration goes too far', *Spectator*, 8 July 2006.
23. Daniel Johnson, 'Terror & Denial: *Londonistan* by Melanie Phillips', *Commentary Book Review*, July/August 2006.
24. Ibid.
25. Charles Moore, 'How Cromwell gave us Joan Collins and other Luminaries', *The Daily Telegraph*, 17 June 2006.
26. Ibid.
27. Ibid.
28. Chris Brooke, 'Couple's Alton Towers Wedding in the Balance after Clash with Muslim Fun Day', *Daily Mail*, 11 July 2006.
29. Rod Liddle, 'Britain's Muslims at Alton Tower', *Spectator*, 8 July 2006.
30. Ibid.
31. Daniel Foggo and Abul Taher, 'Imam backs Terror Attack against Blair: Brighton Mosque Radicalized', *Sunday Times*, 18 June 2006.
32. Ibid.
33. Bernard Lagan, 'Briton backs Imam in "Uncovered Meat" Row', *The Times*, 28 October 2006.
34. 'Law and Orders', *The Daily Telegraph*, 29 June 2006.
35. George Conger, 'BBC Rejects Call to Change Terminology', *The Jerusalem Post*, 29 June 2006.
36. 'Muslims "should stop helping police"', *The Daily Telegraph*, 7 June 2006.
37. Daniel McGrory, Michael Evans and Stewart Tendler, 'Muslims Question Terror Raid Tactics', *The Times*, 6 June 2006.
38. Alice Thomson, interview with Abdul Bari, 'British should try Arranged Marriages', *The Daily Telegraph*, 10 June 2006.
39. 'Voice of the Masses', *The Economist*, 8 March 2007.
40. Thomson, Interview with Abdul Bari, 'British should try arranged marriages'.
41. Amir Taheri, 'Islam in Britain: A Year after the Terrorist Raid', *al-Sharq al-Awsat*, 7 July 2006.
42. Amir Taheri, 'Are British Muslims Really Angry?' *al-Sharq al-Awsat*, 8 September 2006.
43. Ibid.
44. Frederick Forsyth, 'Watch your Language', Letters, *Sunday Telegraph*, 17 September 2006.
45. Olga Craig and Alasdair Palmer, 'What Makes a Martyr?' *Sunday Telegraph*, 13 August 2006.
46. 'Twisted mind of the Agony Sheikh', *Daily Mail*, 21 August 2006.
47. Ben Quinn, 'Bishop Condemned over Imam Warning', *The Daily Telegraph*, 6 November 2006.
48. 'Bishop Criticises "Victim Mentality" of Muslims', *Sunday Telegraph*, 5 November 2006.
49. Christopher Morgan, 'Bishop Attacks "Victim" Muslims', *Sunday Times*, 5 November 2006.

50. Jenny Percival, 'Blair Outlines Curbs on Grants to Religious Groups', *Times Online*, 8 December 2006.
51. Shahid Malik, 'If you want Shari'a Law, you should go and live in Saudi', *Sunday Times*, 20 August 2006; and James Chapman, 'Muslims call for Special Bank Holidays', *Daily Mail*, 14 August 2006.
52. Sean O'Neill and Philip Webster, 'Kelly Penalises Mosques' Failure to Tackle Terror', *The Times*, 12 October 2006.
53. Michael Evans, 'More Britons are Turning to Terror, says MI5 Director', *The Times*, 10 November 2006.
54. Iain Dale's Diary, 'Sir Ian Blair Says New Terror Attack Could Lead to Internment', *iaindale.blogspot.com*, 8 October 2006.
55. 'Terrorist Ringleader Muktar Said Ibrahim: A Robber and a Sex Offender', *Daily Mail*, 9 July 2007.
56. Richard Holt, 'July 21 Bombers Sentenced to Life', *The Daily Telegraph*, 11 July 2007.
57. Philip Johnston, 'Q&A: Britain's Borders', *The Daily Telegraph*, 11 July 2007.
58. Graeme Wilson, 'Young, British Muslims "getting more radical"', *The Daily Telegraph*, 30 January 2007.
59. Sam Coates, 'Extreme Youth: the Muslims who would swap British law for Sharia', *The Times*, 29 January 2007.
60. Daniel McGrory, Stewart Tendler and Dominic Kennedy, 'Muslim Soldiers Faced Kidnap and Beheading', *The Times*, 1 February 2007.
61. Daniel McGrory, Russell Jenkins and Steve Bird, 'Terror Hit-list named 25 Muslim Soldiers', *The Times*, 2 February 2007.
62. David Leppard, 'Al-Qa'ida orders British Beheadings', *Sunday Times*, 4 February 2007.
63. David Leppard and Abul Taher, 'Blair to Launch Spin Battalion against al-Qa'ida Propaganda', *Sunday Times*, 28 January 2007.
64. Jack Malvern, 'British Council Shifts Focus to Muslim States', *The Times*, 26 February 2007.
65. Mark Bridge, 'Ruth Kelly Launches Fund to Fight Islamic Extremism', *Times Online*, 7 February 2007.
66. Tom Harper, 'Preach in English, Muslim Peer tells Imams', *Sunday Telegraph*, 23 July 2007.
67. David Smith, 'Give us a Mufti, say UK Muslims', *Sunday Times*, 10 June 2007.
68. Jonathan Petre, 'New Group for those who Renounce Islam', *The Daily Telegraph*, 21 June 2007.
69. Philip Johnston, 'What happened to Blair's Anti-terror Strategy?' *The Daily Telegraph*, 3 July 2007.
70. 'Cult of Contempt – The Left must Condemn a Fanaticism that is Misogynist and Homophobic', *The Times*, Leader, 3 July 2007.
71. Tim Hames, 'We must Act now to Close this Terror Trail', *The Times*, 2 July 2007.
72. Andrew Pierce, 'The Textbook Terrorists', *The Daily Telegraph*, 7 July 2007.
73. Alasdair Palmer, Roya Nikkhah and Jonathan Wynne-Jones, 'Not in their Name?', *The Daily Telegraph,* 8 July 2007.
74. Ibid.
75. Macer Hall, 'Brown: Don't Say Terrorists are Muslims', *Daily Express*, 3 July 2007.
76. Philip Johnston, 'Offering Sanctuary Threatens our Safety', *The Daily Telegraph*, 10 July 2007.
77. Philippe Naughton, 'Brown Announces Single "Border Force" for UK to Combat Terror', *Times Online*, 25 July 2007.
78. Philip Johnston, 'Balancing our Rights against their Wrongs', *The Daily Telegraph*, 26 July 2007.
79. Michael Burleigh, 'Lawyers sap our Will to Combat Terrorism – We lack the Toughness of our European Neighbours', *Times Online*, 27 July 2007.
80. David Leppard, 'Terror Watch on Mecca Pilgrims', *Sunday Times*, 21 January 2007.
81. 'Muslim Fanatic Works on Trains', *The Sun*, 16 February 2007.
82. John Steele, '4,000 Terror Suspects in UK', *The Daily Telegraph*, 7 May 2007.
83. Ben Leapman, '4,000 in UK Trained at Terror Camps', *Sunday Telegraph*, 15 July 2007.

84. Philip Johnston, 'Foreign Prisoners Clogging Jails cost UK £400m a year', *The Daily Telegraph*, 3 May 2007.
85. John Steele and Duncan Gardham, 'Terror Trial Man was Allowed to Stay after Jail', *The Daily Telegraph*, 5 May 2006.
86. Theodore Dalrymple, 'Our Prisons are Fertile Ground for Cultivating Suicide Bombers', *The Times*, 30 July 2005.
87. Martin Samuel, 'Jailbirds Ripe for Recruiting', *The Times*, 3 October 2006.
88. Robert Winnett, 'Fears that Bin Laden aide is Recruiting in Jail', *Sunday Times*, 5 August 2007.
89. David Conway, 'It is Not Only the Screws Who Are Being Turned in Our Prisons These Days', *Civitas*, 26 February 2007.
90. Richard Ford, 'Muslim prisoners at flashpoint over new imam's interpretation of Koran', *The Times*, 21 November 2006.
91. Steve Bird, 'Sister is Stabbed to Death for Loving the Wrong Man', *The Times*, 17 June 2006.
92. Felix Lowe, 'Honour Killings Linked to Terror Groups', *The Daily Telegraph*, 26 June 2007.
93. Laura Donnelly, 'Doctors Ordered to Act on Forced Marriage', *Sunday Telegraph*, 30 June 2007.
94. Nigel Bunyan, 'Father Killed Family for being too Western', *The Daily Telegraph*, 21 February 2007.
95. Devika Bhat, 'Three found Guilty of Glasgow Race-hate Murder', *Times Online*, 8 November 2006.
96. Stephen Adams, 'Mohammed may Top List of Boys' Names', *The Daily Telegraph*, 7 June 2007.
97. Theodore Dalrymple, 'Time Out Londonistan – A Modest Proposal, or a Radical Plot?', *City Journal*, Summer 2007.
98. Emma Henry, 'Rising Immigration Fuels 26-year Fertility High', *The Daily Telegraph*, 7 June 2007.
99. Iain Martin, 'We must face up to the Truth on Immigration', *Sunday Telegraph*, 5 August 2007.
100. Christopher Hope, 'UK Cities to have White Minorities "in 30 Years"', *The Daily Telegraph*, 15 September 2007.
101. Ruth Gledhill, 'Britain Bars US Clergy under "Anti-terror" Law', *The Times*, 26 May 2006.
102. Bess Twiston-Davies, 'Faith News', *The Times*, 27 January 2007.
103. Olga Craig, 'Time to Fight the Good Fightback', *Sunday Telegraph*, 10 September 2006.
104. Jonathan Wynne-Jones, 'Drive for Multi-faith Britain Deepens Rifts, says Church', *Sunday Telegraph*, 8 October 2006.
105. Jonathan Wynne-Jones, 'Christians ask if Force is Needed to Protect their Religious Values', *Sunday Telegraph*, 5 November 2006.
106. Nigel Bunyan, 'Next Wave of Iraq Suicide Bombers Thwarted', *The Daily Telegraph*, 25 May 2006.
107. David Leppard, 'British Brigade of Islamists join al-Qa'ida Foreign Legion in Iraq', *Sunday Times*, 4 June 2006.
108. Sandra Laville and Hugh Muir, 'Secret Report Brands Muslim Police Corrupt', *The Guardian*, 10 June 2006.
109. Andrew Alderson, Sean Rayment and Patrick Hennessy, 'Terror Cell was Planning Nerve Gas Attack on Capital', *Sunday Telegraph*, 4 June 2006.
110. Yaakov Katz, 'UK Hamas Funder to be Deported', *The Jerusalem Post*, 30 May 2006.
111. Charles Moore, 'Blair's Major Moment: Why Human Rights are like the ERM', *The Daily Telegraph*, 20 May 2006.
112. 'Satanic Verses had more Impact than al-Qa'ida', *The Daily Telegraph*, 23 May 2006.
113. Wynne-Jones, 'Christians ask if Force is Needed to Protect their Religious Values'.
114. Stephen Schwartz, 'A Threat to the World', *Spectator*, 19 August 2006.
115. Lagan, 'Briton Backs Imam in "Uncovered Meat" Row'.
116. Irfan al-Alawi and Stephen Schwartz, 'Ken's Mega-mosque will Encourage Extremism', *Spectator*, 6 January 2007.
117. Don Melvin, 'New Mosque Reflects Changes in Britain's Religious Landscape', *Cox News Service*, 12 December 2005.

118. Philip Johnston, 'The Shadow Cast by a Mega-mosque', *The Daily Telegraph*, 25 September 2006.
119. Melissa Kite, 'Citizenship Test Stumps One in Three Migrants', *Sunday Telegraph*, 15 October 2006.
120. Paul Stokes, 'Four Arrested over "Immigration Scam"', *The Daily Telegraph*, 12 February 2007.
121. Michael Horsnell, 'Family's Fears at East London Terror Protest', *Times Online*, 9 June 2006.
122. Marc Horne, 'Islamic Scout Groups Spark Ghettoist Fears', *Sunday Times*, 21 May 2006.
123. Alasdair Palmer, 'The Day is Coming when British Muslims Form a State within a State', *Sunday Telegraph*, 19 February 2006.
124. Kanchan Gupta, 'Britain Panders to Radical Islam', *Daily Pioneer*, 30 January 2007.
125. Rod Liddle, 'If Muslims Revered Cattle, Shambo would still be Mooing', *Sunday Times*, 29 July 2007.
126. Ruth Gledhill, 'Police Accused of Inaction as Anti-Jewish Alliance Emerges', *The Times*, 7 September 2006; and George Conger, 'UK MPs find Leap in Anti-Semitism', *The Jerusalem Post*, 5 September 2006.
127. Tom Harper and Ben Leapman, 'Jews far more likely to be Victims of Faith Hatred than Muslims', *Sunday Telegraph*, 17 December 2006.
128. David Byers, 'British MP warns Europe of "new Anti-Semitism"', *The Jerusalem Post*, 22 November 2006.
129. Isabel Oakeshott and Chris Gourlay, 'Anti-Semitism Rules come in at Universities', *Sunday Times*, 25 March 2007.
130. Jonathan Petre, 'Judicial System is "Failing Jews"', *The Daily Telegraph*, 29 March 2007.
131. 'UK to begin Recording Anti-Semitism a Hate Crime', *The Jerusalem Post*, 30 July 2007.

CHAPTER THREE

France's Domestic Turmoil

The first French statesman to warn against the impending Muslim threat in Europe was former Gaullist Prime Minister, Michel Debré, who back in the 1980s announced in a Parisian daily that 'The Danger comes from the South', when Algerian school curricula called for the undoing of the Poitiers battle in 732, when Muslim invaders from Spain were arrested by Charles Martel and forced to retreat. Since he had already retired from politics, not many paid heed to what he wrote, and what he would probably never have said in public had he been in office. But as his prediction was not yet massively backed by Muslim immigration from North Africa, it was understandable that the French did not react to what seemed then a remote and intangible danger. The next great alarmist about the Muslim presence in France was Jean-Marie Le Pen, the founder and leader of the far-right Front National, whose message was otherwise rejected by the French, due to his flagrant racism which alienated him from both the right and left of French politics, despite the fact that his prediction about the forthcoming 'invasion' of France by foreigners in general, and Arabs in particular, was nearly justified. But he was heeded by the French people and his weight in local politics mounted, commensurate with the increase in the North African Arab presence and the escalation in inter-communal clashes between them in Paris and its satellite *cités*, to the point of surpassing the Socialists in the 2002 elections and running against second-term candidate Jacques Chirac.

By then it was too late, as the waves of millions of new immigrants, who arrived mainly as foreign workers, settled down, gained French citizenship, produced second and third generations of embittered youth, and caused a near-crisis situation in the only country in Europe where Muslims constitute 10 per cent, and growing, of the general population of sixty million. During Chirac's two terms it was Nicholas Sarkozy, twice his Interior Minister, who attempted courageously to face up to Muslim rage and to tame the crowds of violence-prone demonstrators who repeatedly disrupted the local order in Paris and other cities. Following the example of the institutionalization of the French Jewish community during the Napoleonic era (which did not prevent either the Dreyfus Affair at the turn of the twentieth century, nor the delivery of French Jews to the Gestapo during the Second World War), Sarkozy made a valiant attempt to bring French Muslims under one umbrella, similar to the CRIF and the Consistoire of French Jewry. He thought that by creating a seminary to train French imams, he could exclude Muslim clerics from Saudi Arabia, Egypt, Pakistan or North Africa, who only added fuel to the flame by inciting their followers to embrace radical Islam of the Muslim Brotherhood type. He also hoped that creating an officially recognized Muslim leadership would suffice to push it towards moderation and recognition of its minority status, which would in turn oblige it to defer to the rules of the Republic. But his measures, which were rightly hailed as courageous and far-reaching, produced catastrophic results. For, far from reining in the fanatics, they won the majority of seats during the elections, and confined the government-supported Dalil Boubakeur, Rector of the Great Mosque in Paris, to the margins, kindling tempers in the process.

Sarkozy faced up to the fanatics and brought them under control, but the fiery orators, like Tariq Ramadan, a Geneva-based maternal grandson of Hasan al-Banna (the founder of the Muslim Brotherhood in Egypt), continued to fan the flames, under the civilized guise of 'dialogue' and 'debate'. The Muslim masses have been on a constant threshold of eruption since, which was given full vent at the end of 2005, when for weeks hundreds of cars were burned in the suburbs and young Muslims went on the rampage in city centres. The dismayed government of Dominique de Villepin, who had himself experienced a short stint as Interior Minister between Sarkozy's two terms, before he left the post to his successor and predecessor, had promised economic measures and a 'firm' social policy to close the gaps between the native French and the new immigrants. In the meantime, the disaffection of young Muslims was mounting in the streets of France. They were showing their mettle not only by demonstrating against their government and sinking ever more deeply in their Arab folk culture in search of their lost identity, but also by forcing their agenda in foreign affairs. They imported the Middle Eastern conflict into France, mounted massive events to protest against Israel and in support of the Palestinians, and let their anger spill over into anti-Semitic broadsides against French Jewry – a model of a successful and law-abiding minority, which regards itself as consummately French and is well-acculturated into the system, including among the intellectual, professional, business and artistic elites.

After the intifada began in 2000, a sustained campaign by French Muslims, in apparent coordination with other Muslims throughout the world, was launched simultaneously against Israel and the Jews, where not only Israeli interests and symbols were desecrated, by also the institutions of their Jewish fellow-French citizens. Synagogues and cemeteries, Jewish day schools and Jewish schoolchildren, Jewish worshippers and their private homes, were attacked, burned, threatened, intimidated and ridiculed in public, causing death in some cases. In no instance did any public or clerical figure in the Arab and Muslim worlds so much as raise their voice against this violent and disrespectful conduct, as they would do with vengeance when an innocent blasphemy against their tenets, which hurt no one and threatened no one, unfolded in Denmark five years later. In 2001, a small collective booklet was put together, edited and published in France, under the title of *Les Territoires Perdus de la République* (The Lost Grounds of the Republic),[1] by a group of high school teachers throughout France who could no longer bear the rule of terror introduced into the public school system by Muslim youth. Chapter after chapter, writer after writer, the teachers who were audacious enough to publish their accounts told of their experiences in schools, where every time the word 'Jew' was mentioned the Arabs would hurl anti-Semitic swearing at them and express their regrets that Hitler did not finish them off; and whenever the word 'Holocaust' was uttered, a noisy choir of deniers would shout 'Lie! There was no Holocaust!' The frightened teachers left the classes, afraid for their own safety, and turned to their school principals, who were as intimidated as they were and did not react.

This inaction was replicated all the way up the echelons of 'education' in France, even including the Minister of Education himself, who proved just as inept and helpless. In despair, the teachers decided to publicize their book of protest against the Republic, whose values they tried to teach in schools but were violently prevented from doing so.

Admittedly, the grounds were prepared in Europe for such a manifestation of Muslim protest, which in France took on a particularly vicious and violent anti-Semitic turn. For years, Europe had cultivated among its citizenry the notion of Palestinism, which replaced the other disappointing ideologies of the post-war West and was raised to the level of unassailable truth, as Bat Ye'or brilliantly demonstrated in her epoch-making *Eurabia*, published in 2005. The idea of Palestinism, which was upheld by French (and other European) leftist intellectuals, soon found currency in the restive Muslim youth of Europe, but in France it found the most vitriolic and hostile channels of expression. The idea was that Israel of the pre-1967 War was a democratic and pioneering state, besieged by the Arab world, which won the sympathy of the West. But after 1967, the large formula of the Arab–Israeli conflict in which Israel was by definition the underdog, was superseded by the small formula of the Israeli–Palestinian conflict, as if all the other threats against Israel had vanished. In this new fabricated context which had no logical basis, Israel became the villain occupier while the 'saintly' Palestinians were suffering under the yoke of the cruel Israelis, who were also Jewish. Thus the link between anti-Israeli attitudes and what was falsely called 'Zionism' was established, and since the Jews of Europe were automatically linked with Zionism and the sole Jewish state, the fury was turned against them. That they had no more influence over Israeli policies than their fellow-Europeans was not permitted to get in the way of the new hatred. For many Europeans, it was expedient to divert the anger of their frustrated Muslim populations to anti-Israeli and anti-Jewish channels, in consequence raising Palestinism to the degree of a religious tenet, as reflected in the EU's blind support for Palestinians despite their proven corruption, and the diversion of those funds to terrorist acts against Israel and to inculcating in their children a hatred of Israel and Jews.

These trends were particularly salient in France, where in the 2004 regional election campaign, the Europalestine list of candidates, headed by the notorious anti-Semitic actor Dieudonne (ironically meaning God-given), made a relatively strong showing in some constituencies, gaining more than 50,000 votes. Under huge advertisements in the streets of La Courneuve and other heavily Muslim populated areas of Paris, which declared a link between 'Peace in Europe and Justice in the Middle East', more elaborate statements of faith, hatred, racism and bigotry could not be ignored: 'The martyrdom of the Palestinian people has lasted too long'; 'The Palestinian issue has been shamefully marginalized in the corridors of power, in spite of its strong presence in the minds of thousands of citizens'; 'Jerusalem to the Arabs!'; 'Death to the Jews'; '*Allah Akbar*!'; 'Bush and Sharon got Saddam, but I pray that Bin Laden should escape them.'[2] But when Muslim terrorism transcended the boundaries of Israel (where it was consistently justified and forgiven by the European media, who blamed the victims), and struck western territory, first in America and then in Europe, Israel's predicament started to find more understanding in European public opinion. Some Europalestinians started to complain that 'the media only showed Palestinian [terrorist] retaliation, not Israeli violence', because they suspected that 'journalists were rather pro-Israel. If you watch TV, you will find that all of them are Jewish.' They also accused the Jews of 'splashing mud on us and we do not understand what scares them', insisting that 'Jews have been deeply steeped in victimhood.'[3] The vote for Dieudonne and his group was dubbed 'Muslim' by the French press, which also recognized that the 'discovery' of such voting power attracted many North African Arabs who found in the 'Israeli–Palestinian' conflict an echo of the injustice their parents suffered during the Algerian war. Thus, internal French politics and the anti-Jewish and anti-Israel attitudes of the Muslim youth in France found a way to combine forces.[4] During the five years that preceded the outbreak of the intifada in 2000, sixteen anti-Semitic incidents were recorded in France. In the subsequent five years, there were 672. The French Interior Ministry has found that a Jew's chances of becoming the victim of an attack are forty-four times greater than those of a Muslim or a black.[5]

A case in point was what became a *cause célèbre* in France, of a young girl who served as bait for the kidnappers, torturers and killers of Ilan Halimi, a young telephone salesman, whose body was later found in a wasteland of Paris. She realized what she had done, only when she heard the Muslim thugs, those 'youth of the suburbs', dragging their shrieking prey to his death. She was compensated when the captors paid for a hotel room where she and her boyfriend spent the night. Testimony of this grim event made the French internalize the threat of the 'barbarians at the gate' of their beloved capital city, except that in the modern era, the barbarians were within the city walls and trampling upon the brittle remnants of European civilization. Those same gangs of hooded thugs also attacked and robbed students who attended anti-government demonstrations, thus confirming French fears that the hordes of the suburbs were intent on invading their affluent heartland. Indeed, the gang that the girl worked for was known as *les barbares*, which included blacks, Arabs and whites from Portugal and France. The shocking cruelty they inflicted on Halimi seemed to have little to do with their efforts to extract money from his family, and evoked the sadistic universe of *A Clockwork Orange*, the famous novel by Anthony Burgess, with a massive dose of anti-Semitism appended to it. After his abduction, he was tortured with acid and cigarette burns for more than three weeks. More than thirty neighbours in that dreadful residential block were aware of what was happening, but divulged nothing of the crime, which was only part of an overall wave of attacks against Jews in France. Other women were arrested for their botched attempts to entrap Jews. One admitted that the head of the gang, Yussuf the Barbarian, said expressly that he 'wanted a Jew', because 'Jews are rich, and since they stick together they are willing to pay.' That Jews, or any other group, would pay because they hold life to be precious did not occur to Yussuf. One of the witnesses attracted two victims, one of whom was rejected because he was not Jewish. A member of the family of a girl-victim who was ruthlessly torched, said that 'I want barbarism rejected. We are not in a war. I refuse to live in a country that cannot defend its citizens.' These criminal attacks especially against Jewish victims, by gangs of rapists and robbers, for the most part Muslim, strikes a particularly shameful note among the French who are familiar with France's history of anti-Semitism and of the collaboration with Germans in sending Jews to the death-camps. Some specialists acknowledge the rise in anti-Semitism and attribute it equally to the intifada of 2000 and the Dieudonne episode.[6]

But the murder of Halimi was not the first inflicted on French Jewry since the start of the intifada. On 19 November 2003, Sebastian Sellam, 23, a disc jockey, left his apartment in a modest building of Paris' 10th arrondissement, heading to work as usual. In the underground parking lot, a Muslim neighbour slit Sellam's throat twice, and completely mutilated his face with a fork. Even his eyes were gouged out. Sellam's mother said the killer then mounted the stairs, his hands still bloody, and announced his crime. 'I have killed my Jew. I will go to heaven', he said. Such thinking may have been influenced by a *hadith* (Mishkat al-Messabih): 'When judgement day arrives, Allah will give every Muslim a Jew or Christian to kill so that the Muslim will not enter into hell fire.' Another gruesome murder was committed by a Muslim that evening when Mohamed Ghrib, 37, stabbed Chantal Piekolek, 53, twenty-seven times in the neck and chest while she worked in her Avenue de Clichy shoe store.[7] Both incidents were barely reported at the time, and certainly their anti-Semitic motivation was downplayed.

In some Paris suburbs, where Muslim immigrants abound, the word 'Jew' appears in graffiti on walls and on the tongues of Muslim youth in playgrounds and in the streets, as a degrading epithet, with blacks and Arabs coalescing against Jews and intimidating them. Following the Halimi murder in February 2006, anti-Semitic pronouncements have become yet more widespread among Muslim youths, particularly in the state school system. Even school inspectors, like Jean Pierre Obin, who had written a report in 2004 in which he asserted that anti-Semitism is 'ubiquitous', have no compunction in criticizing their own Minister of Education, who is accused of 'having done nothing to redress this pitiful situation', resulting in the sad fact that Jewish children can no longer go to just any school. One teacher was stunned on the morrow of September 11 to see in a stairwell of his school a spray-painted airplane crashing into the Twin Towers, with the caption reading: 'Death to the US and the Jews'. Even years thereafter, Muslims in his classes still believed that the devastation was caused by Jews. He said that when he mentioned that Hitler had killed millions of Jews, one of his Muslim students blurted out that 'he would have made a good Muslim.' A student who wrote 'Dirty Jew' in one of the class notebooks, was punished by only two hours of detention. Some believe that North African Arabs brought with them an anti-Jewish sentiment and handed their prejudices to the second and third generations, while French guilt for their colonial era in North Africa left them disinclined to discipline the Arab immigrants, unlike the firm stance they took against the local right when it showed signs of anti-Semitism. Meanwhile, imams refused the call of rabbis to go together to problematic neighbourhoods, because they feared they would be seen as 'collaborators'. The only solution, which is not a long-term solution, and therefore unsatisfactory, is for the Interior Ministry to increase security around Jewish institutions. All this has generated an exodus of Jews, some of them for the second time. After their parents had left North Africa for the safety of France, they now find themselves obliged to move on to Israel or the US. Some have chosen the inconvenience of settling their families in Israel and commuting every weekend to visit them. Those who stay avoid wearing any Jewish symbols, after being threatened with knives on the streets of France.[8]

Coverage of manifestations of anti-Semitism, parading as anti-Zionism, gradually found expression in non-Jewish French media which previously would have glossed over the phenomenon and looked the other way. The major French daily, *Le Monde*, unexpectedly came out ferociously against anti-Semitism and racism on the internet and pledged to combat it, following a meeting on the topic in Paris of the Organization for Security and Cooperation in Europe. An article in *Le Monde*, written by Renaud Muselier, the French Foreign Secretary, specified the accusations of the blood libel and the fairy tales of the *Protocols of the Elders of Zion* as the targets of its forthcoming campaign against those websites that were created, nourished, expanded and distributed by Muslims in Europe. To maintain the sacred 'balance', Muslims and blacks were also mentioned in that article as victims of this xenophobic hatred, but it escaped no one's notice that it was Jews who were for the most part targeted. The author advocated vigorous steps against the perpetrators of this incitement in spite of the limitations they might pose on freedom of speech and human rights, simply in view of the high stakes involved, as was the case in the campaigns against terrorism and paedophilia.⁹

An editorial in the French weekly *Le Point*, even before the cartoon affair broke out, sounded the alarm when it announced that 'the expansion of Islam' poses a threefold problem to the West in terms of security, culture and 'methodology'. As far as security is concerned, even if not all Muslim radicals explode their bombs in the streets, they have already laid out the ideological foundation in which terrorism may develop. The cultural or civilizational issue connects with the value system, the political matrices and the life habits the Islamists promote which are different from the West's, in view of the shari'a which does not accord with western legal norms, nor the Qur'an with democracy. On the 'methodological' level, the issue is how to distinguish between Islam and Islamism, the strictly personal domain of belief linked to the former and the organized political agitation that accompanies the latter.¹⁰ The problem is that even as they were launching a wide-ranging and world-encompassing investigation of these phenomena, the French editors of this important medium were still attempting, in vain, to find distinctions between Islam and Islamism, as if they were two different faiths. In fact they are not, the Islamists simply reviving the old vocabulary of jihad, 'infidels', the abodes of Islam and of war, in order to achieve through them everything they can. The concept of jihad, after all, is just as much an Islamic as an Islamist one. But when it came to outbursts of anger against the West, for the Danish cartoons or the van Gogh 'blasphemies' in the Netherlands, for the purported 'desecration' of the Qur'an by Americans at Guantanamo or the 'persecution' of Muslims in India and Kashmir, indistinguishable Muslim masses participated in them without stating that they were Islamists and not simply Muslims. And Muslim governments implicitly collaborate with these masses whom they dare not stop, and when they sometimes take visible steps to control them, it is only because they jeopardize their own rule. For whenever Islamists were allowed to have their say, they made considerable gains on the political scene (including the Taleban in 1996 and more recently Hamas in Gaza and the Muslim Brotherhood in Egypt).

To investigate the roots of Muslim wrath, *Le Point* sent correspondents to the far reaches of Islam. This investigation was not conducted for purely academic reasons, which are not the province of the media, but because the French readership was believed to be anxious to understand the root of the danger that threatened it, especially after the Danny Pearl murder which Bernard-Henri Levy had probed and publicized in France through his book and lectures. While in Pakistan, for example, where the Pearl affair had unfolded, they found that the anger was mainly directed against President Pervez Musharraf for his 'sell-out' to the Americans. The radical preacher Abdul Rashid Ghazi (who was killed in July 2007 when the Red Mosque in Islamabad was transformed into a battleground between government forces and clerics), declared to the French reporter:

> There is no dialogue with the West, because we do not understand each other. Westerners ought to stop speculating, like they did after the London explosions. If as a result of the explosion of a bomb in Islamabad, it was revealed that one of the terrorists stayed for some time in a hotel in Oxford, would Britain be accused of the act? ... For now, hatred to the West is not so bad as to prevent them from circulating freely in our streets, but this could happen, because in spite of what we say in our sermons, our population believes that British and American citizens support their governments. I am often asked after services why did the Americans re-elect Bush, but I have no answer for them ... The war against terrorism that was invented by the US, in fact increases terrorism.[11]

A professor in a private university in Islamabad was even more blunt. He said: 'If I lock up a cat in a room for weeks without providing it with any food, the moment I open the door it will jump on me.' He said that Muslim societies are oppressed and disoriented when they face the two pillars of western ideology, namely individualism and positivism. He emphasized that his society and other Muslims of the region hate the West because they feel they are victims of many injustices: firstly, political systems, such as democracy, which they neither know nor understand are imposed on them; secondly, on the economic level, the views of the EU, the World Bank, the International Monetary Fund and globalization, which is reminiscent of neo-colonialism, are forced upon them. He resented the fact that everything in their lives, even the size of the apples they eat, is decided by the West. Finally, in the socio-cultural domain, they resent being dominated by outside standards in the way they behave, eat and listen to music. He claimed that all these lead necessarily to the realization that he who is not familiar with these standards and ways simply does not exist, and that this generates feelings of revenge and irrational behaviour. There were also complaints that whoever in America visits his native village in Pakistan is suspected of links to al-Qai'da. Some said that while before September 11 many Pakistanis wished to go to western countries due to their civil rights and standard of living, now they feel persecuted and under suspicion there and have come to sense a deepening gap between the two cultures that they call the 'clash of civilizations'.[12] This feedback is of importance to western countries inasmuch as they finally realize, for the first time, that their measures against Muslim outrages in their midst have reached their destination and begun to bear fruit.

The Muslim insistence that the West is at war with Islam has been inadequately challenged. The West could incinerate Islamdom overnight if it so wished, choosing instead to limit itself to preventive operations or pinpoint attacks against terrorists (while absorbing attacks on its own civilians at home). It does not bear thinking what might happen if the tables were turned, and such firepower were in Muslim hands. Similarly, Israel has the firepower to obliterate her enemies, but chooses to expose her soldiers to tremendous risks in order to minimize harm to civilians amongst whom the Palestinian terrorists take cover. Perversely, Palestinian civilian casualties are welcomed by the terrorists and their leaders, in the full knowledge that half the battle is fought on western television screens. They have seen how casualties constitute the ammunition in the propaganda war against Israel in the West.

In the 11,000 madrassas of Pakistan, where 1.5 million students of all ages undergo a systematic Islamic 'education' for a few years, there are thousands of European youth of Muslim extraction or new converts. Their term of study is subsidized by their parents, although Pakistan supposedly prohibits admitting foreign students to its madrassas, which cultivate jihadists of all stripes. In

Pakistan the President pledged to reform the madrassas after 7/7, in which Muslims of Pakistani origin were involved, but their numbers continue to grow. In the madrassas young Muslims are systematically brainwashed and submit totally to the authority of their masters, who often dispatch them for terrorist action after they graduate or even before that. Reports on the madrassas, together with the new emerging reality of riots in the suburbs, were bound to shock the French public who realized that the Islamic threats from within are not an isolated phenomenon, but backed by a vast Islamic world where the revival of jihad ideology is widespread and aims to expand globally. The awakened French, who were at long last 'mugged by reality', to borrow the self-description of the neo-conservatives in America, suddenly read what they formerly considered as innocent messages of their domestic Islam, which they naively thought was only looking for a better life, in a new light. Under the stunning headline of 'France – the Land of Jihad', which was not likely at any time before in the French press, *Le Point* indeed proved its awakening when it reported that imams in France were preaching against democracy and secularism, the two pillars of the French Republic, and some of them were on a collision course with their country of shelter. Scenes that had unfolded unnoticed before their eyes for years suddenly attracted attention and required analysis:

> The 'Umar Mosque of the 11th Arrondissement in Paris, in the Belleville area, is one of the strangest in France ... Inside of it and on the sidewalk outside, some outlandish things happen. On this Friday of Ramadan, 14 October 2005, hundreds of believers are not in the prayer hall, but pray on their small prayer rugs or on pieces of carton board right there on the sidewalk, but loudspeakers transmit to them the sermon of the imam from inside the building. Rue Morand, a main street, is crowded over 150 metres of its length by the crowds who face the direction of Mecca. In the bar opposite the mosque called 'Le Fidele', where no alcohol is served, people assemble barefooted, ready for prayer, while a volunteer dressed in white directs the traffic of the pedestrians on the sidewalk. Some weeks earlier, on 3 October 2005, a 29-year-old Algerian worshipper, Brahim, was seized by sharp

convulsions and the four men who tried to revive him thought that demons had taken hold of him. One of them mounted on top of him and in his attempt to release the sick man from the grip of the demon, stepped on his neck and his stomach violently enough to break some of his bones while the others were reciting verses from the Qur'an ... In a nearby store a book is sold, entitled *The Protection of Men from Demons and Satan*, where the much revered medieval fundamentalist, Ibn Taymiyya, describes how a seizure of epilepsy ought to be treated: 'I held a stick in my hand, I beat him on the arteries of his neck until my hands grew tired.' Did the four men follow this prescription to the letter? But while the epileptic of the book was healed, Brahim died, and his corpse still carried the traces of the beating he took. The four men were arrested for 'involuntary homicide'.[13]

This medieval scene took place in the heart of twenty-first century Paris. It was depicted in great detail by the reporter, apparently in shock and disbelief, but also in embarrassment that such scenes which are part of the life of the Muslim immigrants in the capital of France had been brushed aside for so many years by the French public. Now they were brought to its attention by the media, and there was no longer any escape from them. It had to face them, and what it saw was disturbing. Around the mosque the rapacious 'falcons of radical Islam', as the French reporter dubbed them, kept circling, probably in search of action, while French police were at hand, supposedly to avert a repetition of the July 2005 arrest of a young Algerian Muslim who was preaching jihad at the gate of the mosque. When the curiosity of the reporter was aroused, he found out that even that event was not without precedent, for already in 2002 congregants of that mosque had gone for jihad training and then distinguished themselves in terrorist operations. One of them was detained by the Americans in Guantanamo, another was killed by American bombs in Afghanistan, yet another was arrested in Australia for plotting more terrorism. A terrorist who had come to France to disrupt the soccer Mundial in the 1990s had made that mosque his headquarters, and back in the 1980s two Muslims who were arrested for terrorist attacks in Paris had also been recruited in that mosque.

The imam of the mosque, Hamadi Hammami, who was identified as one of the champions of Tablighi[14] Islam in France, acted as a president of Foi et Pratique (Creed and Practice), one of the numerous French Muslim organizations, and served on the executive board of the French Council of the Muslim Faith (CFCM, Conseil Francais du Culte Musulman).15

The radical discourse, which is spread in posters, videos, CDs, books, newspapers and sermons in the mosques, by necessity creates an ambience of militancy, especially amongst the youth and the deprived, who have more reasons than one to rebel against the existing order, and perhaps replace it in the long run by an Islamic one. But now, the French, like other authorities in Europe, have learned something and are less reluctant to speak in public about the Islamic threat. Jean-Claude Marin, the Chief State Prosecutor in the region of Paris, revealed some of his thoughts and experiences in these matters:

> When we speak about French radical Islam, we are facing its transformation in the form of both the deepening of fundamentalism and the expansion of proselytization. Although we cannot quantify the phenomenon, for we do not dispose of any statistical tool to evaluate the matter, it is certainly on the march. It is fed equally by a geopolitical radicalism connected to the war in Iraq and other regions of the world, and by a strong determination to establish an Islamic world power ... Its mode of expansion is expressed by the take-over of houses of prayer by self-declared imams, around whom an observant population congregates. Unlike mosques, these places of worship of Islam are not declared to the authorities, therefore they cannot be counted. Their continued appearance does not come under any legislation or regulation, therefore they can escape supervision, including by the official Islamic establishment in France. These informal houses of prayer often become centres of an exacerbated proselytization, in which the language of violence is spoken and calls for jihad are heard. It is usually the preacher who determines whether or not his congregation grows problematic. In the regular official mosques, there are sometimes young people who go to war in Iraq. In the cities of Paris, Roubaix, Levallois, for example, they have

attempted to take over the mosques, but having failed, they create their alternative clandestine venues. One has to bear in mind the economic deprivation of these young people, who are frustrated and unemployed and fear for their future. All this pushed them to join fanatic causes, and this is usually done through the large and growing gamut of associations of sport, health, mutual help and the like, which are not part of the establishment and therefore free from any control. This is exactly the advantage of our democratic system and its weakness too ... The non-Arab French who converted to Islam are sometimes the most zealous because they have to prove the authenticity of their conversion. We can find them in the networks of fighters in Iraq, Afghanistan and Chechnya. Very often their knowledge of Islam and their political consciousness are non-existent, all they want is to become Islamikaze and to shoot. But they are dangerous because they grow within groups whose mobility and leadership is constantly in a state of being, and they keep circulating between Italy, Germany, and the Netherlands, without belonging to any one active group or coming under the financial or military direction of anybody. Their numbers are hard to gauge, just like in the economic and fiscal domain, one can know the numbers of tax-evaders who are caught, but not those who are not. The same goes for the Islamists, we only know the numbers of those who were monitored by Intelligence or went through legal procedures. There are probably many dozens of Frenchmen who are ready to combat for jihad.[16]

This not-so-subtle aversion to and fear of Muslim immigrants in France, and the threat they are perceived as posing to French and European society, is seconded by an audacious, if surprising, editorial by Denis Jeambar in the popular French weekly *L'Express,* who wrote, *inter alia,* his comments on the French version of Bernard Lewis's *Islam:*[17]

> Never before in the history of mankind were so many people in search of a scapegoat for their misfortune. Hundreds of millions of Muslims, who are manipulated by religious

fanatics and despotic rulers ... throw at the rest of the world the responsibility for their misery and despair. Here you have the Muslim nuclear programme, and the clash of civilizations that can no longer be denied. The Hamas triumph in the Palestinian elections is only a manifestation of this situation, inasmuch as Palestinian society has imprisoned itself in the movement to backwardness that demands the application of the shari'a of the past as a remedy for the malaise of today. This legal system which rejects any distinction between divine and civil law, the religious and the political, is the fault separating the Muslim world from the developed one. For, beyond the divisions between Sunni and Shi'a, all Muslim nations are contaminated by the Islamic revolution in Iran, and the risks are great that more countries would fall to the Islamists ... It is time for westerners to stop feeling guilty for Muslim bankruptcy, and desist from legitimizing the Islamists' dialectic which targets them. Instead of uniting their efforts and talent in order to revert to what they used to be in medieval times, they have chosen to plunge in the disastrous process of hatred, obscurantism and confrontation.[18]

French and other European critics of Muslim immigration into their countries cannot help comparing the generosity they accord to the incoming strangers with the tightly restricted immigration policies of Muslim, especially Arab, countries – even for other Arabs who would be straightforward to assimilate, let alone non-Arabs. One recalls the 350,000 Palestinians whom 'moderate' Kuwait expelled from its territory after the Gulf War of 1991, when they were suspected of collaboration with Iraq. There, no laws nor human rights considerations can avert massive deportation of their own kin, unlike the painful and prolonged battle for each deported individual that European countries have to endure when they decide to expel a criminal, an illegal newcomer or a terrorist. Several Arab countries refuse to admit Palestinians or Islamists in the first place, not to speak of convicted troublemakers, who can more readily flee to Britain, Holland and Sweden and enjoy refugee status there. Abu Hamza and Abu Qatada were admitted to the UK where they inevitably ended up being implicated with the law, as was Abu Laban in Denmark. It is difficult for any thinking European to understand why their countries admitted the rejects of the Muslim world, or provided sanctuary to dozens of terrorists, like Abdul Rahman in the US or Omar Bakri in London. Political correctness has necessitated the invention of a whole new vocabulary for the illegal migrants: 'undocumented' in the US, *'sans papiers'* in France and Belgium, *'bidoun'* in Arabic (literally 'without'), except that the *bidoun* are bereft of any rights, whereas the illegals of Europe are handily protected by laws and human rights. Arab Gulf states, which need foreign manpower to attend to their pampered lifestyle, are very diligent in hunting down any expatriate worker who overstays his work visa, to prevent him from establishing roots in their countries. These foreign workers can be deported for the most minor of transgressions, or none, depending on the whims of their employers. So while those Muslim countries delegitimize Israel for being a country of immigrants who have returned to their old patrimony, they take for granted that Muslims should have easy access as immigrants to the West. They forget, too, that more than half of Israel's population consists of Jewish refugees who were expelled from Arab lands, and had not migrated voluntarily as the Muslims in Europe. These double standards, which could not be raised in the public square before, are beginning to emerge and exasperate westerners.

These new trends have even taken to task some French authors who have in a perverse way shown 'understanding' to Islamists in order to justify their own and Muslim anti-Americanism. During the autumn of 2005 a major debate erupted in France after Parliament adopted a law requiring school textbooks to recognize the positive aspects of colonialism, but due to the strong objections of 'memory activists' and historians, the law was finally revoked. The French textbooks remain, therefore, ambivalent on the issue, recognizing both the negative and positive aspects of colonialist rule. Many feared that as French teachers are free to choose their books in the marketplace, which is usually anti-American, students may grow to justify Muslim terrorism as a reaction to American 'imperialism', thereby also taking sides in the internal debate regarding European Islam. For in some textbooks Islamic terrorism was dealt with as just the top tier of public protests which begin with mass rallies, continue via 'citizens' action' like that of José Bové who visited Arafat and accused the Mossad of organizing anti-Semitic eruptions in France, and end up with violence, when one of those texts claimed that the destruction of a McDonald restaurant in Millau had earned Bové 'international fame' as he had become the symbol of anti-globalization. Islamic terrorism occupies the top of that scale of protest, inasmuch as it purports to put an end to American domination of the world. In this light (or rather obscurity), one textbook explains Muslim terrorism as the rejection of western civilization, Israeli policy toward Palestinians and the presence of American troops in the Middle East. In another textbook, students are told that terrorism is the weapon of the weak, who are unable to confront major powers, and therefore attempt to destabilize them by attacking their symbols. In sum, Bové and Bin Laden are described as being engaged in the same battle, only differing by the means used, while the entire ideology of jihad, of which they ignore the import, leaves the authors unmoved.[19]

The two authors of this latter textbook attack the trend of thought which implies that France was becoming an ally of the Islamists, by emphasizing its 'multilateralism' and its constant call for dialogue – thus patently manifesting its impotence in applying independent French policies. The authors claim that these trends that supported Islamists in France did not describe the world as it is but as they fantasize it, because given that the hated US is the sole superpower that dominates the world, France is still the only one to stand up bravely to it, speaking for the 'silent majority', and promoting Islamic terrorism as a 'proud reaction of the humiliated Muslims'. But the authors show that contrary to that image of France, the latter has been engaged in fighting terrorism on its terrain as an ally of the US and under its command in Afghanistan where the Taleban and al-Qa'ida are still entrenched. Even the Chief of Staff of the French Army has been on record as fearing that Paris, just like London, may be threatened by terrorism due to its support of the US. The authors specify that the textbooks in France, which have been sobered by the waves of anti-Semitic eruptions that were generated by their violent anti-Zionist and anti-Israeli sentiment, are now treating Israel more fairly and more objectively. For example, Israel is no longer described as the product of the Shoah, and Zionism is now presented as a political means of Jewish emancipation. Nevertheless, a new obsession with 'balance' has become the order of the day, under which every time Palestinian corruption is mentioned, it is ritually mentioned as 'less painful' than 'occupation'; whenever the Holocaust is referred to, the Arab *nakbah* (disaster) goes hand in hand with it; and when Palestinian terrorism is condemned, so is Israeli 'colonization' in the territories as charged by Palestinians. The authors reveal that when their book came out in late 2005, they were told by many parents that they were shocked to discover what their children were learning. They apparently had not seen Brenner's book which had appeared several years earlier and gave a detailed account of the virulent anti-Jewish, anti-Israeli and pro-Islamic learning materials that was forced on school curricula by the Islamists.[20]

Taking time off from America-bashing, the French elite, which is concerned about Islamic inroads into its country, directed its anger at a new target, Algeria – not as a main source of the Muslim malaise, but as the new ally of the US, about which it has entertained a deep paranoia since the Second World War. According to Amir Taheri, the reason is that Algeria, having promised to sign a treaty of friendship and cooperation with France, paradoxically lost interest when its demographic gains in France should have made it more attractive to mend fences with its erstwhile colonizer. The ostensible cause of the Algerians changing course was a decision by the French parliament in 2005 to rewrite the school textbooks to include 'positive aspects of colonialism' in former French colonies. The idea so incensed the Algerians that they downgraded contacts with Paris, and closed more than forty French-language private schools on the grounds that they represented a threat to 'Algerian national identity'. At the same time they authorized a dozen private English-language schools, a tactic calculated to further damage Chirac's final year in power. Many from the Algerian ruling elite now send their offspring to Britain or the US, rather than France, for further education. 'We have lost Algeria for a second time', said a retired senior French diplomat, 'first to the Soviets in 1962, and now to the Americans.' Several factors have contributed to France's loss of influence, which first became apparent in 1993–94, when Algeria faced a murderous Islamist insurrection. Then-President François Mitterrand established contacts with the Islamist leadership. He had deluded himself into believing that the global Islamist movement was largely anti-American and anti-Jewish and that he could negotiate a *modus vivendi* with Europe. Taheri determined that at a time when the Algerian Islamists were massacring women, children and old people wherever they could, Mitterrand was publicly signalling his readiness to work with any Islamist regime that might emerge in Algiers. Mitterrand was not alone in his failure to distinguish friend from foe in the Algerian civil war. The French elite saw those resisting the Islamists as somehow 'inauthentic', suffering from an 'identity crisis' and thus deserving of having their throats slit by the terrorists. By 1995, having overcome the Islamists and exported them to France, the Algerians decided that they had to look elsewhere for friends. Top of their list were the two 'Anglo-Saxon' powers that the French blame for most of the evil in the world: the US and Britain.[21]

As French Algerians watched their beloved land of origin souring its relations with their land of asylum, they were also subjected to the citizenship tests that were conceived by Sarkozy. The idea was that as Islamists counter western democracy by their Islamic theology, it would be imperative to test the Muslim immigrants for their attitudes to democracy, the relations of their countries with France notwithstanding. The very detailed questions really tested basic attitudes to modern society, but also covered a wide range of absurdities despite the sound intentions that lay at their base. The validity of such tests are doubtful, because whatever the attitude of the candidate, he or she knows what the authorities wish to hear, and responds accordingly. For instance, the question of whether a man may be indicted for raping his wife is a notion that would not occur to many Arabs, and in the multiple choice of answers, most men would elect to state that either there is no rape in marriage or that the law should protect the married men. The multiple choice answers in questions on civil liberties, concerning homosexuals living together and family planning, would probably all be perceived as unacceptable. Was then the test calculated to repel all or most Muslim immigrants, or to evaluate their adaptability to European society where the mores are liberal, sometimes even corrupt in the eyes of Muslims? Attitudes towards democracy (tested by such alternatives as strikes, demonstrations and revolutions), and the names of the remaining French colonies, now euphemistically called *Territoires d'Outre-mer* (overseas territories), were all questions worthy of testing the newcomers. It is noteworthy that some incendiary imams were deported for being in favour of beating women or polygamy.[22]

France's immigration debate heated up in July 2006, with opposition Socialists demanding to know how many 'undocumented' immigrants the government planned to deport before the start of the new school year. Under tightened immigration rules, the government began tracking down families lacking residency papers through children registered at French schools, vowing to expel them during the summer holidays – a policy which threatened to split families. To assuage critics and the news media, the government said that it would grant residency papers to a limited number of families on a case-by-case basis. But that brought a crush of anxious immigrants to government offices around the country hoping that they might be granted residence papers before the August deadline. Immigration opponents were concerned that the government was backing itself into a huge regularization programme for tens of thousands of people. Sarkozy dismissed such fears, saying that the number of illegal immigrants granted papers would be very small. 'There isn't a country in the world that believes that you have to give permanent papers because a child attends school', he told reporters.[23] The new immigration law gave the government more control over who is admitted and increased its expulsion powers. France watched for months as the drama unfolded, with newspapers giving prominent play to cases of schoolchildren threatened with expulsion even though they had lived most of their lives in France. Some opponents of the new law even began sponsoring children of immigrants without proper papers in an attempt to protect them from deportation.[24]

The Economist joined the debate,[25] approving of Sarkozy's immigration bill as a sensible change towards a managed, high-skilled, demand-led immigration policy. Until the mid-1970s, most immigrants to France came to work. Since the law was tightened in 1974, the inflows changed. Today, only 7,000 permanent workers arrive a year, down from over 170,000 in the late 1960s. Three-quarters of legal entrants to France are family-related: spouses, children and sometimes extended families of those already in the country. France has a low proportion of skilled immigrants. Sarkozy's bill aimed to reverse this trend, by introducing selective immigration. There would be yearly targets for three categories of incomers: workers, students and families. Skilled migrants would be encouraged through a new three-year 'talent' work permit. The bill included measures to encourage foreign students. But it also required newcomers to take lessons in the French language and civic education; it sought to control family-related immigration, by clamping down on bogus marriages, and restricting the rules to ensure that those bringing in a family have the means to pay for them. Illegal immigration would be checked by scrapping the automatic right to stay, granted after ten years in France, and increasing deportations. Opposition to the bill was fierce, from the Socialist Party and the Council of Christian Churches. Sarkozy was unapologetic about linking France's social troubles, including the autumn 2005 suburban riots, to immigration and the difficulty of integrating second-generation children. To accusations of mean-mindedness, he replied: 'It is not a mark of generosity to create ghettos at the gates of our big towns, where there is only hopelessness and, beyond that, crime.' He argued that, under the pretext of protecting jobs at home, France had created a system that lets in only those who have neither a job nor any useful skills. Sarkozy, who is of Hungarian origin, recognized 'what an open France gave my family', and told parliament that a policy based only on blood ties would be 'synonymous with national decline'.

Muslim anti-Semitism erupts in every demonstration, whether or not it is related to anti-Israel and anti-Zionist sentiment. Non-Muslim anti-Semites also began to indulge in rampages against Jewish individuals, synagogues or even cemeteries. Nidra Poller, an American writer who lives in Paris, wrote about the emergence of the black Ka Tribe in Paris.[26] In May 2006, thirty Africans stormed into the heart of the old Jewish quarter, terrorizing residents, shopkeepers, and Sunday strollers, only three months after the torture-murder of Ilan Halimi. The Ka Tribe is the lunatic fringe of a broad anti-Semitic movement originally inspired by Dieudonne, who became a hero to a segment of black French society by focusing resentment on Jews. But Dieudonne, with a

French mother and Cameroonian father, was not black enough for the Tribe's Haitian and Ivorian leader, who calls himself Fara (pharaoh) Kemi Saba. His interview appeared on the Ka website until the government shut it down two days after the rue des Rosiers rampage. Deftly manipulating the terms and gestures of French intellectual discourse, Kemi Saba presented his latter-day ideology of 'negritude', preaching total separation from leucodermes (anything less than 100 per cent pure blacks). The kemites (the term replaces leucoderm words like blacks, Africans or Antilleans) are the true chosen people, destined to rule the world. Although Fara rejects both Christianity and Islam, he has a soft spot for Islamism.

Frantic calls to the police met with laconic replies: 'Yes, we have been informed.' The men stomped and shouted for what seemed an endless twenty minutes. Men, women and children felt totally defenceless, delivered up to a storm of uncontrollable rage. Some witnesses reported seeing baseball bats, sticks and knives, but the police did not come until the militia had left. The capture of Yussuf Fofana – leader of the gang of barbarians accused of the torture-murder of Ilan Halimi – and his extradition from the Ivory Coast had provoked the Ka's wrath. They sent a message to various Jewish groups and individuals, threatening to kill other Jews if anyone harmed Fofana. Veiled threats led to aggressive action even before the rampage as the Ka went after real or imagined members of Betar (a group that provides security for Jewish events) and the Jewish Defence League, accused of persecuting blacks and Muslims who penetrate their turf – rue des Rosiers – and beating up kemites during the memorial march for Ilan Halimi. A few days earlier, the Ka militia stormed a gym in the 9th arrondissement, looking for members of Betar and the Jewish Defence League. There they terrorized children (non-Jewish ones, as it happened) who were learning an Israeli martial art. In a case of fantasized warfare, the Ka packaged the rue des Rosiers incursion as a prearranged showdown with the 'Zionist extremists' and announced a knockout victory – because the 'extremists' didn't show up. The Interior Minister visited the rue des Rosiers to show his support and promise results, and called for the dissolution of the group after it had been tolerated for many years. One shop owner said, 'It's over for Jews in France.' He continued: 'The police told me … they said it's over for us ... they can't handle this problem ... It's too late."²⁷ Nowhere else in the West did the authorities' impotence to deal with anti-Semitism reach such ominous proportions. Triggered by Islamists, and supported by the Muslim crowds at large and their right-wing anti-Semites and left-wing 'anti-Zionist' allies, it had now been joined by some blacks, threatening to erupt into the violence seen in Germany during the 1930s.

Faced with the impotence of the French police to protect Jewish communities, or the political unwillingness of the French establishment to alienate the Muslims whose votes they need on election day (Jews constitute only one tenth of the number of Muslims, 600,000 compared to six million), the Jewish community had to turn to self-help, within the confines of the law. When the wave of rioting erupted across France in autumn 2005, a Jewish youth group swung into action to guard synagogues and community centres from possible anti-Semitic spillover violence. Many Jews feel that such a reflex is needed in France, home to the largest population of both Jews and Muslims in Western Europe and sporadically simmering with tensions. Formed in 2000, the Jewish Defence League – which has no ties to the US Jewish Defence League – groups about 100 to 150 Jewish teens and young men to protect their community. Group members are unarmed but train in *Krav-maga* (Hebrew for *corps-à-corps* combat), a form of close combat developed by the predecessor of the Israeli Army. Jean-Yves Camus, a researcher with the European Centre of Research and Action on Racism and Anti-Semitism, said the group epitomizes a new generation of young Jews, who refuse to be passive. League leaders fault what they say is the powerlessness of mainstream associations in stemming the periodic waves of anti-Semitism.²⁸

Without the 'M' word being uttered, and all the violence attributed to the 'poor and disaffected youth of the suburbs', Muslim participation in the repeated episodes of rioting is undeniable. Paris youths clashed with police in May 2006, and the latter resorted to firing rubber bullets and stun grenades against masked youths wielding baseball bats. Projectiles and petrol bombs were hurled at police and public buildings, and the rioters attempted to storm the home of Xavier Lemoine, the conservative mayor of Montfermeil. The violence was sparked by the arrest of a suspect in the beating of a bus driver earlier, but the rioters always look for a pretext to ignite a fight, and when they find it, use it to direct the blame on police or on their victims. The Montfermeil violence spread into the edge of neighbouring Clichy-sous-Bois, the flashpoint for the 2005 riots. Two youths were electrocuted there in October 2005 while hiding from police in an electricity substation.[29]

Recalling the 2005 riots, Transport Minister Dominique Perben said: 'The question of the suburbs is a question for the entire political class', without having the courage to identify the culprits. In twenty nights of rioting in nineteen provinces, 2,900 were arrested and the damage bill was estimated by insurers at some €200m. Dozens of police officers were injured. The rioters burned 10,000 cars and torched 300 housing and commercial structures, and the fact that they did not spare their own schools or cultural centres was particularly disconcerting. More than 400 teenagers and young men were sent to prison, but community leaders complained, again euphemistically, that little has been done to 'answer the grievances of the alienated young in the high-unemployment estates'. An onlooker noticed an interesting phenomenon: while the rioting continued, the French bourse continued to rise steadily. The country seemed on the brink of disintegration, if not now, then next time (and there will almost certainly be a next time). Many French companies, among them some of the best in the world, directed by the genuine elite turned out by the *grandes écoles*, were doing extremely well, with record profits. The explanation for this is that they are increasingly shifting their activities abroad: in 2006, France was the largest exporter of capital in the world.[30]

Montfermeil had been a focus of tension since Mayor Lemoine decreed a by-law the month before, that banned teenagers from circulating in groups of more than three, and required those under 16 to be accompanied by an adult in the centre of the town. A court quashed the by-laws after protests from civil liberties groups and the left. The Socialist opposition blamed Lemoine for fostering the violence in his town with his attempt to restrict the movements of youths. 'No act of violence can be excused ... but the Mayor of Montfermeil has created a local situation which is a factor in the violence', said François Hollande, again putting party rhetoric before the urgency needed to tackle rioters.³¹ The rioters remain convinced that they are above the law and that because they are 'frustrated', their rampages should go unpunished. The courageous Lemoine thought otherwise. He had intervened in the assault and later identified some of suspects, who then retaliated against his home. And then came the apologies for the rioters: high unemployment and a sense of hopelessness that pervades their ghettos. It is worth mentioning that just as the 2005 violence had begun after the accidental deaths of two youths in Clichy-sous-Bois in late October, the same pattern had occurred in Gaza in December 1987, where a car accident that resulted in three Arab deaths was found a good enough pretext to trigger the first intifada that lasted five years. That episode killed hundreds of people and caused such great economic dislocation that the Palestinians dubbed it bitterly an *inti-fawda* (the Arabic words for 'you' and 'chaos', respectively).

Some rioters are drawn to Islam less as a faith and more as an oppositional ideology that has replaced Marxism as the intellectual drug of the 'alienated'. In his *Policy Review* article 'The French Path To Jihad', based on interviews with French prisoners, author John Rosenthal notes that Islam's attraction is often less its theological content than an aura of rebellion. 'Islam disturbs people', notes Jacques, a non-Muslim, 'and for me that's a good sign.' One Muslim prisoner said: 'Islam was my salvation. I understood what I was as a Muslim, someone with dignity, whom the French despised because they didn't fear me enough ... That is the achievement of Islamism. Now, we are respected. Hated, but respected.' The Fifth Republic's foreign policy, which sees the Arab world as a counter-balance to US and Israeli power, has unintentionally legitimated some of the violence. French television, its perspective an extension of the nation's ruling elites, has tried to incorporate young Muslims by depicting the conflicts in the Middle East largely from a Franco-Muslim perspective. On many nights, the TV news glorified the intifada against Israel. The Muslim underclass, not surprisingly, identified with the 'youths' attacking Israelis, seeing their own violence as a heroic extension of the battle against the enemies of Islam.³²

The public-housing projects that gradually burgeoned around most French cities in the second half of the twentieth century now serve as strongholds and training grounds for violent gangs. After an incident of organized large-scale stoning by fifty people in October 2006, with private cars attacked on a major road near Grigny, the stone-throwers were rolled back into the neighbouring projects, but there was no further pursuit. One police source confided to *Le Monde* that security forces were actually 'discouraged' from making incursions into those neighbourhoods, except on rare occasions. The source went on: 'It is a terrible mistake. Since we avoid going inside, where they are, they attack us outside, where we are.' Most French suburban public housing was originally designed by talented architects, and could have developed into pleasant neighbourhoods. Mass immigration had an adverse effect on them, turning them into either North African or black African ghettoes. An estimated 15 per cent of the overall French population – one quarter of the population under 20 – is now non-European. Ethnic criminal gangs took over, forcing the last native French inhabitants out. Later, fundamentalist Islamic brotherhoods asserted themselves in the projects, or *les cités*, as they are called. A complex relationship seems to have arisen between these two power centres. On the one hand, the fundamentalists intended to protect the immigrant community against everything the gangs stood for: drugs, alcohol, sexual promiscuity, easy money from crime. On the other hand, they derived benefits from the ethnic enclave status the gangs had secured. A tacit agreement was reached, whereby the brotherhood would ignore or condone as 'holy war' the activities of the gangs outside the neighbourhood; the gangs would help the brotherhoods impose Islamic law on the inside. There was a further division of labour. When the gangs would engage in inordinate violence against the police or non-Muslim communities, the brotherhoods would act as 'wise men' available to mediate between the government and the gangs and to help restore law and order, albeit on their own terms. This is precisely what happened in 2005, when Sarkozy talked of 'thoroughly cleansing' the 800 or so no-go zones that had cropped up all over urban France. Neither the gangs nor the fundamentalists liked that prospect. The gangs masterminded unprecedented 'youth riots'; the fundamentalists then restored civil peace, and won as a reward *de facto* pardon for most rioters, a 'less provocative' police presence in the suburbs, more privileges for Islam as 'France's second and most quickly growing religion', and recognition for themselves as national leaders. Michel Thoomis, the secretary general of Action Police, a conservative union, told *L'Est Républicain*: 'Security is a state prerogative. Inasmuch as the national police fail to provide it, the imams are ready to usurp it.'[33]

In November 2006, the weekly magazine *Le Nouvel Observateur* published a confidential report drawn up by a public service trade union, the CGT, containing scores of eyewitness accounts of brutal attacks on public servants who work in the *banlieues*, from gas board workers to staff from the electricity company. The CGT report painted a graphic picture of violence: blocks of cement dropped on paramedic crews; washing machines pushed off balconies on to fire engines; electricity company agents too scared to cut off customers who have not paid bills, after being attacked with knives, guns and fists. Shortly after the three weeks of rioting that gripped French suburbs, Sarkozy said the violence was above all 'territorial'. Gangs were trying to seize control of a piece of territory, 'and rule it by force'. *Le Nouvel Observateur* found a clear echo in the views of a politician on the opposite end of the spectrum, the communist mayor of Sevran, a poor north-eastern Paris suburb. Youths who burned buses or attacked firemen were only hurting their own families and neighbours, who would be deprived of the few remaining public services, said the mayor, Stéphane Gatignon. 'For them it's a way of showing they exist, that this is their home, their territory.'[34] Those places in France that the French state does not control are referred to by the euphemistic term Zones Urbaines Sensibles, or Sensitive Urban Zones, with the even more antiseptic acronym ZUS, and there are 751 of them as of last count. They range from two zones in the medieval town of Carcassone to twelve in the heavily Muslim town of Marseilles, with hardly a town in France lacking one. The ZUS came into existence in late 1996 and according to a 2004 estimate, nearly five million people live in them. Daniel Pipes commented that a more precise name for these zones would be *Dar al-Islam*, the place where Muslims rule.[35]

There was much support for the rioters among the predominantly white and non-Muslim parties of the far left: the two

Trotskyite parties, what is left of the old Communist Party, and the Greens. Even the far-right activists, for whom hatred of America, Israel, and the 'free-market EU' tends to outweigh any other consideration, support the gangs. Some intellectuals on the left and right relish the prospect of a new French revolution, and welcome the suburban rioters as its spearhead. The possibility of a green–red alliance has a historical precedent in the spread of Islam itself, in the seventh century. The newly founded religious empire from Arabia overran in less than two decades the two mightiest powers of the time, the Christian Byzantine and the Mazdean Persian Empires. In both places, the Arab expansion coincided with a deep ethnic, religious, and social crisis. The Arabs didn't conquer outright Palestine, Syria, Anatolia, Egypt, North Africa, Iraq and the Iranian plateau. They struck alliances with local rebels: Copts, Syriacs, Nestorians, Donatists, Jews and Mardakites, who spoke neither Greek nor Persian nor shared their beliefs. Even the green flag of Islam was borrowed from non-Arabs: it was originally the symbol of rebellion in Byzantium, the equivalent in its day of the red flag in ours.[36]

One year after the riots in the *banlieues*, it was announced that an average of 112 cars a day were torched across France that year and there were fifteen attacks daily on police and emergency services. As burning cars became increasingly routine, the youths progressed onto bus firebombings, leaving one woman passenger with 60 per cent burns. Nearly 3,000 police officers were injured in clashes over the year, particularly in ambushes around Paris. Some police talked of open war with youths who are bent on more than vandalism. 'The thing that has changed over the past month is that they now want to kill us', said Bruno Beschizza, the leader of Synergie, a union to which 40 per cent of officers belong. Car burning has become so routine on the estates that it has been eclipsed in news coverage by the violence against police.[37] Thoomis wrote to Sarkozy warning of an 'intifada' on the estates: 'We are in a state of civil war, orchestrated by radical Islamists. This is not a question of urban violence any more, it is an intifada, with stones and Molotov cocktails. You no longer see two or three youths confronting police, you see whole tower blocks emptying into the streets to set their comrades free when they are arrested.' The union asked the government to provide police with armoured cars to protect officers in the estates.[38] For the Catholic Church in France, it has been particularly disconcerting to see the rise of Islam accompanied by a drop in Catholic observance. Barely half the French population describe themselves as Catholic, sparking a leading religious publication to declare France 'no longer a Catholic country'. A poll published in *Le Monde des Religions* in January 2007 showed the number of self-declared French Catholics had dropped from 80 per cent in the early 1990s to 51 per cent today. The number of atheists has risen steadily to 31 per cent from 23 per cent in 1994. French Catholicism did not begin its real decline until 1905, when pre-war France was declared a secular state, all funding of religious groups was stopped and religious buildings were declared the property of the state. The poll showed that only 10 per cent go to church regularly. *Le Monde des Religions* cited varied reasons for the decline, including the rural exodus, changing values and the rise of individualism.[39] Yet the French authorities offer assistance to accommodate the religious needs of their immigrants. The French Foreign Ministry Religious Affairs Adviser, Laurent Stéfanini, set up a 'French lodge' in Saudi Arabia to help pilgrims with the difficulties they encounter while performing *hajj*, the fifth pillar of Islam. The difficulties include the huge numbers involved, access to sites and 'the cheating atmosphere, lack of time and space', according to the official, who added that 27,000 pilgrims left France to perform the *hajj* in 2005, of whom only 6,000 were French nationals.[40]

Yet every accommodation to the whims of the immigrants has the perverse effect of making integration less likely. France's leading gynaecologists have challenged Muslims to bow to France's secular, 'modern' rules of society, and to stop insisting that their wives are examined by female doctors. The heads of the French National College of Gynaecologists and Obstetricians issued a public declaration, rejecting any moves to undermine the principle that public hospitals are part of a secular state, in which patients must accept being examined by a doctor of the opposite sex. The move came after a consultant in Paris was punched by a Muslim who was concerned that a male doctor wanted to examine his wife after complications in childbirth. The college said: 'Thirty years ago, Muslim women came into our hospitals without any alarm at being taken into the care of doctors, most of whom were men, and there were none of these difficulties. Why are things going backwards? It is for Islam to adapt to the liberties that all must possess in a modern state.' In 2004, there were 145 attacks in hospitals in France, rising to more than 200 in 2006 in which medical staff have been attacked by Muslims.[41]

There is an ongoing debate among doctors over Muslim women who demand operations to 'restore' their virginity before marriage and medical certificates stating that they are virgins – practices said to be commonplace in some Muslim countries. Muslim girls in Europe are more emancipated but still live under rigid codes of family honour. The controversy has flared in France, where gynaecologists say that they are facing a growing number of requests from women desperate to avoid the repudiation that can follow the loss of chastity. The phenomenon is denounced by critics as a sign of social regression driven by Islamic fundamentalists. Jacques Lansac, chairman of the French National College of Gynaecologists and Obstetricians, is leading the campaign against what he describes as 'an attack on the dignity of women'. However, he said that some doctors were ignoring his advice in the hope of protecting patients from ostracization or violent beatings. Jacques Milliez, head of the department of gynaecology and obstetrics at Saint-Antoine hospital, Paris, told *Le Monde*: 'I worked in Algeria as a junior doctor and when I was on call at night I saw these young women whose throats had been slit because they were suspected of having lost their virginity. So if someone asks me, I sign the certificate.'[42] The procedures are legal but shrouded in silence, 'something that passes through non-official channels' via friends or the internet, said Dr Nathan Wrobel. He says women come to him having convinced themselves that the procedure will somehow reverse the irreversible. 'They tell me, "I'll be a virgin again", which in reality is totally false ... It's a secret we share.' Wrobel says he and another doctor at his clinic in a Paris suburb stitch up seven to eight hymens a month in a half-hour operation under general anaesthesia that he likens to plastic surgery. Other doctors issue false virginity certificates or offer such tricks as spilling a vial of blood on the sheets to fool families into believing the bride has passed their purity bar. In Germany, doctors who do hymen repair are easy to find, and Turkish Muslim immigrants are increasingly seeking virginity certificates.[43]

In both Tunisia and France the banning of the hijab has actually helped Muslim women who are subject to Islamic indoctrination. For some Muslims, the imperative to veil women justifies almost any means. Sometimes they try to buy off resistance. Some French Muslim families, for instance, are paid 500 euros (around $600) per quarter by extremist Muslim organizations just to have their daughters wear the hijab. This has also happened in the US. The Syrian-American psychiatrist Wafa Sultan told *The Jerusalem Post* that after she moved to the US in 1991, Saudis offered her $1,500 a month to cover her head and attend a mosque. More often, intimidation is used. A survey conducted in France in May 2003 found that 77 per cent of girls wearing the hijab said they did so because of physical threats from Islamic groups. A series in the newspaper *Libération* in 2003 documented how Muslim women and girls in France who refuse to wear the hijab are insulted, rejected and often physically threatened by Muslim males. Muslim women who try to rebel are considered 'whores' and treated as outcasts. Some of them want to move to areas 'with no Muslims' to escape. So wearing the hijab may or may not be a manifestation of the free exercise of religion. Covering women is a means of social control, and not surprisingly, it is one of the only issues on which Sunnis and Shi'as agree. Unsurprisingly, the hijab really took off after Iran's Islamic regime came to power in 1979. Professor Iqbal al-Gharbi, from the famous Islamic Zaytouna University in Tunis, explained: 'The veil is just the tip of the iceberg. Behind the veil, there is the regressive interpretation of the shari'a. There are the three essential inequalities which define this interpretation: inequality between man and woman, between Muslim and non-Muslim, between free man and slave.'[44]

Another sore issue that concerns the French public (and other Europeans for that matter) is polygamy, imported by Muslims who refuse to renounce it in favour of democracy. Muslims may have their ideas about what constitutes decadent behaviour in the West, but having more than one wife is considered debauched by everyone else's standard. It took a television programme about a patriarch with three wives and tightly scheduled evenings to set off a serious public debate about polygamy. 'Ailat al-Hagg Metwalli' (Hajj Metwalli's family), an Egyptian serial, stirred emotions and sparked a bitter debate about polygamy in the Muslim world during Ramadan in 2001. The drama heats up when 50-something Metwalli Sa'id, long-time husband of three, decides to court a young woman, Samira, in the hope of making her his fourth wife. Unbeknownst to Metwalli, Samira is in love with his own son, who is eventually forced by his father to forsake Samira to marry the daughter of a relative (as is often preferred in Muslim societies). Metwalli's viagra-induced heart attack brings the story to a head. Studying viewer responses to this serial, Norwegian historian of religion Anne Sofie Roald found that assimilated Muslim immigrant women in the West see Metwalli as a dictator: being unfaithful to his wives, forcing them to give up their jobs, forbidding them to leave the house without permission, selfishly forcing his son out of a love marriage, and generally insisting that his word is law. Yet some unassimilated Muslim immigrant women in Europe, and many Muslim men, admire Metwalli for successfully embodying polygamy as authorized by Islam. Metwalli follows the Qur'anic precepts: telling all of his wives that he loves them and materially supporting them well and equally. Even Metwalli's son eventually comes around: affection burgeons in his arranged marriage after his wife bears him a child. This serial served as a reminder that in Muslim immigrant enclaves in Europe, Middle Eastern TV is often the entertainment of choice. In Denmark, for example, Muslim immigrants who might otherwise be watching the local media and absorbing democratic values watch programmes glamorizing polygamy via satellite dish or on the Arabic-language cable channels provided for segregated Muslim communities in Scandinavia. Supporters of polygamy, including the show's creators, argued that it is a religiously proper alternative to adultery, divorce, and remarriage, and a real answer for the many unmarried women who might otherwise have no chance at motherhood. Opponents replied that polygamy opens the way to marital discord, divorce, and the consequent destitution and abandonment of women and children.[45] The French Government estimates that there are somewhere between 8,000 and 15,000 polygamous families within its borders, originating from countries in Africa and the Middle East. These husbands married two or more women legally in their home country, and have, on average, ten children. France declared polygamy illegal in 1993, as problems developed with delinquency and assimilation. Although officially second wives were not allowed to enter the country after that, the authorities have largely looked the other way and allowed many to enter and take up residency. This leniency has created a unique set of problems because these women are not legal residents and have no rights. They are not allowed to work and they are not entitled to any form of social welfare. As a result, they become totally dependent on their husbands. Often they have no access to birth control and are not even allowed to leave the house. In an interview with *The Christian Science Monitor*, Hoiloyo Diop repeatedly called herself 'the second wife'. She is also the mother of eight, and shares a five-room apartment in Les Mureaux, a city west of Paris, with her husband, his first wife, and their combined seventeen children. Living in the West has brought problems not encountered in their home countries. 'Back in Senegal we never had a problem with polygamy. [In France] everything is different', she said. The wives find themselves living in a culture unequipped to accommodate a polygamous lifestyle, and competition and jealousy reign at home. French houses are not built for the numbers involved, and tensions arise with neighbours confronted with such large families. The children are often neglected and play truant from school. The authorities in Les Mureaux started to provide a separate house and financial support for women who entered the country before 1993 when polygamy was outlawed. Marie-Françoise Savigny, social affairs administrator in Les Mureaux, complained, 'Polygamy has been forbidden for more than ten years. But second wives are still being allowed to enter the country. Politicians have kept their eyes shut for the problems they created.' She says politicians are afraid to act, because they fear accusations of racism.[46]

From the earliest history of England polygamy has been treated as an offence against society, for there is a deep connection between monogamy and democracy. The great liberal political philosopher John Stuart Mill attributed the advanced character of western democracies to their social structures. Muslim families arrange marriages to cousins and other kin, thereby reinforcing couples' identification with family and tribe. But from the fourth century through the Middle Ages, the Church fought to protect individual choice in marriage, while prohibiting marriage between cousins and other relatives. That undercut social forms based on kinship and collective identity, ultimately leading to the triumph of democratic individualism in the West. Like Muslims today, Mormons touted polygamy as an alternative to prostitution and out-of-wedlock births, and a boon to women facing a dearth of marriageable men. In Africa, co-wives and their children generally live in separate houses or huts. In extreme cases, children sleep in shifts in their small French apartments, making school attendance all but impossible. Yet raising questions about the real-world effects of family structure was stigmatized as bigotry by civil rights advocates and French Muslims alike. After riots broke out in 2005, Bernard Accoyer, parliamentary leader of Chirac's party, pointed to polygamy as one of several causes of the disturbances. Various prominent politicians and scholars followed suit. 'Anti-racist' groups called the comments 'sickening and irresponsible', threatening legal action against the historian Helene d'Encausse, permanent secretary of the prestigious French Academy, for her suggestion that large families with little parental supervision crammed into small apartments had played a role in the disturbances. (Hate-speech lawsuits are a favourite device of the French left for shutting down public debate.) The attack from the left, and pressure from France's allies in Africa (where public anger at the polygamy remarks ran high), quickly forced Chirac to distance his government from the controversy. When Chirac arrived in Mali for a December 2005 summit, he personally ruled out any connection between polygamy and the riots. Yet Chirac's Government proposed a law that would make it more difficult for French residents to bring in foreign spouses and children. With a critical mass of practitioners on French soil and able to vote (or riot), and with the left seizing on polygamy as a civil rights issue, enforcement of the ban is in doubt.[47]

In Britain, too, polygamous marriage is flourishing as the government admitted for the first time that nearly a thousand men are living legally with multiple wives in Britain. Although the families are entitled to claim social security for each wife, no one has counted how many of them are on benefits. Ministers appear to be ignoring the separate practice of unauthorized polygamy, which is said to have become commonplace. The Ministry of Justice admits that it has no estimates of numbers for these unions, which are often presided over by an Islamic cleric. The government has long reassured Parliament that its policy is to prevent the formation of multiple marriages by refusing to allow second wives entry into the country. Under British law, husbands and wives can have only one spouse at a time. Multiple simultaneous marriages constitute bigamy, a criminal offence. Britain does recognize polygamous marriages that have taken place in countries where the custom is legal, such as Pakistan, Nigeria and India. The Home Office said that multiple wives in polygamous marriages may be allowed into the country as students or tourists. Officials are advised to let extra wives into Britain even if they suspect that a husband is trying to cheat the system by getting bogus divorces. The practice is said to have become commonplace, at least among Kashmiris, a group that accounts for most of the estimated 747,000 Pakistanis in Britain. Opposition politicians are concerned about the burden being placed by polygamy on the social security and tax systems. A husband may claim housing benefit for each wife even if she is abroad, for up to a year. To calculate the amount of income support that is payable to an extra wife, officials subtract the rate paid to an individual from that paid to a couple. This produces the amount that a cohabiting spouse is deemed to need in social security benefits. Women who enter unrecognized multiple marriages in Britain are far more vulnerable. They are effectively regarded as mistresses with no legal or tax rights and can end up being dumped with no safeguards.[48] Opposition MPs are demanding an urgent change in the law, claiming that the government is rewarding a custom which has no legal status and which is 'alien' to Britain's cultural traditions. Muslim couples are only married in the eyes of the state if they undergo a register office wedding as well as a *nikah*, or religious ceremony. A spokesman for the MCB said it was quite common for men here to undergo more than one *nikah* with different wives. This does not count as bigamy since only the first marriage is legally recognized. Some more secular Muslim countries such as Turkey and Tunisia do not allow polygamy at all, while it is relatively common in traditionalist Arab countries such as Saudi Arabia.[49]

France is more riot-stricken than any other European country due to the size of its Muslim population. But it is not free from other Muslim threats, including terrorism. Concurrently with the attacks against the US on September 11, other Muslim groups were planning to attack the American Embassy in Paris and Strasbourg Cathedral. Twenty-five Islamist radicals were convicted by a Paris court in June 2006 for their roles in a plot to bomb French landmarks, and received varying prison terms. The group's alleged chemicals expert, Menad Benchellali, was imprisoned for ten years, but Menad's father, Chellali Benchellali, an imam in the Lyon suburb of Venissieux (*tel père tel fils*, as the French would say), received only an eighteen-month suspended sentence. All but one defendant had been accused of helping Islamic fighters in Chechnya in what prosecutors said underscored the 'globalization of the jihad movement'. Prosecutors were unable to prove strong suspicions that the attack was to have involved chemicals, even though investigators found equipment, including a protective suit, and chemicals including the highly toxic ricin. They were found guilty of criminal association in relation with a terrorist enterprise, a broad charge used by France to sweep wide in bringing terror suspects to justice. The Benchellali family was at the centre of the case, including Menad's mother, Hafsa, and brother, Hafez. The Russian Embassy, a police station and the Eiffel Tower were mentioned as possible targets during interrogations.[50]

Profiling the network, the prosecutor put the origins of the group in Algeria in 1999, where eight members had refused an Algerian Government amnesty plan for Islamic insurgents. They then travelled to Spain, France, Italy and the border region between Pakistan and Afghanistan, while a core group formed in the Paris region in late 2000 to create an Islamic support network in Chechnya. It is beyond comprehension that European countries admit into their territories the families of convicted radical terrorists, who were refused amnesty in their home country. Far from expressing remorse, the convicted terrorists voiced their usual slogans and propaganda. 'These convictions profit the US, Algeria and Russia', said Isabelle Coutant, who represented Merouane Benhamed, one of the convicts. 'They have been convicted because they are Muslims.' While London may be convulsed by controversy over police clampdowns on terror suspects, Charles Bremner, *The Times*'s Paris correspondent, says that the French police take a tougher line without the same public soul searching: 'There is a big difference between the French and British policy and approach to terrorism. The DST, the equivalent to MI5 as well as the police intelligence, keep a very close watch on the housing estates where the majority of the Muslim population live.' Until recently the French were very unhappy with what they regarded as incompetence by the British. The French thought the British were far too lax towards radical Muslim activities on their territory. Abu Hamza was followed by the French investigation service without informing the British because they were so worried by his activities. The shooting of Jean Charles de Menezes in London following the July 7 bombings, and the apology by police to the brothers arrested in Forest Gate, east London, did little for the perception of the British police. In France, house raids happen very often and do not get the same media coverage as in the UK. There have been countless investigations after the conviction of the Algerian network, resulting in the arrests of dozens of suspects. The threat from the Chechen connection has been known in France for some time, predominantly from warnings by one man, Jean-Louis Bruguière, the chief French investigating magistrate for terrorism.[51]

Just prior to the immigration law being passed in June 2006, several arrests once again highlighted the need for firm measures. The arrest of Daw Meskine, secretary general of the French Council for Imams, and his son sent shockwaves across the Muslim minority. Even against this background, the government was the target of relentless criticism from the left-wing opposition and human rights groups, incensed that the new immigration law would skim off the most talented people from countries where they are badly needed while making life harder for ordinary migrants. 'Keeping the best and sending back the worst is not exactly Christian', said Cardinal Philippe Barbarin, the Archbishop of Lyon. So while he himself classified some immigrants as belonging to the 'worst' category, he was unconcerned about the danger they posed to his fellow-citizens.[52]

Zuhir Burik, president of the French Council for Imams, told Islam Online (IOL): 'Meskine (paradoxically meaning 'miserable') is a prominent and respected Muslim figure (they all are, even when caught red-handed), and is well known to French authorities and Interior Minister Nicolas Sarkozy himself.' Interior Ministry sources told IOL Meskine and his son were arrested as part of a probe into the funding of his al-Najah (ironically meaning 'success') school and a farm he owns in northern France, which he had turned into a summer camp for students. (No information was released on what the students were taught. Symbolic names are never chosen accidentally, and always refer to a context of action.) Some twenty members of Meskine's family and aides were arrested in the swoop ordered by Paris prosecutors. The arrests were linked to an investigation into funds coming from Gulf countries and money laundering activities for a terrorist organization. The arrest of Meskine, of Tunisian background, drew fire from officials in his school, France's first private Muslim high school which is located in the northern Paris suburb of Aubervilliers. IOL was told by a 'well-placed source' that the arrest came 'fifteen days before approving state funds for the school', adding it was intended 'to deprive the school from state funding'. Private schools qualify to receive state finances after operating independently for five consecutive years. Sarkozy had said that police would be granted extra powers to expel more radical imams from the country after the London bombings.[53]

Rather than addressing the violent waves of anti-Semitism among them, Muslims in France, as in other parts of Europe, reverse the blame by accusing others of 'Islamophobia'. But these are not two sides of the same issue, because the Jews are attacked by Muslims for no reason, while Muslims cannot claim that their own co-religionists did not earn the 'Islamophobia' that they complain about by their terrorist acts. With financial backing from the French and Qatari Governments, an Islamic institute was planned ostensibly 'to counter the rising Islamophobia'. The government hopes to train qualified imams and preachers on the premises, thereby avoiding the importation of radical imams. The institute, which is affiliated to the University of Lille, 'will project the tolerant image and openness of Islam', said the dean, Mohammad el-Beshari. The institute will admit both Muslim and non-Muslims interested in studying Islamic civilization and culture. Specialized courses will be offered for Muslim imams and preachers working in prisons, the army and hospitals. In July 2003, the French Government approved the establishment of Ibn Rushd (the famous medieval Muslim philosopher Averroes) school in Lille, which became the first secondary Muslim school in France. Muslims make up about 25 per cent of Lille's one million population.[54]

But as in London, while the Muslim leadership spoke words of peace, its followers were preparing for war. In fact, Islamic terrorists operating in France are more agile at plotting attacks than before, better educated, and more ideologically grounded than a decade ago, and their numbers are growing despite advances in methods to track them. French intelligence officials have described changes in how terror cells finance and plan attacks, and how they recruit and train. Terrorist funding is coming from ingenious and often small-scale sources: money laundered through halal butcher shops, cannabis dealing and ATM scams. 'The spider web [of terror] put in place since the 1990s hasn't stopped growing', said Louis Caprioli, former assistant director of the DST, the country's main counter intelligence agency. 'The level of recruitment is rising, with more and more engineers or technicians, or chemists or physicists', he said. A leading anti-terrorism prosecutor described the attackers of 1995 as down-and-out youth from impoverished French suburbs, while today's Islamic terrorists are more of the 'university profile'. He said prison authorities are fighting what is so far a losing battle against terrorist recruitment behind bars. French investigators do not talk of al-Qa'ida, insisting that there is no such convenient, single enemy. Instead they see several small, unconnected terror cells around the world that share a common ideology inspired by Osama Bin Laden. That is the pattern followed by all al-Qa'ida branches in the world, since the backbone of the leadership was broken in Afghanistan, and the remnant act in a decentralized fashion. Dynamic, cross-border intelligence cooperation is crucial. Coordination between European and North African secret services, for example, helped avert a dozen attacks in France since 1996, Caprioli said. For many Islamic terrorists, the target of an attack is secondary, said Jean-François Ricard, a former top anti-terrorism judge and now a Defence Ministry official. 'The objective is fixed at the last moment', he said. French officials have made several adjustments to their anti-terrorism arsenal. A law passed in December 2005 gives authorities new powers to monitor citizens who travel to countries known to have terrorism training grounds, and expands the use of video surveillance and electronic monitoring on French soil. Other changes include an extended detention period from four to six days and a new court for minors accused of terror-related crimes. Defence lawyers and human rights groups say France's new anti-terrorism measures go too far in eroding civil liberties. 'The fight against terrorism is not an easy thing', said Patrick Baudouin, head of the Paris-based International Human Rights Federation. 'One must not cede to the pressure of police who want a maximum free hand. The end doesn't always justify the means.'[55]

Security passes were withdrawn from seventy-two staff at Charles de Gaulle Airport in Paris in November 2006 because of their possible links to terrorism. While the majority were Muslims, ten were Tamils and one was a Sikh. Those affected include baggage handlers, security agents, drivers, cleaners and clerks believed to be 'linked to fundamentalist movements with potential terrorist activities'. One was a friend of Richard Reid, the 'shoe bomber' now serving a life sentence in America for attempting to blow up a Paris–New York flight.[56] Demographics make the workforce of European airports vulnerable to Islamic extremism. In Germany, authorities announced that they had broken up a suspected plot to use an airport employee to plant a bomb on an El Al airline. Airports must maintain stringent standards for their personnel, said Christophe Chaboud, chief of a police anti-terrorism unit, who led the inquiry on workers at Charles de Gaulle Airport. 'You have to choose', he said. 'Either you worship at a radical mosque, you have contacts with radicals, or you work at the airport. You can't do both.'

People who frequent radical environments are vulnerable to being recruited, although it doesn't mean they are terrorists. Charles de Gaulle has about 85,000 employees, about one-fifth of them Muslim. The workforce at De Gaulle has doubled in a decade, increasing the presence of private subcontractors and short-term workers, and authorities have started to lose control. Some ethnic networks recruit in their hometowns in Morocco, so in effect illegal immigrants are hired. A former French anti-terrorism official who investigated airport employees said many are Salafists, the ideology behind al-Qa'ida. Many travelled to study at madrassas in countries such as Yemen, Afghanistan and Pakistan, where religious indoctrination is often accompanied by a paramilitary-training component. Some workers belong to Tablighi Jama'at, a missionary group that organized their trips. Although Tablighis officially shun politics and violence, the group has produced a number of terrorists. Anti-terrorism officials acknowledge wrestling with ambiguities when monitoring extremism that falls short of lawbreaking. 'The risks are often going to be subjective', said Alain Grignard of the Belgian Federal Police, a respected expert on Islam. 'You can't ban someone from a job just because of their religion.' Grignard has long worried that extremists could target airport workers because of the combination of their low socio-economic status and high-security jobs. A Brussels cell dismantled in late 2001 after allegedly plotting to bomb the US Embassy in Paris had associates working in maintenance and security at Brussels airport.[57]

In December 2006, French and American secret services reported that the thirty-one-mile Channel tunnel had been targeted by a group of Islamic terrorists aiming to cause maximum carnage during the holiday season. According to French sources, the plan was put together and directed in Pakistan. The plotters were believed to be Europeans, possibly Britons of Pakistani descent. Staff on the line went on strike in 2006 in protest at what they said were lax security arrangements. The French intelligence services also reported an al-Qa'ida project for a 'wave of attacks in an unidentified European country planned and run from Syria and Iraq'.[58] Jean-Louis Bruguière revealed that France had become more of a terrorist target because an Algerian network that considered Paris its principal enemy had officially linked up with al-Qa'ida. Three significant plots had been averted, including attacks on the Paris Métro, Orly, and on the Directorate of Territorial Security. The link with al-Qa'ida had given the network, the Salafist Group for Preaching and Combat, commonly known by its French acronym GSPC, access to a growing number of jihadists hardened by battle in Iraq. Opting out of the US-led war in Iraq did not shield the country from Islamic terrorism, and Europe is now easier to target than the US. The GSPC appeared in 1998 as an offshoot of another Algerian terrorist organization, the Armed Islamic Group. In 2003, it pledged allegiance to Osama Bin Laden. In September 2006, al-Qa'ida posted a video on the internet in which its deputy leader, Ayman al-Zawahiri, formally endorsed a 'union' which could broaden the Algerian group's recruitment base and access to funds. Zawahiri vowed to target 'American and French crusaders'. Its reach in Europe has also spread beyond France. Several arrests linked to the group have been made in Spain and Italy. 'What is new is that this organization has formally pledged allegiance to al-Qa'ida, and that the relations between al-Qa'ida and the GSPC allow the GSPC to work with the Iraqi branch', Bruguière said. 'The Iraqi branch is fed by the GSPC, and that produces a risk of exporting jihad to North Africa, but also to France, the main target of the GSPC.' Algerian terrorists have long staged attacks in France, first during the eight-year Algerian war of independence that ended in 1962, and more recently in the 1990s, after Paris backed a military coup in Algeria that prevented an Islamic party from winning elections and taking power. Eight people were killed and more than 100 wounded when the Armed Islamic Group exploded several bombs in the Paris Métro in 1995. Since then, Bruguière said, French security forces have foiled one or two plots a year by Islamic terrorists.[59]

In January 2007 the GSPC declared that it would henceforth be known as the al-Qa'ida Organization in the Islamic Maghreb, to unify jihadist factions in Algeria, Tunisia, Morocco and Libya under one banner. The GSPC was identified as the lead group because of its long association with al-Qa'ida (dating back to the Afghan camps of the 1990s) and because it has established highly effective mobile training centres in the Sahara.[60] To European dismay, intelligence services are now admitting that their earlier assumptions that all men act upon the same instincts, are deterred by the same threats and aspire to the same prosperity and well-being as all humans, have collapsed. They have found out, through bitter experience, that if the westerners mean well, they cannot take for granted that the others would too and that if they are offered shelter and welfare, they will not necessarily become grateful and refrain from terror. They also 'discovered' that commitment to religion and doctrine can be much stronger than values of democracy and the safeguarding of human life. Now they realize, after years of denial and of condemnation of those who had issued politically incorrect warnings, that westerners and Muslims have widely different views of world events.

A survey of more than 14,000 people during April–May 2006 in thirteen nations indicates that each group tends to view the other as violent, intolerant and lacking in respect for women. In what the survey, part of the Pew Global Attitudes Project, called one of its most striking findings, majorities in Egypt, Indonesia, Jordan and Turkey, all supposedly 'moderate' Muslim countries with fairly strong ties to the US, said that they did not believe that Arabs were responsible for 9/11.[61]

Overall, Muslims in the survey, including the large Islamic populations in Britain, France, Germany and Spain, broadly blamed the West for the bad relations, while westerners tended to blame Muslims. Muslims in the Middle East and Asia depicted westerners as immoral and selfish, while westerners saw Muslims as fanatical. Support for terrorism declined in some of the Muslim countries surveyed, dropping sharply in Jordan, after it was hit by al-Qa'ida when terrorist bombings killed more than fifty people in Amman in November 2005. Majorities in every country surveyed except Pakistan expressed pessimism about Muslim–western relations, with Germany most strongly viewing the situation as bad (70 per cent), followed by France (66), Turkey (64), Spain and Britain (61), and Egypt (58). Interviews were conducted face to face, except in the US, Britain, France and Germany, where they were done by phone.[62]

In follow-up interviews in countries surveyed about the results, Muslims attributed poor relations with the West to a variety of causes. Pew asked respondents to give their opinions of Christians, Muslims and Jews, and it found anti-Jewish sentiment to be 'overwhelming' in the Muslim countries surveyed. A 'deep attitudinal divide' was found between western and Muslim publics, with Muslims more critical of westerners than vice versa. For the second year running, the survey shows increasing opposition among Muslim populations to violence targeting civilians in the name of Islam. There is, however, no obvious correlation between diminishing support for terrorism and more positive perceptions of the West. Muslims also blame western policies for their countries' lack of economic prosperity. Meanwhile, people in western countries blame Muslim countries for what they perceive to be government corruption, lack of education and Islamic fundamentalism. But 'nothing highlights the divide between Muslims and the West more clearly', the survey found, than clashing views over the controversy about the Danish cartoons. Up to two-thirds of westerners blamed the controversy on Muslim intolerance, while well over two-thirds of Muslims blamed western disrespect.[63] But the pollsters are not UN observers, and therefore have no obligation to avoid judging and to just report what each party stated. There is also a matter called 'truth'. When the majority of Muslims claim that Jews were responsible for September 11, one cannot report such delusions and lies as 'different perceptions' of reality. This is not an assessment of facts nor a commentary upon them, but the very factual basis of events that is being challenged, and any survey has to account for that, so readers may draw the appropriate conclusions about Muslim psychology.

A close corollary of these differences of world views is the preferential treatment that many Muslims on the Continent clamour for, and many Europeans are eager to afford them, as a way to 'compensate' them for their miseries. The Muslims have been trying to introduce 'positive discrimination' policies, or what the Americans call 'affirmative action', because they have been 'wronged' by the West, and therefore they deserve some redress to overcome their backwardness for which they blame the West. But they fail to comprehend that 'positive discrimination' is anything but positive – it is actually patronizing, and points to possibly inherent deficiencies in their characteristics which might make them ill-equipped to contribute to politics, the arts, academe, education, science or the legal system, officialdom or law enforcement. Even in the best of circumstances, a policy of 'positive discrimination' throws up inconsistencies and absurdities which might make it unworkable, but the problems are multiplied in societies where the threat of terrorism, accompanied by incitement, are ever-present. The harm that can result from hiring those who are intent on subversion in government bureaucracy, law enforcement or the military, is incalculable. No country can reasonably be expected to introduce a potential fifth column in sensitive posts in what is a time of war, especially since that war is not of the conventional sort between two armies. Furthermore, there is an element of bigotry in 'positive discrimination', inasmuch as it presupposes that Muslim immigrants can attain a certain level and no more, or conversely that they may only occupy the higher ranks of employment in certain numbers which cannot be exceeded under this policy. Why, for example, predetermine that only one Muslim judge should sit in the Supreme Court, or two Muslim Cabinet ministers ought to be nominated, if by fair competition their numbers could be higher (or lower) according to personal merit? If adopted anywhere in the West, this policy would only perpetuate feelings of discontent and humiliation among Muslims who would stand out as having attained their positions not by individual effort but by the favours of the host society, and resentment in the host society because those who may be better qualified are overlooked in the name of racial hiring practices. Moreover, promoting people on the basis of ethnic origin would destroy incentives to work hard, and induce emigration by those who would justly feel that their opportunities for advancement have been circumscribed – the very people any country can ill-afford to lose.[64]

This realization is slowly filtering to some of the ruling classes in Europe, while others continue to resist it, so much so that Trevor Phillips, chairman of Britain's Commission for Racial Equality, said that race laws must be overhauled to protect national security and fight terrorism, while paradoxically claiming that positive discrimination should be used to recruit more Muslims to the police and security forces. In a speech at the Social Policy Forum, Phillips claimed that Muslim officers are vital to the security of Britain because they understand Islamic culture and can carry out covert surveillance without being compromised. Current legislation bans positive discrimination and a number of police forces that have tried to boost the number of officers from ethnic minorities have fallen foul of the law. Over recent years there have been many campaigns to make the police force more attractive as a career for Muslims, with little success. Based on the experience of some countries that are afflicted with minority relations, the most positive and effective way of attaining integration and avoiding the divisive phenomenon of unions of Muslim parliamentarians, judges, artists, scientists, or the already existing one of police officers in London, is to embrace a programme of long-term education to gradually instil the necessary western values of unbiased learning and research, honest conduct, the sanctity of the public square and public service, democracy, a rejection of violence, the rule of law, the supremacy of state law over religious law, and the like. It may take years, but when implemented and successful, Muslims, like all others, would slip with ease into elite positions without any favours from anyone.[65]

Ideas and ideals apart, the grim reality is that Muslim terrorism not only persists in European streets, but it seems to gain momentum, as each Middle Eastern crisis is superseded by another, the self-awareness and sense of grievance of the Islamic world increase, and the tensions continue to mount between the Muslim populations in Europe and their host societies. A French terrorism trial was thrown into turmoil by a leaked report that French intelligence agents had secretly interviewed the six defendants during their detention by the US at Guantanamo Bay in Cuba. The revelation by the daily newspaper *Libération* embarrassed the French Government, which had long expressed official disdain for the American policy of detaining terrorism suspects beyond the reach of law. Jean-Baptiste Mattéi, the Foreign Ministry spokesman, defended the Guantanamo interrogations, saying they were normal consular visits during which it is routine to 'gather any useful information'. French courts had previously declared the Guantanamo detentions illegal. The six former detainees, seized by the US as they fled the American invasion of Afghanistan in late 2001, were accused of 'associating with terrorist groups'. In 2004, their lawyers asked that their cases be dismissed because the interrogations were 'outside of any legal framework'. A spokeswoman for the prosecutor's office denied that the secret interrogations played any role in their case, saying the accusations were based on information uncovered since the defendants were released from Guantanamo.[66]

During the May 2007 presidential elections, the socialist candidate, Segolene Royal, was perceived as the 'ally' of the Muslims, in view of the traditional French policy that favoured immigration and tempted the new immigrants to join socialist ranks. Sarkozy, by contrast, had an uncompromising image with regard to immigration controls and the preservation of peace and order. The difference between the candidates, however, was not only their respective political affiliations, but stemmed mainly from the proven record of Sarkozy as an Interior Minister in charge of public order and of fighting terrorism, as against Royal who was an unknown quantity and had never undertaken any major national project. Although it is generally assumed there are six million Muslims in France, figures as high as eight million and more have been quoted. It is unknown how many of them are legal residents. Just prior to the elections, it was announced that three million of the forty-five million registered voters were new. Seventy per cent of them are of North African descent, who registered en masse specifically for the elections, casting doubt on the assumed Muslim population figures. The French electorate grows by 2 per cent every election campaign, but in 2007 the growth rate soared to nearly 5 per cent.[67] The election of Sarkozy, by a comfortable margin of 53 per cent, was quickly felt in immigration policy. Brice Hortefeux, who heads the newly created Ministry of Immigration and National Identity, ruled out the possibility of legalizing undocumented immigrants. He said government policy would be firm and pragmatic, and he planned to adhere to the policy of deporting illegal immigrants.[68]

The government also wants to encourage legal migrants to reconsider their decision to stay in France, by paying them to go back home. Under the voluntary scheme, Paris will provide each family with €6,000 to return to their country of origin. A similar scheme introduced in 2005 and 2006 attracted around 3,000 families. Under a 1970s paid repatriation programme, some immigrants took the money and went home, only to return again as illegal immigrants. Biometric identification cards and a firm deportation policy should prevent such abuses, but very few immigrants are accepting the offer. Hortefeux has insisted that 'co-development' will be an important consideration of French immigration policy. He argued that the system of voluntary return can be seen as a means for investment in developing countries, and that the method of transferring funds via returning immigrants to their country of origin was a better policy than providing development aid.[69] In the aftermath of the 2005 riots, a start was also made to encourage immigrants to reach prominent positions in public life. The most revolutionary change occurred in the media, which now has presenters, journalists, entertainers, academics, philosophers and public figures from immigrant origins. A small revolution has also occurred in key government positions, in public administration and industry.⁷⁰ The changes have not reached the inhabitants of the suburbs, and this will be one of the major challenges facing the new government.

Tough numerical goals for yearly expulsions have been set, and quotas for questioning suspected illegal aliens. A group of leftist artists and academics have protested Sarkozy's new Ministry of Immigration and National Identity, objecting to the link between the two, although the French favour the new Immigration Ministry by a margin of three to one. When Sarkozy was Interior Minister, he doubled the number of deportations to 24,000 annually. Now the target for 2007 has been raised to 25,000 expulsions. French-speaking illegal immigrants from Africa now prefer Spain as a destination, avoiding France because of its rigid labour markets, but also because of Sarkozy's tough immigration stance. A law passed in July 2006 requires immigrants to prove they can support family members without welfare. The new bill would require 'reunifying' family members to pass a test on the language and values of the Republic (including 'social solidarity' and fraternity) before entering the country (and offers two months of training for the test). All family members would have to sign a 'contract of integration' and parents would be held responsible for their children's integration – to the point where a family's welfare benefits could be suspended.⁷¹ Throughout the presidential campaign, Sarkozy blamed crime and social breakdown on the failure of immigrant families from the Muslim and black African states to embrace French values. 'If some people are annoyed by being in France, they should not hesitate to leave a country that they do not like', he said.⁷²

In keeping with his pursuit of 'open' government, in which other political parties, women and members of ethnic minorities are represented, Sarkozy recruited so many of the Socialist Party's big names that during a recent European summit he joked he was 'the only non-Socialist in the French delegation'. Some of his white, conservative colleagues have complained of being sidelined, while the best have been snatched from the discredited left. This policy has been viewed as a cunning strategy to encourage the dismantling of the Socialist Party and its removal as a political threat for years to come. He appointed Algerian-born Fadela Amara, 43, a Muslim feminist, as junior Minister for Urban

Affairs. Amara, who still lives in the *banlieues*, rejects descriptions of her appointment, and those of two other women of immigrant origin – Rachida Dati, 41, the Justice Minister and the Senegalese-born Rama Yade, 30, junior Minister for Foreign Affairs – as token gestures, arguing that they have made a big impact. 'The Socialists were always talking about it [diversity] but did nothing. President Sarkozy does what he says.' Sarkozy became a figure of hate in the suburbs, particularly when he referred to violent youths as 'scum' who had to be cleaned from the streets with a power hose. Amara called his vocabulary 'regrettable' but said that since his election as President 'people in the *banlieues* are beginning to look at him in a new way'. At 18 Amara had established her first women's group, complaining that Muslim girls 'must act like submissive but virtuous vassals or be treated like cheap whores' who were often victims of gang rapes, known as *tournantes*. After the murder of a 17-year-old girl who was set on fire by a youth in 2002, she founded the organization 'Ni Putes Ni Soumises' (Neither Prostitutes, nor Submissive), which fights violence against women among immigrants. She is encouraged by initiatives in the Justice Ministry, where Dati has introduced 'anti-discrimination' magistrates; and the defence ministry, where 'affirmative action' plans are being drawn up to make the military's predominantly white officer class more reflective of France's 'rainbow' society. Her urban planning team intends to renovate the decrepit housing estates in the suburbs, improve living conditions and education and bring down unemployment.[73] Dati, the daughter of an Algerian workman and a Moroccan housewife, was battling to salvage her reputation after only weeks in office. Four of her most senior aides resigned, while two of her eleven siblings have been involved in drug-dealing charges. Her appointment was regarded as a master stroke by Sarkozy to counter his image as an intolerant right-winger. No non-white had ever held a senior Cabinet post, let alone a woman from the poor estates. Her critics depict Dati as a ferociously ambitious favourite who has been over-promoted. Dati's legal experience consisted of a few years as a junior provincial magistrate and junior prosecutor and she had never held an elective office.[74]

In *Integrating Islam – Political and Religious Challenges in*

Contemporary France, Jonathan Laurence and Justin Vaisse reaffirm 'the much-maligned French model of integration'. The Muslims in France still exhibit the pathologies that have long characterized the underclass in western societies. Nearly a fifth of French residents with immigrant origins don't have jobs. Unemployment among young people in the projects runs as high as 50 per cent. Muslims make up a majority of the French prison population, and in prisons near urban areas their numbers approach 70 to 80 per cent. Laurence and Vaisse seem to believe that just as France has successfully integrated Armenians and Vietnamese before them, the Muslims will be integrated too. France has Europe's highest rate of intermarriage between Muslims and non-Muslims. Though immigrant birth rates are high, they tend to slow down with each succeeding generation. A Muslim middle class is tiny but emerging. An assimilationist outlook may be emerging as well. According to a Pew Global Attitudes survey published in July 2006, 42 per cent of French Muslims consider themselves French first; 47 per cent, Muslim first. (In Britain, the numbers are 7 per cent British first; 81 per cent, Muslim first). Yet the survey also shows that Islam is putting down roots in France, as it is elsewhere in Europe. The young who were born in France but feel at home neither in the West nor in the birthplace of their parents are the most susceptible to radicalization. Zacarias Moussaoui, the convicted 9/11 terrorist and a French citizen, is the most prominent example of this cohort. The Muslim Brotherhood is certainly active in Frances's suburbs. France's anti-terrorism laws are the toughest anywhere in the western world. French prosecutors can hold terror suspects for years without charge; the definition of 'links to terrorism' is loose. Every mosque in France is monitored. Since 9/11, the government has cracked down on foreign financing and moved to train 'French imams'. The path to integration would run smoother if France could undertake a major economic reform. Little has been done to loosen up the restrictive labour codes that do so much to keep poor immigrants from finding work and integrating themselves into French life.[75]

NOTES

1. Emmanuel Brenner, *Les Territoires Perdus de la République* (Paris: Mille Et Une Nuits, 2001).
2. Didier Hassoux, *Libération*, 15 June 2004.
3. Ibid.
4. Nathalie Segaumes, *Le Parisien*, 15 June 2004.
5. Daniel Ben Simon, 'Segolene hasn't come', *Haaretz*, 28 November 2006.
6. Matthew Campbell, 'Barbarians of Suburbs Target French Jews', *Sunday Times*, 2 April 2006.
7. Alyssa A. Lappen, 'Ritual Murders of Jews in Paris', *FrontPageMagazine.com*, 4 December 2003.
8. Craig Smith, 'Jews in France Feel Sting as anti-Semitism Surges among Children of Immigrants', *The New York Times*, 26 March 2006.
9. Renaud Muselier, 'No to a Racist and anti-Semitic Internet!', *Le Monde*, 14 June 2004.
10. Pierre Beylau, *Le Point*, 1727, 20 October 2005, p.25.
11. Anne Nivat, *Le Point*, 1727, 20 October 2005, p.26.
12. Ibid.
13. Christophe Deloire, 'La France, Terre de Djihad', *Le Point*, 1727, 20 October 2005, p.36.
14. A proselytizing movement created in northern India in the 1920s. It controls some one hundred mosques in France, with its followers distancing themselves from society in keeping with their prescription that 'a good Muslim must speak moderately during his meals, because if he keeps quiet , he acts like Jews, and if he talks too much he resembles the French, while he has to keep apart from both communities'. As quoted by Alex Alexiev ('Tablighi Jama'at: Jihad's Stealthy Legions', *Middle East Quarterly*, Winter 2005), the French Tablighi expert Marc Gaborieau believes the Tablighi's ultimate objective is a 'planned conquest of the world' in the spirit of jihad.
15. Deloire, 'La France, Terre de Djihad'.
16. Denis Demonpion, 'Interview with Jean-Claude Marin', *Le Point*, 20 October 2005, p.39.
17. Bernard Lewis, *Islam* (Paris: Quarto Gallimard, 2006).
18. Denis Jeambar, 'Regression', *L'Express*, 2 February 2006.
19. Eve Bonnivard (a journalist in *AFP* in Paris) and Barbara Lefebvre (a history teacher), who wrote jointly: *Élèves sous Influence* [Students Under Influence] (Paris: Audibert, 2005). The extract from their book was published by *Haaretz* (Tel-Aviv), 29 March 2006.
20. Ibid.
21. Amir Taheri, 'Eye of the Storm: Algeria bids France "au revoir"', *The Jerusalem Post*, 27 April 2006.
22. Multiple Choice French Citizenship Test, *Spiegel Online*, 6 May 2006.
23. Craig S. Smith, 'Furor Over a French Immigration Crackdown', *The New York Times*, 8 July 2006.
24. Ibid.
25. 'France and Immigration – Let the Skilled Come', *The Economist*, 4 May 2006.
26. Nidra Poller, 'The Wrath of Ka', *City Journal*, 7 June 2006.
27. Ibid.
28. 'French Jews set up own Defence League', *The Jerusalem Post*, citing *AP*, 14 June 2006.
29. Charles Bremner, *Times Online*, 30 May, 2006; and Ariane Bernard, 'Rioting by Youths in 2 Paris Suburbs Recalls Violence of November (2005)', *The New York Times*, 31 May 2006.
30. Theodore Dalrymple, 'I want Sarkozy to be right', *Spectator*, 31 March 2007.
31. Ibid.
32. Fred Siegel, 'Fall of the Fifth Republic?', *New York Post*, 1 November 2006.
33. Michel Gurfinkiel, 'Another French Revolution? The Rioters and their Admirers on the Right and the Left', *The Weekly Standard*, 27 November 2006.
34. David Rennie, 'Youths Challenge the French State', *The Daily Telegraph*, 2 November 2006.
35. Daniel Pipes 'The 751 No-Go Zones of France', weblog, 14 November 2006.
36. Gurfinkiel, 'Another French Revolution?'.
37. Charles Bremner , 'Why 112 Cars are Burning every Day', *The Times*, 21 October 2006.
38. David Rennie, 'Muslims are Waging Civil War against us, Claims Police Union', *The Daily Telegraph*, 5 October 2006.

39. Henry Samuel, 'France "no longer a Catholic Country"', *The Daily Telegraph*, 10 January 2007.
40. 'Pilgrimage: "French lodge" in Saudi Arabia to help French pilgrims', *Morocco Times*, 20 September 2006.
41. David Rennie, 'Muslims Challenged by Gynaecologists', *The Daily Telegraph*, 23 October 2006.
42. Adam Sage, 'Doctors face Moral Dilemma over Restoring Muslim Brides' Virginity', *The Times*, 7 May 2007.
43. 'Young Muslim Women in Europe go to Extremes to be Virgins again', *USA Today*, 25 June 2006.
44. Olivier Guitta, 'The Veil Controversy – Islamism and Liberalism face off', *The Weekly Standard*, 4 December 2006.
45. Stanley Kurtz, 'Polygamy Versus Democracy: You can't have both', *The Weekly Standard*, 5 June 2006.
46. Frank Renout, 'Immigrants' Second Wives find Few Rights', *The Christian Science Monitor*, 25 May 2005.
47. Kurtz, 'Polygamy Versus Democracy: You can't have both'.
48. Dominic Kennedy, '1,000 Men Living Legally with Multiple Wives despite fears over Exploitation', *The Times*, 28 May 2007.
49. 'Polygamous Husbands can Claim Cash for their Harems', *Daily Mail*, 17 April 2007.
50. 'Islamists Jailed over Plot to Attack Paris', *Times Online*, 14 June 2006.
51. Charles Bremner, 'Analysis: France's Attitude to Terror', *Times Online*, 14 June 2006.
52. 'France Approves Immigration Law That Favours Skilled Workers', *AFP*, 1 July 2006.
53. Hadi Yahmid, 'French Imam Arrested on Money Laundering', *Islam Online*, 21 June 2006, http://www.islam-online.net/English/News/2006-06/21/01.shtml.
54. Hadi Yahmid, 'French Islamic Institute Fights Islamophobia', *Islam Online*, 15 June 2006.
55. 'Terrorists Operating in France more Agile at Plotting Attacks', *The Jerusalem Post*, citing *Associated Press*, 5 June 2006.
56. Charles Bremner, 'Paris Airport Staff Suspended', *The Times*, 3 November 2006.
57. Sebastian Rotella and Achrene Sicakyuz, 'Charles de Gaulle Airport Handling Cultural Baggage', *Los Angeles Times*, 12 December 2006.
58. Jason Burke, 'Channel Tunnel is Terror Target', *The Observer*, 24 December 2006.
59. Katrin Bennhold and Souad Mekhennet, 'French Counterterror Forces on High Alert', *International Herald Tribune, Europe*, 19 December 2006.
60. Sean O'Neill, 'Algeria could Provide Springboard for European Terror', *Times Online*, 11 April 2007.
61. Meg Bortin, 'Poll Finds Discord Between the Muslim and Western Worlds', *The New York Times*, 23 June 2006; and Delphine Schrank, 'Survey Details "Deep" Divide Between Muslims, Westerners', *The Washington Post*, 23 June 2006.
62. Bortin, 'Poll Finds Discord Between the Muslim and Western Worlds'; and Schrank, 'Survey Details "Deep" Divide Between Muslims, Westerners'.
63. Ibid.
64. Steve Bird, 'Discriminate for Muslims, Police Urged', *The Times*, 19 June 2006.
65. Ibid.
66. Craig S. Smith, 'Leak Disrupts French Terror Trial', *The New York Times*, 6 July 2006.
67. Daniel Ben Simon, 'Redrawing France's Identity Card', *Haaretz*, 22 April 2007.
68. 'France: No Mass Legalizing of Immigrants', *AP*, 21 May 2007.
69. 'A New Broom In Paris, France to Pay Immigrants to Return Home', *Spiegel Online*, 24 May 2007.
70. Daniel Ben Simon, 'Harmony or Guerrilla War?', *Haaretz*, 27 October 2006.
71. Stanley Kurtz, 'Immigration Crackdown – Our Future is Europe', *National Review Online*, 25 June 2007.
72. Charles Bremner, 'Immigrants to Face Exam on being French', *The Times*, 14 June 2007.
73. Matthew Campbell, 'Minister in the Tower Block gives Sarko Street Cred', *Sunday Times*, 29 July 2007.
74. Charles Bremner, 'Sarkozy's Star Minister Flounders', *The Times*, 17 July 2007.
75. Matthew Kaminski, 'To Keep the Banlieue From Burning – Will France ever Integrate its Muslim Immigrants?', *Opinion Journal*, 26 October 2006.

CHAPTER FOUR

Germany's Dilemmas

Post-war Germans, who had taken the lead in importing Muslim labour to rebuild their devastated state and make up for the huge deficits of male manpower due to the millions killed during the hostilities, were among the first Europeans to create the phenomenon of the *gast arbeiter* (guest workers), assuming that when the latter finished rebuilding the country, they could be sent back to their homes. But, as in the rest of Europe, the dynamics of immigration had the upper hand. When immigrants become absorbed in society, accustomed to their new surroundings, and establish families, they are unlikely to leave. Most of the workers in Germany were Turkish, later to be joined by other Muslims, and latterly Eastern Europeans. At that time, secularist Turkey, a member of NATO, was not regarded as a source of Islamic radicalism, which it has become after the Islamist Party of Prime Minister Erdogan won the majority in the Turkish Parliament in 2002. But the rise of Islam across the world has also touched the Turkish immigrants of Germany, many of whom have in the meantime become naturalized Germans. Like the rest of the Europeans, the self-exonerating 'better-than-thee' ultra-liberal attitude of Germans towards immigrants, lest they be accused of racism, has created a climate of denial and a refusal of one government after another to take any action for fear of causing unrest. Like other liberal democracies, they focused on short-term policies of keeping the population contented until the next election. But September 11 and then, to a lesser extent, the cartoon crisis, brought a new awareness to the very heart of Berlin, the renovated capital city of post-Cold War Germany, of the hard facts that they could no longer ignore. Ironically, the Germans, who murdered the 120,000 Jews of Berlin and other cities, who were part of the intellectual, artistic and commercial elite, were well-assimilated, peaceful and posed no threat or burden to the state, came to realize, much to their chagrin, that the departed Jews have been replaced by a thirty-fold larger Muslim community, which not only refuses to acculturate and has become a socio-economic burden, but has also been posing a challenge to the very social system and the security of the state.

In late 2002 reports about terror cells regrouping and targeting Europe were revealed by intelligence papers from across the continent, depicting a growing danger from a widening network of fanatics. One of the suspects, who led a secret life as one of Europe's new terrorist kingpins, had been watched for months. Abderrazak Mahdjoub, a 30-year-old Algerian, had been a key part of a network of Islamic terrorists dedicated to recruiting and dispatching 'suicide bombers' to the Middle East. Several volunteers had wreaked havoc in a series of attacks in Iraq. Many more were on their way, along with bombers focused on targets in Europe. Mahdjoub's arrest was a minor victory in a major war being fought, bitterly and secretly, in cities from London to Warsaw, from Madrid to Oslo. It pits the best investigative officers in Europe against a fanatical network of men dedicated to the prosecution of jihad both in Europe and overseas. It is a war security officials know they cannot afford to lose – and that they know they will be fighting for the foreseeable future. Previously seen as a relative backwater in the war on Islamic terrorism, Europe is now in the frontline. 'It's trench warfare', said one security expert. 'We keep taking them out. They keep coming at us. And every time they are coming at us harder.' Interviews with senior counter-intelligence officials, secret recordings of conversations between terrorists and classified intelligence briefings have shown that they have been able to reconstitute, and even enlarge, their operations in Europe in 2002–03. Britain was still playing a central logistical role for the terrorists, with the alleged mastermind of the 2003 bombings in Morocco, and a leader of an al-Qa'ida cell, regularly using the UK as a place to hide. Other radicals were using Britain for fundraising, massive credit card fraud, the manufacture of false documents and planning. In one intercepted conversation, a senior terrorist said he needed people who are 'intelligent and highly educated', and implied that the UK could, and did, supply them.[1]

Islamic terror cells began spreading eastwards into Poland, Bulgaria, Romania and the Czech Republic for the first time, prompting fears of a new battleground in countries with weak authorities, powerful criminal gangs and endemic corruption. Austria became a central communications hub for Muslim extremists; France has become a key recruiting ground for fighters in Chechnya; and German groups, who often have extensive international links, are developing contacts with Balkan mafia gangs to acquire weapons. Investigators stress that most of the European cells are autonomous, coming together on an *ad hoc* basis to complete specific tasks. To describe them all as 'al-Qa'ida' is simplistic. The man most of these new Islamic terror networks were looking to for direction was Abu Musab al-Zarqawi, the Jordanian Islamic terrorist. Though he followed, until his elimination in 2006 a similar agenda to Osama Bin Laden, the young and ambitious Zarqawi had always maintained his independence from the Saudi-born fugitive. His developing stature in global Islamic militancy was reinforced when he issued his first-ever public statement, an audio-tape calling on God to 'kill the Arab and the foreign tyrants, one after another'. One of his key lieutenants was an Iraqi Kurd known only as Fouad, a cleric based in Syria, who handled the volunteer 'suicide bombers' sent from Europe to launch attacks in Iraq. Italian investigators made the first breakthrough in the hunt for Zarqawi's followers. In June 2002, an unidentified Arab visitor from Germany, arrived at a mosque in the Via Quaranta, Milan. He began by warning the mosque's Egyptian imam, Abu Omar, about increased surveillance, unaware that Italian police were listening to his every word. Transcripts revealed that the visitor spoke of a project needing 'intelligent and highly educated people'. Already, the visitor said, that 'where the jihad part is concerned there was a battalion of twenty-five to twenty-six units'. It is these 'units', believed by investigators to mean potential 'suicide bombers', that the authorities needed to find.[2]

The visitor then began a review of recent developments. He stressed that 'the thread begins in Saudi Arabia', from where the bulk of funds apparently still comes. 'Don't ever worry about money, because Saudi Arabia's money is your money', the visitor said. He then referred to recent 'confidential' meetings in Eastern Europe with Islamic leaders. 'Now Europe is controlled via air and land, but in Poland and Bulgaria and countries that aren't part of the European Community everything is easy', he said. 'First of all they are corrupt, you can buy them with dollars ... [Secondly] they are less-controlled countries, there aren't too many eyes.' The man named Austria as a launch pad for attacks. 'The country from which everything takes off is Austria. There I met all of the sheikhs and all our brothers are there ... it has become the country of international communications. It has become the country of contacts.' Poland is a particularly important location too, he said, and named a 'Sheikh Abd al-Aziz', before boasting: 'His organization is stunning.' Italian investigators immediately relayed the information to counterparts elsewhere in Europe. 'The nerve centre is still London', the man said and hinted that there are many recruits from the UK: 'We have Albanians, Swiss [and] British.' The role of the UK was reinforced when, in April 2003, 29-year-old Somali-born Cabdullah Ciise was arrested in Milan days after arriving from London. The Italians suspected him of financing a terror cell involved in the car bomb attack on Israeli tourists in Mombasa, Kenya in November 2002. According to Italian court documents, Ciise transferred money from Britain to Somalia through Dubai. He was also accused of being an important member of Zarqawi's international terrorist organization. In November 2003 an Algerian-born British national was arrested after travelling to Poland. He was the subject of an Algerian arrest warrant alleging his involvement in a terrorist group. When the Italians arrested Ciise they put him in the same cell as another Islamic radical known as 'Mera'i'. Again, the conversation was bugged; it gives a chilling insight into the mind of a hardened terrorist.[3]

Mera'i told Ciise that he hates their guards: 'They like life. I want to be a martyr, I live for jihad. In this life there is nothing, life is afterward, the indescribable sensation of dying a martyr.' Then the pair talked about the Syrian-based cleric Fouad, whom they describe as the 'gatekeeper' to Iraq. Other transcripts reveal conversations between Fouad and Mera'i about how they had organized the flow of 'brothers' to Iraq via the Syrian cities of

Damascus and Aleppo. One of the network's recruits is believed to have been involved in the rocket attack against the Baghdad hotel where Paul Wolfowitz, the American Deputy Secretary of Defence, was staying.

After 11 September, the Germans had concentrated on rounding up all those connected with the 'Hamburg cell' who had led the attacks on New York and Washington. Soon, however, they came across a group known as 'al-Tawhid' (the unitarians) which posed as grave a threat. Al-Tawhid were loyal to Zarqawi. The link between the Italian network and the German cells was a 30-year-old Palestinian called Mansour Thaer. Another connection was a Turk called Mevluet Tar, who spoke fluent German. Both were quickly picked up. The dossier lists a dozen senior al-Tawhid followers in Germany. Most were involved in the provision of false passports or spent their time raising and transferring funds to fighters in the Middle East. Others were involved in plotting bomb attacks against Jewish targets in Western Europe. In Switzerland a series of raids broke up an alleged support and fundraising network which had connections to the men who set off bombs in Riyadh. In Spain, a favoured entry point into Europe for North African terrorists, investigators continue to chase down those linked to cells rounded up earlier. A Moroccan cleric called Mohammed al-Garbuzi, whom local authorities claim was a key figure in the Casablanca bombings in May 2003, was believed to be at large in the UK. Scotland Yard warned leaders of the Jewish community that the threat 'remained high'. Senior British police officers said they were aware that millions of pounds were being raised in the UK by credit card fraud for Islamic terrorist groups. 'We act when we can', said one police source. 'But we are stretched enough going after the clear and immediate threats, let alone their back-up.'[4]

Speaking to a meeting of Christian Democrats in March 2007, the German journalist and university lecturer Udo Ulfkotte warned that Islam is slowly but surely taking a grip on European culture. Traditional values, customs and judicial standards are gradually customized to meet Muslim requirements. More and more institutions are making allowances for Muslims. Many banks are abandoning the so-called piggy banks, because they are afraid of losing Muslim customers. Muslims regard the pig as an unclean animal. German butchers who sell pork are targeted by Muslim extremists. Muslims occasionally spit on sausages on sale at open-air markets. In some European cities Muslim taxi drivers refuse to transport dogs, even blind persons with guide dogs. Two schools in Berlin have installed two separate entrances – one for German Christians and Jews and the other for Muslim Arabs and Turks. Shari'a law is also beginning to take hold, with some banks offering shari'a-friendly investments. Authorities in Berlin have recognized a shari'a lawyer, who settles family feuds. Many German politicians turn a blind eye to the gradual Islamization, while Muslims show a lack of tolerance. For their integration to be successful they would have to adapt to basic European values. Hindus, Ulfkotte said, are a good example that this is possible. They accept that Europeans eat beef, although Hindus regard cows as sacred animals.[5] Germany's Muslim population is becoming more religious and conservative. Islamic associations are fostering the trend, particularly through their work with the young, accelerating the drift towards a parallel Muslim society. Some of the blame must attach to the state, since under the guise of religious tolerance, German society stood blithely by as segments of its Muslim communities began turning into parallel societies. The experiences of Ekin Deligöz, a member of the German parliament representing the Green Party, underscore the potential dangers. Having called on Muslim women to remove their headscarves, Deligöz faced death threats and now receives police protection.

Some groups truly want to establish a separate world. The Association of Islamic Cultural Centres, known by its German acronym VIKZ, operates a number of children's centres throughout Germany. Critics say the children, who often have no exposure to the outside world, are subjected to religious indoctrination – an allegation the association's leadership denies. A typical centre in Duisberg houses thirty-eight Muslim adolescents between the ages of 12 and 19. The children attend state schools in the morning, but otherwise live and learn in the home with noticeably austere surroundings. Officially they are here to improve their performance at school, but German academics and youth experts have warned that this type of group is widening the gulf between Muslims and the rest of society. The VIKZ has a lot of clout among Muslims in Germany. Some 300 mosque communities count themselves as members. It is the third-largest Muslim organization in the country, representing more people than the Central Council of Muslims. In public, the association's officials are eminently friendly and impeccably dressed, often in stylish pinstriped suits. Although the Duisberg home has German teachers, employing German-speaking teachers is a statutory requirement. Pupils often have no time for leisure activities with their non-Muslim peers. Critics, such as Reverend Rafael Nikodemus, the Islamic Delegate of the Protestant churches in the Duisburg district, have little faith in VIKZ's professed open-mindedness. Getting the representatives of VIKZ to work with local clubs and churches took 'enormous pressure', he said.[6]

University of Marburg professor and VIKZ expert Ursula Spuler-Stegemann was commissioned to review the association's institutions by the region's social services authority in 2004. Despite assertions to the contrary, she found the homes were 'almost exclusively devoted to Islamic teaching and practice of the faith'. They were 'an unequivocal obstacle to integration'. The pupils were 'indoctrinated' into a 'rigidly shari'a-oriented' form of Islam and 'immunized' against Christianity, the West and the German constitution. She described VIKZ as an elitist organization within Islam that made sure its pupils were trained to accept strict obedience and an even stricter gender segregation. VIKZ refutes these censures, defensively adding that it had never been subject to surveillance by Germany's security agencies. Yet the regional government was so alarmed by the concerns that it halted approvals of new VIKZ homes. 'The VIKZ officials are full of promises but end up doing whatever they want', said Hanspeter Pohl, who is responsible for children's and adolescents' homes in Hesse's social services department. Religious instruction took place 'on a much larger scale' than was admitted, and children were regularly woken up in the middle of the night for prayers. A junior-high school teacher from North Rhine-Westphalia, whose school is in the catchment area of an unofficial VIKZ home, has been observing the situation for years. She witnessed how the pupils suddenly adopted 'extremely anti-Semitic and anti-American attitudes'. English was seen as the enemy's language and some refuse to speak it at all, even if it means failing their exams. They reject the theory of evolution in biology lessons, the age of the earth as discussed in geography, and anything remotely satirical in their German classes. Evidence abounds that VIKZ is acting outside the law. Camps and schools are set up without the requisite approval, and are therefore unregulated. Herbert Müller, head of the Islamist Competency Group at Baden-Württemberg's office for national security, said, 'The associations claim to be spearheading the integration of these adolescents into society, but in reality they mean the various Muslim communities.' Milli Görüs is just one example. The group, which the authorities have under surveillance, runs summer camps for some 30,000 Muslim youngsters, according to its own figures. And the Islamic Community of Germany – considered an Islamist organization – devotes much of its work to young people, above all adolescents of Arab origin.[7]

According to Faruk Süen, director of the Centre for Turkish Studies, the boys and girls are increasingly defining themselves by reference to their faith. In his view, this is another consequence of 9/11, since Islam was thenceforth stigmatized by the world at large, sparking a counter-reaction among Muslims. In 2000 Süen's centre conducted a survey. The results showed that 8 per cent of immigrants of Turkish extraction said they were 'very religious'. In 2005, the figure had climbed to 28 per cent, proof that large-scale terrorist attacks in themselves contribute to radicalization. The survey's findings on headscarves are also striking. While only 27 per cent had thought Muslim women should cover their hair in 2000, the number had almost doubled to 47 per cent five years later. The numbers were even higher amongst 18 to 30-year-olds, and amongst VIKZ members. A similar pattern emerged on the topics of dual-sex sports classes and participation in co-educational school trips. Rejected by 19 per cent in 2000, by 2005 the proportion had risen to 30 per cent. Ironically, German judges have often proved the staunchest supporters of Muslim parents, often ruling that the parents' religious freedom is paramount and ignoring the rights of girls to join in normal school activities. As far back as 1993, a federal court found that physical education was not mandatory for a 13-year-old Turkish girl if the classes were not segregated by gender. Bremen's board of education stated that they had already allowed girls to play sports with their heads covered. Allowing further religious exceptions would jeopardize class trips, sex education classes, theatre visits and other extra-curricular activities. It was therefore crucial 'to apply the existing regulations on school attendance ... otherwise the teaching at schools with a high percentage of foreigners would disintegrate completely'.

The judges decided enforced participation represented an infringement of religious freedom, and the school either had to offer single-sex classes or grant the female students a special dispensation. In another regional case, the judges had to decide whether a class excursion was mandatory for a Muslim girl. In their ruling of 2002, they accepted the language of a fatwa issued two years previously. The former chairman of the Islamic Religious Community in Hesse, Amir Zaidan, had stipulated that a Muslim woman not accompanied by a *mahram*, a male blood relative, must not stray more than fifty miles from her home. The opinion came to be known as the 'camel fatwa', because this was the distance a camel caravan could travel in one day during the time of Muhammad. Zaidan's argument was that a woman who travelled farther would run the risk of being raped. The judges recommended sending the 15-year-old brother along as a *mahram*.[8]

Today the impact of Islamic indoctrination is noticeable at almost all schools with a high proportion of Muslim pupils. Fewer and fewer Muslim pupils are taking part in swimming, sports in general, or school trips. In Hamburg this was true of almost half of Muslim girls in 2004. On the Muslim-Markt (Muslim Market) website run by brothers Yavuz and Güerhan Özoguz, parents can download a form for exemption from swimming lessons and find links to key court rulings. In Berlin in 2001, the Islamic Federation, which is believed to be influenced by Milli Görüs, petitioned for the right to give religious instruction in its own institutions, and now teaches some 4,000 pupils. Marion Berning, principal of Berlin's Rixdorf Elementary School, was dismayed by the change in the children: 'The girls hardly said a word and kept their eyes cast downward; the boys were rumbustious.' A teacher at Richard Elementary in the same district gave disturbing evidence to the school committee: German children 'weren't really being tolerated', and 'Christian' was often used as a term of contempt. School is one of the few places where young Muslims come into contact with the non-Islamic environment. As a result, the teachers often see what is happening most clearly.⁹

It is worth examining the ideology of Milli Görüs, both to appreciate the long-term effect of their indoctrination on German Muslim children, and to put the present Turkish leadership in perspective. A Turkish Flash TV interview with former Turkish Prime Minister Necmettin Erbakan (1996–97), who is the founder and leader of the Islamist Milli Görüs, was aired in July 2007. Erbakan is the leader and mentor of the ruling AKP leadership, including both Prime Minister Recep Tayyip Erdogan and President Abdullah Gul – both of whom have in the past been active members of Erbakan's political parties, filling mayoral, ministerial, and parliamentary posts. All of Erbakan's parties have been banned by Turkish court orders. In his campaign to promote his 'Islamist Happiness Party' before the July 2007 elections, Erbakan reiterated his anti-Semitic views. Some of the colourful opinions he expanded upon in intricate detail during the interview include the following: all 'infidel nations' are 'one Zionist entity'; Jews want to rule from Morocco to Indonesia; the Zionists worked for 5,767 years to build a world order in which all money and manpower depend on Jews; the US dollar is Zionist money; the Jewish 'bacteria' must be diagnosed for a cure to be found; Zionists organized the Crusades; Jews founded Protestantism and the capitalist order; and Bush attacked Iraq to build Greater Israel, so Jesus can return.¹⁰

Violence at a Berlin school dominated by Arab and Turkish youths in March 2006, and the nearby slaying of a police officer, fuelled alarm that troubled parts of the German capital are lurching out of control. Police were brought in to help control the situation in the immigrant-dominated Neukölln district, with six officers checking students for weapons. Teachers published a letter saying conditions at their school had become so bad that it should be closed down. They had lost all authority and were now so afraid that they only entered classrooms with a mobile phone so they could call for help in an emergency. 'The mood ... is dominated by aggression, lack of respect and ignorance', said the letter, adding: 'We have reached a dead end and there is no way to turn around.' When reporters went to the school one day, they were pelted with paving stones by masked youths from the schoolyard as the district's mayor stood helplessly at the entrance of the building. 'While sheer chaos dominated behind him, the mayor talked about the failures of the 1968 generation', jeered the *Berliner Kurier* newspaper. Teachers complain that over 83 per cent of the 224 children attending the school are foreigners. The biggest group, 35 per cent, are Arab children mainly from Lebanon and the Palestinian territories. In short, the intifada was imported into Germany, as it was before into the French streets and school system. Turks, with 26 per cent, comprise the second largest group at the Ruetli school. Germany has about 7.3 million foreigners or 9 per cent of the total population, half of them Muslims. A problem in German schools is that Arab male students in particular often refuse to respect the authority of women teachers, education sources told *Deutsche Presse-Agentur*. Peter Struck, education specialist at the University of Hamburg, was blunt about problems posed by foreign students in German schools which separate children headed for university from those who are not, who are educated in less-competitive Hauptschulen.[11]

'It is often Hauptschulen which are hit with difficulties because they have a concentration of problem students and high numbers of foreigners which means that the boys are often being raised in a home environment which glorifies violence', said Peter Struck. Students at the Ruetli Hauptschule were not shy about expressing their views to reporters. 'The German [students] brown nose us, pay for things for us and stuff like that, so that we don't smash in their faces', said a foreign student as quoted by the *Berliner Kurier*. But there are also conflicts between Arab and Turkish students, mirrored in battles between the city's foreign-dominated youth gangs. Integration of foreign youths in Berlin is often poor. Even second and third generation children frequently do not speak fluent German and many fail to complete school – all of which leads to a high jobless rate among immigrant youths. White German families are moving out of districts like Neukölln and into better parts of the 3.4 million metropolis or into new suburbs ringing the city which were swiftly built after the 1989 opening of the Berlin Wall. Unlike the process in Paris, where the Muslim populations live mainly in the *cités* that surround the city, in Berlin it is the German families who escape to the suburbs to avoid the Muslim populations of the city neighbourhoods. The brutal slaying of a police officer in Neukölln shocked the city, where he had been involved in efforts to clean up the notorious drug-dealing. Police arrested two unemployed men of Turkish origin in connection with the killing. Germany has strict gun control laws and the shooting of police officers or use of firearms in murders are both rare.[12]

An Israeli Druze, Samuel Schidem, spoke of his experience in Neukolln, which is also referred to as 'New Gaza' because of the large number of Palestinians who live there. He talked with the youth about their families and each one introduced himself and said where he came from. As Schidem pointed out, 'Even though they were all born in Germany, not one said that he was German. They say that they're from all these Palestinian villages that no longer exist.'[13] European sympathy for the Palestinians in their conflict with Israel has come back to haunt them now that 'integration' of immigrants is perceived as vital for avoiding social unrest and terrorism on their home turf. Four generations have passed since the UN approved the independence of Israel, but Palestinians have yet to be told that no one is regarded as a refugee after the second generation. Their choice is to integrate into their new homes or continue to live off their 'victimhood'.

Many second and third-generation Turks (who constitute some 60 per cent of the Muslim population of 3.5 to four million), Arabs, Bosnians, Iranians, and Afghans, feel alienated from the German mainstream. Part of the alienation emanates from the fact that while Britain, France, the Netherlands and Italy absorbed in their midst Muslims from former colonies who were already somehow versed in their language and culture, the Turks were totally foreign to Germany and its civilization and they recoiled from the sustained efforts of the Germans to Germanize them. Even when both sides realized that Turks were there to stay, the tensions did not relent. Thirty years after 1973, when the Germans put an end to the phenomenon of the 'guest workers' and tried to absorb those already settled in Germany, the high degree of alienation and potential for friction and explosion remains unmitigated. Another reason is the extreme fragmentation of the Muslim community in Germany. Some felt it necessary to have one umbrella organization to bring all the Muslim fragments and factions together, although this creates a two-way problem: no organization can speak for all Muslims; and, conversely, the Federal Government cannot address all Muslims when no single organization represents all of them. In any case, the example of France illustrates that this is not the answer. The French Government established such a structure to represent all the Muslim organizations and imposed elections on them. This proved to be of little value during the 2005 riots. The Muslim Council of Britain, which claims to represent British Muslims, has consistently adopted the most extreme position on most issues.

The major drawback of a Muslim umbrella group is that it serves to perpetuate the Muslims' sense of being on the periphery of society, and fosters 'identity politics' of the worst sort. By finding representatives to act as 'middlemen' in all policy decisions which affect Muslims (although all decisions inevitably affect non-Muslims too), a government in effect politicizes Muslim identity. This has led to the development of identity politics in place of democratic party politics in the UK, to the extent that even after 7/7, Tariq Ramadan called for a reaffirmation of Muslim identity – when it was clear to the entire country that the refusal to identify with the British state first and foremost was a direct contributory factor to the bombings. Western governments should instead aim to stop Muslim immigrants from viewing the affairs of state through an Islamic prism. Since the immigrants themselves chose to make their homes in parliamentary democracies, it is incumbent upon them to express their political views and concerns through party politics, and seek to persuade and influence their fellow-citizens through national rather than separatist channels. There is no shortage of political parties in each western country which immigrants may join. Should they not find a party amenable to their way of thinking, there is nothing to stop them from establishing their own. As things stand in those countries where there are Muslim umbrella organizations, they have become little more than single-issue pressure groups which expect to dictate, for example, the country's foreign policy. Yet their numerical minority status does not justify such expectations. Should a Muslim party participate in national elections, its numerical strength would become apparent, and it would be obliged to submit to the will of the entire electorate. Over the course of a few electoral cycles, the immigrants will learn that politics is conducted via the will of the majority as expressed through the ballot box, and not via threats, intimidation and violence as in their countries of origin.

Efforts were made by the fractious Muslims of Germany to organize so as to maximize their impact and reinforce their demands, and an Islamic Council was established in 2005. But the dichotomies separating the Turks from the Arabs and the Kurds from the Afghanis; the many liberal Muslims, some of whom consider themselves secular and do not even appear in the census figures; and within the Turkish communities, Shi'ite Alevis who constitute 20 per cent of the group and live separately as a constitutionally recognized community, isolated from the rest of the Turks; the gaps between Sufi orders and supporters of the Muslim Brothers; and the vociferous extremists who reject western laws and systems and do not accept the predominance of the German state, versus the majority who do; all that precluded the imposition of some sort of unified structure upon them. They operate over 2,000 houses of prayer, which are in part declared as *waqf* (holy endowment), and manage their own slaughter houses to provide for their halal meat requirements. To circumvent the German custom of recycling cemeteries every thirty years, Turks prefer to send the corpses of the dead to Turkey for burial. Because the first immigrants were blue-collar workers who knew little about religion, the growth of their community had necessitated the importation of clerics from Turkey and other Muslim countries, who bring in their language and culture and are not inclined to let their flock adapt to local circumstances. These imported imams are put at the head of local associations which operate autonomously and contribute to the further fragmentation of the community.

Interior Minister Wolfgang Schäuble brought together his ministry with Islamic groups in pursuit of a 'German Islam'. The Islamic delegation was comprised of representatives from their major organizations, as well as people from 'Islamic civil society', including teachers, entrepreneurs and secular intellectuals. The spokesman of the liberal Islamic group Aleviten wondered why only the conservative Islamic groups were given the privilege of holding a speech during the conference. Schäuble wanted to address religious education and the training of imams. The German Government doesn't financially support Islamic educational institutions, and the majority of the mosques in Germany import clerics from other countries. Since they usually do not speak German, it is difficult for the government to know what they are preaching. Schäuble wanted a new legal relationship between the state and its Muslim citizens that would give Islam more recognition, to persuade them to be more transparent and committed to the constitutional system. Meetings are envisaged every six months to monitor the work of four working groups.[14] But progress will be very difficult to attain. The Central Council of Muslims in Germany accused the secretary general of Chancellor Merkel's Christian Democrats of stoking up prejudices with his remarks in the newspaper *Bild am Sonntag*. Ronald Pofalla wrote that 'It is certainly painful for many Muslims to witness their religion being exploited for violence ... The problem of religiously-motivated violence today is almost exclusively a problem of Islam.'[15]

In April 2007, the leading Muslim organizations joined forces to form an umbrella group, the Coordination Council of Muslims in Germany (KRM). Now the government will have a single negotiating partner on important issues affecting Muslims, assuming the group succeeds in agreeing on a common position. Individual mosques and associations will be welcome to join KRM. The radical Islamic organization Milli Görüs, which has been long under observation by Germany's domestic intelligence agency, is not a founding member of the KRM. However, it is indirectly associated, as an influential member of the Islamic Council.[16] KRM aims to make Islam a 'recognized' religion under federal law, to put Islam 'on an equal footing' with Christian religions in Germany, said Aiman Mazyek, general secretary of the Central Council of Muslims. This could lead to Islamic instruction in German public schools, or even tithing of Muslims through the German tax office, a feature of federal law that provides income for Christian churches. Germany's Jews have received federal funding since 2003. The demand for official recognition of Islam is controversial. Armin Laschet, a conservative Integration Minister in North Rhein-Westphalia, said the new umbrella group simply had too few members to speak for all German Muslims. KRM combines four Islamic organizations – the Islamic Council, the Turkish-Islamic Union for Religious Affairs, the Central Council of Muslims, and the Association of Islamic Culture Centres – but they represent no more than a third of Muslims in Germany. (Some estimates put the number as low as one-tenth.) A spokesman for KRM, Ayyub Axel Köhler, said his group represents a full 85 per cent of German 'mosque associations', but a huge majority of Muslims in Germany aren't listed as members of any association. This lack of organization may be KRM's stumbling block. To tithe Muslims through tax offices in Germany, the group would have to become a public corporation, which – among other prerequisites – requires a membership process. It might be easier to get Islamic instruction into German schools. Köhler has said the point of forming the group was to be 'recognized under German law as a religious association'. Simple federal recognition would be different from public corporation status, and it would force German states to offer classes for Muslim children to match the Christian courses already offered. A spokeswoman for the Interior Ministry said the government will listen to KRM but wants a solution to school integration problems, like the conspicuous absence of girls from swimming or biology classes.[17]

One after the other, European countries have decided to control immigration by putting more obstacles in its way. In March 2006, the German state of Hesse proposed a catalogue of 100 questions to ask prospective immigrants. The idea of a citizenship test is a controversial one in Germany, but instead of the centralized tests of Britain and France, the German federal system permits the states to act individually on such matters, except that if adopted by one of the states, the regulations would have to become practically uniform in all Germany due to the difficulties of enforcing restrictions for passage from one state to the other. The questions that were to confront candidates were considered incomprehensible by many Germans, let alone by immigrants. Unlike the French, who facilitate the entrapment of the naive immigrants, when multiple and 'attractive' options are suggested to them as a matter of choice, the Germans require straightforward positive knowledge, from basic data on their new country (geography, history, political system), to the requisite conditions for becoming a citizen of the country. The tricky questions for

Muslims come when the significance of the Holocaust is evoked or the reaction of the candidate is solicited when the Holocaust is denied in his presence, or when he is asked about the right of Israel to exist. As the immigrants wish to become part of the German economic miracle, they are quizzed about its significance, as they are required to show some basic knowledge about postwar Germany, the circumstances of its partition and unification and the new constitutional arrangements that have emerged to guarantee Germany's civil liberties, democratic system and equality before the law. But the Muslim immigrants are also confronted with the necessity of distancing themselves from limitations on the freedom of movement of women, from discriminatory customs against women, and other traditional mores incompatible with free and democratic societies. Then the mechanics of a working democracy are tested, including the significance of freedom of creed (which is not a matter of course in Islamic lands), tolerance of others' thoughts and expressions even when one's feelings are offended (perhaps a lesson from the cartoon affair), and the obligation to enrol one's children in the public school system for the sake of civic education to absorb these values. Implied in the test is the assumption that the parents have no absolute right to discipline their children by any means they deem fit, and that they cannot force them to marry against their will.[18]

An entire chapter of the questionnaire deals with the political make-up of Germany, including the multi-party system, the transition of government legitimacy and rule – notions that are totally alien to Muslim immigrants. The initiatives of civil society, like lobbies and pressure groups, which seek change via regular political discourse rather than through violence and intimidation, are also almost totally unknown under the authoritarian regimes of the Islamic world. Personal retribution is immediately ruled out by the test, lest imported Muslim mores might wreak havoc on the whole judicial system of fair trial and punishment administered by the state courts. In view of the fact that the new immigrants would be free to circulate throughout the EU, and that European law would also become their own, they are required to show some understanding of that law and of the European institutions which administer it. German literature, culture and science, which are the pride of the nation, must also be reflected in the new candidates' knowledge of the country, a test that even native Germans would find challenging. And finally the immigrants are expected to know the significance of the national colours and the national anthem. Though the test is fair and devoid of attempts to trap the new immigrants, it is no easy trial both of the readiness of the candidate to learn and of his capacity to do so.[19]

Such a test was supported by Chancellor Angela Merkel and other conservatives and, predictably, opposed by leftists who care about their ideology and their liberal pieties more than about the future of their nation. Although drawn up by the state of Hesse, it is being considered for national use. The test is intended to prevent the entry of fundamentalist Muslims, but it is precisely there that it will fail, because a committed Muslim would have every incentive to prepare for it. Coming on the heels of a similar law that was adopted in Holland, this test may become a standard control at the gates of Europe against new Muslim migrants, especially the illegal among them. In Holland, a two-hour video of the test is available and the candidates can view it and even buy it for a mere $80, in addition to the $420 the test costs each time it is taken. In 2000, Germany passed a law permitting German-born children of foreign parents to become citizens if they applied to do so. The law was expanded in 2005, to provide for cultural and linguistic education of applicants for immigration, each of whom is required to take 600 hours of German language instruction and an additional thirty hours in German history, culture and way of life.[20]

In recent years, much has been made of Germany's economic decline. It is certainly true that chronically high unemployment and consistently anaemic growth have long plagued the world's third-largest economy. But for all its problems, the country has remained an extremely comfortable place to live. With German public opinion in early 2006 focused on a strike to protest plans to raise the number of hours worked each week, Muslims were consumed by anger over the printing of caricatures of their prophet in European newspapers. Some of the public discussion turned to the potential for a widening 'clash of civilizations' between the West and Islam. The country's major dailies devoted considerable space to profiling the new head of the Central Council of Muslims in Germany, Ayyub Axel Köhler, a 67-year-old

German convert to Islam. German commentators were generally hopeful that he would serve as a bridge between two cultures. The leftist *Die Tageszeitung* reported that although Köhler condemned the cartoons as 'blasphemous', he called on the world's Muslims not to let themselves be provoked since violence is 'un-Islamic'. Germany's populist daily *Bild* asked the question, 'Must We Fear Islam?', with a massive headline under a photo of angry Iranian protestors burning a German flag. The tabloid then asked Köhler why he preferred Muhammad to Jesus. After diplomatically trying to explain that he didn't find one 'better' than the other, Köhler said he liked the fact that Islam seemed to be more clearly structured than Christianity and didn't have the confusing holy trinity beliefs to deal with. Köhler added that the commotion over the cartoons 'is justified because the caricatures insult Islam'. The conservative daily *Frankfurter Allgemeine Zeitung* called into question his claim that 'humiliation' by the West was the underlying cause of the latest outbreak of hatred, emphasizing that 'this became a cliché long ago. Colonialism is a thing of the past and many Muslim countries never were colonies.' The paper commented that many people in Muslim countries did not have the luxury that Köhler had by living in a democratic western nation where it was perfectly acceptable to change his religion.[21]

A series of press reports reflected the dilemmas that the Federal Government faced, domestically *vis-à-vis* its Muslim population, and externally regarding Muslim countries. *Tagesspiegel* carried a cartoon which depicted the Iranian national team as potential suicide bombers, and the cartoonist had to go into hiding. Another report was carried by *Reuters* from Berlin, concerning a brothel in Cologne which was forced to black out the flags of Saudi Arabia and Iran from a huge World Cup soccer-themed advertising banner after angry Muslims complained and threatened violence. The twenty-four-metre-high by eight-metre-wide banner displayed on the side of the building featured a scantily-clad woman and the slogan: 'The world as a guest of female friends', a variation on the World Cup slogan, 'The world as a guest of friends'. The flags of the thirty-two nations participating in the tournament in June 2006 were displayed. A spokeswoman for the Cologne police confirmed that the Saudis and Iranians 'didn't want these two flags to be associated with this go-go girl on the banner as it's a brothel and it offended their religious feelings. The owner removed the flags even though he wasn't legally obliged to as no crime had been committed.' The problem created resentment among the German population, and was reminiscent of the cartoon affair in that once again 'religious sentiments were hurt' and the Muslims retained sole judgement to pronounce when this was the case. What was worse, they threatened violence and it stands to reason that they would have resorted to it had the brothel owners not given in. Muslims may feel victorious each time the West gives way in this culture war, but in reality it is a Pyrrhic victory which diminishes what is left of their credibility and the respect to which they feel entitled.[22] Muslims may condemn prostitution in the West, but enjoy religiously-sanctioned prostitution themselves. Apart from being permitted to have four wives simultaneously, Sunni Muslims have a practice called *misyar*, common in Egypt and Saudi Arabia. It is a lesser form of relationship between a man and a woman than normal marriage, in which a wife is expected to live with her parents, and her 'husband' can visit her according to an agreed schedule. Shi'as practice *mut'a* in Iran and Iraq. A man and a woman can enter into a temporary marriage, in which they make an irrevocable contract stating the period (which can vary from a day to a number of years) and agree the recompense to the woman.

A German politician from the opposition Green Party triggered a debate by calling for an official Turkish translation of the German national anthem to symbolize how multicultural Germany had become. But conservatives worried it would send the wrong signal about integration. It was hard to imagine many of Germany's 2.6 million or so Turks, even the 840,000 of them with German passports, singing 'Unity, Justice and Freedom for the German Fatherland' on public occasions, even if they have the lyrics in Turkish. But the politician stoked a debate by calling for an official Turkish translation of the third verse of the song – the only verse sung on official occasions because the others, including the first one starting 'Deutschland, Deutschland uber Alles' and the second one ending 'German Women, German Loyalty, German Wine and German Song', are deemed outdated, subject to misinterpretation, and a bit too fervent. The idea echoed the controversial debut of a Spanish version of the US national anthem, 'The Star-Spangled Banner', on some US radio stations in support of millions of illegal immigrants protesting for legal rights. The move was criticized by President Bush who said: 'I think the national anthem ought to be sung in English and I think people who want to be citizens of this country ought to learn English and they ought to learn to sing the national anthem in English.' A leading member of Merkel's conservative Christian Democrats dismissed the idea of a Turkish version of the 'Deutschlandlied'. 'The German national anthem in Turkish would be the opposite of integration. Learning to speak and write the German language is the key qualification. So if we were to offer the German hymn in Turkish, it would give the wrong signal for all immigrants living here.'[23]

A measure of dissonance in western thinking about immigration is discernable in media coverage. In the same breath, readers are told that European countries need new immigrants in order to bolster the workforce – and that many immigrants are dependent on welfare payments or turn to a life of crime. So, where is the benefit in importing people who are dependent on welfare, or become a drain on resources by expanding the prison population? If western governments cannot become resigned to shrinking populations, one solution would be to offer inducements to increase the birth rate (but it is likely that immigrants would also take advantage of this facility). Otherwise, it is necessary to be very discerning with the sources of immigration. Both Hindus and the Chinese are disposed to integrate with enthusiasm, and their religions are neither fanatical nor hateful. They are motivated primarily by economic improvement (which will inevitably benefit their new homes), and not by a religious fervour which is singularly antithetical to western civilization. There are also many minorities who were converted to Christianity in previous centuries by European missionaries, or have been Christians of even longer standing, (in, for example, Iran, Iraq, Egypt, Pakistan, Afghanistan, Indonesia, China, Algeria, Sudan and the Palestinian territories) who are presently persecuted by the Islamic societies in which they live. At times the persecution is meted out by their governments and at others by their neighbours. Yet they have been shamefully abandoned to their fate by Europe today. Coverage of their predicament is extremely limited in the media, since their persecutors are neither American nor European, and are not white. It also attests to the low level of expectations of Muslim societies that they are rarely held to account for the intolerance they evince to their non-Muslim minorities. This is what should be offending Muslims, and not some cartoons about their prophet. The demographic situation in Europe being what it is today, and with very little prospect of change on the horizon, the difficulties abound, the dilemmas of all European governments become increasingly insoluble, and the daily clashes between the host and guest cultures unavoidable.

In Australia, where political correctness has not completely stifled debate, the leader of the Christian Democratic Party, Reverend Fred Nile, said priority in immigration should be given to Christians wanting to flee persecution in Muslim countries. Nile, a member of the New South Wales upper house, has called for a ten-year moratorium on Muslim immigration. There had been no serious study of the potential effects on Australia of the more than 300,000 Muslims who are already here, and he wanted a comparison with the examples of the Netherlands and France, where the Muslim minority has become large enough to 'flex its muscle'. Nile said Coptic Christians from Egypt had approached him on the campaign trail for the March 2007 state election to complain that persecution by Muslims seemed to have followed them to Australia. Muslim embassy staff also often discriminated against Christian visa applicants, he said. 'I don't want Muslims working in our embassies overseas dictating who comes to Australia. Let's give priority to persecuted Christians. Muslims aren't persecuted in Muslim countries, Christians are.'[24]

Government officials argue that Germany must absorb its immigrants rather than isolate them in ghettos where they may fall prey to Islamic fundamentalist groups. 'The government sees it as a security issue', said Tanja Wunderlich, an immigration researcher for the German Marshall Fund think tank. Although there is widespread agreement on the need for more integration, opinion is divided on how to bring it about. Germany has one of the lowest birth rates in the world. Even if the annual influx were to double to 200,000, the population would still shrink by 8.5 per cent by 2050. The children and grandchildren of 1960s 'guest workers' often speak little German and have limited chances of finding a job. Unemployment among immigrants is 26 per cent. Their chances of discovering a role model are just as remote. 'School for them', said Petra Eggebrecht, former director of a school, 'is simply a place to fight for peer recognition, where young criminals become idols.' Young people are also easy targets for Islamic organizations. Children defiantly greet visitors outside their schools in Arabic and not German.[25]

When the government tries to intercede on behalf of Muslim women, its caring measures backfire. Every year, thousands of teenage girls, very few past the age of consent, arrive in Germany from Turkey for arranged marriages and lives of domestic servitude enforced by tradition, isolation and fear. It's a thriving one-way trade that has been going on for more than three decades, and it sits at the core of Europe's greatest predicament today: the widening gulf between an increasingly post-modern society and its often pre-modern immigrants. The subject of foreign brides came to the fore in the German media in 2005 when a 28-year-old Turkish man took his 11-year-old wife to a registry office in Düsseldorf to get her an ID card. On that occasion, the girl was detained by the authorities and deported to Turkey. But according to the Turkish-born German sociologist Necla Kelek, that is more often the exception than the rule. In two bestselling books, *The Foreign Bride* and *The Lost Sons*, she has exposed Germans to the lives of their Turkish community in a way few of her German-born peers would have dared. For obvious reasons, the most prominent Muslim critics of contemporary Muslim societies – Ayaan Hirsi Ali in Holland, Irshad Manji in Canada, Seyran Ates in Germany – are women. 'It's the women who have felt the relapse into shari'a the most', explained Kelek. 'The boys might be slaves to their families, but on the streets they are free, and besides they can always look forward to a wife they can suppress. It's the women who explode.' Kelek herself came to Germany as a child in the late 1960s with her family, which initially sought to integrate into German society. She learned German, made German friends, and followed the German *Leitkultur*, the 'lead culture'. But things changed in the 1970s. Previous Turkish immigrants had generally come from cities and were relatively secular, but later arrivals were overwhelmingly from the countryside and traditional in their outlook. The rise of fundamentalist Islam also had an effect. Religion became the primary marker of individual identity. Codes of family honour and standards of female purity, to which Kelek's family had once been relatively indifferent, became important.[26]

When Kelek was a rebellious 17-year-old, her father abandoned the family after knocking down her door with an axe. It was, she says, one of the happiest days of her life: 'We turned on all the lights and played music. We were free.' A similar scenario between a rebellious daughter and her Turkish father might end differently these days. 'Honour killings' are usually perpetrated by a brother, acting at his father's behest. The Turkish community tends to treat these young killers as heroes. Such violence is integral to what Kelek calls the Turkish community's 'organized self-marginalization'. The tender age of the foreign brides, for instance, isn't just a matter of depraved sexual tastes. 'They want a girl with closed eyes', Kelek explains. The younger the bride, the more likely she is to be submissive to her husband, dependent on his family, ignorant and terrified of the world outside. Today, every second Turkish woman who has a child in a German school is herself a foreign bride. Two-thirds of these children arrive in school not speaking a word of German. The educational system bends over backward for them, providing religious instruction in Turkish or Arabic and excluding girls from physical education, sex education and other subjects where Islamic mores might be offended. The results have been dismal: 60 per cent of Turkish children leave school without any kind of certificate. The Turkish community is not the only party at fault, however. Until 2005, few Turks, including those whose families had lived in Germany for generations, could obtain citizenship. Successive governments compensated for their refusal to grant citizenship by allowing the Turkish community to do more or less as it pleased. This explains the 11-year-old bride, and with a parent's consent, Turkish law will allow even a 9-year-old girl to marry. Had German law applied, the age threshold would have been 16. Furthermore, Kelek says Germans 'want to do everything right that they previously did wrong. This is especially the case with the Muslim community because it's such a different culture, such a different religion. Germans are trying to prove to themselves just how tolerant they are.' This is why Kelek's proposals for legislation that would require foreign brides to learn

German before their arrival and bar entry to those under 21, faced opposition by the Social Democrats and the Green Party. For too many self-described progressives, limitless tolerance of 'the other' has replaced the defence of individual liberty as proof of virtue. Kelek sees it differently. Europe, she says, 'has to fight for its values', not least by putting some hard questions to its increasingly alien and belligerent Muslim communities: 'Why aren't your women free? Why aren't your children free?'[27]

A recent ruling in Germany by a judge in Frankfurt who cited the Qur'an underscores the dilemma the country faces. A 26-year-old German woman of Moroccan origin was terrified of her violent Moroccan husband and wanted a speedy divorce. German law requires a one-year separation before a divorce can be completed, and exceptions for an expedited process are only granted in extreme situations. Judge Christa Datz-Winter refused an expedited divorce, arguing the woman should have 'expected' that her husband, who had grown up in a country influenced by Islamic tradition, would exercise the 'right to use corporal punishment' which his religion grants him. The judge even quoted the Qur'an as grounds for her decision. In Sura 4, verse 34, she wrote, the Qur'an contains 'both the husband's right to use corporal punishment against a disobedient wife and the establishment of the husband's superiority over the wife'.[28] The reactions to the ruling were severe from all sides of the political and social spectrum. 'In my work educating sexist and short-sighted Muslim men', asked Michaela Sulaika Kaiser of the Network for Muslim Women, 'do I now have to convince German courts that women are also people on the same level with men and that they, like any other human, have the right to be protected from physical and psychological violence?'[29]

Out of a sense of misguided tolerance, said women's rights activist and lawyer Seyran Ates, judges treat the values of Muslim subcultures as a mitigating circumstance and thus pave the way for a gradual encroachment of fundamentalist Islam in Germany's parallel Muslim world. Frankfurt family court judge Datz-Winter was removed from the case of the Moroccan couple and the courts thus proved themselves capable of acting responsibly. In many other cases, however, the liberal nature of the constitutional state has been misused. The debate now revolves around the question of how much assimilation the constitutional state can or must demand from immigrants. For far too long, German judges raised little opposition to the strategy employed by Islamic groups to demand their supposed religious freedom in court. But 'giving preferential treatment to groups violates the principle of equal treatment in a secular legal system', argued Johannes Kandel from the centre-left Social Democrat-aligned Friedrich Ebert Foundation. While freedom of religious expression is guaranteed under the German constitution, it is no 'basic right deluxe', in the opinion of Udo Di Fabio, a judge on Germany's Federal Constitutional Court, the country's highest judicial institution. Rather, it is one of many constitutional rights, and one that constantly has to be weighed against other rights. The slaughter of Theo van Gogh highlighted the clash of cultures in neighbouring Netherlands, drawing Germany's attention to conditions that many had preferred to downplay as 'cultural diversity'. Suddenly Germans were waking up to the creeping Islamicization on the fringes of their society, and to the existence of parallel worlds in German cities. Until only a few years ago all of this was happening with the support of the state and its bureaucrats.[30]

German judges were accommodating to Muslims in many minor rulings. In 2002, the state labour court in Hamm ruled that prayer breaks are permissible during working hours, but must be coordinated with the employer. A company had reprimanded a Muslim worker who wanted to pray several times a day, while he demanded his rights, citing religious freedom. Also in 2002, the Federal Constitutional Court issued a landmark decision allowing halal butchering. Muslims can also often count on the support of German courts when it comes to building mosques. As far back as 1992, the Federal Administrative Court ruled that neighbours must 'fundamentally accept' being woken before sunrise with the Muslim call to prayer from minarets in traditional mosques. Attempts by cities to appeal decisions favouring mosques have rarely succeeded. As the courts saw it, the principle of equal treatment also applied to those with little interest in equality. Muslims can also often depend on courts that deal with laws governing the press. In May 2006 a judge barred the ZDF public television network from referring to an imam as a 'hate preacher' on its website. And yet Imam Yakub Tasci had characterized Germans during his sermons as the equivalent of 'stinking infidels'. According to the court, Tasci had not been referring to Germans in particular but atheists in general. In 2003, Fereshda Ludin, a teacher, sued for the right to wear a headscarf in the classroom. The Federal Constitutional Court ruled that it is up to the states to enact the appropriate legislation if they wanted to ban teachers from wearing the headscarf, which hasn't happened. In 1984, a court upheld a Muslim woman's demand that she be allowed to wear her headscarf on photos for official identification documents. In one case, a judge argued that whether the Qur'an does in fact require certain behaviour is immaterial, and that a perceived precept is already sufficient. In 2004, the Federal Ministry for Social Affairs informed German health insurance agencies that, 'polygamous marriages must be recognized if they are legal under the laws of the native country of the individuals in question'. So Muslim men from countries where polygamy is legal – like Morocco, Algeria and Saudi Arabia – could add a second wife to their government health insurance policies without having to pay an additional premium. Such excesses are rare today. Judges are increasingly accepting the responsibility that legal expert and Islam scholar Mathias Rohe demands of them: to use the law 'to signal to a society what is allowed and what is not'. In 2005 a judge ordered that a Muslim boy could be required to attend school swimming sessions together with girls, but fundamental social change has yet to follow.[31]

Muslim organizations are also beginning to establish their own schools, arguing that they are integrative. Domestic intelligence kept a close watch on the King Fahd Academy in Bonn for years. The mosque and associated school, opened in 1995, were criticized because some of the schoolbooks they used glorified jihad. The late King Fahd established academies in London, Washington, Moscow, Bonn and Bosnia, all of which subscribe to the strict Wahhabi interpretation of Islam promoted by the Saudi regime. The London academy has received a good deal of negative exposure recently, thereby providing a window into how all the sister academies currently operate. It was opened in 1985 for the offspring of Saudi diplomats, and is owned, funded and run by the Saudis, charging fees of up to £1,500 annually for day students. But the overwhelming majority of its 750 pupils are now the children of British Muslims, including some of the children of Abu Hamza and Abu Qatada. A former teacher at the academy, Colin Cook, said textbooks used by children as young as 5 describe Jews as 'repugnant' and 'apes' and Christians as 'pigs'. Having poisoned the minds of pupils with lessons in hate, it is not surprising that pupils have allegedly been heard saying they want to 'kill Americans', praising 9/11 and idolizing Bin Laden as their 'hero'. The academy in Bonn, meanwhile, has been singled out by the German intelligence services as a meeting place for activists linked to terrorism. Cook, a Muslim convert, taught English at the school for nineteen years until he was dismissed in December 2006. Cook claimed he was fired after exposing the school for covering up cheating by children in the national 16+ exams and is bringing a tribunal claim for unfair dismissal, race discrimination and victimization. He also alleged that when he complained to school management about the content of the curriculum and questioned whether it complied with British laws, he was told: 'This is not England. It is Saudi Arabia.' The school denied all his allegations and claimed he was dismissed for misconduct. The school, which teaches pupils up to the age of 18, devotes around half of lessons to religious education and teaches almost all classes in Arabic, with boys and girls following different curricula. In the past, parents have claimed that the school is teaching British children fundamentalist Islam while giving girls an inferior education. One such parent is Dr Mai Yamani, the daughter of the former Saudi Oil Minister Sheikh Ahmed Zaki Yamani. Ofsted, which inspected the school in March 2006, made a series of criticisms of its performance and refused to give it full registration as an independent school. Cook said that most of the school's teachers are Saudis who speak little or no English, and that textbooks used on the Saudi curriculum, which are published by the Saudi Government's Ministry of Education, prove that the academy 'is institutionally racist'. Pupils are taught that religions including Christianity and Judaism are 'worthless'.[32]

Mai Yamani, a research fellow at the Royal Institute of International Affairs, had two daughters at the school, but removed them when she became uncomfortable with the education they were receiving:

I moved my eldest daughter at the age of seven. Her new school said that, in their opinion, she had been 'totally untaught' to that point ... The books they taught the girls from kept going on about idolatry and sin and how to avoid it. It was about the fires of hell, torture in the grave and how to make sure that your ways are not those of the 'infidel'. The school is trying to make sure that the Saudis who go there abide by the system of state control in Saudi Arabia. The method is 'loyalty to the system and hostility to the outsider'. Three years ago I interviewed some of the pupils for a book and some of them were talking as if they didn't live in London at all.

Another parent complained that 'only one lesson in six is taken in English. The children would not have the standard to even read the paper by the time they reach A-level [at 18]. It has arrived at a situation where the school seems to be saying: "This is the only correct version of Islam." It's such a fundamentalist approach.' A recent review of the curriculum concluded that almost a fifth of lesson plans contained tracts preaching anti-Western and anti-Semitic views.[33] Between 2004, when these allegations first surfaced, and 2007 when Cook presented fresh allegations, no action was taken. After the new adverse exposure, the school, which receives more than £4 million a year from the Saudi royal family, insisted it had 'ripped out' the offending pages from all textbooks. In one chapter, an early Islamic scholar is quoted as saying 'the monkeys are the Jews and the pigs are the Christian infidels at Jesus's table'. Sumaya Alyusuf, the principal, denied that teachers had used the offensive chapters, which had been 'taken out context'. It has been reported that the school dropped the official Saudi curriculum and now teaches the international baccalaureate, the Swiss-accredited curriculum used worldwide.[34] While the academy sought to clear its reputation as a tolerant faith school, three people claiming to be former pupils accused it of being racist, on the website facebook.com. One contributor, aged 21, claimed he was told that 'people of other religions were not on a par as human beings with us'.[35]

Further controversial details emerged about the King Fahd Academy. In his statement to the employment tribunal, Cook claimed that non-Saudis such as himself were viewed as 'second-class Muslims', adding that in Saudi Arabia, 'non-Saudis have very few human rights'. As chief inspector for schools David Bell had complained, Islamic schools were a potential threat to Britain's sense of national identity – teaching a narrow curriculum that failed to prepare children for life in a multicultural democracy.[36] Even the ordinary Qur'an schools, which exist at practically every German mosque, often forcefully draw their roughly 70,000 children and adolescents back into the world of their grandfathers. Women are brought up to serve and obey. Boys are alternately spoiled and beaten, as custom requires. According to a study conducted by the Lower Saxony Criminology Research Institute, physical abuse of boys is more than twice as common in Turkish families as in their German counterparts. And girls from conservative families say that their fathers and brothers have the right to hit them. Laws and court decisions do send signals, and if the wrong signals are sent, this also affects families.[37]

Young women routinely come to support centres after being married off against their will, but such arranged marriages are neither illegal nor regulated in Germany. According to a 2004 study commissioned by the Federal Ministry for Family Affairs, 17 per cent of Turkish women surveyed considered their marriage forced. German lawmakers have repeatedly considered raising the age at which 'guest workers' are allowed to come to Germany as a way of protecting young girls against forced marriages. Measures other countries established to protect young women are non-existent in Germany. In Britain, for example, women who are worried that they could be forced into marriages while on vacation can leave information with the authorities before leaving the country. If they fail to report back by a prearranged date, officials, including those at the British Foreign Office, begin searching for them. The literature of conservative Muslims demonstrates that it is vulnerable women who are the victims of the accommodations extended to Islam. In his book *Women in Islam*, Imam Mohammed Kamal Mustafa of Spain recommends how women should be beaten. A disproportionately high percentage of women who flee to women's shelters are Muslim. According to the Federal Office of Criminal Investigation on 'honour killings', women are often slaughtered in the most gruesome ways for violating archaic concepts of morality. In 2005, Hatun Sürücü, a young Berlin woman, was killed because she was 'living like a German'. In her family's opinion, this was a crime only her death could expiate. Her youngest brother executed her by shooting her several times at a Berlin bus stop. But because prosecutors were unable to prove that the family had planned the act, only the killer himself could be tried for murder and, because he was underage, he was given a reduced sentence. The rest of the family left the courtroom in high spirits, and the father rewarded the convicted boy with a watch. In 2003 the Frankfurt District Court handed a mild sentence against a Turkish-born man who had stabbed his German-born wife to death. She had disobeyed him and demanded a divorce. The court argued that one could not automatically assume that the man's motives were contemptible. He had acted 'out of an excessive rage', 'based on his foreign sociocultural moral concepts'. The divorce would have violated 'his family and male honour derived from his Anatolian moral concepts'. The court argued that the fact that his actions were based on his Muslim moral concepts served as a mitigating factor. The Federal Constitutional Court reversed the decision in 2004. Family attorneys say that social workers have even been known to turn away girls who have turned to youth welfare officials for fear of being forced into a marriage. The social workers' response to the girls is that that sort of thing is 'normal with you people'.[38]

Lawyer Seyran Ates closed her practice and went underground after receiving death threats for defending Muslim women who have been forced into marriage. Ates said police had refused to protect her despite threats against her life, including a shooting incident in which a colleague was killed and she was seriously injured. Police denied that they had been approached by Ates for protection. Her withdrawal from public life as one of the country's most outspoken critics of the subjugation of Muslim women has been called 'alarming' by politicians. A Turkish Kurd who moved to Germany as a child, she has been the repeated target of insults and attacks by the families of many Turkish and Kurdish women in Germany.[39]

Western commentary on the social ills of Muslims is very tame in comparison to what Muslims themselves are willing to state. In an article entitled 'The Arab Man is the Problem, The [Arab] Woman Is the Solution', Israeli Arab author and poet Salman

Masalha was harshly critical of the situation of women in Arab countries, and argued that women's equality would put an end to the backwardness of Arab and Islamic society. His assessment of 'honour killings' is far more strident than anything published in the western press: 'The Arab man's insistence upon controlling the destiny, and particularly the body, of the woman, is nothing but an attempt to cling to honour that he does not possess and of which he is deprived, socially and politically.' Commenting on the export of 'honour killings' from Arab countries, Masalha added: 'We often hear of so-called 'honour' crimes among the people of the [Arab] diasporas in Scandinavia, Britain, France, and other countries. These crimes, that traverse seas and continents, take place because Arab societies developed within a patriarchal mentality at their primitive, animal stage. And if these things occur in Europe, then they clearly occur with greater frequency in the Arab world.'[40]

EU member states should stop Muslim women from wearing the full face veil, Schäuble has declared. 'The full veil runs contrary to the achievements of the European civilization', he told reporters after a meeting with the European Parliament's Civil Liberties Committee. In an echo of the pronouncement by Jack Straw, the former British Foreign Secretary in 2006, Schäuble said, 'You cannot communicate with the person wearing it [the full veil]. Our communication is also to a great extent non-verbal.' Schäuble said he does not favour introducing European laws on the wearing of a full face veil, but it would be an 'incorrect understanding of tolerance if we were not brave enough to express ourselves on that'.[41]

The *Washington Post* reported a growing number of vocal non-believers in Europe and the US. Many analysts trace the rise of the 'non-religious movement' to the 9/11 terrorist attacks. The sight of religious fanatics killing 3,000 people caused many to begin questioning, and rejecting, all religion. 'This is overwhelmingly the topic of the moment', said Terry Sanderson, president of the National Secular Society of Britain. 'Religion in this country was very quiet until September 11, and now it is at the centre of everything.' Since 9/11, several religiously inspired attacks and plots have shaken Europe. Many Europeans are angry at demands to use taxpayer money to accommodate Islam. Along with calls for prayer rooms in police stations, foot baths in public places and funding for Islamic schools and mosques, expensive legal battles have broken out over the niqab, which some devout women seek to wear in classrooms and court. Attempts to pretend that all religions present a threat are now *de rigueur*, and the *Washington Post* duly mentions 'Christian fundamentalist groups who want to halt certain science research, reverse abortion and gay rights and teach creationism rather than evolution in schools'. Sanderson himself perpetuates this intellectual dishonesty, saying: 'There is a feeling that religion is being forced on an unwilling public, and now people are beginning to speak out against what they see as rising Islamic and Christian militancy.'[42]

One group of human rights activists and non-believers is attracting attention in Europe: the Council of Ex-Muslims. Founded in Germany in February 2007, the group now has a few hundred members and an expanding number of chapters across the continent. Its Iranian-born founder Mina Ahadi is under police protection after receiving death threats. Ahadi set up the group with forty others to highlight the difficulties of renouncing the Islamic faith which she believes to be misogynist, and to help women renounce the Islamic faith if they feel oppressed by its laws. She wants the group to form a counterweight to Muslim organizations that she says don't adequately represent Germany's secular-minded Muslim immigrants. She is critical of Islam in Germany and of the way the German Government deals with it. Many Muslim organizations like the Central Council of Muslims in Germany or Milli Görüs engage in politics or interfere in people's everyday lives. Since she believes it is not possible to modernize Islam, her goal is to form a counterweight to the Muslim organizations.[43]

The latest comprehensive attempt to achieve a modernization of Islam was introduced in December 2006. A ten-point charter urging Muslims to abide by national laws and renounce extremist interpretations of the Qur'an was launched at the European Parliament. The Muslim Charter asks Islamic institutions to revise and amend Qur'anic verses that might be interpreted as promoting jihad against non-Muslims.[44] But the chances of engaging any serious Muslim leadership to undertake such a revolution is equivalent to asking the Vatican or the Chief Rabbinate of Israel to tamper with verses from the Bible. Unlike Judaism and Christianity, however, which do not educate to hatred, terrorism and jihad, in Islam such an unlikely revolution is a prerequisite to change. Even if it is impossible to alter a holy scripture, Muslim revolutionaries who espouse change should and could distance themselves from it.

Hoping to change the terms of debate about Islam in Europe, the Council of Ex-Muslims also launched a Scandinavian group in May and a British chapter in June 2007. The activists, many of them Iranian exiles, support the freedom to criticize religion and the end to what they call 'religious intimidation and threats'. Maryam Namazie, head of the British group, who left Iran in 1980, complained that 'too many things in the media and government policies have been geared to pandering to the political Islamic movements and Islamic organizations'. Namazie said the British group had about twenty-five activists.[45] She and other leaders of the council held a news conference in The Hague to launch the Dutch chapter on 11 September, the sixth anniversary of the terrorist attacks in the US. 'We are all atheists and non-believers, and our goal is not to eradicate Islam from the face of the earth', but to make it a private matter that is not imposed on others, she said.[46] Ehsan Jami, 22, founder of the Committee for Ex-Muslims in the Netherlands, has been forced into hiding after a series of death threats and a recent attack. A Labour Party councillor, Jami said the movement would declare war on radical Islam, adding: 'Shari'a schools say that they will kill the ones who leave Islam. In the West people get threatened, thrown out of their family, beaten up. In Islam you are born Muslim. You do not even choose to be Muslim. We want that to change, so that people are free to choose who they want to be and what they want to believe in.' Shari'a calls for the death of an apostate, and the *hadith* cites a special reward in paradise for the killer of apostates. Jami said the launch date was chosen 'to make a clear statement that we no longer tolerate the intolerance of Islam, the terrorist attacks'. He continued: 'In 1965 the Church in Holland made a declaration that freedom of conscience is above hanging on to religion, so you can choose whether you are going to be a Christian or not. What we are seeking is the same thing for Islam.' Jami, who has compared the rise of radical Islam to the threat from Nazism in the 1930s, is receiving only lukewarm support from his party which traditionally relies upon Muslim votes.[47]

The planned construction of a 2,000-capacity mosque with twin minarets that will reach 170 feet near a major Christian landmark, Cologne Cathedral, has sparked a furious row in Germany. 'It's not a popular plan ... I know about Londonistan and I don't want that here', said Joerg Uckermann, the district's deputy mayor. Ralph Giordano, a prominent historian of the Third Reich, who opposes the mosque, stated that he had received death threats for his opinions, adding: 'What kind of a state are we in that I can face a fatwa in Germany?' For Uckermann, who belongs to Merkel's CDU party, Giordano's comments smashed a long-held taboo in Germany. 'Giordano broke down the wall. Before if you criticized this monstrous mosque you were a Nazi.' Prelate Johannes Bastgen, Dean of Cologne Cathedral, remarked: 'We live in a land of religious freedom. I would be very glad if the same principle existed in Muslim countries.'[48] Giordano has argued that the mosque project sent the 'wrong signal' and claimed that the integration of Muslims in Germany had failed. He objected to women wearing burqas on German streets, whom he described as resembling 'human penguins'. Giordano's remarks provoked accusations that he was making common cause with Nazis and racists, although the 84-year-old's own first-hand experience of Nazi racial persecution as the son of a Jewish mother is the core theme of his writings. But according to the Turkish-born author and Cologne resident Arzu Toker, there are also many opponents of the mosque project to be found among the people whom Germany's Islamic associations are presumed to represent. Toker, a critic of the increasing influence of the Islamic associations in German public life, co-chairs the Central Council of Ex-Muslims of Germany. Asked by the German monthly *Konkret* whether she was surprised that Giordano's remarks provoked such vehement reactions, Toker replied:

> No. In the first place, Germans have a problem with Jews. When a well-known Jewish personality like Ralph Giordano says something, every word is placed under the microscope ... In the second place, Islamists have a problem with Jews.

> If you take a look in the Qur'an, you will find that there are maybe thirty anti-Christian verses, whereas there are hundreds of anti-Jewish verses. Animosity toward Jews is a central element of the Islamic faith.

Toker's primary opposition to the mosque is based on what is taught inside them:

> There is not a single verse in the Qur'an that sets out the requirement of a mosque. Muslims could just as well pray in a park, for example. The building is not necessary. Mosques first came into being when Muslims conquered Christian and Jewish territories where there were already churches or synagogues and they converted them into mosques. What is going on in Cologne is a demonstration of power. The Islamic associations are on the rise. They already have a seat at the negotiating table with the government and now they think they are powerful enough to have a mosque in the middle of town ... Five times a day, one is called to prayer with the words 'There is only one Allah and Muhammad is his prophet.' The call to prayer is thus necessarily tied to the negation of Christianity. How can that be acceptable? The Muslims could say 'No, we don't deny Christianity', but they are completely incapable of critical self-reflection. Besides, nothing positive has ever come out of the mosques: calls for social integration, for instance. On the contrary, what comes out of the mosques is always alienated from the surrounding society.[49]

In an observation that mirrors the British experience with the Muslim Council of Britain, Toker asserts that the image of the German Muslim – thanks in part to Interior Minister Schäuble – is completely and utterly determined by the 30,000 organized Muslims in the Islamic associations. This effectively marginalizes the vast majority of Muslims who live in Germany. Their assertiveness led some Muslim representatives to threaten a boycott of an 'integration summit' in July 2007 in response to a new immigration law which they say discriminates against them. The government is insisting that Muslim wives who join their husbands in

Germany should have a basic knowledge of the language – a demand that has irritated parts of the Turkish community.[50]

Opposition to mosque construction is increasing throughout Europe. In September 2007, an Italian senator called for a 'Pig Day' protest against the planned construction of a mosque in northern Italy. Roberto Calderoli of the anti-immigrant Northern League Party said he was ready to bring his own pig to 'defile' the site where the mosque is due to be built in Bologna. 'I am making myself and my pig available for a walk at the site where they want to build the mosque', Calderoli, who is a deputy speaker of Italy's Senate, said. Tensions flare regularly over the site of new mosques to serve a growing Muslim population, and are becoming more frequent because of the misuse of mosques for non-religious purposes. Locals protested near Genoa over the planned construction of a mosque which they said would be offensive because of its proximity to a church. In December 2006, protesters left a pig's head outside a mosque being built in Tuscany. In July 2007, police arrested an imam on suspicion of leading a terrorism 'training school' in a mosque in central Italy. After that arrest, the Northern League called for all existing mosques – most in old garages or converted factories and warehouses – to be closed for security checks.[51]

Stunning figures from official reports in Germany in May 2006 unsettled many Germans. For while the German authorities seem to believe that they bought immunity by not participating in the Iraq War, and the media needlessly bring Israel into the equation in order to provide 'plausible' explanations, the numbers continue to sound the alarm. A report by Germany's domestic security agency, the Verfassungsschutz, said that the number of Islamic extremists based in Germany increased slightly to 32,100 in 2005, but the country faces a 'far lower threat' of terrorist attacks than states which took part in the Iraq War. The biggest Islamist group is Milli Görüs, a Turkish movement with 26,500 members. Other groups are Hamas with about 300 members, Hezbollah with 900 and the Muslim Brotherhood with 1,300. The Verfassungsschutz did not give figures for the number of al-Qa'ida members based in Germany. 'Even though the degree to which Germany is threatened is clearly lower than for those states which took part in the Iraq War, it must be noted that Germany is still seen ... as a helper of the US and Israel', said the report. Former German Chancellor Gerhard Schröder declined to send troops to Iraq in 2003, a decision kept in place by Merkel.[52] That the German authorities and their European counterparts apologize and justify their policies by pointedly distancing themselves from the US and Israel, only serves to demonstrate how supposedly independent nations have mortgaged their futures to their Muslim minorities.

According to intelligence sources, three women were prevented from travelling to Iraq after one of them planned to self-explode. The women, who have close contacts with Islamists in Germany, came to the attention of intelligence agencies after one of them had announced on an internet site that she intended to blow herself and her child up in Iraq. The women had contacts with sympathizers of Ansar al-Islam, a terrorist group linked to al-Qa'ida and suspected of smuggling 'suicide bombers' from Germany to Iraq. The group is also suspected of raising money to attack the US-led forces in Iraq. While it has become routine for foreign terrorists to be used in Iraq, the introduction of European citizens could become a dangerous trend. In November 2005 a female Belgian convert exploded herself near Baghdad.[53]

Asked by *Der Tagesspiegel* how dangerous the 'Islamist terror' threat was for Germany, Federal Prosecutor Kay Nehm said: 'I have the impression we're sitting on a powder keg. The attacks on Madrid and London showed that dissatisfied migrants living in a country can become radicalized without the threat they pose being recognized in time.' Nehm, whose office is responsible for investigating suspected acts of terror against the state, said there was an increasing tendency for perpetrators to act alone, which made it harder for authorities to apprehend them.[54]

A study published in 2006 referred to a 'spiral of conflict' starting in Germany, with Germans doubting the western and Islamic worlds can peacefully coexist. In spite of official attempts to promote dialogue among religions, distrust of Islam continues to grow. According to an Allensbach study commissioned by *Frankfurter Allgemeine Zeitung*, 'Germans are increasingly of the opinion that a lasting, peaceful coexistence with the Islamic world will not be possible.' Some 56 per cent of Germans said they believed a 'clash of cultures' already exists, according to the survey's authors Elisabeth Noelle and Thomas Petersen. The Germans were also less willing to show tolerance to Muslims. Germans' esteem for Islam has been falling since 9/11, with 83 per cent of the 1,076 Germans questioned in the survey agreeing with the statement that Islam is driven by fanaticism. Seventy-one per cent said they believed Islam to be 'intolerant'. When asked what they associate with the word 'Islam', 91 per cent of respondents connected the religion to the discrimination of women, and 61 per cent called Islam 'undemocratic'. Eight per cent of Germans associated 'peacefulness' with Islam. About 40 per cent of Germans were willing to limit the constitutionally guaranteed freedom of religion if constricting the practice of Islam would lead to fewer violent Muslims choosing to live in Germany. Fifty-six per cent agreed with the statement, 'If some Muslim countries forbid building churches, then it should be forbidden to build mosques here.' There was one encouraging result for those working on intercultural dialogue: two-thirds of Germans said they believed Islam does not pose a threat, but that radical, politically motivated individuals are behind extremist acts.[55]

Germany, like other European countries, does not only fear Muslim rage domestically, but also a possible backlash from the Muslim world at large for any action to contain the Islamic threat within. Hundreds of Islamists took to the streets in Islamabad in June 2006 to protest the death of a 28-year-old Pakistani, Amir Cheema, in German police custody in Berlin. The protesters demanded Pakistan's Government expel Germany's ambassador from the country and announce an economic boycott of Berlin (imagine, poor and deprived Pakistan boycotting one of the wealthiest nations on earth!) as a mark of protest at what they called Cheema's murder at the hands of the German police. Thanks to the limitless endurance evinced by the West, Muslims have become accustomed to a state of affairs whereby they can, brutally and without due process, kill, execute or murder others at will. But any Muslim who is arrested in the West becomes a 'martyr', his prosecutors are 'murderers', and the system under which justice is administered is 'oppressive' and 'Islamophobic'. A protest organized by Jamiat Ahl-e-Sunnat (Society of the Adherents of the Sunna, JAS), a grouping of Pakistani Sunni

Muslims, was told that the German police subjected Amir Cheema to torture in prison. Germany offered Pakistan full cooperation in the inquiry and delayed the autopsy till Pakistani officials could attend. The police said Cheema hanged himself with a noose made from his own clothing, and a pathologist found that the injuries were consistent with suicide. He was arrested in Berlin in March 2006 after he reportedly tried to enter the offices of *Die Welt* and was accused of trying to kill its editor, Roger Koeppel, because the newspaper had printed the Muhammad cartoons. German police said they had also recovered a knife from Cheema. The protesters in Pakistan were told that Cheema should have been tried in a court of law had he really attacked the newspaper editor, but instead, Berlin police officials killed him. Anti-German slogans were shouted at the protest while the JAS leaders delivered fiery speeches. The protestors also burnt German flags, overlooking the fact that it all started with Cheema's attack on an editor. Burning the German flag and thereby insulting the entire German nation is apparently of little consequence.[56] Their eagerness to distance themselves from America's prosecution of the war on Islamic terrorism notwithstanding, European governments, or at least their intelligence services, abetted the American practice of 'extraordinary rendition' without informing their publics. European leaders hypocritically censured the practice – at one point earning a rebuke from US Secretary of State Condoleeza Rice over their duplicity. 'Extraordinary rendition' refers to the kidnapping of terrorism suspects by American agents who then transport the suspects to third countries for interrogation, beyond the jurisdiction of American laws. Any European participation in the extra-judicial seizures and detentions, not to mention the torture that is said to be involved, would constitute a breach of the European Convention on Human Rights. Outrage ensues in Europe when America becomes involved, to the point that no one seems to know what Europe's interests are beyond the hypocritical adherence to the politically correct line. The EU Justice and Home Affairs Commissioner complained that terror suspects had been transferred to US intelligence agents on European territory. Spokesmen from several EU countries asserted that they would never sanction the procedure. However, all fell silent when Dick Marty, a Swiss senator investigating on behalf of the Council of

Europe, concluded that fourteen countries had colluded with US intelligence over secret flights and detention. He said that Britain, Germany, Italy, Sweden, Bosnia, Macedonia, Turkey, Spain, Cyprus, Ireland, Greece, Portugal, Romania and Poland had been complicit in unlawful inter-state transfers of people. Some, including Sweden and Bosnia, have admitted some involvement.[57] In one instance, Germany's external intelligence service, the BND, said that it knew about the American seizure and detention of a German citizen sixteen months before the country was officially informed of his mistaken arrest. Germany had previously maintained that it did not learn of the abduction of its citizen Khaled el-Masri in Macedonia in December 2003, until he returned to Germany in May 2004 after being held in Afghanistan. The government publicly criticized the Bush administration. Masri's name is similar to that of a man wanted in connection with 9/11, and he was released after his captors determined that he was not the man they were seeking.[58]

Perhaps the biggest terrorist events in Germany were those that did not happen when two suitcase bombs failed to explode on separate German trains in July 2006; and planned attacks on the American Ramstein air base and Frankfurt International Airport were thwarted in September 2007. Police suspect the only reason the train bombs didn't detonate was because the gas bottles that were to ignite them were too full and therefore there was insufficient air in the bottle. The terrorists will certainly be grateful for the free advice and they will try harder next time. German officials were investigating links to two unsolved bombings in North Rhineland-Westphalia. The first occurred in Cologne in June 2004, when a nail bomb exploded on a street whose residents were mostly Turks, injuring twenty-two. The second explosion happened in 2000 in Düsseldorf near a local train station. Ten Eastern European immigrants, most of them Jewish, were badly injured.[59]

Youssef el Hajdib and Jihad Hamad came to Germany as students and behaved inconspicuously, until the day they deposited the two suitcase bombs in regional trains. Data was discovered on Hamad's computer that could tie him to al-Qa'ida. Of special concern to investigators is that the duo may not necessarily be members of a 'domestic terrorist organization', but simply Muslim fanatics acting entirely on their own. This presumed new breed of independent terrorists appear out of nowhere and form miniature cells of their own. Instead of a network and commanders, all they need is a reason to strike, bomb-building instructions they can easily download from the internet and the conviction that they are acting on behalf of a greater cause. In some sense, these self-made terrorists may also believe that they are part of al-Qa'ida, which has long since transformed itself from being only a terrorist organization, instead encompassing an entire ideology. They are not members of a large group that can be observed or infiltrated with intelligence agents. Not having learned the terrorist trade in training camps in Pakistan or Afghanistan, they persistently fall through the cracks whenever there is a large-scale crackdown. Finally, because they are self-funded and do not communicate with handlers elsewhere, they provide authorities with few leads to follow. Hamad and Hajdib could well have been precisely such nightmare candidates.[60]

Hajdib, who lived in the northern German city of Kiel, managed to get away. He had apparently grown nervous and called his father, a member of Hizb ut-Tahrir, in Lebanon. The father urged his son to 'get out of Germany immediately' because his picture was on TV. Lebanese intelligence notified German authorities, who arrested him. The Lebanese terrorists did not raise any suspicions during the routine security check that was performed when they applied for visas. On his application for a college in Kiel, Hajdib cited an address in Hamburg which is shared by the Islamic-Albanian Cultural Centre, a residential dormitory for men and the al-Nur Mosque, which domestic intelligence officials in Hamburg have long suspected of ties to Islamist activities. Fellow students say that Hajdib justified violence against what he called the Danish cartoonist 'blasphemers'. His behaviour toward female instructors was condescending and contemptuous, and he once called a German instructor who had given him a poor grade a racist and Muslim-hater. It is disturbing that no suspicions are raised when religious Muslims perceive any criticism as a grave insult and openly display their aversion to the West and its way of life. A perception of normalcy persists because there are many others like Hajdib and no one wants to be called a racist. German educators face a true dilemma. More than 10,000 students of Arab origin are registered at German universities.[61]

The train plot reignited the debate about the nature of the terrorist threat. It had been assumed that Britain was attacked because Tony Blair was Bush's poodle. Spain suffered attacks because José María Aznar helped remove Saddam Hussein from power. But not much consideration was given to Canada, where terrorists sought to attack Parliament and behead the Prime Minister, although Canada, like Germany, was against the Iraq invasion. Al-Qa'ida has murdered innocents in Indonesia, the world's largest Muslim country, which opposed the Iraq War. The German debate about Islamic terrorism had hitherto been irresponsible. Hans Magnus Enzensberger, one of Germany's leading literary figures and social critics, debated the Iraq War with another leading intellectual, Jürgen Habermas. Habermas insisted that Europe, with its superior humanistic values, go its separate way from America. Enzensberger vigorously dissented in the pages of *Frankfurter Allgemeine Zeitung*, and also published *Men of Terror*. Enzensberger blames neither poverty nor Bush for the scourge of Islamic terror. He sees its roots in an intolerant vision of Islam, traceable to the Muslim Brotherhood's founding in Egypt in the 1920s. The essay quotes the UN Human Development Report and concludes that massive deficits in education and self-government in the Arab world have helped create an incubator for the dreadful complexes of inferiority and alienation that produce the 'radical loser'.[62] Playing on European fears, Islamic terrorists threatened to attack Germany and Austria unless they withdrew their personnel from Afghanistan, according to a web statement released by the Voice of the Caliphate, believed to be run by al-Qa'ida. Germany has no troops in Iraq but has troops serving with the NATO-led International Security Assistance Force in Afghanistan, most of them focused in the north of the country. Austria also has no troops in Iraq and has just five officers in Afghanistan.[63]

Three men were arrested in September 2007 – two German converts to Islam and a Turkish resident of Germany, suspected of plotting to attack American targets in southern Germany with car bombs. The federal prosecutor's office said Fritz Martin Gelowicz, 28, Daniel Martin Schneider, 20, and Adem Yilmaz, 28, had undergone terrorist training in Pakistan. After nine months of investigations, during which the suspects' phone calls were monitored and their movements tracked, the authorities concluded that their possible targets included the Ramstein air base, a crucial transportation hub for the American military, and Frankfurt International Airport. The country's sixteen state Interior Ministers, who control the state and local police, promptly called on the Federal Government to make training at a terrorist camp a criminal offence. Ministers remained divided over how to balance the need to protect civil liberties with protecting citizens against possible terrorist attacks. Günther Beckstein, the Interior Minister of Bavaria, said the bomb detonators had come from Syria. There are about 4,400 Islamic extremists under surveillance in the state of Baden-Württemberg, where the arrests took place.[64]

Wolfgang Schaüble gave warning that western countries faced a new threat from home-grown terrorists brainwashed by a radical ideology. 'One thinks that people who have grown up here and who enjoy the benefits of our free society are immune', he said. 'But some are susceptible to radicalization. These are dangerous, fanatical people with a high degree of criminal energy.'[65] A connection between Fritz Gelowicz and Mohammed Atta, who attacked the Twin Towers, dates back to 2000 while the latter was studying in Hamburg and preparing the 9/11 attack. German police reports are vague about the encounter, but it centres around Atta's links with a small mosque in Bavarian Neu-Ulm, which had a reputation for radicalism. Firebrand preachers were passing in and out of the town and it had become a magnet for angry young Muslims. Gelowicz's case has highlighted the curious and sinister role of Neu-Ulm – a small township in the Roman Catholic heart of southern Germany – as a cradle of Islamic extremism. When the Gelowicz family moved to Neu-Ulm in 1983 it was a relatively prosperous community with an American garrison and its big-spending soldiers. Once the US decided to station Pershing missiles nearby, the town became a hub of protest and the national mood swung against America. When the Americans eventually left and took their missiles with them, Neu-Ulm suddenly became much poorer – and the typical contradictions of anti-American leftists meant that declining fortunes made Neu-Ulm even more resentful.[66]

Investigators are still trying to determine how Gelowicz and Schneider became radicalized and how they came into contact with the Islamic Jihad Union, a South Asian network that has asserted responsibility for the planned attack on American targets. In Copenhagen, a convert is among four defendants who went on trial in September 2007 for plotting to blow up political targets. In Sweden, a webmaster who changed his name from Ralf Wadman to Abu Usama el-Swede was arrested in 2006 on suspicion of recruiting fighters on the internet. In Britain, three converts are awaiting trial on charges of participating in the 2006 transatlantic airline plot. Religious converts are sometimes more prone to radicalization because of their zeal to prove their newfound faith. They are also less likely to attract police scrutiny in Europe, and terrorist groups, which used to eye converts suspiciously as potential infiltrators, now recognize their value from both operational and cultural angles. Converts are a tiny subset of the Muslim population in Europe, but their numbers are growing in some countries. In Germany, government officials estimated that 4,000 people converted to Islam in 2006, compared with an annual average of 300 in the late 1990s. Estimates suggest that there are up to 100,000 local converts to Islam. The recent arrests prompted some lawmakers to suggest that police should keep converts under surveillance. The trend is not limited to Europe. In Florida, US citizen and convert Jose Padilla was convicted in August 2006 on conspiracy charges for participating in an al-Qa'ida support cell. In March 2006, David M. Hicks, an Australian convert, became the first prisoner at Guantanamo Bay to be convicted on terrorism charges. Wadih el-Hage, a Lebanese Christian who converted to Islam and became a US citizen, served as an aide to Bin Laden in the 1990s and was convicted for his role in the 1998 US Embassy bombings in East Africa. In May 2006, al-Qa'ida deputy chief Ayman al-Zawahiri released a videotape in which he repeatedly praised Muslim leader Malcolm X and urged African American soldiers to stop fighting in Iraq and embrace Islam. Bin Laden released a videotape in September 2007 calling upon all Americans to convert. Analysts said his speech was probably influenced by Adam Gadahn, a US convert who has become a media adviser for al-Qa'ida. He was indicted in the US on treason charges in 2006.[67]

It was not until October 2007 that Germans showed their impatience with the escalating expectations of their immigrant population. Ashkan Dejagah, an Iranian-born German soccer player, refused to play in a match in Israel, for what he initially claimed were personal and family reasons. However, the German daily *Bild* quoted Dejagah as saying his refusal 'had political reasons'. Although Theo Zwanziger, the president of the German Football Association, initially supported Dejagah's right to refuse to play, the player was permanently suspended. A government spokesman condemned Dejagah's position, saying, 'The interior minister is of the opinion that all members of German soccer teams must agree to play in any nation that Germany has a sports connection with. It is forbidden that political circumstances would influence this.'[68]

Asked by *Der Spiegel* whether western foreign policies were contributing to terrorism, the British novelist Salman Rushdie was firm in his conviction that 'terrorism is not the pursuit of legitimate goals by some sort of illegitimate means. Whatever the murderers may be trying to achieve, creating a better world certainly isn't one of their goals. Instead they are out to murder innocent people. If the conflict between Israelis and Palestinians, for example, were to be miraculously solved from one day to the next, I believe we wouldn't see any fewer attacks.' He agreed with Lenin's description of terrorism as bourgeois adventurism, adding:

> One must not negate the basic tenet of all morality, that individuals are themselves responsible for their actions. Upbringing certainly plays a major role there, imparting a misconceived sense of mission which pushes people towards 'actions'. Added to that there is a herd mentality once you have become integrated in a group and everyone continues to drive everyone else on and on into a forced situation. There's the type of person who believes his action will make mankind listen to him and turn him into a historic figure. Then there's the type who simply feels attracted to violence. And yes, I think glamour plays a role too.[69]

For years, Syrian-born political scientist Bassam Tibi has been urging Muslims to integrate into European societies and Europe to stand up to Islamists. Accusing somebody of racism is a very effective weapon in Germany. Islamists know this, and that as soon as someone is accused of demonizing Islam, the European side backs down. Tibi believes the conflict between the western world and Muslim groups is an 'ideological war', and that the result of a conflict between two sides is that people politicize their cultural backgrounds. In Germany representatives of the Islamic communities try to hijack children born there, along with the entire Islamic community, to prevent them from being influenced by the society which has taken them in. He is emphatic about the error of compromising with Muslim immigrants in order to avoid antagonizing them, since the Islamic officials view this as weakness. Muslims stand by their religion entirely. It is a sort of religious absolutism. Europeans have stopped defending the values of their civilization, confusing tolerance with relativism. Far from defusing the conflict, the western tendency to avoid insulting Muslims has the opposite effect. The weaker the partner is viewed by the Muslims, then the greater the anger which they express. And this anger is often carefully staged. Tibi said the argument over the cartoons was completely orchestrated. Protests like these are weapons in this war of ideas. Tibi gave another example: 'The president of the Iranian parliament was visiting Belgium where he had an appointment with a female Belgian colleague. He refused to shake her hand, so she didn't meet with him. He left Belgium and accused her of racism. The accusation of cultural insensitivity is a weapon. And we have to neutralize it.' Tibi said Germany's Islam Conference will fail because the biggest taboo is that there is a conflict at all. 'Instead people talk about misunderstandings and how these should be resolved. But a conflict of values is not a misunderstanding. Islamic orthodoxy and the German constitution are not compatible.' For Tibi, the solution lies in Muslims giving up three things in order to become Europeans:

> They have to bid farewell to the idea of converting others, and renounce the jihad. The jihad is not just a way of testing yourself but also means using violence to spread Islam. The third thing they need to give up is the shari'a, which is the Islamic legal system. This is incompatible with the German constitution. There are also two things they need to redefine. Pluralism and tolerance are pillars of modern society. That has to be

accepted. But pluralism doesn't just mean diversity. It means that we share the same rules and values, and are still nevertheless different. Islam doesn't have this idea. And Islam also has no tradition of tolerance. In Islam tolerance means that Christians and Jews are allowed to live under the protection of Muslims but never as citizens with the same rights. What Muslims call tolerance is nothing other than discrimination.[70]

The scale of the problem is illustrated by Tibi's belief that only a few thousand of the Muslims living in Germany would agree to these demands. Tibi said that although the organizations at the Islam Conference said they accept the German constitution and that it is permitted to change religion or have no religion at all, even though the shari'a punishes a loss of faith (*ridda*) with the death sentence, he was dismissive, since only representatives of organized Islam went to Schäuble's conference. They told Schäuble they are against terrorism, but that is not a policy. Tibi said that when the Alfred Herrhausen society wanted to invite a German-speaking imam with European ideas to a discussion, no one could be found. Tibi wants imams to be trained locally with the curriculum decided by the state. He advocates the re-education programmes which were carried out in Germany after the Third Reich. Social studies teachers and political science faculties were given the task of turning young people into democrats. Tibi wants a change in German culture too, so that not only those who are born here and have ethnically German parents are seen as German. Almost 20 per cent of the people living in Germany today have a foreign background. Tibi claims the problem is that Germany can't really offer foreigners an identity because, a result of Auschwitz, the Germans hardly have a national identity themselves.[71]

NOTES

1. Antony Barnett, Jason Burke and Zoe Smith, 'Terror Cells Regroup – and now their Target is Europe', *The Observer*, 11 January 2004.
2. Ibid.
3. Ibid.
4. Ibid.
5. Wolfgang Polzer, 'Islam is Taking a Grip on Europe – Why Muslims Object to Piggy Banks', *Journal Chrétien*, 10 March 2007.
6. Andrea Brandt and Cordula Meyer, 'Religious Divisions Within Germany – A Parallel Muslim Universe', *Spiegel Online*, 20 February 2007.

7. Ibid.
8. Ibid.
9. Ibid.
10. 'Anti-Semitism and the Turkish Islamist Milli Görüs Movement', cited by MEMRI, Special Dispatch Series, 1699, 29 August 2007.
11. 'Police Brought in as Teachers Lose Control at Berlin School', *DPA* and *Expatica*, 31 March 2006.
12. Ibid.
13. Anshel Pfeffer, 'Double Vision', *Haaretz*, 6 October 2007.
14. 'Islamic Conference in Berlin, Lowering the Wall Between Mosque and State', *Spiegel Online*, 27 September 2006.
15. 'Merkel Aide Criticized for Comments on Islam', *DPA* and *Expatica*, 2 October 2006.
16. 'Germany's Muslims Band Together – New Umbrella Group Founded', *Spiegel Online*, 11 April 2007.
17. 'Muslim Group's First Mission, Official Recognition of Islam in Germany?', *Spiegel Online*, 16 April 2007.
18. 'Becoming German: Proposed Hesse Citizenship Test', *Spiegel Online*, 9 May 2006. English translation kindly provided by signandsight.com.
19. Ibid.
20. Richard Bernstein, 'Letter from Europe: a Quiz for would-be Citizens tests German Attitudes', *The New York Times*, 29 March 2006.
21. 'The World from Berlin', *Spiegel Online*, 7 February 2006.
22. Ibid.
23. 'Integration Debate: The German National Anthem in Turkish?', *Spiegel Online*, 2 May 2006.
24. 'Keep out Muslims, says Nile', *Herald Sun*, 12 March 2007.
25. Matthew Campbell, 'Migrant Ghettos Anger Germany', *Sunday Times*, 30 April 2006.
26. Bret Stephens, 'The Foreign Brides: Germany tries to Protect Turkish girls from Arranged Marriages', *Opinion Journal*, 7 May 2006.
27. Ibid.
28. Matthias Bartsch et al., 'German Justice Failures – Paving the Way for a Muslim Parallel Society', *Spiegel Online*, 29 March 2007, translated into English by Christopher Sultan.
29. Veit Medick et al., 'Justifying Marital Violence – A German Judge Cites Koran in Divorce Case', *Spiegel Online*, 21 March 2007.
30. Bartsch et al., 'German Justice Failures – Paving the Way for a Muslim Parallel Society'.
31. Ibid.
32. 'Pupils aged five "Poisoned" at Islamic School that "Teaches Hate"', *The Daily Mail*, 5 February 2007.
33. Emma Hartley and Julie Henry, 'Girls at London Saudi School are treated as Inferiors', *The Daily Telegraph*, 29 May 2004.
34. Graeme Paton, 'Islamic School "Rips Pages from Textbooks"', *The Daily Telegraph*, 9 February 2007.
35. Lucy Bannerman, 'Islamic School Pledges to Amend Offensive Books', *The Times*, 8 February 2007.
36. Sian Griffiths, 'We Don't Teach Hate', *Sunday Times*, 11 February 2007.
37. Bartsch et al., 'German Justice Failures – Paving the Way for a Muslim Parallel Society'.
38. Ibid.
39. Kate Connolly, 'Threats Halt Woman Lawyer who Fought Forced Marriages', *The Daily Telegraph*, 6 September 2006.
40. Salman Masalha, 'The Arab Man is the Problem, The Arab Woman is the Solution', www.elaph.com, September 24, 2004, cited by MEMRI, Special Dispatch Series, 807, 28 October 2004.
41. 'German Minister: Muslim Women should not Wear Full Face Veil', *DPA* and *Haaretz*, 24 January 2007.
42. Mary Jordan, 'In Europe and US, Non-believers Are Increasingly Vocal', *The Washington Post*, 15 September 2007.
43. 'Not Possible to Modernize Islam', interview With Founder Of Council Of Ex-Muslims, *Spiegel Online*, 27 February 2007.

44. Bess Twiston-Davies, 'Faith News', *The Times*, 16 December 2006.
45. Tom Heneghan, '"Ex-Muslim" Group Launches in Britain', *Reuters*, 20 June 2007.
46. Jordan, 'In Europe and US, Non-believers Are Increasingly Vocal'.
47. David Charter, 'Young Muslims begin Dangerous Fight for the Right to Abandon Faith', *The Times*, 11 September 2007.
48. Harry de Quetteville, 'Huge Mosque Stirs Protests in Cologne', *The Daily Telegraph*, 25 June 2007.
49. 'Islam in Europe: An Interview With Arzu Toker on the Cologne Mosque', *World Politics Review Exclusive,* 17 August 2007. The interview first appeared in the July 2007 issue of the German monthly *Konkret*, and was translated into English by John Rosenthal.
50. Roger Boyes, 'A Winger and a Prayer: the Latest Way to Settle Religious Divisions', *The Times*, 9 July 2007.
51. Silvia Aloisi, 'Muslims irked by Italian Senator's "Pig" Comments', *Reuters*, 13 September 2007.
52. 'More than 32,000 Islamist Extremists in Germany', *Expatica*, 22 May 2006.
53. Matthias Gebauer and Holger Stark, 'German Women Vowed to Mount Suicide Attacks in Iraq', *Spiegel Online*, 30 May 2006.
54. 'Germany is Terror Threat "Powder Keg" – Top Prosecutor', *Asia News/Reuters*, 13 May 2006.
55. Rainer Sollich, 'German Mistrust of Muslims and Islam Grows', *Deutsche Welle*, 20 May 2006.
56. 'Angry Protests after Death of Pakistani in Germany', *Expatica*, 13 May 2006.
57. 'Countries Named over Secret Terror Transfers', *The Times*, 28 June 2006.
58. Souad Mekhennet and Craig S. Smith, 'German Spy Agency Admits Mishandling Abduction Case', *The New York Times*, 2 June 2006.
59. Stephen Brown, 'German Train Terror', *FrontPageMagazine.com*, 4 August 2006.
60. Gunther Latsch *et al.*, 'Terrorism in Germany – Every Investigator's Nightmare', *Der Spiegel*, 28 August 2006, translated into English by Christopher Sultan.
61. Ibid.
62. Jeffrey Gedmin, 'Der Terror Ist Da – Germany wakes up, sort of', *The Weekly Standard*, 11 September 2006.
63. Salah Nasrawi, 'Islamic Militants Warn Austria, Germany', *AP*, 11 Mar 2007.
64. Judy Dempsey and Katrin Bennhold, 'Germany Debates Security Measures', *The New York Times*, 8 September 2007.
65. Harry de Quetteville, 'German Police Hunt for 10 Terror Accomplices', *The Daily Telegraph*, 7 September 2007.
66. Roger Boyes, 'German Terror Suspect met 9/11 Hijacker', *Times Online*, 7 September 2007.
67. Craig Whitlock, Imtiaz Ali and Shannon Smiley, 'Converts To Islam Move Up In Cells – Arrests in Europe Illuminate Shift', *The Washington Post*, 15 September 2007.
68. Megan Jacobs, 'Germany Suspends Iranian Soccer Player', *The Jerusalem Post*, 11 October 2007.
69. Erich Follath, 'Terror Is Glamour', interview with Salman Rushdie, *Spiegel Online*, 28 August 2006.
70. Cordula Meyer and Caroline Schmidt, 'Europeans Have Stopped Defending Their Values', interview with German Islam expert Bassam Tibi, *Spiegel Online*, 2 October 2006, translated into English by Damien McGuinness.
71. Ibid.

CHAPTER FIVE

The Cartoon Affair and the Failure of Dialogue and Coexistence

As long as there was a dialogue between the West and Muslims, through diplomatic and other channels, many naive people believed that coexistence was possible. Differences could be ironed out peacefully, in an open and civilized debate where the intellectually superior or the spiritually more attractive could win. But the outbreak of the cartoon controversy, in the last months of 2005 and early 2006, dashed those illusions, when it transpired that the Muslim world was not up to a debate, demanding instead a universal recognition of its superiority. In the Muslim rally in Los Angeles on 18 February 2006, one of the slogans waved by the furious demonstrators was 'Islam Shall Dominate!', in other words, that they were not seeking accommodation, but victory; not calming down their own tempers which had reached boiling point, but vindication of their fanatical positions. Many movies and slogans have been produced in the West, which had could be interpreted as 'injurious' to other faiths, but in no case had such a violent uproar exploded, or were other people threatened or attacked as in this alleged 'harm' done to the prophet of Islam. Nothing that the West can do will ever match the volume of abuse the Muslims heap on Christianity and Judaism or their violent attacks against the followers of other faiths. It is Muslims and non-Muslims who flee for their lives from Muslim regimes to western societies, an indication in itself of where persecuted individuals feel safer.

The cartoon controversy, which transcended the boundaries of a religious row, initially looked like a repetition of the Salman

Rushdie affair, with prizes promised to whoever killed the 'blasphemous' cartoonists, clamours for 'vengeance' resounding from one end of the world to the other, journalists dismissed for supporting freedom of the press, politicians resigning or castigated by a frightened Europe, and large-scale violence used by Muslims against European national symbols (including embassies and flags); only a clear death sentence by an authoritative cleric (fatwa) was missing to make the comparison complete. There is nevertheless a world of difference between the two: the Rushdie affair was directed at a Muslim individual who had 'sinned' in Muslim eyes, while the cartoon explosion was directed at a country (Denmark) and expanded into an anti-western wave of abuse and violence. Secondly, in the age of naivety and candour, when the West differentiated between the vast majority of 'peaceful Muslims' and a few 'extremists', political correctness had it that if one could only 'understand' the offence done to Islam and apologize for it, even if that entailed sacrificing one individual (Rushdie) to appease the rest, then peace and tranquillity would prevail. The cartoon affair taught the West that the more apologies and 'understandings' (which are unfailingly directed from Christendom to Islamdom, never the other way round), the more violent the anti-western furies, because Muslims have convinced themselves that all 'infidels' aspire to undermine Islam. Then, in the 1990s, the ascent of oil-rich Islam was at its peak, Muslim immigration to Europe and America was gathering strength, and it seemed that Islam had become unstoppable. Now, a bitter, humiliated Islam that has been repeatedly classified by UN development reports (all written by Arabs), as languishing at the bottom of the world scale, has been rendered more sensitive to its eclipse and is therefore more prone to violence.

Something has happened between the Rushdie affair and the days of wrath over the Danish cartoons some fifteen years later, and that is September 11, which has shocked westerners out of their slumber and illusions about a simple amicable coexistence with Islam. The dogged American determination to pursue the war in Iraq, and then to democratize that country, thereby putting in jeopardy the entire system of dictatorships into which the Muslim world has comfortably settled, is reason enough for the most directly threatened rulers of Syria and Iran to incite their crowds against the West. Iran's 'elected' President Ahmadinejad, who is hugely popular among the Muslim masses due to his bluntness and the challenge he epitomizes toward the West, by both his clear anti-Semitic rhetoric and denial of the Shoah, backed by his persistent programme of going nuclear, has encouraged Muslim crowds worldwide to defy the West and its values and attack westerners when they can do so with impunity. The West has become accustomed to the sight of American and Israeli flags and effigies being burned in the name of 'political protest' throughout the Muslim world and in western democracies where Muslims have settled, without anyone interfering to restrain that outrageous conduct which offends Americans and Israelis no less than what Muslims consider blasphemy when their symbols are desecrated. But no one had imagined that Scandinavian flags would undergo the same disparaging treatment in Muslim hands, unless the cause was the underlying hatred for the cross on Scandinavian flags. In other words, much more than just 'blasphemy' is at stake, and the burning of flags of non-Muslim nations is but one manifestation of a deep resentment against the West, that has been waiting to erupt at the first opportunity.

It is baffling to witness the endless energy and resources Muslims expend at burning flags and embassies, and on desecrating the religious symbols of other faiths, and at the excess leisure time that must represent, which would be better spent on educating, working, building and creating. The impression arises that they are always on the alert to find excuses to feel offended in order to demonstrate their anti-western animus, sinking into inconsolable misery if such occasions for violent demonstrations do not present themselves often enough. But they have no lack of such opportunities, for they manufacture them constantly. At the very height of the cartoon affair, Sunni Muslims blew up a mosque in the ancient capital of Islam, Samarra, just north of Baghdad, which is one of the most hallowed shrines for Shi'ites. It is the burial place of the 10th and 11th Imams in the line of the twelve adulated by the Twelver Shi'ites of Iran and Iraq, just before their descendent, the 12th Imam, went into hiding and assumed the identity of the *Mahdi* Messiah who is expected to return and bring with him peace and justice to the world. The sanctity of the place is evident, judging not only from its objective place in Shi'ite hagiography but also from the fury and outrage that shook the Shi'ite majority in Iraq and was expressed in the equally outrageous outburst of violence in which dozens of Sunni mosques went up in flames. The enmity between Sunnis and Shi'ites is not new. What is striking is that, unlike the cartoon affair where no one was killed or hurt by the act of drawing cartoons, the mosque desecrations and the massacres before and since have brought Iraqi society to the brink of civil war. Yet no outrage was heard in the Islamic world and no massive demonstrations were mounted against these violent acts. The only conclusion is that it is not the 'insult' itself that counts, but who triggers it. The Muslims can kill, desecrate, maim, burn and destroy at will, their own and others' holy places and symbols, but woe betide non-Muslims who dare to draw a caricature.

Symptomatic of all these eruptions of violence, whether 'provoked' by the West, like the cartoon affair, by Muslims themselves against the West like the September 11 horrors, or by Muslims against other Muslims like the ongoing Iraqi carnage between Sunnis and Shi'ites, is that they are all imputed by Muslims to the Jews in general, to Israel and the Mossad in particular, or to western subversion of Islam. Exactly as 9/11 was widely attributed to Jews in the Muslim world,[1] the cartoon controversy that began in Denmark was ascribed by the spiritual leader of Iran, and others following his example, to Israel and the Jews, the 'only ones to benefit from the rift between Islam and Europe'.[2] (But blaming Jews for 9/11 does not stop Muslims from simultaneously praising Osama Bin Laden for the attacks.) Furious Iraqi Shi'ites who demonstrated against the destruction of their mosque in Samarra by their fellow Sunni countrymen, were 'convinced' in their depositions to the world media that it must be the Jews or the Americans who wished to cause civil war between the two factions of Islam in Iraq.[3] What is particularly tragic for coming generations of Muslim society is that they too are coached from childhood to disown any responsibility for their actions, since others are always blamed: the West, imperialism, Israel, Jews, Christians, anybody and everybody, just not Muslims. The 'rationale' is clear: Islam being a religion of peace, harmony and love (never mind about the Muslim infighting around the world), any wrong-doing must be attributed to those most likely to 'benefit' from it, and those are invariably the Jews or their allies – the Americans and sometimes

Europeans. It is a tragedy because with this state of mind there is no incentive to improve or overcome their puerile thought-processes, for, as any child soon learns, it is always much easier to accuse others than to amend oneself. In this shame-based society, anything is better than admitting a mistake or a misdeed; but if it happened and cannot be denied, then attributing it to others is the only way out.

Perhaps no story better encapsulates the 'logic' of Muslim thinking on cause and effect than the destruction of the twenty synagogues left intact in Gaza when Israel withdrew from the Strip in August 2005. The Palestinians promptly destroyed them, and a spokesman for the 'Popular Resistance Committees', Abu Abir, said the area in which the synagogues once stood were used to fire rockets at Israel, their 'ceasefire' notwithstanding. Yet Abir blamed the Jewish state for the desecration of the Gaza synagogues by Palestinian Arabs, claiming the decision to leave the structures intact was part of an Israeli conspiracy. Israel 'left the synagogues behind so the world would see the Palestinians destroying them', he said.[4] It has been suggested that the seeds of Islamic attacks against Denmark, as a stepping-stone for the takeover of Europe, were planted long before the cartoons were even published. On 15 April 2005, Palestinian cleric and Hizb ut-Tahrir (HuT) leader Sheikh Issam Amayra called, from al-Aqsa Mosque in Jerusalem, upon Muslims in Denmark to begin a holy war. Amayra's sermon warned that: 'the 3 per cent of the Muslims in Denmark constitute a threat to the future of the kingdom of Denmark ... it should not be a surprise that our Danish brothers manage to bring Islam to all the homes of the Danes ... the citizens of the Caliphate (which will be raised in Denmark) will wage war on Oslo ... In the next stage, they will wage a holy war and spread the message of Islam to the rest of Europe.' He has travelled widely to Kuwait, Jordan, the Palestinian territories, Iraq, Egypt, the UK and US.

Denmark has in the last few years become a host country for various Muslim radical groups. HuT first started receiving media attention a month after September 11, when more than 1,000 members marched against the military actions against the Afghan Taleban. According to the Swedish daily *Svenska Dagbladet*, they also demonstrated against democracy, human rights, gender equality, and other western threats to what the group considers the true way of Islam. Being labelled a political party conveniently enables the HuT to operate like the Palestinian Hamas, using a political façade to mask their terrorism. Their terrorist activities are usually carried out by a splinter organization, the al-Muhajirun, which was established in 1995. Omar Bakri Mohammed, former leader of al-Mujahirun, who preached in London, also threatened to overthrow the Danish Government, as was reported by the *Copenhagen Post*, on 9 August 2002. HuT's goal is to establish a global Caliphate and force all non-Muslim states to pay a tax or face war. Its members join al-Qa'ida, according to Zeyno Baran, director of Hudson's Centre for Eurasian Policy. Concurrently with the French riots in 2005, Århus, Denmark's second largest city, suffered from rioting Muslims – the immediate pretext being Muslim objections to the police entering their neighbourhoods.[5]

The cartoon affair represented a watershed in the relations between Islam and the West, not so much for its own impact but for the backlash it produced in the civilized world. Not only Muslims worldwide were waiting for another opportunity to explode in anger, but the West, which had been terrorized for years by political correctness and the fear of being dubbed racist, suddenly realized that it was being abused by the very people it sought to protect, and its liberal system was being exploited to instil hatred, hostility, bigotry and insecurity in its midst. While that realization was developing since September 11 with the spread of Muslim violence in Europe, the unjust outburst against Denmark was the final straw. Now, the Danes and other Europeans were ready to spell out the causes of the malaise, to discuss it openly and to give vent to their own counter-grievances against Islam. Many issues that lay beneath the surface were debated, and since cartoons were the trigger of this explosion, yet more cartoons were introduced into the arena. The original cartoonists would have languished in obscurity had it not been for the Muslims themselves. The greater the incitement and violence generated by the Muslim masses (most of whom had never seen the cartoons, and would have remained oblivious to them if it were not for Muslim publicity), the more incensed became the Europeans who saw themselves subjected to an intolerable cultural and civilizational attack. It is this general settling of old accounts, not merely the cartoon controversy, which is worth exploring, because its effects and impact will expand in time and space far beyond the boundaries of the cartoon row.

Indeed, the Islamic outrage for the 'insult' hurled against their prophet, far from gaining them the respect they craved, only depicted them as obscurantist fanatics who have no concern for human life and are driven by violence. Even had they known the outcome of their rampage, they would probably not have refrained from violence, for this is part of their irrational outlook which values the damage that they inflict on perceived adversaries much more than the self-inflicted harm they cause themselves. Anyhow, a tarnished image is what they 'gained' from the staged outbursts of violence which they tried to posit as 'spontaneous', something hardly credible for a series of demonstrations and attacks which began four months after the cartoons were published, voicing the same slogans, emitting the same threats and committing the same acts of arson all over the Muslim world, and burning a considerable stock of Danish flags which could hardly be manufactured instantly. Among the shower of cartoons that targeted Europe in January and February 2006, many were no less offensive than the original Danish cartoons. Under the caption 'drawing the line of free speech', one showed a dismayed Danish cartoonist at work while a Muslim cleric, sabre in hand, draws a line around the cartoonist's neck.[6] Another showed a Muslim handling a sabre and cutting off the right hand (with a dripping pen between its fingers) of a western cartoonist, and exclaiming: 'Maybe now you will learn tolerance and respect for the views of others.'[7] Still another decried the totalitarian regimes that hold Muslim populations under their grip, reproducing a dialogue between Assad of Syria and Ahmadinejad of Iran where they agree to incite violence over the 'blasphemous cartoons', because 'our most sacred texts demand it'.[8] The Iranian nuclear threat that dominated the headlines alongside the Muslim rampage, caused some cartoonists to combine the two themes. A cartoonist is shown at his desk, when an enormous nuclear bomb explodes next to his home, and he exclaims: 'What did I do now?'[9] Another shows Ahmadinejad holding a nuclear missile in his hands facing a Danish cartoonist, under the caption: 'The Battle of the World's Greatest Evil-Doers'.[10]

Europeans finally appreciated their own folly in providing Muslim immigrants with shelter, new homes, generous welfare payments, public services and the freedoms which they could not even dream of in their places of origin. Even those who thought that the publication of the cartoons was wrong, and castigated the cartoonists for it, became exasperated by the Muslim reaction, which died out as suddenly as it began, to be overtaken by other events at a time of the Muslims' choosing. But the instantaneous nature of the debate, with claims and counterclaims being immediately aired in the media and on websites, soon drew Muslim participants into the angry exchanges. At the height of the Muslim fury against Denmark and the West, the Arab-American psychologist, Wafa Sultan,[11] was interviewed by al-Jazeera. In her forthright replies, she said to millions of Arab viewers:

> The clash we are witnessing around the world is not a clash of religions, or a clash of civilizations. It is a clash between two opposites, between two eras. It is a clash between a mentality that belongs to the Middle Ages and another mentality that belongs to the twenty-first century. It is a clash between civilization and backwardness, between the civilized and the primitive, between barbarity and rationality. It is the clash between freedom and oppression, between democracy and dictatorship. It is a clash between human rights, on the one hand, and the violation of these rights, on the other hand. It is a clash between those who treat women like beasts, and those who treat them like human beings. What we see today is not a clash of civilizations. Civilizations do not clash but compete ...
>
> The Muslims are the ones who began using this expression [of clash of civilizations]. The Muslims are the ones who began the clash of civilizations. The prophet of Islam said: 'I was ordered to fight the people until they believe in Allah and His Messenger'. When the Muslims divided the people into Muslims and non-Muslims, and called to fight the others until they believe in what they themselves believe, they started this clash and began this war. In order to stop this war they have to re-examine their Islamic books and curricula, which are full of calls for *takfir* [labelling others 'infidels'

or heretics or apostates in order to justify war against them] and fighting the 'infidels'.

[Some Muslims say] that they never offend other people's beliefs. What civilization on the face of this earth allows them to call other people by names that they did not choose for themselves? Once they call them Ahl-al-Dhimma [protected people under Islamic rule]; another time the People of the Book; and yet another time they compare them to apes and pigs, or they call the Christians 'those who incur Allah's wrath' [in the opening *sura* of the Qur'an, which in this verse refers to Jews]. Who told you that they are People of the Book? They are not people of the book, they are people of many books. All the useful scientific books that you have today are theirs, the fruit of their free and creative thinking. What gives you the right to call them 'those who incur Allah's wrath?' or those 'who have gone astray?' [this is the accepted reference to Christians in the same *sura* of the scripture], and then claim that your religion commands you to refrain from offending the beliefs of others? ... You are free to worship whoever you want, but other people's beliefs are not your concern, whether they believe that the Messiah is God, son of Mary, or that Satan is God ... Let people have their beliefs ...

The Jews have come from the tragedy [of the Holocaust] and forced the world to respect them, with their knowledge, not with their terror; with their work, not with crying and yelling. Humanity owes most of the discoveries and science of the nineteenth and twentieth centuries to Jewish scientists. Fifteen million people, scattered throughout the world, united and won their rights through work and knowledge. We have not a single Jew blow up in a German restaurant; we have not a single Jew destroy a church; we have not seen a single Jew protest by killing people. The Muslims turned three Buddha statues into rubble. We have not seen a Buddhist burn down a mosque, kill a Muslim or burn down an embassy. Only the Muslims defend their beliefs by burning down churches, killing people and destroying embassies. This path will not yield any results. The Muslims must ask themselves what they can do for humankind, before they ask that human kind respect them ...

> Why does a young Muslim man, in the prime of his life, with a full life ahead, go and blow himself up? How and why does he blow himself up in a bus full of innocent passengers? ... In our countries religion is the source of education, and is the only spring from which that terrorist drank until his thirst was quenched. He was not born a terrorist and did not become a terrorist overnight. Islamic teachings played a role in weaving this ideological fabric, thread by thread, and did not allow other sources – I am referring to scientific sources – to play a role.[12]

Of course, Sultan's words, which were circulated worldwide, brought her instant fame. In an interview she gave to the *Los Angeles Times*,[13] she said that in this battle between modernity and barbarism, reactionary Islam is destined to lose. Islamic reformers have praised her for saying out loud what few Muslims dare to say even in private: 'I believe our people are hostages to our own beliefs and teachings; knowledge has released me from this backward thinking.' Shortly after the broadcast, clerics in Syria denounced her as an 'infidel'. One said she had done Islam more damage than the Danish cartoons mocking Muhammad. She said that she was working on a book that would turn the Islamic world upside down if it is published. 'I am questioning every single teaching of our holy book. The working title is, *The Escaped Prisoner: When God Is a Monster*'.[14]

Sultan grew up in a large traditional Muslim family in Syria, and she followed the faith's strictures into adulthood. Her life changed in 1979 when she was a medical student at the University of Aleppo. Muslim Brotherhood terrorists burst into the classroom and killed her professor, shouting, 'God is greater!' She said that at that point, 'I lost my trust in their God and began to question all our teachings. I had to look for another God.' She and her husband left for the US. She started writing for an Islamic reform website called al-Naqed (The Critic). An angry essay on that site by Sultan about the Muslim Brotherhood caught the attention of al-Jazeera, which invited her to debate an Algerian cleric in July 2005. Her remarks set off debates around the globe and her name began appearing in Arabic newspapers and websites. But her fame grew exponentially when she appeared on al-Jazeera again in February

2006, and the interview was translated and widely distributed by the invaluable Middle East Media Research Institute (MEMRI). MEMRI said the clip of her February appearance has been viewed more than a million times. The other guest on the programme, identified as an Egyptian professor of religious studies, Dr Ibrahim al-Khouli, asked, 'Are you a heretic?' He then said there was no point in rebuking or debating her, because she had blasphemed against Islam, Muhammad and the Qur'an. Dr Sultan said she took those words as a formal fatwa, a religious condemnation. Since then, she said, she received numerous death threats.[15]

Sultan was more specific during a visit to Australia in August 2007, saying the West was still underestimating the evil of Islam. She warned that all Muslims needed to be closely monitored and insisted that Australia and the US have been duped into believing there is a difference between the religion's moderate and radical interpretations. In an interview with *The Australian*, Sultan said Muslims were 'brainwashed' from an early age to believe western values were evil and that the world would one day come under the control of shari'a law. She warned that Muslims would continue to exploit freedom of speech in the West to spread their 'hate' and attack their adopted countries, until the western mind grasped the magnitude of the Islamic threat:

> You're fighting someone who is willing to die. So you have to understand this mentality and find ways to face it. [As a Muslim] your mission on this earth is to fight for Islam and to kill or to be killed. You're here for only a short life and once you kill a 'kafir', or a non-believer, soon you're going to be united with your God.

She considered Muhammad to be 'evil' and said the Qur'an needed to be destroyed because it advocated violence against non-believers. Sultan believes Muslims must be exposed to different cultures, thoughts and belief systems.[16]

Wafa Sultan took extraordinary risks in speaking up, and there is some following for her moderate and realistic stance, comparable to other reforming spirits in the Islamic world who can operate openly only in the West. But she and other reformists like her will be persecuted and silenced, and it is doubtful whether scholars and thinkers can pursue any sustained programme of reform in the face of intimidation, threats and excommunication. For Sultan represents one hopeful pole in the Islamic world, which is still dominated by the opposing pole of ignorance, hatred and bigotry. For example, the praise Sultan had for the Jews enraged Muslim clerics no less than the cartoon affair, and they tied both themes together in their reactions. The Saudi Sheikh Muhsen al-'Awaji was interviewed on Ein TV and had this to say:

> Too late now for a Denmark apology. You cannot put back a decapitated head after it decomposes. If Arabs can fight a forty-year war to defend the honour of a female camel, how about the honour of the prophet? ...
>
> When all this began, the people of Denmark insisted, in a premeditated and unprecedented way, on humiliating our prophet ... Incidentally, the Americans have done worse things than the Danes, in degrading the holy Qur'an, the word of God, but they were smarter [because they apologized officially] ...
>
> [We face] a group of people, a gang, which gathered, or more accurately were purged from all the countries of the world. They have become loathsome in European eyes and that is why the Europeans vomited them into our occupied land. They have become loathsome in the eyes of America ... Our brothers all over the Islamic world know that a Jew or a Christian has the right to live there, just like the Arab Muslim has the right to live there. But gathering those Jews from Poland, Russia ... the South Pole, is forcing them like a cancerous tumour into the centre of the Arab and Muslim body. They have no common language with those who surround them, nor do they share their political platform with their surroundings. And then they come with this arrogance and enslave the entire world in order to allow them to violate these rights and commit these official assassinations, approved by the highest-ranking officials, and after all this we are told we must discuss their legitimacy ? No![17]

This sort of statement, capitalizing on European disarray and mood of self-flagellation in the initial stages of the crisis, was tailored to lure Europeans to follow the Muslim line of reasoning and delegitimize Jews as a national minority and deny their right to statehood. It fits in seamlessly with the fact that 'Jews had become the symbolical tool for Europeans to avoid confronting as long as possible the problems posed to them by the Arab and Muslim immigration, since the Middle East conflict had become a means to mediate the complex relationships between Europe and the immigrant population. Condemning Israel is a way for Europe to keep civil peace at home'.[18] Or so it thought, based on the record of European disregard for Muslim attacks against Jewish targets in Europe. Instead of confronting Muslim aggressors, Europeans elected to turn the Jews into scapegoats while the Jewish victims were powerless to face these accusations and, ill-disposed to react to them actively and violently, had to accept them passively. Shmuel Trigano further claims that since Europeans adored Jews provided they are dead, they recognized Jewish peoplehood only in the context of their suffering and elimination in Europe – hence the 'excessively sacral' fashion in which the commemoration of the sixtieth anniversary of the liberation of Auschwitz took place. The contemporary European hostility against Israel and the Jewish communities in the continent, suited exactly the vituperative sentiment being cultivated by Muslims and Arabs for years. For Europeans, identifying with the Shoah was a way to redeem themselves from the Nazi culpabilities and their own collaboration with them, in the process turning the Jewish victim into the executioner by the very fact that he dared to take up weapons and revolt against the state of victimhood assigned to him. This convergence between European feelings of guilt and inveterate Muslim hatred of Jews was somewhat disrupted by the cartoon controversy which vilified the Danes and other Europeans together with the Jews. That process had begun after the Theo van Gogh murder in Holland and prior to the cartoons and London underground explosions when a Danish daily proclaimed, 'Today we are all Israelis.' A Danish retired general declared, in a panel debate he shared with this author in October 2005 in Copenhagen, that 'Europe cannot sustain another Holocaust. If Israel goes down, Europe will go down with it.' But the cartoon crisis put Europeans and Jews/Israelis squarely on one side and the Muslims on the other, once again pitting Muslim civilization against its Judaeo-Christian counterpart.

Sheikh Muhsen's broadside against the West and the Jews was by no means an isolated one. A famous Egyptian actor and singer, Sha'ban Abd al-Rahim, echoing the widespread sentiment in the Islamic world against Danes and Jews, soon entered the fray, adding a popular (in both senses of the word – folkloric and loved by the populace) twist to this affair. He had behind him a rich record of hatred when he recorded a hit in 2000 entitled 'I hate Israel, I love Amr Mussa' (a former Egyptian Foreign Minister and now the secretary general of the Arab League who overflows with hostility towards Israel, despite the 1979 Israeli–Egyptian peace treaty). Al-Rahim followed that up after 9/11, with an album featuring the song: 'Hey people, it was only a tower, and I swear by Allah that they [the US] are the ones who pulled it down.' In view of the cartoon affair, he persuaded his producer to record two new songs, one sending Denmark to hell, (the other about the outbreak of avian flu), for he was convinced that 'we must wake up Islam and write a song right now'. His interview, which was broadcast throughout the Arab world, is most instructive about his and his vast audiences' state of mind, which ought to be understood and heeded by the West:

> I had begun with the song 'I hate Israel' ... Then I started to sing and when the song became a hit and there was such a big fuss, I decided to follow these things so that I could pick up things that people like, and which help angry people to let off steam ... One morning at six, when I finished working, I turned on the TV and heard about those bad cartoons. I got really mad and called my producer and insisted that we must write a song now ...

> We are completely fed up. (2)
> But there are no solutions.
> Humiliation has reached even the religion and the prophet. (2)
> The religion and the prophet.
> Allah's messenger, Muhammad the imam of prophets.
> They want to distort his image – those despicable fools. (2)
> Those despicable fools.
> No religion can be held responsible for the man who humiliated the prophet.

These are crazy people and their top guy is an idiot. (2)
Their top guy is an idiot.
Denmark? They are nothing but pagans.
Who are they to say anything about the prophet? (2)
About the prophet.
Our Islam is innocent of them, and what they say is all lies.
Our Islam is a religion of love, not of injustice and terrorism.
(2)
Not of injustice and terrorism.
When you all meet in hell, the flames will burn your faces.
The flames will burn your faces.
They will burn your faces.
I will speak and won't be silent, and others will say along with me:
We want a total boycott, and even that is not enough.
Why shouldn't we curse them just like they curse us.[19]

Other Muslims, more cynical, ignorant, fanatical and outrageous, even tried to outdo this popular Arab singer by taking their revenge for their fury on the Jews. Arab and Muslim media, who routinely carry hideous anti-Semitic caricatures, noticeably multiplied their output during the cartoon crisis, as if this satisfied their need to channel their hatred where it was least likely to backfire on them. *Hamshahri*, a leading Iranian newspaper, announced, as its way of 'retaliating' (for what?) against Jews, a Holocaust cartoon contest. What do victims of the Holocaust, which the Iranian President denies having ever happened, have to do with Muslim outrage over cartoons? The Arab–European League, a self-proclaimed 'moderate' Belgian–Muslim organization, published, in 'retaliation' to the cartoons, a cartoon showing Anne Frank in bed with Hitler, with the Nazi murderer saying: 'Write this one in your diary, Anne.'[20]

Daniel Goldhagen, a writer on the Shoah, has also detected in the cartoon affair not simply a detached and independent event but a link in a chain of phenomena that express the march of political Islam and its muscle-flexing in the streets, the halls of power and the battlefields, to the extent that a Sunni cleric in Beirut, who organized anti-cartoon protests, declared that the war with the West had already started. Goldhagen claims that the cartoons did not provoke a storm until Iran was about to be referred to the Security Council for its threatening nuclear activities. He found it revealing that Gaza, the hotbed of Hamas, was one of the spots where 'philo-Palestinian Danes and other Europeans were attacked', even though its residents receive more European economic aid than anyone else in the world. European largesse has not and never will buy the Palestinians' goodwill, and is regarded as an 'entitlement' to which they have a 'right'. The same attacks were duplicated in Syria, Iran and Lebanon – other epicentres of Islamic turmoil. Demonstrators in the streets of London held banners proclaiming: 'Massacre those who insult Islam; butcher those who mock Islam; Britain – you will pay, 7/7 is on its way; and Europe – your 9/11 will come.' In Gaza demands were made to amputate the hands of the cartoonists, together with death threats against the publishers. European goods were boycotted, embassies torched and a bounty of a million dollars was offered for the murder of the cartoonists.[21] This is far beyond what can be expected as a proportionate (let alone civilized) reaction in any western society. For Goldhagen, the meek European response of apologies and self-flagellation lent legitimacy to intifada-like eruptions of violence whenever the Muslims felt they were injured.

While the fury over the cartoons spread throughout the Muslim world, Danish, Norwegian, British and even French and Austrian embassies, consulates and humanitarian aid agencies were burned down and Christians were attacked and robbed, bringing the numbers of those directly killed by the protests to 200 (the equivalent of the Bali massacre in 2002). It was evident that the protests were staged and manipulated and not spontaneous. Israel was drawn in when Palestinian Muslims attacked western interests in the West Bank and Gaza, stomped on Danish flags, kidnapped westerners and sent the rest fleeing to Israel for safety. Those who provide shelter to the victims of Muslim fury are, by Muslim definition, accomplices of the 'anti-Muslim' forces, who must be assailed and condemned. On 8 February 2006, in the West Bank city of Hebron, sixty international observers from the Temporary International Presence in Hebron (TIPH) – including twenty Danes and Norwegians – were forced to flee their headquarters, after being attacked by Palestinians. Since the PA police were unable to defend them from the demonstrators, the Israeli army had to be summoned for the job. The irony of the situation lay in the fact that it was the Palestinians who asked for these international observers. Now the TIPH leadership was asking Israeli soldiers for protection from a Palestinian onslaught.[22]

Israel became involved also as a precursor of what was happening to Europe during the cartoon furies. A columnist wrote:

> As long as Muslim demonstrators only shouted 'Death to America' and 'Death to Israel', Europe's and the rest of the world's left found reasons either to ignore the Nazi-like evil inherent in those chants, and the homicidal actions that flowed from them; or to blame America and Israel for the hatred ... But like the early Nazis, our generation's fascists hate anything good, not merely Jews and Americans. And now, the Damascus Embassy of Norway, a leading anti-Israel 'peace at any price' country, has been torched. And more and more Norwegians, and Brits, and French, and Dutch, and Swedes, and the rest of the European appeasers who blamed America for September 11 and Israel for Palestinian suicide bombings, are beginning to wonder whether there just might be something morally troubling within the Islamic world.[23]

Apart from such moralists as Ahmadinejad blaming Israel for the conflict which evolved between Islam and the Christian world independently of either Israel or world Jewry, Israel's name was invoked in any and every demonstration against the cartoons. When Danish flags were burned down throughout the Islamic world, they were always accompanied by the Israeli Star of David and the American Stars and Stripes, and shouts of 'Destroy' or 'Death to' Denmark, Israel, America, or slogans that Bush or Angela Merkel or the American neo-cons were 'stupid Zionists'. Since threats of 'Death to Israel, Zionism and Jews' have become the *delenda est Carthago* of radical Muslims, the cartoon crisis was another occasion for them to express their hateful fury at anything Jewish, including Jewish statehood and the Jewish movement of national liberation. So blatant were these manifestations of anti-Semitism, that European countries, who have been oblivious to them in other contexts, suddenly woke up to the reality of anti-Semitic cartoons in the Muslim media, and of Muslim insults to other religions. Moreover, the western media came to realize that while the cartoon incident was an isolated one, the Muslim deprecation of others is permanent, repetitive, self-sustaining and independent of any particular provocation. So overwhelming was this attitude of the Muslim masses that even such a prominently moderate Nobel Prize winner, the Egyptian Naguib Mahfuz, was cited as having joined the boycotters of Denmark[24] – prompting a comment by the American columnist Charles Krauthammer that what passes for moderation in the Islamic community is nothing of the sort:

> It is simply a cynical way to endorse the goals of the mob without endorsing its means. It is fraudulent because, while pretending to uphold the principle of religious sensitivity, it is only interested in this instance of religious insensitivity ... Have any of these 'moderates' ever protested the grotesque caricatures of Christians and, most especially, Jews that are broadcast throughout the Middle East on a daily basis? The sermons on Palestinian TV that refer to Jews as the 'sons of pigs and monkeys'? The Syrian prime time TV series that shows rabbis slaughtering a gentile boy in order to ritually consume his blood? The 41-part series on Egyptian TV based on that anti-Semitic czarist forgery, *The Protocols of the Elders of Zion*, showing the Jews to be engaged in a century-old conspiracy to control the world? ... Those who don't are not moderates but hypocrites, opportunists and agents for the rioters, using merely different means to advance the same goal: to impose upon the West, with its traditions of freedom of speech, a set of taboos that is exclusive to the Islamic faith. These are not defenders of religion, but Muslim supremacists trying to force their dictates upon the liberal West.[25]

Independently of the way Jews and Israel became unwittingly involved in the cartoon controversy, both Jewish organizations and the State of Israel reacted each in its own way, to the crisis. The Anti-Defamation League (ADL) stated that it was opposed to religious and racial or ethnic stereotyping in the media, and that it found some of the cartoons 'troubling' because they linked

Muhammad with violence. But for the sake of the usual sacrosanct 'balance' it also condemned the use of violence, threats and boycotts as 'inappropriate' for future debates on Islam, democracy and free speech. This kind of balanced statement especially underlines the latent Jewish fear that if 'stereotyping' is not excluded from any debate, then in the future it may be applied against Jewish communities. However, the ADL did not hide its disgust for the 'despicable anti-Jewish caricatures' routinely published throughout the Arab and Islamic world, implying that if Muslims have anything to complain about they cannot occupy the moral high ground if their own hands are not clean. Other Jewish groups argued that while poking fun at religions is permissible because faith is a matter of free choice, ethnicity and persecution cannot become a subject of humour because they are not.[26]

When it comes to Israel, matters are slightly different. Israel has suffered from the Arab boycott for half a century and therefore understood the meaning of Denmark's boycott by the Muslim world. Back in 2002 the Labour Union of Denmark was among the first to call for the boycott of Israeli goods due to the Palestinian intifada. But when the Muslim boycott of Denmark was launched, the partial Danish boycott of Israel backfired, as many refused to join the 'buy Danish' movement because of Danish attitudes to Israel when the latter was confronting the Muslim terrorist threat alone. Since many Muslim countries withdrew their ambassadors from Copenhagen and the Danes had to apologize repeatedly for the 'wrong' they did not do, the Muslims felt vindicated while the 'pro-Zionists', in their parlance, were defeated. It was announced in Riyadh in early April 2006 that Danish Arla dairy products would be back on the shelves of the Saudi Kingdom, after the unofficial boycott was lifted following the recommendation made by five Islamic organizations which participated in the Islamic Conference in Bahrain in March to debate the issue of the 'blasphemous cartoons'. Danish exports to the Middle East had slumped by 15.5 per cent, but this was accompanied by a rise in US exports by 17 per cent after a 'buy Danish' campaign was organized. It was claimed that the boycott was lifted after the Arla group issued a worldwide apology and pledged to 'disseminate awareness about Islam and make donations to Muslim charities'.[27] In their eagerness to promote trade with the Muslim world, the Danish authorities might become even more circumspect in their dealings with Israel, even though the Danish populace and media now understand that they received the same treatment habitually meted out to Israel.

The cartoon controversy had further repercussions elsewhere in the West. The fact that simultaneous and equally vexatious legal complaints were filed by Muslims suggests that some degree of coordination must have existed during this concerted effort by world Islam. A group of twenty-seven Danish Muslim organizations filed a defamation lawsuit against the newspaper that first published the caricatures, two weeks after Denmark's top prosecutor declined to press criminal charges, saying the drawings did not violate laws against racism or blasphemy. The lawsuit sought $16,100 in damages from *Jyllands-Posten* editor-in-chief Carsten Juste and culture editor Flemming Rose. The newspaper said it published the cartoons to challenge self-censorship among artists afraid to offend Islam. Rose had heard that a children's author writing a book on Muhammad was unable to find an illustrator to draw him. So the country's biggest-selling daily decided to commission cartoons mocking the prophet as a way of illustrating the problem of self-censorship. The lawsuit came despite the fact that the drawings were later reprinted in other western media, mostly in Europe, in the name of free speech and news value and that the Danish newspaper apologized for offending Muslims after violent protests erupted throughout the Islamic world – but not for its decision to print the drawings, citing freedom of speech.[28]

The booksellers Borders and Waldenbrooks, based in Michigan, decided not to carry the April/May 2006 issue of *Free Inquiry Magazine* because it contained the Danish cartoons. The company meekly explained that, 'For us, the safety and security of our customers and employees is a top priority, and we believe that carrying this issue could challenge that priority.' Claiming to respect their customers' right to choose what they wish to read and buy, it was a little strange that Borders and Waldenbrooks should prevent them from doing so. While Islamic tradition bars the depiction of Muhammad to prevent idol worship, which is strictly prohibited, Islamic law cannot be made to prevail in non-Muslim countries. 'What is at stake is the precious right of freedom of expression', said Paul Kurtz, editor-in-chief of *Free Inquiry*.

'Cartoons often provide an important form of political satire ... To refuse to distribute a publication because of fear of vigilante violence is to undermine freedom of the press – so vital for our democracy.'[29]

The American bookseller's shameful capitulation was soon reflected in Paris. News is given immediacy by instant reporting, and any 'success' by Muslims anywhere in the western world can immediately be emulated elsewhere. A gang of young Muslims wielding iron rods forced a Paris café to censor an exhibition of cartoons ridiculing religion. Some fifty drawings by well-known French cartoonists were installed in the Mer a Boire café in the Belleville neighbourhood of Paris, as part of an avowedly atheist show entitled, 'Neither God nor god'. The collection targeted all religions, including Islam, but there were no representations of Muhammad such as those which sparked the crisis between the West and Muslims. The youths warned that if the cartoons were not taken down, they would call in the Muslim Brothers who would burn the café down. They repeatedly asserted: 'This is our home. You cannot act like this here.' Refusing to dismantle the exhibition, the owners placed white sheets of paper inscribed with the word 'censored' over the cartoons that were targeted by the gang. Unlike Borders and Waldenbrooks, the café owners recognized that to take down the cartoons would have been a surrender. But not wishing to be exposed to violence, they said the pictures could still be seen by lifting the paper.[30]

For France's Muslim youths, religion has become a mark of identity, and more acts of vandalism and coerced yielding to Islamic customs will inevitably follow, not least because the police remained out of sight during the café rampage. One of the cartoons that aroused the wrath of the youths was a bar scene, in which the barman offers a drink to an obviously inebriated man who says 'God is great.' The caption is: 'The sixth pillar of Islam.[31] The bar pillar'. In France a 'bar pillar' is a drunk. A cartoonist who took part in this exhibition, Charb, told *Le Parisien* daily: 'Putting on this type of show in this place was not in the least a provocation. Unless you think that freedom of expression in itself is a provocation.'[32] Meanwhile, Prince Charles, who has always been uncritical of Islam, raised the issue of reciprocity while on a visit to Egypt, when he was awarded an honorary doctorate from al-

Azhar University in Cairo. Britain's Bishop Michael Nazir-Ali took the opportunity to write a critique of the lack of reciprocity in Islam, against the background of a trial of an Afghan who had converted to Christianity, although this lack of recriprocity extends throughout all Muslim dealings with the West:

> The Prince of Wales enjoys a high reputation in the Muslim world, higher than he has in his country. This is because he has taken Islam seriously and attempted to engage with the various civilizations associated with it. It is true that he repeats various mantras that we have come to associate with him and seeks to find common ground in the face of glaring differences. He is perhaps too apologetic about the history of Christianity in Europe and too uncritical about the history of Islam. But he does for the first time mention the importance of reciprocity. He talks about respect for one another and, specifically, how the treatment of Muslims in Europe, in its positive and negative aspects, is inextricably bound up with how Christian and other minorities are treated in the Muslim world. Again and again Muslim scholars assure us that there is no compulsion in matters of religion and that Islam upholds fundamental freedoms. Yet it remains the case that all existing schools of law prescribe the death penalty for apostasy.[33]

Watching from afar, no longer with indifference but with a growing sense of concern, the US began to suspect that the limitations to speak freely that were imposed on Europe by fear, might come to America's shores if the government does not protect freedom of speech. The Ayn Rand Institute of Irvine, California, raised the issue with 'depressingly many examples' cited from Europe: a painter, Rashid Ben Ali, was forced into hiding after one of his shows 'featured satirical work critical of Islamic militants' violence'; Ayaan Hirsi Ali, originally from Somalia, who became a member of the Dutch parliament, needed round-the-clock protection after it became known that she renounced her Islamic faith; and a film director, Theo van Gogh, was savagely stabbed to death for making a film critical of Islamic oppression of women. When *Jyllands-Posten* published some cartoons to expose and challenge

The Cartoon Affair and the Failure of Dialogue and Coexistence 299

this climate of intimidation, the response was violent. The Ayn Rand report saw all this as precursors of what 'appears that we should now begin to get used to in America'. Citing the reaction of Borders and Waldenbooks stores, the author emphasized that the decision was not based on disagreement with the content of the magazine, but simply due to Borders' capitulation to Islamic thugs that seemed 'understandable' given the 'pathetic response of our and other western governments'. The author complained:

> Has any western government declared that an individual's freedom of speech is sacrosanct, no matter who screams offence at his ideas? No. Has any western government proclaimed each individual's right to life and pledged to hunt down anyone, anywhere, who abets the murder of one of its citizens for having had the effrontery to speak? No – as they did not when the fatwa against Rushdie was issued: American bookstores were firebombed, and Rushdie's translators were attacked and murdered. On the contrary, our government went out of its way to say that it shares 'the offence that Muslims have taken at these images', and even hinted that they should not be published. The British police, Douglas Murray reports, told the editor of a London magazine that they could not protect him, his staff, or his offices from attack – so the magazine removed the cartoons from its website. (A few days later, Murray notes, 'the police provided 500 officers to protect a "peaceful" Muslim protest in Trafalgar Square'.)
>
> In the face of such outrages, we must demand that the US Government reverse its disgraceful stand and fulfil is obligation to protect our right to free speech. Freedom of speech means the right to express one's ideas without danger of physical coercion from anyone. This freedom includes the right to make movies, write books, draw pictures, voice political opinions – and satirize religion. This right flows from the right to think: the right to observe, to follow the evidence, to reach the conclusions you judge the facts warrant – and then to convey your thoughts to others. In a free society, anyone angered by someone else's ideas has a simple and powerful recourse: don't buy his books, watch his movies, or read his

newspapers. If one judges his ideas dangerous, argue against them. The purveyor of evil ideas is no threat to those who remain free to counter them with rational ones. But the moment someone decides to answer those he finds offensive with a knife or a homemade explosive, not an argument, he removes himself from civilized society. Against such a threat to our rights, our government must respond with force. If it fails to do so, it fails to fulfil its reason for being: 'to secure these rights', Jefferson wrote, 'Governments are instituted among Men.' And if it fails to do so, we the people must hold it to account. We must vociferously demand that our government declare publicly that, from this day forward, it will defend by force any American who receives death threats for criticizing Islam – or religion – or any other idea. We must demand that the government protect the stores and employees of Borders, of Waldenbooks, and of any other organization that reprints the cartoons. We must demand this, because nothing less will prevent America's climate of freedom from disintegrating into Europe's climate of fear.[34]

The German *Der Spiegel* devised its own insights to summarize the cartoon affair, contending that because many Muslim regimes are competing with radical Islamists for popular approval, they continue to incite public outrage. While the Danish Cultural Institute in Damascus was being looted and the Danish Embassy was on fire, Omar Bakri was preoccupied sending more than six million e-mails in twenty-four hours from his Beirut apartment – short summaries of Islamic legal opinions on the Islamists' case for blasphemy, as well as calls for demonstrations and tirades against the West. The cartoon controversy gave the jihadist preacher who left Britain after 7/7 a new focus for his animosity. Outside the Danish General Consulate in Beirut, he said: 'At first we felt only pain. But then we realized what a gift the Danes had in fact given us. They woke a sleeping giant – the giant of Islam. You have no idea just how big he is.' Protests, some of them violent, erupted in Iran, Afghanistan, Pakistan, Somalia, India, Bangladesh, Thailand and New Zealand. Other publications in the West, including *Charlie Hebdo*, a Paris-based satirical journal, decided to print the contentious cartoons, attracting condemnation by Jacques Chirac. Meanwhile the Bush administration, which had initially expressed understanding for the Muslim protests, changed its tone. After meeting with Jordan's King Abdullah, President George W. Bush said that the Americans 'reject violence as a way to express discontent with what may be printed in a free press', adding that he had assured Danish Prime Minister Anders Fogh Rasmussen of American 'support and solidarity'. US Secretary of State Condoleezza Rice was more forceful, saying that 'Iran and Syria have gone out of their way to inflame sentiments and to use this to their own purposes. And the world ought to call them on it.' The EU's foreign policy chief, Javier Solana, also voiced his suspicions over the impetus behind some of the protests. His spokeswoman said it was 'very strange' that the demonstrations in Iran, Syria and the Gaza Strip were especially vehement, adding that Arab leaders who value good relations with the West should 'clearly and unmistakably' discuss the deteriorating situation. Those western leaders who condemned the cartoons did not understand that far from calming tempers, more Muslims around the world were encouraged to step up their rage once it had shown its efficacy in generating so many apologies.

Adil Hammuda, editor-in-chief of *al-Fagr*, a liberal Egyptian weekly, was astonished when the storm erupted in January. He had reprinted the cartoons that had been published in *Jyllands-Posten* in his own paper four months earlier, even going so far as to place the most controversial cartoon depicting Muhammad with a bomb in his turban on the front page. *Al-Fagr* is a young paper which became prominent during Egypt's presidential election in September 2006.[35] But the reprinted cartoons failed to attract much attention – another proof, if needed, that it is not the 'profanation' of the prophet that matters, but how it is interpreted to an otherwise unthinking public. Muslim children are educated by being given facts to commit to memory. The inculcation of skills in reasoning and inquiry, so central to the concept of education in the West, is unheard of. The highest pinnacle of achievement for a Muslim is the learning of the Qur'an by rote, and not the interpretation of it. It is therefore not surprising that Muslims wait for directions from their leaders, whether religious or political, before they react to any information. There is no such thing as a spontaneous demonstration in the repressive and authoritarian Muslim world. When those who are ready to incite minds detect that the moment has come to further their ulterior motives, they take advantage of any incident to fan the flames. 'It can't be a coincidence', said Hammuda, 'that the story didn't explode until so much later.' Carl Bildt, a former Swedish Prime Minister, blamed the Egyptians for escalating the reactions, in a fashion that only an ex-politician dare do in Sweden.[36]

The cartoons were published on 30 September 2005, and on 9 October, spokesmen for the local Islamic community demanded an apology from *Jyllands-Posten*. Ten days later, Prime Minister Fogh Rasmussen refused the request for a meeting by eleven ambassadors from Muslim countries about state intervention against the newspaper, saying the cartoons were a matter for the free press. Copenhagen received a stern warning of a 'possible escalation' of the situation, delivered by the Egyptian Government to the Danish ambassador in Cairo. It was after these warnings were ignored by Copenhagen that Cairo circulated the cartoons. A delegation of Danish Muslims had travelled to Cairo in early December, where they met with top officials including Egyptian Foreign Minister Ahmed Abu al-Gheit. He showed the cartoons to attendees at the meeting of the Organization of the Islamic Conference (OIC) in Mecca on 7 December 2005, and then enlisted the support of other Arab governments. It is worth noting that the OIC had outlined its expectations in its 'Declaration of Human Rights in Islam' in 1990: 'All have the right to freely express their opinions in a manner that does not run counter to shari'a law.' Thus freedom of expression in western nations had to conform with shari'a law. On 29 December, Arab League Foreign Ministers publicly criticized Fogh-Rasmussen. Egypt's behaviour exploded once and for all the myth of its 'moderation', 'politics of reason' and 'pro-western stance'. As calls for boycotts began appearing on the internet, first individual ministers, then entire governments and, finally, the entire Jordanian parliament (yet another 'moderate' nation) condemned the drawings.[37] Since an Egyptian paper had published the cartoons just after they appeared in Denmark, the Egyptian Government will have known that the Danish Muslims had added three acutely offensive cartoons to the original drawings. In other words, the 'blasphemy' of the cartoons came from the pens of Danish Muslims and no one else. Arab papers, meanwhile, claimed the Danish media had portrayed Muhammad as a pig, the original twelve cartoons magically became 120 drawings, and the Danish Government was accused of having instigated the crisis. Egypt had another axe to grind. Copenhagen and Cairo had agreed to a Danish–Egyptian 'dialogue forum' in January 2005, and felt slighted when the request for a meeting with Fogh Anders Rasmussen in October was declined.

The Danish Muslim delegation was led by two imams, Ahmed Akkari and Ahmed Abu Laban, who convinced themselves that they had evidence of an 'Islamophobia' and racism that permeated Danish society. Newspapers failed to publish their letters of complaint and politicians seemed unwilling to listen. 'As a group in society, we've simply been ignored', Akkari said. Feeling 'ignored' is the key word, particularly for adherents of a supremacist faith. Akkari said he wanted to draw attention to the racist climate in order to prevent 'a repeat of the Theo van Gogh drama in the Netherlands'. Kaare Quist, a journalist at the Danish daily *Ekstra Bladet*, said the group found a number of highly placed officials in the Arab world keen to listen to its message, including representatives of the Arab League, Egypt's Grand Mufti and other high-level officials. Of the three offensive caricatures added to the original twelve, one showed Muhammad as a paedophile, another as a pig and the last depicted a praying Muslim being raped by a dog.[38] 'We want to internationalize this issue so that the Danish Government would realize that the cartoons were not only insulting to Muslims in Denmark but also to Muslims worldwide', said Laban. He claimed that this strategy was agreed upon by organizations representing Pakistani, Turkish and Arab Muslims in Denmark.[39] Danish Muslim delegations thereafter made repeated trips to the Middle East, taking their forty-three-page dossier on 'Danish racism and Islamophobia'. The delegations were publicly criticized by the Danish Prime Minister, who said he was 'speechless' that his fellow countrymen could tour the Arab world 'inciting antipathy towards Denmark'.[40]

At an EU Foreign Ministers' meeting in Brussels on 30 January 2006, the representative of Luxembourg stated he wasn't just speaking for his own country when he said that the entire affair was 'more a Danish than a European problem', undermining the solidarity which supposedly underpins the EU enterprise. Even the American State Department spokesmen referred to the cartoons as 'unacceptable' and 'offensive'. The diplomats had the situation under control for a few more weeks, but three events helped trigger the outbreak of rage: the success of the Muslim Brotherhood in Egyptian parliamentary elections in November, the reprinting of the cartoons in Norwegian newspaper *Magazinet* on 10 January 2006, and Hamas's victory in the Palestinian elections. 'Then it suddenly became clear that the Arab regimes had their hand in the game', said Jørgen Nielsen, previously employed at the Danish Cultural Institute in Damascus. According to Rami Khuri, publisher of Beirut's *Daily Star*, Arab governments were 'competing for legitimacy', and their reactions to the cartoons varied. Saudi Arabia recalled its ambassador from Denmark on 26 January. Qatar's chamber of commerce cancelled invitations to Danish and Norwegian delegations. The United Arab Emirates permitted demonstrations, a move that would normally be unheard of. 'We have no other choice', said an employee in the country's Ministry of Religion. 'Those who say nothing create the impression that they secretly want to see the prophet insulted.' The Gulf states also started boycotting Scandinavian dairy foods, but that did not last, for 'no sheikh would seriously consider doing without his new [Danish] Bang & Olufsen stereo system'. Other regimes went a step further. 'It would have been easy to block off the entire street where the Danish Embassy is located', said Nielsen, but the Syrian Government chose to incite the mob to riot. Busloads of demonstrators from northern Lebanon went to the Danish consulate in Beirut. As it turned out, seventy-seven of the 192 arrested were Syrian. Mobilizing people onto the streets is a proven tool of Arab rulers. It sends a message to the West: if you didn't have us to control this mob, you'd be dealing with it. Syria, which had come under pressure for its alleged involvement in the assassination of former Lebanese Prime Minister Rafik Hariri, applies this logic, said Khuri – as do Libya and Egypt. 'But the argument is gradually becoming less convincing. After all, the West is already cooperating with an Islamist-tinted government in Turkey, and Washington itself helped put the Islamists in power in Iraq.' The dictators are no longer needed.[41]

A western diplomat in Beirut pointed to a similar motive. He said that Hamas's victory at the polls worried the Arab world's autocrats more than any Islamist bombing attack. 'Until now, the Islamists were a security risk, a problem mainly for the police and intelligence agencies. Now they're a democratic alternative.' Street hooligans are much easier to control than winners in an election. Not all governments derived the same amount of political capital from the cartoon dispute. Lebanon's Cabinet was caught completely off-guard by the protests, prompting it to apologize to Denmark for the violence. In Jordan, a country still in shock over terrorist attacks at three hotels in Amman in November 2005, pressure from the Islamists was relatively light. As a result, King Abdullah II was able to keep his comments about the cartoon affair comparatively mild. The way Iraq's Shi'ite-dominated government played the cartoon crisis is also instructive, using it to mend fences with the Sunni minority. Although Shi'ites generally avoid depicting Muhammad, their prohibition of images isn't nearly as strict as it is in Sunni Islam. Millions of portraits of Ali and Hussein, the most important Shi'ite martyrs, are in circulation. Nevertheless, Iraq froze all economic agreements with Denmark and refused reconstruction aid from Denmark and Norway. Grand Ayatollah Ali al-Sistani, the spiritual leader of Iraqi Shi'ites, took an unusual approach to the cartoon dispute. He condemned publication of the cartoons as a 'despicable act', but also criticized Muslim extremists, saying they are partly responsible for Islam's poor image in the West. 'Misdirected' and 'oppressive' parts of Muslim society, he added, contribute to a distorted image of Islam. Sistani, a Persian by birth, was probably referring more to the leadership of al-Qa'ida than to Ahmadinejad – reflecting the emerging rivalry with Osama Bin Laden over who should be shaping the opinions of Muslim extremists. Iran, already entangled in a row with the West over its nuclear programme, had eagerly inflamed the culture war. Although the contest for the best cartoons about the Holocaust, which Tehran newspaper Hamshahri announced, shocked the West, it impressed men like British fugitive Omar Bakri, a Bin Laden supporter. 'The rhetoric from Tehran is quite impressive', the preacher of hate said from his Lebanese exile, 'but it's nothing more than just rhetoric. What has Ahmadinejad done to America so far?'[42]

On 3 February, a 'Day of Rage' was proclaimed, a device so beloved by the late Palestinian leader Yasser Arafat. It never failed to impress Europeans with the notion that the Palestinians were demonstrating because of the 'despair' and 'injustice' of the Israeli 'occupation'. Now the same tactic was being put to use against Europe. Across the Muslim world, the cartoons were the focus of Friday prayers. Friday mosque sermons are traditionally used by imams to whip their congregations into a Pavlovian frenzy. Hence their governments habitually resort to lining the streets outside mosques with security forces, in case the frenzy is transformed into anti-government riots. In years gone by, an attack on an embassy would have invited a military response, but now the West evinced cowardice and was more concerned about the effect on exports. For their part, the Muslims demonstrated the speed and agility with which they could mobilize their populations.

Celebrated author and Muslim dissident, Ibn Warraq, argued that freedom of expression is part of the western heritage. It must be defended against attacks from totalitarian societies, or else the Islamization of Europe will have begun in earnest. He cited the great British philosopher John Stuart Mill who wrote in *On Liberty,* 'Strange it is, that men should admit the validity of the arguments for free discussion, but object to their being "pushed to an extreme"; not seeing that unless the reasons are good for an extreme case, they are not good for any case.' Ibn Warraq wondered if the West was going to cave in to pressure from societies with a medieval mindset, or defend the most precious freedom, the freedom of expression, for which thousands of people sacrificed their lives. He contended that democracy cannot survive long without freedom of expression, the freedom to argue, to dissent, even to insult and offend. It is a freedom sorely lacking in the Islamic world, and without it Islam will remain unassailed in its dogmatic, fanatical, medieval fortress; ossified, totalitarian and intolerant. He asserted that without this fundamental freedom, Islam will continue to stifle thought, human rights, individuality, originality and truth. He also raised another more general problem, specifically the inability of the West to defend itself intellectually and culturally:

> Do we still have to apologize, for example, for the British Empire, when, in fact, the British presence in India led to the

Indian Renaissance, resulted in famine relief, railways, roads and irrigation schemes, eradication of cholera, the civil service, the establishment of a universal educational system where none existed before, the institution of elected parliamentary democracy and the rule of law? What of the British architecture of Bombay and Calcutta? The British even gave back to the Indians their own past: it was European scholarship, archaeology and research that uncovered the greatness that was India; it was British Government that did its best to save and conserve the monuments that were a witness to that past glory. British Imperialism preserved where earlier Islamic Imperialism destroyed thousands of Hindu temples.'[43]

The same arguments could of course be made for French rule in North Africa, British rule in the Arab world and Dutch rule in the Indies. So, it was strange that of all former colonial powers who had subjugated Islamic lands, but also brought them enlightenment, the Muslims should have picked on Denmark which had no part in that. Ibn Warraq continued:

Should the West really apologize for Dante, Shakespeare, and Goethe? Mozart, Beethoven and Bach? Rembrandt, Vermeer, Van Gogh, Breughel, Ter Borch? Galileo, Huygens, Copernicus, Newton and Darwin? Penicillin and computers? The Olympic Games and football? Human rights and parliamentary democracy? The West is the source of the liberating ideas of individual liberty, political democracy, the rule of law, human rights and cultural freedom. It is the West that has raised the status of women, fought against slavery, defended freedom of enquiry, expression and conscience. No, the West needs no lectures on the superior virtue of societies who keep their women in subjection, cut off their clitorises, stone them to death for alleged adultery, throw acid on their faces, or deny the human rights of those considered to belong to lower castes. How can we expect immigrants to integrate into western society when they are at the same time being taught that the West is decadent, a den of iniquity, the source of all evil, racist, imperialist and to be despised? Why should they, in the words of the African-American writer James Baldwin, want to integrate into a sinking ship? Why do they all want to immigrate to the West and not Saudi Arabia? They should be taught about the centuries of struggle that resulted in the freedoms that they and everyone else for that matter, cherish, enjoy, and avail themselves of; of the individuals and groups who fought for these freedoms and who are despised and forgotten today; the freedoms that much of the rest of the world envies, admires and tries to emulate. When the Chinese students cried and died for democracy in Tiananmen Square (in 1989), they brought with them not representations of Confucius or Buddha but a model of the Statue of Liberty.[44]

After 1945, Europe remade itself on the idea of its refusal of war, after the fatigue of enduring so much bloodshed. European democracy is now centred on a diversified space where life is good, accompanied by welfare from the cradle to the grave. But the contrast is striking between the European society of law, dialogue, mutual respect and tolerance, and the tragedies being endured by the rest of the world. Yet Europe claims to have no adversaries, only partners, and to be a friend to all. And Europe has been haunted by the torment of repentance of its past crimes: slavery, imperialism, fascism, communism. Continuing in the footsteps of the Arabs and the Africans, Europe instituted the transatlantic slave trade. But, following in the footsteps of the British example, it was also the first to put an end to slavery. A civilization capable of the worst atrocities as well as the most sublime creation cannot examine itself only from the perspective of a guilty conscience, and nor is genocide a western specialty.[45]

In contrast, the Muslim Turks refuse to admit that the massacres of Christian Armenians (when 1.5 million perished between 1915 and 1923) amounted to a genocide; and today, the OIC has exhibited total indifference to the Sudanese Arab Muslim genocide against the black Muslims of Darfur that has claimed 300,000 lives.[46] Despite their oil-generated billions, not a single Arab country has sent humanitarian aid to relieve the suffering of their fellow-Muslims in Darfur, nor taken any step to stop the massacres. According to Human Rights Watch, there have been many incidents of government forces and Janjaweed militias destroying mosques, killing those seeking refuge inside mosques and desecrating the Qur'an while attacking civilian villages. Yet the world witnessed Muslim 'outrage' against the West for allegedly defacing the Qur'an at Guantanamo, and publishing 'blasphemous' cartoons in Denmark.

For decades, Europe has dwelt on her dark deeds while undervaluing her successes and values, generating both self-loathing and defeatism. Europe now sees her role as paying off debts. Both the Protestant and Catholic churches have been at the forefront of the periodic waves of 'apologies' to less-developed countries. But the spirit behind such repentance is wasted and worse if other cultures and other faiths fail to admit their errors. It enables them to monopolize 'moral purity' simply by claiming they are humiliated and persecuted, and they are never held to account for the gross injustices they have perpetrated and indeed continue to perpetrate today. Meanwhile, their acts of unspeakable brutality continue unabated, from mass murder by self-implosion in the midst of civilians in the streets of Baghdad or the transport systems of Europe, or the matchless barbarity of the beheading of kidnapped western victims on television as a recruiting tool for yet more jihadists. Their rallying cries of '*Allahu akbar*' as they slaughter their hapless victims on the screen has done more to associate Islam with gratuitous cruelty than anything any westerner could say or do. Indeed, it must be offensive to the average Christian or Jew to have their faiths linked with Islam in a trio of 'monotheistic religions', for the vengeful god of Islam is far removed from the Christian and Jewish deity. Europe's guilt-based policies harm the very people the Europeans focus their guilt on, since they generate inertia or violence instead of motivating them to develop and improve their societies. Instead of dividing the world along the lines of rich or poor or former colonialists and the colonized, it would be more fruitful for all countries to recognize their duty and face up to their own previous misdeeds and current shortcomings. Europe needs to prepare for forthcoming confrontations and recover the spirit of resistance to the ideological successor of fascist and communist totalitarianism.[47]

Not only did the cartoon controversy not open a dialogue of reason between Islam and the West, but the dialogue remained confined to incriminations and accusations. Especially instructive in this regard are the views of Shujaat Ali, the al-Jazeera cartoonist. Commenting on the outrage in the Arab world over the cartoons, and on State Department criticism of his own work, he suggested that it was the responsibility of journalists to be ethical. Religion is a very sensitive issue, he thought, and no truly professional cartoonist in the world would ever try to pick on a religion like this. There's an informal code of ethics among cartoonists in the media, and it includes two kinds of censorship: one is self-censorship; the other is professional censorship. He attacked Islamic parties in Pakistan during elections for steering religion in the wrong direction, leading one Islamic party to attack the newspaper's offices with guns. In response to the accusation by the State Department regarding the insensitive cartoons he published after September 11, he explained that his actual target in those particular cartoons was the US Government and not its people, forgetting that 3,000 Americans, not the government, had perished there. Regarding the anti-Semitic vitriol that pours out of his and other Arab cartoons, he agreed and 'expressed sorrow' about that, but did not pledge to stop that form of incitement himself. He recognized that all members of all religions should be respected and that an ethical code should guide all cartoonists to leave religion alone, and set limitations upon them.[48]

But on the issue of government reaction to breaches of these ethics, Ali was firm, despite the fact that limitations might be perceived in the West as anti-democratic: if the government doesn't take steps to stop the media from attacking a religion, which can lead to a major conflict between people, it could damage their international reputation. He considers freedom important, and said he was fighting for it, but within limits. When artists use this kind of (religious) issue in their cartoons to provoke, and they know that it will hurt the feelings of people in the other religion, then they've crossed the line and this has to go to the higher authorities responsible for this. Ali could not understand that there are no 'higher authorities' for freedom of the press and that the West would rather see abusive uses of this freedom than the use of violence to quell it. For Shujaat Ali, the Muslim reaction was a way of 'correcting the Danish cartoonists and trying to show them the feelings of the masses'. He said explicitly: 'We cannot tolerate any disparagement of the prophet – for whom we have the highest respect.' But he admitted that Muslim extremists should be criticized, for (Muslim) extremism is also bad.⁴⁹ His responses serve to highlight the depth of the gulf between the two cultures. More worrisome is the fact that anti-Semitic and anti-western cartoons continue unabated, and very few questions are asked about whether, to what extent and whom, they hurt.

In the West too, outside Denmark, reactions varied, from papers and magazines in France and Germany which reprinted the cartoons to make their point, to the editor of the Danish paper which caused the controversy, who found it necessary to apologize for causing offence. In a column in the *New York Times*, Flemming Rose argued that the left in Europe is deceiving itself about Islamism and immigration just as 'young hippies' like himself deceived themselves about communism thirty years ago. *Der Spiegel* wondered why the anger and outrage in the Arab world continued to mushroom even after the Danish paper apologized. What began as a family fight in unhappily multicultural Denmark had become a global *cause célèbre*, with the whole affair taking on cartoonish dimensions. EU Trade Commissioner Peter Mandelson, who frequently insists that Europe speak with one voice, informed Saudi diplomats (since the boycott was instigated by Saudi Arabia) that a boycott of Denmark would be handled like a boycott of the entire EU. The EU threatened Arab countries which support the boycott with WTO sanctions. Seventeen Foreign Ministers of the Arab League even called for the punishment of the responsible editors at a meeting in Tunis, while representatives of Denmark's 200,000 Muslims accepted the 'apology' from the paper.⁵⁰ The reality about EU solidarity with Denmark did not match up to Mandelson's assertions. Prime Minister Anders Fogh Rasmussen was asked about attempts in the Arab world by companies associated with Nestlé, the Swiss food giant, and Carrefour, the French retailer, to distance themselves from Denmark. He said that attempts by European companies in the Middle East to disassociate themselves from Denmark or Danish products were 'disgraceful', and attempts to gain commercial advantage at Denmark's expense had struck at the hearts of all Danes. He said the government was re-evaluating relations with local Muslim leaders who stoked tensions by showing the cartoons to Arab religious leaders, adding: 'We are witnessing events with deep sadness and disbelief. We are not used to it in Denmark.' Instead of learning from the way Israel had been treated by the Arabs for decades, Europe chose to look away.[51]

An attempt at 'dialogue' was initiated by the Belgian Foreign Minister, with the Europeans apologizing and the Arabs accusing. He asked the western media to show 'responsibility', and the Arab media to stop broadcasting racist terrorist messages, such as anti-Semitic programmes on Hizbollah's al-Manar channel. The very imbalance inherent in those requests demonstrates that the West disastrously sees itself as a supplicant, setting itself up to be promptly slapped down by Arab speakers. The EU also organized a conference on 'Europe for Mediterranean Journalists'. Such gatherings prove to the Arabs that their views are fit to be taken seriously, that their outlook has merit, and reinforces their hateful and intolerant attitudes. They actually ought to be shunned, and told that they have not earned the privilege of sitting at the adults' table. Only then will they have an incentive to reform. The conference was ostensibly organized to prepare for a training programme for journalists from Syria, Jordan, Lebanon, Egypt, Morocco, Algeria, Tunisia, Turkey, 'Palestine' and Israel, yet no amount of training can overcome the strictures placed on journalists in Arab societies. Simon Wiesenthal Centre's Rabbi Abraham Cooper focused on the internet which has emerged as 'the virtual university of terrorism'. Speaking at the forum on curbing 'hate messages' in the media and on the internet, he urged the Organization for Security and Cooperation in Europe (OSCE) and other international agencies to work together to 'diminish, if not eliminate' websites being used by terrorist organizations to promote their causes. Cooper, the associate dean of the Los Angeles-based centre, said there were up to 600 'problematic sites', some of which carried anti-Semitic and racist messages while others even served as instruction manuals on how to make bombs and carry out terrorist attacks. 'Without any doubt, the internet today has been co-opted by terrorist groups who present to all of us existential threats', he said, 'and I believe we are only at the very beginning in civil society of grasping the enormity of that challenge.'[52]

The keynote address was delivered by Saudi Information Minister Ayad Ben Amin Madani, who preceded his speech with a prayer in Arabic for tolerance, proceeding quickly enough to denounce the 'Islamophobia' of western civilization. He complained that Arab media are always pictured in the West as tools of government and social control. Representatives of the media, including Aidan White, general secretary of the International Federation of Journalists, strongly condemned any attempt by politicians or religious leaders to curb freedom of speech. Wadah Khanfar, director general of al-Jazeera, defended freedom of speech and his network's right to broadcast tapes by al-Qa'ida leaders.[53]

The conservative paper *Die Welt* demonstratively reprinted the cartoons, asking 'Is it possible to satirize Islam? How much humour is compatible with the religion of Islam, this metaphysics of world conquest by an early medieval robber prince, who with his caravan army created a great empire on the basis of polygamy and a strict code of honour?' While the paper agreed that there is a certain 'threshold of shame' in regard to the satirization of religion, 'The standard of measure set by the Muslims nonetheless is a challenge for an open society.' *Die Welt* also regretted what it regarded as the Danish capitulation to pressure, and defended the 'right to blasphemy' against calls not to 'provoke religious minorities'. The left-wing *Berliner Zeitung* took a different approach to the Muslim economic boycott. Noting that the expression of Muslim anger against the cartoons is considered illegitimate since it lacks respect for freedom of opinion, the paper concluded, 'if we really want to protect our values, then we should respect this call for boycott and just accept the sacrifices they will incur, as the sacrifices of a civil, market-oriented way of life'. The business daily *Handelsblatt* concerned itself with the economic consequences of the affair. According to the analysis of the Danish Jyske Bank, a one-year boycott of Danish food products would result in lost revenues totalling €322 million and the loss of 4,000 jobs. In the case of a spillover effect to other branches, 11,000 jobs would be in danger. The centre-left *Suddeutsche Zeitung* described the Danish People's Party's Pia Kjaersgaard as the most powerful right-wing politician in Europe and credited her with the falling acceptance rates of asylum seekers from 53 per cent in 2001 to 9 per cent in 2004.[54]

The cartoons episode was summed up by the Danish editor who triggered the controversy, in a scathing fashion: 'It was worth it!' *Jyllands-Posten*'s employees were flooded with death threats by telephone and post, and its offices endured a number of bomb threats, prompting its spokesman to comment that they 'served to show how relevant the debate that the newspaper unleashed four months earlier is in contemporary society'. He said the paper did not intend to provoke Muslims by running the political cartoons. 'Instead we wanted to show how deeply entrenched self-censorship has already become.' The paper's political editor, Joern Mikkelsen, said the editors remained strong. 'We're not afraid, but this has made us more reflective.' Mikkelsen said the paper had not violated ethics or even the law, but it had nevertheless apologized to all those who were offended by the caricatures. In his view, 'this doesn't have to do with the pictures anymore – I mean, who has even seen them?' Instead, the issue was transformed into a conflict of civilizations.[55] One Danish editor admitted that newspapers would take more time in the future to consider whether stories they publish would hurt people's feelings, and whether the story is important enough to take that risk. Meanwhile, Imam Akkari said it wasn't his intention to introduce censorship or to ban criticism of religious issues, although he disapproved of the Danish media focus on Muslim communities. As a direct result of his own actions, critical reporting on Muslims increased sharply, and Akkari was 'worried that the problem is escalating and that some people might get the wrong idea'.[56]

In France, events backfired unexpectedly, and the controversy surrounding the cartoons continued to expand in unforeseen directions. The publisher of *France Soir* fired his editor, Jacques Lefranc, after he published the caricatures. The paper's owner, Egyptian magnate Raymond Lakah, said he removed the editor 'as a powerful sign of respect for the intimate beliefs and convictions of every individual'. Lakah was infuriated that the front page of *France Soir* depicted Buddhist, Muslim, Jewish and Christian gods telling Muhammad, 'Don't worry Muhammad, we've all been caricatured here.' Officials in Tunisia and Morocco banned the sale of that day's issue of *France Soir*, while the French Foreign Ministry criticized the decision to publish. Even if freedom of expression is important to France, the ministry said, it 'condemns all that hurts individuals in their beliefs or their religious convictions'. Seldom, or never, has the French Foreign Ministry issued any condemnation when anti-Semitic caricatures are published in Arab and European media. Other French media, however, rushed to *France Soir's* defence. Some noted that other books had been ruthlessly satirical in their caricature portrayals of religious leaders like Pope John Paul II. If other religions could be the subject of sarcasm and humour, then why not Islam and Muhammad, too? Meanwhile, on the culture pages of Germany's respected *Frankfurt Allgemeine Zeitung*, the journalist Christian Geyer urged other papers to publish the caricature. 'Only Europe-wide solidarity can show that religious fundamentalists who do not respect the difference between satire and blasphemy have a problem not only with Denmark, but with the entire western world', he wrote.[57]

Some sober views in the world of Islam, fearful of a clash with the West, tried to calm tempers. One of them was Abdullah Hassan Barakat of al-Azhar University. He experiences none of the sentiments of self-doubt, insecurity and feelings of inferiority that western observers attach to Islam. 'The war of cultures is an invention of the West. Islam is about living together peacefully.' He said that al-Azhar is Islam's foremost intellectual centre, and the most influential mosque for Sunnis. No fatwas are more observed than those of al-Azhar, and few have the authority within the Islamic world of the university's professors. With calls from western politicians for a 'cultural dialogue', attention naturally turned to al-Azhar. Barakat wanted the West to say that the caricatures were not protected by freedom of the press and he sought an apology, adding that, 'They are not civilized enough to solve conflicts peacefully.' He mentioned the Iraq War as proof and, without irony, the fact that medieval churches burned scientists at the stake at a time when the Islamic world emphasized research at places like al-Azhar, as though nothing had changed since. He refused to accept the arson at Danish embassies as a counter-argument: 'There is a difference between action and reaction.' The university brings more of its own agenda and more of its own unfaltering self-confidence to the table than many in the West would prefer. While it is ready to discuss terrorism, Barakat said 'western terrorism' must be looked at as well and not just that perpetrated by al-Qa'ida. There had been few marches in Egypt against the caricatures, one of them at al-Azhar, where some demonstrators chanted, 'Osama Bin Laden, explode

Copenhagen', and burned a Danish flag just outside the mosque gates.⁵⁸

Muslims have learnt that they never have to compromise with the West on any matter, however important or trivial. They simply have to stand firm, knowing that in its eagerness to overcome differences, the West can be relied upon to give way. Even toilet facilities in a British prison are being built so Muslim inmates do not have to face Mecca. The Home Office said two new toilet blocks are being installed as part of a refurbishment at Brixton gaol in south London. Faith leaders had told prison bosses it was unacceptable for Muslim inmates to face Mecca while using the toilet. 'The refurbishment has been carried out with due consideration for all faiths', a Home Office spokeswoman said.⁵⁹ No consideration for such banality is known to take place anywhere in the Islamic world, except perhaps Saudi Arabia, and turning western countries into guardians of Muslim whims, which are not respected elsewhere, only makes the West appear subservient to any Muslim caprice, thus justifying Muslim supremacist notions. Some British Muslims themselves admit that this type of deference has gone too far. An MPs' committee recommended more should be done to meet the needs of Muslim prisoners, necessitating the expenditure of thousands of pounds on colour-coded kitchen tools for Muslims to prepare halal meals. However, a Muslim in Wakefield, Yorkshire, said: 'We've all eaten in restaurants where no one cares how food is prepared. None except the strictest Muslims bother to check whether different equipment is used.'⁶⁰ Unsurprisingly, Muslims worldwide have an ever-growing list of demands in the West. On the issue of curtailing freedom of speech, Islamic groups and governments are pressing ahead with a campaign to have international organizations take steps, including legal ones, to provide protection for their religion in the wake of the cartoon controversy. In a drive pursued largely away from the headlines, the OIC has been promoting the issue at the UN and EU, with some success. The executive council of the UN Educational, Scientific and Cultural Organization (UNESCO) approved an agenda item entitled 'respect for freedom of expression, sacred beliefs, values and religious and cultural symbols'. It also directed UNESCO's director general to carry out a 'comprehensive study of all existing relevant international instruments'.

The motion did not refer directly to the cartoon furore, although an 'explanatory note' offered by the OIC members did.[61]

The note stated that respect for religious symbols and beliefs and freedom of expression were 'indissociable'. Muslim demands habitually carry an implicit threat, and this note continued that tradition. 'Given the importance of religion to peoples and to dignity and the way of life in different cultures, respect for different religious beliefs is essential to international peace and security and to the progress of human civilizations', it said. The matter was also taken up in exchanges with the EU, 'as well as with various international and regional inter-governmental organizations and Non-Governmental Organizations (NGOs)'. In February 2006, OIC members had succeeded in pushing through a last-minute amendment to the preamble of a UN resolution establishing a new UN Human Rights Council. The OIC addition to the text referred to the important role of states, NGOs, religious groups and the media 'in promoting tolerance, respect for and freedom of religion and belief' – but made no balancing reference to freedom of speech. Furthermore, not only do these Muslim states deny tolerance and freedom of worship to all non-Muslim religions, but those who adhere to a different sect of Islam to that of their rulers are also persecuted. That the West allows itself to be lectured by the intolerant without asking for a *quid pro quo*, guarantees that the Muslims' next set of demands will become more extravagant.

The Islamic campaign won sympathetic responses from some senior UN and EU figures. 'Your anguish over the publication of insulting cartoons of the prophet Muhammad is clear and understandable', Secretary General Kofi Annan said in a message read on his behalf at the OIC gathering in Istanbul in March 2006. Addressing a meeting of European imams in Vienna, Foreign Minister Ursula Plassnik of Austria – who was then EU president – also referred to the cartoons. 'Freedoms do have limits that should not be overstepped', she told 300 Muslim religious leaders from across the continent. At the same gathering, the head of the EU's official anti-racism body bemoaned what she said was a 'dangerously high' level of anti-Muslim discrimination in Europe. Beate Winkler, head of the European Monitoring Centre on Racism and Xenophobia, said EU Governments should provide time for religious programmes on public broadcasters and support mosque construction. Participant Turfa Bagaghati of the European Network Against Racism – an EU-funded NGO – told Islam Online it was time Muslims pressed 'for their rights, like enacting laws banning aggression on Islam'. EU external relations commissioner Benita Ferrero-Waldner also addressed the Vienna meeting, saying that both freedom of religion and freedom of expression were 'non-negotiable'. But she added a qualifier only in the case of freedom of expression, saying 'it does come with responsibilities and should be exercised with the necessary sensitivity to others'.

In September 2007, the OIC told the Human Rights Council in Geneva that the report of the Special Rapporteur on freedom of religion called for stronger denunciation of violence by Muslim leaders in order to 'de-link' Islam from terrorism. OIC representative Marghoob Saleem Butt, from Pakistan, complained that there had been many such denunciations, but a response had not been forthcoming. 'The ever-growing incidents of religious intolerance and xenophobia in the West were taking the world far from its aim of religious and cultural harmony. The OIC condemned forced religious conversions by majority religious groups, attacks of places of worship, restriction on the display of religious symbols and erosion of rights of parents to ensure moral education for their children', the diplomat added. The dishonesty in such a claim in relation to Saudi Arabia, let alone other Islamic states, is indicative of the value of 'dialogue' with them. Butt stressed that the Islamic countries deplored states that linked freedom of belief with freedom of expression in order to shrug off responsibility. He said efforts were needed to eliminate intolerance and discrimination, including through education and interfaith dialogue – everything which the Muslims themselves fail to abide by.[62]

A summary of the worldwide reverberations of the controversy by Duncan Currie concluded: 'ever since those cartoons in Denmark, the rules have changed. Nobody shows an image of Muhammad anymore.' And he elaborated: 'The cartoon jihad occasioned far fewer robust defences of press freedom than it did craven surrenders to the threats of radicals', adding that even 'South Park', Comedy Central's irreverent powerhouse, has felt the backlash. Its creators Matt Stone and Trey Parker were banned from depicting Muhammad by network executives, although Comedy Central had allowed 'South Park' to broadcast a Muhammad character five years earlier, a few months before 9/11. A source close to the show said: 'It's a vastly different world that we live in right now.' It is a world where terrorists apparently have veto power over American television. Stone and Parker did not take Comedy Central's censorship lightly. In the 'Cartoon Wars' episodes, the screen goes black when Muhammad is poised to appear, and a brief message announces that Comedy Central 'has refused to broadcast' the prophet's image.

At a town meeting, South Parkers hear from a university professor. 'Our only hope', he says, 'is to make the Muslim extremists know that we had no part in the Muhammad episode: that even though the episode aired, we didn't watch it, we didn't hear it, and we didn't talk about it.' How do they do that? 'We bury our heads in sand.' By enlisting some two dozen dump trucks, the professor explains, they can stockpile enough sand for the whole town. By highlighting the network's double standard later in the episode, that offending Christians is permissible while offending Muslims is not, 'South Park' affirmed that free expression may at times lead to hurt feelings. But that's no reason to capitulate, especially not when political correctness becomes physical intimidation. The writer continued: 'The cartoon jihad may be over. But when even "South Park" is stifled by recent world events, it becomes clearer than ever who won.'[63]

An online journal published by a Muslim group in Europe, *Ansar al-Sunna* (which means 'Supporters of the Tradition' of the prophet), issued an indirect call to violence which was unlikely to be misinterpreted by the readership. The message was that the prophet had to be avenged. The online journal listed dozens of European newspapers that reprinted the cartoons, hoping to motivate acts of retaliation. Terrorist leaders orchestrate violence by means of aggressive demagoguery, counting on their followers to act on their own initiative. The remarks on the cartoon crisis in *Ansar al-Sunna* fit the pattern exactly. 'While it may prove difficult to make all Muslims carry out the divine verdict in this matter', the authors wrote, 'the path of jihad against the enemies of God is still available.' The example the authors offered to potential jihadists was particularly cynical. Commenting on the murder of Dutch film director Theo van Gogh, they noted that by making his film *Submission*, which they considered to be anti-Islamic, the director prompted Muhammad Bouyeri to kill him. As usual, the victims of Islam were to blame.[64]

The founder of Ansar al-Islam (the organization out of which *Ansar al-Sunna* developed), Mullah Krekar, fled Iraq and settled in Norway in 1991. The group is one of the most active terrorist organizations in Iraq. Its enthusiasm for the perpetuation of the fight was due to the perceived gains it brought in the face of western squeamish 'sensitivity' and 'tolerance'. Ansar al-Islam has a network of terrorists in Germany, Scandinavia and Italy. Its followers have been caught trafficking terrorists in and out of Iraq from Italy and Germany.[65] Mullah Krekar was judged a threat to national security in Norway by February 2003 and was served with a deportation order. In an interview with al-Jazeera in August 2005, he said that a deportation to Iraq 'is an offence that shouldn't be made without punishment. I defend my rights in their court just like western people defend their rights. I am patient like they are patient. But if my patience runs out, I will react like Orientals do.' He added that jihadists would continue 'until they see Islam's house equipped with Saladin's sable, Muhammad's conquering turban and Osama Bin Laden's vision'. He thus combined three important symbols used by Islamic extremists.[66] Today's terrorist networks are decentralized and don't operate by giving specific orders, preferring to suggest targets, as Ansar al-Islam has done. 'It's our duty to increase our efforts to correct the wayward thinking of some Muslims and show what the religion of democracy really means', according to their journal, adding that the task of every jihadist is 'to follow the way of the prophet and take up the struggle against the enemies of religion'.[67] What this basically amounts to is the following:

> Radical Muslims are determined to terrorize and eliminate any manifestation of democracy, free press or disrespect to the prophet, or even anything they regard as 'insulting' to Islam.
>
> Muslims need not wait for insults to filter through to their countries, since their distribution throughout the West allows them to act immediately against anyone who dares to

speak against them.

Muslim wrath is not likely to be calmed or appeased. Its potential to rekindle is always there, subject only to Muslim considerations.

Islam is impervious to a compromise to allow coexistence with the West, but determined to eliminate all 'crusaders' in order to win an unqualified victory.

The Muslims have declared that they are poised for a long, protracted struggle, on all fronts. Therefore, the excuse for any particular rift is irrelevant, for even if things settle on one issue they are sure to explode on another.

Radical Islam capitalizes on the steady erosion in the steadfastness of the West, which is tormented by bouts of guilt and misplaced sensitivity, fear of being labelled 'racist', a lack of self-confidence, doubts about its fair conduct and moral stature, all the while posturing as the only alternative to the demoralized and vanishing western culture.

After the cartoon controversy fizzled out, curious and outlandish reactions continued to reverberate in the media. A British television station, The Islam Channel, hoped to capitalize on the infamy brought upon Copenhagen by holding a conference called 'Islamophobia: a dilemma in the West', as a way to 'create a dialogue and debunk myths'. Mohamed Ali, president of The Islam Channel, claimed that 'fear of and prejudices about Islam have always been there, but we need to have the courage to talk about things'. Despite being billed as an 'international conference', and the 'largest of its kind since the row over the Muhammad cartoons exploded' the previous winter, the majority of those participating were Muslim. Organizers had invited a broad spectrum of Danish politicians, members of the press and other public figures, but only a handful of ethnic Danes were to be found amongst the 900 people in attendance. 'We had hoped to see more Danes take part in the debate. We invited the prime minister to open the conference and all Danish ministers to participate. We invited political parties, even the Danish People's Party, the mayor of Copenhagen – and the Queen', Ali said.[68]

While western panel members such as Tøger Seidenfaden, editor-in-chief of *Politiken*, nodded in agreement at the call for dialogue, some Muslims were concerned that Middle Eastern Muslims were stealing the show. 'This conference is spectacular, but I don't think it contains anything we can use in our daily lives', said Aziz Fall, the president of an association of Senegalese Muslims in Denmark. Foreign conference participants said they were shocked to see the conditions Muslims in Denmark were forced to accept. 'I thought Denmark was a free and open country, but that's not so', said Yvonne Ridley, a British reporter who converted to Islam after being held hostage by the Taleban. She failed to explain why thousands of Muslims knocked on Denmark's doors to settle there, and why none of them made any effort to return to his country of origin. Ridley, now the political editor for The Islam Channel, claimed Denmark's Muslims were made to feel like outsiders, since Denmark doesn't have a single purpose-built mosque. Ridley added that she and other Muslims were tired of being held responsible for terrorist acts committed in their religion's name. 'I don't demonize all Danes because of the cartoons. And you shouldn't demonize all Muslims on account of al-Qa'ida.' So much for building bridges.[69]

In an interview with *The Jerusalem Post* a few months later, Carsten Juste agreed that it was somewhat accidental that Denmark had become Europe's standard-setter for freedom of expression – sixty-three years after being the only European country whose Jews were rescued from the Nazis. In a revealing aside about the agenda of al-Jazeera, it emerged that Flemming Rose gave the channel an interview, in which he expressed regret over the cartoons, saying his newspaper had not intended to hurt devout Muslims. However, his contrition was not translated into English and widely disseminated. In an editorial on 6 March 2006, entitled 'The Terms of Satire', Juste wrote, 'We had gotten used to the fact that we could say, draw and write whatever we wanted without anybody taking it so seriously that they reacted violently. This affair has turned it upside down. The freedom of expression stood its test. The air has been cleansed.' Juste believed that freedom of expression had not lost the battle, but that self-censorship had been increasingly in evidence. People who shout most loudly and threaten to kill others succeeded in provoking a reticence which is caused solely by fear of reactions. The cartoonists needed constant police protection. Juste expressed shock, resentment and anger at the sight of Danish flags and embassies in the Middle East being burned. He would not have printed the cartoons if he knew the consequences because hooligans endangered peoples' lives. Pointing out that nobody could have anticipated the consequences, he stressed that he cannot be responsible for how hooligans and Middle East dictator-states react to some fully legal Danish newspaper cartoons, adding that no one was forced to read *Jyllands-Posten*.[70]

In an incredible postscript to the cartoon story, Pakistan's English publication *The Nation*, which prides itself for being 'internationally the most quoted Pakistani newspaper', reported on 15 June 2006 that the editor of *Jyllands-Posten* 'was burnt to death when a fire mysteriously broke out in his bedroom'. *The Nation* was itself quoting a Saudi newspaper, which gave the *Jyllands-Posten* editor the wrong name. *The Nation* continued: 'The [Saudi] paper claims that the Danish Government is trying to cover up the news of the death. He was hit by divine retribution, the paper added.' This genre of writing is absolutely typical of the Arab press in general, which routinely fabricates stories purely to 'prove' to the masses that Allah is on their side.[71]

No sooner had the furore over the cartoons abated than Europe was faced with yet more Muslim fury. To place the next major episode in context, it is necessary to appreciate the degree of change in Vatican thinking regarding Islam. The Catholic Church began a dramatic shift from a decades-old policy to protect Catholics living under Muslim rule. The old methods of quiet diplomacy and muted appeasement had clearly failed. An inter-religious dialogue initiated at the second Vatican Council in 1962 had not produced a single document of rapprochement coming from their Muslim counterparts. The estimated forty million Christians in Dar al-Islam, notes the Barnabas Fund's Patrick Sookhdeo, increasingly find themselves an embattled minority facing economic decline, dwindling rights, and physical jeopardy. (The Barnabas Fund is an aid group for persecuted Christian minorities.) There are fifteen million Christians in Indonesia, nine million in Egypt and three million in Pakistan. Most are despised and distrusted second-class citizens, facing discrimination in education, jobs, and the courts (where the witness of a Christian is worth less than a Muslim's). Many have had to flee their ancestral lands for the West. For the first time in nearly two millennia, Nazareth and Bethlehem no longer have Christian majorities. This reality of oppression and decline stands in dramatic contrast to the surging Muslim minority of the West, granted extensive rights and protections even as it wins new legal, cultural, and political prerogatives. This widening disparity caught the attention of the Church, which for the first time is pointing to radical Islam as the central problem facing Christians living with Muslims. Monsignor Velasio De Paolis, secretary of the Vatican's Supreme Court, said: 'Enough now with this turning the other cheek! It's our duty to protect ourselves.' He continued, 'The West has had relations with the Arab countries for half a century, and has not been able to get the slightest concession on human rights.'[72]

The widening imposition of shari'a has meant an increasingly-precarious existence for Christian minorities. In Sudan, the government has imposed shari'a and the Arabic language on the Christian south. The result is three million Christians dead and up to five million refugees. In Nigeria, where twelve of the nineteen states have declared shari'a, 15,000 Christians have been killed in the past few years. Sookhdeo said that long before Bin Laden targeted the West, he was attacking Christian minorities. His training videos feature troops firing on a cross. In Indonesia, the Laskar Jihad has killed about 30,000 Christians. The extremists are putting increasing pressure on Muslim governments, who appease them by restricting Christians further. Because the Christian minorities lack oil or geopolitical significance, western governments are little concerned. Sookhdeo says they feel betrayed by the indifference of the western church, which embraces 'interfaith dialogue' while politicians claim Islam is all about peace. Secularism has neutralized the Christian faith in the West and pluralism has marginalized it, creating a spiritual and moral vacuum that Islam is filling.[73]

The excesses of Islam were also brought much closer to home. Sandro Magister, who covers the Vatican for *L'espresso*, an influential Italian newsweekly magazine, drew attention on his website as long ago as 2003 to incendiary sermons being preached to Muslims in the pope's diocese, pointing out that while this was no isolated case, such sermons were being downplayed in the Vatican to avoid 'compromising dialogue'. The mosque in Rome, which was inaugurated in 1995, is sponsored by the Italian Islamic Cultural Centre and Arab governments, in particular that of Saudi Arabia. The imam was sent by the al-Azhar university in Cairo, the most authoritative university in the Muslim world. Magister wrote:

> The Vatican engages in dialogue with various Muslim representatives, and signs joint messages of peace. But in the meantime, what is going on in the mosques? If the ideas that animate these Friday sermons are like the ones heard in Rome's mosque, is it right to ignore them? In Mecca, the cradle of Islam, a website has for several years been selecting 'the best' of the sermons given in the mosques and sending them to imams all over the world as a guide for preaching. Given what the young Egyptian imam says from the pulpit of the main mosque in Rome, he could be one of the recipients of this service. The ideas are identical: from the defence of crimes of honour to the incitement of jihad against Jews, Christians, and the West.[74]

The change was discernable towards the end of John Paul II's papacy. In 2003, Cardinal Jean-Louis Tauran, the Vatican equivalent of Foreign Minister, stated that 'there are too many majority Muslim countries where non-Muslims are second-class citizens'. Tauran pushed for reciprocity: 'Just as Muslims can build their houses of prayer anywhere in the world, the faithful of other religions should be able to do so as well.' More recently, Monsignor Philippe Brizard, director general of Oeuvre d'Orient, asserted that 'Islam's radicalization is the principal cause of the Christian exodus.' The Danish cartoons crisis offered a typical example of Catholic disillusionment. Church leaders initially criticized the publication of the cartoons. But when Muslims responded by murdering Catholic priests in Turkey and Nigeria, in addition to scores of Christians killed during five days of riots in Nigeria, the Church gave voice to its indignation. 'If we tell our people they have no right to offend, we have to tell the others they have no right to destroy us', said Cardinal Angelo Sodano, the Vatican's Secretary of State. Obtaining the same rights for Christians in Islamdom that Muslims enjoy in Christendom has become the key to the Vatican's diplomacy toward Muslims. The onus is now on western governments to maintain the demand for reciprocity.[75] In September 2005, Pope Benedict XVI convened a two-day conference on Islam, the West and Christianity at Castelgandolfo, which concluded that it was time for a 'more robust' approach to Islam, which in its 'fanatical' or 'violent' form posed a danger to the West. The problem with Islam, the pope told delegates, was that unlike Christianity, which distinguished (in Christ's words) between 'that which is God's and that which is Caesar's', Islam sought to 'integrate the laws of the Qur'an into all elements of social life'. A devout Muslim must aspire to live under shari'a law even in the West. Whereas Jesus and the Gospels offered a model to follow, the Qur'an was imposed rigidly with 'no distinction between civil and religious law'. There was little spiritual or religious common ground, and the main goal of Christian–Muslim discussion has been reduced to the avoidance of conflict. Christianity could engage with Islam only as a 'culture' and remind it to 'respect human rights', including the rights of Christian minorities in Muslim countries. In May 2006, the pope told a Vatican conference on immigration that although he favoured 'dialogue' with Islam it could only be conducted on the basis of 'reciprocity'. Christians should 'open their arms and hearts' to Muslim immigrants, but Muslims in turn had to overcome 'the prejudices of a closed mentality'. He was elected in April 2005 because many cardinals were impressed by his insistence on the need to bolster Christian values not just in the Third World but also in Europe, which he believes is threatened by secularism, loss of faith and Muslim immigration. As a cardinal, he was on record as opposing Turkish membership of the EU.[76]

In a homily on 'Faith and Reason' at the University of Regensburg in Germany on 12 September 2006, Pope Benedict XVI cited one of the last emperors of Byzantium, Manuel II Paleologus, in a dialogue concerning the truths of Christianity and Islam with an educated Persian. Stressing the fourteenth-century emperor's 'startling brusqueness', the pope quoted him as saying: 'Show me just what Muhammad brought that was new, and there you will find things only evil and inhuman, such as his command to spread by the sword the faith he preached.' Benedict didn't endorse the comment that he emphasized was not his own, but as with Rushdie's *The Satanic Verses*, which millions of outraged Muslims didn't bother to read, what he meant or even said was secondary to the insistence by Muslim leaders on proscribing how free societies discuss Islam.[77] For Benedict, 'Violence is incompatible with the nature of God and the nature of the soul', and cannot be justified by any religion. Muslim speakers reject this, insisting that the concept of jihad is one of the central pillars of the Islamic faith. 'Muslims can't eliminate jihad from the Islamic discourse, the same way Christians can't do away with the doctrine of Trinity', said Fauzan al-Anshori, spokesman for the radical Indonesian Mujahideen Council. Although some Muslims understand jihad as the struggle against evil and not a call to arms, the general reaction left little doubt concerning the mainstream interpretation. 'Anyone who says that Islam is intolerant or Islam is spread through use of force shows his ignorance. Islam is a very tolerant religion', said Tasnim Aslam, a spokeswoman for the Pakistan Foreign Ministry, seemingly oblivious to the inherent contradiction of the claim.[78]

The reaction to Benedict's homily was slow to develop, and was stoked by an aggressive internet and e-mail campaign that urged Muslims to take to the streets over what was described as a vile slur on Islam. Pakistan's parliament unanimously adopted a resolution condemning the pontiff. A nun was shot dead in Somalia, an al-Qa'ida-linked terrorist group vowed to kill the pope, churches in Palestinian areas were attacked, effigies of the pope were set alight in Pakistan and hundreds joined protests in countries from Indonesia to Lebanon. In total, six Middle Eastern churches were destroyed. Presidents, Prime Ministers and religious leaders urged the Vatican to issue an apology. To stop any further violence, the pope complied. Yet his original argument deserved to be heard, not least by Muslims. The offending quotation was a small part in a chain of argument that led to his main thesis about the close relationship between reason and belief. Without the right balance between the two, mankind is condemned to political and religious fanaticism. The precondition for any meaningful interfaith discussions is a religion tempered by reason. His request for a 'dialogue of cultures' was accompanied by one condition – that everyone at the table reject irrational religiously motivated violence. The pope was not condemning Islam, but inviting it to join rather than reject the modern world.[79] Writing in *The Times*, William Rees-Mogg highlighted the teaching of the Qur'an on violence against the 'infidel'. That existed in the fourteenth century, and was demonstrated on 9/11. The Qur'an contains a command to spread the faith by the sword, and it has influenced modern terrorists. The so-called Sword Verse from Chapter 9 must have been in the Byzantine emperor's mind: 'So when the sacred months have passed away, Then slay the idolaters wherever you find them.' The consistent Qur'anic teaching that God is most merciful cannot be reconciled with suicide bombing. Further, it is a mistake to think that all the major religions are identical: they have real differences of doctrine that have real impacts on human society. Violence is a fault from which no major religion has historically been free. Yet nowadays Islam is the only major religion in which violence is a serious doctrinal issue. It is true that Roman Catholics and Protestants in Ireland have only recently stopped killing each other and vengeful Sikhs assassinated Indira Gandhi in India, but neither the Catholic nor the Protestant churches believe in terror; nor do the Sikhs. A significant proportion of the Islamic community does believe that suicide bombers are martyrs carrying out a religious duty. There are varying degrees of authority and uniformity in different religions. This pluralism has its own virtues, but in Islam they are outweighed by the disadvantages. Those imams who preach al-Qa'ida's view of the duty of jihad are not required to answer to any authority, even the authority of reason.[80] London's satirical magazine, *Private Eye*, captured the mood well. First Muslim: 'The pope says Islam is a violent religion.' Second Muslim: 'Let's kill him then.'

Cardinal George Pell, the head of Australia's 5.1 million Roman Catholics, expressed impatience at Muslim rage: 'The violent reaction in many parts of the Islamic world justified one of Pope Benedict's main fears. They showed the link for many Islamists between religion and violence, their refusal to respond to criticism with rational arguments, but only with demonstrations, threats and actual violence.' Criticizing the reaction of some Muslim leaders in Australia as 'unfortunately typical and unhelpful', he added: 'Our major priority must be to maintain peace and harmony within the Australian community, but no lasting achievements can be grounded in fantasies and evasions.'⁸¹ The former Archbishop of Canterbury, Lord Carey of Clifton, said that Muslims must address 'with great urgency' their religion's association with violence. He made it clear that he believed the 'clash of civilizations' endangering the world was not between Islamist extremists and the West, but with Islam as a whole. 'There will be no significant material and economic progress [in Muslim communities] until the Muslim mind is allowed to challenge the *status quo* of Muslim conventions and even their most cherished shibboleths.' Lord Carey, a pioneer in Christian–Muslim dialogue, asserted that Samuel Huntington's thesis of a 'clash of civilizations' has some 'validity'. Lord Carey quoted him as saying: 'Islam's borders are bloody and so are its innards. The fundamental problem for the West is not Islamic fundamentalism. It is Islam, a different civilization whose people are convinced of the superiority of their culture and are obsessed with the inferiority of their power.' Lord Carey went on to argue that a 'deep-seated Westophobia' has developed in recent years in the Muslim world. He said he agreed with his Muslim friends who claimed that true Islam is not a violent religion, but he wanted to know why Islam today had become associated with violence. 'The Muslim world must address this matter with great urgency', he said.⁸² Cardinal Cormac Murphy O'Connor, the head of the Roman Catholic Church in England and Wales, questioned whether Turkey should join the EU. He echoed comments previously made by Pope Benedict and Lord Carey that the predominantly Muslim state was not culturally part of Europe. Cardinal Murphy O'Connor questioned the position of Tony Blair who had consistently argued for Turkish membership of the EU on the grounds that exclusion would be damaging, arguing: 'There may be another view that the mixture of cultures is not a good idea.'⁸³

At a special summit meeting with Muslim diplomats in his summer residence near Rome, the pope issued a unique public apology saying that he regretted that Muslims were offended, although he did not actually retract his words. He told them that the future depends on dialogue between Christians and Muslims, and restated the need for 'reciprocity in all fields', including religious freedom. This is a major issue for the Vatican in Saudi Arabia and several other countries where non-Muslims cannot worship openly.⁸⁴ It was left to José Manuel Barroso, the EU Commission President, to express disappointment that few European leaders had defended the pope's right to express his views, adding: 'The problem is not the comments of the pope but the reactions of the extremists.'⁸⁵ His remarks highlighted the quandary faced by liberal democracies in dealing with illiberal minorities. Members of the Turkish Government urged the pope to reconsider his pre-planned visit later that year, with senior officials in Turkey warning that they could not guarantee his safety. A series of assaults on Catholic priests in Turkey left one dead. Salih Kapusuz, deputy leader of the strongly Islamic party led by Recep Tayyip Erdogan, the Prime Minister, said, 'He has a dark mentality that comes from the darkness of the Middle Ages', and compared Benedict to Hitler and Mussolini.⁸⁶ The visit to Turkey went ahead as planned in November 2006. Benedict offered messages of reconciliation to Muslims, including appeals for greater understanding and, despite his known misgivings, support for Turkey's steps to become the first Muslim nation in the EU. The Vatican added a visit to the Sultan Ahmet Mosque to the pope's schedule as a 'sign of respect' to Muslims. The visit to the Blue Mosque followed a highly sensitive tour of the Haghia Sophia museum, a 1,500-year-old complex which was for centuries a centre of Christianity. In 1453 it was converted to a mosque during the Muslim conquest of what was then Constantinople, now Istanbul. The site remained that way until 1935, when it was converted to a museum under the secular Turkish republic proclaimed in 1923. His visit to the complex was interpreted by many Muslims as an attempt to reclaim the building as a bastion of Christianity, setting off more protests.⁸⁷

It was primarily to advance the dialogue between Eastern Orthodoxy and Western Catholicism that the pope visited Turkey. He met with the ecumenical patriarch of Constantinople, Bartholomew I, bishop of the highest and most famous see in the Orthodox Church. And then Islam intruded. After the riots and protests and endless editorials denouncing Benedict, it is easily forgotten that the reference to the violent history of Islam constituted only a small portion of his homily at Regensburg. Through most of the lecture, he spoke of European history and his worries about the decline of belief in reason throughout western culture.

In his first papal address, he warned against the relativism and nihilism that had seized much of the modern world. The success of violent Islamic political movements is an effect of something deeper happening outside the Muslim world. According to the pope's analysis, radical Islam ascendant is a symptom, and western hollowness is the disease. Just as the collapse of European birth rates allowed and even required the immigration of huge numbers of Islamic workers, so nihilism and self-hatred provided an opportunity for radical Islamic political movements to confront the West. The moral and intellectual weakness of western culture encouraged tyrannical governments to flourish in the Middle East, backward cultures to be affirmed as authentic by western intellectuals, and terrorists to believe that victory was possible.[88]

Over the ensuing months, the pope's publicly stated view of Islam underwent a transformation. The clue to the change was enunciated in his pre-Christmas address to the Roman Curia reviewing the events of 2006. Speaking of the threat of conflict between 'cultures and religion', he said that finding the way that leads to peace is 'a challenge of vital importance'. His preferred way of meeting the challenge is dialogue leading to a convergence of faith and reason. While he believes that Islamic terrorism is beyond the pale of civilized behaviour, he fears a cataclysmic clash between extremes, between a secularized West and jihadist Islamic fundamentalism. Hoping to promote entente between reasonable, responsible Christians and Muslims, he thinks Catholicism can be a model to Islam, showing how a traditional faith can adapt to the modern world while remaining true to itself. Pope Benedict told the curia that, 'On the one hand, it is important to avoid a dictatorship of positivist reason that excludes God from community life and public legislation ... On the other hand, it is necessary to welcome the true achievements of the enlightenment: human rights and especially the freedom of faith and of its expression. The Muslim world ... is facing the great task of finding appropriate solutions to these questions.'[89]

In an all-too-familiar pattern, the pope completed his capitulation to Islam shortly afterwards. In May 2007, he restored power and prestige to the Vatican department that oversees dialogue with Islam a year after he downgraded it thanks to its futility. The

Pontifical Council for Inter-Religious Dialogue would again become a separate department. Benedict downgraded the office in March 2006 by putting it under joint presidency with the Vatican's Culture Ministry, which had offended Muslims.[90] In contrast to the Vatican's outlook, for them it is irrelevant whether a 'dialogue' achieves results. In fact, it is preferable that it does not, in order to ensure its continuance. 'Dialogue' with western leaders is *the* goal, since it gives them the respect they believe is their due, whether or not they have earned it, and it is the vehicle by which they assuage their acute feelings of inferiority. At the same time, it is important to Muslim governments and individuals alike that the timing and terms of a dialogue are set by themselves alone, to give them the 'upper hand'. This enables them to postpone the resolution of an intractable problem and buy time, after which they hope the problem will be overtaken by the next set of headlines. The Archbishop of Canterbury, Dr Rowan Williams, suffered a serious setback in his attempts to foster 'Muslim–Christian dialogue' after the Malaysian Government banned the interfaith 'Building Bridges' conference he was due to be chairing in May 2007, with just two weeks' notice. It was the sixth in a series set up in the wake of 9/11 and meant to be an annual meeting of Christian and Muslim academics to find theological understandings that might help prevent future terrorist attacks. The seminar in Malaysia was intended to signal a breakthrough in relations, but some influential Muslims believe that Christianity is 'not a heavenly religion' and therefore opposed inter-religious dialogue. Although the Malaysian Government allowed Dr Williams into the country for another event, it refused to permit the interfaith dialogue to take place. The question ought to be asked whether anything would be worse than it is now should the West studiously avoid all 'dialogue'.[91]

A very public debate took place in July 2007 when the Vatican described the Protestant and Orthodox faiths as 'not proper Churches' in a document issued with the full authority of the pope. Anglican leaders reacted with dismay, saying the new sixteen-page document outlining the 'defects' of non-Catholic churches constituted a major obstacle to ecumenism. Father Augustine Di Noia, a senior doctrinal official at the Vatican, insisted that the Catholic Church was not 'backtracking on ecumenical commitment. But it is fundamental to any kind of dialogue that the participants are clear about their own identity. That is, dialogue cannot be an occasion to accommodate or soften what you understand yourself to be.' Protestants welcomed the honesty of the document. Reverend David Phillips, General Secretary of the Church Society, said: 'We are grateful that the Vatican has once again been honest in declaring their view that the Church of England is not a proper Church. Too much dialogue proceeds without such honesty. Therefore, we would wish to be equally open; unity will only be possible when the papacy renounces its errors and pretensions.' There are lessons here for the future of 'interfaith dialogue' with Muslims, and there is even a possibility that this discussion was conducted so publicly precisely to leave an impression on European Muslims.[92] Soon afterwards, Pope Benedict XVI's private secretary warned of the Islamization of Europe and stressed the need for the continent's Christian roots not to be ignored. 'Attempts to Islamize the West cannot be denied', said Monsignor Georg Gaenswein in the weekly *Sueddeutsche Magazin*. 'The danger for the identity of Europe that is connected with it should not be ignored out of a wrongly understood respectfulness.' Gaenswein also defended Benedict's speech linking Islam and violence, saying it was an attempt by the pontiff to 'act against a certain naivety'.[93]

Pope Benedict re-entered the fray in September 2007, in a speech in 'defence of religious liberty', which, he said 'is a fundamental, irrepressible, inalienable and inviolable right'. He attacked Muslim nations where Christians are either persecuted or given the status of second-class citizens under shari'a. He also defended the rights of Muslims to convert to Christianity, which warrants the death penalty in many Islamic countries. It appears lost on Muslims and their governments that if a death penalty is required to inhibit Muslims from converting out of the faith, it follows that they must be acutely insecure about its 'truth'. Addressing the problem of Islamic extremism, Benedict added: 'Terrorism is a serious problem whose perpetrators often claim to act in God's name and harbour an inexcusable contempt for human life.'[94] An American blogger humorously offered a 'ten-day forecast' for reactions to the pope's latest speech: 'Extended seething, with a 70 per cent chance of rioting and murder by next

Friday'.⁹⁵ On one point there can be little doubt – by their predictably intemperate statements, threats, actions and reactions, Muslims have turned themselves into a laughing stock, the 'court jesters' of old, but spiced up with an element of menace. They have demonstrated themselves to be out of time and out of place in the West.

While most Europeans were cowed into silence for fear of Muslim reaction, some intrepid souls were more outspoken. French intellectuals rallied around a philosophy teacher forced into hiding after he wrote an article describing Muhammad as a ruthless warlord and mass murderer. Robert Redeker needed police protection since threats against him appeared on Islamic websites. His home address was published with calls to murder. 'You will never feel secure on this earth. One billion, 300 million Muslims are ready to kill you', one message said. One threat came from a contributor to al-Hesbah, an internet forum that is viewed as a channel for al-Qa'ida. 'The Islamists have succeeded in punishing me on the territory of the Republic as if I were guilty of a crime of opinion', said Redeker. His supporters, angered by their government's qualified support for him, deplored what they said was cowardice in the face of Islamic extremism. Dominique de Villepin, then Prime Minister, had said: 'Everyone has the right to express his views freely, while respecting others, of course.' Writing in *Le Figaro* on 19 September 2006, Redeker deplored the furore over the pope's references to Muhammad. He called the prophet 'a merciless warlord, a looter, a mass murderer of Jews and a polygamist'. The Qur'an, he asserted, was a book of incredible violence.⁹⁶

Muslim violence in response to comments by the pope fit a pattern that has been building and accelerating since 1989. Six times since then westerners have done or said something that has triggered a wildly disproportionate reaction. In 1989 Rushdie's novel *The Satanic Verses* prompted Ayatollah Khomeini to issue a death edict against him and his publishers, on the grounds that the book 'is against Islam, the prophet and the Qur'an'. Subsequent rioting led to more than twenty deaths, mostly in India. In 1997 the US Supreme Court refused to remove a 1930s frieze showing Muhammad as lawgiver that decorates the main court chamber; the Council on American–Islamic Relations (CAIR) objected, leading to riots and injuries in India. In 2002 American Evangelical leader Jerry Falwell called Muhammad a 'terrorist', leading to church burnings and at least ten deaths in India. An incorrect story in 2005 in *Newsweek* reporting that American interrogators at Guantanamo Bay 'flushed a Qur'an down a toilet' was picked up by the famous Pakistani cricketer Imran Khan, and prompted protests leading to at least fifteen deaths. The last two rounds, of the cartoon controversy and the pope's speech, show a near-doubling in frequency of such incidents, proof that the Muslims have become emboldened by the West's submissiveness.

The edict against Rushdie came as a complete shock, for no one had imagined that a Muslim dictator could tell a British citizen living in London what he could not write about. Seventeen years later, calls for the execution of the pope (including one outside Westminster Cathedral in London) have acquired a too-familiar quality. The outrageous has become routine and predictable. Incidents started in Europe have grown much larger than those based in the US, reflecting the greater efficacy of Islamic aggression against Europeans than against Americans. Islamists ignore subtleties, from Rushdie's magical realism, to the positive intent of the Supreme Court frieze, falsehood of the Qur'an-flushing story, benign nature of the Danish cartoons or Benedict's thesis. What rouses Muslim crowds and what does not is somewhat unpredictable. If no Islamist agitates, the issue remains relatively quiet.[97] These incidents also illustrate a total lack of reciprocity by Muslims. The Saudi Government bans Bibles, crosses and Stars of David, while Muslims routinely publish disgusting cartoons of Jews. Saudi officials arrested Nirosh Kamanda, a Sri Lankan, in Mecca for being a Christian, saying that the city is off-limits to non-Muslims. Similar restrictions apply to the Saudi city of Medina. Highway signs at the entrance to Mecca also direct non-Muslims away from the city's environs. Muslims would be queueing to accuse western countries with such restrictions of 'apartheid' or worse.[98]

Far more worrying has been the West's abject surrender to Muslim sensibilities in several areas of public life. In communist-ruled East Germany, they had a term for it: pre-emptive obedience. This meant guessing the future orders of the politburo and obeying them before they were issued. The German Opera in Berlin decided to cancel its production of Mozart's *Idomeneo* in September 2006 after the managers decided that it might anger Muslims. The opera had already been shown in 2003 without incident. 'Pre-emptive obedience' was also at work when the Whitechapel Art Gallery, one of London's major art exhibition venues, decided to withdraw a number of paintings by the surrealist Hans Bellmer. The management decided that the erotic paintings might 'hurt the sensibilities of the Muslim community' which is strongly present in its locality. The exhibition had already been to Paris and Munich without provoking any protests. Two months after the 7/7 bombings, London's Tate Gallery removed sculptor John Latham's decade-old work 'God is Great', which consisted of a large sheet of glass and torn copies of the Qur'an, the Bible and the Talmud. The pieces are mounted on either side of the glass, appearing embedded in it. In October 2005, the UK's Chief Inspector of Prisons, Anne Owers, banned prison officers from wearing St George tie pins in support of a charity, because they might be 'misinterpreted'. In February 2006, the EU Commissioner for Freedom and Security, Franco Frattini, proposed a voluntary code of conduct to be 'facilitated' by EU officials committing journalists to exercising 'prudence' in reporting on Islam.[99]

A wave of self-censorship has also hit the world of German carnivals. The Düsseldorf carnival banned any gear that might appear 'Islamic' and thus 'hurt Muslim sensibilities'. A work by the Swiss sculptor Fleur Boecklin was withdrawn from public view in Düsseldorf after it was branded 'a misrepresentation of Islam as an aggressive faith'. In Spain, folkloric ceremonies and carnivals marking the expulsion of the Moors from Andalusia have been cancelled in all but a handful of villages, ending a 400-year-old tradition. In Germany, France and Britain numerous illuminated manuscripts of Persian poetry and prose have been withdrawn because they contained images of Muhammad and other historic figures of Islam. Turkish and Iranian museums, meanwhile, continue to display their tableaux containing his images. Further, a clergyman in Westminster, Reverend Phillip Chester, vicar of St Matthew's, advocated abolishing St George as England's patron saint in deference to Muslim opinion, and Blackpool city council threatened to rescind licences from taxi drivers for flying Union

Jacks during the 2006 World Cup soccer tournament. In September 2007, it was reported that the BBC was considering axing a £1million episode of its hit drama 'Spooks' in which an al-Qa'ida terrorist is shot dead, because the actor Shaun Dingwall, who played the terrorist's killer, feared for his life if it was screened. Another manifestation of Europe's pre-emptive appeasement came to the fore in September 2007. Judge Simon Cardon de Lichtbuer of the Brussels civil court ruled that he lacked authority to overturn a decision by the city's mayor, Freddy Thielemans, to ban a demonstration planned for 11 September under the slogan of 'Stop the Islamization of Europe'. The rally had been called to protest what its British, Danish and German organizers call the 'creeping' Islamization of European society, and would have been violating no known law. Thielemans (who had approved a 9 September rally by a group of conspiracy theorists who claim that 9/11 was orchestrated by the Bush administration) feared the possibility of a violent reaction from what he termed 'Muslims', 'peace activists' and 'democrats'. Despite some instances where the authorities have stood firm, it isn't at all clear that Europeans appreciate the long-term threat to their liberties stemming from a growing population of Muslim supremacists.[100]

In most European countries, an official blacklist of books has emerged, containing works deemed to be 'hurtful to Muslim sentiments'. The list includes the names not only of such major European authors as Voltaire and Thomas Carlyle but also of Muslim writers whose work has been translated into European languages. For example, the novel *Haji Agha* by Sadeq Hedayat, translated into French and published in the 1940s, is no longer available. A British publisher cancelled plans to publish *Twenty Three Years*, the translation of a controversial biography of Muhammad by the late Iranian author Ali Dashti. Literary agents and book publishers have no qualms about admitting that they would not touch any manuscript that may stir Muslims into a rage, wary of living under police escort. By submitting to self-censorship, the adepts of 'pre-emptive obedience' display their own soft bigotry. They see Muslims as childish, irrational and incapable of responding to works of literature and art in terms other than passion and violence. This attitude undermines Muslim reformers, by presenting the most reactionary fundamentalists as the sole legitimate representatives of Islam. Self-censorship in Europe also provides the despotic regimes in Muslim countries with an excuse for their systematic violation of the right to free expression.[101] The German Opera House was condemned by senior politicians for the cancellation of Mozart's *Idomeneo* after the Berlin state police had warned of a possible, but not certain, security threat. The premiere in 2003 was criticized over the scene in which King Idomeneo presents the severed heads not only of the Greek god of the sea, Poseidon, but also of Jesus, Buddha and Muhammad. The message is clear: the gods are dead and humans have to take over their own destiny. Interior Minister Wolfgang Schäuble condemned the decision, although the leader of Germany's Islamic Council welcomed it, saying a depiction of Muhammad with a severed head 'could certainly offend Muslims'.[102]

Against a background of acute sensitivity (some would say plain fear) in Europe about offending Islam, police units were established in several EU countries to study potential flashpoints. (In numerous imperceptible ways, the costs of accommodating a volatile population of immigrants continues to mount.) Peter Ramsauer, the head of the conservative Christian Social Union parliamentary faction, described the cancellation as 'an act of pure cowardice. We are opening ourselves up to cultural blackmail.' Not all theatres were ready to make concessions. The respected English Theatre in Frankfurt staged the European English-language premiere of *The Last Virgin*, by Tuvia Tenenbom, the provocative Israeli-American playwright, which makes fun of suicide bombers, and mocks Arabs and Jews in equal measure. Talks were held with the police and sniffer dogs patrolled the aisles before every performance. Despite street protests and pickets by Christian activists, *Jerry Springer, The Opera* went from the Battersea Arts Centre to major productions in London and New York. Tenenbom said: 'This self-censorship shouldn't be happening anywhere, but least of all in Germany. This is where the Nazis burnt books. If you cancel performances because you're scared, then you're burning your own books on behalf of the fanatics.' Christoph Hegemann, of the Berlin Volksbühne (People's Theatre), said: 'The Goethe Institute [the equivalent of the British Council] and the whole business of cultural exchange has failed to create a protected sub-universe between the worldly and the religious.' As a result, religious leaders were unable to distinguish between art, social discourse and an attack on their faith.[103]

Coincidentally, the decision on the production came on the eve of the Islamic summit in Berlin between German ministers, representatives of registered Islamic associations and independent Muslim writers and artists working in Germany. The aim was to reach a mutually acceptable definition of the limits of tolerance. Schäuble made plain that though the tone had been relaxed, there had been no significant breakthrough. 'We made clear for our part that everyone who lives in Germany must respect our constitutional and legal order', he said. One conference sticking point was the reluctance to ban arranged marriages. 'We've still got a long way to go before we can get the Muslim side to agree on our definition of the equality of women', said Günther Beckstein, the Bavarian Interior Minister.[104] The German Opera House finally went ahead with *Idomeneo*, using airport-style security checks. German politicians turned out in force at the performance and newspapers sent their terrorism experts, rather than their music critics. Leaders of the Muslim community, having at first promised to attend, stayed away.[105] Carnival parades in Germany are polemical, provocative and striking, but jokes about Islam were banned in the 2006 carnival. When Jacques Tilly was thinking of how to address the plight of women in Muslim countries, he followed his satirist's instinct. He designed a float with four Muslim women in a row, each more covered than the last. The last woman was tied inside a large trash bag, but his proposal was banned. People in Düsseldorf couldn't resist alluding to the cartoon scandal entirely. One display showed jesters symbolically burying freedom of opinion – the coffin had been pierced by a scimitar. The display's criticism was directed not just at violent Muslim fundamentalists but at overly tolerant westerners as well.[106]

In the Spanish fiestas which celebrate the final *reconquista* of Spain by Catholic kings from the Moors in 1492 after 800 years of Muslim rule, villagers divide into rival 'armies' of Moors and Christians to re-enact the conquest of their towns. But in the era of cultural nervousness after the Madrid train bombings in March 2004 and events since, the end of the 'battle' is accompanied by speeches about civilizations living together in harmony. Several villages have stopped parading giant effigies of Muhammad, which formerly culminated in the burning or blowing up of the figure. Some Muslim leaders have called for the fiestas to be banned, saying they were outdated and triumphalist celebrations with no place in modern Spain. Malik Ruiz, the president of the Islamic Commission in Spain, said Spaniards should not touch some issues that cause visceral reactions, such as the portrayal of Muhammad.[107] A staff revolt at the British tabloid, the *Daily Star*, prevented publication of a spoof Islamic version of the paper called the *'Daily Fatwa'*. Muslim commentators said the newspaper's attempt to mock shari'a law could have sparked international protests similar to those that followed publication of the Danish cartoons. The mock-up *'Daily Fatwa'* promised a 'Burqa Babes Special' and competitions to 'Burn a Flag and Win a Corsa' and 'Win hooks just like Hamza's'. The page also included a spoof leader column under the headline 'Allah is Great', but left blank except for a stamp with the word 'Censored'. But members of the National Union of Journalists called a meeting and passed a motion saying that 'this editorial content poses a very serious risk of violent and dangerous reprisals from religious fanatics who may take offence at these articles. This may place the staff in great jeopardy.'[108]

With attention focused on reverberations from the Benedict episode, the Danish cartoon controversy again hit the headlines after several demonstrators at the Danish Embassy in London were finally charged with soliciting to murder and inciting racial hatred and brought to trial. However, Scotland Yard decided that no criminal offences were committed in another Muslim protest against the pope outside Westminster Cathedral. Police received about twenty-five complaints from members of the public about the protest, which was said to have left worshippers attending the cathedral on 17 September 2006 feeling 'upset' and 'intimidated'.[109] In a startling statement, Anjem Choudary, who helped organize the anti-Danish protests, said outside the courts: 'We should not be surprised at people doing something like 7/7. How else do you expect Muslims to express themselves?' (If Muslims stereotype themselves in this way, they should not be surprised when others automatically link them with terrorism.) Male demonstrators, most wearing scarves across their faces, held placards reading 'Cartoonist free at large, protesters criminalized', and 'Freedom to insult Muhammad, no freedom to defend his honour'. Female protesters, in a separate enclosure from the men and wearing full veils, held placards reading: 'Shari'a – the only option for the UK'.[110]

Mizanur Rahman, 23, a website designer, was among 300 people (including one dressed as a suicide bomber) who protested in London against the Danish cartoons. Rahman was arrested in March 2006 following a public outcry against the provocative nature of the demonstrations the previous month, and convicted of inciting racial hatred.[111] He held placards saying 'Annihilate those who insult Islam' and 'Behead those who insult Islam'. He told the crowd: 'Oh Allah, we want to see another 9/11 in Iraq, in Denmark, in Spain, in France – all over Europe. Oh Allah, destroy all of them.' Referring to British and American soldiers, he added: 'We want to see them coming home in body bags. We want to see their blood running in the streets of Baghdad.' David Perry QC, for the prosecution, said the words were 'clear and unambiguous', adding: 'Annihilate and behead are ordinary English words with the ordinary English meaning of kill.' The court was told many of the crowd became 'hysterical' as they protested outside the embassy. They unfailingly condemn themselves by their irrationality. While these slogans are of course commonplace in the government-staged demonstrations of the Middle East and Pakistan, they and their purveyors are incongruous in the streets of western capitals. Rahman ended his speech chanting along with the crowd. 'There is only one God Allah, Muhammad is His messenger. Bomb bomb France, bomb bomb France, nuke nuke France, nuke nuke France.' Perry said the case against Rahman, of Bangladeshi origin, rested on what he 'intended' when he used the words, adding that freedom of expression 'does not extend to the right to encourage murder or incite racial hatred' because 'to encourage hatred and killing is to deny tolerance'. Rahman claimed he was 'carried away' in front of the crowd and said he was a 'nobody' whose words no one would take seriously.[112]

Police video showed another protester, Umran Javed, 27, leading chants of 'Bomb, bomb USA. Bomb, bomb Denmark'.

Officers in charge of monitoring the demonstration told the court that they did not arrest any of the protesters on the day because of fears that it would lead to violence. Javed said that 'disbelievers' should learn from the murder of the Dutch film-maker Theo van Gogh, and referred to the slaughter of the Jews of Khaybar, which is recorded in the Qur'an. David Perry said that 'If you shout out Bomb, bomb Denmark; bomb, bomb USA, there is no doubt about what you intend your audience to understand.' Javed had continued with his speech as the fifty-strong crowd of demonstrators were joined by 200–300 other Muslims, who had marched from the central mosque in Regent's Park. When police searched Javed's home six weeks after the protest, they found a pamphlet titled *Kill Them by the Sword Wherever They Are*. Police seized nine other documents from his home with titles including *The First 24 Hours of the Islamic State and Britain*. When officers returned to his home two days later to collect copies of the same documents, Javed's wife said that she had destroyed everything touched by the police because they were 'unclean'.[113] Javed, who had links with the recently banned group al-Muhajirun, was found guilty of soliciting murder and stirring up racial hatred. As the verdict was read out a man in the public gallery shouted: 'I curse the judge, I curse the court, I curse the jury, all of you.' Javed said he regretted the chants but described them as 'just slogans, soundbites'. Choudary, a former spokesman for al-Muhajirun, said he was not surprised by the verdict because Muslims were treated as second-class citizens in the UK and denied fair trials. 'When we have peaceful demonstrations, and then slogans that have been used normally, are taken out of context', he said. 'This is a failure of capitalism, of democracy and the freedom of speech.'[114] Again, they condemn themselves with their every word, often without even being aware of it.

Abdul Saleem, 31, was also found guilty of stirring up racial hatred during the protests. The court was told that the British Telecom engineer was the 'cheerleader' of hundreds of protesters at the demonstration. The father-of-five was filmed chanting '7/7 on its way' and 'Europe you will pay with your blood'. Saleem told the trial that while his words could be seen as 'threatening', that was not what he intended and he was repeating slogans 'because everyone else was saying it'.[115] Abdul Muhid, 24, was found guilty of soliciting murder. He led a crowd chanting 'Bomb, bomb the UK', and produced placards with slogans such as 'Fantastic four are on their way' and '3/11 is on its way', referring to the terrorist attacks on London and Madrid. Muhid, a father of two, had a previous conviction for smashing a bus shelter in Walthamstow market which displayed an advertisement which he said 'offended his religious beliefs'. Muhid said that the protest had been intended to show the 'hurt and distress' felt by Muslims after the cartoons were published. Perry said: 'Of course the UK had already been bombed. There was another significance to "Bomb, bomb the UK".' The drawings had not appeared in any UK newspapers. This was supposed to be a demonstration against the publication of drawings in newspapers abroad. This behaviour shows what the demonstration was about – it was an exhortation and encouragement to terrorism.[116] Rahman, Javed and Muhid were each sentenced to six years in prison in July 2007 for soliciting murder, and Saleem was sentenced to four years.

In October 2006, a Danish court rejected a lawsuit by seven Danish Muslim groups against the newspaper that first printed the Muhammad cartoons. The court conceded that some Muslims saw the drawings as offensive, and that some of the drawings could be perceived as linking Islam to terrorism, but said the purpose was to provide social commentary rather than to insult or ridicule Muslims. *Jyllands-Posten's* editor Carsten Juste hailed the court's decision as a victory for freedom of speech. 'Everything but a pure acquittal would have been a disaster for press freedom and the media's ability to fulfil its duties in a democratic society', he said. Once again, Muslims were outraged. 'The dismissal of the lawsuit against the newspaper, which was expected, confirms the ongoing intention to harm our religion and our prophet', said Mahmoud al-Kharabsheh, an independent legislator who heads the Jordanian parliament's legal committee.[117]

The Danish imams' trip to the Middle East in 2006, when they carried a portfolio of cartoons, spread false rumours of the Qur'an being burned on the streets of Copenhagen and otherwise did their best to incite violence against their host nation, came back to haunt them. They were later caught on hidden camera by a French documentary film-maker, bragging about their exploits. If it were not so serious, there would have been an element of farce in these imams posturing as holy warriors while being welfare-state spongers, and constantly tripping up in their own lies. After he lost his lawsuit against *Jyllands-Posten*, Sheikh Raed Hlayhel, who had been in Denmark since 2000 and was the prime instigator behind the cartoon protest, decided to return to his hometown of Tripoli in Lebanon. Having received his fundamentalist religious training in Saudi Arabia, he was admitted to Denmark on humanitarian grounds, to enable his invalid son to receive the medical treatment he needed. Hlayhel did not have Danish citizenship and did not speak a word of Danish. The centre of his activities was the Grimhøjvej mosque in the small town of Brabrand in Jutland. Among the users of the mosque were Slimane Hadj Abderrahmane, the so-called Guantanamo Dane – a jihadi of Danish-Algerian parentage who was caught by American troops in Afghanistan – and Abu Rached, who has been identified by Spanish prosecutors as a member of al-Qa'ida. But intelligence experts warned that Hlayhel can still make mischief from the Middle East. In his last prayer in Denmark, Hlayhel denounced the pope, warned against repetitions of the cartoons, and threatened retaliation: 'We are people who love death and will sacrifice ourselves before Allah's feet. Do not repeat the tragedy, or else it will become a tragedy for you and the whole world.'[118]

Hlayhel's fellow demagogue Laban wrote a book in Arabic, about the travelling imams' achievements, entitled *The Jyllands-Posten Crisis*. Laban's extremist connections were well established. A Palestinian with close connections to the Muslim Brotherhood, he went to Denmark after he was expelled from the United Arab Emirates in 1984 for his fiery sermons and denunciations of local leaders. Laban railed against a new group in Denmark called the Democratic Muslims, which was created in the wake of the cartoon crisis, describing its leader, Naser Khader, as 'a rat' and 'an apostate'. This amounts to a death threat, as in the fundamentalist view apostasy is a capital crime. Democratic Muslims are further characterized in the book as 'such nice people, clean shaven, very clever, who are ready to have sex in the park, whenever they feel like it'. The phrase 'sex in the park' is common Arab code for homosexuality, which in shari'a law also merits a death sentence. (It is worth noting that even words which may appear harmless and uncontentious in European languages may carry a sinister meaning in Arabic; or they may be code-words indicating an entirely different agenda.) Laban's name had been linked to Omar Abdel Rahman, the blind cleric who in 1993 was behind the first bombing of the World Trade Centre; to Ayman al-Zawahiri, one of the planners of 9/11; and to Mohammed al-Fizazi, who was responsible for the 2003 Casablanca bombing. Laban at one point also claimed knowledge of an imminent terror operation on Danish soil. His purpose with the book was to strengthen his own claims to leadership in the highly competitive world of extremist imams.[119] In an interview in September 2006, Laban insisted that the crisis was not his fault. Asked why he doesn't leave Denmark if he does not like it, he replied: 'Denmark is a nice country. It's merely that people have this kind of phobia towards Muslims.'[120]

In a quintessential exercise in *taqqiya* (simulation, cover-up, a tenet in Shi'ite Islam, but used also by other Muslims), Laban, from his mosque in the Copenhagen suburb of Nørrebro, tried to hide his satisfaction with the cartoon crisis. Speaking on Danish television, Laban wept crocodile tears, condemning the boycott of Danish goods and the other consequences of his actions. Yet, interviewed by al-Jazeera, the imam said just the opposite, praising the outrage of the Muslim world at his adoptive country. On 4 February, he even told Islamonline that Danish demonstrators intended to burn Qur'ans in Copenhagen, a falsehood designed to fuel the fire. According to Danish state television, DR, intelligence documents revealed that Laban had been in close contact for years with members of various terrorist organizations, and in particular with leaders of the Egyptian Gama'a Islamiya (Muslim Groups). In the beginning of the 1990s, several leaders of the Gama'a escaped from the Egyptian *mukhabarat* (intelligence service) and relocated to Europe. Copenhagen became the new hometown of two of the group's leaders, Ayman al-Zawahiri, currently serving as Osama Bin Laden's aide, and Talaat Fouad Qassimy. From Copenhagen, the men published *al-Murabitun*, the Gama'a's official publication. Laban worked as a translator and distributor of the publication, which glorified the killing of western tourists in Egypt and urged the annihilation of Jews. He then worked closely with Said Mansour, a Moroccan man charged in Denmark with running a publishing house that distributed jihadi material.[121] Laban's death was reported in February 2007. Another member of the cartoon roadshow was Ahmed Akkari. Akkari was born in Lebanon but obtained Danish citizenship and is fluent in Danish. Among his political prognostications is that the leader of the Democratic Muslims would be blown up, should he ever become a government minister. Most Danes were of the impression that Akkari had left the country to settle with his girlfriend in Lebanon, as he, too, felt insufficiently appreciated in Denmark. But when Denmark arranged for an evacuation of her citizens during the summer 2006 Hizbollah war in Lebanon, he asked to be rescued with his girlfriend and daughter. *Jyllands-Posten* carried a telling photograph from the rescue operation with Akkari seen against the Danish flag gently wafting in the breeze, the very flag that he and his friends had caused to be burned all over the Middle East.[122]

Many of the evacuees from Lebanon were dual-nationals, and were therefore on vacation in the very place from which they had supposedly sought asylum in Europe. Denmark and Sweden evacuated more than 10,000 citizens via Cyprus or Syria, and all services were free. The Danes had a test run in crisis management thanks to the violent cartoon protests against Danish embassies in Muslim countries. Yet some complained of inadequate sleeping and toilet facilities in the locations they were housed before being flown home to Denmark. Lars Thuesen, coordinator of the evacuations for the Danish Foreign Ministry said: 'We also had a few people complaining about the fact that you could not buy tax-free on the planes which we had chartered to take them home.'[123] Danes were astounded by the number of Danish resident aliens found in Lebanon during the evacuation. There were calls to investigate how many were actually living in Lebanon while claiming unemployment benefits in Denmark. Finally, the Danes learned that Abu Bashar, a Syrian cleric living in the regional capital of Odense and working as a prison chaplain, was fired after complaints from inmates at Nyborg State Prison that he was inciting hatred of Denmark, and after his statement in an article in *Fyens Stiftstidende* that 'Denmark is the next terror target.' Bashar's claim to fame stems from the cartoon crisis, when he showed a photograph of a man in a pig's mask on BBC television, and afterwards slipped it in among the material being presented by the touring imams in the Middle East. It turned out to be a photo of a French comedian in a pig-calling contest. Bashar later claimed that he was misinterpreted and that the photo had been sent to him anonymously, showing how Muslims were insulted in Denmark. His forked tongue damaged his credibility, and he claimed that his dismissal from his prison job was political. However, he said he was willing to forget the incident, if he could have his job back part-time, with disability pay because of a troublesome knee. His request was refused. The question remains why the Danish Government puts up with these imams and does not simply deport them. France has rid itself of more than twenty imams, as has Germany, while Spain and Italy each have deported four, and Holland three. Denmark so far has kicked none out.[124]

In his annual New Year's Day speech in January 2007, Prime Minister Rasmussen praised his nation for defending freedom of speech and not yielding to authoritarian forces during the international uproar over the cartoons. 'It made a strong impression on all of us to see the Danish flag being burnt, to see Danish embassies in flames, to hear and see the threats against Denmark and Danes', he said. Throughout the crisis, the government resisted calls to apologize and said it could not be held responsible for the actions of Denmark's independent media. Queen Margrethe also touched on the cartoon crisis in her New Year's speech, saying Danes 'must understand and make an effort to explain what values our society is based on'.[125] Non-Muslims occasionally raise the idea of banning the Qur'an, Islam, and Muslims. A political party called Stop Islamiseringen af Danmark (Stop Islamization of Denmark) demanded the censorship of parts of the Qur'an which 'encourage violence'. It claimed that the 67th and 69th Qur'anic verses violate the Danish constitution and that mosques across the country should be closed in accordance with the 78th article of the Danish constitution. The leader of the party, Anders Graves, said: 'Denmark is our country. Some verses of the Qur'an are filling me with worries about the lives of my children and grandchildren.' Stating that they have no intention of banning Islam across the country, Graves said people living in Denmark should obey the constitution of the country no matter what they believe in.[126]

In August 2007, Dutch MP Geert Wilders, the leader of the Freedom Party which holds nine of the Dutch parliament's 150 seats, repeated the call for the Qur'an to be banned – as a 'fascist book' – alongside *Mein Kampf* because it urges Muslims to kill non-believers. His call came after an alleged Islam-inspired attack on a Labour councillor who had renounced the Muslim faith. Wilders lives under tight security after murder attempts by suspected Islamic terrorists. He said the Qur'an 'calls on Muslims to oppress, persecute or kill Christians, Jews, dissidents and non-believers, to beat and rape women and to establish an Islamic state by force'. Writing in *De Volkskrant* newspaper, Wilders said: 'Ban this wretched book like *Mein Kampf* is banned!'[127] Two Australian politicians, Pauline Hanson and Paul Green, demanded a moratorium on Muslim immigration. Roberto Calderoli, coordinator of Italy's Northern League, in 2005 wrote that 'Islam has to be declared illegal until Islamists are prepared to renounce those parts of their pseudo-political and religious doctrine glorifying violence and the oppression of other cultures and religions.' British MP Boris Johnson pointed out in 2005 that passing a Racial and Religious Hatred Bill 'must mean banning the reading – in public or private – of a great many passages of the Qur'an itself'. His observation prompted a Muslim delegation to seek assurances (which it received) from the Home Office that no such ban would occur. Patrick Sookhdeo called for prohibiting one translation of *The Noble Koran: a New Rendering of its Meaning in English*, because 'it sets out a strategy for killing the "infidels" and for warfare against them'. Norway's Kristians and Progress Party in 2004 and Germany's Bundesverband der Bürgerbewegungen sought to prohibit the Qur'an in 2006, arguing for its incompatibility with the German constitution. Daniel Pipes believes all these efforts and others are too broad, and it would be more practical to reduce the threats of jihad and shari'a by 'banning Islamist interpretations of the Qur'an, as well as Islamism and Islamists'.[128]

A knighthood awarded to Salman Rushdie in June 2007 for services to literature in the Queen's Birthday Honours provoked another dose of feverish responses from Muslims, particularly in Pakistan and Iran. In Pakistan's national assembly, the Religious Affairs Minister, Mohammed Ijaz ul-Haq appeared to justify a suicide bombing attack when he told Pakistani MPs that 'if somebody has to attack by strapping a bomb to his body to protect the honour of the prophet, then it is justified'. He later said he had been misunderstood. The British High Commissioner to Pakistan, Robert Brinkley, was summoned to meet officials in Islamabad to hear Pakistani objections to the honour, but he expressed 'deep concern' at ul-Haq's remarks. An Iranian extremist group raised the bounty on Rushdie's head from $100,000 to $150,000 while the Queen's effigy was burned on the streets of Lahore. An Iranian newspaper called the Queen an 'old crone'. Paul Goodman, the Tory MP for Wycombe, said that the UK should demand an apology from the highest reaches of the Pakistani Government for ul-Haq's comments and compared the government's response to its quiet stand in the protests over Danish newspaper cartoons. Rushdie remains formally sentenced to death for blasphemy in a fatwa decreed by Ayatollah Khomeini in 1989 but in 1998 Iran had promised not to implement it.[129] Despite mounting protests, the Home Secretary refused to apologize for or back down over the knighthood. International protests continued with both the Iraqi Foreign Minister, Hoshyar Zebari, who was then visting London, and protesters in Malaysia, criticizing the UK. John Reid suggested Rushdie's work belonged in a British culture of challenging religious orthodoxies in the arts, and he cited the chorus of Christian complaints when Monty Python made the film *Life of Brian*. Margaret Beckett, then Foreign Secretary, fractured the government's hitherto united front on the issue, apologizing for any 'hurt' caused and stressing that many other Muslims had also been awarded in the British honours system.[130]

Ul-Haq declared his intention to visit Britain alongside a delegation travelling to London to discuss ways of engaging Muslim clerics to clear up 'misunderstandings' over his remarks. But his accompanying statement demonstrated there was no 'misunderstanding'. He said: 'The West always wonders about the root cause of terrorism. Such actions [giving Rushdie a knighthood] are the root cause of it. If someone commits suicide bombing to protect the honour of the prophet Muhammad, his act is justified.' A unanimous resolution passed in the Pakistani parliament deplored Rushdie's honour as an open insult to Muslim feelings.

A senior Labour Muslim peer appealed to ministers to put the award on hold and revealed that Muslim British businesses were trying to organize a nationwide shutdown in protest over the knighthood. He unconvincingly warned that honouring the author put 'Her Majesty the Queen in a very difficult position, as head of the Church of England, as *The Satanic Verses* had offended Christianity as well as Islam'.[131] All his years of living in the UK had not taught him much about British culture and satire. British Muslims burned the flag of St George and called for the Queen to 'Go to Hell' in a furious rally held in London. Muslims rallying at Regent's Park Mosque said that anger over the award could match the fierce reaction to the Danish cartoons. Anjem Choudary, resorting to his usual hyperbole, said: 'Rushdie is a hate figure across the Muslim world because of his insults to Islam. This honour will have ramifications here and across the world.' A group of traders in Islamabad offered a reward of ten million rupees ($165,000) to anyone who killed Rushdie.[132]

With every escalation of their rhetoric, the Muslims achieve little more than devalue the currency of their precious 'anger'. They are increasingly viewed as children incapable of controlling their temper tantrums, and the wisest way to deal with them is to avert one's gaze. Placards outside Regent's Park Mosque said 'May God curse the Queen', while one speaker told followers Tony Blair should be sent back 'in a bag' from his forthcoming role as a Middle East envoy. A Muslim peer compared Rushdie to the 9/11 hijackers. Interviewed by *Le Figaro,* the Labour peer Lord Ahmed offered further evidence of his irrationality by asking: 'What would one say if the Saudi or Afghan Governments honoured the martyrs of the September 11 attacks on the United States?' For Lord Ahmed, writing a book that is critical of the Muslim prophet is akin to murdering 3,000 civilians in a terrorist attack. Leaflets handed out to people leaving the mosque after Friday prayers said: 'The British Government's decision to honour Salman Rushdie is a public demonstration of their hatred and contempt towards Islam.' It is worth noting that this mosque is affiliated to the Saudi Government. Not to be outdone, the MCB accused Tony Blair personally of rewarding an author who had 'vilified' Islam, in a letter to more than 500 mosques. Jo Glanville, editor of *Index on Censorship,* said: 'In terms of censorship we are extremely unhappy at this level of intimidation that surfaces every time there is dissent, criticism or comment on Islam. It's very much a knee-jerk response that whenever Islam appears to be slighted in any way you can be sure that there is going to be political leaders who are going to shout to gain political advantage.'[133]

In the *Sunday Telegraph*, Jenny McCartney asserted that every culture has its emotion of choice. The West in general has developed a mass taste for mawkish sentimentality. The Islamic world has acquired a penchant for self-righteous fury. Their demonstrators demand: 'Give us what we want, because we feel more strongly than you do.' The angrier a person is, the more he is seen as the authentic voice of his community. And yet, if anger were the only valid currency in town, supporters of liberal values could find much to be angry about as well.[134] The kindest comment that can be made is that the Muslim overreaction is indicative of the insecurity of their beliefs. Their shenanigans have had the unfortunate effect of discrediting all faiths, although the twin secular creeds of fascism and communism have wrought more death and destruction than any religion. In an atmosphere charged with the trials and arrests of aspiring bombers, and a furore over the Rushdie knighthood, the premiere of a work by the leading composer Sir John Taverner in Westminster Cathedral provoked discord because it glorified the Muslim deity. Traditionalist Roman Catholics protested against the work, which includes the singing of the ninety-nine names of Allah. Several wrote to the head of the Roman Catholic Church, expressing concern that the Church would be seen to be endorsing the Islamic idea of God. Sir John's new work, *The Beautiful Names*, was commissioned by Prince Charles.[135]

When Muslim organizations sued French satirical magazine *Charlie Hebdo* for publishing the Danish cartoons, everyone posed as defenders of one or another French tradition. *Charlie Hebdo* directs its satire every week against France's right-wing establishment as well as the self-contented 'caviar left'. The wave of anti-western hysteria in the Muslim world led the western media to close ranks in a remarkable way. As a gesture of solidarity, 150 newspapers in sixty countries reprinted the cartoons. *Charlie Hebdo* added its own cartoon on the cover, showing Muhammad in a state of exasperation. 'It's tough being loved by idiots', he complains, face buried in hands. French Muslim preachers complained of Islamophobia, and felt pious believers had been equated with brutal killers. Dalil Boubakeur, who directs the Paris Great Mosque, spearheaded a new movement against 'fomentation of racial hatred'. In 2003 he created the Muslim Council at the suggestion of then-Interior Minister Sarkozy, who had hoped the moderate umbrella association would weaken the influence of extremists. But the cartoon controversy soured relations between the Muslim Council and the Interior Ministry. Pressured by radical council members, Boubakeur began a legal counter-attack, badly miscalculating the outcome. The trial against *Charlie Hebdo* became a tribunal against religious intolerance. *Le Monde* called it a 'trial from another time'. *Charlie Hebdo* editor Philippe Val said the 'limits of liberty must be verified daily', and quoted John Paul II: 'Be not afraid!'

2007 being an election year in France, several politicians came to the defence of the magazine. François Hollande, first secretary of the French Socialist Party, and François Bayrou, presidential candidate from the liberal UDF Party, both supported *Charlie Hebdo*. Even Sarkozy defended *Charlie Hebdo*, although it typically portrayed him as a nightstick-swinging policeman or a rabid pitbull terrier. Sarkozy, the presidential candidate for the conservative UMP Party, characterized himself as a critic of 'every form of censorship' in a written statement to the court, arguing it was better to have 'too many cartoons' than 'no cartoons' and defended the 'right to smile'. The Muslim Council initially threatened that its heads would resign *en masse* in protest, but watching the development of the case, gave in. Boubakeur demanded a 'calming' of the situation and lamented its 'politicization'. The moderate language came too late, and *Charlie Hebdo* was cleared of all charges. The magazine's usual circulation of 60,000 increased to 400,000 for its Muhammad issue.[136] Val had called the case a 'medieval trial', saying religions should be subject to 'critique and to democratic debate'. Terrorism, not Muslims, were the intended target of the drawings. 'Before being Muslim, one is a citizen of the [French] Republic', he said.[137]

A documentary broadcast in October 2007 showed that several of the instigators behind the violent cartoon demonstrations never saw the drawings. Danish director Karsten Kjær's documentary

'Those Damned Drawings' suggests the crisis began when the man many consider to be Islam's most powerful figure, Yusuf al-Qaradawi (a prominent leader of the Muslim Brotherhood), declared 3 February 2006 as a 'Day of Rage' on his TV programme. In the documentary, Kjær shows the Mohammed drawings to al-Qaradawi, who views them for the first time. Kjær also shows the cartoons to Ali Bakhsi (a 'professional demonstrator' employed by the Iranian Government), the Iranian who spearheaded demonstrations in Tehran that led to the burning of the Danish Embassy there. Bakhsi laughingly says the drawings look nothing like Muhammad but rather like an Indian Sikh.[138]

A discussion of the cartoon jihad would not be complete without an analysis of how it was exploited and even advanced by the Muslim Brotherhood, with its long-term worldwide strategy for establishing Islamic supremacy in the West. Acknowledging Qaradawi's role, the pan-Arab daily *al-Sharq al-Awsat*, in London, stated on 8 February: 'The issue disappeared from the radar until Sheikh Yusuf al-Qaradawi, the mufti of al-Jazeera TV, seized upon it and called for Muslims worldwide to protest.' While it was to be expected that the Muslim Brotherhood would inflame the cartoon controversy, the extent of the Brotherhood's deliberate planning for an Islamist takeover of the West is less well known. A book published by Le Seuil in Paris in October 2005, by the Swiss investigative reporter Sylvain Besson, publicizes the discovery and contents of a Muslim Brotherhood strategy document entitled *The Project*. Besson's book, *La Conquête de l'Occident: Le projet secret des Islamistes* (The Conquest of the West: The Islamists' secret project), recounts how, in November 2001, Swiss authorities responded to a request from the White House to investigate Yusuf Nada, who lived on the eastern shore of Lake Lugano in Switzerland. Nada was the treasurer of the Al Taqwa bank, with financial links to al-Qa'ida. In his house, investigators stumbled onto *The Project*, an unsigned, fourteen-page document dated 1 December 1982. Deputy National Security Advisor for Combating Terrorism, Juan Zarate, described the document as the Muslim Brotherhood's master plan for 'spreading their political ideology'. Zarate told Besson, '*The Project* is a roadmap for achieving the installation of Islamic regimes in the West via propaganda, preaching, and, if necessary, war. It's the same idea expressed by Qaradawi in 1995 when he said: We will conquer Europe, we will conquer America, not by the sword but by our *da'wa* [proselytizing].'

The Project calls for 'putting in place a watchdog system for monitoring the [western] media to warn all Muslims of the dangers and international plots fomented against them'. Another long-term effort is to 'put in place [among Muslims in the West] a parallel society where the group is above the individual, godly authority above human liberty, and the holy scripture above the laws'. A European secret service agent interviewed by Besson explains that 'the project is going to be a real danger in ten years. We'll see the emergence of a parallel system, the creation of Muslim Parliaments. Then the slow destruction of our institutions will begin.' Muslims must constantly work to support Islamic *da'wa* and all the groups around the globe engaged in jihad. Also vital is to 'keep the umma [the Muslim community] in a jihad frame of mind' and 'to breed a feeling of resentment towards the Jews and refuse any form of coexistence with them'. On 2 February 2006, *al-Tajdid*, a Moroccan Islamist daily close to the Brotherhood, asserted that the Danish cartoons were 'a Zionist provocation aimed at reviving the conflict between the West and the Muslim nation'.

The Muslim Brotherhood used the cartoon crisis to radicalize Muslims in the West, by continually pointing out the supposed 'Islamophobia' all around them. The Saudi daily *al-Watan* reported that the OIC decided to create a worldwide Islamophobia watchdog organization to lobby for the adoption of 'anti-Islamophobia' laws, as well as promoting a common position against states or organizations it sees as attacking Islam. Under the scheme outlined in *The Project*, the Muslim Brotherhood would seek to become the indispensable interlocutor with western governments on issues relating not only to Islam but also to international issues affecting the Islamic world. The same approach appeared in Qaradawi's 1990 book, *Priorities of the Islamic Movement in the Coming Phase*. He saw the presence of large Muslim populations in the West as a major opportunity. For him, 'the Islamic presence' in the West is necessary 'to defend the interests of the Muslim nation and the land of Islam against the hostility and disinformation of anti-Islamic movements', calling on Muslims in the West to reform their host countries. The cartoon jihad has enabled Muslim lobbies in Europe to push for the adoption of blasphemy laws by the UN, the EU, and the nations of Europe.[139]

In Britain, a television documentary portrayed Jesus as Muslims see him. With the Qur'an as a main source and drawing on interviews with scholars and historians, the Muslim Jesus explores how Islam views Christ as a prophet but not as the son of God. There was no manger, Christ is not the Messiah, and the crucifixion never happened. According to the Qur'an, instead of dying on the cross, Jesus was rescued by angels and raised to heaven. The director and producer, Irshad Ashraf, said the film was an attempt to shift the focus away from extremism to the spiritual side of Islam. Patrick Sookhdeo, an Anglican canon, accused broadcasters of double standards. He asked: 'How would the Muslim community respond if ITV made a programme challenging Muhammad as the last prophet?' He considered the Qur'an's denial of Jesus's divinity as unacceptable, adding: 'On the last day the Qur'an says Jesus will destroy all the crosses. How can we praise that?'[140]

In August 2007, Swedish artist Lars Vilks drew a cartoon with Muhammad's head on a dog's body. He is now in hiding after al-Qa'ida in Iraq placed a bounty of $100,000 on his head (with a $50,000 bonus if his throat is slit). Several galleries had refused to display the drawing, fearing Muslim violence, and it was finally published in the newspaper *Nerikes Allehanda*. Yet again, the world's most repressive governments are attempting to use the controversy to provide legitimacy for their suppression of their critics in the name of respect for Islam. The OIC is seeking to rewrite international human rights standards to curtail any freedom of expression that threatens their more authoritarian members. Ahmadinejad resorted to his mindless default position, accusing 'Zionists' of being responsible. Pakistan complained that 'the right to freedom of expression' is inconsistent with 'defamation of religions and prophets'. The Turkish Ministry of Religious Affairs called for rules specifying new limits of press freedom. Speaking for the OIC, Pakistan's Marghoob Saleem Butt criticized 'unrestricted and disrespectful enjoyment of freedom of expression'. The issues here have less to do with cartoonists' freedom of expression than the repression in much of the Muslim world. Routinely accusations of blasphemy are invoked to repress writers, journalists, political dissidents and reformers. Apart from the severe repression in Iran, Egypt has been unusually active in imprisoning its critics in the name of Islam by arresting several people and sentencing a blogger, Abdel Kareem Soliman, to three years for 'insulting Islam'. Saudi Arabian democracy activists Ali al-Demaini, Abdullah al-Hamed, and Matruk al-Faleh were imprisoned on charges of using 'un-Islamic terminology' such as 'democracy' and 'human rights', when they called for a written constitution. Saudi teacher Mohammad al-Harbi was sentenced to a forty-month prison term and 750 lashes for 'mocking religion' after discussing the Bible in class and saying that the Jews were right. The Indonesian Ulema Council, the country's highest Islamic authority, issued a fatwa banning the Liberal Islamic Network, which teaches an open interpretation of the Qur'an. Repressive laws, supplemented and reinforced by terrorists, vigilantes and mob violence, are a barrier to dissent, and so to democracy and free societies. When politics and religion are intertwined, there can be no political freedom without religious freedom. If free nations do not resist these totalitarian strictures in the name of religious sensitivity, they will condemn reformist Muslims to silence behind what Senator Joseph Lieberman has aptly termed a 'theological iron curtain'.[141]

Sweden's Prime Minister Fredrik Reinfeldt invited the ambassadors from twenty-two Muslim countries to a meeting to calm tensions. Egyptian ambassador Mohamed Sotouhi said they had agreed on a list of measures Sweden needed to take if it was to secure a long-term solution to the controversy. According to Sotouhi, 'comprehensive measures' were required if Sweden was to prevent some 'amateur artist' from reawakening tensions every other month. 'We want to see action, not just nice words. We have to push for a change in the law', he said. Algeria's ambassador to Sweden, Merzak Bedjaoui, said the meeting 'was an excellent initiative taken in a spirit of appeasement'.[142] Sweden's Ambassador to Saudi Arabia, Jan Thesleff, met Ekmeleddin Ihsanoglu, head of the OIC in Jeddah and offered his 'deepest apologies for the controversy created by the publishing of the hurtful depiction', according to an OIC statement. The Swedish Foreign Ministry itself denied that the ambassador had made any apology, saying that he had only expressed regret. Swedish companies lowered their profile in the Middle East amid fears that the cartoon could spark attacks. Ericsson, the telecoms giant, removed the Swedish flag from offices in several countries.[143]

The reaction to the cartoons and the pope's speech served one other purpose. Writing in *The Weekly Standard,* Lee Smith made the obvious riposte to those who believe the war in Iraq is breeding radicals. A war against radicals is going to make some people more radical, but, then again, a papal speech also served as a pretext for arson and murder – as did the publication of Danish cartoons depicting Muhammad, the alleged 'destruction' of a Qur'an at Guantanamo Bay, and the work of Theo van Gogh in Holland, among a host of other 'insults to Islam'. And yet Muslim radicals were engaging in arson and murder long before the war in Iraq. Smith continued:

> After a certain point, people's willingness to be recruited for a cause does not depend on outrage or vengeance, but on whether or not they believe that cause is likely to succeed. Rational people do not generally volunteer for a suicide mission, nor a cause doomed to failure ... Many of these fighters in Iraq have signed up precisely because they want the chance to kill themselves, along with US-led coalition troops, and/or sectarian rivals. Indeed, the suicide bombing – or in Islamic parlance, the 'martyrdom operation' – is the signature act of Islamic radicals across the world, from Baghdad to Bali, and Morocco to Manhattan. By and large then, we are not talking about rational people, but suicidal-homicidal fanatics in search of a theatre where they can exercise their already radical impulses.

Smith quoted from a 1943 letter by Soleyman al-Asad, an Alawite notable: 'The spirit of hatred and fanaticism imbedded in the hearts of the Arab Muslims against everything that is non-Muslim has been perpetually nurtured by the Islamic religion. There is no hope that the situation will ever change.' Sunni leaders themselves recognize the significant potential for fanaticism in the region. The most obvious way to deal with the problem is to kill the radical actors, but the best way is to have someone else kill them lest the regime's Islamic authenticity come into question. And here is where jihad in foreign lands comes in really handy for Arab rulers. The next best thing to using Muslim fanatics as a policy-making tool is just to get rid of them. Arab rulers dispatch their fanatics to such places in the hope that they never return. Thus, Iraq is not a jihadist incubator, but rather a jihadist dumping ground.[144]

NOTES

1. See R. Israeli, *Islamikaze: Manifestations of Islamic Martyrology* (London: Frank Cass, 2003), esp. Chapter 8.
2. In a public speech by Ali Khamenei, 20 February 2006.
3. *CNN World News*, 22 February 2006.
4. Aaron Klein, 'Synagogues Used as Bases To Fire on Israel', *The New York Sun*, 27 February 2007.
5. Rachel Ehrenfeld and Alyssa A. Lappen, 'Europe's Last Chance', *FrontPageMagazine.com*, 16 February 2006.
6. John Branch, *The San Antonio Express-News*, 10 February 2006.
7. John Cole, *The Scranton Times*, 8 February 2006.
8. Eric Devericks, *The Seattle Times*, 10 February 2006.
9. John Darkow, *The Columbia Daily Tribune*, 10 February 2006.
10. Mike Graston, *The Windsor Star*, 10 February 2006.
11. Wafa Sultan, on *al-Jazeera*, 21 February 2006. See MEMRI Special Dispatch Series, 1107, 7 March 2006.
12. Wafa Sultan, on *al-Jazeera*, 26 July 2005. See MEMRI, Special Dispatch Series, 1107, 7 March 2006.
13. *Los Angeles Times*, 10 March 2006.
14. Ibid.
15. Ibid.
16. Richard Kerbaj, 'Warning to West on "Evil of Islam"', *The Australian*, 21 August 2007.
17. *Ein TV* and *al-Manar TV*, cited by MEMRI, 26 February 2006.
18. Shmuel Trigano, in *Post-Holocaust and Anti-Semitism Series*, 42, 1 March 2000, Jerusalem Centre for Public Affairs.
19. *Dream 2 TV*, 1 March 2006. Translated and reported by MEMRI, 1116, 17 March 2006.
20. Many of the insights referred to here are based on Manfred Gerstenfeld, 'The Muhammad Cartoon Controversy, Israel and the Jews: A Case Study', *Post-Holocaust and Anti-Semitism Series*, 43, 2 April 2006, Jerusalem Centre for Public Affairs.
21. Daniel Goldhagen, 'The New Threat', *The New Republic*, 13 March 2006.
22. Richard Oestermann, 'Drawing Conclusions', *The Jerusalem Post*, 15 June 2006.
23. Dennis Prager, *WorldNetDaily*, 7 February 2006, cited by Gerstenfeld, 'The Muhammad Cartoon Controversy, Israel and the Jews', p.6.
24. Cited by Gerstenfeld, 'The Muhammad Cartoon Controversy, Israel and the Jews', p.7.
25. Charles Krauthammer, 'Save us from Moderates', *The Seattle Times*, 13 February 2006.
26. Gerstenfeld, 'The Muhammad Cartoon Controversy, Israel and the Jews', pp.9–10.
27. *Arab News* (Saudi Arabia), 4 April 2006.
28. 'Danish Muslims Sue Newspaper over Cartoons. Lawsuit seeks $16,100, claims Drawings were "defamatory and injurious"', *AP*, 30 March 2006.
29. Carolyn Thompson, 'Borders, Waldenbooks Won't Carry Magazine', *San Francisco Chronicle*, citing *AP*, 29 March 2006.
30. 'Muslim Gang Forces Paris Café To Censor Cartoon Show', *Middle East Times*, 31 March 2006.
31. The faith of Islam is based on five pillars (*arkan*): testimony that Allah is the one God and Muhammad his prophet, prayer, the fast of Ramadan, giving of alms and pilgrimage to Mecca. Adding a sixth pillar in a religion which is taken seriously and frowns upon humour, is in itself a blasphemy.
32. 'Muslim Gang Forces Café to Censor Cartoon Show'.

33. Michael Nazir-Ali, the Bishop of Rochester, England, 'Muslims Demand Respect – but not for Christians', *Sunday Telegraph*, 26 March 2006.
34. Dr Onkar Ghate, a senior fellow at the Ayn Rand Institute in Irvine, CA, 30 March 2006.
35. Bernhard Zand, 'The Cartoon Wars: The Inciters and the Incited', *Der Spiegel*, 13 February 2006.
36. Carl Bildt, 'Egypt of Escalation', *Bildt Comments*, 18 February 2006.
37. Zand, 'The Cartoon Wars: The Inciters and the Incited'.
38. Yassin Musharbash and Anna Reimann, 'Alienated Danish Muslims Sought Help from Arabs', *Spiegel Online*, 1 February 2006.
39. Ayman Qenawi, 'Danish Muslims Internationalize Anti-Prophet Cartoons', *Islam Online*, 18 November 2005.
40. David Rennie, 'A Danish Muslim Activist Speaks', *The Daily Telegraph weblog*, 3 February 2006.
41. Zand, 'The Cartoon Wars: The Inciters and the Incited'.
42. Ibid.
43. Ibn Warraq, 'Democracy in a Cartoon', *Spiegel Online*, 3 February 2006.
44. Ibid.
45. Pascal Bruckner, 'Re-Arming Europe – The Old World needs an Intellectual Revolution to meet the Challenges Ahead', *Opinion Journal*, 3 June 2007, translated from the French by Sara Sugihara.
46. 'Q & A: Crisis in Darfur', *Human Rights Watch*, 29 January 2007.
47. Bruckner, 'Re-Arming Europe – The Old World needs an Intellectual Revolution to meet the Challenges Ahead'.
48. Michael Scott Moore, interview with *al-Jazeera* cartoonist Shujaat Ali, *Spiegel Online*, 3 February 2006.
49. Ibid.
50. Anjana Shrivastava, 'Denmark's Cartoon Jihad', *Spiegel Online*, 1 February 2006.
51. John Vinocur and Dan Bilefsky, 'Dane Sees Greed and Politics in the Crisis', *The New York Times*, 10 February 2006.
52. Steve Linde, 'Wiesenthal Centre official: Internet Co-opted by Terrorist Groups', *The Jerusalem Post*, 4 June 2006.
53. Ibid.
54. Shrivastava, 'Denmark's Cartoon Jihad'.
55. Roman Heflik, 'Editor Reflects on Denmark's Cartoon Jihad', *Spiegel Online*, 2 February 2006.
56. Ibid.
57. 'Muhammed Strikes Back', *Spiegel Online*, 2 February 2006.
58. Yassin Musharbash, 'al-Azhar University in Cairo: In the Heart of Muslim Belief', *Spiegel Online*, 10 February 2006, translated from German by Andrew Bulkeley.
59. 'Jail Toilets Face Away from Mecca', BBC News, 20 April 2006.
60. Julie Moult, 'Muslim-only Kitchen Kit for Jails', *The Sun*, 13 January 2007.
61. Patrick Goodenough, 'Islamic States Press for Limits on Free Expression', CNSNews.com, 23 April 2006.
62. 'OIC urges De-linking Islam from Terrorism', *Kuwait News Agency*, 13 September 2007.
63. Duncan Currie, 'The Cartoon Wars Are Over, We lost', *The Weekly Standard*, 1 May 2006, Volume 11, Issue 31.
64. Yassin Musharbash, 'Militant Islam Online Magazine Hints at Attacks on Papers that Ran Muhammad Caricatures', *Spiegel Online*, 5 May 2006.
65. Ibid.
66. Nina Berglund, 'Krekar threatens Norway', *Aftenposten*, 6 September 2005.
67. Musharbash, 'Militant Islam Online Magazine Hints at Attacks on Papers that Ran Muhammad Caricatures'.
68. 'Islam Conference Fizzles', *The Copenhagen Post*, 15 May 2006.
69. Ibid.
70. Richard Oestermann, 'Drawing Conclusions', *The Jerusalem Post*, 15 June 2006.
71. 'Danish Editor Burnt Alive', *The Nation* (Pakistan), 15 June 2006, http://www.nation.com.pk/daily/june-2006/15/index12.php.

72. Daniel Pipes, 'Quest for Reciprocity', *The Jerusalem Post*, 5 July 2006.
73. Barney Zwartz, 'Stop Appeasing Muslims: Islam Expert', *The Age*, 3 November 2003.
74. Sandro Magister, 'In Rome's Main Mosque, One Imam Is Calling for Jihad', http://chiesa.espresso.repubblica.it/dettaglio.jsp?id=6953&eng=y, 11 June 2003
75. Pipes, 'Quest for reciprocity'.
76. Richard Owen, 'Homily on Faith, Logic and Holy War was seen as a Slur on Islam', *The Times*, 16 September 2006.
77. 'Benedict the Brave – The Pope said things Muslims need to hear about Faith and Reason', *Opinion Journal*, 19 September 2006.
78. Jenny Booth, 'Muslim Leaders Accuse Pope of Bigotry', *Times Online*, 15 September 2006.
79. 'Benedict the Brave – The Pope said things Muslims need to hear about Faith and Reason'.
80. William Rees-Mogg, 'Why the Pope was Right', *The Times*, 18 September 2006.
81. Jenny Booth, 'Police Patrol Churches after Pope Controversy', *Times Online*, 19 September 2006.
82. Ruth Gledhill and Richard Owen, 'Carey Backs Pope and Issues Warning on "Violent" Islam', *The Times*, 20 September 2006.
83. Devika Bhat, 'Catholic Archbishop Questions Turkish Entry to EU', *Times Online*, 21 September 2006.
84. Jenny Booth, 'Pope urges Dialogue in Meeting with Muslim Leaders', *Times Online*, 25 September 2006.
85. Richard Owen, 'Pope sees Islamic Envoys in Attempt to Heal Rift', *Times Online*, 26 September 2006.
86. Richard Owen and Suna Erdem, 'Muslims Vent Fury at Pope's Speech', *The Times*, 16 September 2006.
87. Devika Bhat, 'Pope Visits Famous Mosque on Busiest Day of Turkey Trip', *Times Online*, 30 November 2006.
88. Joseph Bottum, 'Benedict Meets Bartholomew – The Real Reason for the Pope's Visit to Turkey', *The Weekly Standard*, 11 December 2006.
89. Russell Shaw, 'Papal Transformation – Benedict uses Softer Touch to Dialogue with Islam', *Catholic Online*, 16 February 2007.
90. Philip Pullella, 'Pope in About-face over Muslim Dialogue Office', *Reuters*, 28 May 2007.
91. Ruth Gledhill, 'Summit on Religious Harmony is Thrown into Discord by Malaysia', *The Times*, 10 May 2007.
92. Richard Owen and Ruth Gledhill, 'If it isn't Roman Catholic then it's not a Proper Church, Pope tells Christians', *The Times*, 11 July 2007.
93. 'Pope's Private Secretary Warns of Islamization of Europe', *The Jerusalem Post*, citing AP, 26 July 2007.
94. Simon Caldwell, 'Pope in "Freedom" Blast at Islam', *Daily Mail*, 21 September 2007.
95. Charles Johnson, 'Pope Speaks Out About Islamic Repression', *Little Green Footballs*, 21 September 2007.
96. Charles Bremner, 'Philosophers Demand Help for Teacher on run from Islam Threats', *The Times*, 3 October 2006.
97. Daniel Pipes, 'Islamic Law Rules You, Too', *The Jerusalem Post*, 26 September 2006.
98. Michael Freund, 'Saudis Arrest Christian for Entering Mecca', *The Jerusalem Post*, 24 May 2007.
99. Amir Taheri, 'The West's Self-Imposed Censorship', *Gulf News*, 13 October 2006; see also Daniel Mandel, 'Preemptive Appeasement – Europe's New Strategy for the War on Terror', *The Weekly Standard*, 21 September 2007.
100. Ibid.
101. Ibid.
102. Devika Bhat, 'Opera Reignites Islam Row after Cancelling Production', *Times Online*, 26 September 2006.
103. Roger Boyes, 'Opera Boss Censors Mozart over Stage Beheading of Muhammad', *The Times*, 27 September 2006.'
104. Roger Boyes, 'Mozart Censor Faces a Backlash', *The Times*, 28 September 2006.

The Cartoon Affair and the Failure of Dialogue and Coexistence 361

105. Roger Boyes, 'A Fright at the Opera: Champions of Mozart Brave Cultural Divide', *The Times*, 19 December 2006.
106. Philipp Wittrock, 'Carnival in Germany, Islam No Longer Taboo', *Spiegel Online*, 16 February 2007.
107. Thomas Catan, 'Christian Soldiers take a Beating over Battle with Moors', *The Times*, 23 October 2006.
108. Ian Burrell, 'Newsroom Revolt Forces *Star* to drop its "Daily Fatwa" Spoof', *The Independent*, 19 October 2006.
109. John Steele, 'Met backs off over Muslim Protests', *The Daily Telegraph*, 29 September 2006.
110. Duncan Gardham, 'Muslims Arrested in Old Bailey Demo', *The Daily Telegraph*, 2 November 2006.
111. Matthew Moore, 'Cartoon Protester Guilty of Race Hate', *The Daily Telegraph*, 9 November 2006.
112. Richard Alleyne, 'Cartoon Protester Guilty of Race Hate', *The Daily Telegraph*, 10 November 2006.
113. David Brown, 'Muslim on Racial Hatred Charges', *The Times*, 3 January 2007.
114. Elsa McLaren, 'Muslim Protestor Guilty of Soliciting Murder', *Times Online*, 5 January 2007.
115. Richard Holt, 'Cartoon Protester Guilty of Race Hate', *The Daily Telegraph*, 1 February 2007.
116. Ian Evans, 'Cartoon Protest Muslim is Guilty of Soliciting Murder', *The Times*, 8 March 2007.
117. Jan M. Olsen, 'Muslim Groups' Suit over Cartoons Rejected', *AP*, 27 October 2006.
118. Henrik Bering, 'Sex in the Park – The latest doings of the Danish Imams', *The Weekly Standard*, 27 November 2006.
119. Ibid.
120. Luke Harding, 'How one of the Biggest Rows of Modern Times Helped Danish Exports to Prosper', *The Guardian*, 30 September 2006.
121. Lorenzo Vidino, 'Creating Outrage – Meet the Imam behind the Cartoon Over-reaction', *National Review*, 6 February 2006.
122. Bering, 'Sex in the Park – The latest doings of the Danish Imams'.
123. 'Danes, Swedes Lead Evacuation Race', *AP*, 21 July 2006.
124. Bering, 'Sex in the Park – The latest doings of the Danish Imams'.
125. 'Denmark Stood up for Free Speech during Cartoon Crisis', *The Jerusalem Post*, citing *AP*, 1 January 2007.
126. 'A Danish Party Demands Censorship for Qur'an', *Sabah* (Turkey), 25 February 2007.
127. Bruno Waterfield, 'Ban Qur'an like *Mein Kampf*, says Dutch MP', *The Daily Telegraph*, 9 August 2007.
128. Daniel Pipes, 'The Case Against Banning the Qur'an', *The Jerusalem Post*, 28 August 2007.
129. Sam Knight, 'Britain Responds in Rushdie Knighthood Row', *Times Online*, 19 June 2007.
130. Nico Hines, 'Protests Against the Award have been most Heated in Pakistan', *Times Online*, 20 June 2007.
131. Brendan Carlin, 'Minister Accused over Rushdie may Visit UK', *The Daily Telegraph*, 21 June 2007.
132. 'British Muslims Burn St George's Flag in Furious London Rally over Rushdie Row', *Daily Mail*, 22 June 2007.
133. Duncan Gardham, 'Muslim Peer Compares Rushdie to 9/11 Bombers', *The Daily Telegraph*, 22 June 2007.
134. Jenny McCartney, 'The Moral of Rushdie's Story? Anger is a Choice', *Sunday Telegraph*, 24 June 2007.
135. Jonathan Petre, 'Protests at Taverner's Allah in Cathedral', *The Daily Telegraph*, 17 June 2007.
136. Stefan Simons, 'Danish Caricatures on Trial in France – Cartoons 1: Muhammad 0', *Spiegel Online*, 16 February 2007.
137. 'Muhammad Cartoons Case Reaches French Courts', *The Jerusalem Post*, citing *AP*, 7 February 2007.
138. 'Muslims never saw Mohammed Cartoons', *The Copenhagen Post*, 5 October 2007.

139. Olivier Guitta, 'The Cartoon Jihad – The Muslim Brotherhood's Project for Dominating the West', *The Weekly Standard*, 20 February 2006.
140. Riazat Butt, 'TV Airing for Islam's Story of Christ', *The Guardian*, 18 August 2007.
141. Paul Marshall, 'Muzzling in the Name of Islam', *The Washington Post*, 29 September 2007.
142. 'Muslim Ambassadors: "Sweden needs to change its laws"', *The Local*, 6 September 2007.
143. David Charter, 'Cartoonist Shrugs at Islamic Death Threat: "It's good to know how much one is worth"', *The Times*, 17 September 2007.
144. Lee Smith, 'Fighting Them Over There – Iraq is not a Breeding Ground for Terrorists, it's a Dumping Ground', *The Weekly Standard*, 28 September 2006.

CHAPTER SIX

Quo Vadis, Europe?

A Dudley councillor called for plans to create a 'Muslim village' in the town centre to be conducted more openly after it was revealed that the controversial project would receive £150,000 funding from taxpayers. Liberal Democrat leader Dave Tyler said he wanted to see everything about the Pride of Dudley project out in the open. He said: 'People are very agitated at the prospect of having a large mosque on their doorsteps. The problem we've got is we do not know enough about this – it was sprung on us as a community and the public are wary.' Dudley Council confirmed the project, to include a large mosque, sports halls, fitness room, health clinic and IT centres. It would receive the funding over a two-year period from the government's Neighbourhood Renewal Fund.[1] In February 2007, the local planning committee refused permission for the mosque, but the bid to build the mosque is expected to continue. Local Christians were concerned about security issues, community cohesion, and the Islamization of the town. Stephen Green, national director of *Christian Voice*, said: 'I am delighted that this mosque application has fallen at its first hurdle.' It had started off claiming to be the 'Pride of Dudley'. It had a minaret that would have made it the tallest building in Dudley, an important spiritual statement for Muslims with strong political overtones. Even the latest project had a minaret of some sixty-five feet.[2] The plans sparked a protest campaign described as the biggest in living memory after more than 22,000 people signed petitions and wrote 944 letters of objection. The development control committee rejected the £18 million plans. Muslim leader Khurshid Ahmed condemned the decision as 'the death of democracy'. In 2005 the original £15 million proposal, featuring a 110-

foot minaret, generated 2,000 objections after protesters claimed the tower would dwarf other landmarks like the castle. With the issue becoming increasingly political, Ahmed followed council advice and modified the plans, cutting the minaret to sixty-five feet, dropping the Pride of Dudley title and completely separating the community centre from the mosque. Muslim leaders insisted no public money would be spent on the mosque and no council money would be needed for the project as a whole. Funding, it was claimed, would come from Europe, central government grants and money from community organizations and sporting bodies.[3]

A recent study published in the US[4] has come to the conclusion that Muslim groups have been striving to establish enclaves in which they can uphold and enforce greater compliance to Islamic law, and that what has been happening in Europe has now been transplanted to the US. Europe is not the first precedent, however. More than a decade ago the same phenomenon was reported among the Muslim minority in Israel,[5] and other Muslim minorities under non-Islamic rule in Asia.[6] According to the author, David Kennedy Houck, while the US Constitution enshrines the right to religious freedom and the prohibition against a state religion, when it comes to the rights of religious enclaves to impose communal rules, the dividing line is more nebulous. For example, could US enclaves, homeowner associations and other groups enforce Islamic law? Such questions are no longer theoretical. Muslim organizations first established enclaves in Israel and some countries of South East Asia, and then transplanted that model to Bosnia and Kosovo. That trend is now crossing the Atlantic. Some Islamic community leaders in the US are challenging the principles of assimilation and equality once central to the civil rights movement, seeking instead to live according to a separate but equal philosophy. The Gwynnoaks Muslim Residential Development group, for example, has established an informal enclave in Baltimore because, according to John Yahya Cason, director of the Islamic Education and Community Development Initiative, 'there was no community in the US that showed the totality of the essential components of Muslim social, economic, and political structure'. Houck asserts that Baltimore is not alone. In August 2004, a local planning commission in Little Rock, Arkansas, granted The Islamic Centre for Human Excellence authorization to build an internal Islamic enclave to include a mosque, a school, and twenty-two homes. While the imam says his goal is to create 'a clean community, free of alcohol, drugs, and free of gangs', the implications for US jurisprudence of such enclaves are greater: for example, while the Little Rock enclave might prevent the sale of alcohol, can it punish possession and in what manner? Can it force all women, be they residents or visitors, to don the hijab? The group has foreign financial support: it falls under the umbrella of a much larger Islamic group, 'Islam 4 the World', an organization sponsored by Sharjah, one of the constituent emirates of the United Arab Emirates (UAE). Past investments by the UAE's rulers and institutions have promoted radical interpretations of Islam.

Houck believes the permissible parameters of an Islamist enclave are ill-defined. The greater American Muslim community's unapologetic and public manifestation of belief in a separate but equal ideology does not bode well. In September 2004, the New Jersey branch of the Islamic Circle of North America rented a park in New Jersey for 'The Great Muslim Adventure Day'. The advertisement announcing the event stated: 'The entire park for Muslims only'. Houck cites the next-door example of Canada where Islamists took advantage of liberal flexibility and tolerance to their ends. As US authorities are beginning to do now, Canadian legislators decided to give religious groups the benefit of the doubt, assuming that they would still hold national law to be paramount. But when in October 2003, the Islamic Institute of Civil Justice (IICJ) created Muslim arbitration boards and stated its intent to arbitrate on the basis of Islamic law in Ontario, Canadian Muslim women's groups opposed the application of shari'a laws that would supersede their far more liberal and egalitarian democratic rights. In November 2005 the arbitration act was amended to abrogate all religious arbitration. Houck warned that Muslim enclaves within larger US communities may signal that US jurisprudence will soon be faced with a similar situation. Islamist exceptionalism can abuse the tolerance liberal societies have traditionally extended.

What happens in America, Canada, Israel and other liberal democracies, who for fear of being dubbed 'racists', neglect national security to placate an intrinsically hostile minority which disdains local laws, and regards shari'a as superior to them, also happens in many parts of Europe, where law enforcement officers are unable to enforce the law of the land. Prior to the IICJ demands to impose shari'a, the Arbitration Act worked well. Unfortunately for Canadian Jews, the repeal ended state-enforcement of agreements reached over the use of a rabbinical court system called *Beth Din* (house of law) that had for decades quietly settled marriage, custody, and business disputes. Canadian Catholics likewise were stopped from being able to annul marriages according to Canon Law and avoid undue entanglement in civil courts. Rather than soften the edge between religion and state, the IICJ threatened to eliminate it with the imposition of shari'a. The Canadian experience demonstrates how flexibility can backfire when all parties do not seek to uphold basic precepts of tolerance. Houck concludes that a Muslim enclave is uniquely perilous because there are few if any internal enclaves that adhere to a polity dedicated to the active abrogation of secular law and the imposition of a supreme religious law. The concept of shari'a is so fundamental to Islam that prominent Muslim jurists argue over whether a Muslim can fully discharge shari'a obligations while residing in a non-Muslim territory. Yet, he posits, Muslims have resided peacefully in non-Muslim lands since the seventh century. But he is wrong. If he knew of the bloody uprisings of Muslims in nineteenth-century China, and in twentieth-century Asia, he would have avoided this sweeping generalization. Still, the more vocal Muslim communities in Europe are not likely to abandon the territory they have already gained in favour of some utopian and evasive *pax Europeana*.

The American experience offers salutary lessons for Europe as far as the penal system is concerned. Radical Muslim chaplains, trained in a foreign ideology, certified in foreign-financed schools, and acting in coordination to impose an extremist agenda, have gained a monopoly over Islamic religious activities in American state, federal and city prisons. Soon after 9/11, reports American author Stephen Schwartz:

> I and a group of individuals with whom I have worked first began consultations on the problem of radical Islam in prison. We identified change in the prisons as a leading item in the agenda of our nation in defeating the terrorist enemy. Some of us had received letters from American Muslim prison

inmates complaining that radical chaplains had harassed and otherwise subjected moderate Muslims in prison to humiliation, discrimination, confiscation of moderate Islamic literature, and even physical threats. Muslim chaplains have established an Islamic radical regime over Muslim convicts in the American prisons; imagine each prison Islamic community as a little Saudi kingdom behind prison walls, without the amenities. They have effectively induced American authorities to establish a form of 'state Islam' or 'government-certified Islam' in correctional systems.[7]

The prisons have allowed the seizure of a privileged position for missionaries of Wahhabism, the state religious sect in Saudi Arabia, which teaches hatred of all non-Wahhabi Muslims, especially Shi'a Muslims and the spiritual Muslims known as Sufis. Wahhabis serve as chaplains at all levels of incarceration in America. They are mainly certified and trained as religious officials by two groups: The Islamic Society of North America (ISNA) and the Graduate School of Islamic and Social Sciences (GSISS), which moved to Ashburn, Virginia, after renaming itself Cordoba University[8] in 2005. Both are aligned with Wahhabism, and currently under federal investigation for ties to terrorism. Warith Deen Umar is the former chief Muslim chaplain in the New York State Department of Correctional Services (DOCS). Born Wallace Gene Marks, Umar was once an adherent of the Nation of Islam. New York Governor George Pataki barred Umar from prisons in 2003, after the Wall Street Journal reported that Umar had expressed support for the 9/11 terrorists – even stating that Muslims 'who say they are against terrorism secretly admire and applaud' Bin Laden's mass murderers. (According to Umar, the Qur'an does not forbid terrorism even against the innocent. 'This is the sort of teaching they don't want in prison', he said. 'But this is what I'm doing.') Yet the state of New York failed to take further action about the clique of radical clerics he had installed during the more than twenty-five years he worked in the prison system.[9]

In March 2006, Umar Abdul-Jalil, chief Islamic chaplain in the New York City Department of Corrections, was reported to have said in a speech that the 'greatest terrorists in the world occupy the White House', that Jews control the media, and that Muslims are being tortured in Manhattan prisons. New York Mayor Michael Bloomberg, on free speech grounds, refused to dismiss him. Marwan Othman el-Hindi, a Jordanian-born American citizen who had served as imam at the Toledo Correctional Institution, was charged with recruiting terrorists to fight in Iraq. Saudi Wahhabi organizations recognized that the growth of normative Islam (as opposed to groups like the Nation of Islam) offered an extraordinary opportunity for the infiltration of radical ideology. In the US, this normative base lacked a communal or institutional structure. So imams were imported to America, many from, or after training in, Saudi Arabia. Wahhabi radicals and their apologists claim that there is only one Islam, and it is represented by Wahhabism; and that Saudi Arabia is an ally of the US and a target of al-Qa'ida. American judicial and correctional authorities lacked the legal and educational expertise to distinguish between radical and other forms of Islam. The solution is to identify those chaplains who follow and preach Wahhabism and remove them, and establish a programme for training and certification, to include a standard curriculum for chaplaincies.[10] The penetration of European prisons by the same radicals poses similar problems.

Of special interest are the remarks made by Efraim Karsh to *Front Page Magazine*:[11] the 9/11 attacks, and their underlying ideology, he said, tap into a deep imperialist undercurrent that has characterized the political culture of Islam from the beginning. Given the pervasiveness of misconception, the nature of the foremost threat confronting the West at the beginning of the new millennium is largely misunderstood. In *Islamic Imperialism: A History* he challenges the traditional narrative by showing that Islamic history has been anything but reactive. From the prophet Muhammad to the Ottomans, the story of Islam has been the story of the rise and fall of an often astonishing imperial aggressiveness and, no less important, of never quiescent imperial dreams. Even as these dreams have repeatedly frustrated any possibility for the peaceful social and political development of the Arab-Muslim world, they have given rise to no less repeated fantasies of revenge and restoration and to murderous efforts to transform fantasy into fact. These fantasies gained rapid momentum during the last phases of the Ottoman Empire, culminating in its disastrous decision to enter the First World War on the losing side, as well as in the creation of an imperialist dream that would survive the Ottoman era to haunt Islamic and Middle Eastern politics to the present day. If America is reviled in the Muslim world today, it is not because of its specific policies but because, as the pre-eminent world power, it blocks the final realization of this same age-old dream of a universal Islamic empire (or umma). In the historical imagination of many Muslims and Arabs, Bin Laden represents nothing short of the new incarnation of Saladin, defeater of the Crusaders and conqueror of Jerusalem. In this sense, the House of Islam's war for world mastery is a traditional, indeed venerable, quest that is far from over.

The struggle for world domination should not be misconstrued as a civilizational clash, according to Karsh, which has been a far rarer phenomenon than is generally recognized. Conflicts among members of the same civilization have been far more common, and far more intense, than those between members of rival civilizations. More often than not, empires across the civilizational divide have pragmatically cooperated with their counterparts. Of course, throughout history all imperial powers and aspirants have professed some kind of universal ideology as both a justification of expansion and a means of ensuring the subservience of the conquered peoples: in the case of the Greeks and the Romans it was that of 'civilization' versus 'barbarity', in the case of the Mongols it was the conviction in their predestination to inherit the earth, in the case of the British it was the 'white man's burden'. He continued:

> So, I would rather refer to the millenarian confrontation between the worlds of Islam and Christianity as a 'clash of imperialisms' rather than a 'clash of civilizations'. But then, while the West had lost its imperialist ambitions by the midtwentieth century (having lost its religious messianism centuries earlier), the fuel of Islamic imperialism remains as volatile as ever, and this ambition for world domination is the primary threat confronting the West today ... As a universal religion, Islam envisages a global political order in which all humankind will live under Muslim rule as either believers or subject communities and obliges all free, male, adult Muslims to carry out an uncompromising 'struggle in the path

of Allah', or jihad. This duty has nothing to do with 'Islamism'. It was devised by Muhammad shortly after his migration to Medina in 622 CE as a means of enticing his local followers to raid Meccan caravans, and was developed and amplified with the expansion of the prophet's political ambitions until it became a rallying call for world domination. As he famously told his followers in his farewell address: 'I was ordered to fight all men until they say "There is no god but Allah".' This goal need not necessarily be pursued by the sword; it can be achieved through demographic growth and steady conversion of the local populations by 'an army of preachers and teachers who will present Islam in all languages and in all dialects'. But should peaceful means prove insufficient, physical force can readily be brought to bear. This is a vision by no means confined to 'Islamists'. This we saw in the overwhelming support for the 9/11 attacks throughout the Arab and Islamic worlds, in the admiring evocations of Bin Laden's murderous acts during the crisis over the Danish cartoons, and in such recent findings as the poll indicating significant reservoirs of sympathy among Muslims in Britain for the 'feelings and motives' of the suicide bombers who attacked London.

There is a pervasive guilt complex among left-wing intellectuals and politicians, which dates back to the early twentieth century and stems from the belief that the West 'has been the arch aggressor of modern times', to use the words of Arnold Toynbee, one of the more influential early exponents of this dogma. This has resulted in a highly politicized scholarship (especially under the pretentious title of 'post-colonial studies') which berates 'western imperialism' as the source of all evil and absolves the local actors of any blame or responsibility for their own problems. But this self-righteous approach is academically unsound and morally reprehensible. It is academically unsound because the facts tell an altogether different story of Islamic and Middle Eastern history, one that has consistently been suppressed because of its incongruity with the politically correct dogmas. And it is morally reprehensible because denying the responsibility of individuals and societies for their actions is patronizing. It completely ignores regional players, and instead views them, in the words of Lawrence of Arabia, as 'a limited, narrow-minded people, whose inert intellect lay fallow in incurious resignation'.

Karsh believes that whether or not Europe falls under Muslim domination will really depend on whether Europeans will awaken to reality and recognize the real nature of the threat confronting them. Thus far, this hasn't happened, though some developments, such as the 2005 French riots or the violence attending the Danish cartoons, have acted as (admittedly modest) warning signs. Mu'ammar Qaddafi, the Libyan leader, has predicted the imminent Islamization of Europe. 'We have fifty million Muslims in Europe', he stated in a public speech aired on al-Jazeera television. 'There are signs that Allah will grant Islam victory in Europe – without swords, without guns, without conquests. The fifty million Muslims of Europe will turn it into a Muslim continent within a few decades.' He continued: 'Allah mobilizes the Muslim nation of Turkey, and adds it to the European Union', adding, 'that's another fifty million Muslims. There will be 100 million Muslims in Europe.' While this prediction will probably be dismissed as delusional gloating of an eccentric leader, to this day many Muslims and Arabs unabashedly pine for the reconquest of Spain and consider their 1492 expulsion from the country a grave historical injustice waiting to be undone. Indeed, as immigration and higher rates of childbirth have greatly increased the number of Muslims within Europe itself over the past several decades, countries that were never ruled by the Caliphate have become targets of Muslim imperial ambition. Since the late 1980s, Islamists have looked upon the growing population of French Muslims as proof that France, too, has become a part of the House of Islam. In Britain, even the more moderate elements of the Muslim community are candid in setting out their aims. As the late Zaki Badawi, a doyen of interfaith dialogue in the UK, put it, 'Islam is a universal religion. It aims to bring its message to all corners of the earth. It hopes that one day the whole of humanity will be one Muslim community.' To deny the pervasiveness and tenacity of this imperialist ambition is the height of folly, and to imagine that it can be appeased or deflected is to play into its hands.[12]

The figures offered by Qaddafi are not as fanciful as they may sound. A similar number was suggested by the Spanish Justice

Ministry, which oversees religious issues. Spain financed publication of a school textbook, *Discovering Islam*, which it says is unlike any other in the EU – a primer for Muslim first-graders to learn about Islam in Spanish, as a way to integrate better into society. Jose Manuel Lopez, managing director of the Pluralism and Harmony Foundation (part of the Justice Ministry), said: 'Europe has forty million Muslims and governments don't know what to do to assimilate them. This book is a hint.'[13] What can be said with certainty is that the usual figures offered are woefully out of date. The debate within the West between the politically correct and incorrect, with the former sheltering abusive Muslims who challenge the values of the West and the latter courageously standing up to them, has generated an outstandingly insightful and introspective look at the history and soul of Europe. Writing in April 2004, Matthias Döpfner reduced the world view of the average German to seven formulaic sentences, starting with 'Bush is stupid and evil.' Döpfner emphasized that only a twin approach would defeat the jihadists: 'Tough resistance from the outside through the western democracies and a clear distancing of the moderates in the Moslem world, especially among the clerics, from such extremists'. He asked why the non-Islamic world, apart from America and Britain, had little willpower to complete its part of the job. Since 9/11, the day that Islamic terrorists declared a world war, only three nations above all had been grilled morally – America, England and Israel again and again – for protecting themselves and defending the West. Pointing out that 'he who acts, makes mistakes', he said their policy and politics of clear and tough resistance against the enemies of the free world are right. Bush and Blair are 'following their convictions against the general spirit of the times, against resistance, in part within their own parties, and they are doing that which an international alliance of cowardice is not prepared to do.' He continued: 'It is about weighing the balance as to when tolerance for intolerance has to stop. And when doing nothing is worse than defending the western system with military means.' The illusion that the aggressor could be soothed by good behaviour reminded Döpfner of 1936. 'Maybe George Bush is not stupid and evil, maybe one day, looking back on the developments that have just begun, we might even be thankful to him because he was one of the few who acted in accordance with the maxim: "these things must be nipped in the bud" – a phrase often used in Germany to refer to stopping the re-emergence of Nazism."[14]

In November 2004, Döpfner was inspired to respond to a column by Henryk Broder: 'Europe – your family name is appeasement.' For Döpfner, it was an unforgettable phrase because it is so terribly true. Appeasement cost millions of Jews and non-Jews their lives as England and France negotiated and hesitated too long before they noticed that Hitler had to be fought, not bound to agreements. Appeasement stabilized communism in the Soviet Union and East Germany in that part of Europe where inhuman, suppressive governments were glorified as the ideologically correct alternative to all other possibilities. Appeasement crippled Europe when genocide ran rampant in Kosovo and Europeans debated until the Americans did their work for them. Appeasement allowed Europe to ignore 300,000 victims of Saddam's torture and murder machinery and, motivated by the self-righteousness of the peace movement, to issue bad grades to George Bush. He asked what else has to happen before the European public and its political leadership understand that an especially perfidious crusade consisting of systematic attacks by fanatic Muslims is underway, focused on civilians and directed against free, open western societies. The conflict will last longer than the great military conflicts of the previous century, conducted by an enemy that cannot be tamed by tolerance and accommodation but only spurred on by such gestures, which will be mistaken for signs of weakness. Two American Presidents had the courage needed for anti-appeasement. Reagan ended the Cold War and Bush, together with Blair, recognized the danger in the Islamic fight against democracy. For his policies, Bush risks the fall of the dollar, huge amounts of additional national debt and a massive and persistent burden on the American economy. While the alleged capitalistic robber barons in American know their priorities, Europeans prefer to defend their social welfare systems or listen to TV pastors preach about 'reaching out to murderers'.[15]

Remarking that the prevailing feeling among Muslims is that they are being abused by the West, Broder wondered what should be done about it. We might as well surrender, since we're already on our way, he concluded. In 2006, he followed with a book, *Hurra, Wir Kapitulieren* (Hurray! We're Capitulating), which spent a number of weeks atop the *Der Spiegel* bestseller list. Broder evoked the normality of life only a decade ago, when intellectuals killed time by debating whether Francis Fukuyama was right in claiming that we have reached the 'end of history' and whether capitalism had triumphed over socialism. In those days few were aware of the fine distinction between Islam and Islamism. Today, the sensibilities of around 1.3 billion Muslims, many of whom are thin-skinned and unpredictable, are all-pervasive. At issue is freedom of opinion, one of the central tenets of the Enlightenment and democracy – and whether respect, consideration and tolerance are the right approach to dealing with cultures that, for their part, behave without respect, consideration or tolerance when it comes to anything they view as decadent, provocative and unworthy. The controversy surrounding the harmless Danish cartoons amounted to a show of strength – a rehearsal for the kinds of disputes Europe can expect to face in the future if it does not rethink its current policy of appeasement. As was the case in the 1930s, when Czechoslovakia was sacrificed in the interest of peace under the Munich Agreement – a move that ultimately did nothing to prevent the Second World War – Europeans today also believe that an adversary, seemingly invincible due to a preference for death over life, can be mollified by good behaviour, concessions and submission. All the Europeans can hope to gain in this asymmetric conflict is a temporary reprieve of indeterminate length. Critics who only yesterday agreed with Marx that religion is the opium of the masses suddenly insisted that religious sensibilities must be taken into account, giving the fundamentalists a tremendous boost. It completely justifies their view of the West as weak. Psychoanalyst Horst-Eberhard Richter proposed that the West 'should desist from engaging in all provocations that produce feelings of debasement and humiliation. We should show greater respect for the cultural identity of Muslim countries ... For Muslims, it is important to be recognized and respected as equals.' But short of adopting their cultural and religious mores, it would be difficult to show further respect for the cultural identity of Islamic countries.

He contends that those who react to kidnappings and beheadings, to massacres of people of other faiths, and to eruptions of collective hysteria with a call for 'cultural dialogue' don't deserve any better. This determination to disregard the facts or conveniently distort them by referring to Islam as a 'religion of peace' partly emanates from a natural tendency to avoid conflict and from fear. There is no more effective tool than fear to regulate behaviour. Mao famously said: 'Strike one to educate one hundred' – an axiom that helped him solidify his power. The wilder and more brutal the West's adversaries appear to be, the more likely they are to attract attention and gain 'respect'. In March 2004, Romanian-American author Norman Manea told the German daily *Die Welt* that 'nowadays acts of terrorism are not committed for their own sake, but in the name of an ideology one could call Nazi-Islamism'. The only difference is 'that this ideology invokes a religion, whereas the Nazis were mythical without being religious'. Manea believes that what he calls 'World War Three' has already begun, although Europeans are postponing recognition of the conflict that has arrived. The willingness to submit to self-deception is as widespread today as it was in the years leading up to the Second World War. The Berlin office of the International Physicians for the Prevention of Nuclear War published a paper which predicted two million deaths and a million injured if America conducts a nuclear strike against Iran. But it neither poses nor answers the question of the consequences of an Iranian nuclear attack. No one wants to address this question because no one knows how to prevent an Iranian nuclear attack or even influence the Iranians' policies. In contrast, there is a very small but real possibility that public pressure can be used to influence the American Government to move in one direction or another. For similar reasons, one after another concession is demanded of Israel, including funding the same Palestinian Authority which dispatches suicide bombers into her cities.

For those facing a hopeless situation and powerless to change it, self-deception offers at least some succour. Another option is 'change through ingratiation'. Oskar Lafontaine, a one-time chairman of the Social Democratic Party, sees 'commonalities between leftist policies and the Islamic religion'. In an interview with *Neues Deutschland*, he said: 'Islam depends on community, which places it in opposition to extreme individualism, which threatens to fail in the West. The second similarity is that the devout Muslim is required to share his wealth with others. The leftist also wants to see the strong help the weak. Finally, the prohibition of interest still plays a role in Islam, much as it once did in Christianity.' Lafontaine sees this as 'a basis for a dialogue to be conducted between the left and the Islamic world'. He called upon the West to exercise self-criticism, saying, 'we must constantly ask ourselves through which eyes the Muslims see us', and expressed sympathy for the 'indignation' of Muslims. According to Lafontaine, 'people in Muslim countries have experienced many indignities, one of the most recent being the Iraq war. What we are seeing here is resource imperialism.' Lafontaine has forgotten that 9/11 preceded the Iraq invasion. As for 'resource imperialism', the Arabs' need to sell it (which they do at exorbitant rates) does not enter into his thinking. Broder plaintively asked:

> If Muslim protests against a few harmless cartoons can cause the free world to capitulate in the face of violence, how will this free world react to something that is truly relevant? It is already difficult enough to see that Israel is not merely battling a few militants, but is facing a serious threat to its very existence from Iran. All too often it is ignored that Iranian President Mahmoud Ahmadinejad has already taken the first step by calling for 'a world without Zionism', a call that pro-Israel Europeans only managed to condemn with a mild, 'unacceptable'. How would they react if Iran were in a position to back up its threats with nuclear weapons?'

In 1972, Danish lawyer and part-time politician Mogens Glistrup had an idea that brought him instant fame. To save taxes, he proposed that the Danish army be disbanded and an answering machine be set up in the Defence Ministry that would play the following message: 'We capitulate!' Not only would it save money, Glistrup argued, but it would also save lives in an emergency. On the strength of this 'programme', Glistrup's Progress Party managed to become the second-most powerful political party in the Danish parliament in the 1973 elections. Glistrup had the right idea, but he was a number of years premature. Now would be the right time to set up his answering machine.[16]

The battle against terrorism is difficult to prosecute in Britain because the government is hampered by a lack of support from the judicial system. The judicial focus on human rights would be laudable under normal circumstances, but in times of war (especially one fought purely on the terrorists' terms, with the choice of timing and arena in their hands), it is the terrorists who are given the benefit of the doubt. That happens in America, Canada, Europe and Israel, and hampers the legislation and other arrangements that governments wish to put in place. Regulations were introduced by the Home Office to prevent illegal immigrants from using a bogus marriage as a way of staying in Britain, but were declared unlawful by the Appeal Court. Judges said regulations introduced in 2005 to block thousands of alleged 'marriages of convenience' breached human rights laws. Hundreds of couples who say they have been prevented from marrying may now try to claim compensation. Under the regime, non-EU citizens effectively needed government permission to marry. They had to attend designated register offices and pay £135 for a certificate of approval. The Appeal Court – upholding an earlier High Court ruling – said this was a 'disproportionate interference' in the human right to marry. One Whitehall estimate suggested 10,000 marriages a year were bogus. Liam Byrne, the Immigration Minister, said he was considering an appeal. 'Since we introduced these checks the number of suspicious marriage reports has collapsed from 3,740 to less than 300 by the end of May 2005', he said.[17]

Mohmoud Baiai, an illegal immigrant from Algeria, and Izabela Trzcinska, from Poland, brought a case before the English courts which tested Article 12 of the European Convention on Human Rights, which protects the right to marry and found a family. They were banned from marrying in England because Baiai was in the country illegally. But if Baiai, a Muslim, and Trzcinska, a Roman Catholic, had been members of the Church of England the government could not have stopped them marrying. Under the rules, by which immigrants wishing to marry must apply for written permission from the Home Office, the Church of England is exempt. It was excluded because vicars usually meet couples several times before the wedding. Mr Justice Silber, sitting in the High Court, said that the rules discriminated against those subject to immigration rules on the grounds of religion and nationality. Meanwhile, new marriage guidelines are being drawn up by the Church of England amid fears that its clergy may be unwittingly conducting bogus weddings. Officials noticed a sharp rise in the number of migrants seeking church weddings since the government imposed a crackdown on marriages of convenience at register offices. Because Church of England marriages are exempt, the number of applications for 'common licences' – a legal preliminary for church weddings – increased markedly, particularly in London.[18]

Since the Asylum and Immigration Act came into force in February 2005 the number of marriage applications at some offices dropped by 60 per cent in some areas of London, with Birmingham and Leicester reporting reductions of about 25 per cent. Previously, registrars could only report suspicions about marriages of convenience to the Home Office but the new rules have exposed the true number of foreigners marrying to gain citizenship. Karen Knapton, the general secretary of the Society of Registration Officers, said:

> If people really want to get married they will persevere but the new regulations have highlighted the scale of bogus marriages. Register offices, especially in London, have been very quiet. We have been asking what nationality applicants are for two years but we have been aware that crime rings have been making a lot of money out of sham marriages. It has been no fun when we know people have been using marriage to get around immigration laws. It has made a mockery of our job ... We had a massive increase in January 2005 – perhaps four or five times the usual number of people rushing to get married before the new regulations came in ... It is a relief that the decision has now been taken out of our hands.[19]

While the right to marry and start a family is unarguably a fundamental right, the matter is not one of safeguarding civil rights for innocent individuals, but of entire groups who try to circumvent the system and break the immigration limitations, sometimes with the clear purpose of plotting terrorism or pursuing their demographic growth in Europe, or seeking asylum as economic migrants. In such a situation, a democracy has the right to take measures to protect itself. Just as in the Second World War when the Home Secretary had the authority to arrest any citizen who was suspected of collaborating with the enemy, or in America when American nationals of Japanese origin were interned due to the perceived threat posed to national security, the situation today presents security threats. Limitations on sham marriages in Europe are no worse than the trend since 9/11, and more so after Madrid and London, to eavesdrop electronically on civilian suspects and foreigners, by authorities across the continent who are obtaining more powers and meeting less and less public opposition than President Bush over his post-9/11 wiretapping programme. Indeed, as part of a package of EU anti-terrorism measures, the European Parliament approved legislation requiring telecommunications companies to retain phone data and internet logs for a minimum of six months in case they are needed for criminal investigations. In Italy, which is the most wiretapped western democracy, the number of authorized wiretaps more than tripled from 32,000 in 2001 to 106,000 in 2005. Italy's long tradition of electronic snooping goes back to its fight against the Mafia. It passed a terrorism law after 7/7 that opened the way for intelligence agencies to eavesdrop if an attack is feared to be imminent. Only approval from a prosecutor and not a judge is required, but the material gleaned cannot be used as evidence in court. Similar laws have been approved in France and the Netherlands or proposed elsewhere in Europe, prompting some complaints that the terrorist threat is giving authorities a pretext to abuse powers.[20]

Shortly after the Holocaust in Europe, an entire literature of Holocaust denial, elaborated by pseudo-historians like David Irving, Robert Faurisson and Roger Garaudy, undertook to amend the pages of history, and succeeded to a large degree with the help of their Arab and Muslim counterparts, some of whom, like Mahmoud Abbas (current president of the Palestinian Authority), made academic and political careers of Holocaust denial. A similar process of denial begins to loom on the horizon of Muslim circles, who began to rewrite their narrative of terrorism by denying their decisive part in it and imputing it to western 'provocations', to the extent that the horrors of New York, Madrid, London, Bali and elsewhere might be minimized if the West loses its vigilance not only in fighting terrorism but also in educating its populace to recognize its roots and motivations. At the same time that new details are revealed about Muslim terrorist plots – something which should galvanize a spirit of survival – the liberal court systems of Europe refuse to awaken to the dangers and they continue to tie the hands of their own governments which try to raise the consciousness of their constituencies and mobilize their support for the harsher measures that may be required against suspects. 'There is clearly a legitimate role for surveillance. It's a question of what the safeguards are', said Ben Ward, associate director of the European and Asian division of Human Rights Watch. The use of hidden microphones in criminal investigations is routine in Italy, but a Swedish Government proposal to permit such taps has drawn sharp opposition from civil liberties advocates. Still, the complaints are relatively muted compared with the criticisms that have arisen in the US Congress and among civil liberties groups over the Bush administration's surveillance operations. In a 2003 report, the Max Planck Institute for Foreign and International Criminal Law in Germany put Italy at the top of the European wiretapping list, followed by the Netherlands, using figures published by governments or information from parliamentary debates. The Dutch secret service, known by its acronym AIVD, has gained vast powers since September 11. In September 2004, the government passed sweeping measures that lowered the threshold for wiretapping and surveillance. A turning point in Dutch public attitudes came with the 2004 murder of film-maker Theo van Gogh by a Muslim extremist who claimed a film he made insulted Islam. Siebrand Buma, the ruling Christian Democratic Party's spokesman on anti-terrorism and civil rights issues, said that while the Dutch are liberal on drugs and euthanasia policies, 'people see the need to combat serious crime as worth the sacrifice of personal privacy'. A new anti-crime law introduced in 2004 also made wiretapping easier in France. Prosecutors can now apply for wiretaps when investigations are still in a preliminary phase, rather than wait for an investigating magistrate to take over the case.[21]

In France, the harshest critic of America for its 'discrimination' against African-Americans during the August 2005 Hurricane Katrina disaster in New Orleans, the infamous night of 27 October 2005 (when two Muslim youths fled a police identity check and scaled an electric relay station where they were electrocuted) triggered a rampage by Muslims in Paris and its surroundings. Cries of *'Allah Akbar'*, the war cry of Islamists, reverberated everywhere and talk circulated on turning Paris into Baghdad-sur-Seine. An Islamic site informed its readers that 'the cops are petrified of us. Everything must burn', and a young leader of the Arab European League demanded that France allow Arab sections to govern themselves. He said that Arabs rejected integration when it leads to assimilation and emphasized: 'We are at home here, and whatever we consider our culture to be, also belongs to our chosen country. I am in my country, not the country of the westerners.'[22] While Sarkozy called the rioters 'scum', President Chirac imposed a state of emergency, condemned 'racism' in public to calm tempers and declared himself to be aware of the prevailing discrimination and lack of equal opportunity among the youth. The government's inability to create jobs for the young, angry and welfare-intoxicated Muslim youth and to attract internal and external investors, soon triggered the much larger, all encompassing and more violent riots of March 2006, which forced the government to capitulate. The French police seized explosives and firearms from Muslim groups who were said to have links with al-Qa'ida during the riots, something that does not bode well for the future. Demographic projections in France predict that if the current trend continues undeterred, France will become a Muslim state in the twenty-first century.[23] The immigrants, who regard Europe as their territory, and believe it must acquiesce to their culture, language and religion, and not the other way round, will not lay down their arms and the tremendous pressure of their demography before they see their goal accomplished. The rest of Europe, which is still deluding itself that it would do better than France, and is trying to placate Muslim minorities instead of standing up to them, may wake up too late to reverse these trends.

   The riots did not change the perceptions of the French about the suburbs (*les cités*) as different places where things happen independently of what is taking place in the rest of country. The Muslim youth of the suburbs continue to see their neighbourhoods as their own territory and their sole contact with French society as proceeding through its police force. A proposal has arisen out of the riots that the CV of applicants to new jobs should be evaluated by prospective employers without the names or photographs of the applicants attached so as to avoid discrimination against African and Arab Muslims, but it is still estimated that in any category of education Muslims still suffer from double the unemployment rate than the French. The personal contacts between elites (*pistons*) that one needs in order to advance in this closed and over-centralized system is a barrier to the upward mobility of new recruits. The French middle class, eager to preserve its short work week, paid vacations, job protection and elective early retirement, is unwilling to change, and continues to fear that their 'glorious' country might be 'degraded' to the 'negative model' of the US, where the persistent propaganda has led them to believe that, on top of being cruel and imperialistic capitalists, the Americans have no job and health insurance and people are hungry. The Muslim *jeunes* are cultivating hatred towards the country which made them so dependent on it, though young hard-working women among them have learned to struggle out of their state of inferiority and find their place in the economy if not in society. So, while the Muslim suburbs keep to themselves and hardly any Frenchman dare to go there, just like the *favelas* of South America, it is the French bourgeoisie, like their South American counterparts in the opulent city centres, who dread the day when the impoverished suburbs will launch an assault against the prosperous centres, with no one able to stop the onslaught.[24]

Ron Geaves, a British professor, prefers to view the attacks on London as a legitimate 'demonstration' and long-term protest rather than terrorism. As part of his research, Geaves has looked at the history of demonstrations by British Muslims. His work charts the changing nature of Muslim communities from the demonstrations against Rushdie to the anti-war protests after the invasion of Iraq. 'I have included, rather controversially, the events in London as primarily an extreme form of demonstration and assess what these events actually mean in terms of their significance in the Muslim community', Geaves said, adding: 'Terrorism is a political word which always seems to be used to demonize people.' In his lecture at the University of Chester, which was entitled 'Twenty years of fieldwork: reflections on "reflexivity" in the study of British Muslims', he admitted 'the title refers to the personal transformation that has taken place over the last two decades in which I have moved from a position of academic neutrality to one of active engagement with the Muslim community.'[25] Geaves claims to be pioneering what he calls Britain's first Muslim youth work degree programme. Andrew Dismore, the Labour MP for Hendon, described Geaves's claims as 'absolutely barking'. He said: 'What happened on 7 July 2005 fits with every international definition of terrorism. If any of the men behind the attacks had survived the incident they would have quite rightly been tried under the anti-terror laws. I don't think it's helpful that we have a mealy-mouthed academic trying to justify deaths of innocent people. It is ludicrous.'[26]

Fortunately, there are also sober minds like Brigitte Gabriel who refuse to capitulate to Muslims and their supporters on western campuses. The latter have a unique importance as the battleground for the heart and soul of the next generation of leaders. She asserts that 'these are the battlegrounds where we must fight to win back the opinion and allegiance of American college students. This is made harder when Islamists in both the college and local communities try to intimidate us and deny our free speech on campuses.' What applies to the US certainly applies to many European universities too. Gabriel, a Christian refugee from Lebanon who has shrapnel in her body (dating from the time when she and her family were targeted by Muslims during the Lebanese Civil War), has grown accustomed to negative attitudes on the major East and West Coast 'elite' university campuses that harbour radical professors and anarchist students and radical Muslims. Yet she was stunned to find that in the heartland of America, specifically at the University of Memphis, the Muslim community launched a full-scale campaign to stop the lectures which she was invited to present for the Judaic Studies Programme. They demanded the cancellation of her speech. E-mails flooded the administrators from Muslim students on campus and Muslims in the community and mosques. Their comments were largely detached from reality:

> People like Brigitte are plenty in the world, they are the true enemies of Islam. And despite their rubbish talks, the truth about Islam is spreading like a wildfire across Americas and across the globe (All Praise to Allah). Dr Patterson, hosting

of this lady is in orders of magnitude worse than hosting of the Imperial Wizard of the Ku Klux Klan. Do you honestly think the scheduled lecture will serve any useful purpose other than inflaming the Muslims, insulting them and spilling poison in the community?

Gabriel wrote that 'If they would put the same energy into condemning the radical element within Islam and join us in saying that slaughtering people in the name of Allah is murder not jihad, maybe we wouldn't question their loyalty as American citizens.' Dr Patterson, who invited Gabriel, refused to bow to their intimidation, and introduced her by telling the audience what an eye-opener this lecture had become because of the reaction. He stated that he never realized that in Memphis a speaker's safety could be threatened, necessitating a police presence.[27] This sad state of affairs, when speakers need police officers to protect their freedom of speech, has been duplicated in Europe too. America is the country where free speech is protected under the constitution, and so it is in Europe. But when police ignore it for the sake of 'public safety', it provides the break that Muslim activists are seeking to start the process of disintegration and chaos that would facilitate their takeover of a campus. At the end of Gabriel's lecture the Muslims swarmed in front of her, questioning and intimidating her. Police officers quickly moved in and took her to the police cars as the enraged Muslims started shouting.[28] Such behaviour has turned university campuses in the West into testing grounds where this battle will be waged in years to come. As in the cartoon affair, the issue is not an insult to the prophet or disregard of Muslim values, but whether the very concept of freedom will win in the face of coercion that Islamists are trying to enforce.

A British university was accused of 'selling out' academic freedom of speech by scrapping a talk on links between the Nazis and Islamic anti-Semitism after allegedly receiving e-mails from Muslims protesting about the event. Matthias Küntzel, a German political scientist who specializes in the threat of Islamic fundamentalism, was told by the University of Leeds that a talk and a workshop on 'Hitler's Legacy: Islamic Anti-Semitism in the Middle East', had been cancelled because of security fears. Two academics in the Leeds German department, which had organized the event, claimed the university had bowed 'to Muslim protests'. Küntzel said he had given similar addresses around the world without any problems. He added: 'I was told it was for security reasons – that they cannot shelter my person. But I don't feel in any way threatened ... My impression was that they wanted to avoid the issue in order to keep the situation calm. My feeling is that this is a kind of censorship.' Küntzel said the contents of e-mails described to him did not overtly threaten violence but 'they were very, very strongly worded'. The university denied censorship, saying the organizers had not given it enough notice to arrange for stewards to be on duty at what was bound to be a potentially controversial event. One of the protest e-mails, from a student who describes himself as 'of both Middle Eastern and Islamic background', complained that the title of the event was 'profoundly offensive', and 'To insinuate that there is a direct link between Islam and anti-Semitism is not only a sweeping generalization but also an erroneous statement that holds no essence of truth.'[29] Küntzel later accused Britain of being the worst country for stifling debate on Muslim extremism. The cancellation of his lecture came two weeks after students at Oxford University launched a petition demanding the sacking of David Coleman, a professor of demography, over his links to Migrationwatch, the immigration think tank. Küntzel said: 'It is a worrying trend. If I say something which is not positive about a particular brand of Islam, the imposition is that I am inciting hatred of every Muslim. I am very concerned about this – it is an attack on academic freedom.' He added: 'There is nothing wrong with holding beliefs but you must be able to challenge and question them. Academic integrity is all about the exchange of positions and the search for truth – I think this is in danger in the UK.'[30] His lecture finally went ahead in October 2007.

The alarming situation with Islamists in America generated hearings in the American Senate, some of which are worth citing here inasmuch as they might serve as reference and precedent to future European parliamentary inquiries. One of the statements before the committee referred to the relations between the Department of State and the Muslim Brotherhood, which influences Muslim radical movements worldwide. While scores of moderate Muslims and Islamic scholars, the 9/11 Commission, and European security officials point to the Muslim Brothers as the forefathers of modern Islamic terrorism, the State Department had started to flirt with them. The State Department sent its head of counter-terrorism to be the keynote speaker at a conference co-sponsored by the International Institute for Islamic Thought (IIIT), a Brotherhood-linked Northern Virginia organization. Rachel Ehrenfeld reported that the US Embassy in Rome was planning to co-sponsor a high-profile two-day symposium about immigration and integration where the highly controversial Swiss scholar Tariq Ramadan had been invited as a keynote speaker.[31] Shortly after she highlighted the details, it was announced that the conference had been postponed. At the hearing on 'Islamist Extremism in Europe', various government officials outlined their initiatives to 'reach out' to European Muslims. The US Ambassador to Belgium, Tom Korologos, explained how he had been promoting various seemingly laudable initiatives together with the State Department, in which American and European Muslim organizations met with US officials, opening a dialogue to 'break stereotypes and foster networking opportunities'. So instead of initiating a dialogue with non-radical Muslims to empower them, the organizations that have been chosen to participate in his initiative represent the Muslim Brotherhood's network on both sides of the Atlantic.[32]

Ambassador Korologos' main European partner is FEMYSO, the youth branch of the Federation of Islamic Organizations in Europe (FIOE), the umbrella organization for various groups that are closely linked to the Brotherhood. FEMYSO's cofounder is WAMY, a Saudi charity that has been widely suspected of links to terrorism (ironically, the US Senate itself had solicited an inquiry into WAMY's terror ties). And FEMYSO's long-time president, Ibrahim el-Zayat, came under investigation in Germany for having funnelled more than $2 million to an al-Qa'ida-linked charity. The American partners in the initiative are no less worthy of suspicion. One of them is the ubiquitous Council on American–Islamic Relations (CAIR), whose unrelenting apology of radical Islam has become known to most Americans (less known is the fact that several of its members have been convicted for terrorist activities). The other is the Islamic Society of North America (ISNA), a group that, in Senator Chuck Schumer's words, has 'disturbing connections to Wahhabism and terrorism'.

Considering its track record, the State Department's decision to cooperate with these self-proclaimed moderates is not surprising. Among the many cases of its endorsement of radicals, the most famous example is its partnership with Abdulrahman Alamoudi, who in the 1990s served as its goodwill ambassador to Muslim countries, despite complaints from moderate American Muslims. In 2004 Alamoudi was sentenced to a twenty-three-year prison sentence for violating anti-terrorism sanctions, including a plot to kill the Saudi ruler, and his ties to Hamas and al-Qa'ida have since been publicly exposed. Alamoudi, who also served as a representative of ISNA in Washington, personified the double face of the Brotherhood in the West. He spoke one way to Washington's elites in English, but spread a different message in Arabic. In 1996, Alamoudi told an Islamic conference in Chicago: 'Once we are here, our mission in this country is to change it. ... There is no way for Muslims to be violent in America, no way. We have other means to do it ... If we are outside this country, we can say, Oh, Allah, destroy America.'[33]

Time and again, while those westerners eager to begin a 'dialogue' with the Muslim Brotherhood attempt to portray the Islamic supremacist group as 'moderate' and 'non-violent', Muslim Brotherhood speakers themselves call for attacks against western targets. MEMRI translated the weekly sermon of the general guide of the Muslim Brotherhood in Egypt, Muhammad Mahdi Akef, calling for attacks against 'the enemy concealed in Jerusalem, Baghdad, and Kabul, the enemy who thinks itself the only human race with the right to live, even at the expense of abandoning the others'[34]

The spirit of helplessness of the court system in all Europe radiates to the public and governments alike, and does not permit legislatures to interfere more decisively and enact the necessary laws to protect their countries from attack. Nobel Prize Winner Thomas Mann put it best, noting that 'Tolerance becomes a crime when applied to evil.' In London, the High Court deemed the government's anti-terror laws to be 'an affront to justice and breach human rights laws'. Justice Sullivan said that the controversial control order system, which keeps terror suspects under a form of house arrest, were 'conspicuously unfair'. The anti-terror laws denied suspects under control orders the right to a fair hearing and were incompatible with human rights laws, he added, emphasizing that though the government had attempted to apply a 'thin veneer of legality' to the measure, suspects' rights were determined by ministers with no effective oversight by judges. But a fair judiciary system that every democratic society cherishes cannot mean protecting subversive elements that undermine the very foundations of that society. Judges bear no direct responsibility for the security of the country. The government was forced to bring in control orders after the law lords ruled that holding foreign terror suspects indefinitely without trial was unlawful. Ministers immediately announced that they would appeal against the ruling, but control orders would remain imposed on eight foreigners and four British citizens. The ruling came in a challenge by the first British citizen to have a control order imposed on him as a terror suspect by Charles Clarke, then Home Secretary. Civil liberties groups welcomed the verdict.[35]

Uri Dromi, from the Jerusalem-based Israel Democracy Institute, said international law dealing with terrorism is out of date and needs to be re-evaluated to strengthen the ability of western countries to fight terrorism. He is working to create an international 'consortium' of think tanks to consider how well the law is suited to handling terrorism. The consortium would hold meetings and conferences, and gradually craft modern laws to coordinate with the military aspect of the war on terrorism. Before 2000, Israel, like most countries, fought terrorism using criminal law standards: investigating, arresting and bringing people to trial. As the second intifada grew deadlier, the Israeli military wanted to pursue terrorists using methods approved by rules of war, but there was no precedent for a war between a state and non-state actor. As a consequence, Israel developed a different legal strategy for fighting this new 'war'. Out of that process came Israel's controversial 'targeted killings' of terrorist leaders, which the military is authorized to conduct after ensuring certain criteria are met. The Israeli Supreme Court recently validated the targeted killings approach. When Israel approached allies to adopt these new war rules, they baulked until 9/11.[36]

The EU has drawn up guidelines advising government spokesmen to refrain from linking Islam and terrorism in their statements. Brussels officials have confirmed the existence of a classified handbook which offers 'non-offensive' phrases to use when announcing anti-terrorist operations or dealing with terrorist attacks. Banned terms are said to include 'jihad', 'Islamic' or 'fundamentalist'. One suggested alternative is for the term 'Islamic terrorism' to be replaced by 'terrorists who abusively invoke Islam'. An EU official said that the guidebook, or 'common lexicon', is aimed at preventing the distortion of the Muslim faith and the alienation of Muslims in Europe. Details on the contents of the lexicon remain secret, but British officials stressed that it is there as a helpful aid 'providing context' for civil servants making speeches or giving press conferences.[37] A lexicon to frame the debate on radicalization has been a project of long standing. The previous year, an EU official said: 'The basic idea behind it is to avoid the use of improper words that would cause frustration among Muslims and increase the risk of radicalization', adding that, 'Jihad means something for you and me; it means something else for a Muslim. Jihad is a perfectly positive concept of trying to fight evil within yourself.'[38]

The training of imams once again raises the question of whether Europe is sleepwalking into its demise, or simply entertains an unfathomable death wish. Muslim students training to be imams at a British college with strong Iranian links have complained that they are being taught fundamentalist doctrines which describe non-Muslims as 'filth'. *The Times* of London obtained extracts from medieval texts taught to students in which unbelievers are likened to pigs and dogs. The texts are taught at the Hawza Ilmiyya in London, a religious school, which has a sister institution, the Islamic College for Advanced Studies (ICAS), which in turn offers a degree validated by Middlesex University. The students study their religious courses alongside the university-backed BA in Islamic Studies. They spend two days a week as religious students and three days on their university course. The Hawza Ilmiyya and the ICAS are in the same building at Willesden High Road, north London, and share many of the same teaching staff. They have a single fundraising arm, the Irshad Trust, one of the managing trustees of which is Abdolhossein Moezi, an Iranian cleric and a personal representative of Ayatollah Ali Khamenei, Iran's supreme religious leader. Moezi is also the director of the Islamic Centre of England (ICEL) in Maida Vale, a large mosque and community centre which is a registered charity. Its memorandum of association, lodged with the Charity Commission, states: 'At all times at least one of the trustees shall be a representative of the Supreme Spiritual Leadership of the Islamic Republic of Iran.' Both the Irshad Trust and ICEL were established in 1996.[39]

In their first annual accounts, lodged with the Charity Commission in 1997, the charities revealed substantial donations. The Irshad Trust received gifts of £1,367,439 and ICEL accepted an 'exceptional item' of £1.2 million. Around the same time, ICEL bought a former cinema in Maida Vale without a mortgage. Since then it has received between £1 million and £1.7 million in donations each year which, it says, come from British and overseas donors. The centre declined to say if any of its money came from Iran. Since 2000, its accountants have recorded in their auditors' report on the charity's accounts that they have limited evidence about the source of donations. The links between the two charities and Iran are strong. The final three years of the eight-year Hawza Ilmiyya course are spent studying in colleges in Qom, the power base of Iran's religious leaders. The text that has upset some students is the core work in their 'Introduction to Islamic Law' class, written by Muhaqqiq al-Hilli, a thirteenth-century scholar.[40] The Hawza Ilmiyya website states that 'the module aims to familiarize the student with the basic rules of Islamic law as structured by al-Hilli'. Besides likening unbelievers to filth, the al-Hilli text includes a chapter on jihad, setting down the conditions under which Muslims are supposed to fight Jews and Christians. The text is one of a number of books that some students say they find 'disturbing' and 'very worrying'.

Middlesex University, which accredits the ICAS course but not the Hawza Ilmiyya, said: 'The BA in Islamic Studies offered by the Islamic College of Advanced Studies is validated by Middlesex University.' It is the university's responsibility to ensure that the academic standards of this particular programme are appropriate, and also to inquire into the contents of what is taught in all courses. However, the doctrinal details of the curriculum are no less harrowing than the overall programme. They teach that: 'The water left over in the container after any type of animal has drunk from it is considered clean and pure apart from the left over of a dog, a pig, and a disbeliever'; 'There are ten types of filth and impurities: urine, faeces, semen, carrion, blood of carrion, dogs, pigs, disbelievers. When a dog, a pig, or a disbeliever touches or comes in contact with the clothes or body (of a Muslim) while he (the disbeliever) is wet, it becomes obligatory – compulsory upon him (the Muslim) to wash and clean that part which came in contact with the disbeliever.'[41] 'Disbeliever' here refers to Christians and Jews, vividly demonstrating that Muslim ill-will towards Jews pre-dated the Israeli conflict with the Palestinians by fourteen centuries. The oft-cited and resolvable territorial conflict has therefore always been a smokescreen for the intractable religious one. A nation composed of a people who are despised and considered 'filth' would never be recognized by Muslims. Similarly, the Christian society of Europe, to which Muslims have immigrated out of choice, and yet teach their children to hate and despise it, must wonder about the ultimate goals of these immigrants. For their attitude repeatedly demonstrates that they are in Europe in order to undermine it before they take it over.

More pertinently, one must question whether it is possible to educate moderate and tolerant imams, on the basis of such *Sturmer*-like manifestos of hatred and contempt. *The Times* rightly contends that imams play a vital role in the spiritual education of young British Muslims. The example they set to thousands of young people attending mosques out of school hours is of utmost importance. What they teach, what attitudes they inculcate and how they prepare young Muslims for life in Britain, will determine whether attempts to reconcile Islam with life in Britain succeed or whether a new generation is alienated, embittered and religiously adrift, perceiving only conflict with the society and values around it. Much attention has been focused on the role of imams since the London bombings. There is evidence that it was at their mosques and in meetings with radicalized preachers that the young Muslims who attacked London's transport system developed their extremism. It is also abundantly clear, from the trial of Abu Hamza that those wanting to spread a message of hatred focus first on gaining control of their local mosque as a platform to extend their malign influence over the community, especially its impressionable young men. In Muslim countries, training traditionally begins early – at the age of 11 or 12, when boys are sent to Qur'anic schools for education in Islamic jurisprudence and other studies essential to Muslim scholarship. Such schools do not offer a general education beyond 16, and cannot compare with seminaries taking in students at 18. The way is thus open for institutions funded from abroad to establish colleges, leaving ample room for abuse. Any college in this sensitive area must be fully open to inspection and constantly monitored, and closed down if necessary. It is not enough simply to register an institution with the Charity Commission, which has neither the expertise nor the responsibility to vet the courses. These must be approved by the Department for Education, and their teaching materials must not contravene either laws on religious incitement or standards of decency accepted by British society. The funding must be transparent, so that if a country, such as Saudi Arabia or Iran, provides the bulk of the money and inspiration, this should be known by the authorities. No college should be able to produce apparent jihadists.[42]

Security officials from Europe's largest countries backed a plan to profile mosques on the continent and identify radical Islamic clerics who raise the threat of home-grown terrorism. The project will focus on the roles of imams, their training, their ability to speak in the local language and their sources of funding, said the EU Justice and Home Affairs Commissioner Franco Frattini. Italian Interior Minister Guiliano Amato added that Europe had extensive experience with the 'misuse of mosques, which instead of being places of worship are used for other ends. This is bringing about a situation that involves all of our countries and involves the possibility of attacks and developing of networks that use one country to prepare an attack in another.' Adel Smith, a well-known Muslim activist in Italy, said mosques in Italy are already extensively monitored and called the EU plan discriminatory.[43] When Muslim intellectuals in the West who confront extremism, like Wafa Sultan, are receiving death threats,[44] and hit-lists of 'apostates' are circulated by Islamists groups such as the Gama'at (Muslim Brotherhood) in Egypt,[45] capitulating attitudes only incite more violent Muslim reactions, not mitigate them. Muslims regard every western attempt at accommodation as a surrender, something that is not met with gratitude and reciprocity, but with contempt and more outrageous demands.

British teachers have called for a ban on government funding of any faith schools, amid fears of a rise in fundamentalism in the state system. Delegates of the Association of Teachers and Lecturers voted to cut off taxpayers' money to the schools by 2020 and promote integration, as scientists also gave warning of the dangers of teaching creationism in biology lessons. There are 7,000 faith schools in England, of which 600 are secondary.[46] While this may appear to be a routine internal debate within the educational system, the timing of the controversy is not coincidental. The initiators of the debate cannot bring themselves to state unambiguously that they fear Islamic separatism, and choose to cloak their language by reference to fundamentalist 'creationism' – as if the latter killed anybody. This debate raged also against the background of the indictment of twenty-nine Muslim activists, all of them immigrants on European soil, who planned and executed the Madrid train horrors of March 2004 just three days before Spain's general elections. The attack killed 191 people and wounded 1,800.[47]

The details were quite frightening, for they showed how Europe had become vulnerable to its own liberal ways and openness. Jose Luis Zapatero of the Socialist Party won that election and fulfilled his campaign pledge to withdraw Spanish troops from Iraq immediately after taking office. But the tone of the Islamists' demands has not been mitigated by that surrender; quite the contrary, they feel that they can press forward and obtain more. The cell that carried out the attacks was made up mostly of Moroccan radicals, several with ties to al-Qa'ida and to the Moroccan Islamic Combatant Group, which seeks to establish an Islamist state in Morocco. Spanish investigators have said that the cell came together in Spain initially under the guidance of a Syrian named Imad Eddin Barakat Yarkas, also known as Abu Dahdah, who was sentenced to twenty-seven years in prison by a Spanish court for conspiring to commit the September 11 attacks and for leading a Qa'ida cell in Spain. After his arrest, the group reconstituted itself under the leadership of Sarhane ben Abdelmajid Fakhet, a Tunisian graduate. The judge cited a document posted on a website run by Global Islamic Media Front, a group widely seen as a front for al-Qa'ida. The document called for attacks on Spain before the general elections in March, saying they would help drive a wedge between the Spanish public, which overwhelmingly opposed the invasion of Iraq, and the government of former Prime Minister José Maria Aznar, who supported the invasion and contributed troops. While the timing of the attack was dictated by Spain's electoral cycle, the planning phase had long preceded the invasion of Iraq or Spain's contribution to it. But the terrorists deftly succeeded in linking the attack to the Iraq invasion in the minds of the electorate. In effect, the Spaniards allowed the terrorists to dictate the outcome of their election, handing them a propaganda coup of enormous proportions. The Madrid attacks were partly a response to a crackdown on Islamic radical groups by the Spanish police that began in the late 1990s. That crackdown, which included the arrest of Yarkas and the break-up of his cell in Madrid, disrupted a major logistical base for Islamic radicals in Europe.[48]

At the same time that Spain was re-living the Madrid horrors via the trial, the news was released of large numbers of illegal immigrants who had sailed to the Canary Islands from Africa. The sub-Saharan migrants were to be flown to the mainland before being released and most hoped to make their way to Britain, France, and Italy, officials told *El Pais* newspaper. Thousands of illegal immigrants from Mali and Senegal travel to the Canary Islands in small boats, with many drowning during the perilous 500-mile voyage from Mauritania. They risk the journey because migration routes via Morocco were closed off by its improved co-operation with Spain. In the Canary Islands, they are crammed into detention centres and military camps. Spain has repatriated small groups to Mauritania by chartered aircraft. But, under its liberal immigration laws, illegal migrants can be held for a maximum of forty days. If officials then fail to establish their nationality, or discover that they come from a country such as Mali which has no repatriation agreement with Spain, they must be released. Most illegal arrivals are therefore set free. Once released on the Spanish mainland, the migrants can make their way through continental Europe because of the border-free Schengen zone.[49] (Britain opted out of the Schengen zone.) The last thing Europe needs is to facilitate further immigration from North Africa. Yet in March 2007, Spain's Prime Minister Zapatero met King Mohammed VI of Morocco and pledged support for a tunnel project to link Tangier with Spain. A consortium of engineering firms from Morocco, Spain, France and Switzerland has drawn up blueprints for a twenty-five-mile twin-track rail tunnel to ferry vehicles and foot passengers between Tarifa in southern Spain and Morocco. Feasibility studies are due to be completed this year. The project is estimated to cost up to thirteen billion euros, and will need significant EU funding. The number of Moroccan immigrants in Spain has soared in recent years with more than 500,000 living there legally, according to official statistics, while many more are undocumented residents.[50]

A huge increase in economic migration into the EU is being proposed by the European Commission. It wants to relax controls and open the borders to an extra twenty million workers from Asia and Africa over the next two decades. The Commission is drawing up a new 'blue card' scheme – modelled on the American 'green card' work permit – allowing qualified migrants the right to live, work and travel in the EU. The plan marks a renewed push to convince member states to adopt a single fast-track immigration policy, since EU countries still operate their own programmes and quotas. Britain is not signed up to common EU borders, but would still be affected if the plans went ahead. Under the commission's proposals, once overseas migrants had been in an EU state for five consecutive years they would be free to travel where they wished. The new policy was outlined by Franco Frattini, the EU Justice Commissioner. He said Europe needed labour, both skilled and unskilled, because of a fall in the population of working age. America was also attracting more qualified workers than were coming to the EU, Frattini added. 'We have to look at immigration as an enrichment and as an inescapable phenomenon of today's world, not as a threat. We should take more account of what statistics tell us: 85 per cent of unskilled labour goes to the EU and only five per cent to the USA, whereas 55 per cent of skilled labour goes to the USA and only five per cent to the EU. We have to reverse these figures with a new vision.' Despite recent EU expansion pushing the bloc's total population to 490 million, the working population is declining. By 2050, a third of residents in the twenty-seven countries would be aged over 65. EU members states all operate different skilled immigration programmes. Britain is moving to a points-based work permit system aimed at attracting more skilled workers and removing settlement rights from unskilled migrants. Germany requires a job offer with a minimum salary of 85,000 euros a year for migrants who are hoping to get a work permit.[51]

In the Andalusian city of Cordoba, the centre of Islamic civilization in the Iberian peninsula during nearly eight centuries of Moorish rule, a proposal was made for descendents of Muslims expelled in the seventeenth century to be given preferential terms for Spanish citizenship. In 1609, Spain's King Philip III ordered all Muslims to leave his kingdom, leading to the expulsion of about 300,000 people. Their descendents today mainly live in North Africa and still regard themselves as 'Andalusians', after the old name for Muslim Spain, *Al Andalus*. Giving them preferential terms for Spanish citizenship would be an act of symbolic reconciliation, said Mansur Escudero, head of Spain's Islamic Board, the biggest group representing Spanish Muslims. 'The Andalusians who live in North Africa, most of them in Morocco, in Tunisia, in Libya, they're part of those societies and aren't going to want to come to Spain', Escudero said unconvincingly, forgetting that these 'Andalusians' were invaders from North Africa in the first place. 'It would be more of an emotional, moral gesture, a recognition of an historic injustice', he told *Reuters*. In an echo of a tactic favoured by Palestinians in their war against Israel, Escudero added that some 'Andalusian' families still preserved keys to houses they left behind four centuries ago. A small left-wing party, Izquierda Unida, has backed the call for preferential citizenship for descendents of Spanish Muslims. The governing Socialists, who have promoted an 'Alliance of Civilizations' between the West and Islam, have yet to give their response. Former Prime Minister Jose Maria Aznar, a member of the conservative Popular Party, called for Muslims to apologize for invading Spain in the eighth century.[52] Aznar now heads a research institute, and advocates redefining NATO's mission as fighting jihadism. He thinks Israel should join the organization. Israel 'is on the same side as Europe, the US, Japan and Australia. We defend the same values against the same enemies. It's that simple.'

September 2006 saw the publication in Denmark of *Islamists and Naivists*, a book that equates Islamic fundamentalists with Nazis and communists and warns against Europe's complacency in the face of this threat. While Bush has made this analogy for years, in Europe, comparisons of Islamism to Nazism or communism were until recently confined to the fringes. This book's authors, however, are unassailably mainstream: Ralf Pittelkow, once an adviser to former Social Democratic premier Poul Rasmussen, is now a columnist for the paper *Jyllands-Posten*, while Karen Jespersen is a former Interior Minister and Social Affairs Minister. The fact that the Nazi–communist analogy is going mainstream is critical to galvanizing support for the war.[53] In Rome, Cardinal Renato Martino, the president of the Pontifical Council for Justice and Peace, said that the Italian Government should allow the Qur'an to be taught during the hour mandated for Catholic religious instruction. He emphasized that 'if we were to wait until we saw equivalent treatment for the Christian minorities in Muslim countries, I would say that we were placing ourselves on their level'. That statement, which for many may be interpreted as magnanimous in the face of the Muslim onslaught in Europe, by others as capitulation before Muslim demands without reciprocity by Muslim countries which continue to oppress their Christian minorities, will be taken by Muslims as a gradual recognition by Europe of the superiority of Islam.[54]

Pope John Paul II had viewed Islam as an ally in the battle against communism and secularism, and sought to engage Islam to promote world peace through ecumenism, even though Christian minorities in Muslim lands continued to be oppressed. Pope Benedict XVI initially tried to reverse that trend, but has returned to a policy of 'indulgent ecumenism' towards Islam, in part because of the reverberations following his Regensburg speech. Under John Paul, the ebbing of religious faith in the West caused admiration towards Muslim religious devotion, for it was felt to be preferable to believe in something rather than nothing in a Europe deprived of values and consumed by materialism. French scholar Louis Massignon had popularized the ideas of the Qur'an, which he presented as some sort of Muslim bible that belonged to the Abrahamic tradition. A modern French scholar, Alain Besancon, remarked that an entire literature favourable to Islam has been growing in Europe, partly written by Catholic priests, emanating from that Massignonian teaching. Moreover, the disgraced Bostonian Cardinal, Bernard Law, had also created a controversy when in 2002 he bowed toward Mecca and prayed to Allah in a suburban mosque during a Ramadan service. He had explained to the congregants: 'I feel very much at home with my fellow fundamentalists here, who are convinced that God must be at the centre of our lives.'[55] Of course the question was raised whether it is the same God that he and the Muslim congregants were worshipping. Some recent research suggests a wide gap between the two concepts of God.[56] In his first Easter message, Benedict highlighted his approach in an address to the diplomatic corps attached to the Holy See:

> Attention has rightly been drawn to the danger of a clash of civilizations. The danger is made more acute by organized terrorism, which has already spread over the whole planet. Its causes are many and complex, not least those to do with political ideology, combined with aberrant religious ideas. Terrorism does not hesitate to strike defenceless people, without discrimination, or to impose inhuman blackmail, causing panic among entire populations, in order to force political leaders to support the designs of the terrorists. No situation can justify such criminal activity, which covers the perpetrators with infamy, and it is all the more deplorable when it hides behind religion, thereby bringing the pure truth of God down to the level of the terrorists' own blindness and moral perversion.[57]

Besancon has described the irreconcilable differences between Christianity, Judaism and Islam by emphasizing that though all three are monotheistic, Islam rejects the idea of atonement and redemption that define Christianity and Judaism. Islam does not have the concept of a covenant between God and humanity either, but Allah in Islam decrees his law by means of a unilateral pact, in an act of 'sublime condescension' that precludes any notion of imitating God as is urged in the Bible. He also points out that Islam rejects the Catholic doctrines of original sin and the necessity for mediation between God and humanity, while in the Qur'an Jesus appears out of place and out of time, without reference to the landscape of Israel. But most of all, the irreconcilable difference between the two systems is that while Muslims enumerate the ninety-nine names of Allah, the title of 'Father' is missing from their list but is essential in the Judeo-Christian tradition, namely a personal God who has reciprocal relations with men. He concludes: 'It was the sentimental ecumenism of John Paul II and his geo-political agenda which prevented the Catholic Church from effectively confronting barbarism in Allah's name.' Oriana Fallaci went further in excoriating the church for its courting of Muslims, including terrorists among them, in the name of that ecumenical agenda upheld by John Paul. In *Corriere Della Sera,* and in her book, *The Force of Reason,* she lashed out at those policies and declared:

> I find it shameful that the Catholic Church should permit a Bishop [Hilarion Capucci] ... a saintly man who was found in Jerusalem with an arsenal of arms and explosives hidden in the secret compartments of his sacred Mercedes, to plant himself in front of a microphone to thank in the name of God the suicide bombers who massacre the Jews in pizzerias and supermarkets., and to call them 'martyrs'. Who go to their deaths as to a party ...
>
> I find it shameful that *L'Osservatore Romano*, the newspaper of the Pope, the Pope who not long ago left in the Wailing Wall a letter of apology to the Jews, accuses of extermination a people who were exterminated in the millions by Christians, by Europeans. I find it shameful that this paper denies to the survivors of that people (some of whom still have numbers tattooed on their arms) the right to react, to defend themselves, to not be exterminated again.
>
> I find it shameful that in the name of Jesus Christ (a Jew without whom they would all be unemployed), the priests of our parishes or social centres, flirt with the assassins of those in Jerusalem who cannot go to eat pizza or buy some eggs without being blown up ...
>
> I find it shameful that they are on the side of the very ones who inaugurated terrorism, killing us on airplanes, in airports, at the Olympics, and who today entertain themselves by killing western journalists, abducting them, cutting their throats, decapitating them.
>
> This Catholic Church ... gets on so well with Islam because not few of its priests and prelates are the first

collaborators of Islam, the first traitors. This Catholic Church, without whose imprimatur the Euro-Arab dialogue could neither have begun nor gone ahead for thirty years. This Catholic Church, without which the Islamization of Europe, the degeneration of Europe in Eurabia , could never have developed. This Catholic Church remains silent even when the crucifix gets insulted, derided, expelled from hospitals. This Catholic Church never roars against Muslim polygamy, wife repudiation and slavery.[58]

Fallaci sought to awaken Europe from its slumber and illusion that by showing accommodation towards Islam, Europeans would be rewarded by peace. The terrorist scare throughout Europe, emanating from the many hundreds of al-Qa'ida-affiliated Muslims who roam European capitals and wait for their day to be activated, has propelled the rise of right-wing politicians in France, Benelux, Germany and Britain. In the UK, the British National Party has been boosted by this combination of terror and an immigrant population whose increasing numbers creates constituencies that no politician can ignore, thereby affecting the entire political system. Writing in the *The Daily Telegraph*, Simon Heffer echoed the opinion of many in Britain: 'Whether in towns or villages, we are and remain a tolerant, easy-going people. But in south-east England in particular there is the sense that we simply haven't the room for anyone else. Roads, railways, schools, the NHS and housing are all buckling. Unless the pressure is taken off – and only firm restrictions on further immigration can do that – the easy-going nature of our people may soon be forced to snap, with potentially horrible consequences.'[59]

A *Sunday Telegraph* leading article ascribed a new willingness to vote for the BNP to 'the despair felt by many working class voters at the government's failure to address the problems generated by what they perceive to be a policy not just of unrestricted immigration, but of favouritism towards immigrants'. The editorial criticized the government's failure even to think seriously about the problems generated by large-scale immigration, observing that Labour encouraged mass immigration and that since 1997, allowed an average of 157,000 new migrants annually into Britain – almost triple the number admitted in the decade prior to 1997. Labour has tried to conceal that policy, concentrating instead on announcing its policy on reducing the number of asylum seekers – who, in fact, form only 14 per cent of the annual total of new immigrants. The paper claimed that during the 2005 election campaign, Charles Clarke, the Home Secretary, insisted that 'we want more immigration', and that he, like other well-off people, may well want more immigration: it reduces wages for house cleaners, nannies, painters and plumbers, and increases the choice of restaurant cuisines available. Poorer voters, for whom immigration means lower wages, longer queues for social housing, and unwelcome changes to the familiar form of the local community, do not want more immigration. Tony Blair boasted that he had presided over strict controls to reduce both legal and illegal immigration, but the editorial insisted that this was blatantly false and that far from imposing strict controls, Labour increased the number of work permits given to immigrants and their dependents by a factor of four since 1997. More than 1.2 million arrived in Britain from 1997 until 2005 from outside the EU. The drift towards the BNP in some areas is a sign that portions of the electorate see, or believe they see, new arrivals getting preferential treatment in housing, medical care and education. They believe that as established citizens who have paid taxes, they are entitled to any benefits the state may dispense before the new arrivals.[60]

All this leads British and other European writers to put in doubt the whole concept of a multiracial society which, far from enriching the host cultures harmoniously, has produced distrust and disaffection when people see the rate of crime and friction between the host and guest cultures, as well as the import of terrorism. Many Europeans do not want to see their communities fragmented into different and isolated factions; nor do they want their traditional values of tolerance and liberty replaced by conformity to foreign religious diktat. The editorial concluded that the problem is that these people had not been consulted about the vast social experiment in which they have been forced to participate. Nor can they discuss their anger without being labelled 'racist'.[61] All these descriptions from various parts of Europe do not bode well for the future of the continent. Some writers, like Theodore Dalrymple, now speak of Old Europe as 'doomed'.[62] He faults the lack of cultural self-confidence in Europe which, instead of being proud of preserving its heritage and acculturating into it the Muslim immigrants, has on the contrary embraced the slippery road of cultural concessions, in its vain endeavour to accommodate newcomers. The absence of common grounds between the various parts of the population, and the fading away of that social, cultural and historical contract that holds them together, makes conflict inevitable and increasingly more violent, eventually undermining and destroying these societies. Even as far as the national language is concerned, the Europeans (although some changed direction recently), instead of making the knowledge of their languages a prerequisite to immigration and citizenship, on the contrary abdicated their role to integrate immigrants, by a wholesale acceptance of multiculturalism and multilingualism. The examples of Australia and America in the past, and modern Israel in the present, show that one national language is a *sine qua non* for the creation of a unifying national culture. Even in modern countries where it does not exist for historical reasons, as in India and the Philippines, English was adopted as a substitute to total disintegration. Faced with an aggressive, tenacious and self-confident Islam, which does not shy away from propagating its culture, religion and the Arabic language, a supine Europe as a whole must ultimately fall apart as the victim of the suicidal multiculturalism of its component members.[63]

Claire Berlinski, the author of a book that made ripples in the US (*Menace in Europe: Why the Continent's Crisis is America's*), had some harsh words in an interview about Europe under the Islamic menace:

> In brief, Europeans are lazy, unwilling to fight for anything and willing to surrender to anyone; they are fascinated by decadence; they favour bureaucracy over corporations; they are unable to assimilate their immigrants; they no longer have children; they no longer produce much of scientific or cultural significance; they have lost their religious vocation and they no longer hold their lives to be meaningful ... The circumstances I describe have rendered Europeans more or less completely blind and incapacitated when confronting threats to their own civilization. There are two general

categories [of threats]: the first set is what I'll call the Return of the Living Dead, to wit the political, religious and social conflicts of the past two millennia of European history – a history characterized by unrelenting bloodletting, mind you – have never been fully resolved, and we are seeing the consequences of that now ... I am not observing the return of Inquisition, and I am not saying that the Nazis are on the march again, but I am saying that Europe's conflict with the Islamic world, one that dates from the era of the Crusades, remains unresolved ... The conflict between the ideal of European unity and the nationalism of its member states remains unresolved. Grandiose nationalism, ancient hatreds, concentrations of power where power does not belong, pervasive class envy – these have in the period since WWII been repressed. But the repressed returns. It is returning now ...

We are seeing a recrudescence of violent anti-Semitism. The hatred of Jews has been woven through the fabric of European life since the early Middle Ages, We are seeing a violent conflict between Europe and Islam ... This dates from the time of the earliest Caliphs ... The second general category of threat is what I'll call Wild Cards, where entirely new sets of problems figure, ones Europe had never confronted before, the consequences of which cannot be predicted. Europe has imported a massive number of immigrants from its former colonies and failed completely to assimilate them. The post-war welfare states have given rise to utterly unrealistic popular expectations – this is why France, for example, is now routinely crippled by what appears to be entirely pointless labour unrest. Birth-rates of native Europeans have, for reasons not well understood, plummeted (this time by voluntary collective disengagement from the task of perpetuating the human race, and not involuntarily like the Great Plague). I am particularly concerned about the intersection between these two categories: unassimilated immigrants plus unexpurgated anti-Semitism, for example, or class conflict plus the rise of Islamic radicalism ...

Radical Islamic terrorist cells in every major European city ... That is our problem too, in a very direct way. Recall that the September 11 attacks were plotted in Hamburg. European mosques have for years been importing a particularly bellicose strain of Islam – these mosques are funded by foreign money, headed by foreign clerics. Saudi Arabia now provides 80 per cent of the funding of the 1,200 mosques and Islamic centres in France, for example. These mosques teach the rejection of assimilation, the complete subjugation of women, grotesque anti-Semitism, jihad. There has been a proliferation too of radicalizing Islamist media, disseminated through cable and satellite and the internet. Hizbollah's propaganda station, al-Manar, for example, is widely pumped into Europe via satellite.[64]

Berlinski also observes that the Muslims of Europe have become the authors of the worst wave of anti-Semitic crime since the Holocaust, with rabbis assaulted, synagogues torched and Jewish graves profaned, emboldened by European elites whose visceral anti-Semitism takes the form of a hysterical animus towards Israel. She describes in detail the European Muslims' vision of seeing the continent governed by shari'a law, and the fact that there are more practising Muslims in France than baptized Catholics. She found that the most popular name in maternity wards is Muhammad, and that within a generation, many European cities will have a Muslim majority. The Europeans, when asked about this menace, would say that they are more concerned by American imperialism than by Islamic radicalism. She contends that European Islam is more radicalized than its American counterpart, because its rate in the population is higher and more concentrated in the cities, and therefore more ghettoized. Another reason is that Europe does not offer its Muslims any attractive alternative and any future, while Muslims in America have been integrated for the most part. (There is a counter-argument on this point, since other immigrant groups who preceded the Muslims integrated successfully even without the generous welfare assistance which today's newcomers receive.) Though their rate in the population is higher than that of the blacks in America, for example, not one Muslim has attained a place in the 577-seat French Assemblée Nationale. They have become such a big problem because the Europeans refuse to recognize and admit it, and they permanently underestimate its effects.[65]

A bleak vision of European military capabilities was drawn up at the invitation of Defence Ministers by the new European Defence Agency. Traditional ideas of 'victory' will have to be jettisoned in favour of limited, multinational campaigns to restore 'stability' to conflict zones, with the grudging consent of an ageing, ever more casualty-averse European population. The paper, *An Initial Long-Term Vision for European Defence Capability and Capacity Needs*, paints a Europe in which plunging fertility rates leave the military struggling to recruit young men and women of fighting age, at a time when national budgets will be under unprecedented strain to pay for greying populations. At the same time, increasingly cautious voters and politicians may be unwilling to contemplate casualties, or 'potentially controversial interventions abroad – in particular interventions in regions from where large numbers of immigrants have come'. Voters will also be insistent on having backing from the UN for operations, and on crafting large coalitions of EU member states with a heavy involvement of civilian agencies, and not just fighting units. They will also want military operations to be environmentally friendly, where possible.[66]

In a column about Europe's moral crisis in the face of the Islamist threat, Gerard Baker noted that German aircraft are not permitted by their national rules to undertake night flights. Many of the European nations with forces in Afghanistan are operating under similar restrictions. Their governments are fearful of the public reaction should their soldiers suffer significant casualties. European NATO countries declined to strengthen their forces in Afghanistan. In September 2006 Chirac said France no longer thought the UN should impose sanctions if Iran did not end its uranium enrichment programme. Against this background, there was European outrage following Pope Benedict's remarks on Islam. Baker recalled:

> I actually heard a senior member of the British Government chide the Pope this week for what he described as his unhelpful comments. This minister went on to say that the Pope should keep quiet about Islamic violence because of the Crusades. It was a jaw-dropping observation. If it was meant seriously its import is that, because of violence perpetrated

in the name of Christ 900 years ago, today's Church, and presumably today's European governments (who, after all, were eager participants in the Crusades) should forever hold their peace on the subject of religious fanaticism. Taken together, these reactions imply a slow but insistent collapse of the European will. Great civilizations die not in the end because of external *force majeure* but because internally the will to thrive is sapped.[67]

In considering why American birth rates have not matched the fall in birth rates of Europe, demographer Nicholas Eberstadt of the American Enterprise Institute cites three differences: greater optimism, greater patriotism and stronger religious values. There's some supporting evidence. A survey by the National Opinion Research Center at the University of Chicago asked respondents in thirty-three countries to react to this statement: 'I would rather be a citizen of [my country] than of any other.' Among Americans, 75 per cent 'strongly' agreed; among Germans, French and Spanish, comparable responses were 21 per cent, 34 per cent and 21 per cent, respectively.[68]

Political columnist Mark Steyn wrote that with the onset of the Iraq War, Americans reacted severely towards their supposed European allies who criticized America, especially France, and he added some of those nations to the 'list of polities destined to slip down the EUrinal of history'. He said that in the year 2025 the US will still be much as it is today – big and powerful, though in the eyes of sophisticated Europeans 'absurdly vulgar and provincial', while Europe will be an 'economically moribund demographic basket case', because the main seventeen nations of the continent have a low fertility rate of below 1.3 per woman, from which no nation can survive. He saw France as caught between the twin pincers of the fall and spring rioters: those of fall 2005 were Muslim youths from the suburbs, who were said to have become alienated for lack of economic opportunity; while the Spring 2006 rioters were 'pampered Sorbonne deadbeats' who protested against the new labour law because they demanded job protection regardless of how inefficient they are. That is responsible for the immobility of the French economy, and will eventually bring it to its downfall and takeover by the 'successor population already in place', namely the Muslim one. To conclude, he invoked Gibbon's *Decline and Fall of the Roman Empire,* to warn against the new Muslim march on Europe, which could be a repetition of the events of thirteen centuries ago:

> The decline of the French monarchy invited the attacks of these insatiate fanatics. The descendants of Clovis had lost the inheritance of his martial and ferocious spirit; and their misfortune or demerit has affixed the epithet of lazy to the last kings of the Merovingian race. They ascended the throne without power, and sunk into the grave without a name ... The vineyards of Gascony and the city of Bordeaux were possessed by the Sovereign of Damascus and Samarkand; and the south of France, from the mouth of the Garonne to that of the Rhone, assumed the manners and religion of Arabia.[69]

In *America Alone: The End of the World As We Know It,* Mark Steyn began with the legacy of two totalitarianisms. Traumatized by the electoral appeal of fascism, post-Second World War European states were constructed in a top-down manner 'so as to insulate almost entirely the political class from populist pressures'. As a result, the establishment has 'come to regard the electorate as children'. Second, the Soviet menace during the Cold War prompted American leaders, impatient with Europe's (and Canada's) weak responses, effectively to take over their defence. This benign and far-sighted policy led to victory by 1991, but it also had the unintended and less salutary side effect of freeing up Europe's funds to build a welfare state. This welfare state had several malign implications. The nanny state infantilized Europeans, making them worry about such pseudo-issues as climate change, while feminizing the males. It also neutered them, annexing 'most of the core functions of adulthood', starting with the instinct to breed. From about 1980 birth rates plummeted, leaving an inadequate base for today's workers to receive their pensions. The demographic collapse meant that the indigenous peoples of countries like Russia, Italy and Spain are at the start of a population death spiral. All these factors led to a collapse of confidence that, in turn, bred 'civilizational exhaustion', leaving Europeans unprepared to fight for their ways. To keep the economies running meant accepting foreign workers. Rather than execute a long-term plan to prepare for the many millions of immigrants needed, Europe's elites welcomed almost anyone who turned up. By virtue of geographic proximity, demographic overdrive and a crisis-prone environment, 'Islam is now the principal supplier of new Europeans.' Arriving at a time of demographic, political and cultural weakness, Muslims are profoundly changing Europe. 'Islam has youth and will, Europe has age and welfare.' Much of the western world, Steyn predicts, 'will not survive the twenty-first century, and much of it will effectively disappear within our lifetimes, including many, if not most, European countries'. Europe's successor population is already in place and 'the only question is how bloody the transfer of real estate will be'. He interprets the Madrid and London bombings, as well as the murder of Theo van Gogh in Amsterdam, as the preamble to Europe's civil war and states that 'Europe is the colony now.'[70]

There was a lively debate in the US press about the future of Europe. In keeping with his 'Demography is Destiny' theme, Mark Steyn wrote:

> The native European population is split three ways: some will leave, as the Dutch (and certain French) are already doing; some will shrug and go along with the Islamization of the continent, as the ever-accelerating number of conversions suggests; and so the ones left to embrace Fascism will be a minority of an aging population. It will be bloody and messy, as I write in *America Alone*, but it will not alter the final outcome. If you don't breed, you can't influence the future. And furthermore a disinclination to breed is a good sign you don't care much about the future. That's why the Spaniards, who fought a brutal bloody civil war for their country in the 1930s, folded instantly after those Madrid bombings. When you've demographically checked out of the future, why fight for it?[71]

At the other end of the spectrum, Ralph Peters believes predictions of a Muslim takeover of Europe ignore history and Europe's viciousness:

Don't let Europe's current round of playing pacifist dress-up fool you: This is the continent that perfected genocide and ethnic cleansing, the happy-go-lucky slice of humanity that brought us such recent hits as the Holocaust and Srebrenica. The historical patterns are clear: When Europeans feel sufficiently threatened – even when the threat's concocted nonsense – they don't just react, they over-react with stunning ferocity ... The Europeans have enjoyed a comfy ride for the last sixty years – but the very fact that they don't want it to stop increases their rage and sense of being besieged by Muslim minorities they've long refused to assimilate (and which no longer want to assimilate).[72]

Complacent talk of multiculturalism has allowed European governments to ignore the challenge of winning the loyalties and attachments of immigrants. For children of immigrants, who have no strong attachments either to their old or new countries, extremist ideology often fills the void. Steyn warns that Europe is trending toward societies that are not so much multicultural as bicultural – split between a growing minority that embraces Muslim discipline and identity, and a bewildered, ageing population that does not. Bicultural societies are rarely stable. Europeans scoff at the idea that Iraq could become a pluralist democracy, but then imagine that European social democracy can ensure harmony with people fired by some of the same zeal as Iraqi 'insurgents'. In answer to the question whether reform of Islam is likely, he says: 'What if the reform has already taken place and jihadism is it?' Steyn puts the challenge very sharply: 'Those who call for a Muslim reformation in the spirit of the Christian Reformation ignore the obvious flaw in the analogy – that Muslims have the advantage of knowing (unlike Luther and Calvin) where reform in Europe ultimately led: the banishment of God to the margins of society.' And meanwhile, we continue pouring billions of petrodollars into the coffers of Middle Eastern regimes that still seem content to recycle that immense stream of wealth into extremist religion in Europe and around the world.[73] The steady loss of will amongst some European leaders is responsible for incalculable damage. In Holland, the Dutch Justice Minister, Piet Hein Donner,[74] declared he does not object to shari'a law providing it is done 'democratically', while Swedish minister Jens Orback declared: 'We must be open and tolerant towards Islam and Muslims because when we become a minority, they will be so towards us.'[75]

One of the most prominent figures to spread Muslim propaganda in Europe is Tariq Ramadan, a Swiss citizen and grandson of the founder of the Muslim Brotherhood in Egypt, Hasan al-Banna. Ramadan had his US visa revoked by the Department of Homeland Security in July 2004 under the Immigration and Nationality Act, due to his activities, lectures and writings in support of the Islamist agenda. According to a Spanish judge, Balthazar Garzon, Ramadan had 'routine contacts' with Ahmed Brahim, an Algerian believed to be the financial chief of al-Qa'ida and the financier of the 1998 US Embassy bombings in Kenya and Tanzania. In 1995, during a series of terrorist attacks in Paris perpetrated by the Algerian Armed Islamist Movement, the French Interior Minister, Jean Louis Debré, forbade Ramadan to enter France because of his connections with that terrorist group. Moreover, according to the French daily newspaper *Le Monde*, Ramadan is also believed to have organized a 1991 meeting between al-Qa'ida's second-in-command, Ayman al-Zawahiri, and Sheikh Omar Abdel Rahman, who was convicted in the 1993 bombing of the World Trade Centre, which killed six people and injured more than 1,000. Interviewed by the Italian magazine *Panorama* on 23 September 2004, Ramadan's answer to the question of 'whether it is right to kill children and Israeli civilians because they are considered soldiers', was that it is 'contextually explicable'. Indeed, Ramadan has given enough public speeches in mosques all over Europe, varying his message according to his audience, that the founder of Doctors Without Borders, Bernard Kouchner (and now France's Foreign Minister), describes him as a 'most dangerous man'. The Muslim Brotherhood and Ramadan usually refrain from publicly advocating violence. However, as stated on the Muslim Brotherhood charter and its website, it seeks to install an Islamic totalitarian empire, a worldwide Caliphate, through stages designed to Islamize targeted nations by whatever means available.[76]

Brendan Bernhard reviewed Oriana Fallaci's book, *The Force of Reason*, tackling in particular the question she raised about whether Muslim immigration to Europe is part of a well-thought-out plan. Bernhard raises and discusses a series of sub-questions. For example, how is it that Islam, which was until recently a non-factor, has grown to threaten the Christian character of Europe? How can it be that the most popular name for baby boys in Brussels today is Muhammad? Is it true that Amsterdam and Rotterdam are close to becoming Muslim-majority? Why has the US, which saved Europe in two world wars, and most recently came to the rescue of Bosnian Muslims in 1999, become so hated across Europe? Fallaci was particularly infuriated by intellectuals who ignore that the West has been undergoing a cultural, political and existential war with Islam, which had been predicted by some Arabs long ago. Westerners remain oblivious to it because their intellectuals, who often appear in the media, refrain from mentioning it. Fallaci said the Palestinian leader George Habash informed her as far back as 1972 that the Palestinian problem was about far more than Israel. The Arab goal, Habash declared, was to wage war 'against Europe and America' and to ensure that henceforth 'there would be no peace for the West'. He told her that the Arabs would advance 'step by step, millimetre by millimetre, year after year, decade after decade, determined, stubborn, patient, this is our strategy, a strategy we shall expand to the whole planet'. She said he was not only referring to terrorism, but also to cultural, demographic and religious wars, waged by 'stealing countries from their citizens', namely a war waged through immigration, fertility and presumed 'multiculturalism'. Fallaci cited Houari Boumedienne's warning to the UN General Assembly in 1974, in which he straightforwardly announced: 'One day millions of men will leave the southern hemisphere of this planet to burst into the northern one. But not as friends. Because they will burst in to conquer, and they will conquer by populating it with their children. Victory will come to us from the wombs of our women.'[77] His words were repeatedly echoed by Yasser Arafat, who said Israel would be 'destroyed' by the 'Palestinian womb'. Such remarks are now commonplace. Mullah Krekar, a Muslim supremacist living in Oslo, informed the Norwegian newspaper *Dagbladet* that Muslims would change Norway, not the other way around. 'Just look at the development within Europe, where the number of Muslims is expanding like mosquitoes', he said. 'By

2050, 30 per cent of the population in Europe will be Muslim.'[78] Following Bat Ye'or's seminal book *Eurabia: The Euro-Arab Axis*, on which she draws heavily, Fallaci believed Europe was well on its way to being colonized by Arabs, as a result of a deliberate and gradual scheme. According to this theory, the present Franco-Arab and Euro-Arab dialogues, cultural and economic cooperation and political and diplomatic collaboration, have resulted in Europe accepting Arab oil and manpower, disseminating Arab propaganda about the glory of Islamic civilization, providing weapons and turning against Israel and the US. She cited the Venice Conference of 1977, attended by ten Arab and eight European nations, and which ended with a resolution calling for the diffusion of Arabic and affirming the 'superiority of Arab culture'. The Arabs demanded that the Europeans respect the religious, political and human rights of Arabs in the West, without European requests for reciprocity in the Arab and Muslim world. Nor did the Europeans require that Muslims learn about European history, civilization and values. A combination of socialist rulers in Europe, who were impressed by Khomeini in 1979, and then by Saddam and Bin Laden, coalesced to sell off a substantial portion of Europe's cultural and political independence to the Arabs. Even if Fallaci embellished her case with sweeping and biting generalizations, she had been long sounding the alarm over the neglected issue of Muslim immigration. The response of the West to the threat has never been firm enough to confront the root problems of immigration and resolve them systematically.[79]

Authors and public figures who have awoken to the dangers facing Europe, have couched them in various terms: moral, demographic, civilizational. Others who sense those same threats have been struggling for words to articulate that sense of loss when one feels his country, culture, civilization, environment, society, mores and everything familiar is being hijacked. Morton Messerschmidt, a member of the Council of Europe, and of the Danish parliament on behalf of the Danish People's Party, offers yet another original look at this crisis. In an interview with Jamie Glazov, he said, *inter alia*:

> We are seeing over the entire continent how the extreme groups of Islam are trying to impose their fundamentalist

ideology, which has created awful results in the Middle East, to our part of the world. We see it in the mosques, where the imams preach hate towards Western values; we've seen it in the many claims of respect for the Islamic way of life ... And we have seen it in the terror attacks and attempts which in many cases have been organized inside Europe ... It is well known that Muslim immigrants are disproportional in representing crime records; that the hate towards Jews is increasing in Europe, because of these groups. The serious mistreatment of women, which we see in the Muslim world, is now also taking place in Europe. The lack of labour participation, which is connected to these people living on welfare, is an economic threat to the stability of our societies. In many European countries we speak about the necessity of changing the welfare payments, but the truth is that if we did not have the Muslim burden, many of these changes would not be required ... The left wing has an ideological interest in destabilizing the belief in cultural heritage. Therefore the achievement of their ideology goes hand in hand with the multiculturalism that'll break down any cultural starting point.

I believe the main course has to do with an extremely political press. No doubt there are objective journalists in Europe, but the overall picture is that the newspapers will be presenting the US as the problem-maker and the EU as the peace-maker ... Secondly I believe it has to do with power – it is well known that the Muslim minorities in Denmark are voting for left-wing parties. And some politicians – in Denmark as well as in many other European countries – are deliberately campaigning for these votes. Of course you wouldn't like to disturb the people handing you your paycheque ... [The cartoon affair] has played a very good role in exposing the serious trouble we face with the Muslim minorities in Europe, who are also containing the extreme groups that neither respect nor tolerate the fundamental rights of human beings, such as freedom of the press or of free speech ...

Either you are with democracy – or you are against it. There can be no middle way. And if you define yourself as being against democracy, for instance by supporting shari'a legislation, the European continent should not be your home

> ... Only ignorant people believe that we can solve the problems in the Middle East through emigration to Europe – demographically it's an outrageous thought, looking at the fact that the Muslim civilization has a net increase in population of the size of Spain each year. Therefore the only way to help these people have good lives, is to start reforming those regimes in the Middle East which severely violate human rights. Instead of using billions on the impossible integration of Muslims in Europe we should rather be supporting the internal opposition groups in these countries – and even in some cases do the job ourselves – as we've seen in Iraq. Unfortunately the case of Iraq hasn't been as promising as many of us had hoped, but the idea of removing a dictator and thereby giving freedom to the suppressed is indeed a good one ... We must stop paying welfare to people without Danish citizenship – and make much harsher regulations for those only coming for economic reasons.
>
> First, as I have said, we have to get rid of those groups opposing democracy. That can be done be prohibiting organizations like *Hizb ul-Tahrir*, the Muslim Brotherhood, etc. Second, immigration from Muslim countries must be limited ... Europe will – maybe not in twenty, but rather thirty–forty years from now – have a Muslim majority of population, if nothing is done.[80]

When compared to America, the ultimate paradigm of an immigrant nation, Europe seems in total disarray as far as immigration policy is concerned. But America too has been facing vast new waves of immigrants from its own continent which threaten to inundate it beyond its prodigious absorption capacity. It seems the theory of Mao Tse-tung's heir apparent of the 1960s, Lin Piao, that the underdeveloped and overpopulated regions of Asia, Africa and Latin America, are set to take by assault the capitalist bastions of Europe and North America in order to realize the world revolution, is being implemented. Unlike America, few countries in Europe have historically been immigrant destinations. Some invited a large number of 'guest workers' during the 1950s and 1960s, and yet still lack orderly, long-term immigration programmes. Instead, the Europeans have pursued policies that encourage massive illegal immigration and then compound the problem by legalizing it. They do so by providing generous public assistance to illegal immigrants, tolerating large-scale abuse of asylum laws, failing to deport those who are apprehended, and granting periodic amnesties which trigger ever larger inflows. As in the US, every amnesty is accompanied by earnest assurances that it is 'the very last one' and by promises of a severe crackdown on illegal immigration that will solve the problem once and for all. Invariably, the argument is also made that legalizing the 'undocumented' (a new and politically correct euphemism for illegal infiltrators) will bring them into the mainstream economy, providing much needed labour and a major boost in tax revenues for the state. The reality is the exact opposite.[81]

EU countries legalized approximately 1.75 million immigrants up through 2000, and between 3.5 and 4 million since then. Despite that, illegal immigration is increasing dramatically. Spain carried out four amnesties between 1985 and 2000, and yet, in 2003 it had 1.3 million legal immigrants and more than twice as many illegal ones. In 2005 it amnestied yet another 700,000, with no visible reduction of illegal entries. In December 2005, thousands of would-be immigrants stormed the ten-foot-high, razorblade-wire fences surrounding the Spanish enclaves of Ceuta and Melilla (Moroccan towns that were colonized by the Spaniards who refuse to relinquish them) in Morocco. Similarly, between 1986 and 2002, Italy legalized 1.5 million immigrants in five separate amnesties without stemming the yearly inflow of well over 500,000 illegal immigrants. The same is the case in Portugal, Greece, France, and every other country that practises amnesties. And there is no reason to expect anything different if fully two-thirds of illegal entrants eventually obtain legalization, the odds of deportation are negligible, and the wait for legalization can be spent in the relative comfort of the European welfare system or its illegal economy.

The last point is worth pondering, because it is simply not the case that amnesties bring millions from the underground economy eager to pay the exorbitant taxes the nanny state collects from those working in order to nanny those that are not. The reason there is an underground economy to begin with is because neither employers nor employees are eager to hand over payroll taxes that average 36 per cent in the EU. Indeed, with these kinds of confiscatory levies, the often unskilled and uneducated illegal immigrant becomes unemployable in the regular economy. The result is a huge influx of illegal workers in the shadow economy, which is one reason it is rapidly growing both in Europe and North America. According to expert estimates, it has more than doubled in the past twenty years and currently ranges from 8.4 per cent of GDP in the US to 14.5 in France, 16.8 in Germany, and nearly one-third of GDP in high immigration countries like Italy. Figures usually bandied about in amnesty discussions are highly misleading; in practice, legalizing one illegal alien means eventually providing legal entry documents to several times as many. Through family reunification and what demographers call 'chain migration', every legalized immigrant in Europe eventually brings with him three to five of his own immediate family, who in turn bring more relatives. Throw in arranged and fictitious marriages and the migration chain becomes very long indeed. The vast majority of the 1.7 million immigrants who entered the EU legally in 2005 were just such chain migrants. In the US itself, chain migration already makes up close to 70 per cent of all legal immigration.[82]

The fight against terrorism is far from being led jointly by all Europeans, and they often leave much of the work to the US. The Europeans benefit, but withhold the public support and gratitude they owe the US, even if they undermine the American effort in the process. In 2006 the EU declared one of the most basic forms of cooperation with the US in the fight against terrorism 'illegal', because it 'failed to respect human rights'. What had irked the EU regulators was that the US had been allowed access to records of international bank transfers by SWIFT (Society for Worldwide Interbank Financial Telecommunication), the Belgium-based company that oversees most of them. It handles financial message traffic from 7,800 financial institutions in more than 200 countries. SWIFT had thought it was acting responsibly: the point of cooperating had been to help the US in its effort to track down who was transferring money to terrorist bank accounts, and stop them doing it. The American programme, dating from 9/11, was surprisingly successful: US law-enforcement officers managed to identify and freeze well over $200 million in terrorist-related bank accounts, thus preventing the terrorists financing some of the incidents of mass murder that they had planned. The bureaucrats in Brussels insisted that in allowing the US access to some of its transaction records, SWIFT wrongly put 'security interests ahead of norms of human rights'. It is difficult to understand how it can be more important to keep bank transactions private than to prevent mass murder. What makes the EU's stance even more difficult to understand is that it does allow that 'an important public interest' is enough to override the 'right' to keep bank transactions secret: the European Commission's Working Party on the Protection of Personal Data stresses that 'tax and customs administrations' could take a peek at bank transfers without any rights being violated, as could 'the services responsible for social security and the supervisory bodies in the financial services sector'. Michael Chertoff, the US Secretary of Homeland Security, appealed to EU officials on the fifth anniversary of 9/11 to work with the US 'to ease restrictions before another attack like those of 9/11 occurs'.[83]

The service mostly captures information on wire transfers and other methods of moving money in and out of the US, but generally does not detect private, individual transactions in the US, such as withdrawals from an ATM or bank deposits. The American administration expressed concern that newspaper disclosure of the programme undermined efforts to track terrorism-related activities. 'We know the terrorists pay attention to our strategy to fight them, and now have another piece of the puzzle of how we are fighting them', Dana Perino, deputy White House press secretary, said. 'We also know they adapt their methods, which increases the challenge to our intelligence and law enforcement officials.' Disclosure of the programme followed intense controversy over Bush's directive ordering the National Security Agency to monitor – without court approval – the calls and e-mails of Americans when one party is overseas and terrorism is suspected. *The New York Times* and the *Los Angeles Times* defended their decision to publish despite the Bush administration's concern that it would destroy a useful intelligence tool. Some in Congress were briefed on the operations, including members of the House Intelligence Committee.[84]

So while America is leading the battle against international Islamic terrorism, the rest of the West continues to criticize it and simultaneously enjoys its lead and strength; examines to what extent it can live with Islam as a God-given calamity that cannot be altered; and constantly cherry-picks from the vast menu of what needs to be done to confront radical Islam. The impression is given that new policies are constantly being adopted and pursued, while in fact there is neither a concept among western powers of what ought to be done, nor a united, coordinated and streamlined action to fit that concept. Typically of liberal democracies, where leaders are driven primarily by their wish to be re-elected every four years, they rarely tackle a problem vigorously enough to eliminate it, sometimes bequeathing it to the next government in an even more intractable state. At the Brussels summit of June 2006, all the member states agreed to create a pan-European counter-terrorism force by pooling assets – police, civil protection and military – and place them at the disposal of Javier Solana, the EU Foreign Minister-in-waiting. Such a move had been planned in the constitution which was rejected by voters in France and Holland in 2005, and has latterly been introduced under a new guise of an 'EU reform treaty'. The EU presidency has drawn up a 'manual' of forces and assets which can be called on following an attack in any country. But Eurosceptics reacted with outrage. Chris Heaton-Harris, the Tory Euro MP, said: 'This is another example of the Soviet-style regime which rides roughshod over democratic votes in France and the Netherlands.'[85]

A similar level of European hypocrisy that developed over 'extraordinary rendition' also surrounded the issue of detainees at Guantanamo Bay. America endured relentless criticism over the existence of the camp, and was accused of 'torturing' detainees who were claimed to be 'innocent'. The detainees are being gradually released when countries are willing to take their nationals (which does not always happen) or when the detainees are no longer deemed to present a danger. Some prefer to be held at Guantanamo than released into the clutches of their own governments. However, it is known that at least thirty former detainees have been killed or recaptured after taking up arms against allied forces following their release, mostly in Afghanistan and Pakistan. Commander Jeffrey Gordon said the detainees had falsely claimed to be farmers, truck drivers, cooks, small-arms merchants, low-level combatants or had offered other false explanations for being in Afghanistan. 'Common cover stories include going to Afghanistan to buy medicines, to teach the Qur'an or to find a wife. Many of these stories appear so often, and are subsequently proven false, that we can only conclude that they are part of their terrorist training.' An analysis found that 95 per cent of the detainees were a potential threat to US interests. This was based on their affiliations with groups such as al-Qa'ida, their enthusiasm for violent jihad or their willingness to perform a support role for terrorism. But only a third could be definitely identified as a fighter for the Taleban, al-Qa'ida or associated groups, according to the analysis by the Combating Terrorism Centre based at the West Point Military Academy.[86] It was not until 2007 that a British Foreign Affairs Select Committee report concluded that the inmates at Guantanamo are not being systematically abused and are held in facilities broadly equivalent to a high-security British prison. Its report states: 'We recognize that many of those detained present a real threat to public safety and that all states are under an obligation to protect their citizens and those of other countries from that threat. At present, that obligation is being discharged by the US alone, in ways that have attracted strong criticism, but we conclude that the international community as a whole needs to shoulder its responsibility in finding a longer-term solution.'[87]

Bush declared in 2006 that he would like to close Guantanamo and put the detainees on trial. Almost 400 detainees have been released since 2002, and around 380 men still remain. Britain adopted a typically curious approach to the problem, calling for Guantanamo Bay to be closed but refusing to speed that closure process by accepting the return of five British 'residents' until recently. These men have all lived at some point and for varying periods of time in Britain.[88] After Gordon Brown took office, the British Government finally made a formal request for their release in August 2007. They have been named as Shaker Aamer, Jamil el-Banna, Omar Deghayes, Binyam Mohamed and Abdennour Sameur.[89] The Pentagon warned that the five terror suspects have close ties to some of al-Qa'ida's most high-ranking leaders and could pose a risk to the UK if not kept under close scrutiny. Aamer, 38, a Saudi national granted leave to remain in Britain, allegedly lived in Afghanistan on a 'stipend' provided by Bin Laden and was his interpreter. Aamer is also alleged to have ties with Ayman al-Zawahiri, and was associated with individuals who plotted an attack on Parliament in 2005. El-Banna, 44, a Jordanian citizen, is alleged to have had an association with al-Zarqawi when the two men lived in their native country. Al-Zarqawi became al-Qa'ida's chief in Iraq and was behind the murder of Ken Bigley, the British engineer. Deghayes, 37, a Libyan, is a 'jihadi veteran' of the Bosnian War and has links to Salaheddine Benyaich, a leader of the Casablanca suicide bombings that killed forty-five people. He has direct connections to al-Qa'ida followers in Europe.[90]

'Hopeful' news is intermittently circulated about an impending reform in Islam, except that so-called reformers lack the authority to introduce reforms and neither do they have the requisite following. Ehsan Masood instilled just such a hope in the pages of *Prospect Magazine*.[91] Masood wrote that a year after the 7/7 attacks in London, a challenge to the traditionalist, literal reading of the Qur'an started to gather strength, thanks to a younger generation of Muslims seeking a less insular and more western faith. He recounted a scene that he found unforgettable, with Jean-Marie Lehn, the French winner of the Nobel Prize in chemistry, defending his atheism at a packed public conference at the new Alexandria Library in Egypt, even though talking about atheism in public is dangerous in much of the Muslim world. But the Alexandria Library is run by Ismail Serageldin, a Muslim intellectual who has a bold and ambitious project for Egypt. This is to create a place for dissent in public life. He wants to encourage people to become resilient to criticism, and appreciate that if Muslim societies want to return to the forefront of global intellectual life, they need to be comfortable with public dispute. The library is one place where open debate can take place, earning some protection because its board of trustees is chaired by Suzanne Mubarak, wife of Egypt's President. Otherwise, open dissent is not permitted in Egypt, and Serageldin, the 'open reformer', was proved to be a bigot when he permitted the Library to display the infamous *Protocols of the Elders of Zion* as a document of history. Serageldin is not alone.

Masood claims that what he (and others) are trying to do in Egypt is also happening elsewhere. It is happening at the level of the Organization of the Islamic Conference which has embarked on a ten-year reform plan to transform Muslim states into 'beacons of human rights and free speech'. (This is an outright distortion of the truth, when the OIC has been at the forefront of limiting free speech even in the West since the Danish cartoon crisis.) It is also happening, claims Masood, among Islamic 'rationalists' in the West, who are building a case for Muslim societies to change from within. Masood includes the British-Pakistani writer Ziauddin Sardar, and the philosophers Tariq Ramadan (Swiss-Egyptian) and Abdol Karim Soroush (Iranian) amongst the rationalists. In the US, change is being advocated by the evangelist Hamza Yusuf Hanson, who regards himself as more traditionalist than reformer. It is significant that each of these scholar-activists is either based in a western country, or has spent substantial time in western research establishments. But Ramadan issues contradictory messages according to the nature of his audience, and famously suggested only a 'moratorium' on the stoning of women under shari'a instead of its abolition. One area on which all are agreed (at least outwardly) is the need to break with the traditional literal interpretation of the Qur'an. The majority of Muslims are still taught to believe that the Qur'an is the unaltered word of Allah as delivered to Muhammad, while that human agency did not interfere with the process from revelation to transcription. Islam is also regarded as fixed and unchanging. In most schools, Islam's 'easternness' and resistance to western modernization is seen as one of its enduring strengths.

Archaeological evidence at the restoration of the Great Mosque of Sana'a in Yemen in 1972 tells a different story. Fragments of Qur'ans that are among the oldest in existence were found (dating back to the seventh and eighth centuries – Islam's first two centuries).[92] Gerd-R. Puin, a specialist in Arabic calligraphy and Qur'anic paleography based at Saarland University in Germany, discovered unconventional verse orderings, minor textual variations and some versions written over earlier ones. The Yemeni Qur'ans suggested an evolving text rather than simply the Word of God as revealed to Muhammad. The Yemeni authorities did not want a detailed examination, according to Puin, 'since the Muslim position is that everything that needs to be said about the Qur'an's history was said a thousand years ago'.[93]

The world's 1.3 billion Muslims come in many types. The following four-fold categorization is a rough guide to Muslims in

Britain, as well as in Muslim countries. There are Muslims born into the faith, but who do not practise it beyond family events and cultural festivals; more pious Muslims born into the faith and who are serious about Islamic commandments such as regular daily prayers, fasting and giving to charity; Muslims born into Islam who observe the commandments and also believe that it is incumbent on them to spread the message to humankind; and Muslim converts to Islam of all shades and stripes. Within this diversity of practice as well as the different Shi'a and Sunni schools there is much that unites Muslims. All Muslims believe in God, in Muhammad as the seal of a long line of prophets that includes Abraham and Jesus (except that the latter are not prophets, beyond their declaration to be so by Muhammad). The Qur'an is regarded as the final revelation, designed by Allah to supersede the Old and New Testaments. They believe in accountability for actions, in a day of judgement, and heaven and hell. More pious ones also believe in following certain rules of behaviour, both private and public, as laid down in the two primary sources of shari'a: the Qur'an, and the records of the prophet's life and teachings known as the *hadith*. Traditional Muslims shy away, indeed are prohibited, from asking critical questions and tend to have an emotional identification with the prophet himself and the perfection that his life is supposed to represent.[94]

According to Masood, resistance to modernization is not in itself a problem. Some would like the process to take place on their terms, but there is a particular problem with Islam that has made the modernization project more urgent especially since 9/11. Muslim terrorists regard acts of terror as an Islamic duty and often quote the Qur'an to support such acts. Most significantly, the Qur'an is rarely (if at all) taught to be understood in its historical context. Take verse 3:151, often used by terrorists, which says: 'We will put terror into the hearts of the unbelievers. They serve other gods for whom no sanction has been revealed. Hell shall be their home.' According to historians, this is a verse in which God is addressing the prophet on the eve of a crucial battle during Islam's first decade. This is the battle of Uhud, when the leadership of Mecca decided that this new religion needed to be crushed. The Meccan army was large, the Muslim force small and Muhammad feared defeat. The Qur'an reassures him (but it could not have done so, since it did not exist yet, and was made up by Muhammad as he went along, and as needed) and promises that the enemy will not prevail. In other words, this was a specific injunction designed to address a specific situation in early Islamic history. In countries where the legal system is based on a literal reading of Qur'anic injunctions, traditional Islam like other religions based on a divine revelation can lead to the abuse of human rights. Shari'a is the totality of laws based on Islam. Where the Qur'an and the *hadith* are silent, secondary sources, including early Islamic legal scholars, can be consulted. Another secondary source is reasoning by analogy, and is permitted in situations where there is no precedent. Shari'a was the main means of lawmaking in Muslim countries until the collapse of the Ottoman Empire in 1924, but even today it remains a fixture in civil, family and criminal law in many Muslim states. Some countries, such as India and Morocco, are bringing shari'a into line with liberal norms. They have abandoned shari'a-based family laws that discriminate against women. These include the right of men to divorce their wives without going to court, or to inherit twice as much as women. But elsewhere the movement is in the other direction. In Nigeria, the Muslim-majority north has re-introduced shari'a based penalties, such as stoning.[95]

For Islam's rationalists (which sounds like a contradiction in terms in view of the injunction *bila kayf,* meaning 'do not ask how'), literalism in shari'a is just another manifestation of the way that the Qur'an today is taught with little reference to the context of its revelation. Very few translations of the Qur'an bother to provide any historical background, for fear that everyone would find and interpret his own context. All reformers agree (although they carry precious little weight) that the Qur'an needs to be seen as a broad set of guidelines on how to organize a just society, and not a detailed manual of what is or is not permissable (although this is exactly the way it is regarded by Muslims). There is also broad agreement that if isolated verses are lifted out of context, the Qur'an can be used to justify almost any action, as it indeed is. But consensus does not survive if you then ask: Which verses apply as general principles, and which should be read in their historical context? Can interpretation be left to individuals or should it be religious scholars? Who should decide who counts as a scholar and should their interpretations apply locally, nationally or internationally? For Sardar and Soroush, the answers are clear. First, shari'a laws that deny universal human rights are no longer tenable as a source of law, something which invalidates the Qur'an in general, for if a 'Word of Allah' can be ignored on grounds of human rights, why not on others? Secondly, interpretation has to be a matter of individual conscience, rather than some kind of official scholarly consensus, so that individuals are answerable for their own deeds. Drawing on their experience of working in Iran and Saudi Arabia, Sardar and Soroush are convinced that governments which legislate on the basis of ancient and unreformed laws can create gross human rights abuses. This means that Muslims need to be open to new ideas, and introduce critical thinking and scepticism.

Tariq Ramadan now teaches at St Antony's, Oxford, and is also popular with the authorities in Britain, thanks to his talent for telling them what they wish to hear. In France, by contrast, the political classes remain unconvinced of his reformism and have also accused him of anti-Semitism. A popular Ramadan theme is that the West and Islam should stop seeing each other as monolithic. He argues that thanks to the rule of law, western liberal democracies are 'more Islamic' than many Muslim societies, and that Muslims in the West must regard themselves as being of the West and that they should demand their rights as citizens. Masood unconvincingly suggests that Ramadan's call for Muslim civic engagement may overturn the MCB's founding *raison d'être*, which is the promotion of a separate Islamic identity. Masood's inclusion of the MCB leader Abdul Bari in the reformist wing has been disproved by Abdul Bari's invitation to the most fundamentalist of Saudi clerics, Sheikh Sudayyis, to his London mosque, and his warning of two million home-grown Islamic terrorists if the British authorities do not tailor foreign policy to accord with Muslim demands. Hanson dislikes the term 'reform', believing that a desire to reform Christianity is what gave the world secularism, materialism, a collapse in respect for authority and loose morals. Hanson concedes that the Qur'an needs to be understood in context, and chooses to rationalize the Qur'an, rather than to question it. For example, when asked why two women were needed to witness a commercial contract but only one man, Hanson replied that the fact that a woman was mentioned at all had to be seen as significant progress for that time. Hanson did not say whether in Islamic law today, two women would be needed to witness a financial contract if one man could not be found. In Britain, it is Hanson and Ramadan who command the biggest audiences. Their more prescriptive style of speaking is particularly appealing to those Muslims (perhaps the majority) who are used to authority figures telling them how they should live.[96] According to a Danish report, the European Council for Fatwa and Research is working on a constitution for European Muslims which will be above national legislation. This council has close ties to the Muslim Brotherhood. Its spokesman is Ramadan, despite his reputation of representing a more 'liberal' European Islam.[97]

While the few Muslim reformers in Europe are struggling to convince their Muslim and non-Muslim constituencies that change is feasible, alert writers are pointing to the recent research by westerners that sadly indicates the contrary. Bruce Bawer's book, *While Europe Slept: How Radical Islam is Destroying the West from Within*, considered by its reviewer a 'stunner of a book about continental Islam', has two main themes. The first is that Europe has a Muslim immigration and reproduction problem. This radically new and explosive demographic is not being converted to western liberalism or adopting western lifestyles. The shocking claim by Bawer is that well before 2050, most of Europe is likely to become an outpost of Islamdom governed by shari'a. The second theme is that Europe today is a hellhole of leftist multiculturalism, far worse than anything in America, and even far worse than almost anyone in America suspects. American expatriate Bawer – who has lived in various European countries, mostly Holland and Norway – is almost uniformly horrified by every country he resides in or visits. According to him, political correctness and multiculturalism are 'a habit of thought that in America is an annoyance but in Europe is a veritable religion'. Bawer excoriates his European friends for their propensity to display phoney 'respect' and 'understanding' of the various foreigners in their midst. He disparages their cult-like belief in the mantra of multiculturalism and their unlimited 'belief in peace and reconciliation through dialogue', even with Islamists who emphatically reject peace, reconciliation, and dialogue as methodologies or ideals. *While Europe Slept* also makes the interesting observation that there is virtually no American-style 'religious right' to oppose growing Muslim power. Virtually the whole continent is atheist or *de facto* atheist. This leads to some odd political terminology and alliances. Bawer consistently champions what he calls 'the liberal resistance', but he doesn't seem to know where to find it. He describes how much the multicultural left protects Islamism and the evil alliance they have formed in the heart of western civilization. Bawer calls himself a part-time 'libertarian' and is essentially a classical liberal.[98]

While Europe Slept has plenty of documentation for its claims from almost every nation in Europe. Bawer's fluency in Dutch and Norwegian helps provide quotations, incidents, and stories from all over the continent – many based on personal experience. In the end, this book writes off Europe, arguing that America is the last hope for western civilization. Perhaps the most terrifying part of the book is the way Muslims are confidently planning to rule Europe and make it part of the Caliphate. A popular Swedish T-shirt reads simply '2030 – then we take over'. The leading Parisian newspaper *Le Monde* seems to have already surrendered. In 2004, it praised France for 'the fact of its having and accepting the role of the first Muslim country of Europe'. The problem had begun in the late 1960s and 1970s, with a temporary labour shortage and subsequent special 'guest worker' programmes. But the shortage is long gone and the Muslims are still there without being integrated into the various populations. Most Muslims utterly reject their new country and its western liberal ideology. This growing problem is exasperated by a phenomenon unknown in America called 'fetching' marriages. Muslim males use 'family unification' laws to bring in illiterate females they've never met from their former country, and then marry them – usually as uneducated teenagers. The young girls are then kept at home in a virtual prison where they reproduce wildly. These new citizens never learn the local languages or customs but they do qualify for vast welfare benefits and quickly produce more Islamist-oriented males and submissive females, perpetuating the cycle all over again. The effect of all these Muslims on the lifestyles of Europeans is simply remarkable. Homophobia has increased, as has opposition to abortion and divorce. 'Honour killings' are common as is female 'circumcision'. In many parts of Europe all women must cover their face lest they be deemed whores. By 'right', any Muslim or Muslim gang can rape any uncovered girl. Afterwards, the girl is properly killed by relatives to end the 'shame' of her family. The rapists, naturally, go unpunished. And because native Europeans differ on this practice, many Muslims scornfully think of all white men as weak and effeminate for not being able to control their women.[99] Among the nightmare statistics cited by the book are these:

1. Eighty per cent of the women in Oslo's shelter system are Muslims fleeing abusive families, husbands, and boyfriends.
2. Danish Muslims make up 5 per cent of the population but 40 per cent of the welfare rolls.
3. Amsterdam is now majority Muslim.
4. Seventy per cent of all French prisoners are Muslim.
5. The four London bombers who killed fifty-two in July 2005 received almost a million dollars in welfare benefits.

Another concern of Europeans that reflects the fear of further Islamization is manifested in the reluctance to absorb Turkey with its seventy-five million Muslims. After years of single-mindedly championing European integration, the European Commission has finally been told that it must take into account a revolutionary new factor when drawing up policy: public opinion. Instead of brushing aside the views of ordinary citizens as no more than a nuisance, the EU executive has been instructed by Europe's leaders to take account of 'perception by citizens' when deciding whether the EU should be further enlarged. According to the commission's own survey, 52 per cent of people in the EU oppose Turkish membership, with Britain one of the few countries where those in favour outnumber those against.[100]

The growing western impatience with Muslims has highlighted an interesting parallel with the Irish conflict. Monsignor Denis Faul, who died in 2006, was not merely the best-known Roman Catholic parish priest of the Northern Ireland Troubles; his life also contains profound lessons for democracies on how to fight, and not to fight, terrorism. Faul gained prominence in the British press in the 1970s for his exposure of security force excesses. He incurred the wrath of Sinn Fein-IRA for relentlessly criticizing republican human rights abuses which in his view created a more oppressive atmosphere in the Catholic ghettos than had ever existed during the pre-1997 period of British direct rule. He was fond of citing Pastor Martin Niemoller's famous remark about the rise of Nazism: 'First they came for the Communists, and I didn't speak up because I wasn't a Communist. Then they came for the Jews and I didn't speak up because I wasn't a Jew. Finally, when they came for me, there was no one left to speak up.' The consistency in Faul's approach, contends Dean Godson, was also organizational. Faul was one of the key hidden hands behind Families Against Intimidation and Terror, established in the early 1990s by Henry Robinson, a former Official IRA member, to highlight republican punishment beatings and exilings.[101] Faul supplied Robinson with the blueprint that he had employed in exposing the British Army: taking photographs and witness statements and then giving them the widest possible audience. It was a masterpiece of political warfare, exposing 'freedom fighters' for what they were.

For much of his career, Faul had been a schoolmaster, and frequently told those teenagers who seemed seduced by the lure of violent republicanism: 'If you're lucky, you'll spend twenty years in prison. And if you're not lucky, your mother will be handed a folded tricolour at your graveside. And if you go to prison or die it will sooner or later emerge that your commanding officer was a tout, and that his commanding officer was a tout too. And whilst you're rotting away, they will be getting off scot-free.' If only more imams in Britain today spoke like that to young Muslims tempted by jihad, remarked Godson. Faul felt that though the British state was clever, it had cynically sold out the ordinary decent Catholics for the sake of an accommodation with republican fascists. Faul believed that Britain, by unthinkingly accepting trendy narratives of British oppression, had actually underrated its own reformist achievements in Northern Ireland. Justice mattered as much, if not more, than Irish unity. He believed passionately in Ulster's superlative grammar school system, and wanted to erect statues in nationalist areas to R.A. Butler, author of the Education Act 1944, on the ground that he had liberated far more poor Catholic youngsters than a host of republican martyrs. He deplored the Blair Government's decision to phase the local grammars out as another sop to Sinn Fein-IRA. Yet

Faul was rather unappreciated by the British authorities. This was particularly odd, since Whitehall has traditionally liked working with conservative clergyman across the world to stabilize conflict zones. But too many of Britain's clerical partners in Ulster were far more Anglophobic and subversive than Faul. There is a lesson here as the British state is again embarked on a strategy of working with religious reactionaries to becalm the Muslim ghettoes. Who is the real moderate and who is the bogus moderate?[102]

There is no room for doubt about the pernicious influence of Muslim clerics and self-appointed representatives. Events in Jerusalem in the summer of 2007 demonstrate that it is possible for them to calm and restrain their followers, in keeping with the norms and conventions expected of spiritual leaders. A gay pride parade angered Orthodox Jews in the city, and many *yeshiva* (Jewish seminary) students demonstrated to have it banned. Leading Orthodox rabbis and *yeshiva* heads, appalled at the property damage and violence perpetrated by the students, prohibited their followers from holding any more street demonstrations. The rabbis sent out a message to thousands of students that the ends did not justify the means. Stopping the gay parade, a 'violation of the sanctity of the Jewish people's holiest city', was commendable, but it did not justify burning garbage bins, breaking streetlights and smashing windows. An announcement on the front page of a daily belonging to the Lithuanian Orthodox group stated: 'Demonstrating should be done by each person in his place by feeling outrage in the soul, by praying and beseeching God against the loathsome blasphemy.' Further, 'Each yeshiva head is responsible for making sure his students do not demonstrate.' A spokesman for the rabbis said they were concerned about the negative educational message resulting from the demonstrations. He noted, 'We don't want our yeshiva students to get the wrong idea that the Torah permits the destruction of property. Rather, all demonstrations must be conducted in a legal, safe way that conforms with *halacha* [Jewish law], which means no destruction of property, either public or private.' Rabbi Ya'acov Aryeh Alter, who heads the Gur Orthodox sect, the largest in Israel, also opposed demonstrating against the parade, but for different reasons. Alter was convinced that they must distance themselves completely from the issue of homosexuality and simply ignore the parade.[103]

It is instructive for Europeans to compare the behaviour of Arab leaders towards incitement in mosques when their positions are threatened, and the way they add fuel to the incitement when the ire of the Muslim masses is directed towards the West or Israel. The Prime Minister of the Palestinian Authority, for example, warned clerics that incitement against his government will not be tolerated in mosques, in a continuing crackdown on Islamists in the West Bank following Hamas's violent takeover of Gaza. Salam Fayyad summoned 800 preachers from across the West Bank and warned them to keep politics out of their pulpits. 'We won't allow them to be turned into places of incitement and intimidation', Fayyad said. 'It's the responsibility of men of religion to present religion as a way of tolerance, not as a cover for bloodshed', adopting the same approach used in Egypt and Jordan in dealing with militancy. Both those governments have banned Islamist movements and carefully monitor what is said in mosques to distance them from political power. Islamist clerics said they would continue to preach as before. 'If they mean stopping people from expressing their political opinion, it will not work', said Ismail Awawdeh, a Hamas member.[104] In contrast to Denis Faul, Muslim leaders in Europe remain silent or worse in the face of mounting terror as though it were not their problem, even after the attacks that killed 254 people in Madrid, London and Amsterdam. Europeans want to know why. Why have so few of them publicly condemned the train and bus bombings in Madrid and London? Why have so few spoken out against the murder of Dutch film-maker Theo van Gogh? Worse, why have so many of them found it expedient to 'understand' and 'justify' some of those horrors, including the cartoon affair on such flimsy grounds as an 'insult to Islam'?

Talk to Europe's mainstream Muslims privately, however, and it turns out they have a lot to say. If one seeks them out in the neighbourhoods where they live and work, they denounce attacks against civilians. Mohammed Azahaf, a student who runs a youth centre in Amsterdam, said, 'If you kill one, it's like killing the whole of mankind', quoting a line from the Qur'an (which runs counter to the murderous history of Islam since its inception). Yet they remain silent out of a sense of shame, or even guilt, that innocents have been killed in the name of Islam; they say those feelings make them seek to be 'invisible'. For those lucky enough to have jobs, there is little time to protest or even write letters to newspapers. For others, there is fear of being branded anti-Islam in their communities. Hundreds of thousands did protest in London against the invasion of Iraq, carrying banners which read, 'Not In My Name'. But neither the MCB nor any other Muslim groups saw fit to make similar public declarations against the wanton murder of their fellow-citizens on 7/7 by their fellow-Muslims. A Muslim rapper turned down requests by a popular Amsterdam radio station to sing a song against terrorism. 'If you sing that, it's like you choose the Dutch, not Muslims', said Yassine Sahsah Bahida, who is popular among Dutch North African youths like himself for his songs against racism. Muslims sing against racism only when they are in the minority, not in their own countries. But there is another reason for the silence. Why, many Muslims ask, should they speak out against actions of radicals who do not represent them? This is a flimsy pretext because no one is more representative of today's Islam than those ready to sacrifice themselves for its cause, and they are certainly the most popular in the Muslim world. Osama Bin Laden has been elevated to the status of a world-class hero amongst Muslims in Arab lands as well as in the West. We have seen that what makes the young Egyptian singer popular in the Muslim world are his songs of hatred against the Jews, Israel and the West, while Nobel Prize laureate Naguib Mahfuz was stabbed for praising the peace treaty with Israel.[105]

Many find the very idea of being asked or expected to denounce acts of terrorism 'extremely offensive and insulting', said Khurshid Drabu, a senior member of the MCB. It should be the reverse: if those terrorists are usurpers of Islam, they should be denounced and condemned by every Muslim. Why do Muslims protest every time they think that non-Muslims wrong them, while they suddenly detach themselves when Muslims wrong others? And even if they do not think it is their responsibility to denounce acts of other Muslims, at the very least they should refrain from the widespread and repulsive expressions of jubilation when disaster strikes the West. This silence gives the terrorists strength. 'Isn't silence, justification, fear and hesitation in condemning terrorism, a factor in the encouragement of these individuals to appear on numerous platforms and satellite channels and claim that they represent a religion in the absence of active influential groups and institutions?' asked a blog entry by Ahmed al-Rabei, a Kuwaiti journalist who works for London-based newspaper *al-Sharq al-Awsat*. 'Isn't it a tragic crime to label the millions of European Muslims as guilty because of the rhetoric (and horrible deeds) of a few professional lunatics, while the rest remain silent and wallow in self-pity? We have to admit that Islam has been hijacked particularly in European countries.' Again, others are to blame; it is the Islam that was 'hijacked in European countries' that causes the turbulence. Muslim leaders say they and other Muslims have marched in a number of anti-terrorism rallies in Europe, the largest of which was held on the first anniversary of Madrid's 2004 bombings; and Muslims can't be expected to pour into the streets every day. They also say they have condemned the attacks in the media. Surveys indicate a small but significant number of Europe's Muslims actively support the terrorists, in addition to those who support them tacitly. In a poll of British Muslims after 7/7, 6 per cent thought the bombings were justified. Another 24 per cent condemned the attacks but had some sympathy with the bombers' grievances. Other sympathizers did not show up in the polls. Many Europeans blame the continent's Muslim leadership, which they accuse of making ambiguous and qualified condemnations that give the impression they are making excuses for the bombers: grievances over the war in Iraq or the West's support for Israel. 'It's the leaders who are most responsible', said Rory Miller, senior lecturer in Mediterranean Studies at King's College, London.[106]

But the reason most choose not to protest is far simpler – they do not believe that Muslims were responsible for the attacks. A survey of 500 British Muslims taken by Channel 4 News in June 2007 shows that nearly 59 per cent believe that Muslims were not responsible for 7/7, and 24 per cent believe the UK Government staged them. They believe, too, that the government fabricated the 'martyrdom' videos of the killers admitting responsibility for the bombings, and even the CCTV images of the four men en route to London. The survey was released on the same day that Tony Blair attended a conference on Islam and insisted Muslims 'overwhelmingly' wanted to be 'loyal citizens'.

Another facet of the awakening of Europe in view of the Islamic threat against it has been its reconsideration of its Middle Eastern policies, namely lowering the profile of Palestinism that it had been committed to uncritically, and its substitution by a more balanced view of the Arab conflict with Israel. Surveys conducted among 'opinion elites' in Europe show that support for the Palestinians has fallen precipitously, according to a leading international pollster, Stan Greenberg. Greenberg singled out France as the country where attitudes had changed most dramatically. In 2003, 60 per cent of French respondents said they took a side in the Israeli–Palestinian conflict, of whom four out of five backed the Palestinians. Today, by contrast, 60 per cent of French respondents did not take a side in the conflict, and support for the Palestinians had dropped by half among those who did express a preference. At the root of the change, said Greenberg, was a fundamental remaking in Europe of the 'framework' through which the conflict is viewed. The conflict was formerly perceived 'in a post-colonial framework'. There was a sense that Europe could cancel out its own colonial history by taking the Palestinian side. The US was seen as a global 'imperial' power, added Greenberg, and the fact that it was backing Israel only added to the sense of the Palestinians as victims. France, with the largest Muslim population – an entirely Arab Muslim population – with the direct experience of Algeria and the most anti-US positions, was most prey to this mindset. Today, by contrast, the Europeans 'are focused on fundamentalist Islam and its impact on them'. The Europeans were now asking themselves 'who is the moderate in this conflict, and who is the extremist? And suddenly it is the Palestinians who may be the extremists, or who are allied with extremists who threaten Europe's own society.' An increasing proportion of Europeans are concluding that 'maybe the Palestinians are not the colonialist victims', and the question of which side held uncompromising positions had also shifted – to Israel's benefit. The change in attitudes had been accelerated by the fact that former Prime Minister Ariel Sharon, who had been widely regarded as an ideological 'absolutist', had surprised Europe with the unilateral withdrawal from Gaza, while the Palestinians had chosen the 'absolutists' of Hamas as their leadership.[107]

What was initially referred to as the 'Arab–Israeli' conflict was deliberately renamed the 'Israeli–Palestinian' conflict by the Arabs after 1967. This ensured that Israel was no longer perceived as 'David' fighting for her existence against a 'Goliath' of twenty-two Arab states. The roles were switched by the simple expedient of transforming the conflict into one between the Palestinians and Israel. Now that the Muslim agenda is threatening the West, the essence of the conflict in the Levant is finally being recognized as an 'Islamist–Israeli' one. Far from being a territorial problem, Israel's conflict with the Arabs is religious and, by extension, ideological. Israel will never be accepted in the Middle East because she is not a Muslim state, and no amount of 'peace processing' will procure an end to the conflict. (In the words of the American political philosopher Irving Kristol, 'Whom the gods would destroy they first tempt to resolve the Arab–Israeli conflict.') No country can be expected to negotiate away her existence, and the Arabs will not settle for less. As for Europe, the shift in public opinion derives not only from European feelings that they now understand the threats looming on their horizons. There is a gradual realization that they share the same side of the divide with long-menaced and perennially isolated Israel, inasmuch as this is no longer a matter of sympathy for a beleaguered nation, but for a potential partner and ally.

The call to jihad is indeed rising in the streets of Europe, and is being answered, according to counter-terrorism officials. Hundreds of young Muslim men are answering the call of terrorist groups affiliated or aligned with al-Qa'ida. Detecting actual recruitments is almost impossible because it is typically done face to face. And recruitment is paired with a compelling strategy to bring the fight to Europe. Members of al-Qa'ida have proven themselves to be extremely opportunistic, both by splitting the Western alliance and focusing their energies on attacking the big countries so as to scare the smaller states. Some Muslim recruits are going to Iraq, but more are remaining home to join cells that could help with terror logistics or conduct operations themselves.[108]

Despite tougher anti-terrorism laws, the police, prosecutors and intelligence chiefs across Europe are struggling to contain the openly seditious speech of Islamic extremists, some of whom have been inciting young men to suicidal violence since the 1990s. Laws to protect religious expression and civil liberties limit what can be done to stop hateful speech. In the case of foreigners, the authorities are often left to seek deportation, a lengthy and uncertain process subject to legal appeals, when the suspect can keep inciting attacks. Less effective means, such as immigration violations, are followed up in order to enforce a deportation order. Omar Bakri carried on a robust ideological campaign until 7/7 when it was abruptly ended. He spent much of his time regaling his young followers with the erotic delights of paradise – sweet kisses and the pleasures of bathing with scores of women – while he also preached the virtues of death in Islamic struggle as a ticket to paradise. He spoke of terrorism as the new norm of cultural conflict, 'the fashion of the twenty-first century', warning western leaders, 'You may kill Bin Laden, but the phenomenon, you cannot kill it – you cannot destroy it.' He added: 'Our Muslim brothers from abroad will come one day and conquer here and then we will live under Islam in dignity.'[109]

A series of perspicacious articles that explain the extent to which jihad has been declared on Europe, while paradoxically the Old Continent has become a place of refuge for world terrorists, will conclude the views on what will become of Europe as this momentous struggle goes on. Reuel Marc Gerecht, already in 2004, saw the menacing picture more clearly and earlier than others. He recalled that in August 1995, a terrorist Islamic group led by a French Muslim from Algeria named Khaled Kelkal attempted, unsuccessfully, to bomb one of France's high-speed trains. Later that year, other bombs exploded in France: two in double-decked commuter rail cars in Paris, one in a trash can along the very bourgeois Avenue de Friedland, another in a Parisian open-air market, and one more in a provincial Jewish school. In all there were nine attacks in three months, which killed ten people and wounded 114. The bombings in 1995 provoked a widespread awareness for the first time in France that the country had a home-grown radical-Muslim problem. Kelkal became radicalized in a French prison, as have hundreds of French Muslims. Many thoroughly secularized French Muslims, who did not have crime-filled youths, have become Islamic radicals, culturally at war with the society that made them.[110]

A small cadre of European scholars, mirrored by a small group of European internal security and intelligence officials, have followed the growth of Islamic radicalism in Europe for nearly twenty years. They know, even if European politicians do not, that Europe's most fearsome Muslim true believers are not products of the Israeli–Palestinian confrontation, or the first Gulf War, or the American troop presence in Saudi Arabia after 1990, or the Algerian civil war, or the Bosnian War, or the strife in Chechnya, or the war in Afghanistan, or the second American war against Saddam Hussein, or the globalization of American culture. These events are banners that men who are already converted to jihad wave as they march to give battle. The 'holy' warriors in Europe do not want to see peace in 'Palestine' any more than Hamas or Osama Bin Laden or Iran's clerical guide Ali Khamenei want to see Israelis and Palestinians solve their problems in two separate coexisting states. They do not care about Israeli settlements. Europe's jihadis are born from the particular alienation that young Muslim males experience in Europe's post-Christian, secular societies. The European jihadis have absorbed the virulently anti-American left-wing currents of continental thought and mixed it with the Islamic emotions of 1,400 years of competition with the Christian West. The globalization of this virulent strain of largely Saudi-financed Islam is growing.[111]

September 11 could not have happened without a European base of operations. Though the State Department wasn't particularly discriminating in issuing visas to Saudis before 9/11, it is more efficient now. The security review of visas granted to Middle Eastern men will only become more stringent with time, doing enormous injustice to the innocent and greatly complicating the operational lives of the guilty. Western European travel documents – which still allow easy access to the US – are essential for al-Qa'ida and its allied organizations. But obtaining travel-worthy false European passports for non-state-supported terrorist organizations is becoming increasingly hard (this is particularly true since the EU forced the Belgians to implement better control of their passports, which had been 'disappearing' routinely in large numbers). Jihadi organizations need European Muslims who can lawfully obtain passports, prompting al-Qa'ida to focus on Muslims who could travel in the West. If al-Qa'ida cannot enlist and train American Muslims to strike within the US – and the evidence suggests that al-Qa'ida has done a poor job of finding American Muslims who need to kill non-Muslim Americans to express their love of God – then they must enlist European Muslims or risk compromising the most important element in their recruitment call to jihad. America is the cutting edge of western civilization, and modern jihadis want to terrify their enemy's advance guard, not the more lightly armed, less threatening Europeans. While assisting American counter-terrorist efforts (the French have been superb allies since 9/11), Europeans have chosen to distance themselves from the US and promote a pro-Muslim, pro-Arab outlook, and maintain their current official analysis of the Israeli–Palestinian conflict as the crux of all the friction between the Muslim world and the West.[112]

Jihadi war levies an incalculable price on western economies. Hugh Fitzgerald[113] tried at least to ask the right questions, without venturing into gauging the cost. What is the actual expense caused by the large-scale presence of Muslims in the West? What is the cost of guarding every subway train and station, every bus station, every railroad station, every airport, and many planes? What is the cost of guarding synagogues and Jewish day schools, churches and Christian schools, Hindu temples? What is the cost of guarding the outspoken – from Ayaan Hirsi Ali and Geert Wilders to Carl I. Hagen in Norway? What is the cost of protecting pipelines, water treatment plants, nuclear reactors? What is the cost of seeking and monitoring terrorist suspects, whose support may range from active participation and planning, to giving refuge, fundraising and propaganda? What does it cost to investigate, arrest, and try people? What does it cost to pay for a whole network of informers? Some muse that more people make a living from terror than die from it, but this is not far from the truth. But now – is it tens of billions or hundreds of billions a year? The mistake need never have been made in the first place, if Islamic fundamentalism had been understood before admitting their people into the West in large numbers. Added to the vast sums spent on foreign aid to Muslim countries, which for some amounts to *jizya* (the poll tax imposed on *dhimmis)*, and the time spent on security checks, the total is incalculable. In contrast, it would not cost very much to develop and enforce sane immigration policies, based on an acknowledgment that those who want to replace western societies with shari'a states are not welcome. Another aspect of the cost is the propaganda war (*da'wa*) waged against the West in general, which erodes its resilience. Had the authorities heeded a decade ago the counsel to be more circumspect and in absorbing bogus refugees and asylum seekers, the situation would have been different today. Current attempts to counter the threat, to placate public opinion, are largely too little and too late.

Western governments have been far too naive in their recruitment policies in sensitive areas. After the third major Dutch terrorism trial ended in an acquittal, the government approved a large budget increase for the intelligence service to recruit extra staff. However, a newly hired Arabic translator at the agency, Outman ben Amar, was arrested and charged with mailing terrorism suspects copies of their wiretapped conversations.[114] But the more experienced western security apparatuses become, the more the terrorists augment their efforts at recruiting 'white' Muslims, from among imported Muslims of fair complexion like the Bosnians, or European Muslim converts, in order to make suspects more difficult to detect. Tens of thousands of Europeans have embraced Islam in the last decade. Significant numbers of white Britons have been lured into Islamic terrorism, according to a Whitehall report which emerged in the week before the first anniversary of 7/7. The report also revealed that white converts and other British Muslims are joining a 'terrorist career path' after being targeted by radical recruiters at universities or by extremist preachers. The document, entitled *Young Muslims and Extremism*, stated that as many as 16,000 British Muslims 'support' Islamist terrorist acts at home and abroad; up to 208,000 British Muslims defended the terrorist attacks against the US on 9/11; and 416,000 Muslims have admitted that they feel no loyalty towards Britain. The paper disclosed that those Muslims drawn towards terrorism include 'foreign nationals now naturalized and resident in the UK arriving mainly from North Africa and the Middle East, to second and third generation British citizens whose forebears mainly originate from Pakistan or Kashmir'. Whitehall officials confirmed there was a problem of radicalization amongst Muslim converts but have refused to reveal exactly how many were active terrorist suspects.[115]

Western accommodation of Islam, which in itself helps its invasion by Muslims, has produced the adoption of Arabic as a language in its media. Indeed, the media battle for hearts and market share in the Middle East is evolving into a teeming crowd of western news organizations poised to deliver headlines, and geopolitical views, in the language of the Qur'an. Backed by government financing, Germany's public international broadcaster, *Deutsche Welle*, has entered the arena, as have the *BBC World Service* and France's international channel. The state-owned *Russia Today* has plans for a website and Arabic television. The rush of these news organizations reflects a practical approach to the Middle East: conflicts can be influenced by story-telling and a relentless flow of information as well as by missiles and diplomats. But the debate is beginning about whether these foreign broadcasts will create understanding or more bitter conflict. CNN's Eason Jordan admitted in the pages of *The New York Times* that during the Saddam era, his station was careful to report only the accepted Iraqi narrative of the day.[116] The usual potential risks were apparent when about 500 Iraqi followers of a radical Shi'ite cleric attacked the Iranian consulate in Basra, Iraq, in anger over talk show commentary on al-Kawthar, an Iranian satellite television channel that broadcasts in Arabic. In March 2003 the state-owned Spanish news agency EFE started an Arabic service with financing from the Foreign Affairs Ministry, concentrating on reaching African media outlets in some of the countries closest to Spain: Tunisia, Mauritania and Morocco, the latter being the home country of several terrorists involved in the Madrid bombings.[117]

In Denmark, the anti-immigration Danish People's Party is proposing to set up what it calls an Arab version of Radio Free Europe through the national public broadcaster, Danmarks Radio, tapping a 100-million-kroner fund set up in 2003 by an initiative called the 'Danish as an Arab'. Soren Espersen, the Danish People's Party's foreign policy spokesman, said: 'We feel that there is a lack of democracy in Arab countries, and that was the reason for the crisis with the cartoons. It's important that they get discussions about democracy.' For the newcomers, the keys to success are credibility and performance. Already, more than 200 free television channels cover the Arab region on the satellites Arabsat and Nilesat, with 10 per cent devoted to news, according to Judeh Siwady, a media analyst with Arab Advisors Group. That includes the American-backed station *al-Hurra*, which, according to the Arab Advisors surveys, lags far behind the news leaders, the Qatar-based *al-Jazeera* and the Saudi station *al-Arabiya*. *Al-Jazeera* is undoubtedly the most trusted news source, while few western channels are likely to have a following. 'People will have a look' at the new foreign channels, said Nasib Bitar, a Dubai-based producer and media consultant. 'It all depends on content and how they run it. I believe if any broadcaster showed compassion through its programming, people would watch. The problem at this stage is that Arabic broadcasting is growing in numbers, but not in quality.' In other words, only those channels which transmit the Arab viewpoint will make an impact, which rather defeats the purpose. CNN is holding back for a better commercial opportunity, lacking access to government financing available to the BBC and others. The BBC seems best poised to expand into Arabic broadcasting because of its long history, which dates from the start of its Arabic shortwave radio service in 1938. The organization can leverage its established Middle Eastern presence with more than twelve million radio listeners and 1.5 million unique visitors monthly on the BBC Arabic website. New technology is central to the British and French strategies, with television programming designed to be interactive with Arabic websites. Ahmed al-Sheikh, *al-Jazeera's* editor-in-chief, said the new competition was positive, adding: 'Information is becoming more important than diplomacy. Diplomats sometimes screw things up, but if you play it right via television, then you can achieve so much more.'[118]

The internet has become crucial for radical Islamic terrorists, with official and unofficial websites, forums and chatrooms that appeal to supporters worldwide. One security source described the islamic websites as 'virtual mosques', adding that they can pour out 'a stream of hatred against the West into the bedroom of a susceptible young man and they can do it twenty-four hours a day, every day'. Britain's MI5 tries to keep tabs on these websites but even if home-based ones are shut down, foreign ones are often beyond their reach unless an overseas government is prepared to help. Terrorist websites have grown from a dozen in 1998 to an estimated 5,000 today. The structure of the internet reflects the pattern of modern terrorist organizations, with loose-knit networks of cells. The websites can be used to raise funds, recruit members and plan and execute attacks. They can show how to make a bomb and where to plant it to cause maximum carnage.[119] Extremists post messages and images on password-protected sites. From his exile in Beirut, Omar Bakri has discussions with his followers on a webcast. The webcasts can run several times a week, and up to seventy people a night log in, each with an individual password. The growing use of webcasts and websites by extremists has been highlighted by Ed Husain, a former jihadi. 'There is an unchallenged, unreported Islamist underworld in the UK in which talk of jihad, bombings, stabbings, killings and executions is usual. Rhetoric is an indication of a certain mindset and, I think, the prelude to terror. In internet chatrooms ... the Islamists break news of beheadings in Iraq, the downing of US helicopters and discuss who is next on their agenda of killing and destruction.' Husain warned: 'Unless we stem the rising tide of radical Islamist rhetoric in Britain, a prelude to jihadism, then the carnage of Baghdad may well erupt in Bradford and Birmingham.' The EU announced that it wanted to strengthen its monitoring of radical Islamist websites.[120] But free speech on the internet is also under threat from draconian new laws, which could see bloggers imprisoned for up to three years. Europe's Justice Ministers have agreed genocide denial and race hatred legislation that will outlaw remarks on the internet 'carried out in a manner likely to incite violence or hatred'. The legislation goes beyond German or Austrian-style bans on Holocaust-denial to cover those people who question the official history of recent conflicts in Africa and the Balkans.[121]

At a conference of international experts in terrorist use of the internet in Eilat, Israel, Gabriel Weimann of Haifa University explained that terrorists 'narrow-cast' their messages to 'trap' selected audiences of adherents. Taking this further, Boaz Ganor, of the Israeli Interdisciplinary Centre and a specialist in anti-terrorism, showed how the 'captured' adherents are then indoctrinated into radicalization by emphasizing a problem, such as threats posed by a common enemy or humiliation suffered by Muslims at the hands of their adversaries. Emphasizing the religious obligation of Muslims to confront their enemies and the challenge to their faith is the common denominator that binds the audience into their new virtual community. Segments of this community are then activated into a variety of activities on behalf of the terrorist group, such as fund-raising, recruitment, training and warfare. The different types of terrorist activities on the internet require appropriately differentiated responses. As outlined by Weimann, one such response is based on monitoring, using and disrupting. First, terrorist websites need to be monitored to learn about their mindsets, motives, persuasive 'buzzwords', audiences, operational plans and potential targets for attack. These sites will also reveal whom they consider to be their political and religious authorities, as well as moderate religious clerics they regard as particularly threatening. Monitoring also reveals their inner debates and disputes. Second, counterterrorism organizations need to 'use' the terrorist websites to identify and locate their propagandists, chatroom discussion moderators, Internet service provider (ISP) hosts and participating members. Third, terrorist websites need to be 'disrupted' through negative and positive means. In a negative 'influence' campaign, sites can be infected with viruses and worms to destroy them, or kept 'alive' while flooding them with false technical information about weapons systems, circulating rumours to create doubt about the reputation and credibility of terrorist leaders, or inserting conflicting messages into discussion forums to confuse terrorists and their supporters. In a more positive approach, alternative narratives can be inserted into these websites to demonstrate the negative results of terrorism or, to potential suicide bombers, to suggest the benefits of the 'value of life' versus the self-destructiveness of the 'culture of death and martyrdom'.[122]

John Reid, then-British Home Secretary, warned of the 'devastating consequences' of cyber terrorism. He said priority was being given to protecting the country's critical national infrastructure from terrorist attack. Reid said there was an additional threat of a terrorist assault on the West's twenty-first century electronic communication systems. According to the US Federal Bureau of Investigation, cyber terrorism is any 'premeditated, politically motivated attack against information, computer systems, computer programmes, and data which results in violence against non-combatant targets by sub-national groups or clandestine agents'. A cyber terrorist attack is designed to cause physical violence or extreme financial harm. The US Commission of

Critical Infrastructure Protection says possible cyber terrorist targets include the banking industry, military installations, power plants, air traffic control centres, and water systems.[123]

For *The Washington Post* columnist Robert Samuelson, 'Europe as we know it is slowly going out of business.'[124] Political consultant Don Feder is not more optimistic in his analysis. The population theories of Thomas Robert Malthus turned out to be completely erroneous, and the western world now faces the reality of depopulation. Since the 1970s, worldwide fertility rates have been cut in half. In all, fifty-nine nations with 44 per cent of the world's people have below-replacement birth rates. To maintain a stable population requires a birth rate of 2.1 children per woman. Italy's rate is 1.2. In Spain, the average is just 1.15. Russia is losing 700,000 people a year by attrition. If the trend isn't reversed, by 2050, the nation could lose one-third of its current population (146 million). For decades, western society has inculcated an anti-family ethos, under the sway of feminists, environmentalists, and those wedded to zero population growth and other assorted utopias. Selfishness was celebrated. Marriage and children were downgraded to lifestyle options. Women who stayed at home to raise and nurture a family were derided. The importance of fathers was downplayed. Abortion was enshrined as a 'human right'. And contraception was ubiquitous. Exacerbating the trend, in the post-war period, most industrialized nations rapidly secularized. In western Europe, weekly church attendance has fallen to 5 per cent, compared with 30–40 per cent in the United States (which has a replacement-level birth rate of 2.1). Faith is the strongest incentive for family formation and procreation. Mormon Utah has the highest birth rate in America. Worldwide, it is traditional Catholics, Orthodox Jews and evangelical Christians who are having large families.[125] Now, with Europe's population dwindling, talk of a united Europe challenging America is a fantasy, for according to economist Samuelson, 'It's hard to be a great power if your population's shrivelling.' It's also hard to maintain a social insurance system with a demographic deficit. According to the US Census Bureau, about one-sixth of the population in Western Europe is 65 and older. By 2030 that would be one-quarter, and by 2050 almost one-third.[126]

The question remains whether the West will confront the danger growing within before it is too late. Osama Bin Laden did the West an inadvertent favour by attacking America so spectacularly as early as 2001. He alerted the West to the gathering menace posed by a totalitarian ideology, albeit dressed in religious garb, at a time when its adherents had not yet reached a critical mass in Europe. In an age of political correctness and a fetish for 'dialogue', 'negotiation' and 'peace processing' (always concluding with concessions to the more obdurate side to convey the impression of 'progress') as remedies for all friction, westerners had been ill-served by their leaders and media regarding the realities of Islamic aggression. Similarly, all attempts by western governments to encourage 'integration' or 'social cohesion' are doomed to failure. Latterly, the EU announced plans to set up a network of bomb disposal units to share intelligence and to share air passenger data within Europe and track stolen or lost explosives. It also plans to make it a criminal offence to spread bomb-making instructions via the internet. EU Justice Commissioner Franco Frattini will canvass the twenty-seven member states on how they handle religious education to prevent Islamist radicalization. 'The idea under discussion is to have a European Islam', he said.[127] But whether the latest fad is to train imams in Europe, enforce 'positive discrimination' on employers, introduce 'citizenship classes' or policies to 'win hearts and minds', the results are sure to be meagre. 'Winning hearts and minds' is itself a phrase based on muddled thinking. It places the onus for integration on westerners rather than on the shoulders of those who voluntarily made Europe their home. They were welcomed with excessive assistance, in contrast to previous immigrant groups who found a niche for themselves without welfare benefits. If the responsibility for integrating themselves is taken from the Muslims, their host countries cannot expect anything other than a relentless escalation of demands for further 'special treatment', always accompanied by threats of violence or worse. Immigrants may live here, work here, contribute their share towards the welfare state and enjoy the benefits it offers. They may practise their religion in their homes and houses of worship, but the public square is for everyone.

A hijab is acceptable, but fully-veiled women are not because of the security risks. They should be treated like everyone else, and no 'special pleading' should be countenanced for them in any public sphere or public service as a distinct religious group. In Europe, all politics is conducted via the ballot box, and it is through that channel alone that they may seek change. As for the terrorists themselves, there are a number of ways to severely curtail their motivation. Those who plan to murder civilians should know that they will have forfeited their 'human rights', and will be instantly deported in the case of foreign-born terrorists and imprisoned for life if born in Europe. Terrorists and their families who have been naturalized should have their citizenship withdrawn, leading to deportation. Another useful deterrent is the confiscation of assets. There should be restrictions on legal aid for those taking advantage of this facility by unnecessarily prolonging their cases. Treason law should be updated so that those who preach the destruction of their countries can be charged with sedition. In October 2006, a 28-year-old 'loner' became the first American charged with treason since 1952, for appearing in a succession of al-Qa'ida videos under the guise of 'Azzam the American'. He was charged in his absence, and he is thought to be in the tribal areas of Pakistan.[128]

This is a war for supremacy, with occasional 'ceasefires' thrown in by the Islamists in order to help them regroup. Western governments owe it to their citizens, native and immigrant alike, to convey the simple truth that it is not possible to negotiate with those who openly seek your destruction. It is not too late for the West to reverse the tide. The lack of willpower rests with the governments and particularly the unelected bureaucrats of the European Union – their populations have repeatedly shown signs of being far ahead of their rulers in sensing the dangers, although a reticence to forgo welfare benefits remains. In summer 2007, over half of Europeans voiced support for a pre-emptive military strike to prevent Iran from acquiring nuclear weapons (while their governments continue to equivocate), according to a poll released by Open Europe, a London think tank. However, the survey of more than 17,000 Europeans in March 2007 conducted by the French polling firm TNS-Sofres found little support for increasing military expenditures to counter the threat. In response to the statement, 'We must stop countries like Iran from acquiring nuclear weapons, even if that means taking military action', 52 per cent of Europeans agreed, 40 per cent disagreed and 8 per cent stated they were undecided. Questioned as to the threat their countries faced from 'Islamic fundamentalism', European opinion was more varied. While 58 per cent agreed radical Islam was a serious threat, the national responses ranged from 71 per cent in Britain, 66 per cent in Germany, 64 per cent in France, to 24 per cent in Latvia. EU Government budgets reflect public antipathy towards military spending. European Defence Agency statistics show that the EU spent US$255 billion on defence in 2005, less than 4 per cent of all government expenditures, a rate roughly one half of total US figures.[129] In contrast, European Foreign Ministers again displayed their weakness by failing to back Britain in a threat to freeze the €14 billion trade in exports to Iran when British marines were taken hostage. EU Foreign Ministers meeting in Germany called for the sailors to be freed but ruled out any tightening of lucrative export credit rules. The EU is Iran's biggest trading partner. France, Iran's second-largest EU trading partner, cautioned that further confrontation should be avoided. The Dutch said it was important 'not to risk a breakdown in dialogue'.[130]

In a column entitled 'Winning Muslim hearts and minds', Michael Burleigh wrote that the current war will be won or lost not just by soldiers, spies, and policemen, but ultimately by the wider public. He believes the public should expand the circle of what it takes a sympathetic interest in, so that the ongoing debate is not left to the Islamic radicals by default. What happened, for example, to the 5,000 Africans maimed by al-Qa'ida bombs in 1998? Did the children blinded by flying glass get an education? Islamist fundamentalists should not be left to equate western culture with trashy television programmes rather than Bach, Rubens or Mozart, Newton, Pascal or Einstein. As the philosopher Roger Scruton has written, we should be more careful about what image (and reality) the West projects into more traditional societies. Burleigh continued:

> Far too often we concede too much to the terrorists' vision, not only of us, but of themselves. How exactly would the Caliphate of Bin Laden's imaginings be governed? Hardly at all, judging by the carnage that enveloped Afghanistan

under the Taleban. What precisely do the self-appointed emirs and imams know about Islam? How do you subvert the cultural supremacy of Arabic within it? Surely we should be encouraging authoritative voices that regard radical jihadists as heretics rather than kow-towing to useless so-called 'community' leaders? We also unconsciously seem to accept the purity of motive of people prepared to immolate themselves, which is what suicide-homicide is intended to achieve ... How many suicide bombers have dysfunctional pasts involving adultery, criminality or prostitution? How much are the Saudis or Iranians paying posthumously for each 'performance'? ... We are entitled to have accurate information about immigration, with open discussion of its cultural, as well as economic, merits and demerits. Clear lines need to be established about what the majority of people here are prepared to tolerate, for toleration is not some open-ended, one-way arrangement.

Burleigh concluded by asking: 'What do Australian, Dutch, French or Israeli intelligence agencies have to say on these subjects, for our own do not have a monopoly of wisdom?'[131]

When the attacks on a London nightclub and Glasgow Airport were thwarted in June 2007, *The Times* had some stern advice for the government: 'It is time the government admitted that all the compromises forced on it by the provisions in the European Human Rights Convention are inadequate. The legislation, which forbids the return of any suspect to a place where he might face ill-treatment and does not allow any derogation from this clause, is unfit for purpose. Drawn up in another age, it must be replaced by a convention framed for an era of terrorism ... Those who would kill and maim the people who offer them shelter deserve no protection.'[132] Against the background of the thwarted attacks, the Muslim Council of Britain complained that Muslims were being targeted because of the actions of extremists, necessitating an increase in security measures. Muslim spokesmen promptly resorted to their instinctive claims of victimhood. Inayat Bunglawala said 'some people are trying to find a scapegoat for the recent terror attacks we've seen. The very word Muslim seems to be associated with violence and terror.' Shaykh Ibrahim Mogra, the chairman of the Inter-Faith Relations Committee, said he was shocked when worshippers asked him to install security guards at his Leicester mosque. 'But then [with security guards] the place of worship ceases to be that free place where everybody comes to be peaceful.' For years Muslim spokesmen have been allowed to engage in such disingenuous discourse without being challenged, removing their incentive to face up to their responsibilities. Just as Mogra should have been reminded that his fellow-Muslims have imposed heightened security measures on Jewish places of worship for decades, and that few would concur that mosques are places where everybody goes to be 'peaceful', Bunglawala would benefit from hearing that solid empirical evidence underpins the association of Muslims with violence and terror. No western spokesman is allowed to dissemble so blatantly by the media, and journalists owe it to news consumers to introduce some realism into the public debate on terrorism.[133]

The British historian Andrew Roberts drew a distinction between the more muscular response of the English-speaking peoples of the world to terrorism, and that of the rest of the West. He urged the former to unite around their common heritage of values and sacrifice their naivety about the true nature of war – and the losses that inevitably go with it. Otherwise, they could lose the struggle with radical, totalitarian Islam.

> The reason they are under such vicious attack ... is that they represent all that is most loathsome and terrifying for radical Islam. Countries in which English is the primary language are culturally, politically, and militarily different from the rest of the West. They have never fallen prey to fascism or communism, nor were they (except for the Channel Islands) invaded. They stand for modernity, religious and sexual toleration, capitalism, diversity, women's rights, representative institutions – in a word, the future. This world cannot coexist with the implementation of shari'a law. Those who still view this struggle as a mere police action against uncoordinated criminal elements, rather than as an existential war for the survival of their way of life, are blinding themselves to reality. The new British Prime Minister, Gordon Brown, has dropped the phrases 'war on terror' and 'Muslim' or

'Islamic' terrorism from the government's discussion of what Britons are fighting. Car bombs are going off – we just need to find non-threatening ways to describe them.[134]

This panoply of views and concerns emanating from non-governmental circles in Europe points to the backlash that has been rising among thinking Europeans in the face of the bankruptcy of the policies of appeasement and concessions via multi-culturalism, that governments in Europe have followed for too long. By nature, elected governments in liberal democracies must act as firemen who extinguish fires in order to maintain public order and keep their constituencies sufficiently satisfied to re-elect them next time around. Fortunately for the West, its intellectuals and free-thinking agents are there to reflect upon the long term and pull the alarm bells that politicians are too prone to ignore.

NOTES

1. '"Full Facts" Plea on Muslim Village', *ExpressandStar.com*, 4 March 2005.
2. 'Dudley Mosque Refused Planning Permission', *Christian Voice*, 27 February 2007.
3. 'Land Plan becomes Raging Issue', *ExpressandStar.com*, 24 April 2007.
4. David Kennedy Houck, 'The Islamist Challenge to the US Constitution', *Middle East Quarterly*, Spring 2006.
5. See R. Israeli, *Muslim Fundamentalism in Israel* (London: Brassey's, 1993).
6. M. Yegar, *Between Integration and Secession: The Muslim Communities of South-East Asia* (Lanham, MD and New York: Lexington Books, 2002).
7. Stephen Schwartz, 'Islam in the Big House: How radical Muslims took over the American Prison System', *The Weekly Standard*, 24 April 2006.
8. Symbolic of the medieval city of Islamic learning in the heyday of Islam, which was also the blossoming capital of Muslin Spain for centuries.
9. Schwartz, 'Islam in the Big House: How radical Muslims took over the American Prison System'.
10. Ibid. The author Stephen Schwartz is adapted from remarks given to the 'Domestic Security Preparedness Conference' on 12 April, 2006.
11. Jamie Glazov, 'Islamic Imperialism', interview with Efraim Karsh, *FrontPageMagazine.com*, 5 May 2006.
12. Ibid.
13. 'Spain Publishes Public School Primer on Islam', *The Jerusalem Post*, citing *AP*, 18 October 2006.
14. Mathias Döpfner, 'Bush ist dumm und böse', (Bush is stupid and evil), *Die Welt*, 21 April 2004.
15. Mathias Döpfner, 'Europa, dein Name ist feigheit' (Europe, thy name is cowardice), *Die Welt*, 20 November 2004.
16. Henryk M. Broder, 'Hurray! We're Capitulating!', *Spiegel Online*, 25 January 2007.
17. Philip Johnston, 'Rules to Stop "Sham" Marriages Unlawful', *The Daily Telegraph*, 24 May 2007.
18. Jonathan Petre, 'Church Acts to Stem "Sham" Marriages', *The Daily Telegraph*, 23 April 2007.
19. Duncan Gardham, 'Tough Rules Expose Scale of Bogus Marriages', *The Daily Telegraph*, 16 May 2005.
20. Victor L. Simpson, 'Europeans "see need" for Power to Snoop', *AP*, 11 April 2006.

21. Ibid.
22. Stefan Kanfer, 'France vs France: France's Muslim Problem will only get Worse', *City Journal*, Winter 2006.
23. Ibid.
24. Theodore Dalrymple, 'An Update From France', *Wall Street Journal*, 11 February 2006
25. Andrew Alderson and Chris Hastings, 'July 7 Bombs were a "Demo" not Terrorism', *The Daily Telegraph*, 9 April 2006.
26. Ibid.
27. Brigitte Gabriel, 'Muslims Muzzling Memphis', *AmericanThinker.com*, 10 April 2006.
28. Ibid.
29. John Steele, 'Freedom of Speech Row as Talk on Islamic Extremists is Banned', *The Daily Telegraph*, 15 March 2007.
30. Graeme Paton, 'Academic: Extremism Debate is being Stifled', *The Daily Telegraph*, 17 March 2007.
31. Rachel Ehrenfeld , 'When in Rome ...', *The New York Sun*, 19 April 2006.
32. Lorenzo Vidino, 'State Department's Flirting with the Muslim Brotherhood', 20 April 2006; 'Islamist Extremism in Europe', Hearing before the Committee on Foreign Relations, United States Senate, 5 April 2006.
33. Ibid.
34. MEMRI blog, quoting www.ikhwan.com, Muslim Brotherhood website, April 20, 2007.
35. Richard Ford, 'Anti-terror Laws are an Affront to Justice, says High Court', *The Times*, 13 April 2006.
36. Ben Lando and Hilary Leila Krieger, 'The World must Learn from Israel about Fighting Terror', *The Jerusalem Post*, 22 April 2007.
37. Bruno Waterfield, 'Don't Confuse Terrorism with Islam, says EU', *The Daily Telegraph*, 30 March 2007.
38. David Rennie, 'Islamic Terrorism' is too Emotive a Phrase, says EU', *The Daily Telegraph*, 12 April 2006.
39. Sean O'Neill, 'Muslim Students "being Taught to Despise Unbelievers as Filth"', *The Times*, 20 April, 2006.
40. Al-Muhaqqiq al-Hilli is a thirteenth-century Shi'ite philosopher and jurist. For excerpts of his texts, see Andrew Bostom (ed.), *The Legacy of Jihad* (Amherst, MA: Prometheus Books, 2005), esp. Chapter 20, pp.205–12.
41. O'Neill, 'Muslim Students "being Taught to Despise Unbelievers as Filth"'.
42. 'Preacher Training', Leading articles, *The Times*, 20 April 2006.
43. Colleen Barry, 'EU Proposes Monitoring Radical Mosques', *AP*, 12 May 2007.
44. By Munir al Mawry, 'Arab Intellectuals Receive Death Threats', *Al-Sharq Al-Awsat*, 10 April 2006.
45. Dr Rusty 'John Doe' Shackleford, 'Islamists Post Hit List of Apostates', *The Jawa Report*, 11 April 2006, http://mypetjawa.mu.nu/archives/169819.php.
46. Alexandra Blair, 'Teachers Demand End to State Cash for Faith Schools', *The Times*, 12 April 2006.
47. Renwick McLean, '29 Are Indicted in Connection With Attacks in Madrid', *The New York Times*, 12 April 2006.
48. Ibid.
49. David Rennie, 'Spain to Free 1,500 Illegal Immigrants into Europe', *The Daily Telegraph*, 12 April 2006.
50. Fiona Govan, 'The Hole in the Ground that could Connect Africa with Europe', *The Daily Telegraph,* 10 April 2007.
51. Philip Johnston, 'EU told to Open Door to 20m Migrant Workers', *The Daily Telegraph*, 14 September 2007.
52. Jason Webb, 'Citizenship call from Spain's uneasy Muslim past', *Reuters*, 21 June 2007.
53. Evelyn Gordon, 'The War against Islamic Extremism', *The Jerusalem Post*, 4 October 2006.
54. Sandro Magister and Renato Martino, 'A Cardinal Out of Control', *Chiesa*, 14 March 2006.
55. Joseph D'Hippolito, 'How Will Rome Face Mecca?', *FrontPageMagazine.com*, 6 April 2006.
56. See Boris Havel, excellent unpublished dissertation, submitted to the Hebrew University of Jerusalem (2004/5), *Why Western Scholars of Religion Profess that Christians and Muslims Worship the Same God.*

57. Daniel Henninger, 'The Pope's Easter, Benedict XVI takes on the Excesses of Secularization and Radical Islam', *Opinion Journal*, 14 April 2006.
58. Joseph D'Hippolito, 'How Will Rome Face Mecca?'.
59. Simon Heffer, 'So are we the Nastiest People in the World?', *The Daily Telegraph*, 16 June 2007.
60. Lead article, 'Labour is to Blame for the Drift to the BNP', *Sunday Telegraph*, 16 April 2006.
61. Ibid.
62. Theodore Dalrymple, 'Is Old Europe Doomed?', http://www.cato-unbound.org/2006/2/06/theodoreDalrymple/is-old-europe-doomed/cato unbound, 6 February, 2006.
63. Ibid.
64. Claire Berlinski, 'Menace in Europe', an interview with Jamie Glazov, *FrontPageMagazine. com*, 7 April 2006.
65. Ibid.
66. David Rennie, 'EU Defence Strategy Snatches Stability from the Jaws of Victory', *The Daily Telegraph*, 3 October 2006.
67. Gerard Baker, 'Confronted by the Islamist Threat on all Sides, Europe Pathetically Caves in', *The Times*, 22 September 2006.
68. Robert J. Samuelson, 'Behind the Birth Dearth', *The Washington Post*, 24 May 2006.
69. Mark Steyn, 'Wake up, Europe. It may already be too Late: Why the Fall and Spring Riot Seasons are Signs of the Coming Apocalypse', *Maclean's*, 5 April 2006.
70. Daniel Pipes, 'A Devastating Thesis', *The Jerusalem Post*, 14 November 2006.
71. Mark Steyn, 'They Report, You Decide', *PowerLine*, November 26, 2006, http://power-lineblog.com/archives/016028.php
72. Ralph Peters, 'The Eurabia Myth', *New York Post*, 26 November 2006.
73. Jeremy Rabkin, 'Vive La Caliphate – Does European Islam mean Islamic Europe?', *The Weekly Standard*, 20 November 2006.
74. 'Minister Welcomes Sharia in Netherlands if Majority wants it', *NIS News*, 13 September 2006.
75. David Pryce-Jones weblog, 'Leading Europe', *National Review Online*, 15 December 2007.
76. Ehrenfeld, 'When in Rome …'.
77. Brendan Bernhard, 'Oriana Fallaci asks: Is Muslim Immigration to Europe a Conspiracy?', *Los Angeles Weekly*, 15 March 2006.
78. 'Krekar Claims Islam will Win', *Aftenposten*, 13 March 2006.
79. Mark Krikorian, 'American Dhimmitude: The Road from Amnesty', *National Review Online*, 30 March 2006.
80. Jamie Glazov, 'Europe's Suicide?', *FrontPageMagazine.com*, 26 April 2006.
81. Alex Alexiev, 'Continental Amnesties', *National Review Online*, 1 May 2006.
82. Ibid.
83. Alasdair Palmer, 'The Bomber's Privacy is Paramount', *Sunday Telegraph*, 26 November 2006.
84. Jeannine Aversa and Katherine Shrader, 'US Gets Access to Worldwide Banking Data', *AP* (Washington), 23 June 2006.
85. Justin Stares and Patrick Hennessy, 'EU Ignores Constitution Vote to Launch Anti-terror Squad', *Sunday Telegraph*, 18 June 2006.
86. 'Freed Guantanamo Inmates take up Arms', *The Age*, 28 July 2007.
87. Steven Swinford, 'Guantanamo no worse than Belmarsh, say MPs', *Sunday Times*, 21 January 2007.
88. Sean O'Neill, 'Guantanamo: a Prison that won't go away – Uncooperative Countries and the Law are Preventing the Bush Administration from Closing its Notorious Camp in Cuba', *Times Online*, 5 June 2007.
89. Paul Willis, 'Govt Requests Release of Guantanamo Inmates', *The Daily Telegraph*, 7 August 2007.
90. Dipesh Gadher, 'Terror Alert on Freed UK Suspects', *Sunday Times*, 12 August 2007.
91. Ehsan Masood, 'Islam's Reformers', *Prospect Magazine*, 124, July 2006.
92. Martin Bright, 'The Great Koran Con Trick', *The New Statesman*, 10 December 2001.
93. Toby Lester, 'What Is the Qur'an?', *The Atlantic Monthly*, January 1999.

94. Ehsan Masood, 'Islam's Reformers'.
95. Ibid.
96. Ibid.
97. 'Islamistisk forfatning i Europa', *P1 Morgen*, 21 June 2006.
98. Andre Zantonavitch, 'Survey of *While Europe Slept: How Radical Islam is Destroying the West From Within*, by Bruce Bawer, 2006', *FrontPageMagazine.com*, 2 June 2006.
99. Ibid.
100. Justin Stares, 'Public Opinion Matters says EU', *Sunday Telegraph*, 25 June 2006.
101. Dean Godson, 'Sharp Lessons from a Turbulent Priest', *The Times*, 23 June 2006.
102. Ibid.
103. Matthew Wagner, 'Haredi Leaders want Protests to Stop', *The Jerusalem Post*, 20 June 2007.
104. Carolynne Wheeler, 'Imams Warned to Keep Politics out of the Pulpit', *The Daily Telegraph*, 30 June 2007.
105. Scheherezade Faramarzi, 'Muslims Address Silence on Europe Attacks', *AP*, 24 June 2006.
106. Ibid.
107. David Horovitz, 'Exclusive: European Support for Palestinians "Crashes"', *The Jerusalem Post*, 3 June 2006.
108. Patrick E. Tyler and Don Van Natta, Jr, 'Militants in Europe Openly Call for Jihad and the Rule of Islam', *The New York Times*, 26 April 2004.
109. Ibid.
110. Reuel Marc Gerecht, 'Is al-Qa'ida a Eurocentric Organization? Holy War in Europe', *The Weekly Standard*, 29 March 2004.
111. Ibid.
112. Ibid.
113. Hugh Fitzgerald, 'What is the Cost?', *Robert Spencer's Jihad Watch*, 26 May 2006.
114. Mark Houser, 'Trials, Violence Divide Netherlands', *Pittsburgh Tribune-Review*, 22 May 2005.
115. Sean Rayment, 'Whites being Lured into Islamic Terror', *Sunday Telegraph*, 2 July 2006.
116. Eason Jordan, 'The News we Kept to Ourselves', *The New York Times*, 11 April 2003.
117. Doreen Carvajal, 'Big Fish Dive into Arab News Stream', *International Herald Tribune*, 18 June 2006.
118. Ibid.
119. Philip Johnston, 'The Websites', *The Daily Telegraph*, 8 November 2006.
120. Andrew Alderson and Miles Goslett, 'Internet Spreads Terror to Britain', *Sunday Telegraph*, 24 June 2007.
121. Bruno Waterfield, 'Bloggers say EU Law will End Free Speech', *The Daily Telegraph*, 20 April 2007.
122. Joshua Sinai, 'Defeating Internet Terrorists', *The Washington Times*, 9 October 2006.
123. George Jones, 'Cyber Terror Threat is Growing, says Reid', *The Daily Telegraph*, 26 April 2007.
124. Robert Samuelson, 'The End of Europe', *The Washington Post*, 15 June 2005.
125. Don Feder, 'Facing the Population Bust', *GrassTopsUSA.com*, 31 May 2006.
126. Ibid.
127. 'Terror-spooked EU: Don't say Muslims', *Daily Mail*, 4 July 2007.
128. Tim Shipman, 'US Loner helps Bin Laden to Taunt Bush', *Sunday Telegraph*, 9 September 2007.
129. George Conger, 'Europe: Majority Supports Strike on Iran', *The Jerusalem Post*, 8 April 2007
130. Tom Baldwin, Dominic Kennedy and David Charter, 'EU Refuses to Back Britain over Call to Threaten Exports Freeze', *The Times*, 31 March 2007.
131. Michael Burleigh, 'Winning Muslim Hearts and Minds', *The Daily Telegraph*, 30 November 2006.
132. 'More than Vigilance, The Government must look anew at the Laws to Defeat Terrorism', *The Times*, Leader, 30 June 2007.
133. Fiona Hamilton, 'Mosques Hire Guards to Protect Worshippers as Imam is Attacked', *The Times*, 13 August 2007.
134. Andrew Roberts, 'At Stake in the Iraq War: Survival of a Way of Life', *The Christian Science Monitor,* 12 July 2007.

Bibliography

Newspapers, Journals, Websites, Broadcasters and Press Agencies
Aftenposten
The Age (Australia)
Agence France-Presse (AFP)
al-Ahram Weekly
American Thinker
Arab News
Associated Press (AP)
Atlanta Journal-Constitution
The Atlantic Monthly
The Australian
BBC News
Catholic Online
Channel 4 (British)
Chiesa
The Christian Science Monitor
Christian Voice
City Journal
Civitas
CNN World News
CNSNews.com
The Columbia Daily Tribune
Commentary Book Review
The Copenhagen Post
Cox News Service
Daily Express
Daily Mail

Daily Pioneer
The Daily Telegraph
The Daily Telegraph Weblog
DPA (German Press Agency)
Deutsche Welle
Dream 2 TV
The Economist
Ein TV
European Magazine
Expatica (News for expats in Germany)
ExpressandStar.com
Financial Times
FrontPageMagazine
GrassTopsUSA.com
Gulf News
Gulf Daily News (Bahrain)
The Guardian
Haaretz
Herald Sun
Human Rights Watch
The Independent
International Herald Tribune, Europe
Islam Online
The Jawa Report
al-Jazeera TV
The Jerusalem Post
Journal Chrétien
Konkret
Kuwait News Agency
Le Point
The Local (English News in Sweden)
L'Express
Little Green Footballs
Los Angeles Times
Los Angeles Weekly
Maclean's
Mail on Sunday
Manar TV
MEMRI (Middle East Media Research Institute)

Middle East Quarterly
Middle East Times
Military Review
Morocco Times
The Nation (Pakistan)
National Review
National Review Online
The New Republic
The New Statesman
New York Post
The New York Sun
The New York Times
The Observer
Opinion Journal
P1 Morgen
Pittsburgh Tribune Review
PowerLine
Prospect Magazine
al-Quds al-Arabi
Reuters
Robert Spencer's Jihad Watch
Sabah (Turkey)
San Antonio Express News
San Francisco Chronicle
The Scranton Times
The Seattle Times
al-Sharq al-Awsat
Spectator
Spiegel Online
The Sun
Sunday Telegraph
Sunday Times
The Times
Times Online
USA Today
Wall Street Journal
The Washington Post
The Washington Times
The Weekly Standard

Die Welt
The Windsor Star
WorldNetDaily
World Politics Review Exclusive
Ynetnews

Books

Bonnivard, Eve and Lefebvre, Barbara, *Élèves sous Influence* (Paris: Audibert, 2005). An extract from the book was published by *Haaretz* (Tel-Aviv), 29 March 2006.

Bostom, Andrew (ed.), *The Legacy of Jihad* (Amherst, MA: Prometheus Books, 2005), esp. Chapter 20, pp.205–12.

Brenner, Emmanuel, *Les Territoires Perdus de la République* (Paris: Mille Et Une Nuits, 2001).

Burns, Robert, *The Crusader Kingdom of Valencia* (Cambridge, MA: Harvard University Press, 1967).

CIA World Factbook (Washington, DC: US Government Printing Office, 2007), 'World Population Statistics', July 2007.

De Aristegui, Gustavo, *The Jihad in Spain: The Obsession to Reconquer al-Andalus* (Madrid: Plaza Edición, 2005).

De Mesquita, Ethan Bueno, *Correlates of Public Support for Terrorism in the Muslim World* (St Louis, MO: Washington University in St Louis, 2006).

Etzioni, Amitai, *From Empire to Community* (New York: MacMillan, 2004).

Eurostat (The Statistical Office of the European Communities, 2007).

Havel, Boris, *Why Western Scholars of Religion Profess that Christians and Muslims Worship the same God* (unpublished Masters Dissertation, submitted to the Hebrew University of Jerusalem, 2004/5).

Heinsohn, Gunnar, *Sohne und Weltmacht: Terror im Aufstieg und Fall der Nationen* (Zurich: Orell Füssli Verlag, 2003).

Huntington, Samuel, *The Clash of Civilizations* (New York: Free Press, 2002 New Edn).

Israeli, Raphael, *Muslim Fundamentalism in Israel* (London: Brassey's, 1993).

Israeli, Raphael, *Islamikaze: Manifestations of Islamic Martyrology* (London: Frank Cass, 2003).

Laqueur, Walter, *The Last Days of Europe: Epitaph for an Old Continent* (New York: Thomas Dunne Books, 2007).

Lewis, Bernard, *Islam* (Paris: Quarto Gallimard, 2006).

Mawdudi, abu al-'Ala', *The Nationalism in India* (Malihabad, 1948).

Phillips, Melanie, *Londonistan: How Britain is Creating a Terror State Within* (London: Gibson Square, 2006).

Rehov, Pierre, Interview with several failed Islamikaze for his documentary 'Suicide Killers'.

Spencer, Robert and Bostom, Andrew, *The Myth of Islamic Tolerance: How Islamic Law Treats Non-Muslims* (Amherst, MA: Prometheus Books, 2005).

Yegar, Moshe, *Between Integration and Secession: The Muslim Communities of South-East Asia* (Lanham, MD and New York: Lexington Books, 2002).

Articles

'A Danish Party Demands Censorship for Qur'an', *Sabah* (Turkey), 25 February 2007.

Adams, Stephen, 'Mohammed may Top List of Boys' Names', *The Daily Telegraph*, 7 June 2007.

al-Alawi, Irfan and Schwartz, Stephen, 'Ken's Mega-mosque will Encourage Extremism', *Spectator*, 6 January 2007.

Alderson, Andrew and Hastings, Chris 'July 7 Bombs were a "Demo", not Terrorism', *The Daily Telegraph*, 9 April 2006.

Alderson, Andrew and Goslett, Miles, 'Internet Spreads Terror to Britain', *Sunday Telegraph*, 24 June 2007.

Alderson, Andrew, Rayment, Sean and Hennessy, Patrick, 'Terror Cell Was Planning Nerve Gas Attack on Capital', *Sunday Telegraph*, 4 June 2006.

Alexiev, Alex, 'Tablighi Jama'at: Jihad's Stealthy Legions', *Middle East Quarterly*, Winter 2005.

Alexiev, Alex, 'Continental Amnesties', *National Review Online*, 1 May 2006.

Alleyne, Richard, 'Cartoon Protester Guilty of Race Hate', *The Daily Telegraph*, 10 November 2006.

Aloisi, Silvia, 'Muslims irked by Italian Senator's "Pig" Comments', *Reuters*, 13 September 2007.

Almond, Peter, 'Beware: the New Goths are Coming', *Sunday Times*, 11 June 2006.

Amr, Wafa, 'Palestinians say fed up with Gunmen', *Reuters*, 7 June 2007.
'Angry Protests after Death of Pakistani in Germany', *Expatica*, 13 May 2006.
Anthony, Andrew, 'A Muslim at Bay: Panorama Programme, BBC1', *The Observer*, 28 August 2005.
'Anti-Semitism and the Turkish Islamist Milli Görüs Movement', cited by MEMRI, Special Dispatch Series, 1699, 29 August 2007.
'A New Broom in Paris, France to Pay Immigrants to Return Home', *Spiegel Online*, 24 May 2007.
Arfa, Orit, 'The Nexus', *The Jerusalem Post*, 12 July 2007.
Attenhofer, Jonas, 'Youth Bulge Violence', *The Jerusalem Post*, 10 April 2007.
Atwan, abdul Bari, TV Clip, MEMRI, 1506, 27 June 2007.
Aversa, Jeannine and Shrader, Katherine, 'US Gets Access to Worldwide Banking Data', *AP* (Washington), 23 June 2006.
Baker, Gerard, 'Confronted by the Islamist Threat on all Sides, Europe Pathetically Caves in', *The Times*, 22 September 2006.
Baldwin, Tom, Kennedy, Dominic and Charter, David, 'EU Refuses to Back Britain over Call to Threaten Exports Freeze', *The Times*, 31 March 2007.
Bannerman, Lucy, 'Islamic School Pledges to Amend Offensive Books', *The Times*, 8 February 2007.
Bar'el, Zvi, 'The Arab Version of the Citizenship Law', *Haaretz*, 1 June 2005.
Barnett, Anthony, Burke, Jason and Smith, Zoe, 'Terror Cells Regroup – and Now their Target is Europe', *The Observer*, 11 January 2004.
Barry, Colleen, 'EU Proposes Monitoring Radical Mosques', *AP*, 12 May 2007.
Bartsch, Matthias *et al.*, 'German Justice Failures – Paving the Way for a Muslim Parallel Society', *Spiegel Online*, 29 March 2007, translated into English by Christopher Sultan.
'Becoming German: Proposed Hesse Citizenship Test', *Spiegel Online*, 9 May 2006. English translation kindly provided by signandsight.com.
Bell, Thomas, 'Malaysia Considers Switch to Islamic Law', *The Daily Telegraph*, 1 September 2007.

Ben Simon, Daniel, 'Harmony or Guerilla War?', *Haaretz*, 27 October 2006.
Ben Simon, Daniel, 'Segolene hasn't come', *Haaretz*, 28 November 2006.
Ben Simon, Daniel, 'Redrawing France's Identity Card', *Haaretz*, 22 April 2007.
'Benedict the Brave – The Pope Said Things Muslims Need to Hear about Faith and Reason', *Opinion Journal*, 19 September 2006.
Bennhold, Katrin and Mekhennet, Souad, 'French Counter-Terror Forces on High Alert', *International Herald Tribune, Europe*, 19 December 2006.
Berglund, Nina, 'Krekar Threatens Norway', *Aftenposten*, 6 September 2005.
Bering, Henrik, 'Sex in the Park – The latest doings of the Danish Imams', *The Weekly Standard*, 27 November 2007.
Berlinski, Claire, 'Menace in Europe', an interview with Jamie Glazov, *FrontPageMagazine.com*, 7 April 2006.
Bernard, Ariane, 'Rioting by Youths in 2 Paris Suburbs Recalls Violence of November (2005)', *The New York Times*, 31 May 2006.
Bernhard, Brendan, 'Oriana Fallaci asks: Is Muslim Immigration to Europe a Conspiracy? ', *Los Angeles Weekly*, 15 March 2006.
Bernstein, Richard, 'Letter from Europe: A Quiz for would-be Citizens tests German Attitudes', *The New York Times*, 29 March 2006.
Beylau, Pierre, *Le Point*, 1727, 20 October 2005, p.25.
'Beyond the Vacuum', *al-Ahram Weekly*, 13–16 April 2006.
Bhat, Devika, 'Catholic Archbishop Questions Turkish Entry to EU', *Times Online*, 21 September 2006.
Bhat, Devika, 'Opera Reignites Islam Row after Cancelling Production', *Times Online*, 26 September 2006.
Bhat, Devika, 'Pope Visits Famous Mosque on Busiest Day of Turkish Trip', *Times Online*, 30 November 2006.
Bhat, Devika and *PA News*, 'Three Found Guilty of Glasgow Race-hate Murder', *Times Online*, 8 November 2006.
Bildt, Carl, 'Egypt of Escalation', *Bildt Comments*, 18 February 2006.
Bird, Steve, 'Sister is Stabbed to Death for Loving the Wrong

Man', *The Times*, 17 June 2006.

Bird, Steve, 'Discriminate for Muslims, Police Urged', *The Times*, 19 June 2006.

'Bishop Criticises "Victim Mentality" of Muslims', *Sunday Telegraph*, 5 November 2006.

Blair, Alexandra, 'Teachers Demand End to State Cash for Faith Schools', *The Times*, 12 April 2006.

'Blair calls on Moderate Muslims to do more to Combat Terror', *The Daily Telegraph*, 4 July 2006.

Blair, David, 'Anti-Americanism Helps Fuel Terror, Warns Australia', *The Daily Telegraph*, 9 February 2007.

Blair, David, 'UN Predicts Huge Migration to Rich Countries', *The Daily Telegraph*, 15 March 2007.

Blair, Tony, Speech to the Los Angeles World Affairs Council, *The Times*, 1 August 2006.

Blakely, Rhys, 'The week on the web', *The Times*, 1 September 2007.

Booth, Jenny, 'Muslim Leaders Accuse Pope of Bigotry', *Times Online*, 15 September 2006.

Booth, Jenny, 'Police Patrol Churches after Pope Controversy', *Times Online*, 19 September 2006.

Booth, Jenny, 'Pope urges Dialogue in Meeting with Muslim Leaders', *Times Online*, 25 September 2006.

Bortin, Meg, 'Poll Finds Discord between the Muslim and Western Worlds', *The New York Times*, 23 June 2006.

Bottum, Joseph, 'Benedict Meets Bartholomew – the Real Reason for the Pope's Visit to Turkey', *The Weekly Standard*, 11 December 2006.

Boyes, Roger, 'Opera Boss Censors Mozart over Stage Beheading of Muhammad', *The Times*, 27 September 2006.

Boyes, Roger, 'Mozart Censor Faces a Backlash', *The Times*, 28 September 2006.

Boyes, Roger, 'A Fright at the Opera: Champions of Mozart Brave Cultural Divide', *The Times*, 19 December 2006.

Boyes, Roger, 'A Winger and a Prayer: the Latest Way to Settle Religious Divisions', *The Times*, 9 July 2007.

Boyes, Roger, 'German Terror Suspect Met 9/11 Hijacker', *Times Online*, 7 September 2007.

Branch, John, *The San Antonio Express-News*, 10 February 2006.

Brandt, Andrea and Meyer, Cordula, 'Religious Divisions Within Germany – A Parallel Muslim Universe', *Spiegel Online*, 20 February 2007.
Bremner, Charles, *Times Online*, 30 May 2006.
Bremner, Charles, 'Analysis: France's Attitude to Terror', *Times Online*, 14 June 2006.
Bremner, Charles, 'Philosophers Demand Help for Teacher on run from Islam Threats', *The Times*, 3 October 2006.
Bremner, Charles, Why 112 Cars are Burning every Day', *The Times*, 21 October 2006.
Bremner, Charles, 'Paris Airport Staff Suspended', *The Times*, 3 November 2006.
Bremner, Charles, 'Immigrants to Face Exam on being French', *The Times*, 14 June 2007.
Bremner, Charles, 'Sarkozy's Star Minister Flounders', *The Times*, 17 July 2007.
Bridge, Mark, 'Ruth Kelly Launches Fund to Fight Islamic Extremism', *Times Online*, 7 February 2007.
Bright, Martin, 'The Great Koran Con Trick', *The New Statesman*, 10 December 2001.
'British Muslims Burn St George's Flag in Furious London Rally over Rushdie Row', *Daily Mail*, 22 June 2007.
Broder, Henryk, 'Hurray! We're Capitulating!' *Spiegel Online*, 25 January 2007.
Brown, David, 'Muslim on Racial Hatred Charges', *The Times*, 3 January 2007.
Brown, Stephen, 'German Train Terror', *FrontPageMagazine.com*, 4 August 2006.
Browne, Anthony and Erdem, Suna, 'Education Clash holds up EU Talks', *The Times*, 8 April 2006.
Bruckner, Pascal, 'Re-Arming Europe – the Old World needs an Intellectual Revolution to meet the Challenges Ahead', *Opinion Journal*, 3 June 2007, translated from the French by Sara Sugihara.
Bunyan, Nigel 'Next Wave of Iraq Suicide Bombers Thwarted', *The Daily Telegraph*, 25 May 2006.
'Father Killed Family for being too Western', *The Daily Telegraph*, 21 February 2007.
Burke, Jason, 'Channel Tunnel is Terror Target', *The Observer*, 24

December 2006.

Burleigh, Michael, 'Winning Muslim Hearts and Minds', *The Daily Telegraph*, 30 November 2006.

Burleigh, Michael, 'Lawyers Sap our Will to Combat Terrorism – We lack the Toughness of our European Neighbours', *Times Online*, 27 July 2007.

Burrell, Ian, 'Newsroom Revolt Forces *Star* to Drop its "Daily Fatwa" Spoof', *The Independent*, 19 October 2006.

'Bus Driver Speaks of his Mental Torment', *The Daily Telegraph*, 7 July 2006.

Butt, Riazat, 'TV Airing for Islam's Story of Christ', *The Guardian*, 18 August 2007.

Byers, David, 'British MP warns Europe of "new Anti-Semitism"', *The Jerusalem Post*, 22 November 2006.

Caldwell, Christopher, 'Youth and War, a Deadly Duo', *Financial Times*, 5 January 2007.

Caldwell, Simon, 'Pope in "Freedom" Blast at Islam', *Daily Mail*, 21 September 2007.

Campbell, Matthew, 'Barbarians of Suburbs Target French Jews', *Sunday Times*, 2 April 2006.

Campbell, Matthew, 'Migrant Ghettos Anger Germany', *Sunday Times*, 30 April 2006.

Campbell, Matthew, 'Minister in the Tower Block gives Sarko Street Cred', *Sunday Times*, 29 July 2007.

Carlin, Brendan, 'Minister Accused over Rushdie may Visit UK', *The Daily Telegraph*, 21 June 2007.

Carvajal, Doreen, 'Big Fish Dive into Arab News Stream', *International Herald Tribune*, 18 June 2006.

Catan, Thomas, 'Christian Soldiers Take a Beating over Battle with Moors', *The Times*, 23 October 2006.

'Channel 4 TV Complaint "Politically Motivated"', *The Daily Telegraph*, 17 August 2007.

Chapman, James, 'Muslims Call for Special Bank Holidays', *Daily Mail*, 14 August 2006.

Charter, David, 'Young Muslims Begin Dangerous Fight for the Right to Abandon Faith', *The Times*, 11 September 2007.

Charter, David, 'Cartoonist Shrugs at Islamic Death Threat: "It's good to know how much one is worth"', *The Times*, 17 September 2007.

Chittenden, Maurice and Baird, Tom, 'MPs don't now their Sunnis from Shi'ites', *Sunday Times*, 7 January 2007.
Coates, Sam, 'Extreme Youth: the Muslims who would Swap British law for Shari'a', *The Times*, 29 January 2007.
Cole, John, *The Scranton Times*, 8 February 2006.
Conger, George, 'BBC Rejects Call to Change Terminology', *The Jerusalem Post*, 29 June 2006.
Conger, George, 'UK MPs Find Leap in Anti-Semitism', *The Jerusalem Post*, 5 September 2006.
Conger, George, 'Europe: Majority Supports Strike on Iran', *The Jerusalem Post*, 8 April 2007.
Connolly, Kate, 'Threats Halt Woman Lawyer who Fought Forced Marriages', *The Daily Telegraph*, 6 September 2006.
Conway, David, 'It is Not Only the Screws Who Are Being Turned in our Prisons These Days', *Civitas*, 26 February 2007.
'Countries Named over Secret Terror Transfers', *The Times*, 28 June 2006.
Cowell, Alan, 'A Suicide Bomb, a Dead Daughter and a Test of Faith', *The New York Times*, 6 May 2006.
Craig, Olga, 'Time to Fight the Good Fightback', *Sunday Telegraph*, 10 September 2006.
Craig, Olga and Palmer, Alasdair, 'What Makes a Martyr?' *Sunday Telegraph*, 13 August 2006.
'Cult of Contempt – The Left must Condemn a Fanaticism that is Misogynist and Homophobic', *The Times*, Leader, 3 July 2007.
Currie, Duncan, 'The Cartoon Wars are Over, We lost', *The Weekly Standard*, 1 May 2006.
Dale, Iain (Diary), 'Sir Ian Blair Says New Terror Attack Could Lead to Internment', *iain-dale.blogspot.com*, 8 October 2006.
Dalrymple, Theodore, 'Our Prisons are Fertile Ground for Cultivating Suicide Bombers', *The Times*, 30 July 2005.
Dalrymple, Theodore, 'Is Old Europe Doomed?', *www.cato.unbound.org/2006./2/06/theodoreDalrymple/is-old-europe-doomed/cato*, 6 February 2006.
Dalrymple, Theodore, 'An Update From France', *Wall Street Journal*, 11 February 2006.
Dalrymple, Theodore, 'I want Sarkozy to be right', *Spectator*, 31 March 2007.
Dalrymple, Theodore, 'Time Out Londonistan – A Modest

Proposal, or a Radical Plot?', *City Journal*, Summer 2007.
'Danes, Swedes Lead Evacuation Race', *AP*, 21 July 2006.
'Danish Editor Burnt Alive', *The Nation* (Pakistan), 15 June 2006, www.nation.com.pk/daily/june-2006/15/index12.php.
'Danish Muslims Sue Newspaper over Cartoons. Lawsuit Seeks $16,100, claims Drawings were "defamatory and injurious" ', *AP*, 30 March 2006.
Darkow, John, *The Columbia Daily Tribune*, 10 February 2006.
de Bruxelles, Simon, 'Refugee's Counter to Political Correctness', *The Times*, 31 March 2006.
Deloire, Christophe, 'La France, Terre de Djihad', *Le Point*, 1727, 20 October 2005, p.36.
Demonpion, Denis, 'Interview with Jean-Claude Marin', *Le Point*, 20 October 2005, p.39.
Dempsey, Judy and Bennhold, Katrin 'Germany Debates Security Measures', *The New York Times*, 8 September 2007.
'Denmark Stood up for Free Speech during Cartoon Crisis', *The Jerusalem Post*, citing *AP*, 1 January 2007.
De Quetteville, Harry, 'Huge Mosque Stirs Protests in Cologne', *The Daily Telegraph*, 25 June 2007.
De Quetteville, Harry, 'German Police Hunt for 10 Terror Accomplices', *The Daily Telegraph*, 7 September 2007.
Devericks, Eric, *The Seattle Times*, 10 February 2006.
D'Hippolito, Joseph, 'How Will Rome Face Mecca?', *FrontPageMagazine.com*, 6 April 2006.
'Dispatches, Unholy War', Channel 4, 17 September 2007.
Donnelly, Laura, 'Doctors Ordered to Act on Forced Marriage', *Sunday Telegraph*, 30 June 2007.
Döpfner, Mathias, 'Bush ist dumm und böse'(Bush is stupid and evil*)*, *Die Welt*, 21 April 2004.
Döpfner, Mathias, 'Europa, dein Name ist feigheit' (Europe, thy name is cowardice), *Die Welt*, 20 November 2004.
Doward, Jamie, 'Revealed: Preachers' Messages of Hate – Muslim Worshippers are being Urged by Radical Clerics to Ignore British Law', *The Observer*, 7 January 2007.
'Dudley Mosque Refused Planning Permission', *Christian Voice*, 27 February 2007.
'Egyptian Girl Dies From Circumcision', *The Jerusalem Post*, citing *AP*, 12 August 2007.
Ehrenfeld, Rachel, 'When in Rome ... ', *The New York Sun*, 19

April 2006.
Ehrenfeld, Rachel and Lappen, Alyssa A., 'Europe's Last Chance', *FrontPageMagazine.com*, 16 February 2006.
Elliott, Francis, 'Tory move to Protect Young Foreign Brides', *The Times*, 25 May 2007.
Evans, Ian, 'Cartoon Protest Muslim is Guilty of Soliciting Murder', *The Times*, 8 March 2007.
Evans, Michael, 'More Britons are Turning to Terror, says MI5 Director', *The Times*, 10 November 2006.
Faramarzi, Scheherezade, 'Muslims Address Silence on Europe Attacks', *AP*, 24 June 2006.
Feder, Don, 'Facing the Population Bust', *GrassTopsUSA.com*, 31 May 2006.
Fitzgerald, Hugh, 'What is the Cost?', *Robert Spencer's Jihad Watch*, 26 May 2006.
Foggo, Daniel and Taher, Abul, 'Imam Backs Terror Attack against Blair: Brighton Mosque Radicalized', *Sunday Times*, 18 June 2006.
Follath, Erich, 'Terror is Glamour', interview with Salman Rushdie, *Spiegel Online*, 28 August 2006.
Ford, Richard, 'Anti-terror Laws are an Affront to Justice says High Court', *The Times*, 13 April 2006.
Ford, Richard, 'Muslim Prisoners at Flashpoint over New Imam's Interpretation of Koran', *The Times*, 21 November 2006.
Ford, Richard, 'Visa Rules will Raise Marriage Age to 21'*The Times*, 29 March 2007.
Forsyth, Frederick, 'Watch Your Language', Letters, *Sunday Telegraph*, 17 September 2006.
'France and Immigration – Let the Skilled Come', *The Economist*, 4 May 2006.
'France Approves Immigration Law That Favours Skilled Workers', *AFP*, 1 July 2006.
'French Jews set up Own Defence League', *The Jerusalem Post*, citing *AP*, 14 June 2006.
'France: No Mass Legalizing of Immigrants', *AP*, 21 May 2007.
'Freed Guantanamo Inmates Take up Arms', *The Age*, 28 July 2007.
Freund, Michael, 'Saudis Arrest Christian for Entering Mecca', *The Jerusalem Post*, 24 May 2007.
Fukuyama, Francis, 'The Wrong Kind of Freedom Endangers the

West', *Sunday Times*, 28 January 2007.

'"Full Facts" Plea on Muslim Village', *ExpressandStar.com*, 4 March 2005.

Gabriel, Brigitte, 'Muslims Muzzling Memphis', *American Thinker.com*, 10 April 2006.

Gadher, Dipesh, 'Terror Alert on Freed UK Suspects', *Sunday Times*, 12 August 2007.

Gardham, Duncan, 'Tough Rules Expose Scale of Bogus Marriages', *The Daily Telegraph*, 16 May 2005.

Gardham, Duncan, 'Muslims Arrested in Old Bailey Demo', *The Daily Telegraph*, 2 November 2006.

Gardham, Duncan, 'Muslim Peer Compares Rushdie to 9/11 Bombers', *The Daily Telegraph*, 22 June 2007.

Gebauer, Matthias and Stark, Holger, 'German Women Vowed to Mount Suicide Attacks in Iraq', *Spiegel Online*, 30 May 2006.

Gedmin, Jeffrey, 'Der Terror ist Da – Germany wakes up, sort of', *The Weekly Standard*, 11 September 2006.

Gerecht, Reuel Marc, 'Is al-Qa'ida a Eurocentric Organization? Holy War in Europe', *The Weekly Standard*, 29 March 2004.

'German Minister: Muslim Women should not Wear Full Face Veil', *DPA* and *Haaretz*, 24 January 2007.

'Germany is Terror Threat "Powder Keg" – Top Prosecutor', *Asia News/Reuters*, 13 May 2006.

'Germany's Muslims Band Together – New Umbrella Group Founded', *Spiegel Online*, 16 April 2007.

Gerstenfeld, Manfred, 'The Muhammad Cartoon Controversy, Israel and the Jews: A Case Study', *Post-Holocaust and Anti-Semitism Series*, 43, 2 April 2006, Jerusalem Center for Public Affairs.

Ghate, Dr Onkar, Ayn Rand Institute of Irvine, CA, 30 March 2006.

Gillerman accuses Moderate Muslims of Silence in Face of Islamic Terrorism', *Ynetnews*, citing *AP*, 22 May 2007.

Glazov, Jamie, 'Europe's Suicide?', *FrontPageMagazine.com*, 26 April 2006.

Glazov, Jamie, 'Islamic Imperialism', interview with Efraim Karsh', *FrontPageMagazine.com*, 5 May 2006.

Gledhill, Ruth, 'Britain Bars US Clergy under "Anti-terror" Law', *The Times*, 26 May 2006.

Gledhill, Ruth, 'Faiths Unite Against Terrorism', *The Times*, 7 July 2006.

Gledhill, Ruth, 'Police Accused of Inaction as Anti-Jewish Alliance

Emerges', *The Times*, 7 September 2006.

Gledhill, Ruth, 'Summit on Religious Harmony is Thrown into Discord by Malaysia', *The Times*, 10 May 2007.

Gledhill, Ruth and Owen, Richard, 'Carey Backs Pope and Issues Warning on "Violent" Islam', *The Times*, 20 September 2006.

Godson, Dean, 'Sharp Lessons from a Turbulent Priest', *The Times*, 23 June 2006.

Goldhagen, Daniel, 'The New Threat', *The New Republic*, 13 March 2006.

Goodenough, Patrick, 'Islamic States Press for Limits on Free Expression', *CNSNews.com*, 23 April 2006.

Gordon, Evelyn, 'The War against Islamic Extremism', *The Jerusalem Post*, 4 October 2006.

Govan, Fiona, 'The Hole in the Ground that could Connect Africa with Europe', *The Daily Telegraph*, 10 April 2007.

Graston, Mike, *The Windsor Star*, 10 February 2006.

Griffiths, Sian, 'We Don't Teach Hate', *Sunday Times*, 11 February 2007.

Guitta, Olivier, 'The Cartoon Jihad – The Muslim Brotherhood's Project for Dominating the West', *The Weekly Standard*, 20 February 2006.

Guitta, Olivier, 'The Veil Controversy – Islamism and Liberalism face off', *The Weekly Standard*, 4 December 2006.

Gupta, Kanchan, 'Britain Panders to Radical Islam', *Daily Pioneer*, 30 January 2007.

Gurfinkiel, Michel, 'Another French Revolution? The Rioters and their Admirers on the Right and the Left', *The Weekly Standard*, 27 November 2006.

Hall, Macer, 'Brown: Don't Say Terrorists are Muslims', *Daily Express*, 3 July 2007.

Hames, Tim, 'We must Act now to Close this Terror Trail', *The Times*, 2 July 2007.

Hamid, Tawfik, 'The Trouble With Islam – Sadly, mainstream Muslim teaching accepts and promotes violence', *Opinion Journal*, 3 April 2007.

Hamid, Tawfik, 'How to End Islamophobia', *Opinion Journal*, 25 May 2007.

Hamilton, Fiona, 'Mosques Hire Guards to Protect Worshippers as Imam is Attacked', *The Times*, 13 August 2007.

Hammond, Andrew, 'Muslims Gaining Strength in United States

– Cleric', *Reuters*, 5 August 2007.
Hanscom, Aaron, 'A Fatwa in Spain', *FrontPageMagazine*, 4 September 2006.
Hanson, Victor Davis, 'Why Radical Islam – and Why Now?', *victorhanson.com*, 26 December 2006.
Hanson, Victor Davis, 'A Borderless World: The Immigration Problem is Global', *National Review*, 31 May 2007.
Hanson, Victor Davis, 'Endemic Madness', *The Washington Times*, 23 June 2007.
Harding, Luke, 'How one of the Biggest Rows in Modern Times Helped Danish Exports to Prosper', *The Guardian*, 30 September 2006.
Harper, Tom, 'TV "Preachers of Hate" Escape Police Action', *Sunday Telegraph*, 21 January 2007.
Harper, Tom, 'Preach in English, Muslim Peer tells Imams', *Sunday Telegraph*, 23 July 2007.
Harper, Tom and Leapman, Ben, 'Jews far more likely to be Victims of Faith Hatred than Muslims', *Sunday Telegraph*, 17 December 2006.
Hartley, Emma and Henry, Julie, 'Girls at London Saudi School are treated as Inferiors', *The Daily Telegraph*, 29 May 2004.
Hassoux, Didier, *Libération*, 15 June 2004.
Hastings, Chris and Jones, Beth, 'BBC Mounts Court Fight to Keep "Critical" Report Secret', *Sunday Telegraph*, 15 October 2006.
Hay, William Anthony, 'Misplaced Faith', *Opinion Journal*, 22 February 2007.
Heffer, Simon, 'So are we the Nastiest People in the World?', *The Daily Telegraph*, 16 June 2007.
Heflik, Roman, 'Editor Reflects on Denmark's Cartoon Jihad', *Spiegel Online*, 2 February 2006.
Helm, Toby, 'Amnesty Call for 500,000 Immigrants', *The Daily Telegraph*, 31 March 2006.
Henderson, Mark, 'People in Ethnically Diverse Area less Trusting than Others', *The Times*, 30 August 2007.
Heneghan, Tom, '"Ex-Muslim" Group Launches in Britain', *Reuters*, 20 June 2007.
Henninger, Daniel, 'The Pope's Easter, Benedict XVI takes on the Excesses of Secularization and Radical Islam', *Opinion Journal*, 14 April 2006.
Henry, Emma, 'Rising Immigration Fuels 26-year Fertility High',

The Daily Telegraph, 7 June 2007.

Herman, Ken, 'Bush Insists on Islamic Fascists', *The Atlanta Journal-Constitution*, 12 August 2006.

Hines, Nico, 'Protests Against the Award have been most Heated in Pakistan, *Times Online*, 20 June 2007.

Holt, Richard, 'Cartoon Protester Guilty of Race Hate', *The Daily Telegraph*, 1 February 2007.

Holt, Richard, 'July 21 Bombers Sentenced to Life', *The Daily Telegraph*, 11 July 2007.

Hope, Christopher, 'UK Cities to Have White Minorities "in 30 years" ', *The Daily Telegraph*, 15 September 2007.

Horne, Marc, 'Islamic Scout Groups Spark Ghettoist Fears', *Sunday Times*, 21 May 2006.

Houser, Mark, 'Trials, Violence Divide Netherlands', *Pittsburgh Tribune-Review*, 22 May 2005.

Horovitz, David, 'Exclusive: European Support for Palestinians "Crashes" ', *The Jerusalem Post*, 3 June 2006.

Horsnell, Michael, 'Family's Fears at East London Terror Protest', *Times Online*, 9 June 2006.

Houck, David Kennedy, 'The Islamist Challenge to the US Constitution', *Middle East Quarterly*, Spring 2006.

Ibn Warraq, 'The Genesis of a Myth', in Robert Spencer and Andrew Bostom, *The Myth of Islamic Tolerance: How Islamic Law Treats Non-Muslims* (Amherst, MA: Prometheus Books, 2005).

Ibn Warraq, 'Democracy in a Cartoon', *Spiegel Online*, 3 February 2006.

'Integration Debate: The German National Anthem in Turkish?', *Spiegel Online*, 2 May 2006.

'Islam Conference Fizzles', *The Copenhagen Post*, 15 May 2006.

'Islam in Europe: An Interview with Arzu Toker on the Cologne Mosque', *World Politics Review Exclusive*, 17 August 2007. The interview first appeared in the July 2007 issue of the German monthly *Konkret* and was translated into English by John Rosenthal.

'Islamic Conference in Berlin, Lowering the Wall Between Mosque and State', *Spiegel Online*, 27 September 2006.

'Islamist Website Instructs Mujahideen in Using Popular US Web Forums to Foster Antiwar Sentiments Among Americans', MEMRI, Special Series,1508, 20 March 2007.

'Islamistisk forfatning i Europa', *P1 Morgen*, 21 June 2006.

'Islamists Jailed over Plot to Attack Paris', *Times Online*, 14 June 2006.

Ivens, Martin [meets] Cohen, Nick, 'You've lost it, Guardianistas', *Sunday Times*, 4 February 2007.

Jacobs, Megan, 'Germany Suspends Iranian Soccer Player', *The Jerusalem Post*, 11 October 2007.

'Jail Toilets Face Away from Mecca', BBC News, 20 April 2006.

Jacque, Philippe, 'The Challenge is to Adapt our Societies to Islam', *Café Babel, The European Magazine*, 16 December 2004 (translated from French by Veronica Newington).

Jay, Anthony, 'Confessions of a BBC liberal', *Sunday Times*, 12 August 2007.

Jeambar, Denis, 'Regression', *L'Express*, 2 February 2006.

'Jihadists' Return Worries Europe', *The Washington Times*, citing AFP, 18 May 2006.

Johnson, Charles, 'Pope Speaks Out About Islamic Repression', *Little Green Footballs*, 21 September 2007.

Johnson, Daniel, 'Terror and Denial: *Londonistan* by Melanie Phillips', *Commentary Book Review*, July/August 2006.

Johnston, Philip, '1 Million new British Citizens under Blair', *The Daily Telegraph*, 24 May 2006.

Johnston, Philip, 'Asylum Cheats get £3,000 to go Home', *The Daily Telegraph*, 6 June 2006.

Johnston, Philip, 'The Shadow Cast by a Mega-mosque', *The Daily Telegraph*, 25 September 2006.

Johnston, Philip, 'The Websites', *The Daily Telegraph*, 8 November 2006.

Johnston, Philip, 'Foreign Prisoners Clogging Jails cost UK £400m a year', *The Daily Telegraph*, 3 May 2007.

Johnston, Philip, 'Rules to Stop "Sham" Marriages Unlawful', *The Daily Telegraph*, 24 May 2007.

Johnston, Philip, 'What Happened to Blair's Anti-terror Strategy?', *The Daily Telegraph*, 3 July 2007.

Johnston, Philip, 'Offering Sanctuary Threatens our Safety', *The Daily Telegraph*, 10 July 2007.

Johnston, Philip, 'Q&A: Britain's Borders', *The Daily Telegraph*, 11 July 2007.

Johnston, Philip, 'Balancing our Rights Against their Wrongs', *The Daily Telegraph*, 26 July 2007.

Johnston, Philip, 'EU Told to Open Door to 20m Migrant

Workers', *The Daily Telegraph*, 14 September 2007.

Jones, George, 'Blair Admits he has no Policy on Population', *The Daily Telegraph*, 5 July 2006.

Jones, George, 'Cyber Terror Threat is Growing, Says Reid', *The Daily Telegraph*, 26 April 2007.

Jordan, Eason, 'The News we Kept to Ourselves', *The New York Times*, 11 April 2003.

Jordan, Mary, 'In Europe and US, non-Believers are Increasingly Vocal', *The Washington Post*, 15 September 2007.

Kaminski, Matthew, 'To Keep the Banlieue From Burning – Will France ever Integrate its Muslim Immigrants?', *Opinion Journal*, 26 October 2006.

Kanfer, Stefan, 'France vs France: Frances's Muslim Problem will only get Worse', *City Journal*, Winter 2006.

Katz, Yaakov, 'UK Hamas Funder to be Deported', *The Jerusalem Post*, 30 May 2006.

'Keep Out Muslims, says Nile', *Herald Sun*, 12 March 2007.

Kennedy, Dominic, '1,000 Men Living Legally with Multiple Wives despite fears over Exploitation', *The Times*, 28 May 2007.

Kerbaj, Richard, 'Warning the West on "Evil of Islam"', *The Australian*, 21 August 2001.

Kite, Melissa, 'Citizenship Test Stumps One in Three Migrants', *Sunday Telegraph*, 15 October 2006.

Klein, Aaron, 'Synagogues Used as Bases to Fire on Israel', *The New York Sun*, 27 February 2007.

Knight, Sam, 'Britain Responds in Rushdie Knighthood Row', *Times Online*, 19 June 2007.

Krauthammer, Charles, 'Save us from Moderates', *The Seattle Times*, 13 February 2006.

'Krekar Claims Islam will Win', *Aftenposten*, 13 March 2006.

Krikorian, Mark, 'American Dhimmitude: the Road from Amnesty', *National Review Online*, 30 March 2006.

Kurtz, Stanley, 'Polygamy versus Democracy: You can't have both', *The Weekly Standard*, 5 June 2006.

Kurtz, Stanley, 'European Lessons – The Last Days of Europe show how Immigration is at the Root of Europe's Current Problems', *National Review*, 6 June 2007.

Kurtz, Stanley, 'Immigration Crackdown – Our Future is Europe', *National Review Online*, 25 June 2007.

Kurtulu, Mustafa, interviewed by *Times Online*, 30 March 2006.
'Labour is to Blame for the Drift to the BNP', lead article, *Sunday Telegraph*, 16 April 2006.
Lagan, Bernard, 'Briton Backs Imam in "Uncovered Meat" Row', *The Times*, 28 October 2006.
'Land Plan Becomes Raging Issue', *ExpressandStar.com*, 24 April 2007.
Lando, Ben and Krieger, Hilary Leila, 'The World must Learn from Israel about Fighting Terror', *The Jerusalem Post*, 22 April 2007.
Lappen, Alyssa, 'Ritual Murder of Jews in Paris', *FrontPageMagazine.com*, 4 December 2003.
Lappin, Yaakov, 'UK Islamists: Make Jihad on Israel', *Ynetnews.com*, 2 July 2006.
Latsch, Gunther *et al.*,'Terrorism in Germany – Every Investigator's Nightmare', *Der Spiegel*, 28 August 2006, translated into English by Christopher Sultan.
Laville, Sandra and Muir, Hugh, 'Secret Report Brands Muslim Police Corrupt', *The Guardian*, 10 June 2006.
'Law and Orders', *The Daily Telegraph*, 29 June 2006.
Leapman, Ben, '4,000 in UK Trained at Terror Camps', *Sunday Telegraph*, 15 July 2007.
Leapman, Ben, 'Abu Hamza Bullied in Prison, says Wife', *Sunday Telegraph*, 29 July 2007.
Leppard, David, 'More than 230 Terror Suspects free to stay in Britain', *Sunday Times*, 21 May 2006.
Leppard, David, '400 Terror Suspects on loose in UK', *Sunday Times*, 9 April 2006.
Leppard, David, 'British Brigade of Islamists join al-Qai'da Foreign Legion in Iraq', *Sunday Times*, 4 June 2006.
Leppard, David, 'Terror Watch on Mecca Pilgrims', *Sunday Times*, 21 January 2007.
Leppard, David, 'Al-Qai'da orders British Beheadings', *Sunday Times*, 4 February 2007.
Leppard, David and Taher, Abul, 'Blair to Launch Spin Battalion against al-Qai'da Propaganda', *Sunday Times*, 28 January 2007.
Lester, Toby, 'What is the Qur'an?', *The Atlantic Monthly*, January 1999.
Lewis, Bernard, 'Was Osama Right? Islamists always believed the US was weak. Recent political trends won't change their

views', *Opinion Journal*, 16 May 2007.

Liddle, Rod, 'Britain's Muslims at Alton Towers', *Spectator*, 8 July 2006.

Liddle, Rod, 'When Toleration goes too far', *Spectator*, 8 July 2006.

Liddle, Rod, 'If Muslims Revered Cattle, Shambo would be still be Mooing', *Sunday Times*, 29 July 2007.

Linde, Steve, 'Wiesenthal Center official: Internet Co-Opted by Terrorist Groups', *The Jerusalem Post*, 4 June 2006.

Lowe, Felix, 'Honour Killings Linked to Terror Groups', *The Daily Telegraph*, 26 June 2007.

Magister, Sandro, 'In Rome's Main Mosque, One Imam is Calling for Jihad', http://chiesa.espresso.repubblica.it/dettaglio.jsp?id=6953&eng=y, 11 June 2003

Magister, Sandro and Martino, Renato, 'A Cardinal Out of Control', *Chiesa*, 14 March 2006.

Malvern, Jack, 'British Council Shifts Focus to Muslim States', *The Times*, 26 February 2007.

Malik, Shahid, 'If you Want Shari'a Law you should go and live in Saudi', *Sunday Times*, 20 August 2006.

Mandel, Daniel, 'Preemptive Appeasement – Europe's New Strategy for the War on Terror', *The Weekly Standard*, 21 September 2007.

Marshall, Paul, 'Muzzling in the Name of Islam', *The Washington Post*, 29 September 2007.

Martin, Iain, 'We must face up to the Truth on Immigration', *Sunday Telegraph*, 5 August 2007.

Martin, Nicole, 'BBC Drops Casualty Suicide Bomb Plotline', *The Daily Telegraph*, 20 August 2007.

Martin, Nicole, 'Anger over Jesus quote left on BBC website', *The Daily Telegraph*, 20 August 2007.

Masalha, Salman, 'The Arab Man is the Problem, The Arab Woman is the Solution', *www.elaph.com*, 24 September 2004, cited by MEMRI, Special Dispatch Series, 807, 28 October 2004.

Masood, Ehsan, 'Islam's Reformers', *Prospect Magazine*, 124, July 2006.

al Mawry, Munir, 'Arab Intellectuals Receive Death Threats', *al-Sharq al-Awsat*, 10 April 2006.

McCallum, Mark, 'Muslim call to thwart capitalism', BBC News,

12 July 2003.

McCartney, Jenny, 'The Moral of Rushdie's Story? Anger is a Choice', *Sunday Telegraph*, 24 June 2007.

McGrory, Daniel, Evans, Michael and Tendler, Stewart, 'Muslims Question Terror Raid Tactics', *The Times*, 6 June 2006.

McGrory, Daniel, Jenkins, Russell and Bird, Steve, 'Terror Hit-list named 25 Muslim Soldiers', *The Times*, 2 February 2007.

McGrory, Daniel, Tendler, Stewart and Kennedy, Dominic, 'Muslim Soldiers Faced Kidnap and Beheading', *The Times*, 1 February 2007.

McLaren, Elsa, 'Muslim Protestor Guilty of Soliciting Murder', *Times Online*, 5 January 2007.

McLean, Renwick, '29 are Indicted in Connection with Attacks in Madrid', *The New York Times*, 12 April 2006.

Mekhennet, Souad and Smith, Craig S. 'German Spy Agency Admits Mishandling Abduction Case', *The New York Times*, 2 June 2006.

Melvin, Don, 'New Mosque Reflects Changes in Britain's Religious Landscape', *Cox News Service*, 12 December, 2005.

Meo, Nick, 'Islam's War on Sin Dims Bright Lights in a Nation Torn Between Cultures', *The Times*, 18 August 2007.

'Merkel Aide Criticized for Comments on Islam', *DPA* and *Expatica*, 2 October 2006.

Meyer, Cordula and Schmidt, Caroline, 'Europeans Have Stopped Defending Their Values', interview with German Islam expert Bassam Tibi, *Spiegel Online*, 2 October 2006, translated into English by Damien McGuinness.

'Minister Welcome Shari'a in Netherlands if Majority Wants it', *NIS News*, 13 September 2006.

Moore, Charles, 'Blair's Major Moment: Why Human Rights are Like the ERM', *The Daily Telegraph*, 20 May 2006.

Moore, Charles, 'How Cromwell Gave us Joan Collins and other Luminaries', *The Daily Telegraph*, 17 June 2006.

Moore, Charles, 'Stirring up Racial Hatred – not the Medium', *The Daily Telegraph*, 11 August 2007.

Moore, Matthew, 'Cartoon Protester Guilty of Race Hate', *The Daily Telegraph*, 9 November 2006.

Moore, Michael Scott, interview with *al-Jazeera* cartoonist Shujaat Ali, *Spiegel Online*, 3 February 2006.

Moore, Molly, 'With End of French School Year Comes Threat of

Deportation', *The Washington Post*, 15 June 2006.
'More than 32,000 Islamist Extremists in Germany', *Expatica*, 22 May 2006.
'More than Vigilance, The Government must look anew at the Laws top Defeat Terrorism', *The Times,* Leader, 30 June 2007.
Morgan, Christopher, 'Bishop Attacks "Victim" Muslims', *Sunday Times,* 5 November 2006.
Moult, Julie, 'Muslim-only Kitchen Kit for Jails', *The Sun,* 13 January 2007.
'Muhammed Strikes Back', *Spiegel Online,* 2 February 2006.
'Muhammed Cartoons Case Reaches French Courts', *The Jerusalem Post,* citing *AP,* 7 February 2007.
'Multiple Choice French Citizenship Test', *Spiegel Online,* 6 May 2006.
Muselier, Renaud, 'No to a Racist and anti-Semitic Internet!', *Le Monde,* 14 June 2004.
Musharbash, Yassin, 'Al-Azhar University in Cairo: In the Heart of Muslim Belief', *Spiegel Online,* 10 February 2006, translated from German by Andrew Bulkeley.
Musharbash, Yassin, 'Militant Islam Online Magazine Hints at Attacks on Papers that Run Muhammad Caricatures', *Spiegel Online,* 5 May 2006.
Musharbash, Yassin and Reimann, Anna, 'Alienated Danish Muslims Sought Help from Arabs', *Spiegel Online,* 1 February 2006.
'Muslim Fanatic Works on Trains', *The Sun,* 16 February 2007.
'Muslim Gang Forces Paris Café to Censor Cartoon Show', *Middle East Times,* 31 March 2006.
'Muslim Group's First Mission, Official Recognition of Islam in Germany?', *Spiegel Online,* 16 April 2007.
'Muslim Ambassadors: Sweden needs to change its laws', *The Local,* 6 September 2007.
'Muslims never saw Muhammed's Cartoons', *The Copenhagen Post,* 5 October 2007.
'Muslims "should stop helping police"', *The Daily Telegraph,* 7 June 2006.
'Muslims and socialists – with friends like these', *The Economist,* 8 February 2007.
Nasrawi, Salah, 'Islamic Militants Warn Austria, Germany', *AP,* 11 March 2007.
Naughton, Philippe, 'Brown Announces Single "Border Force" for

UK to Combat Terror', *Times Online*, 25 July 2007.

Nazir-Ali, Bishop Michael, 'Muslims Demand Respect – but not for Christians', *Sunday Telegraph*, 26 March 2006.

'News From Everywhere', *The Daily Telegraph* Leader, 8 July 2006.

Nivat, Anne, *Le Point*, 1727, 20 October 2005, p. 26.

'Not Possible to Modernize Islam', interview with Founder of Council of Ex-Muslims, *Spiegel Online*, 27 February 2007.

Oakeshott, Isabel and Gourlay, Chris, 'Anti-Semitism Rules come in at Universities', *Sunday Times*, 25 March 2007.

Oestermann, Richard, 'Drawing Conclusions', *The Jerusalem Post*, 15 June 2006.

'OIC urges De-linking Islam from Terrorism', *Kuwait News Agency*, 13 September 2007.

Olsen, Jan, 'Muslim Groups' Suit over Cartoons Rejected', *AP*, 27 October 2006.

O'Neill, Sean, 'Muslim Students "being Taught to Despise Unbelievers as Filth" ', *The Times*, 20 April 2006.

O'Neill, Sean, 'Algeria could Provide Springboard for European Terror', *Times Online*, 11 April 2007.

O'Neill, Sean, 'Guantanamo: a Prison that won't go away – Uncooperative Countries and the Law are Preventing the Bush Administration from Closing its Notorious Camp in Cuba', *Times Online*, 5 June 2007.

O'Neill, Sean and McGrory, Daniel, 'Blunders that Left Abu Hamza Free', *The Times*, 30 May 2006.

O'Neill, Sean and Webster, Philip, 'Kelly Penalizes Mosques' Failure to Tackle Terror', *The Times*, 12 October 2006.

Owen, Richard, 'Homily on Faith, Logic and Holy War was Seen as a Slur on Islam', *The Times*, 16 September 2006.

Owen, Richard, 'Popes Sees Islamic Envoys in Attempt to Heal Rift', *Times Online*, 26 September 2006.

Owen, Richard and Erdem, Suna,'Muslims Vent Fury at Pope's Speech', *The Times*, 16 September 2006.

Owen, Richard and Gledhill, Ruth, 'If it isn't Roman Catholic then it's not a Proper Church, Pope Tells Christians', *The Times*, 11 July 2007.

Palmer, Alasdair, 'The Day is Coming when British Muslims Form a State within a State', *Sunday Telegraph*, 19 February 2006.

Palmer, Alasdair, 'The Bomber's Privacy is Paramount', *Sunday*

Telegraph, 26 November 2006.

Palmer, Alasdair, Nikkah, Roya and Wynne-Jones, Jonathan, 'Not in Their Name?', *The Daily Telegraph*, 8 July 2007.

Paton, Graeme, 'Islamic School "Rips Pages from Textbooks" ', *The Daily Telegraph*, 9 February 2007.

Paton, Graeme, 'Academic: Extremism Debate is being Stifled', *The Daily Telegraph*, 17 March 2007.

Percival, Jenny, 'Blair Outlines Curbs on Grants to Religious Groups', *Times Online*, 8 December 2006.

Peters, Ralph, 'The Eurabia Myth', *New York Post*, 26 November 2006.

Petre, Jonathan, 'Judicial System is "Failing Jews" ', *The Daily Telegraph*, 29 March 2007.

Petre, Jonathan, 'Churches Act to Stem "Sham" Marriages', *The Daily Telegraph*, 23 April 2007.

Petre, Jonathan, 'Protests at Taverner's Allah in Cathedral', *The Daily Telegraph*, 17 June 2007.

Petre, Jonathan, 'New Group for those who Renounce Islam', *The Daily Telegraph*, 21 June 2007.

Pfeffer, Anshel, 'Double Vision', *Haaretz*, 6 October 2007.

Pierce, Andrew, 'The Textbook Terrorists', *The Daily Telegraph*, 7 July 2007.

'Pilgrimage: "French lodge" in Saudi Arabia to help French pilgrims', *Morocco Times*, 20 September 2006.

Pipes, Daniel, 'More Converts to Terrorism', *FrontPageMagazine.com*, 7 December 2005.

Pipes, Daniel, 'Quest for Reciprocity', *The Jerusalem Post*, 5 July 2006.

Pipes, Daniel, 'Piggybacking on Terror in Britain', *The New York Sun*, 29 August 2006.

Pipes, Daniel, 'Islamic Law Rules You Too', *The Jerusalem Post*, 26 September 2006.

Pipes, Daniel, 'A Devastating Thesis', *The Jerusalem Post*, 14 November 2006.

Pipes, Daniel, 'The Case Against Banning the Qur'an', *The Jerusalem Post*, 28 August 2007.

Pipes, Daniel and Chadha, Sharon, 'CAIR: Islamists Fooling the Establishment', *Middle East Quarterly*, Spring 2006.

'Police Brought in as Teachers Lose Control at Berlin School', *DPA* and *Expatica*, 31 March 2006.

'Polygamous Husbands can claim Cash for their Harems', *Daily Mail*, 17 April 2007.
Poller, Nidra, 'The Wrath of Ka', *City Journal*, 7 June 2006.
Polzer, Wolfgang, 'Islam is Taking a Grip on Europe – Why Muslims Object to Piggy Banks', *Journal Chrétien*, 10 March 2007.
Poole, Patrick, 'New Study: Political Islam Correlated to Support for Terrorism', *American Thinker*, 15 June 2007.
'Pope's Private Secretary Warns of Islamization of Europe', *The Jerusalem Post*, citing *AP*, 26 July 2007.
Porter, Henry, 'Tolerating Intolerance is still this Country's Besetting Sin', *The Observer*, 4 February 2007.
Portillo, Michael, 'The Bloody Truth is that Israel's War is Our War', *Sunday Times*, 23 July 2006.
Prager, Dennis, *WorldNetDaily*, 7 February 2006, cited by Gerstenfeld, 'The Muhammed Cartoon Controversy'.
'Preacher Training', leading articles, *The Times*, 20 April 2006.
Pryce-Jones, David, weblog, 'Leading Europe', *National Review Online*, 15 December 2007.
Pullella, Philip, 'Pope in About-Face over Muslim Dialogue Office', *Reuters*, 28 May 2007.
'Pupils aged Five "Poisoned" at Islamic School that "Teaches Hate"', *Daily Mail*, 5 February 2007.
'Q & A: Crisis in Darfur', *Human Rights Watch*, 29 January 2007.
Qenawy, Ayman, 'Danish Muslims Internationalize Anti-Prophet Cartoons', *Islam Online*, 18 November 2005.
Quinn, Ben, 'Bishop Condemned over Imam Warning', *The Daily Telegraph*, 6 November 2006.
Rabkin, Jeremy, 'Vive La Caliphate – Does European Islam Mean Islamic Europe?', *The Weekly Standard*, 20 November 2006.
Raved, Ahiya, 'Ex-Mossad Chief warns of Muslim European Cities and of World War Three', *The Jerusalem Post*, 4 June 2006.
Rayment, Sean, 'Whites Being Lured into Islamic Terror', *Sunday Telegraph*, 2 July 2006.
Rees-Mogg, William, 'Why the Pope was Right', *The Times*, 18 September 2006.
Rennie, David, 'A Danish Muslim Activist Speaks', *The Daily Telegraph weblog*, 3 February 2006.
Rennie, David, '"Islamic Terrorism" is too Emotive a Phrase, says EU', *The Daily Telegraph*, 12 April 2006.
Rennie, David, 'Spain to Free 1,500 Illegal Immigrants into

Europe', *The Daily Telegraph*, 12 April 2006.

Rennie, David, 'EU Defence Strategy Snatches Stability from the Jaws of Victory', *The Daily Telegraph*, 3 October 2006.

Rennie, David, 'Muslims Challenged by Gynecologists', *The Daily Telegraph*, 23 October 2006.

Rennie, David, 'Muslims are Waging Civil War against us, Claims Police Union', *The Daily Telegraph*, 5 October 2006.

Rennie, David, 'Youths Challenge the French State', *The Daily Telegraph*, 2 November 2006.

Renout, Frank, 'Immigrants' Second Wives find Few Rights', *The Christian Science Monitor*, 25 May 2005.

Roberts, Andrew, 'At Stake in the Iraq War: Survival of a Way of Life', *The Christian Science Monitor*, 12 July 2007.

Rotella, Sebastien and Sicakyuz, Achrene, 'Charles de Gaulle Airport Handling Cultural Baggage', *Los Angeles Times*, 12 December 2006.

Rubin, Barry, 'The Region: East and West', *The Jerusalem Post*, 5 August 2007.

Sage, Adam, 'Doctors face Moral Dilemma over Restoring Muslim Brides' Virginity', *The Times*, 7 May 2007.

Samuel, Henry, 'France "no Longer a Catholic Country" ', *The Daily Telegraph*, 10 January 2007.

Samuel, Martin, 'Jailbirds Ripe for Recruiting', *The Times*, 3 October 2006.

Samuelson, Robert, 'The End of Europe', *The Washington Post*, 15 June 2005.

Samuelson, Robert, 'Behind the Birth Dearth', *The Washington Post*, 24 May 2006.

'Satanic Verses had more Impact than al-Qa'ida', *The Daily Telegraph*, 23 May 2006.

'Saudi Police "Stopped" Fire Rescue', BBC News, 15 March 2002.

Sayyed, Tashbih, 'The Plea of a Genuine Muslim Moderate', *FrontPageMagazine.com*, 6 October 2006.

Schrank, Delphine, 'Survey Details "Deep" Divide Between Muslims, Westerners', *The Washington Post*, 23 June 2006.

Schwartz, Stephen, 'Islam in the Big House: How radical Muslims Took Over the American Prison System', *The Weekly Standard*, 24 April 2006.

Schwartz, Stephen, 'A Threat to the World', *Spectator*, 19 August 2006.

Scruton, Roger, 'Islamofacism – Beware of a religion without irony', *Opinion Journal*, 20 August 2006.

Segaumes, Nathalie, *Le Parisien*, 15 June 2004.

Shackleford, Dr Rusty 'John Doe', 'Islamists Post Hit List of Apostates', *The Jawa Report*, 11 April 2006, http://mypetjawa.mu.nu/archives/169819.php.

Shaw, Russell, 'Papal Transformation – Benedict uses Softer Touch to Dialogue with Islam', *Catholic Online*, 16 February 2007.

Shipman, Tim, 'US Loner helps Bin Laden to Taunt Bush', *Sunday Telegraph*, 9 September 2007.

Shrivastava, Anjana, 'Denmark's Cartoon Jihad', *Spiegel Online*, 1 February 2006.

Siegel, Fred, 'Fall of the Fifth Republic?', *New York Post*, 1 November 2006.

Simons, Stefan, 'Danish Caricatures on Trial in France – Cartoons 1: Mohammed 0', *Spiegel Online*, 16 February 2007.

Simpson, Victor, 'Europeans "see need" for Power to Snoop', *AP*, 11 April 2006.

Sinai, Joshua, 'Defeating Internet Terrorists', *The Washington Times*, 9 October 2006.

Smith, Craig, 'Jews in France Feel Sting as anti-Semitism Surges Among Children of Immigrants', *The New York Times*, 26 March 2006.

Smith, Craig, 'Leak Disrupts French Terror Trial', *The New York Times*, 6 July 2006.

Smith, Craig, 'Furor over a French Immigration Crackdown', *The New York Times*, 8 July 2006.

Smith, David, 'Give us a Mufti, say UK Muslims', *Sunday Times*, 10 June 2007.

Smith, Lee, 'Fighting them Over There – Iraq is not a Breeding Ground for Terrorists, it's a Dumping Ground', *The Weekly Standard*, 28 September 2006.

Smith, Robert, 'Islam will be Dominant UK Religion', *Gulf Daily News* (Bahrain), 10 March 2004.

Sollich, Rainer, 'German Mistrust of Muslims and Islam Grows', *Deutsche Welle*, 20 May 2006.

'Spain Publishes Public School Primer on Islam', *The Jerusalem Post*, citing *AP*, 18 October 2006.

Stalinsky, Steven, 'Hamas TV Prepares for Intifada III', *The New*

York Sun, 12 April 2007.

Stares, Justin, 'Public Opinion Matters, says EU', *Sunday Telegraph*, 25 June 2006.

Stares, Justin and Patrick Hennessy, 'EU Ignores Constitution Vote to Launch Anti-terror Squad', *Sunday Telegraph*, 18 June 2006.

Starkey, David, 'Henry was Wrong. Put Religion back in its Box – Our Outdated Link between Church and State is Dangerous in a Fundamentalist Era', *Sunday Times*, 12 November 2006.

Steele, John, 'Suicide Bomber's Video won't frighten us, say July 7 Families', *The Daily Telegraph*, 7 July 2006.

Steele, John, 'Met backs off Over Muslim Protests', *The Daily Telegraph*, 29 September 2006.

Steele, John, 'Freedom of Speech Row as Talk on Islamic Extremists is Banned', *The Daily Telegraph*, 15 March 2007.

Steele, John, '4,000 Terror Suspects in UK', *The Daily Telegraph*, 7 May 2007.

Steele, John and Gardham, Duncan, 'Terror Trial Man was Allowed to Stay After Jail', *The Daily Telegraph*, 5 May 2007.

Stephens, Bret, 'The Foreign Brides: Germany tries to Protect Turkish girls From Arranged Marriages, *Opinion Journal*, 7 May 2006.

Stewart, Frank H., 'The Biased Broadcasting Corporation', *The New York Times*, 15 March 2007.

Steyn, Mark, 'Wake Up Europe. It may already too Late: Why the Fall and Spring Riot Seasons are Signs of the Coming Apocalypse', *Maclean's*, 5 April 2006.

Steyn, Mark, 'They Report, You Decide', *PowerLine*, 26 November 2006, http://powerlineblog.com/archives/016028.php.

Stokes, Paul, 'Four Arrested over "Immigration Scam" ', *The Daily Telegraph*, 12 February 2007.

Sultan, Wafa, interviewed by al-Jazeera, 26 July 2005, MEMRI, Special Dispatch Series, 1107, 7 March 2006.

'Sunni Sheikh Yussuf al-Qaradawi Heralds the Coming Conquest of Rome', al-Jazeera, 24 January 1999, cited by MEMRI, Special Dispatch Series, 447, 6 December 2002.

Swinford, Steven, 'Guantanamo no worse than Belmarsh', *Sunday Times*, 21 January 2007.

Taher, Abul, 'Hamza May Go Free as Witness Backs Down', *Sunday Times*, 19 August 2007.

Taheri, Amir, 'Abu Hamza: Unanswered Questions', *Arab News*, 18 February 2006.
Taheri, Amir, 'Eye of the Storm: Algeria bids France "au revoir" ', *The Jerusalem Post*, 27 April 2006.
Taheri, Amir, 'Islam in Britain: A Year after the Terrorist Raid', *al-Sharq al-Awsat*, 7 July 2006.
Taheri, Amir, 'Are British Muslims Really Angry?', *al-Sharq al-Awsat*, 8 September 2006.
Taheri, Amir, 'The West's Self-Imposed Censorship', *Gulf News*, 13 October 2006.
'Talking of Immigrants: America's Debate on Immigration may be Painful, but Europe's is Dysfunctional', *The Economist*, 1 June 2006.
Taranto, James, 'Best of the Web', *Opinion Journal*, 27 August 2007.
'Terror-Spooked EU: Don't Say Muslims', *Daily Mail*, 4 July 2007.
'Terror Victims are BBC Licence-payers too', *The Daily Telegraph* Leader, 20 August 2007.
'Terrorist Operating in France more Agile at Plotting Attacks', *The Jerusalem Post*, citing *AP*, 5 June 2006.
'Terrorist Ringleader Muktar Said Ibrahim: A Robber and a Sex Offender', *Daily Mail*, 9 July 2007.
Thompson, Carolyn, 'Borders, Waldenbooks Won't Carry Magazine', *San Francisco Chronicle*, citing *AP*, 29 March 2006.
Thomson, Alice, interview with Abdul Bari, 'British should try Arranged Marriages', *The Daily Telegraph*, 10 June 2006.
Trigano, Shmuel, in *Post-Holocaust and Anti-Semitism Series*, 42, 1, March 2000, Jerusalem Center for Public Affairs.
Tugend, Tom, 'Letting Suicide Bombers Speak for Themselves', *The Jerusalem Post*, 26 November 2006.
'Twisted mind of the Agony Sheikh', *Daily Mail*, 21 August 2006.
Twiston-Davies, Bess, 'Faith News', *The Times*, 16 December 2006.
Twiston-Davies, Bess, 'Faith News', *The Times*, 27 January 2007.
Tyler, Patrick and Van Natta, Jr, Don, 'Militants in Europe Openly Call for Jihad and the Rule of Islam', *The New York Times*, 26 April 2004.
'UK Panel tells Brown Boycott of Hamas is Counterproductive', *Haaretz*, citing *Reuters*, 13 August 2007.
'UK to begin Recording Anti-Semitism a Hate Crime', *The*

Jerusalem Post, 30 July 2007.

Ungoed-Thomas, Jon, 'The "Hearts and Minds" Battle for British Muslims that Failed', *Sunday Times*, 13 August 2006.

'US Envoy to UN: ME Conflicts could lead to Conflagration', *The Jerusalem Post*, 27 August 2007.

Veit, Medick *et al.*, 'Justifying Marital Violence – A German Judge Cites Koran in Divorce Case', *Spiegel Online*, 21 March 2007.

Vidino, Lorenzo, 'Creating Outrage – Meet the Imam Behind the Cartoon Over-reaction', *National Review*, 6 February 2006.

Vidino, Lorenzo, 'State Department's Flirting with the Muslim Brotherhood', 20 April 2006; 'Islamist Extremism in Europe', Hearing before the Committee on Foreign Relations, United States Senate, 5 April 2006.

Vinocur, John and Dan Bilefsky, 'Dane Sees Greed and Politics in the Crisis', *The New York Times*, 10 February 2006.

'Voice of the Masses', *The Economist*, 8 March 2007.

Wagner, Matthew, 'Haredi Leaders want Protests to Stop', *The Jerusalem Post*, 20 June 2007.

Walters, Simon, 'We are Biased, Admit the Stars of BBC News', *Mail on Sunday*, 21 October 2006.

Waterfield, Bruno, 'Don't Confuse Terrorism with Islam, says EU', *The Daily Telegraph*, 30 March 2007.

Waterfield, Bruno, 'Bloggers Say EU Law will End Free Speech', *The Daily Telegraph*, 20 April 2007.

Waterfield, Bruno, 'Ban Qur'an like *Mein Kampf*, says Dutch MP', *The Daily Telegraph*, 9 August 2007.

Webb, Jason, 'Citizenship Call from Spain's Uneasy Muslim Past', *Reuters*, 21 June 2007.

Wheeler, Carolynne, 'Imams Warned to Keep Politics out of the Pulpit', *The Daily Telegraph*, 30 June 2007.

Whitlock, Craig, Ali, Imtiaz and Smiley, Shannon, 'Converts to Islam Move Up In Cells – Arrests in Europe Illuminate Shift', *The Washington Post*, 15 September 2007.

Wildman, Sarah, 'Europe Rethinks its Safe Haven Status', *The Christian Science Monitor*, 24 May 2006.

Willis, Paul, 'Government Requests Release of Guantanamo Inmates', *The Daily Telegraph*, 7 August 2007.

Wilson, Graeme, 'Young British Muslims "getting more radical" ', *The Daily Telegraph*, 30 January 2007.

Winnett, Robert, 'Fears that Bin Laden aide is Recruiting in Jail',

Sunday Times, 5 August 2007.

Wittrock, Phillip, 'Carnival in Germany, Islam no Longer Taboo', *Spiegel Online*, 16 February 2007.

Woolsey, James, 'West Bank Terrorist State: The folly of Israeli Disengagement', *Opinion Journal*, 29 May 2006.

Woolsey, James and Shea, Nina, 'What about Muslim Moderates?', *Opinion Journal*, 15 July 2007.

'The World from Berlin', *Spiegel Online*, 7 February 2006.

Wynne-Jones, Jonathan, 'Drive for Multi-faith Britain Deepens Rift, says Church', *Sunday Telegraph*, 8 October 2006.

Wynne-Jones, Jonathan, 'Christians Ask if Force is Needed to Protect their Religious Values', *Sunday Telegraph*, 5 November 2006.

Yahmid, Hadi, 'French Islamic Institute Fights Islamophobia', *Islam Online*, 15 June 2006.

Yahmid, Hadi, 'French Imam Arrested on Money Laundering', *Islam Online*, 21 June 2006.

'Young Muslim Women in Europe go to Extremes to be Virgins again', *USA Today*, 25 June 2006.

'Zahar: Qur'an Forbids Recognizing Israel', *The Jerusalem Post*, 20 April 2007.

Zand, Bernhard, 'The Cartoon Wars: the Inciters and the Incited', *Der Spiegel*, 13 February, 2006.

Zantonavitch, Andre, 'Survey of *While Europe Slept: How Radical Islam is Destroying the West from Within*, by Bruce Bawer, 2006', *FrontPageMagazine*, 2 June 2006.

al-Zawahiri, Ayman *et al.*, 'Knights Under the Banner of the Prophet', *Military Review* (US Army CGSC) 85, 1 (January 2005).

Zwartz, Barney, 'Stop Appeasing Muslims: Islam Expert', *The Age*, 3 November 2003.

Index

Abbas, President Mahmud, 80, 128
Abd al-Aziz, Sheikh, 230
Abd al-Rahim, Sha'ban, 290
Abdullah, Bilal, 136
Abdullah, Daud, 138
Abdullah, King, 301, 305
Abdul-Rahman, Sheikh, 190
Aberdeen, 162
Abode of War / *Dar al-Harb*, 68, 182
Abu al-Gheit, Ahmed, 302
Abu Fattah, Amira, 196ff
Abu Laban, Sheikh Ahmed, 189, 303, 344–5
Abu Omar, 229
Abu Qatada, 143, 189, 254
Abu Usama al-Suede, 271
Abu Yussuf, 4
Accoyer, Bernard, 208
Action Police, 200
Afghanistan, 1–2, 17, 26, 28–9, 44, 57, 70, 74, 93–4, 99–100, 103, 105, 110–12, 114, 120, 130–1, 133, 136, 140–1, 144, 152, 154, 186, 188, 191, 210, 213–14, 216, 238, 240, 247, 267, 269, 300, 405, 418, 446
   'Afghanis', 17
Africa, 17, 39, 54, 78, 85, 91, 99, 120, 195–6, 200, 206–8, 222, 394, 441, 446,
   Black, 26
   Horn of, 57
   North, 20, 26, 54, 85–7, 151, 174–5, 178, 181, 200, 202, 213, 216, 221, 231, 307, 438
   South, 71
   West, 82
Ahl al-Hadith, 121
Ahl al-Sunna wal-Jama'a, 161
Ahmadinajad, President Mahmud, 2, 11, 15, 278, 283, 293, 305, 355, 376,
Ahmed, Khurshid, 132, 162, 363–4
AIDS, 15, 39
Akkari, Ahmed, 303, 314, 346
Al-Ahram, 2

Al-Aqsa (mosque), 23, 281
   Brigades, 80
Alawite, 357
Al-Arabiya, 36, 440
Al-Azhar, 22, 298, 315–6
Albania, 120, 160, 230
Al-Eqtisadiah, 67
Aleppo, 231
   University of, 286
Al-Fajr, 301
Algeria, 3, 17, 26, 28, 36, 48, 60, 81, 133, 174, 185–6, 192–3, 204, 210–11, 215–16, 222–3, 228–30, 247, 253
   Archbishop of, 36
Al-Hurra, 36, 439
Ali, Ayaan Hirsi, 58–9, 249, 298, 437
Al-Jazeera, 12, 23, 36, 44, 129, 284, 309, 313, 322, 440
Al-Manar, 312
Al-Masri al-Yaum, 46
Al Muhajirun, 29
Al-Noor School (Germany), 39–40
Al-Quds al-Arabi, 23
Al-Sharq al-Awsat, 353
Al-Sheikh, Abdul Aziz, 39
Al-Tajdid, 354
Alton Towers, 108
Al-Watan, 354
Amarya, Sheikh Issam, 281
America (see also US), 70, 91, 354
   North, 365, 416
   South, 165
Amman, x, 217, 305
Amsterdam, 411
Anatolia (see also Turkey), 202, 257
ANB TV, 23
Andalusia, ix, 21, 336, 396
   Andalusian Syndrome, 21
Annan, Kofi, 317
Anne Frank, 291
Ansar al-Islam, 264, 320
Ansar al-Sunna, 319–20

Anti-Defamation League, 294–5
Anti-Semitism, 3–5, 13, 15, 17, 32, 37, 56, 106, 166–9, 176–81, 190, 192, 195–7, 233, 236, 255, 279, 291, 293, 312, 403–4, 424
Antwerp, 60
Arab, ix, 2, 7, 20, 26, 57, 61, 66, 88–9, 102, 139, 174, 176, 178, 181, 189, 217, 232, 234, 238, 240
  Democracy, 28
  History, 120
  Human Development Report, 41
  Israeli Conflict, 48, 102, 177, 433
  League, 90, 290, 302, 311
  Nation, 26
  Pan, 26
  Soil, 17
  World, 26, 41, 91, 196–7, 199, 258
Arabia, 103, 202, 371, 402
Arabic (language), 36, 137, 162, 166, 206, 250, 439
Arafat, Yasser, 6, 27, 190, 306
Archbishop
  of Canterbury, 114, 128, 132, 150, 329, 332
  of Lyon, 211
  of Westminster, 132
  of York, 102
Arhus, 282
Arístegui, Gustavo, 21–3
Armenians, 65, 224, 308
Asia, ix, 17, 54, 91, 116, 146, 152, 217, 364,
  Central, 57, 86, 131
  East, 57
  South-East, 57, 364
Assad, President Bashar, 283
Association of Chiefs of Police Officers (ACPO, British), 167
Association of Islamic Cultural Centers (VIKZ, German), 232–4
Association of Muslim Social Scientists (British), 156
Auschwitz, 274, 289
Ates, Seryan, 249, 251, 257
Atlantic Ocean, 37, 82, 105, 364, 386
Atwan abd al-Bari, 23
Atta Muhammed, 270
Aubervilliers, 212
Australia, 29, 55, 57, 70–1, 111–12, 158, 186, 248, 271, 287, 328–9, 348, 402, 447
  The Australian, 287
Austria, 58–9, 74, 229–30, 269, 292
  Foreign Minister, 317
Aznar, Jose Maria, 269, 394, 396

Baader-Meinhof, 139
Ba'ath, 26
Badawi, PM Abdul, 66

Baden-Wurttemberg, 234, 270
Baghdad, 29, 130, 135–6, 231, 264, 271, 309, 441
Bahrain, 88–9, 90
Bakri, Omar Muhammed, 38, 93, 119, 135, 190, 282, 300, 305, 435, 441
Balen, Malcom, Report, 36
Bali, 292
Balkans, 21, 54, 229, 441
Baltimore, 364
Bangladesh, 57, 60, 75, 115, 117, 165, 300, 341
Banna, Hassan al-, 4–5, 175
Banu Quraiza, 103
Barborin, Cardinal Philippe, 211
Bari, Muhammed abdul, 114–15, 118, 121, 125, 424
Barroso, Jose Manuel, 330
Bat Y'eor, 177
Bavaria, 270
  Interior Minister, 339
Bayrou, François, 352
BBC 1, 45–6,101, 106,
BBC News, 33ff, 67,113–14, 121, 138, 145, 337, 440
Beirut, 300, 441
Belgium, 3, 57, 61, 87, 190, 264, 273, 291, 312, 436
  Arab-European League, 291
  Federal Police, 215
Belize, 95
Belleville, 185 297
Ben-Ali, Rashid, 298
Benchellali, Chellali, 210
Benedict XVI, Pope, 326–8, 331–5, 397–8,
Berlin, 32, 61, 167, 227, 232, 235–6, 245, 257, 265
Berliner Kurier, 237
Berliner Zeitung, 313
Bible, 35, 150, 260, 335–6
  New Testament, 41, 422
  Old Testament, 41, 422
Bild, 245 272
Bild am Sonntag, 241
Bildt, PM Carl, 302
Bin Laden, Osama, 11–12, 15, 17–19, 27, 35, 45, 104, 120, 131, 191, 213, 215, 229, 254, 271, 280, 305, 316, 320, 345, 370, 431, 435, 443, 446
Birmingham, 11, 39, 42–3, 99, 129, 147, 152, 441
Blacks (see also Africa), 152, 195–7
Blackpool, 98
Blair, Sir Ian, 106,125
Blair, PM Tony, 16, 24, 27, 31, 37–8, 95, 98, 105–6, 109–10, 118–19, 123, 132–3, 136, 138, 142, 154–5, 161, 163, 165, 169, 351, 372, 432

Index

Blood Libel, 15, 181
Bologna, 263
   Mosque in, 263
Bonn, King Fahd Academy in, 253–4
Borders and Waldenbrooks, 296, 299–300
Boumedienne, Houari, 411
Bosnia, 17, 119, 125, 151, 238, 253, 267, 364, 411, 420, 436
Boubakeur, Rector Dalil, 175, 352
Bové, José, 190–1
Bradford, 142, 441
Brazil, 72, 86
Bremen
   University of, 80
   Board of Education, 234
Brent, 11
Brighton, 37, 110–11, 158
Bristol, 101
Britain/UK/England, x, 9, 15–16, 27–8, 31, 33, 35ff, 44, 47, 57, 61–2, 65–6, 72, 76, 82–3, 85, 91, 93ff, 183, 189, 207, 208–9, 217, 228–9, 231, 238, 258, 267, 446
   Army and Police, 129–30
   Commission for Racial Equality, 219
   Crown Prosecution Service, 41, 43
   Government, 23, 122, 134
   Foreign Office, 158, 168, 256
   Home Office, 98, 127, 136, 141–3, 148, 151, 161, 401
   House of Commons, 50, 107
   Jews of, 3, 102, 106–7, 166–7
   Ministry of Defence, 85, 130
   Muslims of, 38, 61, 93ff
   Palestine Parliamentary Group, 11
   Stop the War Coalition, 30
British Council, 131, 156
British Muslim Forum, 132, 162
Brook, Dr Yaron, 9–11
Brown, PM Gordon, 134, 136, 138–9, 141, 419, 448
Bruguiere, Magistrate Jean-Louis, 211, 215–16
Brussels, 79, 215, 388, 417
   Airport, 215
Buddhist, 26, 48, 138, 285, 308, 314
Bulgaria, 229–30
Bunglawala, Inayat, 45, 104, 122, 128, 447
Burleigh, Michael, 75, 139, 446–7
Burgess, Anthony, 179
Burma/Mianmar, 57
Bush, President George W., 9, 16, 23, 30–1, 105, 120, 178, 183, 236, 247, 267, 269, 293, 372–3, 417, 419
Byzantine, 202, 327–8

Cairo, 4, 19, 37, 298
Calderoli, Roberto, 263, 348
California, 9, 19
Caliphate/Islamic State, 7, 21, 103, 131, 136, 281–2, 371, 403, 426, 446
   Voice of the Caliphate, 269
Cameron, David, 129, 139
Cameroon, 195
Camous, Jean-Yves, 197
Canada, 26, 55, 71, 81, 249, 269, 365, 407
Canary Islands, 82, 394
Capitalism, 20–1, 76, 236
Caprioli, Louis, 213
Carcassonne, 201
Cardiff Airport, 166
Carter, President Jimmy, 2
Cartoon Crisis (2006), 1–2, 17, 63, 65, 72, 103, 115–16, 163, 182, 217, 227, 245–6, 266, 277ff, 370, 374, 421
Casablanca, x, 231, 420,
Cassarino, Jean-Pierre, 59
Catholics, 34, 37, 94, 116 ,132, 149, 202–3, 270, 309, 323, 328, 351, 397, 399, 400
Catholic Herald, 149
CBS News, 5
Center for Turkish Studies, 234
Ceuta and Melilla, 415
Central Council of Muslims (Germany), 233, 241, 244, 259
CGT (Trade Union in France), 201
Chamberlain, Neville, 51
Channel 4 (Britain), 14, 38–40, 432
Channel Tunnel, 215
Charity Commission, 110–11, 390
Charlie Hebdo, 300–1, 351–2
Chatham House, 125
Chechnya, xii, 17, 19, 20, 28, 81–2, 100, 131, 151, 188, 210–11, 229
Cheema, Amir, 265–6
Chief Rabbi, 102, 106, 132, 259
Ciise, Cabdullah, 230
China, 19–20, 27, 30, 57, 66, 71–2, 86, 247, 308
   East, 86
   North, 86
Chirac, Jacques, 174–5, 208, 300
Choudary, Anjem, 161, 340, 350
Christ, Jesus, 37, 41, 102, 157, 236, 245, 255, 326, 355, 398, 422
Christmas, 159
Christians, 12, 14, 20, 22–3, 26, 35, 39–40, 47, 54, 61–2, 64–6, 73–4, 84, 102, 107, 109, 114, 116, 119, 128, 138, 143–4, 148–9, 150, 158, 162–4, 202, 217, 233, 245, 247, 363, 436
   Anti, 39, 45, 121, 180, 196, 232, 235, 254–5, 259, 262, 325, 391
Christendom, 64
   Institute, 150
   People's Alliance, 159

Gospels, 107
Pieta, 1–2
'Sunday people', 23
Christian Democrats (Germany), 231, 241, 247, 261
Christian Democratic Party (Australia), 248
Christian Science Monitor, 207
Church of England, 34, 40, 122, 148–9, 159, 207, 350, 378
Churchill, Winston, 51
CIA, 25
  World Factbook, 7
Cités/Banlieues, 174, 201–2, 222–3, 237, 380–1
City Journal, 146
Clarke, Charles, 142, 401
Clash of Civilizations, 184, 189, 329
Clichy-sous-Bois, 198–9
CNN, 439–40
Colonialism/Colonization, 48, 54–5, 66, 70, 73, 78, 85, 181, 190, 192, 245
  Neo, 183
Cologne, 245, 267
  Cathedral, 261
  Mosque, 261–3
Commission on Cohesion and Integration (UK), 150, 335
Communism/Marxism, 26, 28, 30, 73, 199, 201, 308–9
  Communist Party (France), 201
Constantinople/Istanbul, ix, x, 23, 122, 330
  Haghia Sophia, 330
Congress (American), 11, 25, 83, 417
  House Intelligence Committee (see also US), 11
Congressional Quarterly, 11
Conseil Francais du Culte Musulman (CFCM), 187
Consistoire and CRIF, 175
Conversions to Islam, 114, 188
Cooper, Rabbi Abraham, 312
Coordinating Council of the Muslims of Germany (KRM), 241–2
Copenhagen, 271, 289, 295, 316, 343
  Copenhagen Post, 282
Copts, 20, 202, 248
Cordova, Mosque of, 22
Corriere della Sera, 399
Council of Christian Churches, 195
Council of Ex-Muslims, 260
  of Britain, 260
  of Germany, 259, 261
  of Netherlands, 260
  of Scandinavia, 260
Croats, 119
Cromwell, 107
Crown Prosecution Service (CPS, see also Britain), 145, 167, 169
Crusades, 12, 20, 47, 129, 215, 236, 369, 403, 406
Cuba, 220
Cyprus, 72, 99, 120, 267, 346
Czech Republic, 229, 374

Daily Star, 304, 340
Daily Telegraph, 38, 41, 97, 104, 106, 133, 138–9, 153–4, 159, 400
Dalrymple, Theodore, 143, 146
Damascus, 231, 293
Danmarks Radio, 439
Darfur, 26, 120, 308
Darul Uloom School, 39
Dati, Rachida, 222–3
Day of Judgement, 13
Da'wa, x, 70, 354
Debré, Michel, 174
Deghayes, Abubaker, 109–11
  Omar, 110–11
Deligoz, Ekim, 232
Democrats (US), 11
Denmark, 17, 83, 189, 206, 280ff, 346, 396, 439
  Anti, 1, 103, 176, 278
  Embassy, 140, 301
  Labor Union, 295
  Parliament, 412
  People's Party, 313, 321, 412, 439
Der Spiegel, 272, 300, 311, 374
Derby, 43
Deutsche Presse Agentur, 237
De Villepin, Dominique, 175, 334
Dewsbury, 129, 159
Dhimmi, 3, 12, 48, 88, 285, 437
Di Fabio, Udo, 252
Dialogue (with Muslims), 13, 49–50
Diaspora, 86
  Jewish, 3
  Muslim, 85
Die Presse, 74
Die Tageszeitung, 245
Die Welt, 266, 313, 375
Dieudonne, 178, 180, 195
Directorate of Professional Standards, 152
Downer, Alexander, 29
Dreyfus Affair, 175
Dubai, 230
Druze, 238
Dublin, 122
Dudley, 363–4
Duisberg, 232–3
Duncan-Smith, Ian, 163
Dundee, 162
Dusseldorf, 249, 267, 336

Index

East Europe, 227, 229–30, 267
Economist, 81, 194–5
Edgware Road (London), 44, 101
Edinburgh, 162
Education Without Borders (France), 77, 228
Eggelbrecht, Petra, 249
Egypt, 2–3, 6–8, 14–15, 17, 20, 22, 26, 46, 60, 70, 89–90, 103, 122, 137, 145, 168, 175, 182, 202, 205, 217, 229, 246–8, 269, 281, 301, 316, 356, 420, 430
Eiffel Tower, 210
Ekstra Bladet, 303
El-Al Airline, 214
El Pais, 394
Equal Opportunities Commission (Britain), 123
Erbakan, PM Necmettin, 236
Erdogan, PM Recep Tayyip, 227, 236, 330
Eritrea, 126–7
(l)'Espresso, 324–5
Essex, 39
Est Republicain, 201
ETA, 49, 139
Ethiopia, 126
Etzioni, Amitai, 63
Europe, ix, x, 1–2, 6, 13, 17, 20–1, 23, 26–7, 29–30, 32–3, 50, 54, 57, 70–1, 81, 91, 103–4, 131, 227, 371
   Council of, 266, 412
   Court of Justice of, 154
   Colonies of, 6–7
   Convention of Human Rights of, 136, 139, 155
   Exchange Rate Mechanism of, 154
European Center of Research and Action on Racism and anti-Semitism, 197
European Council on *Fatwa* and Research, 124, 425
European Monitoring Center on Racism and Xenophobia, 76–7, 317
European Parliament, 258–9
European Society, 188
European Strategic Intelligence and Security Center, 79
European Union, 61, 65, 81–2, 97–8, 120, 177, 183, 201, 230, 243, 266, 311, 371, 388–9, 392, 444
Eurabia, 177, 400, 412
Europalestine List (for the European Parliament), 178
Evangelical Alliance, 148, 150–1
Eweida, Nadia, 151
(l)Express, 188
Fallaci, Oriana, 410–12
Far East, 54
Fascism, 9–10, 26, 31, 73
Fatah, 24, 26–7, 80

Fatwa, 14, 106, 122, 168, 261, 278, 349
Faurisson, Robert, 15, 379
Fara Kemi Seba, 195–6
   Kemites, 196
FBI, 25, 94
Feder, Don, 443
FEMYSO (Youth Branch of Federation of Islamic Organizations in Europe), 386ff
Fernandez, Yussuf, 21
Fischer, Joschka, 23
Flemish, 60
Florence, 59
Florida, 271
Foi et Pratique (France), 187
Forest Gate (London), 114–15, 153, 160, 211
France, ix, 3, 11, 21, 36, 57–9, 61–2, 72, 77, 82–3, 87, 134, 139, 142, 151, 157, 174ff, 210, 217, 229, 238, 258, 292, 311, 439, 447
   Academie Francaise, 208
   Army of, 191
   Assemblée Nationale of, 58, 192, 404
   Education Ministry of, 180
   Fifth Republic of, 199
   Foreign Ministry of, 203, 220
   Front National, 83
   Government of, 82
   Immigration Ministry of, 221–2
   Intelligence and DST of, 79, 188, 210, 213, 215
   Interior Ministry of, 78, 175, 178, 181, 196, 211, 220
   Media of, 178, 199
   National College of Gynecologists and Obstreticians, 203–4
   Prime Minister of, (see also De Villepin), 175
   Renseignements Generaux of, (see also Intelligence above), 63
France Soir, 314–15
Frankfurter Allgemeine Zeitung, 245, 264, 269, 315
Frankfurt, 251, 338
   District Court, 257
   International Airport, 267, 270
Free Inquiry Magazine, 296
Freedom of Information Act, 36
Fregosi, Frank, 86–8
French Muslim Council, 87
Friedrich Ebert Foundation, 252
Front National, 174
Fukuyama, Francis, 83, 374

G-8, 120
Gabriel, Brigitte, 383
Galloway, George, 110, 114
   Respect Party, 116
Gama'at, 70, 392

Islamiyya, 345
Ganor, Boaz, 441
Garaudy, Roger, 15, 379
Garbuzi, Muhammed, 231
Garzon, Baltazar, 79
Gast Arbeiter/Guest Worker, 227, 238, 248
Gaullisme, 174
Gaza, 4, 24, 26, 60, 80–1, 182, 199, 292, 433
  Strip, 90, 153, 301
Geneva, 175
  Conventions, 59
  Human Rights Council in, 318
Genoa, Mosque in, 263
Genocide, 15, 24, 26, 80, 120, 308
Georgetown University, 25
Germany, x, 23, 26, 30, 57, 61, 71, 78, 87, 119, 139, 157, 179, 188, 197, 204, 214, 217, 227ff, 285, 311, 320, 386, 439, 446
  Administrative Court, 252
  Bundestag, 232
  Domestic Security of, 263
  Federal Constitutional Court, 252–3, 257
  Federal Ministry of Family Affairs, 256
  German Marshall Fund, 248
  Intelligence (BND) of, 254, 267
  Interior Ministry of, 241–2
  Media of, 294
Gestapo, 175
Gharbi, Prof. Iqbal, 205
Ghazi, Abdul Rashid, 183
Gillerman, Dan, 47
Giordano, Ralph, 261
Glasgow, 101, 134, 138, 146, 162–3
  Airport, 136
Globalization, 183, 191, 210
GLORIA (Global Research in International Affairs), 66
God/Allah, 8–9, 12, 23, 29–30, 43, 67, 101, 107–9, 116, 124, 135, 144, 147, 168, 229, 262, 285, 290, 314, 398, 421
  Allah Akbar!, 178, 309, 340, 381
Goldhagen, Daniel, 291–2
Goth/Visigoth, 85–6
Gough, Steve, 95, 143
Grade, Michael, 35
Granada, ix, 20
Grandes écoles, 198
Greece, 41, 65, 267, 415
  Greek language, 202
Green Party, 201, 232, 246
Guardian, 34, 105, 152
Guantanamo, 110, 130, 182, 186, 220, 271, 309, 335, 357, 418
Gul, President Abdullah, 236
Gulf, Arab/Persian, 36, 161
  States, 17, 20, 26, 36, 61, 70, 190, 212, 304
  War (see also War), 189, 436

Gupta, Ganchan, 165
Guyana, 163

Habash, George, 411
Habermas, Jurgen, 269
Hadith, 13, 23, 43, 100, 180, 260, 422–3
Haiti, 195
Halal (food), 77, 108, 164, 252, 316
Halevy, Ephraim, 78
Halimi, Ilan, 60, 179–80, 195–6
Hamas, 4, 6, 9, 11, 15, 20, 24, 26–7, 38, 42, 45, 50, 78, 80, 102–3, 106, 137, 153, 182, 189, 263, 282, 292, 304–5, 430, 433
Hamburg, 235, 268, 270, 403
  Cell, 231
  University of, 237
Hamid, Tawfik, 47–8
Hammami, Hamadi, 186
Hanbalite (Cult), 4
Handelsblatt, 313
Hanafite, 4
Hanson, Victor Davis, 26–7
Haramain Foundation, 143–4
Hariri, Rafik, 304
Harrods, 94
Hart, Rev. David, 149
Hart, Commissioner James, 99
Harvard University, 57
Hawai
  University of, 80
    Populations Studies at, 80
Hawza Islamiyya, 389–90
Hebron, 292
Heinsohn, Gunnar, 80–1
Hennessy, Professor Peter, 125
Hesse, 235, 242
Herzliya, Inter-Disciplinary Center at, 66
Hicks, David, 271
Hijab/Veil, 38–9, 72, 77, 87, 108, 124, 128, 151, 205, 234, 253, 258, 261, 444
  'jilbab', 117
Hilali, Sheikh Taj Din al-, 112, 158
Hindus, 54, 66, 72–3, 124, 146, 149, 152, 159, 166, 232, 247, 307, 437
Hitler, 15, 26, 31, 105, 176, 180, 291
Hizbullah, 11, 24, 27, 37, 169, 263, 312, 346, 404
Hizb-ut-Tahrir, 106, 134, 136, 268, 281–2, 414
Hollande, François, 198, 352
Holy Land, 20
Hormuz, Straits of, 23
House of Commons (see also Britain), 134, 155–6, 208
  Foreign Affairs Committee of, 50
  Liaison Committee of, 95
  Parliamentary Committees of, 166–7, 169

Index

Hungary, 71, 195
Human Rights, 112–13, 139, 148, 154–5, 318
Humiliation, 6, 8, 191
Huns, 86
Huntington, Samuel, 79–81
Hussein, Saddam, 18, 31, 120, 269, 412, 436
Husseini, Haj Amin, 26

Iberia, ix, 21, 73
Ibn Taymiyya, 4, 186
Ibn Warraq, 7, 306–8
Iddon, MP Brian, 11
Ilford, 39
Immigration, Asylum and Nationality Bill, 133–4
Imperialism, 9, 26, 66, 190, 280, 307–8, 370, 376
  'Moral', 31
India, 20, 26, 28, 54, 57, 60, 66, 72–3, 86–7, 98–9, 136, 158, 165, 182, 209, 300, 306, 402
Indonesia, 25, 28, 57, 50, 86, 217, 236, 247, 269, 323
  Ulema Council of, 356
Institute for Public Policy Research (Britain), 83, 96
International Federation of Journalists, 313
International Human Rights Federation, 214
International Institute of Strategic Studies (London), 79
International Monetary Fund, 183
Interpol, 131
Intifada, 176, 178, 180, 202
  First, 199
IRA (see also Ireland), 37, 95, 106, 116 427–8
Iran/Persia, 2, 7, 11, 20, 22, 4, 26, 54, 57, 60, 67, 70–1, 79 86, 107, 119, 133, 166, 168, 202, 205, 238, 245–7, 259, 272, 278, 291, 300, 349, 436, 439, 445–6
  Plateau, 202
  Revolution, 11, 189
  language, 202
Iraq, 1–2, 4–6, 11, 17, 19, 25–6, 29–31, 44, 48–9, 70–1, 79–80, 86, 99–100, 105, 110, 112, 115, 119–21, 123, 126, 130–1, 135–6, 151–2, 187–9, 202, 215, 228–30, 246–7, 263, 439
Ireland, 37, 106, 116, 267
  Irish Republican Army (see also IRA), 106
  Northern, 135, 437
Irving, David, 15, 379
Islam
  Channel, 321
  Friends of, 11
  Islamdom, 48, 60, 184
  Islamic Human Rights Commission, 158

Islamic state (see also Caliphate), 103, 132
Islamofascism, 10–12, 15, 21, 31
  O*nline*, 211–12
Islamabad, 183, 265, 349
Islamic Commission (Spain), 340
Islamic Community of Germany, 234, 240
Islamic Conference, ix, 66, 302
  Organization of (OIC), 73, 158, 302, 308 316–18, 355–6, 420
Islamic Council of Europe, 164
Islamic Federation, 235
Islamic Happiness Party, 236
Islamic Jihad Union, 271
Islamic Mission (see also *da'wa*), 38
Islamic Relief Worldwide (IRW), 153
Islamic Society of Britain, 164
Islamikaze/Martyrdom, ix, x, 9, 13, 42, 44, 79–81, 106, 110, 121–2, 125, 137, 140, 149, 152–3, 188, 228–30, 264, 338, 357
Islamophobia, 3, 16, 45–7, 75, 84, 95, 104, 125, 129, 156–7, 158, 164, 212, 265, 303, 313, 354
Israel, 15, 19, 23, 37–8, 44–5, 47–8, 71–2, 91, 154, 169, 243, 388–9, 402, 433
  Anti, 1, 3–5, 14, 17, 25–6, 36, 66, 89, 102–3, 105, 166, 176, 191–2, 230
  Armed Forces, 197
  Greater, 236
  Palestinian Dispute, 113, 178, 238, 437
  Shin Bet in, 153
Italy, 21, 30, 61, 82, 139, 188, 210, 216, 229–31, 238, 263, 267, 320, 392
  Islamic Cultural Center in, 325
Ivory Coast, 195–6

Jakarta, 166
Jama'ah Islamiyya, 47, 161
Jama'at Ahl al Sunna, 265
Janjaweed, 308–9
Japan, 9, 153
Jeddah, x, 356
Jerusalem, 178, 429
  Wailing Wall in, 399
Jewish Chronicle, 102
Jews, 16, 20, 22–3, 31, 37, 40, 42, 47, 54, 84, 100, 102–3, 116, 124, 138, 202, 217, 232, 373
  Anti, 2, 4–6, 13, 26, 32, 39, 34, 45, 48, 65, 103, 121, 140, 164, 166, 175–6, 178, 180, 227, 254, 262, 375, 391
  Jewish Conspiracy/Lobby, 170
  Jewish Defence League, 196–7
  Jewish State, 177
  Migrations of, 75, 106–7
  'Saturday People', 23
Jihad, x, 4, 17–18, 20–21, 23, 25, 38, 42, 44, 47, 79, 93, 102–3, 106, 112, 114, 129,

131, 136, 139, 143–4, 151, 157, 160, 167, 182, 184–8, 191, 210, 215–16, 229–30, 259, 273, 318, 320, 325, 327, 354, 358, 370, 389, 434–6, 441
Mujahid, 9, 17, 29, 86, 131
Camp, 113
'Soft', 56
Jizya, 438
John Paul II (Pope), 315, 325, 352, 397, 399
Johnston, Philip, 133, 138–9, 159
Jordan, 2–3, 6, 15, 17, 70, 80, 89–90, 133, 136, 168, 217, 229, 281, 343, 430
Joseph, Sarah, 62
Judaism (see also Jews), 156
Judeo-Christian, 54, 149
Judeophobia (see also anti-Semitism), 3–4, 13, 15, 17
Juste, Carsten, 296, 322, 343
Jutland, 344
Jyllands Posten, 296, 299, 301, 314, 323, 343–4, 346, 397

Ka Tribe, 195–6
Kabul, 4
Kafir/Infidel, 39, 40, 108–9, 121, 182
press, 108
Karachi, 4
Karsh, Efraim, 368–70
Kashmir, 40, 119, 182, 209
Kazakhstan, 131
Kelly, Ruth, 124–5, 131–2
Kennedy, President John, 16
Kenya, 19, 25, 230, 410
Khalilzad, Zalmay, 74
Khamena'I, Ayatullah Ali, 389, 436
Khan, Imran, 335
Khayam, Omar, 140
Khaybar, 100, 342
Khobar, 19
Khomeini, Ayatullah Ruhollah, 106–7, 334, 412
Khuri, Rami, 304
Kiel, 268
King Fahd Academy, 254–6
King's Cross (London), 44
Kingsway International Christian Charity Center, 160
Kohler, Ayyub Axel, 242, 244–5
Konkret, 260
Kosovo, 40, 120, 123, 364, 373
Kouchner, Bernard, 410
Krauthammer, Charles, 294
Krekar, Mullah, 320, 411
Kurds, 65, 71, 120, 145, 229, 240, 257
Kurtuldu, Mustafa, 99–101
Kuwait, 18, 89, 189, 282, 432

Labour (England), 11, 83, 98–100, 123–4, 129, 260, 350, 383
New, 154
La Courneuve, 178
Lancashire, 148
Lansac, Jacques, 204
Laqueur, Walter, 73–5
Latinos, 83
Latvia, 446
Law and Religion Research Center (Strasbourg), 87
Lebanon, 6, 17, 19, 24, 26, 28, 133, 169, 237–8, 271, 305, 344, 346, 383
Leeds, 44, 99
University, 147
Le Figaro, 334, 350
Lefranc, Jacques, 314
Leicester, 147, 448
Lemoine, Xavier, 197–9
Le Monde, 63, 181, 200, 204, 352
Le Monde des Religions, 203
Le Parisien, 297
Le Pen, Jean-Marie, 174
Le Point, 182, 185–6
Levallois, 187
Levy, Bernard-Henry, 183
Lewis, Bernard, 18–19, 188
Liberals (UK), 11
Libération, 205, 220
Libya, 17, 110, 133, 151, 216
Lille,
Ibn Rushd School, 212
University of, 212
Liddle, Rodd, 108–9, 166
Liverpool, 99
Anglian Cathedral in, 159
Livingstone, Mayor Ken, 138, 165
London, 1, 23, 37, 39, 72, 99, 191, 228, 230, 253, 255, 379
bombings, x, 33, 38, 40–1, 44, 47, 50, 61, 63, 93, 95, 98, 115, 125, 134, 138, 140, 150, 153, 156, 161, 165, 167, 183–4, 211, 239, 264, 292, 427, 432
Brixton Gaol, 316
Stansted Airport, 154
University
Queen Mary College, 127
Londonistan, 103–6, 261
Long Lartin Prison, 143
Lord Carey of Clifton, 329
Los Angeles, 277
Times, 286, 417
World Affairs Council of, 27
Lower Saxony Criminology Research Institute, 256
Luton, 117, 147
Luxemburg, 303
Lyon, 210

Archbishop of, 211

Macedonia, 99, 267
Madani, Ayad Ben-Amin, 312
Madagascar, 19, 77
McDonald Restaurant, 191
Madhhab (School of Law), 4
Madrasa, 27, 123, 140, 163, 184–5, 214
Mafia, 229, 379
Madrid, x, 1, 7, 28, 41, 49–50, 61, 110, 228, 264, 340, 379, 393–4, 432
Magazinet, 304
Maghreb (sse also Africa/North), 103
Mahfudh Naguib, 294
Mahmood, MP Khalid, 11
Major, PM John, 11, 154
Malaysia, 57, 66–7
Mali, 60, 208
Malik, MP Shahid, 124, 129
Malmo, 62
Ma'mun, Caliph, 41
Malthus, Thomas Robert, 443
Manchester, 30, 99, 151–2, 167
Manji, Irshad, 249
Manningham-Buller, Eliza, 123
Maqreze Center for Historical Studies, 95
Marburg, University of, 233
Marin, Jean-Claude, 187
Marseille, 62, 201
Martel, Charles, ix, 174
Mary, St, 102, 285
Masalha, Salman, 257
Masri, Abu Hamza, 38, 93ff, 103, 111, 117, 133, 165, 189, 211, 254, 340, 391
Mattéi, Jean-Baptiste, 220
Mauritania, 394, 439
Mawdudi, Abu al- Ala' al-, 4–5, 42, 73
Mayzek, Ayman, 241
Mecca, 121, 185, 302, 335, 397, 422
  Pilgrimage (*Hajj*) to, 73, 140, 203
Media, 3, 29, 31, 33ff, 40, 49, 156, 163, 168, 248, 313
  Arab, 5, 13, 36, 166
  British, 98–9, 100, 113, 115, 126, 132, 157
  French, 181–3, 185–6, 194
  German, 249
  Jihadi, 29
  Kufr, 108
  War, 29–30
  Muslim, 15, 129
  Western, 5, 33ff, 36, 46, 95, 120, 132, 156, 178
Medina, 100, 335
Mediterranean, 21, 85
Mein Kampf, 166, 348
Merkel, Chancellor Angela, 241, 244, 247, 261, 264, 293

Methodist Church, 148
MI5, 98–9, 125, 127, 130, 140–2, 151, 153, 210, 440
MI6, 141
Mian, Dr Ijaz, 39
MEMRI (Middle East Media Research Institute), 29
Merkazi Jamiat Ahl al-Hadith, 45
Metropolitan Police (London), 114–15, 141, 148, 152, 158
Michigan, 296
Middle Ages, 20, 22, 207, 330, 403
Middle East/Levant, 2, 11, 25–8, 36, 54, 57, 74, 78, 85, 91, 102–3, 113, 131, 140, 165–7, 169, 176, 178, 191, 199, 206, 217, 227, 231, 289, 294, 311, 322–3, 327, 341, 343, 357, 370, 413, 434, 436, 439
  Conflict (see also Arab-Israeli), 56, 220
Middlesex, 144, 389
  University, 390
Midlands, West, 41–3, 129
Migration Policy Institute, 82
Migration Watch UK, 99 127
Mikkelsen, Joern, 314
Milan, 139, 229
Mile End Group, 125
Mill, John Stuart, 165, 207, 306
Milli Gorus, 234–6, 241, 259, 263
Milosevic, Milovan, 120
Mishkat al-Masabih, 180
Mitterand, President François, 192–3
Mogadishu, 19
Moghul, 54
Mogra, Sheikh Ibrahim, 162, 447–8
Muhammed VI, 394
Mohammed, Ramzi, 126–7
Mombasa, 230
Monfermeil, 197–8
Moniquet, Claude, 79
Moors, 336, 339
Moore, Charles, 41–3, 106–7, 154–5
Mormons, 208
Morocco, 6, 60, 214, 216, 228, 236, 251, 253, 314, 346, 393, 415, 439
  Islamic Cobatant Group, 393
Moscow, 253
Mosque, 38, 42, 49, 56, 62, 72, 77, 87, 106, 109–10, 116, 119, 121–3, 125, 134, 137, 158, 187, 205, 225, 229, 232, 252–3, 256, 259, 403
  Brighton, 110–11
  Cologne, 261
  Dudley, 363–4
  East London, 42, 115, 159
  Finsbury Park, 94, 111, 165
  Great, (Paris), 175, 352
  Green Lane, 39, 43
  Grimhovej, 344

London Markaz, 158–9
Morden, 159
Red, 183
Regent's Park, 39, 350
Sparbrook, 38–9
Umar (Paris), 185
Undercover, 40, 42
Mosque Association (Germany), 242
Mosque and Community Affairs, 161
Mossad, 6, 16, 78, 190, 280
Mosques and Imams National Advisory Body (Britain), 161
Moussawi, Zacarias, 224
Mozakka, Nader, 44
  Benhaz, 44
Mubarak, President Husni, 420
  Suzanne, 420
Mugabe, President Robert, 31
Mufti, 134
  Grand, 39
Muhajirun, 134, 161, 282, 342
Multiculturalism, 10, 14, 22, 32, 35–6, 38, 51, 56–8, 76, 83–4, 104, 106, 123, 129, 149, 159, 165
Munich
  Agreement / Appeasement, 374
Muntada Islamic Forum, 103
Murabitun, 21
Musharraf, President Pervez, 183
Muslim (see also Islam), 217
  Brotherhood, 30, 70, 110, 168, 175, 182, 240, 263, 269, 304, 344, 353–4, 385, 387, 392, 410, 414, 425
  and Christian, 120
  countries, x, 6, 17, 28, 46, 54, 61, 100, 124, 131, 144, 159, 189
  Parliament, 39, 72, 114, 140
  parties, 2, 227
  rule, ix
  world, 1–2 4, 6, 13–14, 16, 26, 54, 66, 79, 130, 176, 185, 220
  Youth, 38, 40, 76, 125, 131, 386
Muslim Association of Britain (MAB), 30, 129
Muslim Council of Britain (MCB), 45, 104, 106, 112, 114–15, 121–2, 125, 128, 132–3, 137, 139, 157, 209, 239, 262, 351, 424, 431, 447
Muslim Council for Religious and Racial Harmony (Britain), 110,158
Muslim Public Affairs Committee (MPAC), 108–9
Muslim News, 136
Mussa, Secretary General Amr, 290
Mustafa, Muhammed Kamal, 256

Nablus, 153
Al-Najah School, 211

Namazie, Maryam, 133, 260
Napoleon, 175
Nasser, President Gamal abd al, 26
(*The*) *Nation* (Pakistan), 323
Nationalism, 102, 403
  European, 65, 83
  Muslim, 73, 105
National Front (France), 36
National Party (Britain), 400
National Secular Society (Britain), 258
NATO, 120, 227, 269, 396
Nazir, Azhar, 144–5
Nazir Ali, Michael, 122, 298
Nazism, 9, 30, 166, 261, 289, 293, 322, 338, 373, 428
  Neo-, 167
  Third Reich, 261
Nepal, 86
Nestorian, 202
Netherlands, 1, 57–9, 61, 83–4, 182, 188–9, 238, 244, 248–9, 252, 260, 289, 298, 379–80, 418, 425, 446
  Church in, 260
  Freedom Party in, 348
  Supreme Court in, 59
Network for Muslim Women, 251
Neues Deutschland, 375–6
New Scientist Magazine, 58
New South Wales, 248
New Ulm, 270
New York, 7, 19, 47, 214, 231, 379
  Times, 36, 311, 417, 439
  University, 31
New Zealand, 300
Nicholson, Rev. Julie, 101
Nielsen, Jorgen, 304
Nigeria, 25, 57, 70, 98, 209, 325
Nikomemus, Rev. Rafael, 233
Nile, Rev. Fred, 248
Nobel Prize, 294, 420
Noelle, Elisabeth, 265
Northampton, 11
North Rhine, Westphalia, 233, 241, 267
Northern League Party (Italy), 263
Norway, 292–3, 304, 329, 425
Nouvel Observateur, 201
Nyborg State Prison, 346

Observer, 40, 45–6
O'Connor, Cardinal Murphy, 329–30
Odysseus Network, 58
Ofcom, 41
Office of National Statistics, 147
Oil, 26, 74, 278
  wells, 23
  prices, 2, 17, 26
Omar, Millah, 120

Omar, Yassin, 126
OPEC, 74
Oregon, 94
Organization for Security and Cooperation in Europe (OSCE), 158, 181, 312
Oslo, 228, 281, 411, 427
Osservatore Romano, 399
Ottomans, ix, x, 22, 54, 368–9
Oxford, 183, 424
Ozoguz, Yavuz, 235

Padilla, Jose, 271
Pakistan, 6, 14–15, 17, 28, 57, 69, 70, 72, 99, 104–5, 127, 129–30, 135, 140–2, 144–5, 152–3, 157–8, 165, 175, 183–4, 209–10, 214–15, 217, 247, 265–6, 269, 300, 303, 327, 341, 349, 418, 445
Palestine, 3–4, 9, 11, 14–15, 24–6, 28, 38, 40, 60, 80–1, 89–91, 102, 118–19, 128, 153, 169, 176, 189, 191–2, 202, 231, 237–8, 247, 281, 433
  Authority, 2, 17, 50, 81, 135, 379, 430
  Foreign Minister, 50
  Israel Conflict, 178, 434, 436
  Palestinian state, 90, 103, 120
  Palestinian terrorism, 1, 24, 184
  Palestinism, 177
Papua New Guinea, 139
Paris, 32, 60, 62, 111, 174–5, 178–81, 185, 187, 191, 195, 197, 202, 214, 237
  Charles de Gaulle Airport, 214
  Directorate of Internal Security, 215
  New York Flight, 214
  Orly Airport, 215
Parry, Admiral Chris, 85–6, 88
Partido Popular, 21
Pasha, Sayed Aziz, 124
Patel, Yaseen, 108
Pax Islamica/Dar al-Islam, 7, 22, 67–8, 73, 88, 182, 201
Peace, 47, 50, 64, 73, 101
  with Israel, 13, 24–5, 290
Pearl, Daniel, 183
Pell, Cardinal George, 328–9
Pew Global Attitudes Project, 217, 224
Philippines, 25, 57, 72, 402
Phillips, Melanie, 103–4, 106
Phillips, Trevor, 219
Piekolek, Chantal, 180
Pipes, Daniel, 47, 165, 201, 348
Pirkei Avot, 107
Plassnik Ursula, 317
Pohl, Hanspeter, 233
Poitiers, ix, 174
Poland, 229–30, 267, 288
Political Correctness Corrective Party, 96
Policy Review, 199

Politiken, 322
Poller, Nidra, 195
Portillo, Michael, 23–4
Porter, Henry, 40–1
Portugal, ix, 19, 179, 267, 415
Prince of Wales, 118, 122–3, 297–8, 351
Prison Officers' Association (Britain), 95, 143
Prison Service (Britain), 145
Private Eye, 328
Prokop, Liese, 58
Prophet, 41
  of Islam, 12, 23, 43, 65, 75, 100, 103, 109, 146, 235, 245, 248, 262, 277ff, 422
Protestant, 82, 236, 309, 328
Protocols of the Elders of Zion, 15, 167, 181, 294, 420
Psaradakis, George, 33

Qaddafi, President Mu'ammar, 371
(al) Qa'ida, 9, 11, 17, 19, 25, 29, 44, 47, 79, 87, 94, 105, 110, 115, 125–6, 128, 130–1, 135, 140–1, 151–3, 156, 184, 191, 213–17, 228–9, 263, 267–9, 271, 282, 305, 313, 315, 327, 334, 353, 381, 393, 410, 419, 434, 445–6
  Organization in the Islamic Maghreb, 216
Qaradawi, Yussuf, 5, 23, 122, 165, 353–4
Qatar, 212
  University of, 122
Quayum, Sajid, 162–3
Qur'an, 7, 12–13, 19–20, 35, 50, 100, 109, 112, 118, 121, 137, 143–4, 146, 163–4, 182, 186, 206, 251, 253, 256, 259, 262, 285, 287, 309, 326, 328, 343, 348, 355, 357, 391, 397–8, 421–3, 430, 439
Qut'b, Sayyed, 4–5 137

Racism, 14, 26, 32, 40, 62, 75, 83, 94–5, 104, 133, 152, 164, 169, 174, 178, 181, 207–8, 227, 254–5, 261, 268, 272, 282, 303, 312, 365
Radio Ramadan, 163
Ralison, Andiriamina, 77
Ramadan, 185, 205, 397, 424
Ramadan, Tariq, 175, 239, 386, 410, 424
Ramstein Air Base, 267
Rand Ayn Institute, 9–11, 298–9
Rasmussen, PM Fogh, 301–2, 311, 347
Rather, Dan, 5
Reagan, President Ronald, 16, 18, 373
Reconquista, ix, 339–40
Regensburg, 330
  University of, 326–7
Rehov, Pierre, 8
Reid, Secretary John, 98, 159, 349, 442
Reinfeldt, PM Fredrik, 356
Republicans (US), 30

Return Migration to the Maghreb Movement, 59
Reuters, 245, 396
Reyes, Congressman Silvestro, 11
Riaz, Muhammed, 145
Rice, Secretary Condoleeza, 266, 301
Ridda/Apostasy, 133
Ridley, Yvonne, 114, 322
Riyadh, x, 19, 43, 231, 295
Robert Schuman Center for Advanced Studies (Florence), 59, 87
Rochester, Bishop of, 122
Rodinson, Maxime, 11
Rohe, Mathias, 253
Romania, 229, 267
Rome, 23, 325, 397
  Roman Curia, 331
  Roman Empire, 85–6
  Romiyya (Europe), 23
  scenario, 86
Rose, Fleming, 311
Rosiers, Rue de (Paris), 196
Roubaix, 187
Royal Institute of International Affairs, 254
Royal, Segolene, 220
Rubin, Barry, 66
Rushdie, Salman, 27, 45, 63, 106, 272, 277–8, 299, 327, 334–5, 348–51, 382
Russia, 19–20, 57, 210, 288, 407, 443
  Embassy, 210
  Federation, 78

Sacks, Dr Jonathan (see also Chief Rabbi), 102, 106
Sacranie, Iqbal, 45, 104, 106, 109, 115, 117, 121
Sadat, President Anwar, 90
Sahara, 216
Sa'id Metwalli, 205–6
Sajid, Dr Abdallah, 110–12, 158
Salafism, 47–9, 143, 214, 216
Samarra, 279
San Ramon Valley Herald, 19
Sanabel Relief Agency, 151–2
Sanderson, Terry, 258
Santorum, Senator Rick, 9
Sarkozy, President Nicolas, 59–60, 77, 193–4, 200–2, 211, 220–3, 352, 381
Saudi Arabia, 7, 14–15, 17, 20–1, 38–40, 60, 67, 79, 89–90, 103, 107, 117, 121–2, 124, 131, 133, 140, 143–4, 153, 157–8, 175, 203, 205, 209, 229–30, 245–6, 253–5, 289–90, 308, 312, 318, 335, 344, 354, 356, 419, 424, 436, 447
  Grand Mufti of, 39
Savigny, Marie-Françoise, 207
Sawt al-Khikafa, 131

Scandinavia, x, 61, 206, 258, 279, 320
Schengen, 394
Schauble, Wolfgang, 240–1, 258, 262, 270, 274, 338–9
Schily, Otto, 139
Schindler's List, 15
Schroder, Gerhard, 264
Schwartz, Stephen, 157–8
Scotland Yard, 44, 98, 231, 340
Scriptuaries (People of the Book, see also Jews and Christians), 20
Scout Association (in Britain), 162
Seattle, 94
Sellam, Sebastian, 180
Senegal, 207, 223, 322, 394
Sentamu, Dr John, 102
September 11, ix, x, 1–2, 4–7, 9, 12, 16, 20, 25, 28, 41, 45, 50, 77, 87, 110, 115, 117, 122, 130, 141, 156, 167, 180, 184, 209, 217–18, 225, 227, 231, 234, 254, 258, 260, 265, 267, 270, 278, 280–2, 292–3, 310, 328, 350, 370, 403, 436
Serbs, 119
Serious Fraud Office (Britain), 140
Shah (see also Iran), 2
Shahid, Imran, 146
Shanmugam, Johannes, 96
Shari'a, 4, 7–8, 27, 38, 40, 42, 48–9, 66, 73, 103, 124, 128, 132, 160, 163–4, 182, 189, 232–3, 249, 260, 274, 287, 324, 333, 341, 365–6, 424
  Court, 67
  Council for the UK, 166
Sharon, PM Ariel, 178, 433
Sharq al-Awsat, 432
Sheffield, 160
Shi'a, 4, 11, 48, 88–9, 132, 144, 189, 205, 246, 279–80, 305, 439
  Alevis, 240
  Twelver, 279
Shoah/Holocaust, 2, 14–15, 26, 106, 124–5, 176, 191–2, 243, 279, 285, 291, 305, 441
Sicily, 19
Sidique Khan, Muhammad, 44, 105
Siddiqui, Ghayasuddin, 39–40, 114, 140
Sierra Leone, 119
Sikhs, 124, 146, 152, 214, 328
Sinai, x
Sistani, Ayatullah, 305
Slough, 147
Social Forum Movement, 30
Socialist Workers Party, 30
Socialists (in France), 174, 194–5, 198, 220, 222–3, 352
Social Democrats (Germany), 251–2, 375
Sodano, Cardinal Angelo, 325–6
Solana, Javier, 301
Somalia, 25, 58–9, 126–7, 142, 230, 298,

300
Sookhdeo, Dr Patrick, 149–50, 163–5, 323–4, 348, 355
Soviet, 71, 192, 418
  Communism (see Communism)
  Empire, 17–18
Spain (see also Madrid), ix, 19–23, 41, 49, 61, 78–9, 82, 87, 94, 119, 174, 210, 216–17, 222, 231, 246, 256, 267, 269, 371–2, 393, 415, 443
  Interior Minister, 139
  Socialist Government, 139
Spanish Federation of Islamic Religious Entities, 21
(The) Spectator, 108, 166
Spuler-Stegerman, Ursula, 233
Sri Lanka, 98
Sriskandarajah, Danny, 82
St Louis, 17
Staffordshire, 108
Stalin, Joseph (see also Soviet), 30
Stanmore, 126
Stéfanini, Laurent, 203
Stein, Jeff, 11
Strasbourg, 87, 155
Staw, Jack, 43, 143, 258
Streeter, MP Gary, 11
Struck, Peter, 237
Sudan, 17, 26, 70, 133, 247, 308
Sudayyis, Sheikh abdul Rahaman, 121, 424
Suddeutsche Zeitung, 313
Sudeten, 71
Suen, Faruk, 234
Sufism, 48, 240
Sultan, Dr Wafa, 205, 284–8, 392
Sunday Telegraph, 120, 167, 351
Sunday Times, 11, 31, 124
Sunni, 4, 11, 48, 88–9, 132, 144, 157, 189, 205, 246, 279–80, 305
Surucu, Hatun, 256
Sussex,
  Muslim Society Charity, 111
  Police, 110
  University of, 59
Svenska Dagbladet, 281
Sweden, 82, 189, 267, 271, 281, 302, 346, 355–7, 380, 410
Swiss, 230, 231, 255, 266, 311, 353
  Nestlé, 311
Synagogue, 32, 107, 176, 197, 262, 437
Syria, 2, 6, 16–17, 22, 24, 26, 60, 70–1, 79, 89, 202, 205, 215, 229–30, 270, 278, 283, 286, 301, 304, 346, 393
  Syriac, 202

Tablighi Jama'at, 63, 158–9, 186, 214
Tagespiegel, 245, 264
Taheri, Amir, 94, 118–20, 192–3

Taleban, 17, 27, 38–9, 94, 114, 120, 123, 141, 157, 182, 191, 281, 322, 419, 446
Tamil, 214
Tanzania, 19, 25, 410
Tanweer, Shehzad, 44
Taqiyya, 41, 345
Taqwa Bank, 353
Tasci, Imam Yakub, 252–3
Tatchell, Peter, 99
Tauran, Cardinal Jean Louis, 325
(al) Tawhid, 231
Tehran, 4, 19, 305
Tel Aviv, 24
Ten Commandments, 128
Terrorism, 17–18, 22, 25–7, 32–3, 37–8, 40–1, 44, 46–7, 50, 56, 61, 63, 78–9, 82, 99ff, 112–15, 134
  Anti-, Laws, 112–13
  Counter, activities, 114–16, 121, 133, 136, 138, 181, 183
  International, 1
  Islamic, x, 2, 7–8, 10–13, 15, 26–7, 31, 48–9, 51, 74, 93ff, 116, 128, 130, 138, 140, 178, 186, 228
  Palestinian, 24, 27, 89, 153, 184
Thaer, Mansur, 231
Thailand, 26, 40, 48, 57
Thames University, 145
Thatcher, PM Margaret, 33
The Hague, 260
Theater, MP Sarah, 11
Thielemans, PM Freddy, 337
Third World, 85, 91, 326
Thompson, Damian, 149
Thoomis, Michel, 200, 202
Tibi Bassam, 272–4
Time Out, 146
(The) Times, 94, 166, 210, 328, 389, 391, 447
Toker, Arzu, 261–2
Tories/Conservatives, 11, 23, 37, 83, 98, 129, 138, 154, 167
Tottenham, 146
Trafalgar Square, 23
Transylvania, 71
Trigano, Shmuel, 289
Trotsky, 201
Tunisia, 9, 12, 124, 161, 204, 209, 212, 216, 314, 393, 439
  Zaytuna University in, 205
Turkestan, Eastern, 71
Turkey, 2, 57, 60, 65–6, 71, 79, 87, 99, 119, 124, 139, 204, 209, 217, 227, 231–2, 234, 236, 238, 240, 246–7, 249, 256–7, 267, 269, 303–4, 355, 371, 427
  Parliament, 227
  Turkish language, 250
Turkic, 71
Tuscany, Mosque in, 263

Twin Towers (see also September 11), 112, 180, 270

Uckermann, Joerg, 261
Uighur, 20
Ujaama, James, 94–5
UK Islamic Heritage Foundation, 157
'Ulama, 72
Ulfkotte, Udo, 231–3
Umayyad, 73
Umma, 74, 103, 105, 369
UN, 16, 24, 41, 47, 91, 151, 218, 238, 317, 355, 405
 Ambassador, 74
 Arab Human Development Report, 41, 269, 278
 Human Rights Council, 317
 Secretary General of, 317
 Security Council, 292
 UNESCO, 316–17
 World Health Organization, 39
Union Jack, 36
Union of the Muslim Organizations of the UK and Ireland, 124
United Arab Emirates, 89, 304, 344, 365
 Sharjah, 365
Urdu, 162
US, ix, 1–2, 5, 7, 10, 13, 16, 18, 22, 26–8, 44, 55, 57–9, 71, 78, 81, 86, 95, 105, 112, 114, 120, 151, 185, 246–7, 436
 Anti, 18–19, 26, 29, 35, 49, 79, 104, 180, 190, 233, 254, 270
 Ambassador/Embassies, 74, 209, 215
 Muslims, 25
 Territory, 17
 Senate (see also Congress), 82, 143
 Treasury, 151
US Institute of Peace, 17
USS Cole, 19

Vadillo, Umar Ibrahim, 21
Valencia, 73
Van Gogh, Theo, 1, 59, 182, 289, 298, 303, 320, 342, 357, 380, 430
Vandals, 85–6
Vatican/Holy See, 259, 323–7, 330–3, 398
Venezuela, 22
Venissieux, 210
Verdonk, Rita, 58–9
Versi, Ahmed, 136–7
Vienna, ix, 54, 76, 317
Vietnam, 224
Voivodina, 71

Wahhabi, 4, 20, 38, 63, 135, 143–4, 253, 367, 386
Wakefield, 148
Wales, 99, 147, 167
 Prince of Wales (see entry)
 Welsh Assembly, 168
Wall Street, 21
Wandsworth Prison, 144
Waqf, 240
War, 10, 28, 48, 74, 80–1, 104, 184
 in Afghanistan, 17 (see entry)
 Civil, 120
 Cold, 17, 140, 227, 373
 Gulf, 189, 436 (see entry)
 in Lebanon, 169
 1948, 6
 1967, 80, 177
 1973, 2, 74
 in Iraq, 49, 126, 151, 263 (see entry)
 on terror, 40, 136
 World, I, x, 16, 54, 369
 World, II, 9, 16, 34, 54–5, 59, 75, 175, 192, 374, 378, 403
 World, III, 78, 375
Ware, John, 45–6, 121
Warsaw, 158, 228
Washington, 7, 11, 29, 35, 82, 231, 253, 304,
 Institute for Near East Policy, 124
 Post, 77, 258–9, 443
 University, 17
Webb, Justine, 35
Weekly Standard, 357
Weinmann, Gabriel, 441
West, 1–2, 4–8, 10–11, 14, 16, 18, 20, 22, 24–6, 30–1, 41, 47, 50, 55, 67, 86, 88, 90, 119, 182, 184, 277, 374
 Anti, x, 2–4, 13, 17, 23, 28, 36, 46, 128, 217
 power, 54
 Western culture, 54–5, 64, 133, 128, 135, 183, 205
 Western Intelligence, 105, 135, 140, 215, 216, 228
 Western policy, 131
West Bank, 23, 60, 80, 292, 430
White, Aidan, 313
Wikipedia, 16
Wilders, Geert, 348
Wilkinson, Guy, 150
Williams, Rowan, 150, 332
Winkler, Beate, 76–7, 317–18
Wolfowitz, Paul, 231
Woolas, Phil, 168
Worcestershire gaol, 143
World Bank, 183
World Cup, 245, 337
World Trade Center (see also September 11 and Twin Towers), 11, 19, 410

Index

World Trade Organization, 120
Wright, Ian, 169
Wrobel, Dr Nathan, 204
Wunderlich, Tanja, 248

Yade, Rama, 223
Yahya, Adel, 126
Yaqoub, Salma, 165
Yale University, 167
Yamani, Dr Mai, 254
　Dr Ahmed Zaki, 254
Yasin, Sheikh Ahmed, 39, 45
Yemen, 19, 26, 94, 133, 214, 421
Yones, Heshu, 145
Yorkshire, 105, 316
Youtube, 29
Yussuf the Barbarian, 179

Zahar, Dr Mahmoud, 50
Zaidan, Amir, 235
Zakat, 147

Zapatero, PM Jose Luis, 393–4
Zarqawi, abu Mu'sab, 79, 120, 229, 230–1, 420
Zawahiri, Ayman, 21, 44, 47, 215, 345, 410, 419
Zimbabwe, 31, 71
Zionism, 168, 177, 196, 236, 295, 355
　Anti, 3, 9, 37, 106, 123, 181, 191, 195, 197, 293
　-conspiracy, 106
Zoroastrians/Mazdeans, 54, 202
Zones Urbaines Sensibles (ZUS), 201
Zwanziger, Theo, 272

Vallentine Mitchell is a long established international publisher of books of Jewish interest, both for the scholar and the general reader. Subjects covered include Jewish history, culture and heritage, religion, modern Jewish thought, biography, reference and the Holocaust. We hope that among our past and present titles you will find much of interest. Vallentine Mitchell also publishes the two journals *Jewish Culture and History* and *Holocaust Studies: A Journal of Culture and History*.

Our new and forthcoming publications include several important and eagerly awaited titles.

Visit our website
www.vmbooks.com
to read blurbs, see jackets and journals and more.
Vallentine Mitchell